Colonialism and Homosexua

Colonial lands, which in the late nineteenth and early twentieth century included most of Africa, South and Southeast Asia, and the islands of the Pacific and Indian Oceans and the Caribbean, provided a haven for Europeans whose sexual inclinations did not fit neatly into the constraints of European society. Certain colonies became known as sites of homosexual licence. Bonds between men in the colonial world ranged across a wide spectrum – from friendship with other Europeans to relationships with native men or boys. Robert Aldrich argues that homosexual inclination exercised a profound influence on the political attitudes and artistic works of many Europeans in the colonial world.

Colonialism and Homosexuality is a thorough investigation of the connections between homosexuality and imperialism from the late 1800s – the era of 'new imperialism' – until the period of decolonisation. Aldrich reconstructs liaisons, including those of famous men such as Cecil Rhodes, E.M. Forster and André Gide, and their historical contexts. Each of the case studies is a micro-history of a particular colonial situation, a sexual encounter and its wider implications for cultural and political life.

Robert Aldrich teaches European and colonial history at the University of Sydney. He is the author of *The Seduction of the Mediterranean* (1993) and co-editor of *Who's Who in Gay and Lesbian History* and *Who's Who in Contemporary Gay and Lesbian History* (both published in 2001).

Colonialism and Homosexuality

Robert Aldrich

 Routledge
Taylor & Francis Group

LONDON AND NEW YORK

First published 2003
by Routledge
11 New Fetter Lane, London EC4P 4EE

Simultaneously published in the USA and Canada
by Routledge
29 West 35th Street, New York, NY 10001

Routledge is an imprint of the Taylor & Francis Group

Typeset in Goudy by Taylor & Francis Books Ltd
Printed and bound in Great Britain by TJ International Ltd,
Padstow, Cornwall

British Library Cataloguing in Publication Data
A catalogue record for this book is available from the British Library

Library of Congress Cataloging in Publication Data
Aldrich, Robert F.
Colonialism and Homosexuality / Robert Aldrich
p.cm. Includes bibliographic references and index.
1. Homosexuality – Europe – Colonies – History. 2. Gay men – Europe –
Colonies – Sexual Behaviour. 3. Interpersonal relations – Europe –
Colonies. 4. Gay men – Africa – Social conditions. 6. Africa –
Colonization. 7. Asia – Colonization. I. Title.

HQ76.2.E9 A43 2002
306.76'6–dc21

ISBN 0–415–19615–9 (hbk)
ISBN 0–415–19616–7 (pbk)

To Clive Faro and Garry Wotherspoon

Contents

Acknowledgements

Many scholars have provided useful leads and helpful suggestions, or have kindly read and commented on the manuscript for this book, and I would like to thank them most sincerely. Clive Faro kindly read the entire manuscript, Roger Bowen and Christopher Robinson read most of the chapters and discussed the project with me at great length, and David Higgs provided a useful appraisal. Laurence Brown, John Connell, Clive Moore, Mark Seymour, Michael Sibalis and Garry Wotherspoon have read some individual sections, and helped in many ways. Patrick Ferry did invaluable research work on Melanesia. Ronald Hyam, whose own work gave me inspiration, helped with his counsel. Jacques and Françoise Miel provided much insight and warm hospitality during my research on Jean Sénac, and Hamid Nacer-Khodja sent me useful material on the poet. Chloë Green and A.D. Maclean graciously discussed G.F. Green with me. Paul Snijders translated material from Dutch, and Wilhelm von Rosen translated a passage from Danish. Edward Lucie-Smith answered a query on homoerotic art; J.G.P. Delaney responded to my questions on Glyn Philpot. Anne Holliday provided generous and indispensable help with Hubert Stowitts. Paul Stringer carefully read the chapter on Stowitts and art. Shyam Selvadurai and Trevor Shearston responded to questions about their novels. The Modern Archive Centre of King's College, Cambridge, gave me access to E.M. Forster's papers, and Jacqueline Cox guided me through the material. A number of contributors to the Routledge *Who's Who in Gay and Lesbian History*, which I co-edited, alerted me to particular figures. I would like to pay tribute to Australian colleagues whose work has made the homosexual history of this country the best documented of all colonies.

I would also like to express my appreciation to the staff of the Inter-Library Loans department of the Fisher Library at the University of Sydney, who were able to get for me a number of essential, but often obscure, sources. Ruth Williams provided splendid secretarial assistance and computer help during various versions of the manuscript. Victoria Peters, my publisher, awaited the manuscript with enthusiasm and patience, and Sünje Redies at Routledge also provided help. Mark Edwards, Stephen Cupper and David Highton, as well as others already mentioned, provided friendship, moral support and good cheer. To all of them, I am grateful.

For permission to quote from the published and manuscript works of E.M. Forster, I would like to thank the Provost and Scholars of King's College, Cambridge, and the Society of Authors; for permission to quote from the stories of G.F. Green, I would like to thank Vivian Cox.

Illustrations have been reproduced by permission of the National Portrait Gallery, London; King's College, Cambridge; the York City Art Museum; and the Hubert Stowitts Museum and Library.

Maps

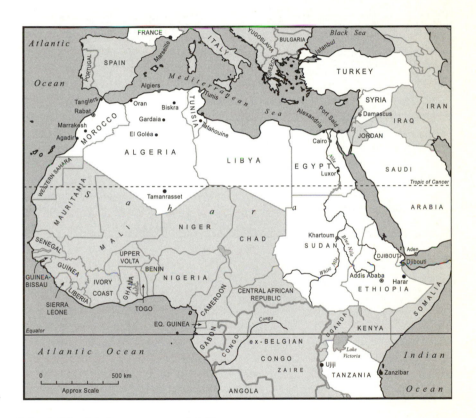

Map 1 The Mediterranean and Africa

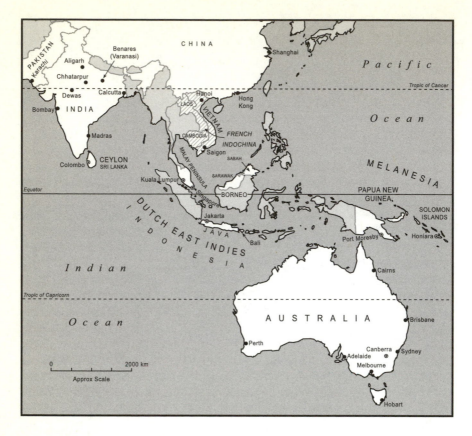

Map 2 Asia and the Pacific

Introduction
The seduction of the colonies

A number of famous men associated with European imperialism had sexual and emotional proclivities oriented towards intimacy with other men. Cecil Rhodes kept company with a series of young assistants, as did Henry Morton Stanley (whose one novel, *Kalulu*, is a love story between two African men). Lawrence of Arabia dedicated *The Seven Pillars of Wisdom* to a young Bedouin who had captured his heart, and E.M. Forster dedicated *A Passage to India* to an Indian with whom he had fallen in love. Hector Macdonald, British commander in Ceylon, committed suicide when superiors alleged that he was homosexual, and Roger Casement was executed for treason after revelations of his homosexuality thwarted moves to pardon the Irish nationalist. On the French side, Arthur Rimbaud, poet turned trader on the horn of Africa, left his worldly goods to a young male protégé. André Gide wrote about his homosexual initiation in Algeria. Marshal Lyautey, France's premier imperialist, enjoyed the companionship of virile military subalterns and rhapsodised about handsome North Africans.

Certain colonies gained fame as sites of homosexual licence. Indeed, in French slang, '*faire passer son brevet colonial*' (literally, to give someone an examination for a colonial diploma) meant to initiate him to sodomy.[1] Europeans fantasised about 'vice' in the Islamic world, and writers from Gustave Flaubert to Paul Bowles were seduced by the hammam, the kasbah and the desert. Officials worried about sodomy in France's disciplinary battalions in North Africa and the Foreign Legion, just as the British expressed concern about homosexual behaviour in penal colonies in Australia. Sydney in the mid-1800s was called the 'Sodom of the South Seas'. A homosexual scandal wracked the Netherlands East Indies in the 1930s, and another scandal was hushed up in British Malaya. Islands such as Bali and Ceylon attracted homosexual writers and painters throughout the colonial era.

Homosexual misbehaviour was not a matter just of private life, as scandals, tragedies and court cases illustrated. Explorers channelled energies into expeditions and homoerotic friendships rather than 'normal' married life. Wilhelm von Humboldt left Germany for South America after what appears the failure of a relationship with a man, while Russia's most famous Central Asian explorer, Nikolay Przhevalsky, preferred the camaraderie of male assistants to the pleasures of a wife. The imperial vocations of Rhodes, Lyautey and James Brooke, the Rajah of Sarawak, owed much to sexual ambivalence. Edward Carpenter's and Forster's interest in India grew from friendship with South Asians in Britain. The anti-colonial sentiments of Jean Genet and the *pied-noir* poet Jean Sénac were bound to their homosexuality. Those writers, as well some other leading men of letters inspired by the colonial experience – Melville, Loti, Couperus – transposed homoerotic overseas experiences into literary classics.

This book explores connections between male homosexuality and European imperialism through the lives and careers of selected figures, primarily in the British and French empires, in the hundred years after the mid-nineteenth century. The aim is neither to 'out' imperialists or colonials, nor to argue that homosexuality forms the pivot for conquest and rule of foreign domains (or opposition to European domination). By looking at homosexual aspects of imperial and colonial history, and at imperial and colonial aspects of the history of homosexuality, it suggests that sexual ambivalence and the desire of certain men for emotional and physical union with male partners produced a direct and identifiable influence on their public lives, whether in political actions, philosophical beliefs or artistic and literary creations. It also illustrates the variety of homosexual relationships in colonial contexts, from lofty and ostensibly innocent evocations of male beauty in speeches or memoirs to outright pornography, from stories of love to cases of rape, from long-lasting and heart-felt romances to promiscuity and prostitution.

My approach is historical and biographical; sources include archival documents, court records, unpublished manuscripts, autobiographical writings, works of fiction and poetry, paintings and photographs, as well as secondary sources. Exoticism, Orientalism and imperialism are linked, and I have not tried to untangle them. However, geographically, I have concentrated on areas of formal European imperial control, though with one or two pertinent other examples.

Following an explosion of work on the history of sexuality, and renewed interest in colonial and imperial history, recent years have seen increased research on sexuality and imperialism, gender and empire, and non-Western sexualities. Ronald Hyam's pioneering *Empire and Sexuality*, published in 1990, analysed British attitudes and policies towards sexuality at home and abroad, and argued that colonies provided opportunities for diverse sorts of sexual licence. Hyam indeed suggested that a sexual imperative formed part of the imperial exercise.[2] Subsequent monographs, written from traditional, archives-based approaches or using literary deconstruction, post-modernism and post-colonialism, have examined the gendered nature of overseas expansion, the ways in which sexual identities were constructed, evolving patterns of masculinity and the representation of sexuality in literature and art.[3] Most scholars agree, despite methodological and doctrinal disputes, that sex and gender, as well as 'commerce and Christianity', were important factors in the colonial equation.

The general connections between travel and sex have also been explored, notably by Ian Littlewood, though he largely excludes the colonial world from his discussion. Since the Grand Tour, connoisseurs, pilgrims and rebels – Littlewood's three categories of tourists – have journeyed abroad, with sex as one of the goals of travel; for tourists such as Americans in Paris in the 1920s, 'travel was itself a form of sexual expression'. Travel, Littlewood argues, was a great source of unease for moralists at home as foreign experiences undermined moral absolutes, the perceived 'immorality' of the Mediterranean and destinations further afield providing ideological challenges, cultural inspiration and liberating influences. To homosexuals, such sites as Tangier appeared the 'antithesis' of a straight-laced middle-class Western civilisation that rebels fled, and their pent-up urges were more likely to be vented overseas than at home. 'It is the homosexual tourist,' Littlewood adds with reference to figures ranging from Gide to Joe Orton, 'more than any other, who has promoted the interplay of sex, travel and subversion.'[4]

The colonies provided many possibilities of homoeroticism, homosociality and homosexuality – a variety of perspectives and experiences by which men expressed attraction to other men (or male youths). Some European men found sexual partners, whether for casual encounters or longer-term relationships, among fellow Europeans or indigenous men. Others enjoyed the homosociality of predominantly male expeditions, military barracks, trading outposts and missionary stations. The gendered nature of expansion, in which men monopolised many imperial activities, and where manly virtues were championed, created situations congenial to intimate male bonding. The imbalance in the sex ratio between European men and women, and the limited range of sexual partners in some outposts, encouraged 'situational' homosexuality. The world outside Europe, as well, provided ample material for portrayal of exotic men in literature and art.

Having homosexual proclivities does not necessarily imply sexual (or, more specifically, genital) relations with someone else. Obstacles inhibiting physical expression of sexual desire include psychological repression, religious vows or beliefs, fear of disease, lack of reciprocated affections or opportunities, pressures from the police, religious officials and medical authorities (and punishments for contravening accepted mores), and distance from or absence of a beloved. In the late nineteenth and early twentieth centuries, when many Europeans considered sexual continence a virtue, lack of physical relations should not be surprising. This does not mean that sexual needs and desires were not present. Furthermore, boundaries between homosexuality, intimate friendship, male bonding and paternalistic or avuncular sentiments were extremely porous, and mateship could and did veer off into sexual intimacy.

Restricting discussion of homosexuality to cases in which incontrovertible evidence of physical intercourse can be found narrows the range of human emotions, and imposes a burden of proof on students of the history of homosexuality not expected from those studying heterosexuality. Indeed, demand for 'proof' of homosexuality is a contestable exigency, even though many writers go to great lengths to show that their subjects were *not* homosexual (sometimes by simply ignoring evidence). Moralists fear that implications of homosexuality tarnish esteemed figures, or that a focus on the sexual life of public figures is inappropriate.

For some Europeans abroad (and non-Europeans), homosexual encounters were circumstantial, because of lack of female partners, the result of chance meetings or pent-up frustrations, or part of the violence perpetrated throughout the colonial world. Others first realised or accepted their homosexual inclinations while overseas, different cultures and climates stimulating desires and liberating libidos. Still others went overseas intentionally to seek out homosexual encounters, heading for countries where traditions tolerated or fostered such relationships.

Colonialism and imperialism, in theory, aimed to set up respectable, loyal and profitable European outposts overseas, and to impart European (generally Christian) virtues to 'savages' and 'heathen'; in this design, homosexuality had no place. Paradoxically, however, colonialism – to the horror of stay-at-home moralists – encouraged sexual irregularity, heterosexual and homosexual. Male bonding proved essential to the colonial adventure, especially on the frontier, during warfare and in the pioneer period preceding arrival of large numbers of European women. Confinement of lusty young men to military cantonments (or other same-sex milieux) created a hothouse of sexual urges, with trespassing across sexual borders bound to occur. Hierarchical relations – master to slave, entrepreneur to employee, officer to subaltern, colonist to houseboy – facilitated sexual expectations and demands. The relative wealth of Europeans overseas made the exchange of sex for money or other advantages easy.

The frequency of homosexuality in the colonies is difficult to judge. Some contemporary observers, and many later historians, minimised the extent of homosexuality, seeing it as an unfortunate consequence of harsh conditions, the 'perversion' of a few individuals, the vice of 'natives'. Other commentators opined (with little evidence) that hot climates favoured homosexual vice, and that colonials prey to the *cafard* – a general malaise induced by hot weather, rough conditions, loneliness and boredom – were prone to sexual excess. Statistics on arrests and trials for homosexual offences from late colonial Papua New Guinea (to use one example) suggest that the incidence of homosexuality was far from trivial, and an enquiry in Australia in the 1830s highlighted with consternation the alarming frequency of sodomy in prison colonies. Folk wisdom has always proclaimed that homosexual practices were rife in North Africa.

Homosexuality in the colonies regularly troubled administrators and commentators, though historians differ on their interpretations. Robert C. Young remarks that 'concern about racial amalgamation tended if anything to encourage same-sex sex (playing the imperial game was, after all, already an implicitly homo-erotic practice)'. Better to enjoy the pleasures of homoerotic sex than the dangers of heterosexual miscegenation, thought the colonialists. Young adds that 'feminisation' of indigenous peoples encouraged illicit attractions.[5] Ann Laura Stoler, by contrast, suggests that in the Dutch case, at least, 'concubinage between European men and native women was considered an alternative, albeit an unattractive one, to homosexuality among the ranks'.[6]

Calculating whether there were proportionately more homosexuals among expatriate populations than in Europe is impossible because of incomplete records, lack of criminalisation of homosexual practices in many colonies, the clandestine and 'closeted' nature of encounters, and the necessity to restrict homosexuality to 'proven' cases of physical contact in order to total sums. Lack of documentation has generally limited research on colonial homosexuality. Two illustrations suffice. Stoler, a specialist of the East Indies, remarks that the

> absent presence of the dangers of homosexuality…is striking. What is more, in the Dutch archives, the threat of homosexual desire among stolid Dutch agents of empire, of the colonial *middenstand*, is rarely if ever mentioned. When homosexuality is breached, it is always in the form of a *deflected* discourse, one about sodomitical Chinese plantation coolies, about degenerate subaltern European soldiers, never about respectable Dutch men.

Stoler admits that 'my silence on this issue…reflects my long-term and failed efforts to identify any sources that do more than assume or obliquely allude to this "evil"'.[7] Christian Henriot, writing on Shanghai, justifies not covering male prostitution by saying that 'the case of homosexual prostitution is still more revealing about the evident trouble that this subject caused both authorities and Chinese society and its elites: the silence is almost total, although the existence of such prostitution is admitted'.[8]

By the late nineteenth century, a widespread belief circulated in Europe that homosexuality (and other sexual deviance) was endemic in the non-European world. The perception, and (to a limited extent) the reality, of the empire as a homosexual playground must not be underestimated. Homosexual men fleeing legal persecution in Britain, Germany and the Netherlands (and cultural disapprobation, if not criminal prosecution, in France) often found a warm welcome in the colonies, though when behaviour became too indiscreet, they suffered condemnation and conviction. Itinerancy has remained a prime trait of modern homosexuals, migrating from countryside to city, leaving the provinces for *fin de siècle* Paris or Weimar Berlin, journeying to Capri, Taormina and other mythic Mediterranean sites. Colonies provided further destinations, at a time when imperial propagandists, popular writers and newly established travel agencies promoted overseas journeys, while the colonial administration, the military and private businesses offered jobs to those willing to tempt their chances abroad.[9]

According to Françoise d'Eaubonne, 'The colonies had the privilege of seeing a great many men flourish in this domain [of homosexuality].'[10] For Jean-Edern Hallier, 'Homosexuals, pure, heroic and martial, were the spearhead of this childish dream which constituted French colonisation.'[11] Christian Gury makes an ambit claim: 'Homophilia represents a common trait of all of the great colonials, whether British or French, and the connecting thread which makes sense of their destinies.'[12] Theorising about the 'discourse of effeminacy' in colonial writing, Sarah Suleri locates a homophile common denominator in European expansion: 'Both the desire and the disempowerment implicit in such a formulation [about effeminate Asian 'natives'] underscore the predominantly homoerotic cast assumed by the narrative of colonialism.'[13] Ashis Nandy identifies an 'unconscious homo-eroticized bonding' linking British colonial men and their Indian male subjects, and hypothesises about ways in which this facilitated Indian strategies of resistance to British rule.[14] Nandy also points out that homosexuality (especially when the Oscar Wilde affair burst in Britain) came up against the sexual norm, 'a basic postulate of the colonial attitude in Britain', which mandated heterosexuality, marriage, monogamy, child-rearing and family life as essential values of civilised society. A figure such as Wilde was 'an unself-aware, but more or less complete, critic of the political culture which sired colonialism'.[15] In short, homosexuals – and homosexuality – played a far more significant and diverse role in colonialism than many would allow.

Writing about homosexuality and imperialism

In 1970, d'Eaubonne remarked on the lack of scholarly work on homosexuals in the colonies.[16] A quarter of a century later, Madeleine Rebérioux, in a preface to an anthology of writings on *Amours coloniales*, which conspicuously included no homosexual instances, regretted the lacuna and again pointed to the subject as one deserving attention.[17] Yet a number of well-known recent books on gender in colonies still elude discussion of homosexuality.[18]

Few historical studies have been published on homosexuality and European expansion. Hyam's book is a notable exception because of the considerable attention it pays to colonial men with homosexual inclinations, one of the first (and still only) books by mainstream colonial and imperial historians to address the issue in a direct and extended fashion. Many other historians of the British Empire, and almost all colonial historians of France, have remained reticent about homosexuality, though hidden in a few books are brief descriptions or anecdotes – a priest dismissed for homosexual dalliance in Tahiti, a bishop forced into retirement in the Solomon Islands, an administrator suspected of homosexuality in Nigeria. Historians of homosexuality, too, have paid surprisingly little attention to colonial homosexuality. The most comprehensive body of work on settler colonies comes from Australia; other British dominions await comparable treatment.[19] Also largely uncharted, other than the case of Tangier, are expatriate communities in other colonial outposts.

Biographers have a mixed record on homosexuality. Tim Jeal's biography of Baden-Powell and John E. Mack's of Lawrence of Arabia, which dared to discuss their sexual dissidence, provoked considerable criticism for doing so; a book on the homosexuality of Marshal Lyautey, by contrast, attracted little attention in France. Among other biographers of imperial political figures, Frank McLynn is one of the few to face head on the question of homosexuality. Recent writers on Lord Kitchener and Arthur Rimbaud have gone out of their way to exculpate them from allegations of homosexual behaviour overseas. Only biographies of men of letters, such as Gide or Forster, are more expansive. Homosexuality remains a delicate issue in studying the colonial great and good, and even the marginal and suspect.[20]

Anthropologists have shown greater energy in investigating same-sex behaviour in indigenous cultures, a welcome addition to scholarly literature. Books on homosexual practices in Melanesia, Japan, China, the Islamic world and sub-Saharan Africa are now available, although gaps remain. In examining the construction of sexuality outside the West, ethnologists have been less interested, however, in interactions between local and foreign cultures. Their aim has been to understand sexual dynamics in traditional societies, outside the context of Judeo-Christian and Western ideologies. One historical anthropology that does look at the interaction is Rudy Bleys's study of Europeans' discovery, from the 1500s through to the 1800s, of (to them) non-standard same-sex practices, including initiation rites, male 'marriages', intimate bonding and transsexual and transgender behaviour. Bleys's excellent work demonstrates how such discoveries profoundly upset Europeans' sexual outlooks, and provided challenges paradoxically both to 'moralise' the rest of the world and to reassess Western sexual verities.[21]

Relationships between Europeans and 'the other' have become a staple for scholars interested in Orientalism. Edward Said had little to say about homosexuality, and he and others have been taken to task for, in the words of Joseph Boone, the 'conspicuously heterosexual interpretive framework'.[22] The most detailed treatment of homosexuality in colonial fiction from the post-colonialist perspective is Christopher Lane's *The Ruling Passion*.[23]

Two seminal cross-disciplinary articles represented path-breaking work on colonialism and homosexuality. A subtly reasoned and rich study by Joseph Boone examines the 'homoerotics of Orientalism' by canvassing the writings of British and French novelists of Egypt, the Maghreb and the Middle East. He explores the ways in which travellers came into contact with homosexual practices in the Islamic world, and what their experiences meant for their lives and works. Boone analyses the economy of sexual barter in the Near East, the ways in which Europeans exercised fantasies about foreign men, yet maintained a blinkered vision of Islamic realities, and how Western and Muslim sexualities colluded and collided.[24] Rudi Bleys has looked at the 'textuality of the imaginary paradise', the nomadic instinct of homosexuals and the complex but 'profound relation...between travelling in other cultures and the experience of a homosocial or homosexual sensibility' from 1800 to 1980. Bleys thus links European discovery of different sexualities with colonial encounters and post-colonial experiences.[25]

This book differs from earlier studies in several ways. Its geographical focus is broader than the British imperial experience, as it examines the French colonial empire, Australian rule in Papua New Guinea and, to a limited degree, the Dutch epoch in the East Indies. In addition to North Africa, South and South-East Asia and Polynesia, it provides extended case studies of Australia and Melanesia. The book is also broad in its sexual spectrum, looking at homosexual sex *per se*, and at homoeroticism and homosociality, including representations in art and literature. It also looks at a larger group of individuals than is sometimes the case. While some of the figures discussed are well known, others – G.F. Green, Jean Sénac, François Augiéras, Hubert Stowitts – have received little previous attention. Finally, this study gives greater space than is usual to the 'native' partners and friends of European men, with as detailed a portrait as possible of Kalulu, Athmann ben Saleh, Ponnambalam Arunachalam, Mohammed el-Adl and Syed Ross Masood.

This study, however, is not primarily about the colonised 'other' and his emotional commitments and sexual behaviour. I try to provide the context in which local men, for whatever motivation, contracted intimate relationships with foreigners, but I do not claim to see into the 'native' mind. I do not have the pretension of expounding in a detailed manner, and from an 'indigenous' point of view, on sexual imperatives and options in non-Western society. As interesting as such a project on the foreign perspective on inter-ethnic encounters would be, that is the not the object of the present work.

Two other caveats must be noted. This book is not concerned with lesbians overseas, another undoubtedly fascinating topic. Only exceptionally do I discuss European lesbians, for example, Annemarie Schwarzenbach. The attraction of the colonies to such heterodox women as Isabelle Eberhardt and Odette de Puygaudeau, the emergence of lesbian identities and networks in settler societies, and scientific and literary discussions of 'native' lesbianism would make an interesting and important study. I can only hope that some scholar will soon undertake that research.

Finally, partly because of constraints of space, I do not look in depth at post-colonial sexual tourism and inter-ethnic homosexual relations in the contemporary world. I have given rather short shrift to sexual travellers and expatriates even during the last decades of the imperial period, preferring to concentrate on the high age of imperialism. Many themes and characteristics that appear in this study of colonialism and homosexuality nevertheless persist in the period after colonies gained independence. That, too, would make an arresting subject for research.

Colonial homosexuality

Aimed at both the general reader and the academic specialist, the present book brings together well-known and new material on colonial homosexuality in diverse situations. It follows from my earlier study on homosexuals in the Mediterranean. I have suggested that, particularly before the emergence of a self-identified, affirmative and militant 'gay' identity from the mid-twentieth century onwards, European homosexual desire manifested itself in certain identifiable but coded fashions, for instance, a vogue for aestheticism or a fascination with working-class men.[26] A particularly important connection was identification between Northern homosexuals and the European Mediterranean, both the Mediterranean of the classical world, where homosexuals found legitimation for reprobate desires, and the latter-day Mediterranean, where travellers visited ancient ruins, Renaissance galleries and baroque churches, enjoyed the sea and sun, and found sexual partners.[27] *Colonialism and Homosexuality* represents another case, *mutatis mutandis*, of homosexual men looking for sexual and emotional companionship away from home, the ways their desires melded into public actions and political beliefs, and how art and writing reflected experiences: the seduction of the colonies, or perhaps the seduction of the tropics, the desert and exotic islands. It is no surprise that, even in 'darkest Africa' or 'primitive Oceania', homoerotic writing described a comely local man as Ganymede or Antinous, and harked back to paradigms of 'Socratic love'; some travellers felt that they had discovered a homosexual Eden or equatorial Athens overseas.[28]

Several issues need addressing at this point. Almost all men discussed in this book, though to much varying degrees, accepted ideas current in the colonial age about 'natives'. Racialist and racist stereotypes abounded. Romanticisation and idealisation of foreign cultures – or, conversely, denigration of them – were common, along with wild fantasies about the luxuriance of the hammam, Africans' generous genital endowments, Asians' passivity and the beauty and virility of half-naked 'savages'. Homoerotic writing and art lauding the physical attributes of foreign men participated in race-based stereotyping.[29] Furthermore, travellers and expatriates assumed that almost any foreign man was available to a passing European, and money could buy sex, if not love. Relations of power permeated colonial sexual culture. Non-European men were regularly and systematically 'objectified' and 'commodified' (to use currently fashionable terms). European homosexuals were more often interested in their partners' bodies than their minds. With notable exceptions, few made real attempts to understand the cultures of men they bedded; some remained blithely unconcerned about the political disenfranchisement, economic exploitation and cultural alienation to which colonialism had reduced subject populations. A nostalgic thought and a wistful wave were sometimes, though not always, the only indications that Europeans felt much regret about their return to a world of privilege and power, leaving their barefoot partners in countries ravaged by conquerors.

The personal histories recorded here must be seen in the context of European expansion, an enterprise based on arrogation of Europeans' right to rule the rest of the world, establishment and maintenance of unequal relations between colonialists and colonised peoples, extraction of human and natural resources, and the racist ideologies that underpinned imperialism. Lack of deep concern for colonised people by many figures, and the unabashed sabre rattling and flag waving of a few, make more poignant the courage of those who raised voices against imperialism, and the extreme effort of ones who attempted to breach barriers of race and class. Examples of long-standing friendships – Carpenter and Arunachalam, Forster and Masood – and cases of men, like Sénac, who cast their lot with anti-imperialists, are powerful reminders that homosexual proclivities led to opposition to colonialism as well as promotion of expansion, to mutually beneficial relationships as well as exploitation.

A second issue is paedophilia, or, more properly, inter-generational sexual relationships. A number of the figures were attracted to, or had sexual relations with, young men, generally in their late adolescence; only rarely did a European man show sexual interest in a pre-pubescent boy. Desire of adult men for younger partners has been widespread in Europe and overseas, with antecedents reaching back to Antiquity. Present-day laws make sexual relations with minors illegal, but ages of consent have varied widely. In Britain, the age of consent for girls was twelve until 1875, and there was none for boys; in most continental European countries, it remained below sixteen for both sexes – thirteen for girls and boys in early twentieth-century France, twelve in Italy. During the late 1800s and early 1900s, there was no legal age of consent for males in India, Ceylon, China, Japan and parts of Australia.[30] Not all sexual encounters that would now be criminal acts with 'minors' were then legally penalised. Furthermore, in many cultures, sexual initiation, sexual relations (of various sorts) and marriage generally occurred at precocious ages, especially where there was no premium on male chastity before marriage. Many adolescent males in Africa, Asia and the Pacific would probably have been sexually active, whether their relations were with compatriots or foreigners.

Another sensitive issue is prostitution. Male prostitution existed in Europe and abroad – London had half a dozen brothels with men in the mid-twentieth century. Male brothels in Tientsin, China, employed 800 sex workers around 1900, and there were half a dozen male brothels in Singapore.[31] Institutionalised male prostitution existed elsewhere as well. Furthermore, areas where sailors and soldiers congregated were generally known as fertile ground for men searching out partners for pay. However, the phenomenon of prostitution is awkward to delimit. Many people provide some material benefit for bedfellows – money, food, accommodation, employment or preferment. This was particularly common, for both female and male partners of Europeans, in the colonial world, where racial and class differences were marked. The transactional nature of these arrangements might or might not be exploitative.

A final issue is misogyny. Several men discussed here clearly did not care for women, either as sexual partners or social companions, and many seemed uncomfortable in dealings with women. The ethos of the colonial world (and indeed of much European public life in the imperial age) was masculine, with women excluded, and a current of misogyny underlay European life. Colonial homosexuals, however, were not necessarily women-haters, and facile links between homosexuality and misogyny are spurious. Quite a number were married and bisexual; others had close women friends and confidantes. Most 'natives' who had sex with European men, or bonded intimately with them, became husbands and fathers. In societies and in an age where private or public affirmation of an exclusively homosexual identity was rare (and that very concept was a modern Western construct), many men, easily or with difficulty, moved across the continuum between what we consider homosexuality and heterosexuality.

These comments point to the complexity of understanding sexual, social and other cleavages in past times and foreign places. They also indicate – as with the imprecise differences between homosexual erotic desire, intimate friendship and avuncular sentiments – the porosity of boundaries: between adolescence and adulthood, free and paid sexual favours, exclusive homosexuality and exclusive heterosexuality, situational behaviour and confirmed identities. The age of imperialism, not coincidentally, marked the time when many of these definitions and differences were being articulated.

A brief word on nomenclature is necessary. I generally use colonialism (which, in English, refers more specifically to establishment of settler societies while, in French, it often means acquisition and administration of formal colonies) and imperialism (which, particularly in French, refers to a more general process of foreign domination in both 'formal' and especially 'informal' spheres of influence) synonymously, although differences should at places be clear. 'Homosexual' (and homosexuality), coined in the late nineteenth century, achieved wider currency than 'Urning', 'Uranian', 'invert', 'homophile' and other labels, but gradually gave way to 'gay' and, latterly in some quarters, to 'queer'. Particular socio-economic and cultural conditions patterned, or constructed, sexual behaviour, and a homosexual identity immutable across history and geography is improbable. This is even more certainly the case in non-European societies. Recognising the permutations of sexuality in different epochs and places, I nevertheless use 'homosexual' for convenience, preferable to the cumbersome 'same-sex' or similar expressions. 'Homosocial' and 'homoerotic' are used in their standard, more general, senses.

After a prologue, on a world tour of 'the art of colonial love' by a French military doctor, the five chapters in the first section of this book look at groups of men with homosexual inclinations active in the colonies: explorers, military officers, civilian settlers, writers and artists. There is then a chapter on men who paid the price for sexual indiscretion through scandals and tragedies. The second section, on sites of colonial homosexuality, focuses on case studies of Australia and Melanesia, and then on the British in South Asia and the French in North Africa, with E.M. Forster providing a connection between the last two areas. The final section comprises a chapter on homosexuality and anti-colonialism, with an epilogue on homosexual travellers in the last years of empire.

Notes

1 François Caradec, *N'Ayons pas peur des mots: Dictionnaire du français argotique et populaire* (Paris, 1988), p. 132.
2 Ronald Hyam, *Empire and Sexuality: The British Experience* (Manchester, 1990).
3 See Malia B. Formes, 'Beyond complicity versus resistance: Recent work on gender and European imperialism', *Journal of Social History*, Vol. 23, No. 3 (1995), pp. 629–41, and Linda Bryder, 'Sex, race, and colonialism: An historiographical review', *International History Review*, Vol. 20, No. 4 (1998), pp. 806–54.

4 Ian Littlewood, *Sultry Climates: Travel and Sex since the Grand Tour* (London, 2001), quotations from pp. 20, 127 and 129.

5 Robert J.C. Young, *Colonial Desire: Hybridity in Theory, Culture and Race* (London, 1995), pp. 26, 29.

6 Ann Laura Stoler, *Race and the Education of Desire: Foucault's History of Sexuality and the Colonial Order of Things* (Durham, NC, 1995), p. 129, footnote 96.

7 *Ibid.*

8 Christian Henriot, *Belles de Shanghaï: Prostitution et sexualité en Chine au XIXe–XXe siècles* (Paris, 1997), p. 15.

9 See James Buzard, *European Tourism, Literature, and the Ways to Culture, 1800–1918* (Oxford, 1993).

10 Françoise d'Eaubonne, *Eros minoritaire* (Paris, 1970), quoted in Christian Gury, *Lyautey–Charlus* (Paris, 1998), p. 14.

11 Quoted in Gury, p. 111.

12 Gury, p. 62.

13 Sara Suleri, *The Rhetoric of English India* (Chicago, 1992), p. 16.

14 Ashis Nandy, *The Intimate Enemy: Loss and Recovery of Self under Colonialism* (Delhi, 1983), p. 10.

15 *Ibid.*, p. 44–5.

16 D'Eaubonne, *op. cit.*

17 Alain Ruscio (ed.), *Amours coloniales: Aventures et fantasmes exotiques de Claire de Duras à Georges Simenon* (Brussels, 1996), p. 7.

18 Among such works are Rana Kabbani, *Europe's Myths of Orient: Desire and Rule* (London, 1986), Anne McClintock, *Imperial Leather: Race, Gender and Sexuality in the Colonial Context* (New York, 1985), and Julia Clancy-Smith and Frances Gouda (eds), *Domesticating the Empire: Race, Gender, and Family Life in French and Dutch Colonialism* (Charlottesville, VA, 1998).

19 See Robert Aldrich, 'Homosexuality and colonialism', *Thamyris: Mythmaking from Past to Present* (Amsterdam), Vol. 3, No. 1 (1996), pp. 175–91.

20 See, *inter alia*, the discussion of works on Kitchener, Rimbaud and Rhodes in Chapter 2, below.

21 Rudi Bleys, *The Geography of Perversion: Male-to-Male Sexual Behaviour outside the West and the Ethnographic Imagination, 1750–1918* (New York, 1995).

22 Joseph A. Boone, 'Vacation cruises; or, The homoerotics of Orientalism', *PMLA*, Vol. 110 (1985), pp. 89–107.

23 Christopher Lane, *The Ruling Passion: British Colonial Allegory and the Paradox of Homosexual Desire* (Durham, NC, 1995).

24 *Ibid.*

25 Rudi Bleys, 'Homosexual exile: The textuality of the imaginary paradise, 1800–1980', *Journal of Homosexuality*, Vol. 25, No. 1/2 (1993), pp. 165–82.

26 Robert Aldrich, 'Die mediterrane Besessenheit: Ein Beispiel zur Frage der Homo-Imagination', in Maria Kalveram and Wolfgang Popp (eds), *Homosexualitäten-literarisch* (Essen, 1991), pp. 13–21.

27 Robert Aldrich, *The Seduction of the Mediterranean: Writing, Art and Homosexual Fantasy* (London, 1993).

28 *Colonialism and Homosexuality* builds, as well, on earlier papers in which I sketched out ideas more fully developed here. 'White and black men: Travel, colonialism and homosexuality' discussed literary traces of overseas encounters, in both the colonial and post-colonial age, and in a second article I attempted a historiographical critique, focused more particularly on colonialism and homosexuality in Oceania. Another article looked at homosexuality in the French Empire. The present work also provides considerably broadened treatment of many personalities profiled in a biographical dictionary of gay and lesbian history (Robert Aldrich, 'Weisse und farbige Männer. Reisen, Kolonialismus und Homosexualität', *Forum:*

Homosexualität und Literatur, No. 7 (1989), pp. 15–24, and 'Colonialism and homosexuality', *op. cit.*, 'Homosexuality in the French Colonies', in Jeffrey Merrick and Michael Sibalis (eds), *Homosexuality in French History and Culture* (New York, 2001), pp. 201–18, as well as entries in Robert Aldrich and Garry Wotherspoon (eds), *Who's Who in Gay and Lesbian History: From Antiquity to World War II* and *Who's Who in Gay and Lesbian History: From World War II to the Present Day* (both London, 2001).)

29 On fantasies about Africans' genital endowments, see David M. Friedman, *A Mind of Its Own: A Cultural History of the Penis* (New York, 2001), Ch. 3.

30 Hyam, p. 62.

31 *Ibid.*, pp. 63, 141, 145.

Prologue
The art of colonial homosexual love

In 1893, a book entitled *L'Art d'aimer aux colonies* by Dr Jacobus X was published in Paris. The author, clearly writing under a *nom de plume*, identified himself as a medical doctor in the French Navy with years of colonial experience. He was also a disciple of Ambroise Tardieu, a sexologist famous for medico-legal study of sex crimes who asserted that it was possible to find physiological evidence of homosexuality. Jacobus was a member of the Société d'Ethnographie and the Alliance Scientifique Universelle, and an officer of the Légion d'Honneur and the Ordre le l'Instruction Publique. He published several books on sexuality, as well as a study of the Marquis de Sade (who, he argued, was a 'degenerate invert', or homosexual).[1] *L'Art d'aimer aux colonies*, his first book, Jacobus declared, was 'not an obscene work but a psychological document on the general history of Love in the human race' – a noble purpose somewhat compromised by the inclusion of sixteen illustrations of naked 'native' women. In almost 400 pages, he discussed sexual behaviour in Indo-China, the French West Indies, Oceania and Africa, basing his statements (he claimed) on clinical observations and on evidence provided by colleagues (though the book contains no scholarly apparatus).[2]

L'Art d'aimer aux colonies provides an inventory of sex as practised in indigenous non-European societies, and a catalogue of liaisons contracted between Europeans and colonised people. In voyeuristic detail, Jacobus describes the genitals of women and men, and was especially assiduous in phalloplethysmography, measuring the size of penises and comparing dimensions across races. He lists the various positions assumed in sexual intercourse, discusses brothels and other venues of sexual pleasure, speculates as an amateur anthropologist on the causes of particular practices and reveals the sexual life of French men overseas. He quotes from the works of such novelists as Pierre Loti to evoke the sexual ambience of exotic lands. Jacobus's cultural preferences – he especially enjoyed the Antilles and Oceania – are evident, though his sexual proclivities and indulgences remain veiled.

Most of Jacobus's study is devoted to heterosexuality, but more of it than might be expected focuses on homosexuality, despite the good doctor's statement that he finds homosexual practices repulsive. Jacobus judges homosexuality most prevalent in South-East Asia. In Cochin-China, homosexuality appeared endemic among Vietnamese and Chinese during his first visit in the 1860s. Jacobus denies that Europeans introduced homosexuality to Indo-China:

> The Annamite is a pederast because he is lascivious. Here is a sophisticated old race, which was already corrupted....[Pederasty] is an innate stigma, which the European discovered in full bloom and from which a few (a small number, let us hope) have profited.

In slightly tortured logic, Jacobus argues that soldiers of the French expeditionary forces to China in the mid-1800s did not acquire unnatural habits there and bring them to Cochin-China, because they had already been introduced by Chinese migrants. The Frenchman in Indo-China, however, 'was able to become a sodomite or a pederast because he found, without even having to search for them, men and children who presented him the opportunity'. Indeed, Indo-Chinese had corrupted Europeans, especially in the early colonial period when there was a scarcity of European women:

> Formerly, the European pederast was far from a rarity and a goodly number of men, including some of the most respectable, still had this sad reputation. However, they were not despised, or even thought badly of, because of it. In the cafés when the most scandalous stories were told about them, everyone laughed.

In the 1860s, those who enjoyed sodomy and opium gathered openly to indulge their pleasures. A quarter of a century later, Jacobus remarks on an improvement in morals. Fewer European men smoke opium. 'As for European pederasts,' he observes,

> they hardly exist except as a memory. Those who have kept this reputation are old traders or bureaucrats....They are regarded as a curiosity by new arrivals. It is [nevertheless] possible that among this latter group, there are those who have a penchant for Greek love, since they exist in Europe, too.

According to Jacobus, *boys* (youths employed as household servants) or younger *nays* (porters or errand-boys), in the early days of French conquest but also at the end of the century, were widely available for sex. Such youths engage in fellatio and anal intercourse, proving versatile in the services they provide for a modest sum of money. One speciality is oral sex:

> One must not think that the depraved Asiatic feels any repugnance whatsoever to engaging in this turpitude. He has even less than the *belle de jour* who performs the same operation. Whether the European reclines in a long planter's chair or lies on his bed, the *boy*, kneeling or squatting, *inguina osculatur, sugit, emissumque semen in bucca recipit, usque ad ultimam guttam* [*sic*].

Jacobus claims to find physical evidence of homosexual practices in the distended mouths and anuses of youths who had indulged – colonial proof for Tardieu's theory that those who engaged in passive sodomy develop 'funnel-shaped' anuses. He had found only two cases of passive sodomy among Europeans, curing two men of anal gonorrhoea, one a 17-year-old who initially claimed that he had contracted the disease from a woman prostitute. Jacobus notes in the 1890s that *boys* are still available at more or less open meeting places, including brothels-cum-opium dens in the Saigon suburbs. He also mentions an old school friend, a navy officer in Indo-China, who developed a 'deplorable reputation because of his too little concealed taste for boys'.

Jacobus observes similar morals elsewhere in Indo-China – 'The Tonkinese race…is basically lascivious, lubricious, pederastic and sodomitical. Let us note this and continue on.' By contrast, in French Guiana, there is little sodomy among Africans and *métis*. He treated a 15-year-old black boy who had 'accepted the impure offers of an Arab', who got him drunk and took advantage of him, leaving the youth with an anal fissure. (The boy's mother pretended that he had been struck by the horn of a goat chasing him.) The reason for lack of sodomitical activity, he suggests, is 'the ease of procuring women in this fine country'. The story is altogether different with the South Asians brought to the Caribbean and French Guiana as indentured labourers, and with many European and North African prisoners transported to Devil's Island. Some homosexuality among prisoners is situational, because of lack of women, but for others it is 'hereditary'. Almost all Indian 'coolies' between fifteen and twenty indulge in pederasty, often with European or Arab partners, in return for money: 'The depraved man can thus satisfy his passions in Guiana.' As for the North Africans convicts, 'The Arab is an inveterate pederast, even in his own country, where women are not lacking.…All the travellers writing about morals in Arabia and Turkey have commented on this fact.'

In sub-Saharan Africa, Jacobus concentrates on the genital endowment of men, the large size of whose penises he attributes, curiously, to circumcision. He finds heterosexual sodomy uncommon: 'The reason is perhaps that the practice of anal coition, because of the size of the Negro's penis, would be a real torture, a sort of empaling.' Homosexual activity is not frequent, except among slaves and *tirailleurs sénégalais* (French African troops). He blames this, predictably, on lack of women partners; two *tirailleurs*, 'a true Negro Castor and Pollux', had constituted an enduring 'unnatural' relationship until they found a woman partner, whom they then shared.

On his last stop, in the South Pacific, Jacobus notices homosexual contacts among Melanesians in New Caledonia, once again when no women are available, and remarks on male homosexuality and lesbianism among prisoners transported to the colony: the 'vices of Sodom and Gomorrah [are] in full flower'. Sometimes lasting partnerships are formed among convicts and emancipists, unions marked by jealousy, violence and revenge for infidelity. Melanesian labourers from the neighbouring New Hebrides engage in sodomy, though Jacobus says that, unlike Orientals, they are ashamed of their activities, and he had to use bribery to extract confessions. In Tahiti, homosexuality is rare, although the Tahitian in his twenties, Jacobus admits, is 'a superb man and, in my opinion, one of the most perfect specimens of human beauty'.

L'Art d'aimer aux colonies is specious anthropology and sexology, marked by imperialist assumptions, racialist scientific views and the author's personal prejudices, voyeuristic soft porn masquerading as scientific study. Yet it remains valuable for several reasons. It shows that French observers were well aware of homosexual practices in their colonies among 'natives', indentured labourers and migrants, transported prisoners and free men, middle-class settlers and even European adolescents. Homosexual sex was available for money, or for free, and could be obtained from youths encountered on the street, domestic servants, fellow prisoners or 'sex workers' in brothels. Known networks of contacts and places of sociability – signs of emerging homosexual identities – existed in such cities as Saigon by the end of the nineteenth century. The gamut of sexual acts, including fellatio and active and passive anal intercourse, could be easily obtained.

Jacobus's book also illustrates typical late nineteenth-century attitudes, popularised by Tardieu, about homosexuals and the ways to identify them. He had manifestly not read Freud or other sexual theorists of the *fin de siècle*. Furthermore, his work reflects stereotypes about the small genitals, sexual licentiousness (and, often, sexual passivity) of Asians, the oversized genitals and carnal prowess of Africans, and the widespread penchant of Arabs for sodomy. He posits that 'natives' could corrupt the French, and affirms that Europeans did not introduce homosexuality to the colonies. He admits that, among indigenous and migrant populations, situational homosexuality flourishes. However, Jacobus adds that some men, including Europeans, are naturally given to homosexual 'vice'. Nevertheless, though homosexual activities did occasionally cause medical problems (such as venereal disease), and even if Jacobus found them revolting, he hardly mounted a campaign against sexual immorality.

Jacobus's book – still in print in new editions the late 1920s – became something of a classic, to judge by citations of the volume. In 1922, for instance, Jean Hervez paid homage to Jacobus, quoting long passages from *L'Art d'aimer aux colonies* without attribution. (Indeed, Hervez seems to have no other source for his work.)[3] Ten years later, Anne de Colney's *L'Amour aux colonies* depended even more on Jacobus's work without mentioning either the doctor or his book.[4] The very similar title and organisation of the later study, and entire sentences lifted from *L'Art d'aimer aux colonies*, suggest either that de Colney's work is simply plagiarised, or that de Colney and Hervez are later pseudonyms for Jacobus himself.

These books reinforce Jacobus's observations, sometimes with further information. Hervez states that a *nay* in Indo-China often proposes sexual services when delivering goods to a European's house: '*Captain...moa bocou conaite chouchou banane*' ['Captain, I know a lot about eating a banana'], they say in pidgin, and then add, '*Moa conaite l'ablic*' (using, he claims, a Frenchified Vietnamese word for sodomy). The offer accepted, he sneaks into the European's house during the siesta. *Nays* also await clients outside cafés or restaurants. *Boys* (between sixteen and twenty), however, ply their services from nine p.m. to midnight, arranging rendezvous in carriages, parks or brothels. Hervez identifies another source of homosexual partners, former school-boys. In Saigon and the interior, the French teach youngsters reading and writing, geography and arithmetic, but only the best find jobs, generally as court interpreters. The others, educated but unemployed, wander around searching for work, willing to engage in the same 'turpitude' as houseboys. They frequent areas containing brothels, offering themselves as guides, translators and sexual partners. 'Unfortunate is the European novice who falls into their clutches,' for the Vietnamese youth will plead for a job as secretary or scribe. If the Vietnamese gets invited home, he will rob the European and, if the foreigner threatens to contact the police, the lad will himself threaten to report the European for compromising his virtue: 'He, too, has learned the value of blackmail.'[5]

Hervez elaborates on inter-racial homosexuality in Guiana, where Arab prisoners often have sex with Indians or Europeans. When released, they frequently become shop-keepers or foremen (prized because of their abstention from alcohol):

> Those who employ them know their vice, and this will sooner or later bring them to court when they use violence on a partner who is recalcitrant not because of prudishness but for fear of being empaled [by the large penis, Hervez says, that characterises Arabs].[6]

Hervez also writes about homosexual practices in such colonies as New Caledonia and, unusually, devotes a chapter to 'sapphism' in the West Indies.

De Colney, repeating details about *nays* and *boys*, indicates yet another reservoir of homosexual partners in Indo-China:

> One should also number among the devotees of this [male] prostitution the employees of business houses, tailors and cobblers, because it is rare for a Chinese of these occupations to refuse the advances of a European pederast. This is not a question of money but of sexual pleasure. Nevertheless, if a European happens on someone who sells trinkets…he has to agree to a few purchases which subsequently he will need to make at regular and short intervals.

Chinese merchants, 'who have a taste for pederasty', often maintain homosexual relationships with their employees – one was so notorious that respectable Europeans avoided his shop. 'With an eclectic taste, the Chinaman searches out the European affected by the same sexual perversion.' De Colney describes a homosexual bordello where young men, aged twelve to twenty, 'richly attired in silk outfits of pastel colours fill the role of Ganymedes. Cubicles, similar to horses' stalls, instead of feed troughs, contain beds that allow the amorous couples' to consummate their encounters.[7]

Whether imitators of Jacobus or reincarnations of him, Hervez and de Colney propagated similar stereotypes. Voyeurism, pseudo-science and racism are even more flagrant in these later books than in Jacobus's study in the 1890s, with the implication that non-European races (particularly Asians) are immoral and lascivious. Such attitudes formed the stock-in-trade of most colonial propagandists. Yet Jacobus, Hervez and de Colney do provide, in a rudimentary fashion, geographical and sociological perspectives on homosexual activities, especially in Vietnam.[8] A European planter, bureaucrat or merchant so inclined could find sexual companionship with a porter, houseboy, shop assistant or unemployed graduate, whom he might cruise outside a café or restaurant, in a shop or brothel. Money generally changed hands, and risks of theft, blackmail or notoriety awaited. Efforts to control 'pederastic' activities seem not to have been very intensive in the French Empire. (The British attitude towards homosexuality, as will be seen in the following chapters, was considerably harsher.)

Notes

1   His other works included *De l'Amour. Etude physiologique de l'amour normal et de ses abus, perversions, folies et crimes dans l'espèce humaine* (Paris, 1901), *Le Marquis de Sade et son oeuvre devant la science médicale et la littérature moderne* (Paris, 1901) and *L'Acte sexuel dans l'espèce humaine. Etude physiologique complète de l'amour normal et des abus, folies et crimes relatifs à l'instinct génital à travers les peuples et les âges* (Paris, 1931).

2   Jacobus X, *L'Art d'aimer aux colonies* (Paris, 1927 [1893]), especially pp. 54–62 and 67–78 (Cochin-China), 97–8 (Tonkin), 129 (Cambodia), 156 and 163–7 (Guiana), 255–6 (Africa), 300–7 *passim* (New Caledonia), 384 (Tahiti).

3   Jean Hervez, *Le Baiser: Baisers d'Orient* (Paris, 1922).

4   Anne de Colney, *L'Amour aux colonies* (Paris, 1932).

5   Hervez, pp. 52–3.

6   *Ibid.*, pp. 84–6.

7   De Colney, pp. 15, 18.

8   French doctors did worry about venereal disease in Vietnam, and traced some of it to homosexual practices. See, e.g., Dr Michaut, 'Syphilis et pédérastie, fumeurs d'opium et climat', *Bulletin général de thérapeutique médicale*, Vol. 61, No. 1 (January 1893), pp. 274–9.

Part I

Colonials and homosexuality

1   The sex life of explorers

Explorers, hardy adventurers on an unending quest for the unknown, and with remarkable endurance in the face of adversity, counted among the most famous heroes of imperialism. An eager public followed their expeditions in newspapers and rushed to buy accounts of their journeys, geographical societies fêted them and governments engaged them to 'push back the frontier' of imperialism and to collect intelligence for diplomatic manœuvres. Battling malaria and other tropical fevers, fighting head-hunting cannibals and bloodthirsty chieftains (as they would have put it), racing with imperial rivals to reach the fabled city of Timbuktu or to discover the source of the Nile, these men were quintessentially romantic figures of the imperial age. Scientific interest, a desire for fame and taste for adventure lured them overseas, and sometimes took them to their deaths.

Most explorers did not exactly fit into traditional European moulds. Some fled Europe, rejecting societies they considered degenerate, compatriots whom they judged flaccid, or political regimes at odds with their ideals. Private demons haunted others. By necessity, they gave up the comforts of European life for the ardours of exploration, most content when 'on the road'. They were, in general, solitary men, more at home in camp tents than drawing rooms, happier in the company of the men they recruited for their expeditions, and the porters, guides and bearers in their entourage, than among the armchair travellers who celebrated their exploits.

Explorers often married late and left their wives for long periods of solitude and worry before they came home. Some explorers declined marriage entirely and avoided entangling alliances with women. A few were certainly homosexual – Eigil Knuth, a great Danish explorer of Greenland, 'in his old age privately regretted that he did not at some point in his earlier life come out publicly as a homosexual'.[1] Evidence suggests that others were homosexually inclined, or that their most significant emotional attachments lay with men.[2] This chapter examines five of them, a German in South America, an Englishman in the Indian sub-continent, a Russian pioneer of Central Asia, another Englishman, who trekked through the Libyan Desert and the 'Empty Quarter' of Arabia, and one of the most famed of all explorers, Henry Morton Stanley. In each case, attraction to the company of other men contributed to the timing, itineraries or motivations of their imperial ventures.[3]

Humboldt and his friends

One explorer always involved in intense friendships with men, and the timing of whose departure for the overseas explorations that made his fame was determined by the failure of plans to settle down with his most intimate friend, was Alexander von Humboldt. 'The greatest scientific traveler who ever lived', according to Charles Darwin, Humboldt was a geographer, anthropologist and general man of science, author of thirty volumes of field studies and a five-volume *magnum opus*, *Cosmos* (1845 to 1862), an attempt to catalogue all human knowledge about the physical world.

Born into an aristocratic family in Berlin in 1769, Alexander's brother was Wilhelm von Humboldt, a renowned comparative linguist. The death of their father when Alexander was nine, and a difficult relationship with their distant, cold mother, marred the brothers' childhoods. Alexander studied in Freiburg, Frankfurt, Göttingen and Hamburg, and during a university holiday hiked around Europe with George Forster, the illustrator who accompanied Captain Cook to the South Seas. At twenty-two, Humboldt took a job as a government mines inspector in Franconia; his mother's death five years later left him with the money to pursue his desire to explore.

Humboldt frequented fashionable salons as a young man, flirting with young women who found him handsome and charming. He also formed close attachments to fellow male students. In 1794, he met Reinhardt von Haeften, a 21-year-old lieutenant who was stationed in Bayreuth, where Humboldt was working. Humboldt soon developed a fascination – 'crush' would be an appropriate term – with the young officer, revealed by the first extant letter he sent to his 'good dearly beloved Reinhardt' on 19 December: 'I hope on Christmas night to wrap my arms around your neck.' First, however, he had to visit Goethe, whose company he enjoyed and with whom he could have spent the holidays. But then,

> I would see you six days later, and such a loss I would not like for the whole world. Perhaps other men cannot understand this…I know, I live only for you, my good and unique Reinhardt, only in your company am I completely happy.

The next spring, Humboldt and Haeften travelled to Munich and Innsbruck, then on to Venice, Vicenza, Verona, Milan and Switzerland, a trip that Humboldt said he had organised largely for Haeften's benefit. He confessed to a woman friend his 'affinity' with this 'unique and excellent man', adding that he had experienced with Haeften such 'scenes of human existence as one lives through [only] one or two times'. Humboldt exulted in the 'sea of beatitude for me' that Haeften had expressed in a letter after their return.[4]

Humboldt concocted a plan to spend more time with Haeften, despite the lieutenant's romantic interest in a woman, then marriage. In 1797, Humboldt decided that he, his brother, Alexander's wife and three children, with Haeften and his wife and two children, should live together in Italy for several years. In January, he wrote to Haeften that over two years had passed since they had first met. Happy was the day that Haeften had expressed his friendship to Humboldt, who saw in him 'a man of such delicacy of sentiment and purity of soul [that] since that time I feel myself in full communion with you, united as by an iron lock'. More florid words followed about the strength and depth of a friendship that only death could end.

> With such shared sentiments we are working together for our common happiness. The most satisfying days of my life have been the last two years in that I was given this closeness to you, and even now feel growing in me each day this happiness.

Again he wrote:

> I never cease to bless the day when, for the first time, you opened yourself to me, and told me what a comfort you felt from it. I felt better myself in your presence and I was thenceforth linked to you by chains of steel. Even if you were to reject me and treat me coldly and disdainfully, I would still like to remain close to you, and I could thank heaven for having let me know, before my death, what two human beings can mean for one another. From day to day, my love and my attachment to you grow....The love I have for you is not just friendship or brotherly love, it is veneration, the recognition of a child, and devotion to your will is my most exalted law.[5]

Humboldt nevertheless empathised with Haeften's marital contentment:

> Now Christine [Haeften's wife] is yours, you have that which fundamentally characterises human happiness, a fine wife whom you love, and a friend [Humboldt himself] who would be happy to sacrifice his life if by doing so he could assure your perpetual tranquillity.

His feelings clearly stated, Humboldt detailed his plan. 'I know from experience that for you the greatest pleasure of all the delights in life is travel, the best way to cultivate the capacities of man and to give his mind new experiences of the world.' He suggested that the entourage of Haeftens and Humboldts spend six to eight months in Rome, Florence and Naples, then pass the cooler months travelling around the Italian peninsula and Sicily, staying on as long as Haeften would agree. The sojourn promised an idyllic time:

> What could be more important for you, my good and dearly beloved Reinhardt, that this experience in the fullness of your youth, broadening your mind by contact with excellent fellows? When you will meet noble delights, when the senses are stimulated by new objects and the character develops, raising itself to a feeling for the great and the morally beautiful, in a word, assuring us the sentiment of noble humanity. Oh! These years living with us in Italy will remain the richest in pleasure of your life.

Humboldt's letter also announced that he planned an expedition to America, but 'I will undertake it when you have decided whether to remain in Italy or to return to Germany after – as I hope – two or three years'.

Wilhelm von Humboldt was at first dubious about the arrangement, but Alexander convinced him to join the venture. As Alexander wrote to Haeften: 'My brother depends more on me than I do on him, and although he may not yet have found interest in you, nevertheless the thought that he cannot have me near him without you will bind him gratefully to you'.[6] So Haeften and his wife, and Wilhelm and his spouse, gathered their caravan of servants and carriages in Jena later in 1797. They proceeded to Dresden and Vienna, where they had to delay their trip because of unrest and war in Italy – a product of the French Revolution's shock effects. Wilhelm and his family continued on to Switzerland and France, while Alexander and the Haeftens spent the winter in Salzburg. By May 1798, the group reunited, the journey started again, but the party soon separated, though the reasons are unclear. Wilhelm's wife wrote enigmatically to a friend who had asked after the Haeftens: 'I have nothing new to say about them; they remain unchangeable people.'[7] Haeften and his wife returned to Germany. By October, Humboldt was in Spain to arrange his trip to America. The failure of the plan to live in Italy with Haeften pushed forward the expedition to America, where Humboldt would remain for the next five years.

Humboldt wrote to Haeften warmly before he left in early 1799 and continued to correspond with him afterwards, though many of his letters were lost on the way from South America to Europe. Those that remain testify to Humboldt's abiding affection for Haeften, although he was now being seduced by the new world:

> Believe me, my dear friend, man should not live just in Goch and in Bayreuth and in Erpath [Haeften's stomping-ground], but also in the tropics. What a delight! With each day I am more and more happy at having made the trip to this continent.

He described the landscape, his excursions into the jungle, the exoticism of the Indians, the pleasures of research, the collaboration with budding Spanish-American researchers, the fun of nightly dancing with the blacks. Humboldt's letters overflow with the transcendental delights of the tropics:

> My God! What a world of plants, birds with the most beautiful plumage, forests of mahogany, ebony, cedar, palm and brazilwood! What wonderful aromas! Butterflies as big as our Sperling, spiders that the hummingbirds devour....If you could just see, dear Reinhardt, the brightly-coloured hummingbirds, flamingos, all sorts of parrots, screamers and troupials that we can see in flocks around the gardens.[8]

While Humboldt was still in America, Haeften died in 1803, at the age of thirty. Humboldt only learned of his death some time afterwards, and wrote a rather stilted letter to his widow, in which he rambled on about Greek and Hebrew philosophies of life and death. Wilhelm, who read the message, told his own wife that he found his brother's letter moving but could not understand a word of it – 'You can gather from the contents of this letter that one is not closer to nature when one has retired from the civilised world,' he joked; Wilhelm added that his brother had acidly asked if Haeften's widow had already remarried.

Meanwhile in Ecuador, in 1802, Humboldt had taken up with a young American-born Spaniard, Francisco José de Caldas, an amateur astronomer. Humboldt was impressed with his work, and Caldas travelled for a while with Humboldt and his fellow scientist, Aimé Bonpland, helping them with geography and map-making. Caldas was overjoyed when Humboldt decided to use a map that he had drawn, and enthused to a correspondent about his ecstatic happiness in Humboldt's friendship. Caldas hoped to join Humboldt on the continuation of his expedition to Peru and Mexico, but his hopes were dashed when Humboldt refused to let him accompany the party. Caldas gathered that the refusal was because either the other explorers feared that he was not fit enough for the journey or that Humboldt found his company tedious – Caldas confessed that his reserve, shy temperament and pious sentiments separated him from the ebullient, light-hearted and irreverent Humboldt. Outwardly, the two remained on good terms. Humboldt continued to treat his protégé well, and Caldas accompanied him for a climb up a volcano – bragging that he thus proved himself strong and adventurous, no matter what others might think about him. In private Caldas impugned Humboldt's morals, accusing him of frequenting houses of 'obscene, dissolute love' in Quito (establishments 'where impure love reigned'), making friends with 'obscene, dissolute youths', giving vent to the 'shameful passions of his heart', 'mixing his debilities with the sublime efforts of science'. He complained that Humboldt had replaced him on the planned expedition by a young man who was 'ignorant, without principle and dissipated' – Humboldt had taken off 'with Bonpland and his Adonis'. Caldas did not give more details, but allusions to 'Venus having moved from Cyprus to this city [Quito]' suggest sexual misbehaviour, dissolution that offended the puritanical and dour young man. The denunciation, and the reference to the 'Adonis' whom Humboldt chose for his expedition instead of the rather plain Caldas, hint that Humboldt was keeping very suspect company indeed.

After returning to Europe, Humboldt spent several years teaching in Germany, then lived for two decades in France, working with a young scientist, François Arago (later director of the Paris Observatory). They met when Arago was twenty-five and Humboldt almost forty, and the relationship was intense, professionally and personally. When he travelled to Germany, Humboldt became distressed when Arago did not write often enough. After Arago was arrested for his radical politics following Louis Napoleon's *coup d'état* in 1851, Humboldt tried but failed to secure permission to visit him in prison; before his death in 1853, one of Arago's last expressed wishes was to see his German friend again. By then, Humboldt was an old man, living in Berlin and tended by a servant, Johann Seifert, and his wife. They had met earlier when Seifert, a well set-up former soldier, was a young man, and he accompanied Humboldt to Asia in 1829. The familiarity with which Seifert treated his master surprised visitors, and rumours circulated that one of his daughters was fathered by Humboldt. This was improbable, and it has been suggested that Seifert was Humboldt's lover.[9]

Was Humboldt homosexual? As for so many men of his age, a definite answer is impossible. A dream that he carefully recorded indicated, at least, sexual ambivalence. Humboldt dreamed that he had been reflecting on Alcibiades' maxim 'Reason and Virtue should be respected in men and venerated in women'. A handsome old man shook his hand, and asked Humboldt to follow him to a marvellous city, where he saw people wearing long cloaks that made it impossible to identify their sex. Humboldt was attracted to three who did look masculine. Two of the figures fled, and he then noticed that they were women. Afterwards, Humboldt saw on a roadway a child who had been raped by bandits. Strangers came to help the naked and injured creature, taking off their cloaks to cover it. Humboldt tried to look at one of the women and felt a transport of happiness, but turned away. The old man who had accompanied him told Humboldt that if he really wanted to see the woman, he should look at a picture he held, saying that Nature had made a mistake. The picture revealed the old man transformed into a young man, whom Humboldt said he wanted to clasp in his arms – but the vision vanished.[10]

Humboldt's most significant friendships were with men, particularly Haeften, and he nourished a veritable 'cult of friendship'.[11] His letters expressed a depth of affection remarkable even in a period of epistolary floridness.[12] Affairs with women, marriage, children – the usual markers of heterosexuality – are missing in Humboldt's life. Humboldt denigrated marriage for men like himself:

> I am convinced that the man who agrees to the yoke of marriage is a fool, and I would even say, a sinner. A fool because he gives up his own freedom, without gaining any corresponding compensation. A sinner because he then gives Life to children without being able to give them the certainty of happiness'.[13]

Whether he had sexual relations with Haeften will never be known. It is unlikely Humboldt envisaged a continuation of any physical relationship if they lived together in Italy surrounded by Haeften's wife and children. Perhaps Haeften had 'given in', later to shift his attentions to Christine. The end of the grand Italian plan remains mysterious. Did Haeften or his wife, or both of them, tire of Humboldt's overwrought affections and cloying patronage?

Mystery also surrounds Humboldt's life, as related by Caldas, in Quito. Exactly what sort of dissolute company was he keeping and why did Caldas find it so shocking? Why did Humboldt choose a handsome travelling companion rather than the worthy Caldas? Were Caldas's letters an attempt (though, in gentlemanly fashion, in private) to blacken Humboldt's reputation because of the slight, or might they bespeak the agony of one whose affections for Humboldt had been spurned? Back in Europe, how far did the intense emotional ties Humboldt have with Arago or Seifert go?

The timing of Humboldt's departure for America had a great deal to do with his plans for Haeften falling apart; had there been no political difficulties in going to Italy, or had the Haeften family not decided against following through with the plan, his expeditions would, at least, have been delayed. Humboldt's letters from South America, with lyrical descriptions of tropical nature, suggest that the disappointments at separation from Haeften were superseded by the pleasures of exploration. When Humboldt was most infatuated with Haeften, he put aside science for friendship. Before the first voyage to Italy with Haeften, he wrote: 'I am following him...obligingly enough. I would prefer to neglect certain of my scientific objectives rather than not being fully available to him during the first part of the trip.'[14] Yet Humboldt had written, presciently, at the age of twenty: 'I am ready to take my first steps in the world, without a guide and as a free man....No strong passion will drag on me. Serious subjects and above all the study of Nature will be a bullwark against sensuality.'[15]

It would be facile to argue that desire for the world of Nature replaced 'unnatural' desires that Humboldt felt, but the jungles of South America clearly gave Humboldt the elation he seemed not to find with women or a physical fulfilment consummated with men. As with other explorers, the terrain of travels – flora and fauna, the exotic locales, the often weird but fascinating habits of native populations, masculine camaraderie during the expedition – replaced the comforts of home and hearth, while close friends and the occasional 'Adonis' provided emotional plenitude.

Richard Burton and the Sotadic Zone

With Humboldt, friendship was privileged over sex, and the issue of homosexuality is implicit. With another figure, sex – at least observation and description of it – turned into an obsession, and discovery of exotic homosexuality was one of the results of exploration. Captain Sir Richard Francis Burton (1821–90) was one of the great imperial adventurers, his life spanning the nineteenth century, his travels covering South Asia and South America, the Middle East and Africa. Reputed to know twenty-five languages, famous for rivalry with John Hanning Speke to reach the source of the Nile, author of sixty books, recipient of numerous awards, a British consul, Burton was:

> the paradigm of the scholar-adventurer, a man who towered above others physically and intellectually, a soldier, scientist, explorer, and writer who for much of his life also engaged in that most romantic of careers, undercover agent.[16]

Contemporaries and present-day writers have found it hard to pin down Burton. For Frank McLynn he was an imperialist who took British culture to the globe, but did not hold a high view of imperialism. He entered fully into other cultures, but retained violent prejudices, particularly hatred of Africans. He travelled incessantly, yet did not seek financial reward or try to 'discover' new places – the journey more than the destination presented the major challenge and pleasure. He liked disguise, and left corners of his private life hidden.[17]

Burton's connection with homosexuality is twofold. When Burton served in India in 1845, the British commander of the Sind, General Sir Charles Napier, asked him to investigate certain rumours. In Burton's words:

> It was reported to him that Karachi…supported no less than three lupanars or bordels, in which not women, but boys and eunuchs, the former demanding nearly a double price, lay for hire.…Being then the only British officer who could speak Sindi, I was asked indirectly to make enquires and to report upon the subjects.

Napier expressed concern that some of his own officers frequented these brothels. Burton agreed to undertake the investigation, providing that his report not be sent to Napier's superiors in Bombay; he feared that his reputation with officials of the East India Company, in whose employ he served, would be compromised. Disguised as an Arabic merchant and benefiting from his linguistic abilities, Burton 'passed many an evening in the townlet, visited all the porneia and obtained the fullest details which were duly despatched to Government House'.[18] He found that many of the brothel clients were Indian princes, and that a full gamut of illicit sexual pleasures were on offer. Napier had the establishments closed. Burton later claimed that Napier had filed his report in his private papers.

Once Napier had left the Sind, Burton's rivals and enemies suggested that he had carried out his investigation a bit too enthusiastically, and Governor Auchmuty wanted him cashiered on grounds of moral turpitude. Burton was indeed denied the position of official East India Company interpreter for which he was clearly the most accomplished candidate. Disappointed, he left India in 1849 after seven years of residence. Accusations of improper conduct had besmirched Burton, though they may have had no basis. McLynn, taking the most interest of Burton's biographers in his sexual make-up, judges that:

> Burton seemed to enjoy his assignment to the Karachi brothels, which the average male would have shrunk from. More seriously, it seems a reasonable inference that Burton would not have obtained his detailed knowledge of the more lubricious varieties without participating himself'.[19]

Sexual practices, particularly non-standard ones, certainly fascinated Burton, as became most apparent in his rendition of *The Thousand and One Nights*. The vision of the sensual delights of the East made it a classic, but publication caused some to accuse Burton of translating filth. Only four episodes concerned homosexuality, but Burton appended a now famous 'Terminal essay', of which the fourth section, 'Pederasty', developed his notion of the Sotadic Zone. Burton argued that the cause of pederasty was 'geographical and climatic'. He located the Sotadic Zone in a band stretching from 43 degrees north of the equator to 30 degrees south, encompassing southern France, the Iberian peninsula, Italy and Greece, as well as the North African coast, running eastward to embrace Asia Minor, Mesopotamia and Chaldea, Afghanistan, the Sind, Punjab and Kashmir, thence broadening to include China and Japan, the South Sea Islands and the Americas.

> Within the Sotadic Zone the Vice is popular and endemic, held at the worst to be a mere peccadillo, whilst the races to the North and South of the limits here defined practice it only sporadically amid the opprobrium of their fellows who, as a rule, are physically incapable of performing the operation and look upon it with the liveliest disgust.[20]

Burton's essay constitutes an omnium gatherum of classical references and quotations, psychological speculation about masculine and feminine temperaments, linguistic pedantry and amateur anthropology. The idea of warm climates breeding sexual irregularity was not new nor was the association of pederasty with the Arabic and Asian worlds. His arguments lacked clarity – homosexuality was variously caused by temperament or climate, but Burton also blamed classical imperialism for having spread Greco-Roman mores: 'Roman civilization carried pederasty also to Northern Africa, where it took firm root, while the negro and negroid races to the South ignore the erotic perversion, except where imported by foreigners into such kingdoms as Bornu and Haussa.'[21] Much of Burton's material was second-hand, as when he reported a French traveller's accounts of the pederastic morals of the eighteenth-century Indian ruler Ranjit Singh.

Burton hardly expressed approval of 'the vice', either overseas or in Europe, although his account was free of the 'Bible-bashing' denunciation that homosexual behaviour provoked in many observers. His arguments continued, and promoted, ethnological speculations about diverse sexualities disseminated since the first age of exploration. The idea that homosexuality was endemic and climatically caused implied that, at some level, it was a natural occurrence rather than wilfully sinful behaviour. The publication of the 'Terminal essay' in 1885, just as sexologists were focusing on the issue of homosexuality, made a distinct contribution to discussions about sexual variance. By developing a hypothesis about the Sotadic Zone, Burton suggested that, for better or worse, many areas conquered by European imperialists were marked by the behaviour. Also implied, though Burton did not belabour the point, was the possibility that Europeans might themselves indulge when in the Sotadic Zone. Burton – repeating traditional rumours of white travellers being savaged by Oriental perverts – noted that 'a favourite Persian punishment for strangers caught in the

Harem or Gynaceum is to strip and throw them and expose them to the embraces of the grooms and negro slaves'. He cited the case of:

> a well-known missionary to the East during the last generation [who] was subjected to this gross insult by one of the Persian Prince-governors, whom he had infuriated by his conversion-mania; in his memoirs he alludes to it by mentioning his 'dishonoured person'.

Another case involved the Governor of Bushire, who 'used to invite European youngsters serving in the Bombay Marine and ply them with liquor till they were insensible. Next morning the middies mostly complained that the champagne had caused a curious irritation and soreness in la parte-poste' [*sic*]. Europeans could be raped, but they might simply be tempted to try renegade pleasures. Burton quoted a French nobleman describing the 'frightful pederastic excesses' among soldiers that followed the conquest of Algiers in 1830, fearing that the contagion might spread to civilians. [22]

With his personal investigation of male brothels in the 1840s and the insistent presentation of Sotadic sodomy forty years later, the obvious question is whether Burton was homosexual. He married a strait-laced, respectable and piously Catholic woman, Isabel Arundell, who, immediately after his death, burned Burton's journals and an almost completed 1,200-page manuscript, a translation of a Persian classic, *The Perfumed Garden*. Burton had said this was to be 'the crown of my life', and even Isabel admitted it would have been his *magnum opus*. The sexual nature of the work horrified Isabel, who throughout her marriage had been uncomfortable with Burton's interest in sexual matters around the world and worried by his notoriety. Only one chapter of the translation concerned homosexuality, but (as with *The Arabian Nights*) the manuscript included lengthy notes and commentaries on the subject, inspired by Burton's reading of Karl Heinrich Ulrichs, a German sexologist and homosexual emancipationist.

McLynn argues convincingly that Burton was bisexual. He was little socialised by his parents, and displayed a marked misogyny. Burton's writings made plain his view that women were evil sexual temptresses. The union with Isabel was a marriage of convenience and convention rather than love; she was a plain and appropriate wife rather than a seductive beauty, and tension fraught their relationship. Earlier in life, Burton had claimed to have been romantically struck by a young woman in India, and then to have planned to elope with a postulant at a convent in Goa; McLynn conjectures that Burton invented many details of these episodes. When he arrived in India, he had taken a concubine, as was the custom, but his sexual experiences were less than satisfactory.

By contrast, Burton enjoyed close friendships with men, beginning with his brother, then associates in India – Walter Scott, a dashing young soldier (nephew of the novelist), General Napier and John Steinhaeuser, an amateur Orientalist whom he met in Karachi and who suggested that he translate *The*

Arabian Nights. Burton regarded homosexual intercourse as natural, quoting an obscene quatrain to prove it: 'The penis smooth and round was made / with anus best to match it. / Had it been made for cunnus' sake, / it had been formed like a hatchet.' He preferred male to female beauty, writing in Africa:

> The male figure here, as all the world over, is notably superior, as amongst the lower animals, to that of the female. The latter is a system of soft, curved and rounded lines, graceful, but meaningless and monotonous. The former far excels it in variety of form and in sinew. In these lands, where all figures are semi-nude, the exceeding difference between the sexes strikes the eye at once. There will be a score of fine male figures to one female, and there she is, as everywhere else, as inferior as is the Venus de Medici to the Apollo Belvedere.[23]

Burton's interests in sexual practices were somewhat 'kinky', as well, with life-long fascination with genital size, circumcision, clitoridectomy and sado-masochism. His sexual practice was probably minimal. For McLynn, he 'sublimated his own feelings of inadequacy by turning sex into an academic and anthropological subject, something to be studied and discussed rather than practiced or participated in'. However, he despised 'the puritanism, igno-rance and Mrs Grundyism of Victorian society'.[24] Burton's sexual inadequacies and bisexuality, for McLynn, were repressed and transferred into explorations, writings and friendships: 'Many of the enigmas in Burton's life resolve them-selves plausibly on this hypothesis, his marriage, his male friendships and much else.'[25]

Burton's proclivities played a crucial role at several turning points in his life – investigating Indian brothels (and having career advancement thwarted because of it), writing about homosexuality and articulating a theory of Sotadic love. McLynn also hypothesises that sex (in repressed form) might have been connected with Burton's friendship, then rivalry, with Speke. Speke, according to McLynn, was a repressed homosexual and there was an 'unconscious homo-sexual attraction initially drawing Speke and Burton together'. After their falling out, 'Speke seemed to sense that the unconscious bond between himself and Burton was sexual. In a masterpiece of projection he later claimed that Burton had made advances to him during the expedition to the lakes in eastern Africa'. As further evidence, McLynn cites the work of Laurence Oliphant – a 29-year-old travel writer, whom McLynn conjectures was also homosexual. Oliphant:

> listened to Speke's embittered account of his turbulent relationship with Burton, and persuaded the older man that Burton's actions were evidence of a desire for a sexual relationship with him. Jealous of the motives he attributed to Burton by transference – for it was Oliphant who *consciously* wanted such a liaison with Speke – he turned the screw of Speke's Burtonmania a notch tighter.[26]

This led Speke to mount a campaign against Burton, and to claim for himself his discoveries in Africa, from 1859 onwards; Oliphant goaded Speke into denigrating Burton, attacking him as un-English and hinting that Burton was homosexual.

McLynn's analysis of Burton, and his relationship with Speke, relies on extrapolations from fragmentary evidence, as well as acceptance of the notions of psychological repression, sublimation and projection. (Perhaps more controversial is McLynn's assumption that both Speke's and Burton's childhoods, marked by strong mothers and ineffectual fathers, helped determine their sexual orientations, and that the failure of Burton's love-making with a Gujerati concubine turned him towards masculine friendships.) The account is nevertheless hardly implausible and cogently links episodes in Burton's life with the destruction of his private papers by an unloved and scandalised Isabel.

Burton remains a prototype of the nineteenth-century explorer with an obsessive desire to visit places unknown to Europeans, interest in the habits (including sexual behaviour) of natives, delight in living in foreign places – and also, like Humboldt, in ambivalent sexuality. His Karachi brothel-visits illustrated the temptations European men faced in the tropics, and concerns that right-minded officials held about their men giving in to temptation. Burton's academic work resurrected exaltation of same-sex attraction in Eastern poetry,[27] while his notion of the Sotadic Zone provided an important (though now discounted) contribution to the widespread theorising at the end of the nineteenth century about the aetiology of homosexuality.

The Russian explorer: Nikolay Przhevalsky

The third example of a sexually ambivalent explorer is a racist and misogynistic 'closet case' whose selection of travelling companions, more than choice of destinations, betrays his homosexual inclinations. Nikolay Przhevalsky (1839–88) was born in Russian Poland. An army officer, he explored Siberia, then made seven arduous expeditions to Central Asia, exploring China, Mongolia and Tibet (though he never realised his dream of visiting Lhasa, the Tibetan capital). Przhevalsky published several books, gave popular lectures, brought back 16,000 specimens to St Petersburg and discovered a new species of Mongolian horse (named in his honour). Medals and grants came from the Imperial Geographical Society and the Russian government, and Tsar Alexander II enthusiastically supported his work. On Przhevalsky's death, in Central Asia, Chekhov wrote: 'One Przhevalsky or one Stanley is worth a dozen polytechnics and a hundred good books.'[28] Characterised as a 'ruthless conquistador and misanthropic scientist', Przhevalsky was one of Russia's greatest explorers.[29]

Przhevalsky had no great love for the Asians among whom he travelled. He particularly disliked the Chinese, finding in Beijing 'unimaginable filth and stench' and rejecting Chinese food as unpalatable. 'In my opinion only rifles and cannons of the Europeans can do any good here,' he concluded, and considered fomenting a Buddhist and Muslim rebellion against the Confucian government. From Central Asia, he wrote:

> Here you can penetrate anywhere, only not with the Gospels under your arm, but with money in your pocket, a carbine in one hand and a whip in the other. Europeans must use these to come here and bear away in the name of civilisation all these dregs of the human race. A thousand of our soldiers would be enough to subdue all Asia from Lake Baykal to the Himalayas....Here the exploits of Cortez can still be repeated.[30]

Central Asia would provide *Lebensraum* for Russian colonists, and the tsar should challenge the British in the Indian sub-continent, establish bases in East Asia and even provoke war with China if necessary to secure Russia's interests. As Russia fought Turkey in 1878, played the Great Game with Britain in the Himalayas and pressed into Manchuria, Przhevalsky stood as a major promoter and agent of Russian imperialism.

Przhevalsky never married and disliked women, except for his mother and a beloved and ever-faithful nanny. On his travels, he was always accompanied by young assistants, from whom he demanded absolute loyalty but on whom he showered attention. Przhevalsky recruited a 17-year-old, Robert Koecher, for his first expedition in 1866 (when he was twenty-seven), but dismissed him a year later when Koecher announced plans to marry; according to Donald Rayfield, 'It was not the last time that a woman unwittingly deprived Prezhevalsky of his travelling companion; he never forgave the sex.'[31] The replacement was Nikolay Yagunov, a poor 16-year-old typography apprentice, whom Przhevalsky later sent to a military college in Warsaw. His next companion, Mikhail Pyltsov, became so close that he spent Christmas with Przhevalsky and his mother in 1873; Przhevalsky took his marriage with better grace that that of the earlier companion. The successor was Fyodor Eklon, an 18-year-old museum technician whom Przhevalsky taught to ride, shoot and prepare specimens. Przhevalsky planned to take Eklon and Yagunov on a further expedition, but Yagunov's death in a swimming accident left the explorer badly shaken. He recruited a new assistant, Yevgraf, and warned Eklon: 'I know you'll be great friends, but then you will be thrashed together. Of course that won't happen often, but all the same it will occur – nobody's perfect.'[32] In kinder moments, he wrote affectionate letters to Eklon when they were separated, counselling him to take walks, not to skimp on spending the money Przhevalsky provided and not to deny himself sweets. Unfortunately, the new companion proved incompetent, and Przhevalsky sent him home, recording that 'I found it hard to take the decision. Yevgraf is very fond of me personally and he is a good soul....Yesterday evening and this morning I cried several times like a child.'[33]

The expedition successful, Przhevalsky and Eklon returned home in 1880, and Eklon recommended military studies. Their correspondence continued, with Przhevalsky's letters, according to Rayfield, 'full of awkward tenderness and solicitude'. Przhevalsky cautioned Eklon: 'Carriages, fast horses, beaver coats, familiarity with ladies from the demi-monde – all this, by progressive stages, can lead to an undesirable, if not lamentable, end.'[34] Eklon nevertheless drifted away from Przhevalsky, and begged off from the next expedition on account of his mother's ill health; Przhevalsky sent a fond but formal letter of commiseration. When Eklon told Przhevalsky of plans to marry, the explorer rushed to visit and a row ensued; after eight years, their partnership ended with a farewell letter from Eklon and a terse note from Przhevalsky agreeing to pay Eklon for the expedition materials he had accumulated.

Przhevalsky found another companion, thanks to the help of his nanny. Pyotr Kozlov, who had been working in a distillery, was soon ensconced at Przhevalsky's house, and became 'the young man who had been eluding [Przhevalsky] all his life: alert, submissive, loyal and handsome'. Kozlov, later a well-respected explorer himself, recalled his mentor in words bespeaking his attachment: 'At the sight of that man from afar, having him close to me, something extraordinary used to happen. His figure, his movements, his voice, his aquiline head were not like other people's; the deep gaze of his strict, handsome blue eyes seemed to penetrate right into your soul.'[35] Other comrades entered Przhevalsky's entourage as well. For one, he set aside a room in his house; he burst into tears when he bade another good-bye. Kozlov, however, was with Przhevalsky when he died in 1888, and in 1905 realised Przhevalsky's dream of meeting the Dalai Lama in Lhasa.

Przhevalsky's English-language biographer reveals no evidence of sexual relations with his companions, and the explorer, even from student days, was puritanical. His dislike of women, emotional reactions when his companions abandoned him for wives, the gifts and money he lavished on a succession of handsome young men and the highly emotional attachment he showed to them suggest strong and exclusive commitment to his protégés. Whether he was physically homosexual, heterosexual, bisexual or – as may well be the case – asexual, liaisons with young men clearly counted among his most important relationships.

Stanley and Kalulu

The choice of companions, both European and foreign, indicates homosexual emotional desires in the case of Henry Morton Stanley, while the sole novel he wrote provides a *mise-en-scène* of an exotic homosexual romance. No explorer was so famous in the late nineteenth century as Stanley, the man who 'found' Dr David Livingstone, helped carve out an empire for the King of Belgium, won a knighthood from Queen Victoria and served in parliament; his accounts of expeditions became instant best-sellers, and for thirty years he was a worldwide celebrity. This represented an extraordinary accomplishment for someone born, in 1841, in Wales, the illegitimate son of a woman of suspect morals and an unknown father. John Rowlands (his real name) was left in the care of a grandfather, on whose death the 6-year-old was boarded out, then cruelly told that he was going to live with an aunt but dumped in a workhouse. His experiences there were probably not so awful as Stanley made out – he got a reasonable education and was a favourite of the director – but life in the establishments made infamous by Dickens was lonely and hard. Upon leaving the workhouse, Stanley worked at odd jobs, before finding employment as a cabin boy on a ship to North America. In New Orleans, he was befriended by a Mr Stanley, whose name he adopted, and his fortunes took a turn. After a few adventurous years travelling and serving in both the Confederate and Union armies during the American Civil War, Stanley landed a job as a journalist, winning acclaim for reports from the American West. The editor of the *York Herald* in 1871 assigned him to 'find Livingstone', to search for the famous Scottish missionary in Central Africa. The mission was accomplished – and probably the best-known words in colonial history uttered – when Stanley reached Ujiji and asked, 'Dr Livingstone, I presume?'

Fêted in Europe and America, Stanley within a few years set out on an even more ambitious expedition that, from 1874 to 1877, took him from the eastern to the western coast of Africa along the Congo River, a trek so arduous that all three of his English fellow travellers, and several African porters, paid with their lives. The journey added greatly to geographical knowledge of equatorial Africa, and paved the way for King Leopold II to establish a personal colony more than seventy times the size of Belgium. In the late 1880s Stanley again led a major expedition, this time in the Sudan, to rescue an Austrian adventurer, Emin Pasha, who had got himself appointed as a local governor, and then got himself into strife. Lecture tours, honours and what might now be called imperial 'consultancies' followed before Stanley's death in 1904.

Stanley charted his explorations in diaries and journals, and wrote up his adventures in fast-paced, highly descriptive books – *How I Found Livingstone*, *Through the Dark Continent* and *In Darkest Africa* – which brought home the 'darkest continent' to armchair travellers, recounting battles against cannibals and fierce warriors, tsetse flies and leeches, raging rivers and murderous water-falls, malaria and smallpox, almost unbearable fatigue and gut-wrenching scarcities of food and water. So popular were the books that Thomas W. Knox put together a one-volume condensed version of *Through the Dark Continent*, called *The Boy Travellers on the Congo*, part of a successful series for juveniles. Two chums, Frank and Fred, on a ship from America to England, are able thus to read the highlights of Stanley's work to their enthralled companions, watched over by another passenger, none other than Stanley himself.

One book that Stanley wrote, however, is now forgotten. Even biographers devote only a few lines to the volume, and some cite its title wrongly. The book, a novel, was *My Kalulu: Prince, King and Slave*, sub-titled *A Story of Central Africa*, published in 1873. Stanley wrote it after his return from finding Livingstone, partly during a lecture tour in the United States, where he was accompanied by a young African whose name, Kalulu, Stanley gave to his novel.

The first pages introduce Selim, a 15-year-old Zanzibari 'Arab', 'whose appearance at once challenged attention from his frank, ingenuous, honest face, his clear complexion, his beautiful eyes, and the promise which his well-formed graceful figure gave of a perfect manhood in the future'. Selim wants to accompany his father Amer on a three-year expedition to East Africa to hunt for ivory and slaves; and Selim 'fled unregretfully the pleasant days of the harem, memories of his romps with girls, days upon days of effeminate life'. Adventures begin with an encounter with a crocodile, then an attack by intruders; Simba the slave saves Selim, who pledges his friendship. Soon battles rage between Zanzibaris and Africans, who kill Selim's father and take him prisoner. They strip and beat him, and the African leader takes Selim as his slave. During a march through the jungle, Selim escapes and manages to kill a lion before collapsing with fatigue, hunger and thirst. Meanwhile, Simba and another Zanzibari slave, Moto, also escape and seek help; by chance the son of a chieftain, Kalulu, is a young man whom Moto once saved in battle. Kalulu embraces Moto, and his father agrees to intercede for the release of Selim and the other Arabs.

Stanley devotes more than two pages to a description of 'Prince' Kalulu, cast in the mould of Antiquity:

> Kalulu was one of the best specimens which the ancient sculptors would have delighted to imitate in stone. His face or head may not, perhaps, have kindled any very great admiration, but the body, arms, and limbs were unmistakeably magnificent in shape. He had not an ounce of flesh too much, yet without the tedious training which the modern athlete has to undergo, and following nothing but the wild instinct of his native tribe, he was a perfect youthful Apollo in form. The muscles of his arms stood out like balls, and the muscles of his legs were as firm as iron.

Repeating the word 'Apollo', Stanley emphasises the ideal embodied in this new black god decorated with ivory bracelets, ostrich plumes and beaded hair.

The narrative resumed, a search party sent out by Kalulu's father comes upon the exhausted Selim and brings him back to the camp. Kalulu nurses him until he regains consciousness. The two become instant friends, their mutual attraction expressed in lyrical outbursts, and after five days the friendship is consecrated by a ceremony of blood brotherhood.

Lion hunts and comradely bliss follow, but Kalulu has new duties when he inherits his father's throne. Kalulu offers Selim anything he desires, including a wife, but the Zanzibari says that he must return home. A distraught Kalulu importunes him to stay a little longer. As the young men engage in daily amusements and talk late into the night, Ferodia, erstwhile ally of Kalulu's father, in a surprise *coup*, seizes the village, captures the two friends and vows to kill Kalulu. The Arabs' faithful slaves, including ever-loyal Simba, free Kalulu and Selim, who invites his friend to visit Zanzibar so that he can meet Selim's mother. The pair first sail to another island for an Arcadian idyll that gives them a chance for a philosophical discourse on beauty. Suddenly a hostile tribe attacks and takes them prisoner, but they escape during a flood. They brave attacks by leopards and yet another belligerent tribe.

During a peaceful interlude, when the party go fishing, Kalulu wanders off and is taken captive by a group of Arabs; he protests in vain that he is Selim's 'brother' and is sold into slavery. Back at camp, Kalulu's friends, especially Selim, are alarmed at his disappearance. Fearing Kalulu lost forever, Selim delivers a eulogy and instructs his entourage that they must move on. Selim eventually reaches Zanzibar, where joyful reunion with his mother is tempered by sadness at the loss of his friend. Then a miracle occurs – Selim sights Kalulu, 'King of Watuta', for sale in a slave market. Selim has Kalulu freed and, in scenes of ecstasy, invites him to stay in the family palace until they can marshal forces to fight Ferodia and reconquer Kalulu's realm. The book closes with Selim's presentation to his mother, 'Behold my brother, MY KALULU!' Initially dubious, she is won over, 'To thee, knowing as I do that thou hast suffered much, I shall be as a mother, and thou shalt be MY KALULU!'

High adventure, an improbable plot and maudlin verbiage mark Stanley's book, which is intended as a moral fable, as he announced in the preface: 'This book has been written for…those clever, bright-eyed, intelligent boys, of all classes, who have begun to be interested in romantic literature, with whom educated fathers may talk without fear of misapprehension.' The imperative for soft boys to turn themselves into strong men, values of bravery and endurance, and the sacredness of loyalty and friendship are lessons young readers are meant to learn. The evils of slavery – the book is dedicated 'to all those who have aided in the suppression of slavery on the east coast of Africa' – and the implicit mandate for Europeans to stamp out barbaric practices are the political lessons imparted. Europeans are nevertheless absent in the book, highlighting the savage nature of a continent filled with warriors and slave-traders, lions and leopards, jungles and floods – visions that Stanley's career and writing did much to create.

Stanley's descriptions of male characters linger on their physical beauty, though he carefully points out that both Selim and Kalulu are handsomer than many Arabs and Africans – Selim has a lighter coloured skin ('like unto that of rich cream') than most Zanzibaris. As for Kalulu:

> If I give him such praise for his elegance of form and free graceful carriage, I may not continue in the same strain in the description of his face. Kalulu was a negro, but his colour was not black by any means, it was a deep brown or bronze. His lips were thick, and, according to our ideas, such as would not lend beauty to his face; his nose was not flat, neither was it as correct in shape as we would wish it.

Such words embody typical racialist ideas, but Stanley nevertheless endows his heroic characters with strength of both body and character.

The descriptions suggest ambiguity in Selim. In Zanzibar, a foreigner remarks: 'Thou appearest to me to be like a little girl whose mother bathes her in new milk every day to preserve her complexion'; eager for adventure, Selim quits his mother's quarters 'happy as he had been with his feminine playmates, proud as he had been of his golden tassels and embroidery'. Before meeting

Kalulu, Selim is 'the dreamy boy with the poet's head, who chose solitudes, forests, and the depths of tall corn-stalks to indulge in reverie'. When black slaves praise his beauty, another boy mocks, 'Is Selim, the son of Amer, turned a girl, that his ears court such music?' Selim, in the mean time, shows himself sensitive to the beauties of nature, begins to question the institution of slavery and fraternises with slaves to a greater degree than seems appropriate. Emotional traits that Stanley paints on Selim's portrait differ little from characteristics associated with mother's boys, sissies, artistic types and others considered sexually suspect at Stanley's time (and later). Even at the end of the book, having proved himself a warrior and wise man, Selim returns to his palace and his mother, bringing home his companion.

Simba, 'the embodiment of a black Mars' and 'the bronze Achilles of war', exemplifies rough-hewn masculinity; after saving Selim in an ambush, 'The boy turned his large bright eyes upon Simba's face, which glowed with honest pride and affection, and then they measured the giant limbs, the tremendous arms, and the broad heaving chest.' Kalulu represents physical perfection (except, perhaps, for that African face), an antique statue incarnated. In a passage that both recapitulates Greek ideas and ennobles the African, Stanley says:

> Since ancient Greece displayed the forms of her noblest, finest youth in Olympic games, and gave her Phidias and Praxiteles models to immortalise in marble, all civilised nations have borrowed their ideals of manly beauty from statues left to us by Grecian and Roman sculptors, because civilised nations seldom can furnish us with models to compete with superexcellent types designed by Greece…[but] the centre of Africa teems with finer specimens of manhood than may be found in this world; such types as would even cause the marble forms of Phidias to blush.

Long lyrical passages about African warriors, coupled with the absence of women, create a homosocial and homoerotic ambiance.

Episodes of homoerotic voyeurism occur throughout the novel. After the Africans capture and strip the Zanzibaris, 'when they saw the pale and clean colour of their bodies, the fierce Watuta gathered about them'. Naked, roped together with his companions, indignant Selim complains of being 'stripped of my clothing to have my modest youth shocked by the unbelievers' rude gaze'. When he first meets one of the Arabs, an African king 'placed his hand on his shoulders, and marvelled at their softness; and then toyed with the boy's hair'. The king replies to Kalulu's requests for clothing for the still unclad Selim: 'What needs he cover his nakedness, boy? He looks fair and clean enough without anything. He is not a girl.'

The relationship between Selim and Kalulu, even given the overwrought prose, is remarkable. The youths complement each other in physique and character, weather extraordinary difficulties and save each other's lives. Through Kalulu, Selim learns about the horrors of slavery and the slave-trading practised by his own family; Kalulu will gain an introduction to Arabic culture, and may regain his throne, thanks to Selim. Their continual embracing, and the exclusive nature of their bonds, point towards a union surpassing the usual bounds of friendship. The ceremony of brotherhood between Selim and Kalulu takes the form of boys' secret oaths, but also mimics a Christian wedding with vows and an exchange of presents. Stanley introduces the ceremony:

> Here the author may remark, for the benefit of the younger readers, that a close brotherhood among men or boys, unrelated by blood, birth, or marriage, is in no way singular. I need but mention David and Jonathan, Achilles and Patroclus, Damon and Pythias, as examples among men; and what boy of any nation, in any public school, has not some friend who is as dear to him as a born brother?

Reference to public school mateship and its subliminal sexual tension is blatant, and the allusion to classical couples taken as models of homosexual partnerships is even more patent. At his investiture ceremony as king, Kalulu 'stood before them in the now bright moonlight, graceful as a dusty Ganymede', another reference to a quintessential homosexual hero. Selim and Kalulu's adoption into each other's cultures, and the ways in which they phrase their new kinship – '"I shall love all Arabs for thy sake for ever....Where I shall be, there shalt thou be"' – recall the biblical bonds between Ruth and Naomi, and Selim's mother's adoption of Kalulu as her son echoes Christ's request from the cross that his mother take his 'beloved disciple' John as her son. Such evocations were hardly unfamiliar to Victorian readers.

My *Kalulu*, an edifying tale for Victorian boys, may be read as an idealised homosexual love story in an exotic setting, filled with recognisable classical and biblical allusions, and complete with a 'they lived happily ever after' conclusion. Perhaps it represented the ideal romance that Stanley never found in his own life.

Stanley's other writings give little hint of the romantic and sexualised nature of the novel. Young European companions on his adventures, such as John and Edward Pocock, are described no more daringly than as 'stalwart...adventurous lads...two very likely-looking young men'. The occasional mention of 'half-naked porters' or an African singer, a 'young, handsome, and stalwart Corypheus', would hardly have raised a Victorian eyebrow, nor (except to initiates) would a slightly more *risqué* evocation of a chieftain's beautiful sons: 'The sculptor might have obtained from any of these royal boys a dark model for another statue to rival the classic Antinous.'[36]

Though transformed in the novel, Kalulu and Selim were real figures from Stanley's African trips. Selim was one of Stanley's bearers or interpreters, a sturdy-looking fellow he recruited in Zanzibar. Stanley identified Kalulu in the preface to his novel as the boy 'who accompanied me from Central Africa to England', adding that some features in his fictional character derived from a chieftain whose exploits were related by a guide. The fictional Kalulu is significantly older than the real one, a strapping adolescent, almost an adult.

Stanley's diaries contain little on Kalulu and Selim – the diaries, incidentally, have nothing on his novel. Selim, possibly a Christian Palestinian from Jerusalem, was paid one pound a month for his work. Stanley occasionally became annoyed with Selim, whose tasks were carried out 'with his usual carelessness'; Stanley had Selim flogged on one occasion 'for stealing the sugar, and then aggravating the offence by the most obstinate lying'. A few days later Selim again suffered a flogging for eating forbidden fruit, which prolonged an attack of dysentery; Stanley was worried enough about his illness to record Selim's condition regularly over a fortnight. Stanley also directed another employee to sew a pair of twill bags for Selim, who 'wants some clothes very badly'.[37]

Kalulu joined Stanley in Tabora (on his way to find Livingstone), a young slave given as a present by an Arab merchant. Not finding his original name, Ndugu M'hali ('my brother's fortune'), attractive, Stanley asked for help selecting another name. One African, 'after looking at his quick eyes, and noting his celerity of movement, pronounced the name Ka-lu-lu [the name for the young of the blue-black antelope], "because" said he, "just look at his eyes, so bright! Look at his form, so slim! watch his movements, how quick! Yes, Kalulu is his name".' Stanley agreed and, 'water being brought in a huge tin pan, Selim, who was willing to stand godfather, holding him over the water', Stanley performed a mock baptism, 'Let his name henceforth be Kalulu, and let no man take it from him.'[38] Kalulu quickly displaced other servants as his favourite:

> He understands my ways and mode of life exactly. Some weeks ago he ousted Selim from the post of chief butler by sheer diligence and smartness. Selim, the Arab boy, cannot wait at table. Kalulu – young antelope – is frisky. I have but to express a wish and it is gratified. He is a perfect Mercury, though a marvellously black one.

Kalulu became an adopted son for Stanley, who nevertheless once referred to him as 'my infant cannibal'.[39]

In 1872, Stanley took Kalulu to Europe and America. Because of a missed ship connection, they stayed for a month in the Seychelles and there, and later in London, Kalulu was photographed with Stanley. The posed studio photographs are stiff and heroic compositions with Stanley dressed in tropical gear and holding a gun. Kalulu, barely tall enough to reach Stanley's shoulder, is barefoot and dressed in a colourful floor-length sarong-type garment. In one photograph, he holds onto a gun standing on the floor next to him, shyly turning away from the camera; in another, he looks directly at the lens and in yet another, which includes Selim, the African and the Palestinian carry guns on their shoulders, while Stanley shoulders a reversed rifle.

Stanley recorded two 'amusing experiences with the black boy' in Europe. As the train from Marseilles to Paris entered a tunnel, a frightened Kalulu hid under the seat: 'Kalulu thought that the white man's country was very strange in this abrupt ending of day and thunderclap fall of darkness.' Kalulu's reaction to shrieking train whistles 'proved that his nerves were being severely tried'. Stanley and Kalulu dined at the train station in Lyons, and, recorded Stanley, 'He behaved very nicely and handled his knife and fork remarkably well. He was rather too free with the mustard, so much so that his eyes watered profusely.' Kalulu was even more shocked with his first taste of ice cream: 'He bravely swallowed it and then complained that it was too hot. "Gently, Kalulu, take it little by little, and drink some water." The curious expression on his face and manifest distrust of ice cream created merriment among every passenger.'[40]

Kalulu was a hit in Paris, talking about Africa and showing off to society ladies. According to one contemporary,

> Kalulu never allows his admiration to overstep his patriotism. His native Chambezi is ever to him the finest of rivers, and his description of its beauties and amenities represent it to be vastly more civilised than the most advanced districts of England. Since his introduction to French society his mental powers have been rather taxed but so far he has proved equal to the occasion. His first taste of wine, combined with the excitement of travelling by express, made him a decidedly hilarious companion.[41]

After their success on the Continent, Stanley and Kalulu moved on to England. Stanley was mortified to see his unloved and intoxicated half-brother and a cousin awaiting them when their ship docked: 'What little Kalulu must have thought of my drunken relatives I do not know.' Nevertheless, Stanley was a celebrity and Kalulu sat on stage during his lectures, attended banquets (dressed in European clothes), modelled for a statue in Madame Tussaud's museum, took tea with titled personages and otherwise provided a colourful accompanist. When Livingstone died, Kalulu walked with Stanley behind the coffin at the funeral service in Westminster Abbey.

Stanley's lecture tour continued in America, where Kalulu 'would obligingly perform parlour tricks, such as imitating a Muslim at prayer, performing tribal dances, and singing in Swahili' at dinner parties.[42] After the transatlantic return, Kalulu visited Wales with Stanley, who was embarrassed when his protégé lost a footrace to their hosts' daughter. In 1873, when Stanley went to Spain on assignment for the *New York Herald*, he placed Kalulu in a private school operated by a clergyman in Wandsworth; the master reported that Kalulu was clever and making progress reading English. The next year, Stanley and Kalulu were reunited, and Stanley took him on expedition back to Africa. Kalulu once tried to desert, a heinous crime in Stanley's eyes; Stanley sent a servant after him and briefly put Kalulu into slave chains when he was recaptured. The boy soon returned to Stanley's good graces. By 1877, Stanley wrote to a friend: 'You would wonder to see how tall he is grown, he has shot up like a palm tree.' Later in the expedition, along with several of Stanley's other companions, both European and African, Kalulu accidentally died when a boat drifted into rapids in the Congo River. Stanley wrote:

> My heart aches sorely...but it is such a dangerous career we now run, accidents are so numerous and daily, and I myself run daily three or four startling adventures, that we scarcely have space or time to wail or weep. Peace to them, and I pray we may have it (for it is a sad life) when we die.[43]

Stanley named Kalulu Falls in his young companion's honour.

Stanley's attitude towards Kalulu was stern and paternal, though ambivalent – he took his 'adopted son' overseas, like a good father, though most fathers do not put their sons into chains, even if only as a brief punishment. The tone of Stanley's writing about the youth in his non-fiction is parental, while in My *Kalulu* it is eroticised. Stanley's own sexuality is clouded, but has fascinated biographers, who, however, have not generally commented on the homoerotic nature of his novel. For Frank McLynn, Stanley never lost his shame at being an illegitimate child and this 'led to his later notorious difficulty in coming to terms with sexuality'. It is probable that he was sexually assaulted, or raped, by the headmaster in the workhouse where he spent part of his childhood.[44] Indeed, an 1847 report of the Board of Education about St Asalph's home remarked that adult male inmates 'took part in every possible vice', and added that children, generally sleeping two to a bed, an older with a younger one, 'from the very start...were beginning to practise and understand things they should not'.[45] Not unusually Stanley became attached to school fellows, writing fondly of one – who died when they were in school together – in particular. In New Orleans, a friend took Stanley to a brothel, but he fled when prostitutes entered. In his autobiography, Stanley recounted sharing a room and bed with a cabin boy he did not realise was really a girl, but McLynn suspects that Stanley may have concocted the story. 'The true significance of the tale,' McLynn comments, 'is Stanley's uncertainty about his *own* sexual identity.' Stanley never got on with women, and even disliked them, confiding:

> To me who to tell the truth never was a great admirer of women, who looked upon them as natural enemies to mankind, idlers of valuable time, pretty excuses for man's universality, toys to while slow time, heirs to a man's fame, to me who regarded them with that special concern a man should look upon movable talkable trifling human beings.[46]

When Stanley eventually married, as appropriate for a Victorian gentleman, it was a companionate union.

Throughout his life, Stanley made close friends of men his age or younger. On the first trip to America, he took up with another shipboy, Lewis Noe, whom he convinced to desert. After spending time in New York, they parted company and Noe enlisted in the Union Army. They met again in 1866, and Stanley suggested a tour to Turkey and Central Asia, India, China and the Pacific. A third young man, William Harlow Cook, joined them. The adventurers sailed to Izmir, Turkey, and set out, but soon encountered difficulties. Noe apparently set fire to some brush, which angered local peasants, and the men had to flee. Stanley, angered at his friend's antics, punished him – 'a few strokes of a switch', in Stanley's words were, according to Noe, more rigorous: Stanley stripped him to the waist, tied him to a tree and 'scourged me with a whip until the blood ran from my wounds'. Soon another misadventure befell the travellers. Stanley's version was that they were attacked by ruffians, whose leader made sexual overtures to Noe; Stanley then hit the Turk with the flat of his sword, and the ruffians dragged Noe and him to captivity. According to Noe, however, Stanley tried to murder a Turk whom they met on the highway, with the intention of stealing his horses. The Turk escaped to ambush Stanley and Noe, taking them prisoner. Whatever the true account, they agreed on what happened next, though they explained it differently. Noe recounted: 'The first night of our imprisonment I was taken out by three of the Turks and treated in a shocking manner'; Stanley confided to his diary, 'Mr. Cook and myself were beaten, Louis [*sic*], a boy of 17, was —', scratching out the final word. Elsewhere, he said that the Turks 'had no pity or remorse but one by one they committed their diabolical crime which is, I think, or I hope, unknown to civilized nations, especially Christian America'. In short, it appears, Noe was raped. The traumatised travellers (whose money and belongings had been lost) made their way to Constantinople, where the American minister came to their aid. Soon Stanley and Noe left Cook to testify in the trial of their abductors, and took a ship to Marseilles, abandoning the plans for a world tour.[47]

The experience, understandably, may have made Stanley view homosexual physical relations with horror, but did not daunt his enthusiasm for young companions. In 1869, only a few years after the Turkish incident, he became attached to Edwin Swift Balch, the 13-year-old son of a host in Paris. He disliked Paris, but enjoyed trips to the tourist sites in Balch's company: 'One is bound to wonder whether it was Paris or Edwin that Stanley really wanted to see,' one writer has commented. Stanley invited Balch to the Middle East and India, but his parents refused to consent.[48] Stanley did find other travel companions – not surprisingly, considering the rigours of African journeys, they were young and robust. Later, in London, Stanley, then in his forties, shared a flat with a Congolese boy named Baruti (about whom little is known) and a 17-year-old Englishman, William Hoffman, who would join him on the expedition to rescue Emin Pasha. Another member of that expedition was an Anglo-Irish man, Arthur Mounteney Jephson, whose aunt, the Countess of Noailles, had contributed a thousand pounds to the expedition. When Stanley married, he took Jephson with him and his wife on the honeymoon in Switzerland (where, incidentally, they met Richard Burton).

Such companionship does not prove that Stanley was homosexually inclined. He was uncomfortable with matters sexual, never wrote about sex and seems to have felt horror at physical relations. His first potential adult experiences with the opposite sex – finding that a cabin-mate was a female, and being taken to a brothel – left him shocked (but probably still a virgin). McLynn interprets this as a response to Stanley's guilt about his mother's promiscuity and his own illegitimacy.[49] Stanley had three broken engagements to women, in situations (McLynn argues) where he would not go through with the marriages. He finally wed only late in life and never fathered children. Unpleasant experiences at St Asalph's and witnessing a companion's rape in Turkey, as well as the strict Protestant sermons he heard as a youth, also made him uneasy with sexual contact between men.

McLynn psychobiographically analyses Stanley as a 'schizoid personality', a chronic liar in many of his reminiscences (although he was largely accurate with geographical descriptions of Africa), who refused to accept facts of his background and personality (for instance, long denying that he was Welsh). He sees Stanley as a repressed figure, 'inhabit[ing] the limbo between homosexuality and heterosexuality'. Although attracted to women, Stanley 'could not integrate sexuality into his perception of them', and 'his relations with women therefore remained at the superficial level of idealisation and courtly love'. Comradeship with men, especially those inferior to him in age, status or race, was easier. 'Nevertheless, his homosexual feelings towards them remained at a passive level.' When his sexuality emerged, it occasionally surfaced as sado-masochism, evidenced by his beating Noe. Later he flogged his African porters, not excluding those whom he held in high regard, for instance, Selim. 'Stanley's young male companions were ever the focus for the repressed homosexual side of his personality.'[50]

My *Kalulu* is a key example of his transforming thwarted personal feelings into a book. Stanley, according to McLynn, sublimated his sexuality. As a young man, when he read voraciously, one method was through fantasy and literature: 'His obsession with books as the perfect barrier between himself and the physical world, especially the world of sexuality, became almost fetishistic.'[51] Another avenue to resolve troubled sexuality was travel and adventure, even the privations they produced: 'The alternation of redemption through the suffering of swamp, starvation and disease with the deprivation of pleasure from infliction of cruelty tends to make Stanley's journeys almost a classic story of externalisation.'[52] Stanley himself wondered: 'Why is man so feeble and weak, that he must tramp, tramp hundreds of miles to satisfy the doubts his impatient and uncurbed mind feels?'[53]

Stanley's relationship with Selim and Kalulu marks a sometimes happy, sometimes less felicitous effort to attain emotional satisfaction. The fantasy of My *Kalulu*, with its comely young men, daring adventures, blood-bound union and happy ending, became a wish-fulfilment, the two 'lovers' (in spirit if not in deed) returning to the mother and childhood home that Stanley never enjoyed, after successfully braving the obstacles that Stanley had endured. My *Kalulu* was written before the real Kalulu's death, while he was working and travelling with Stanley. The 'noble savage' of the novel was a portrait of the companion Stanley hoped that his 'infant cannibal', suitably civilised by English schools, might become. After Kalulu's death, Stanley never again attempted to write a novel, nor did he develop the sort of patronage he had with the African boy. Just as 'civilised nations seldom can furnish us with models to compete with superexcellent types designed by Greece', perhaps Africa remained the only place where Stanley could find the masculine camaraderie and emotional happiness for which he yearned. Stanley cast himself in real life as Selim in his novel, exploring Africa (in theory, stamping out slavery rather than engaging in slaving), forging alliances (or at least enforcing submission) and bringing civilisation. Stanley obsessively continued to mount expeditions, traversing the continent, abetting conquests and rescuing stranded Europeans. His affair with Africa – paternalistic, sado-masochistic and yet genuinely amorous – mirrored his relationship with the flesh-and-blood Kalulu. The quest for fame replaced or triumphed over longing for love, and he left behind the African love story, which proved too personal, too revealing even to discuss in his autobiography.

Wilfred Thesiger and the pleasures of the desert

The last case study is of an avowedly asexual man whose emotional identification and satisfaction have derived from the desert and the male companions with whom he explored its expanses. One of the last, most legendary of the great explorers, now in his nineties a relic of the imperial age, Sir Wilfred Thesiger was born in 1910 in Addis Ababa, where his father headed the British legation in Abyssinia (a posting his parents could reach only after nearly a month's mule trek from Djibouti). Thesiger's background was aristocratic and imperialist – his grandfather was a baron, and his uncle, Lord Chelmsford, was Viceroy of India. Thesiger spent his childhood in Abyssinia (Ethiopia), then returned to Britain for schooling at Eton and Oxford, where he took a third-class degree in history and won sporting medals in boxing. In 1930, in a mark of friendship for Thesiger's father, Haile Selassie invited him to Addis Ababa as a guest at his coronation as Emperor of Abyssinia. The visit confirmed Thesiger's admiration for the ruler to whom he dedicated his autobiography, as well as his love for Ethiopia and for travel in difficult terrain. Thesiger spent several years in Ethiopia, moving among the Danakil (or Afar) people, a group until then little known, and much feared, by outsiders, and locating the source of the Awah river. Thesiger subsequently joined the British colonial service in the Sudan as an Assistant District Commissioner, and also travelled in the Tibesti desert (in British and French Sudan). When Mussolini invaded Ethiopia, Thesiger, among many others, raised his voice in protest against the Fascist imperialism that had forced Haile Selassie from his throne.

During the Second World War, when he served in the British Army, Thesiger saw action against the Italians in Ethiopia and was posted to Arabia, which immediately captured his attention. After the war, Thesiger spent five years exploring the Empty Quarter (Rub-al-Khali) of the southern Arabian peninsula. In incredibly harsh conditions, he crossed the desert accompanied by young Arab companions and the camels on which the explorers travelled, suffering heat and cold, lack of water and supplies – hardships in which Thesiger gloried. His account of the monumental trek, *Arabian Sands*, published in 1959, became an immediate classic of travel writing. (Meanwhile, during the hot Arabian summers, Thesiger had gone on holiday to Pakistan and

Afghanistan, returning regularly to his London flat for visits to his beloved mother.) In the late 1950s, Thesiger began further exploration in Iraq, and his book on *The Marsh Arabs* won renewed acclaim. From the late 1960s until 1994, Thesiger lived mainly in a Kenyan village, repatriated to England as age and physical problems, as well as the deaths of his two closest African companions, made it increasingly difficult to remain there.

On travels and in Kenya, young men always surrounded Thesiger. There was Idris, who journeyed with him in the Sudan (and was rewarded with a trip to Mecca), followed by a 16-year-old Druze, Faris, in Syria. In Arabia, Thesiger recruited two particularly close companions. One was a 15-year old goatherd, Salim bin Kabina: 'We were watering camels in a wadi, and I remember he came up wearing this red loincloth and he had this long hair. He asked if he could come with me, and I asked the Sheikhs and they said he would be useful to me, so I said yes, if he could get a rifle and a camel.' Thesiger considered bin Kabina as an assistant more than a domestic: 'There was no question of bin Kabina being a servant or being paid. He wouldn't have risked his life for me under those circumstances. The last thing in the world I wanted was a master–servant relationship with the Bedu.' When bin Kabina fell ill, Thesiger became greatly distressed, and when another expeditioner questioned where they would be headed on the morrow, he replied, 'There will be no tomorrow if bin Kabina dies.'[54] Thesiger's photographs show a lean, taut young man with fine features and shoulder-length hair, looking regal in a formal pose, and flashing an engaging smile in a casual snapshot.

Thesiger's other close companion in Arabia was Salim bin Ghabaisha, bin Kabina's cousin. According to Michael Asher,

> He was no more than fifteen or sixteen, with an unusually husky voice, and the spare, linear, almost feminine figure which Thesiger admired. He had a grace and quiet dignity that contrasted with the boisterously energetic bin Kabina, although a physically stronger, more staid, more ruthless character....Thesiger waxed over his appearance in *Arabian Sands*, likening him to 'Antinous' when first seen by Hadrian in the Phrygian woods.

Thesiger addressed the implication that the Arab might have been his lover:

> Bin Ghabaisha was a very beautiful boy. One can appreciate beauty without doing anything physical – I mean to have slept with bin Kabina or bin Ghabaisha would have been impossible – you'd probably have got knifed at once. Obviously bin Ghabaisha's beauty, or whatever word you like to use, had an effect on me. I liked him because he was so beautiful.[55]

In Iraq, Thesiger found another comely partner, Amara, described by Thesiger's friend Gavin Maxwell as 'a handsome, self-possessed youth...fine-boned, disdainful as an Arab stallion, often moody and withdrawn'.[56] When Amara got into trouble with a sheikh, Thesiger threatened that if harm befell his protégé, he would make certain the attacker was killed. Later in Kenya, where he lived in a house with an African, his wife and various hangers-on, Thesiger took up with 14-year-old Erope, a young boxer called Sunguna, and Lopago, the 16-year old 'bodyguard' with whom he shared his bed. 'Of course, people find it curious that I live in Maralal with these people,' Thesiger said somewhat defensively.

> Let them....It's not a sexual relationship at all....If people want to think I'm sexually attracted to them, let them think it. It isn't true anyway. I mean I think they are attractive – just as bin Kabina and bin Ghabaisha were attractive....I have Lopago sleeping on my bed, but at eighty-three you can't be said to have any sexual feeling anyway, especially when you've had your prostate out....It's a personal pull on the part of these people that draws me back. I like being with them. Otherwise what?[57]

Thesiger never married or fathered children, and holds a very traditional view of women: 'A woman's job is to stay at home and look after the kids.' His need for companionship has always been satisfied by young men in the countries where he lived or travelled:

> All of my life I have felt the need of human company, and wherever possible have avoided solitude....I have, however, been most content when I have established a close friendship with individuals....Strangely, I have found this comradeship most easily among races other than my own. Perhaps this trait could be traced back to the hurtful rejection I suffered from my contemporaries at preparatory school when I was a small boy freshly arrived from Abyssinia in an alien English world.

The series of companionships continued in Kenya where 'Lawi Leboyare has been with me for the past fifteen years, ever since he left his village school at the age of ten,' Thesiger wrote in 1987, 'and is as dear to me as a son.'[58] Again confronting the suggestion that these relationships were homosexual, he has stated: 'I'm not saying there is anything sexual in it, but certainly you have this feeling of love for them and there you are.'[59]

Thesiger seems to dislike physical sex, but has a narrow definition of homosexuality. Reminiscing about Eton, he commented, 'I never heard of anyone being sodomized, which is what homosexuality is. I can conceive of nothing more unpleasant than sodomy. To me it would be absolutely appalling.' 'Sex has been of no great consequence to me, and the celibacy of desert life left me untroubled,' he confessed in his autobiography.[60] His appreciation of male beauty is more aesthetic than sexual, his physical pleasures ones of enduring the challenges of desert expeditions rather than luxuriating in erotic gymnastics. Perhaps his only genital contacts came from the countless circumcisions he performed on adolescents in Iraq; when local men discovered that circumcision performed with instruments in Thesiger's medical kit was safer than when done using rusty razor-blades, Thesiger's skills at circumcision were much in demand. Neither Thesiger nor his biographers imply that he obtained sexual satisfaction from these operations.

Thesiger was not unaware that sexual relations took place among men he was familiar with, and alludes to these activities without shock or disapprobation. In Iraq, for instance, male dancers who parodied the sex act were considered homosexual. 'The comments I overheard...left no doubt about his other proclivities,' Thesiger remarked of one, and then straightforwardly, if discreetly, discussed homosexual behaviour among the Marsh Arabs. In general, however, Thesiger's writings seldom mention sex, for such was not his interest, either personally or as an explorer. Even descriptions of young men, though emphasising their beauty, are restrained. 'He had a powerful, virile face, clean-shaven except for a close-clipped moustache with dark bushy eyebrows which nearly met over a prominent fleshy nose,' Thesiger describes one Iraqi. His friend Amara was 'slightly built and remarkably handsome' – Thesiger's descriptions do not become more erotic.[61] His interest was more with his friends' rough lives than their bodies or minds. In the critical but apt words of Ian Buruma, 'Thesiger is in love with racial macho.'[62]

Thesiger has often expressed his appreciation for male beauty, agreeing with the 'ancient Greek ideal that the young male is the symbol of human beauty'. His companions were fit and handsome young men, and his bonding with them, if not physical, was nevertheless intense. About the relationship with Idris, Thesiger commented: 'There was nothing physical in it...but I was very fond of him because we were shoulder to shoulder and side by side in many dangerous situations, and he was loyal to me.'[63] Thesiger preferred virile and even rough young men – one companion had been in prison – and he remained friends with some for years. A trip to the Gulf in 1977 reunited Thesiger with bin Kabina and bin Ghabaisha, by that time middle-aged men with adult sons. Bin Kabina had settled down as owner of a large camel herd. Bin Ghabaisha's career had been rather more dramatic. After Thesiger's departure, he became a notorious bandit in the Trucial States, shooting up trucks on the Oman road. Captured in a gunfight and gaoled, he won release through the interventions of an Englishman. British SAS soldiers occasionally spotted him during the Dhofar war in 1957. Bin Ghabaisha then gained employment as overseer of a well. He remarried, and raised a second family, after the death of his first wife. He bought a Land Rover and told Asher in the early 1990s, 'I can't say when I last rode a camel. Not for years. I go by car now' – a sentiment that horrified Thesiger. Both bin Kabina and bin Ghabaisha, in photographs from the 1990s, remained handsome and distinguished, now grey-bearded men.[64]

The Arabs remembered Thesiger with affection, pointing to the benefits they secured from his patronage. For bin Ghabaisha, 'He was generous, and he gave us the things we were interested in: money, rifles, camels. He was canny, he was loyal, he was tireless, and he was afraid of nothing.' Bin Ghabaisha added, 'A lot of people talked about his journeys, and I wanted to become famous among the tribes like the ones who went with him.' For bin Kabina,

'These trips with the Englishman, we considered a chance for the whole tribe to benefit.' Bin Kabina did admit, however, resentment at the long years of Thesiger's absence from Arabia, and noted that 'in the end he only came because they [government officials] invited him'. Despite the warmth of their reunion in the 1970s, bin Kabina lamented, 'He wasn't like before.'[65] Thesiger's patronage had aided his Arabian companions and similarly, in Kenya, he found Lawi a job with a safari company, and set up the would-be boxer as a shop-keeper. Thesiger revealed that he had given his Kenyan friends 'hundreds of thousands of pounds. I don't regret it unless I feel it has gone on something that has achieved nothing....Of course they are exploiting me...I've no idea if there's real affection for me. I think some of them feel it.'[66]

Thesiger dislikes modernity, reserving particular hatred for automobiles (though he travels by both car and aeroplane), and regrets the incursions of modern life into the Middle East and Africa; he is a self-confirmed nostalgic for the era of camel-caravans, ocean-liners and rustic life. He is also an unrepentant apologist for the British Empire: 'The Empire was absolutely outstanding, and I was proud to have something to do with it. It was out of this world compared with any other Empire except possibly the French.' Somewhat paradoxically, Thesiger's greatest admiration is for the 'traditional' life of the nomads among whom he lived in the 1950s, yet he sees British rule as benevolent. 'This country benefited enormously from British rule,' he remarked in Kenya: 'I'd like to see it as it was in the old days when the British were here. I think undoubt-edly people were a lot happier.'[67] Seemingly contradictory views find reconciliation in Thesiger's romanticisation and idealisation of both the British Empire and desert (or village) culture. The attractive companions who accom-panied him on his explorations, and with whom he enjoyed the camaraderie of desert camps, were embodiments of the Greek male ideal of beauty, courage and endurance to which he subscribed. Sharing experiences – horsing about with canoe-boys in Iraq, dossing down in camps with strong young Arabs, sharing a house with 'foster-sons' in Kenya – contributed to the pleasure of voyages: 'It's not the people as a whole that draw me back....It's individuals.'[68]

Links between the emotional draw of young companions, exotic countries and the vocation of explorer are manifest in Thesiger. He is a late incarnation of the imperial explorers of the age of Stanley, the very model of an anti-modern aristocrat idealising the world of the natives, and upholding the banner of the British Empire while enjoying inherited wealth, elite education and valu-able contacts. His anthropological musings may seem amateur, his political opinions dangerously authoritarian, his understanding of world politics naïve. His avocations (including delight in hunting, which let him brag about killing eighty lions and thousands of other animals) are rightly out of fashion. The boldness of his sentiments – 'Inevitably these Bedu had little veneration for human life....I soon acquired the same attitude, and if anyone had killed one of my companions I would unquestionably have sought to avenge him: I have no belief in the "sanctity" of life'[69] – are sometimes shocking. He could easily be characterised as a severely repressed homosexual, sadly deluding himself about his real interests in Arabic or African men. The same charges could be laid against General Gordon and Lawrence of Arabia – two of Thesiger's heroes – but they indict an age more than individuals. Such a judgement, even if merited, misses the genuine empathy between Thesiger and his young friends, and between Thesiger and the countries that he explored, an empathy in which the homosexual (in a broad sense) and the imperial were intertwined.

Sex, companionship and exploration

The sexual and emotional trajectories of these five explorers, spanning the nineteenth and much of the twentieth centuries, leaves an ambiguous legacy. Letters and diaries reveal the excitement of Humboldt anticipating life with Haeften, Stanley's affectionate pride and amusement in the company of Kalulu, Thesiger's admiration for the forbearance and camaraderie of the Arabs, emotional bonding hardly foreign to latter-day readers. In an age when a premium is placed on the physical pleasures of sex – a good sex life – lack of consummation in these relationships evokes less empathy. The men's unsatisfied yearnings may seem pathetic; their reticence about and fears of sex, ridiculous. That Humboldt or Przhevalsky could have died virgins, that Thesiger has been admittedly asexual, that Burton and Stanley may have realised their fantasies in books not in the flesh now appears rather pitiable. That we perhaps think that they should have 'let go', that they should have 'done it', says much about the gap in sexual expectations and realities between their times – from the Enlightenment to the years just after the Second World War – and our own. Seeing sex as the end of the game suggests more about present-day obsessions than historical priorities. Even if Humboldt, Przhevalsky, Stanley and Thesiger did not have sex with their companions, they did have companionship, affection, collaboration in their ventures and inspiration for their work. The pleasures of the company of a virile Arab or African, attractive young German or Russian, cannot be discounted.

Specific connections between apparent sexual inclinations and exploration appear in all these lives. Humboldt left Europe after plans to set up house with Haeften were aborted. Burton's assignment to investigate brothels provoked interest in variant sexual activities, and launched his career, and rivalry with Speke may have embodied sexual tensions. The end of Stanley's planned world tour with Noe after his friend's rape represents a happenstance that changed the course of a life. The choice of travelling companions and fellow investigators reflected self-accepted or repressed longings – Humboldt's replacement of Caldas with an 'Adonis', Przhevalsky's run through a succession of protégés, Stanley's choice of the sturdy Pocock brothers and patronage of Kalulu, Thesiger's bonding with bin Kabina and bin Ghabaisha. In a more general sense, these men's sexual ambivalence and uncertainty – whether best categorised as bisexual, asexual or homosexual – made them ill at ease with the conventions of Europe, willing to leave the cosy familiarity of Berlin, London or St Petersburg, drawn to the hardships and excitement of jungles and deserts.

Perhaps Stanley spoke for all of them in his autobiography when he listed the personal benefits of exploration. Among them were visiting new and unexplored regions and big-game hunting. At the head of the list, however, he placed three more philosophical rewards. Stanley mused,

> No luxury in civilisation can be equal to the relief from the tyranny of custom. The wilds of a great city are better than the excruciating tyranny of a small village. The heart of Africa is infinitely preferable to the heart of the world's greatest city.

He continued,

> One of the first sweet and novel pleasures a man experiences in the wilds of Africa is the almost perfect independence; the next thing is the indifference to all things earthly outside his camp; and that, let people talk as they may, is one of the exquisite, soul-lulling pleasures a mortal can enjoy....The other enjoyment is the freedom and independence of mind, which elevates one's thoughts to purer, higher atmospheres.[70]

From the Arabian sands, the Gobi desert, the South American jungle, fellow explorers could have seconded Stanley's words. Such sentiments might well have been cheered, too, by the most predictably conventional men with wife and children back at home, or native concubine by their side, but for these heterodox travellers, 'relief from the tyranny of custom' and fulfilment of 'the most perfect independence' took on added meaning.

Notes

1 Wilhelm von Rosen, 'Count Knuth, Eigil', in Robert Aldrich and Garry Wotherspoon (eds), *Who's Who in Contemporary Gay and Lesbian History: From World War II to the Present Day* (London, 2001), p. 233.

2 See, for instance, the letters written by Matthew Flinders to George Bass, a fellow explorer of Australia, which indicate intimate friendship and hero-worship, if not sexual interest (Matthew Flinders, *Personal Letters from an Extraordinary Life*, ed. Paul Brunton (Sydney, 2002)).

3 These four represent a selection among explorers who appear homosexual. Details of private lives of many others remain unknown. An example is Luigi Maria D'Albertis (1841–1901), Italian explorer of New Guinea in the 1870s. He collected zoological specimens for an Italian museum, and wrote about his travels in Melanesia. D'Albertis was a flamboyant personality, and in his last years, living in Rome, he kept a pet python and fox. He may have had an affair with one woman, though he remarked, 'I do not care for their company, for women are always an impediment.' He admired young men, such as a chief described as 'a fine man, strong, tall and robust...his classical features strongly reminded [me] of those of the ancient Roman emperors'. D'Albertis was 'invariably accompanied by at least one attractive young man, usually aged twenty or less, and often from a country where homosexuality was not considered abnormal in the nineteenth century'. Arnold and John, two Sinhalese, served as companions in New Guinea; Xavier, a New Caledonian, became a later travel companion. D'Albertis's own 'accounts give no clue to his homosexual inclinations, or to other "skeletons" that he deliberately concealed from biogra-

phers', but he was probably bisexual (John Goode, *Rape of the Fly* (Melbourne, 1977), pp. 73–4, 57, 11).

4 Albert Leitzmann, *Ein Jugendfreundschaft: Alexander von Humboldt* (Berlin, 1915), quoted in Gerardo Paz Otero, *Vida sentimental de Alejandro Humboldt* (Bogotá, 1978), pp. 55–6. Neither Leitzmann, nor Paz Otero, a psychiatrist who takes a Freudian approach in his introduction, says that Humboldt was homosexual, but Paz Otero's comments imply that he was, at least, bisexual.

5 Quoted in Douglas Botting, *Humboldt, 1769–1859: Un Savant démocrate* (Paris, 1988), pp. 50–1.

6 Quoted in Paul R. Sweet, *Wilhelm von Humboldt: A Biography* (Columbus, OH, 1978), p. 177.

7 Sweet remarks that 'for two years Haeften and Alexander formed one ménage. It was the kind of situation that cause people to write: "I won't go into details here, but will tell you about it when I see you"' (p. 177).

8 Quoted in Paz Otero, pp. 63, 65

9 Botting, p. 277, speculates that Humboldt may have been in debt to Seifert, to whom he left his belongings.

10 *Ibid.*, pp. 46–7.

11 Jean-Paul Duviols and Charles Minguet, *Humboldt: Savant-Citoyen du monde* (Paris, 1994), p. 69.

12 Botting, p. 47.

13 Quoted in *ibid.*, p. 116.

14 Quoted in Botting, pp. 49–50.

15 Quoted in Duviols and Minguet, p. 17.

16 Edward Rice, *Captain Sir Richard Francis Burton* (New York, 1990), p. 1.

17 Frank McLynn, *Burton: Snow upon the Desert* (London, 1990).

18 Richard Burton, *The Sotadic Zone* (Boston, 1977); quotations from 'Terminal essay', in Brian Reade (ed.), *Sexual Heretics: Male Homosexuality in English Literature from 1850 to 1900* (New York, 1970), p. 158.

19 *Ibid.*, p. 152.

20 *Ibid.*, p. 159.

21 *Ibid.*, p. 170.

22 *Ibid.*, p. 179.

23 Quoted in *ibid.*, p. 180.

24 McLynn, p. 176.

25 *Ibid.*, p. 16.

26 *Ibid.*, pp. 106, 138, 163–4.

27 Another example of interest in Arabic and Persian poetry manifested by someone with probably homosexual proclivities is Edward Fitzgerald, translator of the *Rubáiyát of Omar Khayyám*. See Robert Bernard Martin, *With Friends Possessed: A Life of Edward Fitzgerald* (London, 1985).

28 Quoted in Donald Rayfield, *The Dream of Lhasa: The Life of Nikolay Przhevalsky (1839–88), Explorer of Central Asia* (London, 1976), p. 203.

29 *Ibid.*, p. 201.

30 Quoted in *ibid.*, pp. 52, 69.

31 *Ibid.*, p. 18.

32 Quoted in *ibid.*, p. 88.

33 Quoted in *ibid.*, p. 196.

34 Quoted in *ibid.*, p. 153.

35 Quoted in *ibid.*, p. 154.

36 As quoted in Thomas W. Knox, *The Boy Travellers on the Congo* (London, 1888), pp. 8, 12, 39, 93.

37 Diary entries of March 1872, 12–26 September 1871 and 21 November 1870, Stanley Diaries, Musée Royal de l'Afrique Centrale, Tervuren, Belgium (hereafter MRAC).

38 H.M. Stanley, *How I Found Livingstone* (London, 1890 [1872]), pp. 230–1.
39 Quoted in Frank McLynn, *Stanley: The Making of an African Explorer* (Oxford, 1991), p. 131.
40 Diary entries of 20 January and 27 July 1872, MRAC.
41 Quoted in McLynn, p. 205.
42 John Bierman, *Dark Safari: The Life Behind the Legend of Henry Morton Stanley* (London, 1990), p. 141.
43 Quoted in McLynn, p. 205.
44 *Ibid.*, p. 18
45 *Ibid.*, p. 8.
46 Notebook BL/PR 2435, MRAC.
47 Bierman, pp. 39–42.
48 *Ibid.*, p. 68.
49 McLynn, p. 29.
50 *Ibid.*, 36, 54, 65.
51 *Ibid.*, p. 36.
52 *Ibid.*, p. 201.
53 Quoted in *ibid.*, p. 138.
54 Quoted in Michael Asher, *Thesiger: A Biography* (London, 1994), pp. 277–8, 325.
55 Quoted in *ibid.*, pp. 323–4.
56 Quoted in *ibid.*, p. 403.
57 Quoted in *ibid.*, p. 510.
58 Wilfred Thesiger, *The Life of My Choice* (London, 1987), p. 432.
59 Quoted in Asher, p. 277.
60 Thesiger, *The Life of My Choice*, p. 295
61 Wilfred Thesiger, *The Marsh Arabs* (London, 1964), pp. 123–4, 169.
62 Ian Buruma, 'Wilfred Thesiger, Wilfred of Arabia', in *The Missionary and the Libertine: Love and War in East and West* (London, 1996), p. 48.
63 Quoted in *ibid.*, p. 130.
64 Asher, pp. 12–13.
65 Quoted in Asher, pp. 18, 324, 385.
66 Quoted in Asher, p. 516.
67 Quoted in *ibid.*, pp. 131, 512, 503.
68 Quoted in *ibid.*, p. 277.
69 Quoted in Dennis Drabelle, 'The frontier comes for the explorer', *Outside Magazine*, October 1998 (www.outsidemag.com).
70 H.M. Stanley, *The Autobiography of Henry Morton Stanley*, ed. Dorothy Stanley (London, n.d.), pp. 533–4.

2 Captains of empire

At the early stages of exploration, conquest and rule, empire was largely men's business. There were women explorers – only now are they receiving due attention and credit – but most Europeans who charted distant seas and trekked into unknown jungles, climbed unscaled mountains or crossed deserts were men. Sailors and soldiers who conquered new lands were men. So were the majority of traders, colonial business employees and colonial administrators. Only among missionaries – Roman Catholic nuns, Protestant pastors' wives – and as spouses of settlers did women join the early colonial ranks. European women long remained rare in the colonies; military officers were often not permitted to take their wives along with them, merchants frequently left families at home, and the East India Company did not allow employees to marry until well into the nineteenth century.

The ambiance of early colonial adventures was decidedly masculine, the social promiscuity of expeditions, camps and barracks, the camaraderie of the ocean voyage, the safari, the trading post. The virtues seen as necessary for the success of the colonial endeavour – bravery, endurance, loyalty, a winning spirit and a sense of fair play – were those ascribed to men. Such ideals were inculcated at all-male boarding schools and military academies, in the predominantly male environment of universities, and on the playing fields where boys competed against each other in preparation to fight for empire. The 'games spirit', viewed as a primarily masculine trait, provided a quasi-spiritual basis for God and country. Many imperialists served their apprenticeship in hothouse environments where male bonding, mateship and manly solidarity were ideal and practice.[1]

In settler societies, or wherever Europeans wanted to establish a permanent presence, women were necessary as wives and mothers, and useful as a 'civilising' influence on the rough and rowdy world of the frontier. Political authorities continually bemoaned the lack of women in the colonies, the enormous imbalance between men and women. Private associations tried to recruit women settlers, promising marriage and prosperity to those willing to quit Europe for the colonies. Officials devised schemes for shipping orphans, widows, female prisoners and even women of suspect virtue to overseas domains, there to find redemption from their sorrows and to bear children to populate

European settlements. European women, they hoped, would also draw men away from the charms of native women and the perils of irregular sexual encounters, for the very absence of women, it was feared, created a temptation to enjoy unchristian liaisons.

The European men working as isolated traders or representing their countries, whether humble district agents or grand governors, generally saw sexual opportunities as one of the benefits of empire. Companionship was easily found, a 'perk' of the job. During the nineteenth century men took concubines, frequented prostitutes and occasionally married native women. Religious and government authorities hardly approved, but could do little, and colonial officials even set up brothels to satisfy the cravings of lusty young troopers. By the early 1900s, inter-racial contacts provoked increased opposition from moral and political superiors, at least in the British case, and the arrival of larger numbers of European women promoted the reproduction of more standard European families.[2] Yet prostitution and concubinage flourished until the end of empire, and only the more reticent old 'colonial hands' did not confess to sampling exotic sexual pleasures overseas.

Not all European men sought the sexual and emotional companionship of women, whether indigenous or European. The gender imbalance pushed some into 'situational' homosexual relations. Others intentionally looked for male bedmates and soul mates among either compatriots or natives. An unknown number escaped condemnation of homosexuality in Europe to take advantage of laxer moral strictures in the wider world. Perhaps many more (including heterosexuals) found their most significant emotional partnerships not with the prostitutes or concubines who passed through their lives, but with the fellow men with whom they explored, fought, ruled and preached the Gospel. Homosociality, sometimes veering to homosexuality, was inescapable in the early colonial world. If the full gamut of emotional and sexual contacts between men are included, it is probable that a considerable cohort had feelings or experiences not strictly conforming to European and Christian precepts of sexual propriety.

Judging the full extent of homosexual encounters is difficult – memoirists are noticeably unwilling to reveal physical affection for other men, much less to recount mutual masturbation, fellatio and anal intercourse. Later writers frequently remain silent on the private lives of public men, as if sexual desires and experiences (or the lack of them) held no significance. Traditional biographers, often ill at ease with homosexuality or the possibility that their subjects *might* have been homosexual, try to prove their heroes not so tainted. A recent biography of Lord Kitchener, for instance, includes an appendix arguing that he could not possibly have been homosexual,[3] and a study of Rimbaud in Africa is at pains to show that the French poet turned colonial trader did not have a sexual affair with a male African servant.[4] Some other writers betray a distaste for homosexuality itself. The esteemed biographer of Sir Edmund Backhouse, who wrote a memoir on sex in China, understands homosexuality only in terms of the decadence and effeminacy of his subject, refers to

Backhouse's 'abnormality' and 'perversions', and remarks on the 'revolting details' of homosexual encounters in Backhouse's writings. After a few paragraphs, he says that the 'reader will have had more than enough' of such horror, and finishes his comments on descriptions of homosexual brothels in Beijing in Backhouse's memoir, 'We read on, and, with some relief, find ourselves in the cleaner air of mere conspiracy and murder.'[5]

Such attitudes recall fears during the imperial age about the temptations of homosexuality (or indeed the frequency of it) among Europeans overseas, the dangers to European morals from native behaviour and the inability of European men to resist the seductions of the tropics or to withstand the pressures and demands of physically taxing and lonely colonial service. Concerns about sexual irregularity in the French Army provide an illustration, and case studies of Marshal Lyautey and Lawrence of Arabia illustrate different sorts of homoerotic experience in the colonial military.

In the army

Gérard Zwang argues that throughout history 'a certain type of career officer was absolutely homosexual', a phenomenon among Roman centurions, Janissaries and French marshals. 'The choice of such a profession,' he continues, 'is made knowingly, and those who enlisted in the [French Foreign] Legion, the African rifles or the "Colo" [the colonial army], were not unaware of what they were getting into.'[6] A French criminologist in 1894 observed a homosexual orgy among soldiers in Algeria and worried about the lasting impact of such excess.[7] Colonel Weygand, a former Legionnaire and a famous general's son, said that commanders had to turn a blind eye to what went on between Legionnaires during rest stops in desert oases.[8] Writers around 1900 mentioned that homosexuality was frequent in remote regions, where *girons* (pretty young boys) became objects of desire for Legionnaires; one corporal committed suicide when his lover cheated on him.[9]

In 1911, two writers (one an army doctor) remembered:

> When we arrived in Algeria, because of the effect of the climate and because of the total lack of [European] women…[soldiers] could not resist imitating the ways of indigenes, and soon their bad reputation for having 'African morals' had reached France.…Homosexuality in the [French] African army corresponded to a physical necessity, but not, in general, to a form of erotic madness.'[10]

Another psychologically inclined writer classified homosexuality with 'psychoses' induced by hot climates; Dr Dautheville, however, worried about the 'exhaustion' that soldiers overseas suffered because of strong sexual urges.[11] A Dr Berthulus expressed fear that France might suffer defeat in North Africa since its troops proved less immune to homosexual temptations than were Italian soldiers – a curious psychological and political analysis.[12]

Another concerned about the effects of North Africa on military morals, and possible spread of vice to general society – with a wink, again, at the Italians – was the Marquis de Boissy, whom Richard Burton quoted:

The conquest of Algiers had evil results....He complained *sans ambages* of *moeurs arabes* in French regiments, and declared that the result of the African wars was an *effrayable débordement pédérastique*, even as the *vérole* resulted from the Italian campaigns of that age of passion, the sixteenth century. From the military the *fléau* spread to civilian society and the Vice took such expansion and intensity that it may be said to have been democratized in cities and large towns.[13]

Like the plague, sodomy might spread from the army to civilian society, from military camps to cities, from the colonies to the motherland.

Indeed colonial soldiers in the *métropole* sometimes attracted homosexual attention. The novelist André du Dognon compared Pigalle, centre of Paris's nightlife and prostitution in the 1930s, to Marrakesh because of the assortment of young men for sale – 'and you must not forget the presence of the colonial soldiers'. Edouard Roditi added that French homosexuals of the time, like young women,

had a rather nationalist taste for uniforms....The *spahis* and *zouaves* [colonial soldiers] also wore those cumberbunds [of red flannel, thought to provide protection from tropical diseases] but there were *aficionados* of more exotic accoutrements who spent their weekend in Senlis, where Moroccan *goumiers* [troopers] were garrisoned....At Saïd's Hôtel du Saumon in the Passage du Saumon behind Les Halles [in Paris], you could find [French] Legionnaires, *spahis*, a little of everything. They played cards while waiting for clients, whom they took away to the bedrooms.[14]

One 1908 writer on homosexuality in the army nevertheless commented that only when it involved criminal offences to public decency (*outrages à la pudeur publique*), abuse of authority or violence did it incur punishment. Military police pursued those involved in irregular activities solely if they would have been the object of criminal proceedings in civilian life.[15] (Homosexual practices had been decriminalised during the Revolution.) Scandal, however, occasionally erupted. For instance, in 1891, Lieutenant Boyer, a *spahi* medical doctor in Algeria, denounced Captain Bouïs for having 'brutalised his soldiers, stolen from them and committed immoral acts on them'. Authorities tried to hush up the affair, announcing that Bouïs would be removed, and Boyer transferred. Bouïs then insulted Boyer, trying to provoke a duel. Boyer refused, 'saying that he would not fight a thief and a pederast', but that he would fight against any other officer who cared to take Bouïs's place. No one offered to do so. A council of enquiry judged that Boyer had forfeited his honour by refusing to fight, and he was forced out of the army.[16] Bouïs's violence seemed of greater concern than pederasty, and his accuser suffered punishment: dishonourable conduct was more serious than immoral behaviour.

Several senior officers of repute appear to have been homosexual. General Lamoricière, one of the conquerors of Algeria, is quoted as having remarked matter-of-factly, 'There [in Africa] we were all [pederasts]', adding that, unlike others, General Changarnier remained so. General Nicolas Gallieni, a leading colonial officer in Indo-China and Madagascar, was rumoured to be homosexual. In the last years of the empire, General de Lattre de Tassigny was probably bisexual.[17] According to one reporter in Indo-China, he had 'very liberal morals...and did not hide his admiration for handsome and courageous young men'.[18]

Homosexuality in the *bataillons d'Afrique* provoked particular concern. The 'Bat' d'Af', established in 1832, were composed of men who, in general, had been twice convicted of crimes (in civilian life or after conscription) with sentences involving at least six months in prison, including morals offences such as *outrage à la pudeur publique*, theft, fraud or pimping. At the beginning of the twentieth century, five companies in the Bat' d'Af' totalled 6,000 men with headquarters at Tatahouine in the Tunisian desert. Most of the soldiers hailed from modest backgrounds and held the lowest military rank; officers treated soldiers with harsh discipline, and they were generally assigned to frontier posts. The battalions had a bad reputation for drink, gang warfare and moral turpitude, and thus retained a special place in French imperial mythology. A popular song around 1911 evoked the long marches, the hunger and thirst, isolation and sexual torments of men in a distant fortress. The 'Complainte de Biribi' hints at sexual irregularities: 'In Biribi, that's where they groan, / They groan on heat, / At night you hear the cry of the male / Who would have thought / That one day he'd have to know / Mam'zell' Biribi? / Because sooner or later you have to / in Biribi.'[19]

René Jude, an army medical doctor posted to Tunisia and author of a 1907 book on 'degenerates' in the *bataillons d'Afrique*, wrote at length about sexual activities. At Tatahouine, out of eighty men, only one or two a week visited local prostitutes: 'In reality, the Joyeux [as soldiers in the battalions were ironically called] do not try to frequent these women. They have picked up unnatural habits (generally in civilian prisons) and do not change when they are in service.' Two-thirds of the soldiers, he estimated, were pederasts, and in the Bat' d'Af's own disciplinary company, almost all were. Soldiers lived in tents, and, in each, Jude saw 'households' (*ménages*) of male couples with a clear division of roles: 'The "woman" shined the shoes, made the bed, sewed on buttons, cleaned', while the 'husband' smoked and kept a look-out for guards. If an officer passed by, the 'husband' made a pretence of working; when heavy-duty chores presented themselves, such as shifting blocks of stone, the 'man' would spring into action 'to show his strength and save his companion such strenuous efforts'. Jealousy marked these partnerships, and fights settled quarrels between men for partners. However, when a 'man' became a 'widow', his mates would lend their 'wives' to do housework for him, and sometimes a 'wife' would be shared between two men, an arrangement soldiers referred to as 'exchanging tickets' (*balancer les tickets*). Men showed great attachment to their partners, and would often go to hospital to stay with them (feigning illness themselves), if they fell sick, or even get assigned to a disciplinary brigade in order to join favourites.[20]

Jude described 'active' partners as generally vigorous and muscular, intelligent and adroit. The 'passive' men were softer, lighter skinned and sometimes rather effeminate in gestures (and sported fewer tattoos than 'active' men). Jude also remarked on men who were not *en ménage*, and generally lived apart. Called 'vultures' or 'Moroccans' by the other soldiers,

> these unfortunate men, who are passive in every respect, have not even been able to find partners. Many of them have descended to the basest stage of moral decrepitude and are really prostitutes manipulated by their pimps through threats of violence.

They specialised in fellating other soldiers. Homosexuality seemed omnipresent in the prisons maintained by the *bataillons d'Afrique*, where twelve to twenty men were confined together in particularly poor accommodations. Some soldiers forced comrades to perform fellatio on them, although others, Jude added, seemed perfectly happy to render this service, and many developed a taste for such activities: men claimed initially to have been forced into sex, but ended up enjoying their debasement.[21]

Jude's book intended to diagnose problems obtaining in the *bataillons d'Afrique*, and denounced the living conditions that drove soldiers to vice. He analysed homosexuality as one element in the general moral degradation produced by social circumstances, using case studies to prove his point. One soldier had a grandfather who committed suicide, and a father who abandoned his mother for a prostitute; at the age of thirteen, he was already living with a girl, and then became a pimp. After entering the army, he was convicted for theft and sent to the Bat' d'Af'. Violent, intelligent and proud, he was a passive homosexual despite his hunky build. In another case, a soldier from a disturbed family – an alcoholic father and mentally unstable uncle – was given to alcohol and 'debauchery' by the age of fourteen. He joined the colonial infantry, but deserted; captured, he committed theft and was also convicted of inflicting grievous bodily harm (the latter offence carried out in the very courtroom where he was standing trial). He recounted to Jude that four days after his arrival in the Bat' d'Af', he had met a handsome soldier of eighteen, whom he helped to set up his bed and invited for a drink. The two men were punished for singing at night (no doubt after drinking sessions) by being locked up together, and they began an intense sexual and emotional relationship – 'I passed him on to one of my mates for several days just to get some rest'. The older man was later killed in gang warfare. A third case history concerned another son of an alcoholic father; he never liked girls and masturbated regularly while in a civilian prison. In the Bat' d'Af', the physically robust but timid man 'offered to render the most ignoble services to his comrades', who nevertheless treated him with disrespect – 'they take him, then they kick him out'. Yet another man had begun engaging in passive homosexuality at the age of eight, sodomised by an older friend every second or third day for three or four years; he then had sex for money with other men. He confessed that the sight of smooth young men excited him more than did women, and that he cruised the barracks to find partners to fellate. 'G.' was a 'passive pederast', one of the 'Moroccans', though he complained to Jude that he had been harassed when he refused to be sodomised. 'G.' claimed to masturbate six or seven times a day, a record about which Jude remained sceptical. Jude categorised the various cases as 'normal', 'unbalanced', 'degenerate' or 'morally insane' men, identifiable by certain traits – 'degenerates' often had funny ears, asymmetric faces and small testicles, and usually stuttered.[22]

Two years after the publication of Jude's book, Dr Rebierre devoted a chapter to homosexuality in another study on the Joyeux. He found 'all forms of sexual inversion', including anal and oral intercourse, among soldiers in the Bat' d'Af'. Rebierre, more than Jude, placed such activities into historical and comparative context, citing Ulrichs and Kraft-Ebbing among sexologists who discussed homosexuality, as well as classical examples of friendships between Orestes and Pylades, and Patroclus and Achilles. He concluded that pederasty is found everywhere, though most often observed among Orientals.

> Uranian practices, which have always incurred some disapproval in the Occident, are openly practiced in the Orient. Among the natives of Persia, Turkey and Egypt, homosexuality is certainly as common as heterosexuality. In Algeria and Tunisia, Muslims do not always live with women, whom they are obliged to purchase from their fathers. Even those who do hardly make any difference between the two sexes. In many Tunisian cities, Arab merchants do not have wives, but keep for all purposes a young man in their shops. In the streets, one often sees adolescent couples holding hands or entwined like lovers. The Arabic and Jewish youth of Tunis readily prostitute themselves to foreigners. This 'pederastic atmosphere' naturally has an effect on the morals of our indigenous troops and on our elite units composed of men who are inclined to let themselves be tempted.[23]

Rebierre isolated four reasons for soldiers engaging in 'perversity': a wish to experiment with new pleasures, lack of 'normal pleasures', fear of impotence or venereal diseases, and simple interest. Soldiers in the Bat' d'Af' were young men 'who have experienced a life of precocious debauchery, who are always on the look out for new types of pleasure and who have often abused sexual pleasures since puberty'. Without sufficient income, soldiers could not afford women prostitutes, and enjoyed the services of comrades, or sometimes Arabs, for free. Three-quarters of the men were sexually 'active'; two-thirds of 'passive' partners engaged in sex under threat of force. Some soldiers' tents became veritable 'theatres of violent orgy', with gang rapes of soldiers. Male prostitution flourished among:

born inverts…and former prostitutes who, in civilian life, used their rectum as a means of earning a living. [Yet] these latter avoid practicing their art in the army, because military prostitution is not well paid enough. One of them told me that he had declined his comrades' solicitations 'in order to preserve my capital for civilian life'.[24]

Homosexual acts, concluded Rebierre, were particularly common in 'predis-posed' army units – the *bataillons d'Afrique*, the Foreign Legion, disciplinary units, the colonial infantry, the navy and units of native soldiers – a lengthy list comprising most French colonial forces. They appeared more frequent during military campaigns than during respites from warfare. However, Rebierre argued that it was not possible to 'treat' homosexuality in the army, and authorities should only react when cases involve violence, prostitution, disobedience or offences to public morality.[25]

The two doctors who studied crime and illness among the Joyeux adopted standard notions about 'inverts', and about the effects of lack of women and harsh climates in pushing men inevitably into homosexual activities. They shared stereotypes about 'active' and 'passive' homosexuals, and the physical traits that characterised each type. They connected pederasty with social prob-lems, such as alcoholism, and linked it to the early onset of sexual activity, regular masturbation and a penchant for debauchery. Furthermore, they agreed with the idea that sodomy was an 'Oriental' vice, endemic in the Arab world where France established colonial outposts – the term 'Moroccans' for the most flagrant homosexuals underlined the notion of Eastern luxuriance. Taking as case studies soldiers who had committed offences and were assigned to particu-larly notorious battalions, they not surprisingly linked homosexual practices with a criminal record and military punishment. Jude's and Rebierre's accounts thus reflect late nineteenth-century ideas about the aetiology of homosexuality, but they also view homosexual practices as only one of the psychological and social problems affecting colonial soldiers.[26]

Isolation, harsh climate, brutal discipline and the hardship of overseas post-ings provoked vice among ordinary soldiers, and units such as the Bat' d'Af' incorporated troopers prey to vice and degeneracy. Many of the men were allegedly unbalanced – Jude stated that the majority of soldiers in the *bataillons d'Afrique* were 'mentally infirm, hysterics and epileptics' – and their conditions worsened during military service.[27] He pointed out, however, that qualities which handicapped degenerates in civilian life came in useful in the army; an innate instability fitted men for the nomadic life of the soldier, lack of affective sentiments gave them courage in warfare, and the intelligence that allowed them to survive in private life helped them survive in the colonies and indeed 'to develop new lands'. Such men, just as their fellow citizens, had a right to protection, justice and leadership. Degenerates – whether men in the Bat' d'Af' or Jesus Christ (whom Jude did not hesitate to label a sexual degenerate because of his lack of a 'normal' sex life) – could also be geniuses. Jude even suggested that dissident sexual urges might not be inappropriate for some careers: 'Many men of genius turned away from the pleasures of women and the distractions which they provide to man's soul. Was not this perversion perhaps useful to them?' Though without connecting such 'perversion' directly with the military, Rebierre went on to say that traits found in Napoleon – lack of affection, absence of altruistic desire, vanity, pride, moral stigmas – could also be identified with 'degenerates'.[28]

Jude's psychological speculations, provocative and daring observations, remain intriguing, even if both he and, with greater outrage, Rebierre deplored sodomitical activities in the *bataillons d'Afrique*. Though material on homosexuality in the French Army remains fragmentary, commentators were clearly aware of homosexual practices among colonial troops. These activities could hardly avoid engendering moral censure and medical concern. The impression nevertheless remains that attending to the problem of homosexuality was hardly a priority, and even senior officers admitted that non-standard sexual practices caused no harm to the army or the nation.

The Bat' d'Af' showed one extreme of homosexual life – overt and indiscriminate sexual intercourse of every sort, prostitution, occasional violence. The physical and promiscuous nature of those practices disconcerted observers. In other conditions, where a superior officer enjoyed the homoerotic and homosocial company of clean-cut young lieutenants, rather than engaging in orgies in camp tents, disapprobation would be muted, an indication not only of different standards for rankers and officers, but of varying views towards base sodomy and noble platonic love.

Marshal Lyautey

The most interesting case of a top-ranking officer with homosexual inclinations in the French army is Marshal Hubert Lyautey, France's greatest colonial soldier. Lyautey was born in 1854 in Nancy, his father a prosperous engineer, his mother a Norman aristocrat. Although sustaining a serious injury as a child, when he fell while watching the baptismal procession of the Prince Imperial, Lyautey determined to pursue a military career and, in 1873, entered the French military academy. As a young lieutenant on holiday, he spent six weeks in Algeria in 1878, a visit that created a life-long love of North Africa. From 1880 to 1882, he was posted to Algeria, but subsequently had to spend the rest of the decade, to his disappointment, in metropolitan garrisons. Lyautey attracted attention to himself (not all of it positive) when, in 1891, he published 'The social role of the officer', outlining the duties and opportunities soldiers possessed to regenerate France, and their potential for an impact on the nation far beyond military life.

In 1894, Lyautey asked to go to Tonkin, in northern Indo-China, where French colonial troops were attempting to 'pacify' rebels, commonly considered Chinese 'pirates'. Lyautey became chief of staff to General Gallieni and acting head of the occupation forces. The meeting with Gallieni proved propitious, as the elder officer, a kindred spirit in his social vision (and, it was said, sexual tastes), became Lyautey's mentor. When Gallieni was made military commander of Madagascar in 1897, Lyautey followed him, and ruled over a third of the island (an area equivalent to a third of France) as veritable proconsul. In 1903, now a general, Lyautey was given command of a large region of Algeria bordering Morocco, whetting his and France's appetite for the still independent sultanate. In 1912, after years of incursions, and jousting with European rivals, France established a protectorate over Morocco. Lyautey was appointed French Resident-General, virtual governor of the country, a position he held until 1925 (except for a brief period as Minister of War in 1916). In his last years as an active soldier, Lyautey turned somewhat bitter at being sidelined by younger officers, despite having been made a marshal, the highest rank in the French Army. He spent the final decade of his life in France, honoured with decorations and election to the Académie Française, and served as Commissioner-General of the grand international Colonial Exhibition in Paris in 1931. He died three years later, and, at his request, was buried in Morocco; his remains were repatriated to Paris in the 1960s and interred in the Invalides, where his tomb bears inscriptions in French and Arabic.

Lyautey had married in 1909, at the age of forty-five, but this was a companionate union rather than an affair of love or lust. Many assumed Lyautey to be homosexual, and jokes circulated about his proclivities. No less a person than Georges Clemenceau, the prime minister, was supposed to have said: 'He is an admirable, courageous man, who has always had balls between his legs – even when they weren't his own.' Madame Lyautey was rumoured to remark to a group of Lyautey's subalterns one morning, 'Ah, Messieurs, last night I cuckolded you.'[29] Homosexual contemporaries, such as Jean Cocteau, Julien Green, Roger Martin du Gard and René Crevel, considered him one of their own. Alain Daniélou, a scholar of India and also homosexual, said that his grandfather, General Clamorgan, had been one of Lyautey's favourites. Others hinted in more guarded terms about his orientation, Abel Bonnard, for instance, remarking that 'instead of excusing his differences, he deployed them almost insolently...disguising nothing of his beliefs, his ideas or his tastes'.[30]

French biographers, who have handled Lyautey gently, generally prove reticent to snoop into his private life, careful not to tarnish his reputation. However, by the 1970s gay publications often spoke of Lyautey as homosexual.[31] Outsiders did not mince words. The respected American military historian Douglas Porch not only takes Lyautey's homosexuality as a given but connects it with his career. 'The social role of the officer' had established Lyautey as a renegade, and his monarchist views and aristocratic manner ruffled fellow officers; a colonial posting in the early 1890s provided a convenient way to use his undisputed talents, while keeping him at a distance. However, says Porch,

> There was another reason why Lyautey was exiled abroad, why, ten years, later, General O'Connor protested formally when he heard that Lyautey was to take command of Aïn Sefra: He was a homosexual. He made no attempt to disguise it. It was well known in later years that he kept one or

two catamites on his large staff, which was more like a court than a military entourage. But Lyautey never took his homosexual affairs seriously. He was too much the professional. If he favored young sublieutenants in bed, he promoted them strictly on the basis of their military merits.

Overseas assignments, Porch continues, suited Lyautey: 'In the 1890s, European homosexuals, outcasts in their own lands, might find more tolerance, and a more accessible selection of young boys, in North Africa.' Porch further links Lyautey's political outlook with his sexuality:

> It was Lyautey's attitudes, rather than his career, that seem to have been most deeply affected by his homosexuality. His sexual preferences certainly offended most of his brother officers, which is one of the reasons why he sought the company of writers, artists and left-of-center politicians with whom he shared relatively few political views. It also helps to explain why, after 1894, he was so enthusiastic about colonial service....The French Empire collected misfits and restive characters....It is perhaps ironic that this deeply conservative and even snobbish man felt far more at home in this world of rebels and social castoffs than in that of the provincial aristocrats and soldiers into which he had been born and educated. Lyautey was a romantic, a man of protest in constant revolt against the mediocrity of life and the restraints of society. His homosexuality confirmed him in his attitudes, for it condemned him to be a perpetual outcast, a man on the margin of many worlds but belonging to none. In a real sense, this was also his strength: part of his originality sprang from the fact that he stood personally on both sides of so many frontiers.[32]

Information on Lyautey's sexual attitudes and behaviours must be sought circumstantially, although there seems no doubt at least about what Daniel Rivet nicely calls Lyautey's 'homophile sensuality'.[33] Christian Gury, a Paris lawyer, has convincingly argued that not only were Lyautey's inclinations homosexual, but that he served as model for Baron Charlus in Marcel Proust's *A la recherche du temps perdu*. As a first item of evidence, Gury cites the opinions of novelists and politicians who affirmed that Lyautey's interests were not heterosexual. Gury also puts forward some of Lyautey's personal tastes and habits, which place the marshal in the camp of *fin de siècle* aesthetes, dandies and decadents – natty dress and punctilious deportment, overwrought decoration in his houses, frequenting of artistic circles, consorting with known homosexuals such as Proust, Reynaldo Hahn and Cocteau.[34]

The most persuasive evidence – which ties Lyautey's sexual and emotional bent with his colonial vocation – comes from his own writings. Even in public utterances, Lyautey made a point of championing the tolerance and latitude for individuality provided by colonial society, and of praising the young folk whose company he enjoyed. In *Paroles d'action*, a generally dry collection of speeches delivered in Algeria and Morocco, Lyautey confessed that 'it was not only

because of a taste for adventure and travel that I became a convinced colonial',
but also because of disenchantment with a France eaten away by fratricidal
conflicts and stymied by sterile words:

> I found in our colonies in Asia, in Africa, here [in Algeria], the finest
> school of energy in which our race is immersing and remoulding itself, as in
> a cauldron. The Frenchman who emerges does not perhaps always conform
> to the familiar type, moderate in his needs and tastes, to the 'regular' ideal
> of our fathers, but he is better – he is 'irregular', the 'glorious irregular', that
> is, one who bucks routines and superannuated regulations to make way for
> the new roles necessitated by eternal evolution.

In the colonies,

> We overlook, in uniform or dress clothes, the misunderstandings, the
> barriers which elsewhere, in an ineluctable way, separate men of different
> professions....The superiority of colonial life is that, with the distance that
> it provides, it engenders a wider, more tolerant, more comforting concep-
> tion of things.[35]

Lyautey is talking about general colonial life and its revivifying influence, but
nevertheless suggests that empire provided a congenial environment for many
who, for whatever reason, did not fit into conventional moulds.

In speeches to soldiers, Lyautey spoke admiringly of the young men whose
courage and virility supported colonial and national endeavours; for instance18-
year-olds in Casablanca were 'fine-looking young men, vigourous and healthy.
They are a tribute to the French race which is growing up in this land.'
Mentioning a Bronzino painting of a young lord he had seen in Florence, 'handsome as a classic', and the ruins of Olympia, 'the sanctuary of beauty and
physical strength', Lyautey confessed how much he loved youth.

> If I like to surround myself with youths, it is not, of course, because I want
> joyful talk and frivolity – which, by the way, is no longer their custom – but
> because the young act with youthfulness and with action, and before
> ending the day, after the heavy quotidian tasks, nothing equals this happy
> bath of fertile and creative sap (*rien ne vaut ce bain d'allégresse, de sève
> féconde et créatrice*).[36]

Whether sexual metaphors were intentional or subliminal – Lyautey often
referred to 'colonial sap' – he expounded a need for and delight in the youths
whom he met and whom he appointed to his staff.

Lyautey indulged in many homoerotic descriptions of young Frenchmen and
'natives' in the colonies where he worked. He also lingered on antique statues
he admired on his holidays: a marble ephebe was 'a triumphal evocation of
voluptuous and strong beauty'.[37] As Gury concedes, Lyautey's profession – with

natural admiration for strength and physical fitness – authorised appreciation of male beauty, yet his prose often went beyond necessary sentiments.[38] A French sub-lieutenant was a 'heart-warming young man, twenty years old, so fecund, his sap, his faith, his hopes, all that, is a rare and exquisite gift'. Another subaltern, who appeared in Lyautey's diary in 1886, was:

> this sub-lieutenant…who pleases me so much…[and] who came from ten p.m. to two a.m. to warm up my old thirty-year-old self with his hot and rich sap. What a young, vigorous and generous nature! I regret his departure. I have always loved the young, when they are apt; they are good companions for work and dreaming, with whom one holds on to the supreme pleasure (*jouissance*) of command.[39]

On his way to Indo-China, Lyautey remarked on 'a handsome black Nubian, silent, supple and shiny', and in Ceylon noticed:

> in this fairy garden…beings who are almost naked, graceful, undulating their bronze bodies…their eyes, huge big eyes which dream with the depths of the sea and then, their smile, soft, engaging, which thanks you and asks for nothing.

Returning to Zanzibar, he noted 'the beautiful bodies, the fine teeth, the grand gestures near the fountains! A trove of colours and poses; and I am eating all this up, leaving behind the scrawny Annamite in his dun-coloured sack'. (Lyautey little appreciated the physiques or manners of the Indo-Chinese.) He waxed lyrical about North Africans. There was an Arab horseman, 'well mounted, well harnessed, well equipped, a good-looking guy…graceful in his mauve burnous'. In 1904, Lyautey took up with the sons of an Arabic official; 'my favourite' was nineteen years old,

> he attached himself to me like a medieval vassal and would not leave me, [he] led me, holding his gun aloft in difficult places, the first one to come to my tent to ask me how I spent the night, making my coffee, arranging my burnous: a young Sarrasin warrior…radiating youth and elegance: what fine chivalrous mores![40]

Enjoyment of the company of French subalterns and Moroccans, whose country and culture Lyautey admired and loved, clearly connected with a colonial vocation. Lyautey's experience of North Africa, and the desert in particular, was transcendental. On his first visit, he wrote to his father about one outing:

> With my brigade I am leading the campaign…; the moon rose an hour ago, it is a beautiful night, one of those bright and clear nights that you will remember, dear father.…What exquisite delight! On the southern route, in front of me, are five horsemen, the pearl white haunches of their small

horses glistening in the light: I am letting myself be taken in by all the dreams that can be imagined by a twenty-seven year old lieutenant…who is crossing the desert….Hosanna! Here is my Africa![41]

Lyautey had no greater happiness than keeping company with his brave young officers in their starched uniforms or young Arabs in colourful burnouses, as they rode across the North African desert.

Lyautey pursued imperial policies of pacification and warfare against rebels. He promoted economic development and the emergence of an export-oriented economy. Despite his nominally advisory role as Resident-General in a protectorate (rather than as governor of a colony), he ruled Morocco with an iron hand. Yet Lyautey gained a reputation (and criticism in some quarters) for his 'progressive' colonial stance, and an obvious interest in Islam and in Moroccan civilisation. He forbade missionaries from evangelising Muslims, and both in Morocco and when presiding at the foundation of a mosque in Paris, spoke with great respect of Islam. He dissuaded large-scale settlement of Europeans in Morocco. He sponsored the building of administrative and residential quarters in an architectural style borrowing from and complementing local traditions. Lyautey's policies were heralded as more enlightened and humane than those of many contemporaries. Gury connects his cultural, political and sexual sympathies: 'Indigenophilia, Islamophilia, homophilia: a classic triangle.'[42] He hypothesises that, in the colonial context, Lyautey's humaneness and humanism linked to his sexuality.[43] A connection between the pleasures of young men, the excitement of North Africa, Lyautey's colonial vocation and the policies he pursued seems a proven case.

The British Army

Similar to Lyautey, several British military greats connected with empire may have had homosexual penchants. Major-General Frank M. Richardson includes Brigadier John Nicholson (1821–57), General George Gordon (1833–85) and Earl Kitchener of Khartoum (1850–1916) among profiles of 'some homosexual generals'.[44] Nicholson, 'the hero of Delhi', played a vital role in putting down the Indian Mutiny of 1857. Richardson characterises Gordon as a prig and sadist: he 'personally administered both corporal and capital punishment and kept the heads of executed criminals on his desk'.[45] He had no interest in women but was obsessed with his military profession. Richardson quotes another biographer, Michael Edwardes, saying that Nicholson was 'a violent manic figure, a homosexual bully, an extreme egotist…a homosexual, a repressed homosexual, disgusted by his own inclination and one who translated his disgust into a violence manic in its manifestation'.[46] Such an analysis indicates Nicholson's extreme self-hatred, sexual repression and psychological transference. General Gordon, who took part in campaigns against the Taiping rebels, then served as governor of the Sudan, where he was killed when Khartoum was besieged by the Mahdi in 1885, became one of the most celebrated imperial martyrs. Various biographers have identified a sadistic streak in his character, too, a death wish and desire for martyrdom, a penchant for remorse and penitence, a neurotic disposition and alcoholism. Gordon had a self-given mission to help poor and orphan boys, whom he took into his home and to whom he ministered with unusual personal attention. He mended their clothes and took pleasure in washing the youths whom Lytton Strachey called 'ragged street arabs and rough sailor lads'.[47] A suggestion that he was a repressed homosexual is not implausible.

Another officer attracted to young men was General Sir Robert Baden-Powell (1857–1941), whose defence of Mafeking during the Anglo-Boer War earned him fame. Baden-Powell went on to found the Scout movement and was rewarded with a barony. Tim Jeal makes a convincing case that he was homosexually inclined. Baden-Powell's attitudes towards women 'ranged from companionable neutrality to outright hostility', and he married only at the age of fifty-five. His sentiments about the male sex were typified by a pithy assertion: 'A clean young man in his prime of health and strength is the finest creature God has made in the world.' Baden-Powell had a long and intense friendship with Kenneth McLaren, 'the Boy', 'my best friend in the world', as Baden-Powell described him, a relationship that might have encompassed a physical side (though Jeal thinks not). Baden-Powell surrounded himself with handsome subalterns and assistants, and admired a team of African gymnasts as 'magnificent specimens'. He counselled Scouts to control their sexual urges, avoid fantasising about women and refrain from 'self-pollution'; he thought that, so curbed, sexual passion could disappear among noble-minded young men. Female nudity revolted him, but he took pleasure in watching young males swimming nude. He also enjoyed peeks at 'those wonderful photographs' of a friend, pictures of naked boys. Scouting, like military life, provided opportunities to watch, socialise with and live in close physical and emotional contact with young men. Jeal concludes: 'The available evidence points inexorably to the conclusion that Baden-Powell was a repressed homosexual.'[48]

Yet another officer reputedly homosexual was Lord Kitchener. Richardson has no qualms in suggesting that Kitchener was at least emotionally homosexual, even if he did not have physical relations with men. The evidence, predictably, draws on his lack of interest in women or recorded sexual adventures with them, which led Queen Victoria to remark, 'They say he dislikes women, but I can only say he was very nice to me.' Furthermore, Kitchener had enduring attachments to young and handsome lieutenants, his 'band of boys', including Frank Maxwell, whom Kitchener called 'Brat', and Oswald Fitzgerald, an unmarried man who served as Kitchener's companion for nine years, and with whom he perished when the ship on which they were passengers hit a mine in the North Sea during the First World War. Jad Adams says that 'this man was truly Patroclus to Kitchener's Achilles, combining good looks and bravery'. Some contemporaries did not doubt that Kitchener was homosexual; the Reuters correspondent in Beijing told another journalist, George Morrison (himself once accused of being homosexual), that Kitchener 'has the failing acquired by most of the Egyptian officers, a taste for buggery'. Kitchener's love of fine fabrics, neatly set tables and pretty porcelain – regarded as feminine interests – have also been taken to suggest his homosexuality. [49]

Kitchener's most recent full-scale biographer, John Pollock, testily denies allegations about Kitchener's sexuality, saying that the 'band of boys' had no sexual connection and that his entourage included married associates in addition to bachelors like Fitzgerald. Pollock points out that Kitchener himself was once unofficially engaged to be married, although his fiancée died of typhoid, and that he congratulated a cousin on her marriage, noting his 'not having been in the happy state you are now', and adding, 'I cannot help envying his good fortune'. [50]

Contrasting conclusions about Kitchener reveal the hazards of surmising from scanty details. Lack of interest in women, close association with other men or an inclination to 'feminine' pursuits do not prove homosexuality. On the other hand, neither an engagement (or even marriage) to a woman, nor strongly held and publicly expressed religious beliefs preclude homosexual interests. Military officers do, of necessity, associate closely with fit young men, but that in itself does not guarantee either homosexual or heterosexual tastes. Evidence can be read either way. Pollock, the first volume of whose biography of Kitchener is dedicated to the third Earl Kitchener, is eager to prove that the hero of Khartoum was not homosexual, just as Richardson wants to include him among his homosexual generals, although he admits that Kitchener probably never had a physical relationship with a man. Adams concurs, remarking sagely that 'evidence of sexual activity is not required for a categorisation; if he was not a "practicing" homosexual, in terms of "sexual proclivity", Kitchener almost certainly was a homosexual'. [51]

Lawrence and Dahoum

A more fully documentable example of a homosexual bent among heroes of empire is T.E. Lawrence (1888–1935). [52] Leader of the Arab revolt during the First World War, British government adviser on Middle Eastern policy, author of the best-selling *The Seven Pillars of Wisdom*, victim of a motorcycle accident, subject of a famous film, Lawrence of Arabia remains one of the most popular imperial figures. Yet Lawrence was a person of contradictions, well respected but born illegitimate, a puritan with violent masochistic urges, a promoter of Arab liberation from the Turkish empire and an agent of British imperialism, as secretive about his private life as he was unabashedly a public figure.

Lawrence remained for long an almost sacrosanct, if enigmatic, character, whose biographies told very little about his personal life, let alone sexual interests. Since the publication of John E. Mack's biography in 1976, it has been well known that Lawrence had a troubled sexuality and never established a long lasting and fulfilling sexual and emotional relationship. More recently, Michael Asher has retraced Lawrence's life and travels, speaking forthrightly about what he calls Lawrence's 'love' for a young Arab. [53]

Lawrence did not smoke, drink or dance, and avoided sexual situations while a student at Oxford and afterwards in the Royal Air Force. Physical sexual relations revolted him; in his own word, sex was 'dirty'. He confessed to ignorance about the sexual act, and said that 'I hate and detest this animal side' of the human personality. He wondered about the value of what he calculated as less than two minutes of physical pleasure. By his own admission, he experienced an inordinately close relationship with his mother – who beat him as a child – and 'knowledge of her will prevent my ever making any woman a mother, and the cause of children'. He stated forthrightly: 'I take no pleasure in women. I have never thought twice or even once of the shape of a woman: but men's bodies, in repose or in movement – especially the former – appeal to me directly and very generally.' His brother remembered that Lawrence was less repelled by the idea of homosexual than heterosexual contact.[54]

For the last eleven years of his life, Lawrence created an elaborate charade to hire a young Scotsman (and eventually another man) to beat him regularly. Lawrence pretended that he had committed some offence, hinted to involve financial impropriety, against an uncle who, instead of having Lawrence arrested, would pay for him to be beaten. A friend, and a doctor, were recruited to inspect Lawrence's body after the floggings to ascertain that he had been sufficiently punished and to report, by letter, to the uncle. Lawrence himself wrote the letters from the 'uncle' to acknowledge the reports and arranged for the Scotsman to be paid. He required the man to beat him across his naked buttocks until he ejaculated, although he undertook no sexual activity directly with the man. Mack judges Lawrence's masochism an expression of his sexual guilt and expiation for having been raped by Turkish soldiers during the war, but also as a sign of immature and neurotic sexuality.

Lawrence's introduction to sexuality came during his time in the Levant, first working at an archaeological dig in Carchemish, Syria (now located in Turkey), then as a soldier. He experienced sexual situations in several different ways. He became familiar with local sexual practices, including intimacy between men (and realised that women partners were also available). Lawrence wrote in his diary, for instance, about a conversation with an 18-year-old sheikh 'with a sharp, rather rapacious and mobile face, and dark curling hair', with whom he had 'a long talk on all subjects in the evening, especially politics; the sheikh ended by going to sleep with his head on my knee!' Later the sheikh offered Lawrence two women, a proposal he declined.[55] He wrote disapprovingly about an Arab 'who regarded our comic reproductive process not as an unhygienic pleasure, but as a main business of life'.[56]

In the first pages of *The Seven Pillars of Wisdom*, surprisingly as an introduction, Lawrence writes, with a mixture of voyeuristic interest and moral disapproval, about sexuality among his Bedouin companions, his prose revealing the sensuality of desert experiences and the temptations they offered. 'Some of the evil of my tale,' begins the first chapter, may have been inherent in our circumstances....For years we lived anyhow with one another in the naked desert, under the indifferent heaven. By day the hot sun tormented us; and we were dizzied by the heated wind. At night we were stained by dew, and shamed into pettiness by the innumerable silences of stars.

The men 'were drained of morality, of volition, of responsibility', strained and punished by the hardships of their campaign. Lawrence averred that:

> Gusts of cruelty, perversions, lusts ran lightly over the surface without troubling us; for the moral laws which had seemed to hedge about these silly accidents must be yet fainter wounds. We had learned that there were pangs too sharp, griefs too deep, ecstasies too high for our finite selves to register.

He said too that the pain of work forced a man to 'abandon' his body as 'rubbish': 'We left it below us to march forward, a breathing simulacrum, on its own unaided level, subject to influences from which in normal times our instincts would have shrunk.' Yet if Lawrence weathered the pain stoically, his Arabic companions were less resistant:

> The men were young and sturdy; and hot flesh and blood unconsciously claimed a right in them and tormented their bellies with strange longings. Our privations and dangers fanned this virile heat, in a climate as racking as can be conceived. We had no shut places to be alone in, no thick clothes to hide our nature. Man in all things lived candidly with man.[57]

The emphasis on the sexual tensions of the campaign is remarkable, with Lawrence tacitly subscribing to the idea that hot climates breed unnatural lusts and that Arabic men (and perhaps all men without women partners) ultimately seek to satisfy their desires with their fellows. The vocabulary – 'dizzied' men, 'stained' at night and 'drained' by exertions in the 'naked' desert – reinforces Lawrence's sexual fascination (at what he still considered an 'evil'). This mixes with obvious yearning for the 'young and sturdy' comrades, 'hot flesh and blood' on show in the 'virile heat'. Indeed the experience of the desert, the military campaign, itself becomes sexual.

Straight from this sexualised description of the pleasure and pain of the desert, Lawrence launches into an explicit paragraph about sexual play among his companions: 'The Arab was by nature continent; and the use of universal marriage had nearly abolished irregular courses in his tribes.' The next sentence describes women prostitutes in unappealing fashion: 'The public women of the rare settlements we encountered in our months of wandering would have been nothing to our numbers, even had their raddled meat been palatable to a man of healthy parts.' Lawrence then talks about other sorts of 'strange longings':

In horror of such sordid commerce our [Arab] youths began indifferently to slake one another's few needs in their own clean bodies – a cold convenience that, by comparison, seemed sexless and even pure. Later, some began to justify this sterile process, and swore that friends quivering together in the yielding sand with intimate hot limbs in supreme embrace, found there hidden in the darkness a sensual co-efficient of the mental passion which was welding our souls and spirits in one flaming effort. Several, thirsting to punish appetites they could not wholly prevent, took a savage pride in degrading the body, and offered themselves fiercely in any habit which promised physical pain or filth.

Given Lawrence's propensity, according to biographers such as Asher, to embroider or invent stories, his descriptions might be less than literal: it would have been highly unlikely for young men to engage in open sexual antics with the wild abandon that Lawrence's account suggests. (If they were 'hidden in the darkness', how did he get such a good view?) In any case, Lawrence's attitude to what he claimed to witness is obviously confused and ambivalent, suggesting both troubled reaction to sex, and licence in recording the scenes. The youths' sexual play was cleaner than commerce with prostitutes, yet was filthy, and sex and pain merged. Were they engaging in mainstream homosexual practices or did they take part in other activities involving 'physical pain or filth'? If there was pain and filth, how could Lawrence characterise such actions as 'pure'? Intercourse was first 'a cold convenience', yet also 'a sensual co-efficient of the mental passion which was welding our souls and spirits'. How were 'hot limbs' intertwined for 'cold convenience'? Were the men 'friends', or did they 'indifferently' engage with one another in an orgy? The passages remain hallucinatory.

Lawrence witnessed the 'friends quivering together in the yielding sand with intimate hot limbs in supreme embrace' – a melodramatic and almost pornographic description. But he then confesses,

I was sent to these Arabs as a stranger, unable to think their thoughts or subscribe their beliefs, but charged by duty to lead them forward and to develop to the highest any movement of theirs profitable to England in her war. If I could not assume their character, I could at least conceal my own.

Did Lawrence regret that he could not be like them, or did he desperately want to take part in their frolics? British reticence replaces Arabic passion, duty comes before pleasure; the Englishman – despite learning Arabic, dressing in Arabic robes and identifying with the Bedouins – remains 'a stranger' standing on the sidelines as these very scenes take place.

Lawrence, after these extraordinary pages, moves on to recount his military feats, but the place these orgiastic scenes (and his reactions) occupy in his book testifies to the priority he accorded them in his Arabian experiences. He remarks, writing in retrospect:

In my case, the effort for these years to live in the dress of Arabs, and to imitate their mental foundation, quitted me of my English self, and let me look at the West and its conventions with new eyes: they destroyed it all for me. At the same time I could not sincerely take on the Arab skin: it was an affectation only.[58]

Lawrence found himself in a limbo of identity, no longer an Englishman, not an Arab; no longer a puritan, not a hedonist; not a respectable heterosexual, reluctant to embrace his homosexual desires.

Lawrence could not join in Arabic sensuality, the sodomitical tumbling in desert sands, but – and this formed his second sexually charged experience – he could fall in love with an Arab. In 1911, Lawrence met Selim (or Sheikh) Ahmed (or Ahmad), a 14-year-old whose mother had nicknamed him Dahoum (a form of an Arabic word meaning 'dark', referring to his burnished skin). A friend of Lawrence described him as 'beautifully built and remarkably handsome', and Lawrence caused eyebrows to be raised when he sculpted a limestone likeness of a nude Dahoum that he attached to the roof of his house. Lawrence's diary makes regular reference to Dahoum, although in unsurprisingly discreet terms. On 30 July, 'Dahoum came to see me. Slept about 9.30, badly.' (Why did Lawrence sleep badly after Dahoum's visit?) The following day, 'Dahoum came to see me: slept about 9 p.m.', a note repeated the following day. Dahoum soon became indispensable: 'The boy was necessary' for a journey, Lawrence noted on 3 August, and he 'swam across [a river] to bring a boat to help me and the horse over'. Lawrence had already, in June, written to his mother about 'the donkey-boy', who:

> is an interesting character: he can read a few words....of Arabic, and altogether has more intelligence than the rank and file. He talks of going into Aleppo to school with the money he has made out of us. I will try and keep an eye on him, to see what happens.[59]

When Lawrence fell ill with dysentery, Dahoum visited him daily; when Dahoum caught malaria, Lawrence nursed him. Lawrence recounted that he and Dahoum spent an idyllic summer one year sailing along the Syrian coast. For Asher, Lawrence with Dahoum 'was able to open up completely as he could not do with anyone of his own age, race and status. With Dahoum, he felt unthreatened.'[60] Two years after they met, Lawrence took Dahoum (and another Arab whom he had to invite along to persuade Dahoum to make the journey) on a trip to England. He introduced them to his mother and brother in Oxford; Lawrence's friends were much taken with Dahoum's beauty, and one commissioned a portrait of him. Lawrence's (implausible) claim that Dahoum was of Hittite ancestry – like the antiquities he shipped to the Ashmolean Museum and which Dahoum helped him unpack – added to his allure. Dahoum toured London and Oxford, and apparently had a pleased, if slightly bemused, reaction to Britain.[61]

Lawrence's attitude to Dahoum was paradoxical. Lawrence mentioned him as part of a joke, when the youth was forced to drink Seidlitz powder and, according to Asher, 'declares, in a good impersonation of Crusoe's Man Friday, that the white man's sorcery is "very dangerous for by it men are changed suddenly into the forms of mares or great apes"'. Yet Dahoum rapidly became more than a figure of fun as Lawrence grew attached to him. Lawrence found him intellectually promising, but regretted that he wanted to go to school and would thus turn into the vulgar Europeanised native whom the Englishman despised. Lawrence admired 'better a thousand times the Arab untouched' than the Europeanised Bedouin, but admitted that desert life was a 'hideous grind' suitable only for 'the low level of village minds'. He bought schoolbooks for Dahoum and considered him ripe for improvement, although he disdained the civilising mission of other colonialists. He criticised foreigners who wielded influence in the Middle East, but then took pride in having taught Dahoum to reason like a Westerner. Dahoum was a 'savage' (as Lawrence called him), but that was part of his attraction. Lawrence professed esteem for Arabic life and culture, yet took Dahoum to England partly to awe him with British achievements. He gave his friendship to the youth but enjoyed unquestioned authority over him. In Asher's words: 'He may have believed that it was Dahoum's mind that interested him, but in fact he was attracted physically to the boy.'[62]

It is difficult to gauge Dahoum's feelings for Lawrence. He earned an income by working as Lawrence's cook and guide, but obviously enjoyed the Englishman's company and went out of his way to help him. He posed for Lawrence to sculpt him naked, and allowed Lawrence to borrow his clothes to disguise himself. He agreed to make the voyage to England and seemed to like his stay. Indeed, says Asher, he spoke of admiration for Lawrence, telling another Arab in 1912 that there was nothing that the Arabs could do that Lawrence could not do. 'He takes such an interest in us and cares for our welfare....We respect him and greatly admire his courage and bravery; we love him because he loves us and we would lay down our lives for him.' When Dahoum encountered an Egyptian nationalist, an Oxford undergraduate who claimed, 'Soon we will cut the throats of these [British] dogs!', he and his travelling companion proclaimed that they were willing to shoot the Egyptian.[63]

When Lawrence left Carchemish to undertake some research in Oxford in 1914, Dahoum found a job as guard at the archaeological site. Soon war broke out, and Lawrence was posted to Cairo, where he spent two years. Meanwhile, at Carchemish, half of the workers died from sickness and famine during the war. Dahoum presumably perished at this time, though Lawrence only learned (perhaps from Syrian recruits) of his death after he had returned to foment the Arab revolt.

Lawrence, in 1919, scribbled movingly on a flyleaf of a book of poetry, 'I wrought for him freedom to lighten his sad eyes: but he had died waiting for me. So I threw my gift away and now not anywhere will I find rest and peace.'[64] Lawrence was then working on *The Seven Pillars of Wisdom*, and it contains a poem dedicating the book 'To S.A.', whom Robert Graves identified as

Dahoum, the only person, Lawrence told him, with whom he had ever been in love. The poem stands as an exceptional statement of how Lawrence's personal feelings for the Bedouin donkey-boy merged with his political campaigns and leadership of the Arab revolt. Sadness at the death of his companion marks the poem. It reads:

> I loved you, so I drew these tides of men into my hands
> and wrote my will across the sky in stars
> To earn you Freedom, the seven pillared worthy house
> that your eyes might be shining for me
> when we came.
> Death seemed my servant on the road, till we were near
> and saw you waiting:
> When you smiled, and in sorrowful envy he outran me
> and took you apart:
> Into his quietness.
>
> Love, the way-weary, groped to your body, our brief wage
> ours for the moment
> Before earth's soft hand explored your shape, and the blind
> worms grew fat upon
> Your substance.
>
> Men prayed me that I set our work, the inviolate house,
> as a memory of you.
> But for fit monument I shattered it, unfinished; and now
> The little things creep out to patch themselves hovels
> in the marred shadow
> Of your gift.

The poem is a declaration of love, romantic but also erotic. It provides a justification for Lawrence's mission, an obituary for his dead friend and a *mea culpa* about his inability to save Dahoum or truly to win freedom for the Arabs. Asher rightly characterises the verses as 'one of the most moving tributes to young love ever written'.[65]

Lawrence's third encounter with Middle Eastern homosexuality was radically different from his three-year friendship with Dahoum. In 1917 Lawrence donned Turkish garb to reconnoitre a rail crossing – connecting lines from Hejaz to Damascus, and from Haifa to Damascus, a vital link on the Arabs' path to the Syrian capital. An auxiliary purpose (or the possible motive) was probably to search for Dahoum (who may have still been alive). Lawrence was captured by Turkish soldiers, who (seeming to mistake him for a Turk) charged him with having deserted from the Turkish army, and took him to the Bey (Governor), although Lawrence (still in disguise) protested that he was Circassian and exempt from military service. The Bey, in Lawrence's account, put his arms around him and tried to pull him onto his bed; when Lawrence refused his advances, the Bey had him stripped and grabbed his genitals, whereupon

Lawrence elbowed him in the groin. The Bey slapped him with a slipper and stuck a bayonet through the skin of his belly before propositioning him again. When Lawrence refused, the Bey ordered soldiers to take him away and teach him a lesson. They beat him viciously – Lawrence said that he lost count of the lashings after twenty strokes – and raped him repeatedly. He was also kicked with hobnailed boots, and his testicles were slashed. Lawrence's wounds were dressed, however, and he managed to escape. During the experience he had felt that 'a delicious warmth, probably sexual, was swelling through me'.[66]

Questions have remained about the incident, for instance, about how Lawrence could have survived, escaped and with painful injuries managed to ride a camel almost 300 miles to safety in three days. Asher points up other problems with the account in *The Seven Pillars of Wisdom* – it is not substantiated by reports in British intelligence or any corroborating evidence (including scars from the beating), the relevant pages from Lawrence's diary have been torn out, and there is confusion with the dating, which suggests that Lawrence was not actually in Dera'a when the incident was supposed to have occurred. Asher also points to Lawrence's propensity to lie about his activities (including the lies concocted to arrange his later beatings), and concludes that Lawrence probably fabricated the episode: 'The Dera'a incident was true only in the sense that it deliberately revealed the unseen Lawrence lurking in the shadows.' He explains:

> Lawrence was a masochist with a homosexual nature, who had from a very early age fantasized about being dominated by other men, especially in the ranks of the army. As he wrote repeatedly, the degradation of such a life appealed to him.[67]

Asher concedes that it may never be known whether Lawrence was captured, beaten and raped. Even if the incident was real, it is impossible to know if the suffering (and the sexual feeling) took place as Lawrence described. In either case, the Dera'a incident suggests that Lawrence's experience of the Arab and Turkish world (whether real or imagined) was dramatically sexual. He had observed the sexual play of his companions with mixed emotions of attraction and fear, voyeurism and horror. He had become so fond of a young Arab that he recorded daily encounters with him, carved a naked statue of him, took him to England, risked his life to search for him in the middle of a war, confessed that he had been unable to replace him in his affections, and dedicated his major literary work to him. Then Lawrence, who may well not have yet had physical experience of sex, either suffered, imagined or possibly simply exaggerated a horrible serial rape, which left him bloodied but with a perverse feeling of sexual satisfaction. Not surprisingly Lawrence later avoided sexual entanglements but had beatings inflicted on him either to expiate guilt at the rape or to relive it. Dahoum remained the innocent companion, the symbol of the noble Arab people whom Lawrence had tried to help. Yet – a point which has not occurred to his biographers – might not Lawrence have had himself beaten because he felt that he had failed Dahoum, failed to protect or save him, desiring to be punished, not just to relive, expiate or actualise the Dera'a incident, but to atone for the death of the beloved Dahoum?

According to Jeffrey Meyers, 'much of Lawrence's life was an unsuccessful attempt to subjugate his body' through starvation, asceticism, masochism, flagellation and denial. Opposition between body and will, in Mayer's psycho-biographical view, extended to an inability even to accept the physiological 'facts of life' and related to Lawrence's hatred of the body, his fear of his mother, revulsion at heterosexuality, and denied homosexuality. Private agony inspired public performance, as 'by disciplining and subjecting his corporal self he was able to channel his libido into war, achieve the outstanding feats of physical endurance and earn the respect of the Bedouin, which was vital to his leadership'. The incident at Dera'a marked a turning point:

> The assault by the despised Turkish enemy on his point of greatest weakness, his sexual core, subverted his will and powers of endurance, betrayed the high ideals of the dedicatory poem to S.A. ('the inviolate house as a memory to you'), ravished his bodily integrity and precious virginity, and set him on a path of renunciation and destruction.[68]

Sexual desire and political vocation came together for Lawrence, but sex and love could not.

Speculation about Lawrence's sexuality moves into the realm of psychohistory, but what is significant here is how, for yet another military officer, colonial experience provided exposure to different sexualities and the opportunity for appreciation of male camaraderie and affection for a young companion. If his descriptions of Arabic youths' sexual play appear fanciful, and the veracity of the account of his rape remains open to doubt, the reality of his emotional relationship with Dahoum is well established and goes some way towards explaining Lawrence's identification with the Arab struggle.

Homosexuality and the military

The conclusion of the following chapter will articulate some general comments on homosexuality among Europeans overseas – explorers, soldiers and civilians. Here several specific observations suggest themselves about homosexuality and the military. The ethos of the army (and navy) was profoundly homosocial with men sharing barracks, dressing and bathing in promiscuity, and living and fighting in close physical proximity, their minds necessarily focused on physical fitness and, after battle, the nursing of the injured and the burial of the dead. Officers drilled military and manly virtues of courage, bravery and endurance into soldiers. Physical punishments, including floggings, sanctioned disobedience. Army life encouraged, indeed necessitated, close friendships amongst men in the line of danger. Rest and recreation involved immoderate drink, a lowering of inhibitions and the search for sex, wherever it might be found.

Homoeroticism also played a role in military life with handsome young soldiers portrayed on recruiting posters and sculpted into war monuments. Colourful uniforms, the spit-and-polish of military decorum, and the exhibitionism and voyeurism of parades and turning-out ceremonies displayed the physical prowess of men in their prime. Senior officers looked with pride on the attributes of their recruits and subalterns, and rankers competed with each other to develop their bodies, hone their skills and prove their vitality.

Such circumstances provided a congenial environment for homosexuality, even if the military ostensibly did not welcome homosexuals and damned homosexual practices among its members. Camaraderie, mateship and solidarity might slide off into physical expressions of loyalty and affection; absence of women in remote outposts could encourage men to take advantage of young and comely colleagues; soldiers who were innately homosexually oriented could easily sublimate sexual feelings through fraternising with men or find partners who shared their proclivities.

If observers suspend disbelief that red-blooded military officers – quintessentially 'real men' and macho warriors – could be homosexually inclined, and if homosexuality is understood to mean more than genital sexual relations, then the men profiled here are cases of homosexual inclination, openly expressed or repressed. There is no proof that Gordon, Kitchener, Baden-Powell, Lawrence, Lyautey or the others had physical relations with other men – given beliefs that promoted continence, the illegality of homosexual practices in the British (if not French) Army, and a fear of discovery and dishonour, it is likely that the British officers (and Lyautey) did not bed other men. Yet their interests – Gordon's bathing urchins, Baden-Powell's Scouting for boys, Lawrence's love for Dahoum, Lyautey's intense enjoyment of manly young colleagues – all point to a distinct homosexual orientation. The colonies provided locales where soldiers' desires to enjoy the company of men could safely, even acceptably, be enacted.

Notes

1 See J.A. Mangan, *The Game Ethic and Imperialism* (Harmondsworth, 1985), and Graham Dawson, *Soldier Heroes: British Adventure, Empire and the Imaging of Masculinities* (London, 1994).
2 See Ronald Hyam, *Empire and Sexuality: The British Experience* (Manchester, 1990).
3 John Pollock, *Kitchener: The Road to Omdurman* (London, 1998).
4 Charles Nicholl, *Somebody Else: Rimbaud in Africa, 1800–91* (London, 1997).
5 Hugh Trevor-Roper, *A Hidden Life: The Enigma of Sir Edmund Backhouse* (London, 1976), pp. 243, 249, 255, 256. On Backhouse, see Ch. 3.
6 Gérard Zwang, *La Fonction érotique* (Paris, 1975), quoted in Christian Gury, *Lyautey–Charlus*(Paris, 1998), p. 61.
7 Rudi Bleys, *The Geography of Perversion* (New York, 1995), p. 149.
8 Quoted in Gury, p. 64.
9 Douglas Porch, *The French Foreign Legion: A Complete History of the Legendary Fighting Force* (New York, 1991).
10 Dr Tranchant and Lieutenant Desvignes, in *Les Condamnés militaires du pénitencier de Bossuet*, quoted in Gury, p. 248.

11 Louis Dautheville, 'Le Cafard ou psychose des pays chauds', *Archives d'anthropologie criminelle*, Vol. 26 (1911), pp. 5–27, as summarised by Wayne R. Dynes, *Homosexuality: A Research Guide* (New York, 1987), p. 418. Cf. Dr Jacquot, 'Des Abbérations de l'appétit génésique', *Gazette médicale de Paris*, 28 July 1889, p. 9, quoted in Bleys, p. 127.

12 Dr Berthulus, 'Considérations sur les causes de dégénérescence physique et morale du peuple dans les grandes villes', *Gazette médicale de Paris*, 1847, pp. 800–1, quoted in Bleys, p. 127.

13 Richard Burton, *The Sotadic Zone* (Boston, 1977), p. 94.

14 Quoted in Gury, p. 65.

15 Paul Clavigny, 'L'Homosexualité dans l'armée', *Revue d'hypnotisme*, Vol. 23 (1908), pp. 39–40, as summarised by Dynes, p. 417.

16 'Médecine militaire: Déni de justice', *Le Bulletin médical*, Vol. 6 (1892), pp. 65–7.

17 See Michel Larivière, *Homosexuels et bisexuels célèbres* (Paris, 1997).

18 Jules Roy, *Etranger pour mes frères* (Paris, 1982), p. 103. Cf. his *The Battle of Dien Bien Phu*, 'Wasn't there something improper about a [woman] secretary of this sort [the assistant to General de Castries]? In Indochina, since de Lattre's time, free morals had been common currency. After all, wasn't this war rather like Atlantis?' (London, 1984, p. 121) I am grateful to Katharine Thornton for these references.

19 Quoted in Francine Dessaigne, *Tatahouine m'était contée* (Ivry-sur-Seine, 1996).

20 Dr R. Jude, *Les Dégénérés dans les Bataillons d'Afrique* (Vannes, 1907), pp. 33–6.

21 *Ibid.*, pp. 36–8.

22 *Ibid.*, pp. 57–66.

23 Dr Paul Rebierre, *'Joyeux' et demi-fous* (Paris, 1909), pp. 48–9.

24 *Ibid.*, pp. 50, 55, 59.

25 *Ibid.*, p. 68.

26 The most common problem was *cafard*, a state induced by isolation, unfamiliar climate (particularly during the sirocco windstorms) and periods of inactivity during siestas and rest days. It led to melancholy thoughts and vague fears, a feeling of uselessness and loss of individuality. *Cafard* often resulted in obsessive performance of chores, or sometimes manifested itself as a violent urge to break things, attack people or even kill (Jude, p. 86 ff., Rebierre, p. 102 ff.).

27 Jude, p. 126.

28 *Ibid.*, pp. 161–2.

29 Quoted in Gury, p. 102.

30 Quoted in Gury, p. 89; for other contemporary views, see, e.g., pp. 43, 74, 79, 88.

31 Gury, p. 90.

32 Douglas Porch, *The Conquest of Morocco* (New York, 1983).

33 Daniel Rivet, 'Lyautey l'Africain', in *Le Temps des Colonies*, special issue of *L'Histoire*, No. 11 (2001), p. 22.

34 Gury, *op. cit.*

35 Hubert Lyautey, *Paroles d'action* (Paris, 1995), pp. 78–9.

36 *Ibid.*, pp. 221, 111–12.

37 Quoted in Gury, p. 28.

38 Gury, p. 21.

39 Quoted in *ibid.*, p. 51.

40 Quoted in *ibid.*, pp. 48–53.

41 Quoted in Robert Aldrich, *Greater France: A History of French Overseas Expansion* (London, 1996), p. 135.

42 Gury, p. 63.

43 Gury, p. 32.

44 Frank M. Richardson, *Mars without Venus: A Study of Some Homosexual Generals* (Edinburgh, 1981).

45 *Ibid.*, p. 129.

46 Michael Edwardes, *Bound to Exile* (London, 1969), quoted in *ibid.*, p. 131.
47 Richardson, pp. 110–15.
48 Tim Jeal, *Baden-Powell* (London, 1989), Ch. 3; quotations from pp. 55, 83, 104 and 103.
49 Jad Adams, 'Was "K" gay?', *History Today*, November 1999, pp. 26–7.
50 Pollock, pp. 225–27.
51 Adams, p. 27.
52 Another example, Hector Macdonald, will be discussed in Ch. 6.
53 Michael Asher, *Lawrence: The Uncrowned King of Arabia* (London, 1998), p. 89.
54 Quoted in John E. Mack, *A Prince of Our Disorder: The Life of T.E. Lawrence* (London, 1976), , pp. 422, 423, 421, 418, 415.
55 T.E. Lawrence, *The Diary Kept by T.E. Lawrence while Travelling in Arabia during 1911* (Reading, 1993), p. 10.
56 Quoted in Mack, p. 421
57 T.E. Lawrence, *The Seven Pillars of Wisdom* (New York, 1935), pp. 30–1.
58 *Ibid.*
59 Lawrence, *Diary*, pp. 28–30, 42–3.
60 Asher, p. 102.
61 *Ibid.*, pp. 109–11.
62 *Ibid.*, p. 88.
63 *Ibid.*, pp. 114, 111.
64 Quoted in Mack, p. 98.
65 Asher, p. 103.
66 Quoted in Asher, p. 284.
67 Asher, pp. 282–95; quotations from pp. 295, 292–3.
68 Jeffrey Meyers, *Homosexuality and Literature, 1890–1930* (London, 1977), pp. 115, 129–30.

3   The company of men

The barracks and the parade ground proved congenial to homoerotic voyeurism and exhibitionism. Military campaigns and expeditions promoted homosocial comradeship. Homosexual inclinations might be expressed in the reveries of thoughtful generals, or the rough-and-ready intercourse of troopers in isolated cantonments. Different colonial situations also facilitated intimate bonding, perhaps between a merchant and an assistant in a trading outpost, between a pastor and a parishioner at a mission station, between an expatriate and the denizens of a male bordello or between settlers looking for companionship in a new land. The previous chapter looked at same-sex relations and desires in the colonial military. Here the lives of men outside the army will be examined, though the fragmentary nature of documentation, the unwillingness of men to confess to homosexual desires and deeds, and the reluctance of biographers to reveal suspect skeletons in the closets mean many colonials' private lives remain secret.

Homosexuals appear among all groups of Europeans who sojourned in the colonies. Some men travelled overseas in the course of their professional lives as public servants, diplomats, missionaries or members of the liberal professions. Their sexual activities while overseas are not always known, and probably were often not particularly relevant to their public lives. The very presence of homosexuals in the colonies nevertheless suggests that the later liberation slogan of 'we are everywhere' applies as well to imperial situations. Sir Harold Nicolson, the bisexual British diplomat, for instance, served in postings in Persia and Morocco, though his homosexual activities remained discreet.[1] Freya Stark, the explorer, married – but never consummated the marriage – a homosexual diplomat at the British embassy in Baghdad.[2] Kurt Haijby, who gained notoriety as the lover of the Swedish king, and for indecent behaviour with teenaged boys in Stockholm, spent a short time in the French Foreign Legion in the 1920s.[3] António Botto, one of the most important homosexual poets in twentieth-century Portugal, spent two years working in a Portuguese African colony, also in the 1920s.[4] Three French Catholic priests were disciplined for sexual contacts with young men in Tahiti in the late nineteenth century.[5]

Other homosexuals spent brief periods abroad visiting friends and relatives, and often searching out other pleasures. The young British writer Denton Welch travelled to the British concession in Shanghai, where his family maintained business interests, and amused himself chatting up British soldiers in a public park. He invited one home for tea, and plied the shy soldier – ill at ease in the Welch family's posh apartment – with whisky and soda, and cigarettes. The soldier, laughing at Welch's own attempts with a cigarette, offered to teach him to smoke like a real man, which involved Welch nestling on the sofa next to him. 'He grabbed my hand, and scraping it down the buttons on his tunic, banged it at last on his stomach, which he had made tight as a drum', ostensibly a demonstration of how to inhale properly. Before things went further, Welch's brother walked in and the soldier fled.[6] The Spanish entertainer Miguel de Molina got luckier; although coy about his sexual adventures, the exception was 'a youth he met on a short trip to Africa: a night of love is fondly remembered'.[7] Travel writers had a ready-made excuse to voyage around the world, and homosexual or bisexual ones – Richard Haliburton, Bayard Taylor and Norman Douglas – no doubt enjoyed a variety of sights and experiences in their line of work. Anthropologists with homosexual inclinations and a professional interest in foreign sexual practices around the world – including Edward Westermarck, Ferdinand Karsch-Haack and Colin Turnbull – found much fieldwork in countries that had come under colonial rule.[8]

Some homosexuals chose expatriation to escape the climates (and constraints) of Europe, moved because of political and cultural convictions, or were forced by circumstances to flee. Valery Pereleshin, born in Siberia, escaped to Harbin, China, after the Bolshevik Revolution of 1917, though he lost his teaching job there when the Japanese invaded Manchuria. After the Second World War, Pereleshin went to Rio de Janeiro, where he spent the rest of his life. His books 'offer fascinating examples of cross-cultural dialogue, describing his relationships with Chinese and Brazilian men'.[9] A less felicitous fate awaited the Dutch author Jacob De Haan, the son of a rabbi. De Haan moved to British-mandated Palestine after the First World War to teach law and work as a journalist; 'in one of his poems, he asks himself if he visits the Wailing Wall for God or for the Arab boys. His involvement with both Arabs and orthodox Jews made him critical of Zionist positions.' He was murdered by radical Zionist terrorists – one of those implicated was a future president of Israel – although 'Zionists spread the rumour that Arabs killed him because of his sexual relations with Arab boys.'[10]

Men also moved in the other direction, from the colonies to European countries. The bisexual Jamaican-born novelist and poet Claude McKay, thanks to the aid of an English mentor, left his island home for the United States and subsequently lived in Britain and Morocco, and travelled widely in Europe and Africa.[11] (His 1932 novel *Banjo* brings together British and French West Indians, Senegalese and African Americans in the port of Marseilles, where they seek work, play jazz, talk politics and frequent women, among them

Algerians and *métisses*. Once character, Ray, based on the author, nevertheless refuses the women's overtures, writes fiction and becomes the best mate of macho Banjo.) The French designer Yves Saint Laurent, an Algerian *pied-noir*, like almost a million other Europeans in North Africa, fled to France after the Algerian war of independence.[12] Guilherme de Melo, born in 1931 in Mozambique, lived through the protracted war of independence in the Portuguese colony in the 1960s and 1970s. His novel *A Sombra dos Dias* is:

> a remarkable account of growing up gay in the privileged environment of a white family in colonial Mozambique before the outbreak of war and of leading an openly gay lifestyle against the background of an increasingly bitter anti-colonial war….The most gripping part of the novel is the description of the dramatic events which brought all this to an end and led to the Portuguese exodus.[13]

Melo himself was repatriated to Portugal.

Melo painted a picture of an intense colonial homosexual life in Mozambique, but traces of homosexuality appear in almost all colonies, waiting only to be discovered by historians. In Palestine, for instance, troops frequented prostitutes, but 'relations with males were also, if less openly, available from among the locals, and certain venues became well known for facilitating these encounters, notably the beach front in Tel Aviv'.[14] The availability of partners for homosexual dalliances in Cairo worried General Montgomery during the Second World War, even if Montgomery himself invited young boys home to parade nude in front of him.[15] Officials worried about the temptations of homosexuality in the Sudan, though old colonial hands admitted only to close male friendships.[16] In Malta, a prominent lawyer, judge, professor and politician, Guglielmo Rapinett, was arrested in 1884 after trying to seduce a young British soldier in Valletta. Rapinett admitted to starting up a conversation with the soldier, who he said had asked him for a shilling. Rapinett claimed that when he refused, the soldier arrested him for indecent and immoral proposals and assault. Rapinett was distressed at the 'sneers and jibes of the evil-minded, the innuendoes of friends and enemies, the political capital which the opposition papers [make]'. Nevertheless, the courts convicted Rapinett and suspended him from his position as magistrate, though three thousand fellow citizens, including legislators and the local archbishop, petitioned for his release.[17]

These are examples of the diversity of sexual itineraries in the overseas world, encounters in Asia, Africa, South America and the Mediterranean, cases involving priests, a magistrate, writers and artists: homosexuality was not limited by place or profession. The remainder of this chapter will explore the lives – and links between private and public lives – of a British scholar in China, colonial rulers in the East Indies and South Africa, and two businessmen, a Briton in Western Africa and a Frenchman on the horn of Eastern Africa.

The queer life of Edmund Backhouse

Sir Edmund Backhouse (1873–1944), a Lancashireman of prosperous Quaker ancestry (but who converted to Catholicism before his death), was educated at Oxford, though he did not take a degree; he did spend lavishly, leading to bankruptcy. After disappearing from circulation for several years, Backhouse in 1898 turned up in China, speaking fluent Mandarin. He found work translating documents for George Ernest Morrison, *The Times's* correspondent in Beijing (the same man who spread the rumour that Lord Kitchener was homosexual). By 1901, Backhouse held a part-time appointment as Professor of Law and Literature in the new university in Beijing, and undertook private work for American and British companies as well. During the First World War he worked as a British secret agent, trying (unsuccessfully) to buy rifles from the Chinese for the British army. Backhouse achieved renown for a book written in 1910 with J.O.P. Bland, a journalistic rival of Morrison. *China under the Empress Dowager* recounted palace life and court intrigues in the last years of the Manchu dynasty; the book was based on the diary of Ching-Shan, Assistant Secretary of the Imperial Household, which Backhouse claimed that he had discovered (in the very house into which he had moved) during the Boxer Rebellion. Four years after this book, Backhouse and Bland published *Annals and Memoirs of the Court of Peking*, which consolidated Backhouse's position as an accomplished Sinologist and helped secure his election to a chair in Chinese at King's College, though he never took up the University of London professorship. Meanwhile, in 1913, he donated 17,000 Chinese books and manuscripts to the Bodleian Library at Oxford, and presented the university with 10,000 more works over the next eight years.[18]

Almost thirty years after Backhouse's death in 1944, a Swiss doctor, who had befriended Backhouse in Beijing at the end of his life, gave to the historian Hugh Trevor-Roper two unpublished autobiographical manuscripts, *The Dead Past* and *Décadence Mandchoue*, which Backhouse had written just before his death. In the works, Backhouse claimed acquaintance with many great men (such as the poet Paul Verlaine). He said that he had been the Dowager Empress's lover and chronicled his sexual adventures in Beijing. According to Trevor-Roper, 'Both volumes are grossly, grotesquely, obsessively obscene. Backhouse presents himself as a compulsive pathological homosexual who found in China opportunities for indulgence which, in England…could be only dangerously and furtively enjoyed.' His home country had nevertheless provided pleasures before his departure for the East, as Backhouse recounted the 'carnival of unbridled lust' he had enjoyed at Winchester College (including sex with Lord Alfred Douglas), recalled chats about homosexuality with Walter Pater at Oxford, told about raising money for Oscar Wilde's defence and even claimed to have slept with Lord Rosebery ('my readers will agree that when a young man is privileged to have sexual intercourse with a Prime Minister, any proposal regarding the *modus operandi* must emanate from the latter').

Trevor-Roper argues that, though Backhouse clearly knew a great deal about China, its language and culture, many of his claims were fraudulent, and documents on which he based his works, including the key diary of Ching-Shan, were fake. Backhouse himself forged the diary, Trevor-Roper suggests, just as he forged some (though not all) of the Chinese manuscripts he presented to Oxford. It seems impossible that he was the lover of the Dowager Empress or Rosebery, and unlikely that he knew Verlaine. However, Backhouse did take part in the defence of Wilde.

Roland de Margerie, a French diplomat in Beijing who knew Backhouse in his waning years, called him 'an old salacious profligate' who was 'obsessed with homosexuality' and happily recalled his homosexual adventures: 'The assurance with which he spoke, and the extreme dignity of his appearance, were in perfect contrast with his known morals, of which he boasted freely.'[19] Earlier in life, however, Backhouse claimed that he had been slandered as '*homosexual*, the basest of untruths' because he had known Wilde and 'admired his wit, knowing nothing of his perverted tastes'. Indeed, he said that his former mentor, Morrison – who had charged that the diaries Backhouse supposedly translated were forgeries, thereby earning his bitter dislike – was himself that way inclined:

> I blame Morrison, that *improbus cinaedus* and *pathicus dévergondé* for most of these unspeakably false stories. I know what he was morally from certain things he said to me, things which I indignantly rejected, to say nothing about the stories of him at the race-course…and of his debauches *à l'instar de Tibère à Capri*.[20]

Décadence Mandchoue, a typescript of more than four hundred pages, begins with a chapter entitled 'Peking interlude, or Cassia Flower', set in a male brothel called the Hall of Chaste Pleasures, to which Backhouse is introduced by a homosexual Chinese prince. The attendant carefully lists the services offered, and their prices, and introduces the visitor to the handsomest young man, known as Cassia Flower, although he already has an engagement for the evening with a duke. Backhouse is invited to watch their intercourse, which includes fellatio and anal sex, sado-masochistic activities and tea drinking, then takes his turn with Cassia Flower. He learns words for various types of pleasure – 'turning the bun' for reciprocal copulation, 'cinnamon leaves' for analingus – of which he partakes, and also enjoys a bout of beating. Cassia Flower's ample endowments and varied skills are described in meticulous detail over thirty pages, complete with the Chinese characters for the various acts of love making performed. After hours of coition,

> Before sleeping the sleep of the just (or should it not be the sleep of the carnally minded) Cassia and I performed ablutions in scented medicated waters and cleansed 'nos fondements et nos parties sexuelles' from taint of impurity; then we lay down to rest.

They subsequently see each other on a regular basis: 'Everyone who saw him was attracted by his charm…and he was indeed an Amour, a Cupid, as beautiful as the morning star or as Hadrian's Greek favourite, the giton Antinous.' In another erotic chapter, 'The hammam and the intrusion', Backhouse describes a homosexual bath-house, to which the Dowager Empress herself pays a visit, commanding the men present to perform all manner of sexual connection for her enjoyment before whisking Backhouse away to a tryst with her at the royal palace.[21]

The incidents recorded in Backhouse's manuscript are hardly believable as such, though he insists with emphasis in the preface that there is *'no romance nor embroidery'* in his text. The scenes may well be based on real homosexual establishments in imperial Beijing, and the manuscript is dedicated 'to Kuei Hua, my own Cassia Flower', a suggestion of a real-life model for the youthful beauty.[22] The manuscript – though clearly not to Trevor-Roper – is uproariously funny, as Backhouse, clearly inspired by Victorian pornography and the writing of aesthetes, evokes remarkable sexual activities, quotes Greek, Latin, French and Italian writers, and both creates and caricatures sexual fantasies about Asia. He admits at the end of the Cassia Flower chapter, 'When souls turn bodies and unite in the ineffable, the whole, rapture of the embodied soul; it may all be a mirage, an illusion of the senses.'[23] Perhaps the whole manuscript should be viewed as a mirage, the 70-year-old author's last lubricious laugh and one of the most amusing pieces of homosexual erotic fiction set in the Orient. 'He who should survive the perusal of my Décadence Mandchoue may not impossibly be driven to a conclusion,' Backhouse joked, 'that, if the Manchu regime were decadent, I was still more so.'[24]

Backhouse remains a curious figure. He carefully covered traces of homosexuality early in his life, but boasted to later visitors of his exploits, both homosexual and heterosexual, and then supposedly told all in the unpublished manuscripts. Trevor-Roper treats Backhouse's memoirs as a 'pornographic novelette', a case of 'pathological obscenity' and the 'morbid eruption of senility'.[25] He concludes that Backhouse was clinically 'sane', but that his writings (including ones purporting to be Chinese documents) were fantasy. Comparing him to Baron Corvo, another travelling writer who invented various personae for himself, Trevor-Roper argues that Backhouse created his own world of sexual and political fantasy with himself at its centre. He connects this with Backhouse's character and milieu, '"aestheticism", the febrile eroticism, the aggressive, insolent deviation of the 1890s', the 'etiolated world' in which he lived in the *fin de siècle*, the 'aesthetic, narcissistic, homosexual côterie' in which he moved.[26] Backhouse's attraction to decadent China is, Trevor-Roper suggests, directly linked to his emergence from the decadence of turn-of-the-century Europe:

> He saw himself as one of the aesthetes of the 1890's – one who, by the accident of his linguistic genius, had transplanted himself from 'la décadence anglaise' to 'la décadence mandchoue'....Only in the purulent atmosphere of the decaying Manchu court could a pale reflection of English decadence linger on.[27]

Trevor-Roper's simplistic understanding of homosexuality, and manifest discomfort at even reading the more salacious passages of Backhouse's manuscript, make his judgement questionable. Stripped of the commentaries on 'perversion', Trevor-Roper does convincingly establish a link between the environment in which Backhouse lived in the England of Oscar Wilde and the China of the Dowager Empress. In Beijing, Backhouse could create his fantasy and, except for suspicious contemporaries, such as Morrison, and historical detectives, such as Trevor-Roper, possibly live it out. The world of court eunuchs, homosexual brothels and male hammams suited his fevered imagination and his scholarly interests. Whether he actually had the sexual adventures he claimed is not so important as that China provided a congenial site to conjure up these fantasies. China for Backhouse, like the Middle East for Lawrence, provided a terrain for sexual imagination and passion.

Colonial potentates: governing passions

In addition to such eccentrics as Backhouse, European outposts played host to administrators, the men who ran the colonies. As the colonial infrastructure became more entrenched, they were increasingly civil servants with diplomas from colonial training schools, professionals who climbed the ranks from district officer to governor, expected by superiors to manage colonies efficiently and to be models of probity and respectability. In the earlier decades of imperialism, however, potentates were often men of adventure who carved out domains for themselves and enjoyed great latitude of political manœuvre. For some, as well, the colonies provided margins of sexual dissidence. Two cases provide examples of political might and sexual ambivalence – and incidences of men whose biographers long ignored or refuted their sexual inclinations.

James Brooke (1803–68) was founder of the dynasty of 'white rajahs' who ruled Sarawak, part of the island of Borneo in the East Indies, as a private domain from the 1840s until they ceded it to the British Crown in 1946. Brooke was born in Benares, India, son of an East India Company official, who sent him to England for schooling at the age of twelve. Brooke ran away from school and, in 1819, joined the Bengal Army and returned to the East, where he was wounded in the Anglo-Burmese War in 1825. For the next few years, he travelled around South-East Asia, ending up in Borneo in the 1830s; in 1841, he seized control of Sarawak from its nominal ruler, the Sultan of Brunei, whom he persuaded to invest him as Rajah of Sarawak. Brooke also gained appointment as British Confidential Agent to the Princes of Borneo and Consul-General in Labuan, although he resigned his commissions in 1854. The unmarried Brooke remained Rajah of Sarawak until his death, passing on his title to his nephew.[28]

A carefully documented study by J.H. Walker has investigated Brooke's sexuality, a subject skirted by earlier researchers despite rumours about his wayward affections; commentaries on Walker's study by other scholars suggest that many fellow specialists of Borneo still regard the suggestion that Brooke was homosexual as an outrage or, at best, unnecessary concern with minor details of

Brooke's private life.[29] Brooke, not unlike many schoolboys, appears to have had a particularly intense crush on one of his fellows; indeed, when the friend left school, an inconsolable Brooke ran away. On his first voyage East, Brooke formed close friendships, evidenced by highly emotional letters, with four ship-mates, establishing a pattern of searching out younger protégés on whom he lavished attention. 'I am interested in him and like him very much,' he wrote of Harry Keppel, a midshipman for whose promotion he lobbied and who remained a long-time friend. Another young man whom Brooke took under his wing was 13-year-old Willie Brereton, nephew of the Bishop of Calcutta, whom he described as 'a delicate and gentlemanly boy'.[30] In Sarawak, in 1839, he entered into a friendship with a Malay (the only example of such intimacy with a 'native'), Pengiram Budrudeen, brother of the Viceroy of Sarawak and a kinsman of the Sultan of Brunei. Brooke's letters describe Pengiram admiringly, and Brooke gave him his signet ring as a sign of friendship. As Brooke worked to gain control of Sarawak, the presence of Brunei royalty proved inconvenient, and he sent Pengiram (and his brother) home, where they became involved in court intrigue, whereupon Brooke vowed that if anything happened to the brothers he would 'burn Borneo from end to end'. Another faction of the royal family bested Budrudeen and his supporters, and the Malay was killed, though just before he died he was able to return Brooke's signet ring. Brooke wrote to Keppel: 'To me personally, nothing can make up the loss of Budrudeen', and he proceeded to attack Brunei and rout the Sultan.[31] A connection between loss of his friend and imperial venture seems obvious.

Brooke next focused his attentions on a young English midshipman who, in different circumstances, historians might not hesitate to call the 'love of his life'. Brooke met Charles Grant, whom he nicknamed 'Hoddy Doddy' (because of his diminutive stature), probably in 1845, when Grant was 14 years old. Soon Brooke was pursuing Grant, entreating him to write from England and assuring that their friendship would 'be of service to you and afford me pleasure'; a watch and silver-plated pistols betokened Brooke's budding interest. The young man reciprocated the affections, and the Rajah and the midshipman became fast friends. By 1847, Brooke sent to Grant a twenty-page letter, which, according to Walker, 'resonate[s] with the companionable intimacy James and Charles shared'. Brooke persuaded Grant to return to Sarawak with him, arranging a berth on Keppel's ship and paying his passage. On board, Brooke enjoyed the company of Grant and other young men – 'six or seven of them', his assistant recalled, 'would throw themselves on the bed, careless whether Mr Brooke was there or not, and skylark over his body as if he were one of themselves.' Brooke's antics, including playfully making Grant his aide-de-camp, caused the ship's officers to raise eyebrows, but Brooke was elated to have Grant with him. He wrote to the young man's father, suggesting that Grant leave the navy to become his private secretary, and Grant wrote home how 'fond' he was of the Rajah. They enjoyed a blissful interlude in Singapore where Brooke wrote that 'I know nobody that does suit me except one or two far removed from me by years' and gave his favourite horse to Grant.

With approval from his parents for Grant to enter Brooke's employ, the two settled in Sarawak in 1848 and remained inseparable for the next few years. After a trip to England in 1853, Brooke named the 21-year-old Grant governor of the Lundu district; when he fell ill at the remote post, Brooke hurried to nurse him personally. As Grant aged, however, he grew more distant from Brooke, showing an interest in women and assuming responsibility for family property in Scotland after the death of an elder brother. In 1855, he left Sarawak for Britain, travelling with the Rajah's nephew and heir apparent, John Brooke Brooke, but promising to return. The Rajah soon reproached him for not writing and learned from his nephew that Grant was courting a girl; Brooke wrote dismissively to Grant about the prospects of marriage, remarking that his affections would soon move on to someone else. Grant did marry, and went back to Sarawak with his wife in 1857; Brooke Brooke meanwhile married Grant's sister. Contacts between the Rajah and both his protégé and his nephew became increasingly strained, leading to the Rajah disinheriting and banishing Brooke Brooke in 1863, leaving his title to Brooke Brooke's younger brother. Relations with Grant were severed, though he showed no harsh feelings, and Grant attended the Rajah's funeral.[32]

Brooke and Grant may well never have consummated their relationship, but their friendship reads like a love story played out over almost two decades – a chance meeting and courtship, complete with long letters and costly gifts, the reunion and 'honeymoon' in an exotic destination, the rearrangement of lives despite differences in background, age and profession so that they could live together, the years of steady and emotionally charged companionship, the waning of one person's affections and his choice of another partner, the tensions and break-up, and the memories and affections that endured. Brooke's emotions and actions may have been paternalistic or avuncular, the interest of an older man in a worthy and aspiring protégé. However, except to those horrified by the very idea of homosexuality, the relationship between Brooke and Grant looks like a romance.

Similar to Brooke, though with personal ambitions and an international importance on a greater scale, was Cecil Rhodes (1853–1902). Conqueror of Rhodesia, diamond magnate, Prime Minister of the Cape Colony, imperialist extraordinaire, Rhodes shared with the Rajah of Sarawak an affinity for agreeable young men, with whom he developed close emotional relationships and whose departure left him in utter distress. Rhodes, like Brooke, never married and did not much enjoy the company of women, though rumours whispered about liaisons with Coloured or Zulu women in South Africa and a thwarted engagement to an Englishwoman. Queen Victoria, who took an interest in the private lives of her statesmen, wondered about Rhodes, just as she later puzzled about Kitchener's alleged misogyny. 'Is it true, Mr Rhodes, that you are a woman-hater?,' she was said to have asked, to which he replied diplomatically: 'How could I possibly hate a sex to which Your Majesty belongs?'

Rhodes clearly did not hate the blue-eyed, blond-headed young men with whom he surrounded himself (and who typified the youths whose education at

Oxford he would later fund). Rhodes's 'lambs', or 'apostles', as they were known in South Africa, appear in photographs as sturdy, handsome young men. Rhodes had no stronger relationship in his life than the one with Neville Pickering. Born in South Africa in 1857, the son (like Rhodes) of an English clergyman, Pickering gained employment as a commercial clerk to a company in Port Elizabeth. From there he was transferred to Kimberley, where a contemporary described the young man – well made if somewhat severe looking – as 'a remarkably pleasant and promising fellow with everything before him'. Biographers do not know when Rhodes and Pickering met, but at the age of 23, Pickering became secretary of Rhodes's De Beers Company. Within several years, and Rhodes's return from study at Oxford, they were close friends. Indeed, Rhodes and Pickering moved into a modest house together in Kimberley, and contemporaries remarked on the intimacy of the two men sharing a corrugated-tin cottage. The deputy to Sir Hercules Robinson, governor of the Cape Colony, described the relationship between Rhodes and Pickering as 'an absolutely lover-like friendship'.[33]

Rhodes provided proof of his dedication to Pickering when, in 1882, he left negotiations with the Sotho leader to make a three-day ride back to Kimberley to celebrate Pickering's twenty-fifth birthday. He took the opportunity to rewrite his will, leaving his entire fortune to Pickering. Pickering continued to serve Rhodes as a conscientious secretary, but, according to Antony Thomas, 'his importance to Rhodes transcended the qualities of a virtuous and reliable company secretary. For probably the first time in his life, Rhodes was personally fulfilled and happy.' The idyll ended when Pickering became seriously ill in 1886, after a fall from a horse, just at the time that Rhodes was involved with crucial business activities in the Rand. When Pickering's condition worsened, Rhodes determined to be at his side, though no seats were available on the coach, and there was no alternative for the 'ranting, pathetic creature who begged to be allowed to travel to Kimberley' (in Thomas's words) except to ride, dangerously and miserably, atop the coach, wedged between mail bags, for a 500 kilometre journey. Rhodes nursed Pickering for six weeks, refusing to answer telegrams from associates and thus losing an option on gold mines later worth three million pounds sterling. Pickering's condition proved fatal and, after whispering to Rhodes, 'You have been father, mother, brother and sister to me', he died in Rhodes's arms. Rhodes wept hysterically at his burial, and continued to cry for days afterwards. He never returned to the cottage that he and Pickering shared, and would not speak about the dead protégé with whom he had spent five years.[34]

Rhodes formed friendships with other young men, though never of the same intensity. Harry Currey was an especially favoured successor, serving Rhodes as secretary, accompanying him to London and organising his daily life. Currey eventually decided to marry, an announcement Rhodes greeted with fury though Currey promised to remain his secretary; witnesses recalled that 'Rhodes raved and stormed like a maniac'.[35] Rhodes forced Currey to choose between work and wife, and he opted for marriage; Rhodes attended the wedding but remarked to the bride, 'I am very jealous of you'. Another associate, Jack

Grimmer, was less successful as secretary but nevertheless retained Rhodes's interest. Rhodes said that Grimmer's demeanour had a restful effect on him. When Grimmer was bit by a scorpion, Rhodes sat with him for a day, and when he came down with fever, Rhodes gently bathed his feet.[36]

Rhodes's last companion-secretary was Philip Jourdan, a 24-year-old, and in this case the young man seemed infatuated with his employer. Jourdan confessed in his autobiography,

> An uncontrollable desire took hold of me to be his private secretary....Sometimes I would lie awake half the night working myself up into a state of delirious excitement, speculating on the joy and pleasure which would be mine....when I should be always with him and would go wherever he went....I worshipped him and had an intense desire to work for him and to please him....I used to take long solitary walks, sometimes extending over several hours, thinking of nothing but Rhodes, Rhodes, Rhodes and my devotion towards him.[37]

Thomas calls this 'a frank declaration of love', although he judges that Rhodes was physically asexual. He emphasises Rhodes's unremitting attachment to male youths, and the adolescent tomfoolery he enjoyed with them, as an important facet of his psychology, 'the hidden side of responsibility, self-discipline and the ruthless will to succeed. Without that balance it is doubtful whether Cecil Rhodes could have continued to function.'[38] Intimate masculine companionship formed the necessary complement to Rhodes's imperial endeavours.

The business world

Explorers, military officers, administrators, but what of businessmen? Few biographies reveal the homosexual proclivities of colonial traders, planters and other men of business. Most did not leave memoirs, scholars have focused on company histories rather than private lives, and homosexuality was hardly something to boast about among businessmen. Two examples, however, provide illustrations of liaisons involving European businessmen-cum-writers – one a French coffee and arms merchant, the other a British palm-oil trader.

Arthur Rimbaud (1854–91) is one of the most famous figures in modern French letters, the poet of adolescent rebellion and lover of Paul Verlaine. Before he had reached the age of 20, Rimbaud abandoned both Europe and poetry, and boarded the '*bateau ivre*' that eventually took him to the horn of Africa. Rimbaud lived in the British outpost of Aden, working for a coffee merchant, then moved to Harar, an Islamic city in still uncolonised Ethiopia, where he dealt in guns and, according to some accounts, in slaves. Rimbaud remained in Africa for the rest of his life, only serious illness forcing him to be evacuated to Marseilles, where he died.

Rimbaud had little regard for either colonialists or natives. He found Aden hot, airless and dry, an 'awful hole', and the locals appealed little more: 'One's only company consists of local Bedouins, so one becomes a complete idiot within a few years.' In Harar, he wrote home, he was:

> lost in the midst of these negroes, whose lot one would like to improve and who try, for their part to exploit you....obliged to chatter their jibberish, to eat their filthy messes, to endure the thousand and one annoyances that come from their idleness, their treachery, and their stupidity.

As for his compatriots, who had just established a foothold in Djibouti, Rimbaud railed:

> France...occupied the whole Bay of Tajoura, so as to be able to command the starting-point of the trade route to Abyssinia and to Harar. But the coast is completely desolate, and all the money spent here is squandered if she does not soon advance to the highlands in the interior....I do not believe that any nation in the world has a more inept colonial policy than France. If England makes mistakes and squanders money, she has, at least, serious interests at stake and important prospects. But no country equals France in pouring away her money, at a dead loss, in the most impossible places.[39]

In Aden, Rimbaud had a relationship with a young Coptic Ethiopian woman, 'tall and slim, with a rather pretty face'. They lived together for about 6 months, then he sent her away, writing to a friend: 'I have ruthlessly sent the woman packing. I shall give her some thalers [coins] and she may go where she wishes. I have had to deal with this sham long enough.' A longer-lasting, and more intense, friendship was his relationship with Djami Ouddei, his servant. Around 1883, Rimbaud had hired the Muslim Harari youth, then between 14 and 16 years of age, and the two lived in constant companionship; Rimbaud even took Djami with him to Egypt and Yemen. According to Enid Starkie, more expansive about the liaison than most biographers,

> Rimbaud's sole friend and comforter seems to have been Djami....Are critics right in seeing here further proof of his alleged homosexual tendencies? Who can say? No material exists that will to [sic] help us form an opinion. All we know is that Djami was one of the few people in his life whom he remembered and talked of with affection, the only friend of whom he spoke on his death-bed, when the thoughts of other men usually turn to those whom they have known in their early youth. It was Djami's name that was always on his lips when he finally sank into unconsciousness.

Starkie points out that when Rimbaud was dying in Marseilles, after the amputation of a leg, he talked at great length to his beloved sister Isabelle about Djami, even confusing their names. One of his last thoughts was to leave his fortune – about 55,000 francs in today's currency – to Djami. Starkie summarises Isabelle's letter to the French consul in Aden after Rimbaud's death:

With loving care he asked that Djami be told, as the last order and injunc-
tion of his master, who had loved him dearly, to make good and wise use of
this money; to invest it perhaps in some honest and prudent enterprise, but
that the money was not to be a pretext for idleness and intemperance.

Isabelle faithfully carried out her brother's instructions, enlisting the help of the
consul, a French bishop and the father of the future emperor Haile Selassie to
track down Djami. However, they discovered that he, too, was now dead,
perishing 'in the famine of 1891 or killed in some savage raid, or perhaps even
through grief at the loss of his beloved master'. Djami's wife and infant son
received the money Rimbaud had left to him.[40]

Starkie, writing in the 1930s, underlines the strength of the relationship
between Rimbaud and Djami, and certainly his legacy to the African (and
Rimbaud's sister's efforts in tracing him) confirm its significance. Some writers
refute any insinuation that Rimbaud might have been in love with Djami, or
that the African might have been a sexual partner. In a fine recent book on
Rimbaud in the colonies, for instance, Charles Nicholl argues that there is not
enough evidence to suggest a sexual relationship, though he concedes 'a sense of
unexpected affection, of an intimacy in the midst of solitude'.[41] He seems keen,
by contrast, to prove that Rimbaud might have had a sexual relationship with
an Ethiopian woman who worked as another of his servants during his last years
in Harar. Graham Robb, another recent biographer, mentions Djami only in
passing to note that he lived with his wife in a house next to Rimbaud's own
dwelling, and says that he never became the 'son' Rimbaud desired – somewhat
cursory treatment of the relationship.[42] One French biographer, Alain Borer,
noting that Rimbaud called for Djami on his death bed, concludes that Djami
was 'the only being from whom Rimbaud received marks of fidelity or affection'.
Borer adds that 'rather than a hidden passion, this young man from a distant
country was the "mate" [*copain*], just as in a work by Kipling'.[43] Jean-Luc
Steinmetz concurs that 'we know nothing of Rimbaud's sexual desires and
demands during this period of his life', but agrees that Djami was a devoted
companion to the poet-turned-businessman.[44]

The indications of Rimbaud's affections for Djami support the conclusion that
his relationship with the young man, whether physical or not, was far stronger
than any relationship with the Ethiopian concubine or indeed anyone else overseas. Rimbaud, for obvious reasons, would hardly have advertised a sexual
relationship with Djami, though one with a woman would have neither surprised
nor offended other Europeans. His precipitate sending away of a woman
companion in Aden, after a 'sham' relationship, implies that he did not expect or
need a female partner. Djami's own marriage would not have precluded him
having (or having had) an intimate relationship with Rimbaud. It remains impossible to say whether either (or both) Djami or the woman was Rimbaud's
bedmate, though the death bed legacy and his conversations with Isabelle about
his male servant, as well as his earlier history of homosexual activity, hardly
preclude a possibly physical as well as an evident emotional attachment to Djami.

Another colonial businessman and poet, though of far lesser stature than Rimbaud, was John Moray Stuart-Young. Born in Manchester in 1881, he survived a Dickensian childhood – his father, a warehouse labourer, beat him sadistically, his long-suffering mother took in washing to make ends meet, and his sister died of tuberculosis. Stuart-Young left school at 13 and struggled at jobs as office boy and clerk, earning meagre wages. He began to swindle money from a gas-mantle works, was arrested and spent six months in jail. After release, in 1900, he decided to try his fortunes overseas and sailed to West Africa, ending up in the British colony of Sierra Leone, 'the white man's grave-yard'. For three years he worked as an accountant and secretary to a trader.

Except for regular visits to England, Stuart-Young spent the rest of his life in Africa, moving from Sierra Leone to Conakry in French Guinea, then Onitsha on the Niger River. In Onitsha, he set up as a palm-oil trader, bartering European goods for export products:

> The natives brought along their palm-oils or kernels, their rubber or goat-skins or mahogany, and took in exchange what both contracting parties esteemed to be a fair value in commodities like soap, tobacco, cotton-goods, kerosine oil, salt and a modicum of alcohol!

He made enough money, despite competition from the huge Royal Niger Company, to live in comfort. (He tried to diversify his activities in 1935 by selling in England a patent medicine, 'The Young Stimulator', branded as beneficial for 'Conditioning the Nervous System; Brightening the Brain; Soothing the Spirit'.) He died in Port Harcourt, Nigeria, in 1939, and was given a grand funeral by African friends and employees.[45]

During his life as a colonial trader, Stuart-Young had a second career as a writer, publishing a dozen books of poetry, sketches of African life, novels and autobiography. He sought fame with a poem, 'Osrac, the Self-Sufficient', about Oscar Wilde, whom he claimed to have known; one edition included two facsimile letters that Stuart-Young claimed Wilde had written to him. The letters are almost certainly forgeries, according to Timothy d'Arch Smith, and it is unlikely that Stuart-Young ever knew Wilde (much less that he was one of his lovers, as he hinted). Stuart-Young's poems fall into the 'Uranian' tradition of the *fin de siècle*, decadent verses exuding emotion and lauding the love of lads. He was, according to d'Arch Smith, the 'most menial' of the poets; his *œuvre* includes truly awful poems, as well as an amusing 'Ode to a Mosquito (*Anophiles*)'.

Stuart-Young's autobiographical writings form a ramble of poems, details about his painful childhood, philosophising about politics and culture (including interesting comparisons of British, French and German colonialism), trenchant diatribes against Christianity and memoirs of exploits in Africa, sprinkled with Latin and French phrases for due effect. Specific information on his private life (given his penchant for fabulation) is probably not always reliable. It appears that Stuart-Young was once married to an Englishwoman, but he possibly also wed an African (with whom he may have lived in Britain); his novel *Merely a Negress* recounts such a union. However, he confesses straight-forwardly to interest in males and characterises himself as an Urning. Schoolboy romances, and fantasising about men, preceded an obsession with Wilde. In exclamatory phrases, he reveals,

> I was a man, physically and mentally before I began to ponder seriously the complex question of sexuality! I sensed, – how, when or wherefore I could not have satisfactorily explained – that every human being possesses *both male and female elements*!...For, if I had any sex-desires at all (and I some-what doubt the fact!) I was strongly aware of passionate attachment to certain of my male companions.

Humans are, he says, hermaphrodites on 'the *spiritual* plane of being', but for Stuart-Young, 'I find myself persuaded that my contradictory nature is congen-ital. Ever since I can remember, my beauty-loving impulses have always been in the direction of the male sex!' Realisation of his desires made him miserable, and he 'grew into manhood an enigma to myself, and a source of perplexity to everyone who knew me!' Yet, 'once the Urning...has discovered the meaning of his divergence from the type, he is *unafraid* of public opinion!'[46]

D'Arch Smith says that the love of Stuart-Young's life was an Englishman named Tommy Todd. Africans also attracted him; indeed, a photograph of an African had awakened his interest in men and the tropics. As a schoolboy,

> Once I came across a wonderful photograph by Baron Corvo. It had been taken somewhere in Cairo, and it showed a nude boy sitting astride an earthenware jar. This picture (it appeared in the *Sketch*) aroused in my spirit the first ardent impulse to make a home of the tropics. I knew nothing of either Egypt or Nigeria in those days. But I like to think that the impetuosity of desire, aroused in the heart of a youth of fourteen, was due to some psychological infusion of influence into the simple photographic study: a message of the arts to the art-student! That Egyptian child of the tropics was (and is) as well-known to me as if I had met him in the flesh!

The photograph was actually a picture taken by the German Baron von Gloeden, probably in Tunis, not by Frederick Rolfe, the self-styled Baron Corvo, in Cairo, but its influence was marked, and Stuart-Young continued: 'Speculation apart, and notwithstanding the adverse criticism of people who do not understand eroto-culture [*sic*], I continue to meet Beauty everywhere, – here in Onitsha as much as in England or France!'[47]

Stuart-Young's *The Coaster at Home*, the cover of which shows the ungainly looking, slender, cross-eyed blond Englishman, dressed in tropical whites, cradling a naked African infant on his thigh, is reticent about his African liaisons, though the author exudes (in his odd prose style) about the physique of men in the marketplace:

A gang of laborers [sic] breaks through the bending groups, to continue their work of transport of cargo from waterside to farther store. They are fine specimens, of men, – strong and athletic. They carry on their heads loads under which a mule might stagger....The lords of creation make ninepence or a shilling a day with their splendid muscles.[48]

Referring specifically to a group of African children, Stuart-Young says that he is witnessing 'Arcady in ebony'.[49] Elsewhere he cries, referring to naked youths of 15 and 16, 'Alas, alas! For the joys of Greece!'[50] Did Stuart-Young find Africans to provide him friendship and companionship? He seems rather diffident about physical relations, remarking curiously: 'Celibacy can only be defended when the Urning temperament has been evidenced. In that event, Love can assert itself in Platonic friendships, like those of David and Jonathan, Damon and Pythias, Socrates and Alcibiades'.[51]

The Coaster at Home lingers on Stuart-Young's houseboy, Worsu, stating that the two men shared a bedroom (though the African servant slept at the foot of his master's bed). *The Soul Slayer*, a novel dedicated to Edward Carpenter and published in 1920, the best of his works, according to d'Arch Smith, is an allegory with autobiographical and sexual overtones. Stuart-Young's own father serves as model for the stepfather of a beautiful and youthful Ibra, illegitimate son of a European trader and an African princess. He is called 'The Unkissed' because of resistance to the sexual play of fellow students at a Catholic mission school. An English boy tries to seduce Ibra, he watches animals copulate and he looks at obscene drawings that other schoolboys pass around. When Ibra is wrongly accused of having drawn the pictures, his stepfather beats him brutally, discovering his own sexual excitement at incestuous sadism. Ibra kills his step-father, but dies of the wounds with which he was inflicted.[52]

The story perhaps casts Stuart-Young in the role of righteous martyr, but his real-life friendships lacked the horror of the fictional portrayal. In 1905, he kept company with a mixed-race boy, Ibrahim, about 14 years old, whom he took for a visit to England. D'Arch Smith extrapolates from *The Soul Slayer* that Stuart-Young first saw Ibrahim (or Ibra) on an African boat that rowed out to meet his ship in Conakry, as recorded in one of Stuart-Young's poems: 'And then among the sails of speeding ships / I see thy form. (The flashing water's green, / The dusky boatmen, and the oil that drips / From the full casks!) Ay, there in tunic clean / White from the neck, with feet that peep below, / And soft brown shoulders, gleaming teeth, red lips, / (Of honey'd sweetness, shaped like Cupid's bow, – / I know them well!) and undulating hips! / But rarer than these treasures superfine, / Thine eyes, indifferent to the girls, in sweet response to mine'.[53] By 1908, Stuart-Young had another companion, an 11-year-old servant, Bosa, whose stories of African folklore he hoped to publish. In 1911, Bosa accompanied him to England.

Stuart-Young's attachments to young men – whether as foster (or substitute) sons, protégés or sexual partners – illustrate the porous boundaries between different types of colonial relationships. Europeans engaged servants who often lived in their houses and travelled with them, cooked their meals, washed their clothes and served as guides and interpreters. The proximity and constancy of contact necessarily created physical intimacy, especially as servants helped their masters wash and dress, and sometimes slept in their bedrooms. Ample opportunities for sexual intercourse thus existed.

The example of Stuart-Young also suggests the latitude in the colonial era for behaviour that would now raise suspicions. For almost forty years, Stuart-Young, a self-confessed Urning, lived in peace in Africa, unharassed by other expatriates for his sexual orientation. Most would not have read his London-published books, and he might not have discussed his sexual orientation with fellow Europeans. On two occasions, he travelled to Britain in the company of teenage Africans – just as Stanley and Lawrence invited youthful acquaintances for European visits. Neither in Africa nor at home did the British see anything odd in such companionable travel, presumably considering the boys innocent wards of a kindly businessman.

Stuart-Young's life – the distressing childhood, the flight to the colonies, his commercial and literary efforts – reads like a novel and typifies some themes of those who sought fame and fortune, or escape and refuge, outside Europe. 'Most of us have been driven to West Africa because we were not strong enough to combat social conditions at home,' he remarked.[54] His views on the Urning temperament, and references to Carpenter and Wilde, place him in the context of evolving notions of homosexual identity. Companionship with youths – clearly emotional, possibly sexual – mirrors fascination with ephebes common to those who, inspired by classical culture, travelled to the Mediterranean or further afield. West Africa provided Stuart-Young's Arcadia. 'There is a premium on license out here,' he wrote in a manifesto against missionary efforts to impose Christian sexual behaviour on natives, adding 'Morality is more a matter of Locality and Custom than of Divine Inspiration.'[55]

Homosexuality and empire-building

The number of men considered in this and the preceding chapters is small, yet they include some of the leading figures in the imperial pantheon – British imperial heroes did not come much greater than Stanley and Rhodes, Gordon and Kitchener, and Lawrence of Arabia. Lyautey was the quintessential French imperialist and Thesiger, arguably, is the most famous surviving explorer. Humboldt was the leading German explorer of the early 1800s; Przhevalsky, the premier Russian explorer of his time. Figures about whom convincing, if somewhat limited, indications suggest a homosexual inclination appear well represented (even overly so) in the gallery of the imperial great and good, although the very possibility of their being 'sodomites' would have horrified many contemporary compatriots (and some later biographers).

Englishmen have been more numerous than Frenchmen in this chapter. There is no reason to presume, however, that there were fewer men with homosexual inclinations in the French colonies than in Britain's possessions. Less material is available on the sexual lives of French colonial figures, and French biographers have been noticeably reluctant to poke around in their subjects' closets. The French, however, were rather more tolerant of sexual misbehaviours than the British; homosexual activities, after all, were not criminal in France, while the British made a greater effort than their imperial rivals to crack down on illegitimate sexual activities such as miscegenation. The illegality of homosexual acts in Britain – and opprobrium attached to sentiments or actions suggesting homosexuality – might have provided an incentive for men with reprobate desires to tempt their fortunes overseas; paradoxically, however, law codes in British colonies generally included sanctions against homosexual behaviour replicating those at home. Many Britons serving in commanding positions overseas were products of the hothouse atmosphere of public schools and single-sex colleges, where intimate male-bonding, homosociality and homoeroticism veered off towards homosexuality. These conditions, and the emotions they engendered, continued overseas during expeditions, military campaigns and administrative postings. Feverish male friendships at home came to a head abroad for some British men, as indeed for some Frenchmen, despite (or because of) long-lived Victorian pressures in favour of physical continence, disapproval of irregular heterosexual unions and promotion of the clean and hearty 'games spirit' much valued by imperialists. Moreover, the power relations inherent in the colonial order made it possible for European men to attain their desires with subalterns, servants and others over whom they lorded.

The private lives of the men considered here remain enigmatic, with no concrete proof that most of them had homosexual relations (or, for that matter, that many of them ever had heterosexual relations). Their own writings and the reminiscences of colleagues do not leave traces of intercourse, though circumstantial indications hint at physical contacts with protégés. Men such as these might be considered 'closet cases' who repressed or hid their homosexuality, never acting physically on their desires. Such a conclusion, implying sterile lives of fearful frustration, tortured celibacy or assignations so clandestine as to go unrecorded, places overly great weight on physical (particularly genital) satisfaction. A demand for physical consummation may not have been felt strongly by all of these men, especially in an age that valued chastity and sexual abstention. Emotional traumas linked to intimate companionships appear in some biographies – Rhodes's and Lawrence's heartbreak at loss of companions, Lawrence's contortion of his experiences at the hands of Turkish soldiers into later masochistic practices, the fictional happy ending to Stanley's search for a young friend. Others, by contrast, such as Thesiger, appear not to have felt deprived of physical sexual fulfilment, and Lyautey's life and writings hardly bespeak a tortured soul. Perhaps, therefore, emphasis needs to be transferred from physical intercourse to emotional ties.

For these men, primary emotional attachments consisted of intense and generally exclusive bonding with other men in relationships whose intimacy surpassed the usual style of manly friendship or avuncular patronage. They did not marry, or did so only late in life, and fathered no children. In general, they have not left accounts of sexual adventures with women. A number disavowed marriage – Rhodes admitted that he was not the marrying type, and Przhevalsky acknowledged that 'my profession isn't right for marriage'.[56] Yet they enjoyed highly charged relationships with younger male associates: Rhodes with Neville Pickering, James Brooke with Charles Grant, Przhevalsky with a series of assistants. They reacted badly when protégés married, or became extremely (and publicly) distressed when misadventure befell their companions. Their writings and actions vaunt male beauty, and express an appreciation of the masculine camaraderie of colonial life.

In several cases, the men's writings display a bent towards fabulation. Lawrence, Stuart-Young and Backhouse, in particular, seem unreliable, though to different degrees. Others dissimulate sexual desires in heroic descriptions of muscular companions or godlike natives, as with Lyautey, or invent a whole scenario of homosexual love, as in Stanley's novel. Lawrence almost 'comes out' in his poem about Dahoum, but only Stuart-Young admits to being an Urning. Gordon, Baden-Powell, Kitchener and others remain silent about their contrary sexual leanings. Autobiographical silence, dissimulation or confusion, however, should not mislead. An Englishmen could not confess to homosexual practices without risking arrest, and even admission of homosexual sentiments, in the era of Oscar Wilde, proved dangerous. 'Coming out' in Germany in the era of Humboldt, or in Russia at the time of Przhevalsky, was almost unknown. With the chequered background that he tried to put behind him in Africa, Rimbaud would not have been eager to admit to sex with Djami Ouaddei. Few Frenchmen dared be straightforward in affirming their homosexuality. Hints, half-confessions, coded phrases, references to Ganymede, Antinous and other Greek figures, and praise for virile bodies and manly souls: such were ways that homosexual inclinations might be revealed to fellow initiates while concealed from the disapproving majority. Lack of more explicit traces of homosexuality should not be surprising.

The European men who might be considered homosexual directed their affections to a succession of young companions. Przhevalsky replaced one young assistant by another, while Brooke 'went through' shipboard companions and a Malay prince before falling for Charles Grant (and then formed friendships with several rough lads back in England in the last years of his life). Rhodes had a series of young associates, though never one so intimate as Pickering. Serial 'monogamy' (of an emotional sort) with younger men seemed the rule.

Most (though not all) of the empire-builders discussed here were attracted to other Europeans – Baden-Powell and Gordon took an interest in British boys, Kitchener and Lyautey enjoyed the company of subalterns, Rhodes and Przhevalsky bonded with European assistants. T.E. Lawrence and Wilfred Thesiger, by contrast, focused intense emotions on Arabs, and Rimbaud engaged with an African. Though the sample is small, promoters of imperialism seem more likely than critics of colonialism to focus emotional and erotic attentions on fellow Europeans. The two imperialist figures who formed the most intense emotional links with non-Europeans, Lawrence and Thesiger, were also most identified with the 'native' societies in which they lived. Both learned Arabic and occasionally dressed in Arabic clothes, taking great pride in an ability to survive in the desert and live off the meagre fruits of the parched land. 'I experienced the longing to share this life and to be more than a mere spectator,' Thesiger wrote about Iraq. Lawrence would not have disavowed such identification with the Arabic world and the men who lived there. (It is impossible to imagine Rhodes 'going native' or wanting to do so, and Lyautey limited himself to throwing a burnous over his military uniform.) They are also two of the more paradoxical figures – Lawrence and Thesiger opposed Turkish and Italian imperialism, respectively, and promoted the British Empire, but hoped, in vain, for survival of the supposedly immutable non-Western cultures that obsessed them and which they idealised. Though no less imperialist than many others who were sexually ambivalent, their manifest interest in the people and cultures among whom they ventured differs markedly from the views of men such as Baden-Powell, Kitchener, Rhodes and Przhevalsky, whose emotional links lay with fellow Europeans.

The time and place in which the men pursued their careers vary, as does the exact nature of their attitudes towards European expansion, though all supported imperialism. At one extreme stands Przhevalsky, who expressed little but disdain for the foreigners among whom he moved, and who proclaimed the carbine and whip the only instruments for extension of Russian power. At the other is Lyautey, no less an exponent of the *mission civilisatrice*, but with sincere admiration for Islamic culture and an abiding respect for Maghrebin institutions. These men travelled hand in hand with their young comrades-in-arms across desert and jungle, battling what they saw as forces of darkness and savagery. The European explorer and his protégé, the military commander and his subaltern, the administrator and his assistant were the Achilles and Patroclus of imperialism, the Theban Band of European expansion.

Links between sexual ambivalence, colonial careers and particular actions are manifest. In several cases, specific twists and turns clearly hinged on emotional and perhaps sexual flashpoints. Rhodes's devotion to Pickering led him to forgo an option on gold mines 'which might have made Rhodes absolute master of the world's chief source of gold. It was as if fate itself had intervened, and had made Rhodes for once obey his heart instead of his pocket.' William Plomer adds, 'Nothing in his life is more distinguished than his devotion to the dying Pickering'. Pickering's death may have changed Rhodes's outlook on life and imperial policy:

> It may possibly have had something to do with his tendency to cultivate more and more a hardness and even brutality of manner which, it was supposed by some, was not really natural to him but served to hide his susceptibilities.[57]

Among Rhodes's other close friends was an unmarried surgeon, Leander Starr Jameson, with whom he also shared a house; Jameson led an ill-fated raid, promoted by Rhodes, to the Transvaal in 1895. The failure of the military expedition led to Rhodes's downfall as prime minister of the Cape Colony; 'some historians have plausibly argued that the emotional bonds between Jameson and Rhodes clouded the latter's political judgment in one of the most notorious incidents that led to the outbreak of the South African War in 1899'.[58]

John Walker suggests that in the case of Rajah Brooke, the sexual may have become political at several junctures. British officials maintained distinct coolness to Brooke, perhaps linked to concern about his private behaviour, such as his frolicking with young midshipmen on Royal Navy vessels. Brooke's promotion of the ill-fated Budrudeen over his opponents at the court of Brunei was not unrelated to Brooke's attachment to the Malay prince. Moreover, Brooke may well have found one nephew, Charles, a more attractive young man, and a more worthy successor to rule Sarawak, than his other nephew, Brooke Brooke, the brother-in-law of his former companion.[59] Lawrence's actions in Arabia also show the link between homosexuality and empire. Derek Hopwood argues 'that sex and sexual attitudes played a significant role in the relationship between Britons, the French and the Arabs', though perhaps a psychoanalyst is needed to unravel all of the sexual threads binding Lawrence to the Middle East. Hopwood, however, draws back from finding in sex a direct cause for Lawrence's commitment (though Lawrence himself remarked, 'I prostituted myself in Arab service'): 'It is impossible to take seriously the claim that a British officer would fight against the Turks in order to give the present of freedom to a young Arab boy [Dahoum].'[60] Yet that is exactly what Lawrence confessed in the dedicatory poem of his memoir. There seems no reason to doubt his self-analysis.

These three examples show precise occasions in which strong emotional relationships – homosexual, homoerotic or homosocial – inspired particular political decisions. In a more general sense, Lyautey's and Lawrence's Arabophilia, and their personal affections, can be connected with their military and political manœuvres. Backhouse's fantasies about China reflect his sexual fabulations. Rimbaud and Stuart-Young fled a Europe they considered inhospitable. The link between private and public lives, between sexual desires and imperial actions, showed itself constantly in the colonial world.

Notes

1 A.M. Wentink, 'Nicolson, Sir Harold (1886–1968)', in Robert Aldrich and Garry Wotherspoon, *Who's Who in Gay and Lesbian History: From Antiquity to World War II* (London, 2001), pp. 326–7.
2 Derek Hopwood, *Sexual Encounters in the Middle East: The British, the French and the Arabs* (Reading, 1999).
3 Jens Rydström , 'Haijby, Kurt (1897–1965)', in Aldrich and Wotherspoon (eds), pp. 196–7.
4 Robert Howes, 'Botto, António (1897–1959)', in *ibid.*, pp. 54–6.
5 Pierre-Yves Toullelan, *Missionnaires au quotidien à Tahiti: Les Picpuciens en Polynésie au XIXe siècle* (Leiden, 1995), pp. 274–5.

6   Michael De-la-Noy, *Denton Welch: The Making of a Writer* (Harmondsworth, 1984), pp. 71–5.
7   Alberto Mira, 'Molina, Miguel de (1908–1993)', in Aldrich and Wotherspoon (eds), pp. 315–16.
8   See, e.g., Roy Richard Grinker, *In the Arms of Africa: The Life of Colin M. Turnbull* (New York, 2000).
9   Vitaly Chernetsky, 'Perelshin, Valery (1913–1992)', in Aldrich and Wotherspoon (eds), pp. 324–5.
10 Gert Hekma, 'De Haan, Jacob Israël (1881–1924)', in *ibid.*, pp. 120–1.
11 Wayne F. Cooper, *Claude McKay: Rebel Sojourner in the Harlem Renaissance* (Baton Rouge, LA, 1987), p. 30.
12 Roger Leong, 'Saint Laurent, Yves', in Aldrich and Wotherspoon (eds), pp. 363–4.
13 Robert Howes, 'Melo, Guilherme de', in *ibid.*, pp. 273–5.
14 A.J. Sherman, *Mandate Days: British Lives in Palestine, 1918–1948* (London, 1997), p. 169.
15 Hopwood, pp. 74, 82, 210.
16 *Ibid.*, p. 198, 177.
17 Joseph Chetcuti, 'Rapinett, Guglielmo (1843–1912)', in Aldrich and Wotherspoon (eds), pp. 364–5.
18 Hugh Trevor-Roper, *A Hidden Life: The Enigma of Sir Edmund Backhouse* (London, 1976).
19 Quoted in Trevor-Roper, p. 234.
20 Quoted in *ibid.*, p. 205.
21 Edmund Trelawny Backhouse, *Décadence Mandchoue*, manuscript, Bodleian Library, University of Oxford, MS. Eng. misc d. 1223; quotations from pp. 18 and 20. *The Dead Past* details Backhouse's adventures in England.
22 R. Hoeppli, editor of the Backhouse's manuscript in the Bodleian library, says that Backhouse was 'confused' and 'mixed incidents from his reading with reminiscences', but thinks that the manuscript was based on fact. Postface to *The Dead Past*, p. 607.
23 Backhouse, *Décadence Mandchoue*, p. 30
24 Backhouse, *The Dead Past*, introduction.
25 Trevor-Roper, p. 274.
26 *Ibid.*, pp. 279, 280, 281.
27 *Ibid.*, p. 296.
28 This section is based on J.H. Walker, '"This peculiar acuteness of feeling": James Brooke and the enactment of desire', *Borneo Research Bulletin*, Vol. 29 (1998), pp. 148–222.
29 See the various commentaries published as an annexe in *ibid.*
30 Quoted in Walker, pp. 162, 163, 164.
31 *Ibid.*, p. 165.
32 *Ibid.*, pp. 169–78.
33 Rhodes's relationship with Pickering is discussed in Antony Thomas, *Rhodes* (London, 1996), pp. 222–33.
34 *Ibid.*
35 *Ibid.*, p. 228.
36 William Plomer, *Cecil Rhodes* (London, 1993) p. 48.
37 *Ibid.*, p. 229.
38 *Ibid.*, p. 233.
39 Quoted in Enid Starkie, *Arthur Rimbaud in Abyssinia* (Oxford, 1937), p. 132.
40 *Ibid.*, pp. 28, 144.
41 Charles Nicholl, *Somebody Else: Arthur Rimbaud in Africa, 1880–91* (London, 1997), Ch. 15; quotation from p. 170.
42 Graham Robb, *Rimbaud* (New York, 2000), p. 310.
43 Alain Borer, *Rimbaud en Abyssinie* (Paris, 1984), p. 147.

44 Jean-Luc Steinmetz, *Arthur Rimbaud. Une Question de présence* (Paris, 1999), p. 329.
45 Timothy d'Arch Smith, *Love in Earnest: Some Notes on the Lives and Writings of English 'Uranian' Poets from 1889 to 1930* (London, 1970), pp. 202–19.
46 J.M. Stuart-Young, *The Coaster at Home: Being the Autobiography of Jack O'Dazi, Palm Oil Ruffian and Trader Man, of the River Niger* (London, 1916), pp. 286–7, 290.
47 *Ibid.*, pp. 168–9.
48 *Ibid.*, pp. 44–5.
49 *Ibid.*, p. 49.
50 *Ibid.*, p. 153.
51 *Ibid.*, p. 183.
52 D'Arch Smith, p. 217.
53 *Ibid.*, pp. 207–8.
54 Stuart-Young, p. 277.
55 *Ibid.*, pp. 133, 173.
56 Quoted in Donald Rayfield, *The Dream of Lhasa: The Life of Nikolay Przhevalsky (1839–88), Explorer of Central Asia* (London, 1976), p. 184.
57 Plomer, pp. 41–2.
58 Nick Southey, 'Cecil John Rhodes', in George Haggerty, *Encyclopedia of Homosexuality* (New York, 2000) , p. 744.
59 Walker, pp. 185–8.
60 Hopwood, pp. 211–14.

4   Writers' lives and letters

Homosexually inclined writers, just as explorers, soldiers and colonists, were drawn overseas, and traces of their experiences (or fantasies) appear in both their lives and works – the example of Henry Morton Stanley's real-life companionships, and his fictional love-story of Kalulu and Selim, discussed in an earlier chapter, is a case in point. Professional novelists had even greater licence to incorporate colonialist homoeroticism into plots and characterisations, and the ways in which they did so provide the subject for this chapter.[1] It first examines how homoeroticism, or homosociality or outright homosexuality, appears indirectly, in a colonial or exotic setting, in a variety of genres – boys' own yarns and stories of friends and castaways, 'decadent' tales with happy endings and works with tragic climaxes. It then looks at five writers who followed their sexual star to the East: the Italian Giovanni Comisso in Ceylon and China, the Frenchman Claude Farrère in Vietnam and his compatriot Henri Fauconnier in British Malaya, and the Dutchman Louis Couperus in the Netherlands East Indies, as well as an armchair American traveller, Frederic Prokosch, in an imagined journey from Port-Said to Saigon. The South Pacific provided journeys and inspired writings for two other Americans, Herman Melville and Charles Warren Stoddard. The chapter closes with consideration of two of the most famous colonial writers and globe-trotters, John Buchan and Pierre Loti, and sexual ambivalence in their novels of Turkey and Africa.[2]

The world overseas, with the latitude provided by travel and the tolerant mores of 'native' populations, afforded opportunities for portrayals of sexual desires and behaviours considered reprobate in Europe. Imperialism formed the backdrop to writers' own adventures, and those of their heroes, facilitating encounters, remoulding local cultures and creating new needs. Yet most of these authors were also ill at ease with imperialism; their works question, criticise and sometimes subvert the imperial project, while at the same time often reaffirming European stereotypes. In each author's life and work lies a personal quest – for adventure, erotic satisfaction and self-actualisation.

Same-sex relations in different genres

Glimmers of homosexuality appear, with varying degrees of brightness, in the fiction of several canonical writers associated with colonialism. Even in boys' own stories, bonding between youths – bosom buddies braving adversity for the sake of derring-do adventure – verges on adolescent sexuality. The absence of women, combined with the hero-worship of older boys or gallant adult men, replicates the male camaraderie of public schools with at least the possibility of the sexual experimentation for which boarding schools were notorious.[3] Narrative insistence on the strength of 'naked savages' creates a homoerotic titillation of the sort presented in Stanley's novel and the 'Two Boy Travellers' abridgement. Sexuality is seldom explicitly an issue in juvenile literature of the imperial age, except that chastity is usually recommended, miscegenation condemned and irregular liaisons damned as dangerous to morals and health. According to Peter J. Hugill, 'homosexuality was never mentioned, although repressed homosexuality is often evident in juveniles [i.e. literature for juveniles]'. The British weekly of boys' stories, *Chums*, 'was full of idealized homoerotic illustrations of males rescuing each other in situations of mortal peril'.[4] Physical closeness and intense emotional bonding would make suitably imperial men of British boys, while it reinforced a heroic, virile comradeship not too distant from sexual intimacy.

Homosexuality echoes in less inchoate form in adult fiction, including several classics of colonial literature. Joseph Conrad – who shared a hut with Roger Casement in the Congo, though he later turned against Casement because of his Irish nationalism – is one such writer. Several of his works centre on enigmatic friendships. In *Lord Jim* (1900), the story of an Englishman who, like Rajah Charles Brooke, becomes ruler of an East Indian state, Jim Denver hides a mysterious but disgraceful issue in his past. The narrator, Marlow, is much taken with the good looks of Jim, who has been on trial for dereliction of duty at sea. Marlow invites Jim to dinner, and entertains him in his room. He later finds Jim a job with an elderly bachelor and plantation owner, who is also attracted to the fine-looking young man. Jim improves the outlook of the old bachelor, who writes to Marlow of being thrilled when Jim took hold of his arm. The planter reacts with depression and bitterness when Denver departs.

Two other works focus on mysterious friendships at sea. In *The Shadow Line* (1915), on a vessel sailing across the Gulf of Siam, the captain pals up with a broad-chested, well-proportioned cook named Ransome – 'soul as firm as the muscles of his body'. When the ship lands in Singapore, Ransome leaves, much to the captain's chagrin. 'The Secret Sharer' (1909) tells of a shipboard relationship in which a captain shares his room and bed with a stowaway, whom he helps escape as the ship approaches the Cambodian coast. Intimacy in the captain's quarters and an emotionally charged farewell authorise a homosexual reading.[5] In the liminal world of the sea, and in the mysterious East Indies, unexpected and highly intense, if brief, friendships between men provide solace and pleasure.

Conrad's works illustrate how homosexuality can be read into a story, although the extent to which an author intentionally or unconsciously wished it evident could be debated. The male world of colonialism encouraged situations where slippage from friendship to love, from emotional to physical intimacy, and from the frustrations of *dépaysement* to the consolations of sex might easily occur.

Another genre, stories of castaways on islands, was pregnant with homosexual potential. Daniel Defoe's classic island novel intimates close male bonding between Robinson Crusoe and Friday, and retellings of the tale by Michel Tournier, Bernard Malamud and Muriel Spark suggest ambiguous links between two men adrift without other companions, one a sturdy sailor, the other an exotic younger man. For Gregory Woods, islands strip away inhibitions and provide places of polymorphous sexuality. The *mises-en-scène* of island stories re-enact an Edenic state of grace, or a savage place of perdition, both hospitable to diverse sexual expressions.[6]

'Decadent' works also prove conducive to intimations of homosexuality; Ronald Firbank's novels provide illustrations. One female character in *Valmouth* (1919) has as a lover a sailor cruising the West Indies, 'big, handsome, strong *and* delicate!' His affections, however, are divided. 'That little lad,' he says, talking about a 15-year-old cabin boy, 'upon a cruise, is, to me, what Patroclus was to Achilles, and even more.' Dick Thoroughfare returns home to Hare-Hall accompanied by the cabin boy, now a lieutenant, who 'resembled singularly some girl masquerading as a boy for reasons of romance'. 'I'm one of those who, at the last Trump, would run their hand across their hair,' confesses young Whorwood. Thoroughfare's betrothed, Thetis, realises that she cannot marry the sailor because he prefers other sorts of companions. An English priest and a *métis* banana inspector also display suspicious morals, and Mrs Yajñavalkya, an exotic masseuse working in England, reveals, 'In the Happy East you live untrammelled by the ghouls of our insular convention.'[7]

In Firbank's *Prancing Nigger* (1925), young Vittorio eventually seduces a girl though his earlier affectations – carrying a perfumed handkerchief and jewelled cigarette-case, composing 'Five Phallic Dances for Pianoforte and Orchestra', hiring dancing boys, and singing 'Little mauve nigger boy, / I t'ink you break my heart' – suggest at the least an effetely aesthetic sensibility. As for the white archbishop in the Caribbean island where the novel is set, 'Rumour had it he was fond of negresses, and that the black private secretary he employed was his own natural son, while some suspected indeed a less natural connection.' Esmé, the novella's *femme fatale*, dreams of a beau, 'who seemed to imagine that to be a dress-designer to foreign Princesses would give his several talents a thrice-blessed harvest'. Charlie Mouth, son of a socially climbing planter, who migrates from village to town, is a handsome fellow known for 'acquaintance with several young men', including the 15-year-old son of a jazz-hall owner ('who was destined to enter the Church'). When Charlie, lagging behind the family as they move, arrives in Cuna-Cuna, he is asked by a customs inspector, 'Have you nothing, young man, to declare?'; the youthful lepidopterist answers, with Oscar Wilde aplomb, '...[*sic*] Butterflies!' Charlie soon establishes a reputation: 'Ever so lovely are the young men of Cuna-Cuna...but none so delicate, charming, and squeamish as Charlie Mouth.' Charlie refuses one girl's overtures, but enjoys twilight promenades where 'incipient Cupians, led by vigilant blanched-faced queens, youths of a certain life, known as bwam-wam bwam-wams, gaunt pariah dogs, all equally were on the prowl'. He frequents 'a notorious Bar with its bright particular galaxy of boys'. Charlie is 'easy of habit, as tropical animals are apt to be'.[8] Such camp figures and not-so-veiled hints of homosexuality emerged from Firbank's own 1922 trip to the Caribbean.[9]

More serious, and darker, stories also feature homosexuals, often based on authors' personal experiences. Annemarie Schwarzenbach transformed her experiences of Asia Minor into bleak accounts of lost homosexual love. Born in 1908 into a wealthy family of Swiss industrialists, in the late 1920s Schwarzenbach spent a year in Paris, and then in 1931 went to Berlin (where she met Klaus and Erika Mann, with whom she fell in love). The following year she journeyed to Persia, which she would visit six times in the next four years, occasionally working with archaeologists. Thus began travels, and work as newspaper reporter and photographer, which took her to Russia, the Middle East, Afghanistan and the Congo.

In 1934, Schwarzenbach began writing stories set in the Levant and filled with sexually dissident characters. In 'Farewell', a French officer is unaccountably jealous of a handsome Algerian, while in 'Van's Engagement' the ambivalent hero, clearly not cut out for marriage, breaks up with his fiancée. In 'A Single Woman', a Danish adventurer refuses to return home, has a scandalous affair with a local man and 'goes native'. 'Much Patience' tells the story of Dr Rieti, who has fled Fascist Italy for Persia. He cannot take his mind off his old friend Mario, who has gone to France, or Charles, the black servant he had employed in Kenya. A one-night stand with an Italian woman fails, as it is against his nature, and he continues to pine for Mario and Charles. 'The Promised Land' is about a lesbian in the Middle East. Schwarzenbach's characters have escaped Europe with great but often thwarted expectations, for the liberty to be found overseas. 'Here one can love and drink without the least qualm. Here one can march towards the future without dragging the weight of the past behind,' a character in 'The Return Home' says, but another cautions, 'We must not stay too long in this part of the world.'[10]

Schwarzenbach's partly autobiographical *Death in Persia* – a rare example of lesbian Orientalism – is set in an archaeological dig, and centres on a woman who had fled Europe, but finds it impossible to live happily in Persia. Filled with despair, in Teheran, she meets a woman named Yalé, the daughter of a Turkish father and a Circassian mother. Yalé, recently released from a Swiss tuberculosis sanatorium, has been taken to Persia by her father. The European woman falls in love with Yalé, whose father disapproves, so she returns inconsolably to the dig site. Falling ill with malaria and delirious, she asks for Yalé, who comes to visit. As the European recovers, Yalé falls ill and is taken to hospital, but her father forbids visitors. The European returns to the bleak countryside, where she is visited by an angel, who tells her to give up her longing. In the meantime, Yalé dies. A doctor offers general advice: 'In this heat, you should not put stress on your heart.' [11]

Orientalist fables offered a chance to portray, often in coded fashion, homosexual liaisons. Two examples are works by William Beckford and Thomas Mann. Beckford, who was born in 1760 into a family with colonial connections (wealth derived from Jamaican plantations), gained a reputation as an eccentric writer and personality (and constructed a 'ruined' Gothic abbey on his estate). *The Episodes of Vathek*, appendages to Beckford's most famous work, *Vathek* (1787), are suffused with sexual ambiguity in a setting of harems, incense and houris. The story of Prince Alasi tells of a young man who falls in love with 'an angelic form, in a boy's dress'; 'the true heart's-friend' later turns out to be a girl, whom Alasi continues to love in spite of, not because of, her femaleness – and her parallel turn from innocence to evil. *Histoire du Prince Ahmed* (1782), originally written in French, recounts a triangular relationship between best friends, Ali and Ahmed, and the woman whom Ahmed loves. Ali ends up with a wife as well, though 'I could never resolve to separate myself from my dear Ahmed, who is the other half of myself', and the happy ending keeps them together.[12]

A century and a half later, Thomas Mann, author of *Death in Venice*, published 'The Transposed Heads' (1940), a long story ostensibly about the clash of mind and body, but which is a very queer tale about two Indian buddies, thoughtful Shridaman and hunky Nanda. Shridaman falls in love with Sita, whom he marries, but she soon lusts after his robust friend. Shridaman suffers a traumatic experience in a temple; driven wild by the sight of statues of gods and animals, hallucinations of 'sperm and sweat and tears and ropy rheum', he decapitates himself. A distraught Nanda, seeing his friend dead, cuts off his own head. The gods take pity on Sita, and allow her to reattach the heads to bring the men back to life, but she mixes up heads and bodies, then faces the question of which of the cobbled-together men is really her husband. After some twists and turns, a three-way *Liebestod* resolves the conflict. Shridaman and Nanda have been the complement to each other, they become literally linked bodies, join each other in death and live on in the son who can claim both fathers. Mann warned the reader 'not to fall prey to a misconception of [the work's] real character', and the story is another example of a triangle in which love between males is at least as important as a 'normal' sexual and emotional relationship. For Mann, as for Beckford – both authors who struggled with homosexual inclinations – the fantastic East provided the scene for thinly disguised homosexual romances.[13]

Homosexual Orientalism also appeared in poetry, for instance verses by Jacques d'Adelswärd-Fersen, French aristocrat, notorious homosexual, decadent writer and denizen of Capri (where he lived with a Ceylonese companion). *Hei Hsiang* (1921) consists of odes to opium smoking (one of d'Adelswärd-Fersen's addictions), mixed with evocations of Oriental boys. 'Cadences pour un mourant' conjures up a young juggler: 'I will take him, naked, onto my soporific sampan / His silken body I will caress amidst the pink / Peonies: My kiss will part his closed hands / He will submit to the assault of his vanquisher'. In 'Amour' (which also speaks about Oscar Wilde), the poet dreams about a youth emerging from the sea, dried by the sun on the beach, his body fragrant with 'the perfume of tropical lands / The incense of Benares around your eyelids / Ceylonese jasmine on your opal torso', his breath smelling of vanilla, his eyes blue as the night, 'Your breast, the new porch of a mosque / Where the verses of the Prophet will be recited', 'Your legs, they might say, the gates to Baghdad, / Lead, O my Bey, to the silky cushion / When my folly lies at the foot of a pure cypress'. This 'unforgettable voyage among the most beautiful voyages' uses baroque homoerotic imagery from the Levant, the Orient and tropical islands to describe the quest for love: 'You know how much I have suffered, looking / Around the world for a heart that will understand my soul' – a poetic and homosexual world tour.[14]

Orientalism inspired pornographic send-ups of itself, as authors speculated about the carnal enticements of Eastern youths. The enduring attraction of the Orientalist fantasy is illustrated by a curious little volume called *Le Livre des Beaux*, published anonymously in Paris in 1909. Attributed to Pierre Loti, Pierre Louÿs and André Gide – all authors known for an interest in Levantine love – as well as to lesser-known writers, the book was printed in only 350 copies. By reproducing stereotypes of Eastern male love, it pokes fun at images current in Europe; like *L'Art d'aimer aux colonies*, it provides a guide to the boys of the East. The book pretends, not very convincingly, to be the work of one Fazyl Bey, a contemporary of Louis XVI and Napoleon, translated by 'The Three-Legged Pasha'. It presents forty-three sketches of young men of the 'Orient', from Morocco to China, their attributes and proclivities, a catalogue of sodomitical specialities. The Moroccan has 'an iron-hard member', but fickle loyalties and a taste for reward; the Algerian, 'pale fine hands, an intelligent face, a mouth soft to the touch as worn silk'. The Chinese is a professional *mignon*, the Persian knows how to entertain coquettishly, but a boy from Borneo may bite a lover with gold-encrusted teeth. The Basra beau haunts 'a harem always filled with torrid voluptuousness, a fountain of aphrodisiacs and a lawn which welcomes nonchalant fantasies'. As for the Egyptian, 'at the first view of a *sik* [male member], he dilates like a vale in springtime', and would not disdain intercourse with a donkey or a horse. The Abyssinian is 'proportioned like a genie'. Beware of the Damascene, 'a tamed Bedouin', who dances well but hides a dagger or pistol under the pillow. A lad from Aleppo sports a scar on his cheek – 'whoever sees him feels a wound in the depths of his heart that will never heal'. An Albanian masseur, too, will leave a broken heart, but 'a mountain savage' from Bosnia will not be tender: 'Let him serve as a mattress for an orgy of devils on heat.' A Montenegrin 'is solid as a rampart – one must be a strong ram to breach his gates'. An Istanbul boy displays the loyalty of 'a ruined minaret, ready to fall at the first breeze. But he joins the majesty of Alexander to the grace of Joseph and the fragrance of a rose garden', and he has 'philosophical genius: at thirty, he surpasses Plato'. A Georgian will change religion as quickly as his lover. A Circassian remains faithful to religion and lover, an amorous ideal, generous and happy, modest but with the virtues of antiquity: 'The saints admire him. Even if a slave, he has the character of a Sultan.'[15]

Whoever the author might have been, *Le Livre des Beaux* reflects knowledge of Middle Eastern and Asian geography and history, familiarity with the classics and an ability to write an amusing send-up in the form of a lost manuscript with an appropriately scholarly 'bio-bibliographical preface'. The book plays on Western perceptions of sexual luxuriance and sodomitical perversion in countries stretching from North-Western Africa to South-Eastern Asia: the Sotadic zone. It alludes to received idea: the beauty of the Circassian, a trope going back to Hadrian's Antinous; the pleasures of the harem, a stock-in-trade in European travelogues since the Middle Ages; the notion that Moroccan boys were all available, but at a price, a view circulated with increased European intercourse with North Africa. The virile, but rough Balkan and the svelte, feline Malay represented standard racialist stereotypes.

Le Livre des Beaux might have been passed with knowing smiles among the *cognoscenti* of the *belle époque*, including some who had read Dr Jacobus X.'s treatise, readers familiar with Flaubert's letters from Egypt, Gide's *L'Immoraliste* or the ambisexual works of Loti, men who knew the paintings of the Orientalists. Some might have studied learned works of ethnology and history, and many would have read newspaper accounts of distant places. They might have sailed across the Mediterranean to Algiers or Tunis, or visited the pyramids of Giza or the Topkapi palace in Istanbul. In 1909, few would have been unfamiliar with the Wilde scandal across the Channel, and some might have rubbed shoulders with Marcel Proust, Robert de Montesquiou, d'Adelswärd-Fersen or other homosexual aesthetes. Perhaps some had met Marshal Lyautey at a Parisian soirée.

Le Livre des Beaux, which both satirises and perpetuates European erotic images of the East in the style of soft-core pornography, sums up European homosexual fantasies about foreign lands. By the beginning of the twentieth century, links between foreignness and sodomy were well established in the European mind, whether neo-classical pleasures awaiting men in Capri or Taormina, or exotic delights further afield. Colonialism was government policy, travel was in fashion and homosexuality seemed to flourish in decadent quarters of European cities. The book – though known only to a few initiates – brought together strands of European attitudes, behaviour and desires, exoticism and eroticism, fantasy and the promise of reality. Other writers developed these themes more fully.

In Asia

Asia provided a propitious location for reflection on homosexual practices by natives and colonial expatriates; one pertinent example is *Gioco d'infanzia* by Giovanni Comisso (1895–1969), a homosexual who travelled in the East (and also took part in Gabriele D'Annunzio's short-lived conquest of Fiume after the First World War).[16] The novella, set in the inter-war period, tells of Alberto, a wealthy but world-weary and solitary 30-year-old who leaves Europe for Asia, with the more immediate hope of locating a former male lover during a stop in the Italian colony of Eritrea. Two years previously, Alberto and Pietro's affair ended when another man seduced Pietro and secured him a position in Africa. Alberto harbours hopes of rekindling their love and settling together on the Asmara plateau in colonial bliss, complete with a plantation and slaves.

Aboard ship, Alberto lusts for a muscled blond sailor, but never finds the appropriate moment to proposition him. He reluctantly keeps company with a young German, Hans, who is making his way to Thailand to become a Buddhist, and a junior officer, who seems to share Alberto's interests.

At the first port of call, Port-Said, Alberto lets a guide drag him to a sordid brothel, but consents only to watch a scruffy lad having sex with a fat whore. He then races off to a hammam, but refuses to take up a masseur's offer of sex. At Messawa, Eritrea, Alberto receives a letter from Pietro, who is recovering from illness in a hospital in Asmara, and is unable to join him during the 24-hour layover. Peeved, Alberto sets out to explore. A young black man proposes his services as a guide, then offers sexual favours, which Alberto rejects, only to go to a brothel for sex with a black woman, while fantasising about both Pietro and the blond sailor. He then goes off with his officer friend and others – including another blond, to whom Pietro is immediately attracted – to hunt gazelles, although Alberto refuses to shoot. The blond hunter disappears, and the officer becomes distraught, fearing that he has accidentally shot the man, who he implies is his lover. The party return to ship, later receiving word that their missing companion is alive and well.

The novel concludes in Colombo, where Alberto disembarks, having agreed to meet the officer later one evening. He does not show up, and an infuriated Alberto comes upon Hans, who takes him through luxuriant jungle and past handsome youths to a temple. The novice Buddhist guides him to a house where boys are on offer. Through a crack in the wall, they spy the ship's officer having sex with the blond sailor after whom Alberto lusted. Alberto is beside himself, but Hans calms him: 'My dear friend, you suffer too much, let me look after you. I promise that you will enjoy yourself; the people here are available for pleasure.' They catch a rickshaw to a garden, and Alberto chooses a young man with whom he wanders into the woods. The next morning, on the beach, he tells Hans that 'my pleasures are nothing more that the pursuit of my childhood games'. [17]

Alberto's trip charts sexual elation and disappointment, and the varieties of homosexual pleasure to be found in the East: a potential reunion with a lover, the attractions of a lusty sailor, boys for hire in brothels, parks and bath-houses, and intimate friendships with fellow Europeans. The East is a hothouse of sensuality and licence – the winding fetid streets of Port-Said, the incense-perfumed ports on the horn of Africa, the male camaraderie of the hunting safari, and the verdant landscape of Ceylon. Assaulted by heat and dust, smells and sights, the visitor is importuned by sexual partners at every turn, whether grubby Arab youths, black adolescent guides or sleek bronze-skinned Ceylonese.

In the Orient, Alberto can fulfil his boyhood sexual fantasies, once he sheds inhibitions that force him to deny his sexual pleasures and, too, once he has abandoned the romantic dream of life with Pietro and yearnings for an unavailable European sailor. Sexual pleasure lies with the natives, and a man inspired by the tolerance of Buddhism can lead one with the weight of European culture to realisation of his desires. 'It is strange,' Hans tells Alberto. 'You and I are following the same route to the Orient. You to satisfy your sensuality, and I to satisfy the desires of my soul.' 'But do you think that you can make a distinction between them?' Alberto asks and smiles.

> After all what is your soul and what is my sensuality? What is certain, for you as well as for me, is that we no longer believe in our Europe. As for me, I couldn't care less for the laws, religion, philosophy and the art of the West.

Though Alberto takes a while to develop his philosophy, he can now state: 'Only beauty and the pleasures of the senses count: a moment of light in the dark night of everything.' Alberto must seize the moment, and only in exotic climes can he do so. As the novel ends, with Alberto relaxed in post-coital satisfaction, 'The light grew stronger, lively and impetuous, with the wind between the sea and the palms. On their barques the natives raised their little white sails and drifted out. The order of things appeared inalterable to him.'[18]

Alberto regularly comes into contact with the colonial order during his travels: tiresome tourists chattering about the heat or the beauty of the sunsets, the busy life of ports, the Italian outpost in Eritrea, drunken English soldiers crowding into taverns in Colombo. In the colonies, pleasures are not difficult to find, and European money procures the luxuries of a first-class stateroom, hunting and whoring. Alberto leaves behind the traditions and family responsibilities of bourgeois Europe, and discovers the bustling markets, louche gambling dens and bordellos of the foreign world. The colonies provide an escape for those who reject European conventions (and whose morals are damned by fellow Europeans): a fickle Italian in a colonial backwater, an officer with a man in every port, sailors keen for new experiences, an effeminate steward who clucks happily over an attractive passenger, and a thoughtful European searching for himself – and the mythical romantic other.

With Comisso, a reader has a unique chance to compare two versions of travels to the East in the early 1930s. *Gioco d'infanzia*, with its clear homosexual theme, reflecting the author's own proclivities, was only published in 1965, late in Comisso's life. In the 1930s he had published an ostensibly more heterosexual version. Translated into English in 1954 as *Loves of the Orient*, the dust jacket of the American edition is ornamented with a shadowy photograph of a naked woman, portrayed as part of a yin-yang symbol; the other half might represent another silhouette. On the rear cover is a stylised portrait of Comisso with a naked woman superimposed on his cheek and neck. Drawings throughout the text show pith-helmeted travellers eating, drinking and visiting heterosexual brothels. The book's cover thus advertises a blatantly heterosexual novel. The blurb hints at the licence of the East, but is reassuring about the virtue of the West. John [*sic*] Comisso, it says, tells of 'the adventures of Lorenzo in a world which knows none of the restrictions and inhibitions of ours – a world we should know so that we may understand the comparative beauty and safety of our own'. A casual reader might finish the book with that opinion reinforced, convinced that the evil of the Orient has led to the hero's moral degradation. Many would perhaps not grasp how fully Comisso's text subverts the heterosexual publicity and much of the heterosexual plot, and how Lorenzo's eventual succumbing to homosexual sex, after multiple delays and refusals, for him represents liberation rather than degradation, pleasure instead of sin.

The route of the voyage is much the same in this version but Lorenzo, the hero, sails on from Ceylon to China. The plot of *Loves of the Orient* is not altogether different from *Gioco d'infanzia*: a well-heeled young Italian goes in search of adventure (though in the earlier version he is not looking for a lost boyfriend). In Egypt, he becomes aware of the 'easy exhibitionism on the part of the Arabs of their prowess in love', and, in a house of ill repute, he watches two Egyptian men who 'dance with one another with shameless movements'. An ensuing brawl excites Lorenzo, and a fellow Italian mutters, 'They don't do these things where we come from.' In Eritrea, a boy propositions him – 'I be your friend,' he says, and shows Lorenzo a fistful of silver. Lorenzo, however, pays him for showing him to a straight brothel; 'his small lachrymose eyes glare[d] savagely. "Women hurt you"'.[19]

Lorenzo (unlike Alberto) avoids homosexual entanglements, though he is befriended by the same savvy German as in *Gioco d'infanzia*. The aspiring Buddhist monk eagerly shows Lorenzo the sights; the Italian looks but does not touch. He notices that local men are 'slender and flexuous', and remarks on pictures at a police station:

> There was a majority of very beautiful youths who were simply designated with the word 'dangerous'. He asked for explanation from his guide [the German] and he learned that these youths made a commerce of their beauty. Brothels being completely illegal since the island was a direct colony of the English crown, this surrogate species had come to the fore which when linked with an able pimp ended always in a dangerous ambush.

Lorenzo picks up a woman, but is disgusted, then a Ceylonese asks,

> 'You like boys?' At that very moment some boys issue forth from the shadows and surround them invitingly, sweetishly, resembling those seen on the photographs at the police post. By glance and gesture they became suppliant so as to be picked.

The two men stand firm against temptation.

Quickly they freed themselves from them by climbing into two coaches, but one ran after them....In the center, at every corner other youths with bare chests stood still, vigilant in glance. The German said, 'There are others.' 'But this must be an equatorial Athens,' added Lorenzo, laughing.[20]

Lorenzo keeps up the heterosexual side, and sails on, only to be confronted with other examples of illicit love. In a Saigon park,

Lorenzo noticed some youths dressed in black who stood immobile. But when one saw him pass by, he hastened to have himself seen under a street light. He asked the porter [rickshaw driver] what they were doing there. Slowing his pace the porter answered, 'L'amour avec les hommes.'

Lorenzo wants to see one hustler close up, and the driver hails the boy. Lorenzo asks how much he charges, laughs and rides away. In Guangzhou, a hotel servant approaches him. Shanghai, someone tells him, 'offers you all the possibilities of pleasure'. Li, Lorenzo's guide, talks about a transvestite actor: 'He is much better than a woman.' Later, Lorenzo discovers Li in bed with a naked boy. Boys in Beijing make rude gestures at Lorenzo, and he learns that male assistants in a silk shop are the owner's catamites. An American sailor pursues bath-house attendants. In a park, a vendor tries to sell Lorenzo dirty postcards of young men and proposes that:

if Lorenzo were willing he could make him acquainted with some most beautiful young men, and one in particular who was the son of a Mandarin imprisoned for debt, and whom he had already brought to the French Legation....He wanted to see this youth immediately.

Lorenzo remarks philosophically, thinking of his life in Europe, 'Down there he had lived one life, here he lived another completely different': an apt summation of the difference between home and abroad.

Giovanni (an Italian-speaking Chinese) introduces a youth to Lorenzo, and they fix a rendezvous. The rickshaw driver warns Lorenzo that the meeting could be dangerous and offers to show him other entertainments. Lorenzo does not go to the assignation, and Giovanni takes him to a brothel. The Italian finds the boys unattractive and goes off with a girl, but then says that he really wants to meet the boy from the park. The next night Giovanni helps him find the boy, but they argue after he asks for money for the missed rendezvous. Then Giovanni offers himself to Lorenzo; once again, Lorenzo backs off.

A fellow Italian tells Lorenzo about a German whose affair with a beautiful houseboy of wandering affections made his life miserable. Europeans are innocents abroad, particularly in the face of the Chinese. 'They manage to make even vices virtuous, and we always play the role of barbarians.' Undeterred, Lorenzo confesses, 'Since I have learned to appreciate Chinese food, our cooking now seems insipid to me. I hope it will not be the same with everything else.' His friend counsels: 'Don't think about it....Abandon yourself to the yellow wind.' Lorenzo flirts with a half-caste boy in a jade shop, and then takes on over another youth (himself intrigued by Lorenzo's hairy arms). Lorenzo later goes to a brothel with a silk seller; they ask to share a woman, but the madam refuses. Eventually Lorenzo and the Chinese silk vendor go to a hotel, where they have a bath together: 'There was no difference between them, the young Chinese seemed to gratify a deep curiosity long repressed, and Lorenzo abandoned himself with the instinct of obtaining what had been impossible before.' Finally, the reader might sigh in relief, he has 'done it', and the denouement is swift. Lorenzo buys a rug from his companion, and bids a sad Giovanni good-bye – Giovanni, he realises, has been in love with him – to return to Italy when he learns that his bank has failed. Home, he laments in the closing pages, is but a tomb or prison compared to the Orient.

Loves of the Orient is a pot-boiler, an adventure story verging on porn, but nevertheless a 'coming-out' story, remarkable in the 1930s (made more extraordinary because of the clash between cover and text in the American edition). Try as he might to resist temptation, as often as he goes with women, as many opportunities as he refuses, Lorenzo cannot forever repudiate his true nature. He toys with the idea of homosexual sex, chats up hustlers, gives out money, makes an assignation, yet it takes a trek from Egypt to China, and many missed opportunities, before he falls into the arms of another man. The Orient has introduced him to new love, what he really desires despite heterosexual philandering. Only by going overseas, and being confronted countless times by alternative sexual activities in societies where they are tolerated, is Lorenzo able to free himself from sexual and cultural repression.

Comisso's novel suggests that the world outside Europe offers unlimited homosexual liaisons. An American sailor chases bath-house boys, a German has an affair with a houseboy, a French diplomat sleeps with an actor, lewd dancers entertain in cabarets, hustlers haunt public parks, brothels sell the services of males and females, rickshaw drivers offer sex, and shop assistants seek assignations. Locals and colonials take a live-and-let-live attitude. The book confirms the stereotype of Oriental luxuriance, the sexual ambiguity of the East and the moral laxity of Asian societies. Decadence and degradation this appeared to some readers, while to others it proposed an *invitation au voyage*.

For a contemporary French writer, the goal of self-revelation and pleasure also lay in the East. Claude Farrère, a much honoured novelist during his lifetime, but now little known, may have been homosexual. In 1905, he published *Les Civilisés*, a novel that some critics found both pornographic in its plot and libellous in the portrayal of French colonists.[21] Set in Indo-China, it juxtaposes two colonial groups – the 'barbarians', people of impeccably good morals, and the *civilisés* or 'sophisticates', men and women who indulge in opium, alcohol and debauchery. The main character is Comte Fierce, ADC to the commander of the French fleet, who falls in love with a beautiful and innocent woman, to whom he cannot remain faithful, and then dies in an almost-suicide in battle. Dr Mévil, also heterosexual, cannot get the two women he loves, and perishes in an accident. Another character is Torral, a 30-year-old mathematician and engineer, who is homosexual. His sexuality causes no concern to his friends, but he inwardly detests many fellow colonials, and chooses to live in the native quarter rather than a European neighbourhood. He straightforwardly affirms: 'The woman question is not in my field of competence.' 'I've chosen for my lot,' says Torral, 'the splendour of perfect numbers and transcendent forms. And so, I do mathematics, and my private boy takes care of settling my nerves when it's necessary – and I don't have to worry about anything.' Torral, who announces happily, 'We're in Sodom here' in Saigon, 'calculated his pleasures according to Epicurean arithmetic...even in broad daylight he paraded his masculine liaisons, and walked about with his intimate boys Ba and Sao'. His open homosexuality provides a way of showing off his 'condescending hatred of those whom he scandalised', and after a night out with heterosexual friends, he chooses 'an Annamite boy' for comfort. Fierce asks him: 'Do you not wish for anything better? Is that enough – to sleep, eat, drink, smoke cigarettes and opium, make love to women – that is, to boys?' Torral answers grandly, 'Yes', and takes his leave. At the end of the novel, Torral, however, is arrested and flees, paying the price for a debauched life.[22] For Farrère, the colonies may be hospitable environments for excess, but such living does not come cheaply.

The Soul of Malaya was the work of another Frenchman, Henri Fauconnier, a pioneer rubber planter in the British colony. His only novel won the prestigious Goncourt Prize in 1930 and was translated into English the following year. The book tells the story of two men who first meet in the trenches during the First World War. Rolain, like the author, is a planter in Malaya, and the unnamed narrator goes out to Asia during the 1920s. By chance, he meets up with Rolain, who hires him to run his estate. Rolain, a solitary, philosophical character, admits, 'I don't live quite like everybody else', and admits that he might be mad, 'if madness consists in acting differently to other people'. Unmarried, his only companion is a loyal Malay servant, Smail. The novel hints that the two may be sexually intimate. Rolain states that 'I don't see any difference between loving a dog, a mother, a friend, or a mistress.' He expresses admiration for Tiresias, man and woman in turn; he cites Theocritus, author of homoerotic verses; he complains about 'the European mania of confusing love and lechery'.[23] He advises his young European protégé to abandon social conventions and jettison the notion of evil. The narrator meanwhile finds a concubine, but refers to her off-handedly as his plaything, and develops a closer relationship with Smail's brother, Ngah, whom he hires as his servant. The narrator is also clearly attracted to Rolain, though whether as father figure, close friend, spiritual guide or something else remains unclear. Rolain stays distant and mysterious, but grows fond enough of the narrator to present him with the deed to his estate.

The Europeans and their servants go for a holiday trip to the seashore. They bathe and sunbake, Smail and Ngah wrestle on the beach, they stroll around in happy nudity. A British District Officer arrives and breaks the spell. 'You're playing at Eden,' he remarks, 'When I am married I shall regard your conduct

here as shocking. An Eden without an Eve or a serpent is truly shocking.'
Rolain replies:

> It is you who are the serpent when you come and talk to us about morals.
> But we shall not taste the fruit of the Tree again. How was it I had never
> realised that the fabled fruit, which contained the knowledge of good and
> evil, was morality.

The narrator later recalls the time at the beach as 'the happiest days of my life'.
Yet the situation deteriorates, as Smail falls ill and runs amok, killing a rajah. At
the end of the novel, Rolain himself stabs Smail with a *kris*, then comforts the
narrator, who takes flight in the company of Ngah.

Erotic phallic verses, scenes of male servants tending to their masters in the
bath, brothers dancing together – all reinforce the homoerotic aspects of *The
Soul of Malaya*, though the novel's central theme concerns the enigmatic
culture of the country and the ways that it transforms men, though in different
ways. Planters make money and get drunk at pukka clubs, the District Officer
administers his domain, but more sensitive souls undergo a metamorphosis in
the tropics, surrounded by the sounds of the jungle, which forever threatens to
reclaim areas cleared for houses and plantations. Ultimately the tropical world
has its own dynamics, different from those of the West, in which spirits prowl at
night and where a young man, for no seeming reason, becomes a frenzied
murderer. Yet 'every land in which a man cannot live naked all the year round
is condemned to work and war and morality', Rolain remarks, suggesting that
the lure of the East is a call to a life of pleasure.[24]

Another novel set in colonial South-East Asia is by Louis Couperus
(1863–1923). Couperus came from a particularly distinguished Dutch colonial
family. His great-grandfather was Governor of Malacca, his grandfather
Governor-General of the Netherlands East Indies, and his father an official in
the colony's legal office. Couperus, born in The Hague, grew up in Batavia
(Jakarta), later living in Italy and the Netherlands. His many novels were best-
sellers in the Netherlands and widely appreciated in translation, though
present-day readers find them overly effusive and filled with *fin de siècle* clutter.
'A dandy, a homosexual and a romantic, Couperus understood the sensuality of
colonial life perfectly,' according to Ian Buruma:

> He was attracted to the sun – in the Mediterranean, as well as the East – for
> just that reason. He cultivated the image of torrid indolence. His rooms in
> Europe would be heated to a tropical temperature, as though he were an
> orchid, and he pretended to spend most of his time dreaming.

Couperus was not just a hothouse decadent: 'For Couperus celebrated the ambiguity he himself personified: a Dutchman grown up in the Indies; a homosexual
married to a devoted mother/wife; a master of the Dutch language, but an exotic
outsider in Holland.'[25]

Couperus's homosexual interests appear in passing in some works, such as a travelogue, *Eastward*. Only in admiring remarks about muscular boatmen, robust young Dutchmen and bare-chested Balinese with flowers in their hair did he give a clue to his proclivities. Word portraits nevertheless evoked the ambivalence of the Indonesians and the mystery of their country. The Sundanese:

> have soft, almost feminine faces, even though their build is muscular sometimes. They have dreamy eyes, round chins and swaying hips....They seem to live in a continuous dream. It calls up an atmosphere of mystery....This is the land of Java, the island of hidden forces, which either slumber or reveal themselves – to the Westerner at any rate – wrapped in an almost opaque cloak of Oriental enigma.[26]

Couperus there alludes to his most famous work, written almost a quarter-century earlier, 'one of the masterpieces to come from the colonial experience'.[27]

The Hidden Force (*De Stille Kracht*), published in 1900, is suffused with tropical sensuality. Set largely among the Dutch settler community in the provincial Javanese capital of Labuwangi, the story revolves around the lives and loves of the stern but conscientious colonial governor, Van Oudijck, his flighty but beautiful and seductive wife, Léonie, and the two men with whom she has affairs, her stepson Theo, and Adrien de Luce, her stepdaughter's suitor. The underlying theme is the disorientation and impotence of European colonialists faced with the tropical environment, East Indian politics, local religion (including magical practices that undo the Dutch families) and resistance to foreign overlordship. Readers judged the novel scandalous, both for its critical portrayal of Dutch colonialism and for the unbridled sexual behaviour of Léonie and other characters, extending to incest and inter-racial sex – a thorough degeneration of European morals in the East Indies.

Homosexuality does not as such appear in *The Hidden Force*; indeed, sexual and romantic liaisons are blatantly heterosexual. Yet Couperus clearly eroticises the two young men who sleep with Léonie, Theo, robust, blond-haired and fair-skinned, physically a perfect Dutchman despite a native mother, and the more exotic Adrien, son of a Solo princess and a French adventurer from Mauritius. Addy, as he is known, is brainless but has almost hypnotic beauty. His mixed ancestry:

> had given him the physical beauty of a young *sinjo*, with something of the Moor about it, something southern and seductive, something Spanish. ... Addy did not seem to possess a modicum of intellect or imagination, and was incapable of uniting two ideas into one composite thought. He merely felt, with that vague good nature that had settled on the entire family. For the rest, he was like a beautiful animal, degenerate in soul and brain, but degenerated to nothing, to one great nothing, to one great emptiness, while his body had become like a renewal of the race, full of strength and beauty,

while his marrow, his blood, his flesh, and his muscles had become one harmony of physical seductiveness, so perfectly and stupidly beautiful, that its harmony had for a woman an immediate appeal. The boy had only to appear, like a beautiful, southern god, and all the women would look at him and take him down into the depths of their imagination, only to recall him mentally again and again. The boy had but to go to a ball in Ngadjiwa for all the girls to fall in love with him.

This Oriental Adonis seduces with:

> his comely, slender sensuality and the glow of the tempter's eyes in the shadowy brown of his young Moorish face, the curve of his lips meant only for kissing, with the young down of his moustache; the feline strength and litheness of his Don Juan limbs.

He conquers the resident's wife and daughter, and many local women, with the 'irresistible power of his comely Moorish virility'. [28] Addy thus is a composite of many tropes of masculine attractiveness – French sophistication, Eastern mystery and raw Moorish sexuality. More animal than human, he is reduced to empty beauty and unbridled seductiveness by the mixing of his ancestral bloods heated in the tropics.

Even if Addy is rampantly heterosexual, Couperus cannot but suggest ambivalence. He is a beautiful Southern god, like Antinous (and his name recalls Antinous's lover, the emperor Hadrian). Perhaps, as had sometimes been believed, as a *métis*, he would be able to have sex but not father children. He is a 'degenerate', a label often applied to sodomites. If there is something Moorish about him, maybe he engages in sodomitical practices thought to be common among Arabs. His 'feline strength and litheness of...limbs' is a touch effeminate. Women flock to him, but he does not seek them out.

In Léonie, Addy's lover, Couperus creates a person of voracious, unhidden and predatory sexual appetite. The editor of the English translation of *The Hidden Force* comments that Léonie reflects aspects of Couperus's own personality – birth in the East Indies, high social position, elegance, but also lust for men. Léonie represents Couperous's own desires. She is drawn to both blond Theo and dark Addy, creating rivalry between them for her affections, and forming a triad of sexual tension that sets up an implicit homosexual link between the two men ostensibly jousting for her attentions.

One scene in *The Hidden Force* implies a curious (but perhaps unrequited) desire between the men. Upon learning that Addy has seduced Léonie, Theo bursts into Addy's bedroom in fury, 'where he was lying quite naked, as was his habit during this siesta, with the magnificence of a bronze statue, sublime as an ancient sculpture'. Theo threatens to strike him, but Addy so disarms him by his indifference, laughing 'so serenely at the idea of fighting over a woman, that Theo quieted down and came and sat on the edge of his bed'. They begin exchanging confidences. Addy 'patted him on the shoulder with almost fatherly compassion'. They are soon fast friends.[29] Later Addy takes Theo to a village to meet his until then unknown half-brother; Theo, basking in discovery of his kinsman and his newly found friendship, strides off with Addy, who exclaims, 'almost angrily: "Oh, you...[*sic*]; you'll never be anything but a skirt chaser!"'[30] By the end of the novel, Addy is safely married to the Resident's daughter, partly to conceal his affair with Léonie, but Theo has mysteriously disappeared back to a job in Holland. Just in the nick of time, the right order is more or less restored; hearty Theo the skirt-chaser returns to dull and predictable Holland, while Addy remains in the mysterious Orient.

A first reading of the novel suggests that 'normal' heterosexuality is entrenched. Closer consideration reveals doubts. Theo returns to Europe, rejected by the man-hungry Léonie, but not averse to intimate conversation with a naked man, nominally his bitter rival. Addy makes no attempt to cover himself or move away when Theo interrupts his siesta, and indeed initiates physical contact. Addy tells him that fighting over a woman is a waste of time, yet – after Theo does not react more positively to his overtures? – dismisses him as a womaniser. Addy may end up with a wife, but that arrangement is a marriage of convenience. Perhaps Léonie will tire of her toy-boy, or maybe he will first lose interest in an ageing and capricious lover. 'Hidden forces' may eventually cast a different spell.

Farrère, Fauconnier and Couperus wrote about the homoerotic delights of the Malay world, based on personal acquaintance with the East. For Frederic Prokosch, author of *The Asiatics*, the geographical horizons were far broader, but his own experience of Asia, at the time of writing, was nil.

Prokosch was born in Wisconsin in 1906. His father, an Austrian philologist and linguist, became a professor at Yale University. Prokosch graduated from Haverford College, where he was as successful academically as athletically. He spent a year in the late 1920s at King's College, Cambridge, then completed a doctorate at Yale in 1932 with a thesis on the 'Chaucerian apocrypha'. Prokosch taught at Yale and New York University for five years, meanwhile writing novels and poetry, before giving up teaching. He thereafter mostly lived abroad, primarily in Italy, France and Portugal. He published half a dozen novels, set in Central Asia, Yemen, Europe and America, and died in 1989.[31]

The Asiatics, Prokosch's first and best-known novel, appeared in 1935. The plot moves from Lebanon across Asia to Vietnam, and it was a very popular work, its fast-paced adventures and exotic locations appealing to readers confronting the Depression and the political conflicts of the 1930s.[32] André Gide commented that it was 'an astonishing feat of the imagination', 'poetic in its sensuality, witty in its melodrama, urbane in its misanthropy, incandescent in its imagery'. Even more fulsomely, Thomas Mann called it 'a book which has stimulated, haunted and enthralled me....I count it among the most brilliant and original achievements of the young literary generation.'[33] Even if later critics proved less enthusiastic, *The Asiatics* remained in print for three decades.

Prokosch admitted, enigmatically, that parts of *The Asiatics* were autobiographical, although he had not visited any of the locations it describes. He also claimed that it was a 'picaresque novel' in the tradition of Voltaire, Montesquieu, Fielding and Defoe. J.R. Ackerley's *Hindoo Holiday* may have inspired one character. Prokosch wrote the work as a series of relatively discrete episodes (and several chapters found initial publication in magazines). Set in the inter-war period, it follows the exploits of the unnamed narrator, an American robbed in Port-Said as he prepares to sail to Japan to visit a wealthy uncle. He decides instead to make his way to Asia by an overland route. His travels take him from Beirut to Damascus and on to Turkey, then to Soviet Georgia, Iran, Afghanistan, Pakistan and India, from where he sets off to Ceylon, and then visits Burma, Malaya and Cambodia, before finishing his peregrinations in Indo-China. A handsome, well-meaning, but naïve fellow, he weathers diverse misadventures. He is imprisoned in Turkey and threatened with arrest in Georgia. He survives a plane crash in Iran, capture by bandits in Afghanistan and a plague in Malaya. Later trials include fire aboard a ship, falling prisoner to outlaws in Burma and seeing a friend poisoned. By good fortune, an appealing personality that attracts friends and benefactors, and sheer perseverance, he escapes all the dangers and generally manages to enjoy himself in the process. He consorts with a remarkable assortment of people – a French adventurer, a Russian Communist, a Georgian priest, a Dutch smuggler, a French countess, an Indian rajah. *The Asiatics* is a grown-up boys' adventure story with the vast expanses of Asia as backdrop, the whole punctuated with the philosophical musings of the narrator's companions and the political troubles in which he becomes implicated.

Asia is a continent of dramatic scenery, enchanting natives and real dangers for Prokosch's hero. It is, as well, the playground for Europeans who for motives fair or foul traverse it. White men and women are objects of intrigue but reign supreme in countries of formal or informal colonialism. The narrator attends garden parties at a rajah's palace in India, and frequents French cafés in Saigon. He enjoys the hospitality of expatriate aristocrats and the beneficence of foreign criminals. He has a stint as assistant to an English doctor in Penang. He rides trains and cruises on ships that the Europeans have exported to Asia. He listens to expostulations about European imperialism and Soviet Communism. He kits himself out in tropical whites when he has the money. At the end, he seems imbued with the legendary wisdom of the East.

The hero of *The Asiatics* is ostensibly heterosexual, proving himself in several brief liaisons. The novel, however, is suffused with homoeroticism, and the narrator finds European and native men highly desirable. A few outright references speak of homosexuality predictably as an Asiatic vice, though an appealing one. In a prison cell in Turkey, the narrator sleeps in the arms of fellow Russian and Dutch prisoners, in principle, because of the cold, but 'never, certainly, did I see so bawdily displayed the difference between love and lust'; the men feel a 'leaning toward sexual viciousness [that] grew softly powerful….There was no point in behaving like a prig.' From the window, he can see the 'grayish place near the baths where the degenerates gathered. Down along the shore, in the shadow of the bridge. We could see them there, hovering in the darkness in nervous pairs, coming and going pointlessly....We grew vaguely excited.' A Circassian tells of a city in Azerbaijan where he 'will find fair boys and fair maidens, whichever he prefers. Many and many of them, all of them voluptuous and willing.' One travelling companion, a Nestorian priest, goes off in search of boys. The Indian rajah at whose court he stays is homosexual. In Benares, a man exposes himself at a public urinal. Later a youth in a hotel offers himself to the hero. In Bangkok, he is the guest of a nobleman who, 'like many of the Siamese princes', is in love with a boy attendant. The narrator asks a young man, captured by Kachins in Burma, about his fate: '"Sahib," he said softly and sadly, like a true Asiatic, "it is sad to be a pretty boy."'[34]

Many of the native men whom Prokosch's hero meets are described homo-erotically, either as effeminate – an elegant, mysterious prince, for instance – or as handsome hunks. In Baalbeck, Moroccan guards in the service of the French have 'bodies strong and [as] supple as tigers', while at Smyrna, 'bronze-skinned bare-breasted sailors' carry cargo. He is massaged in India by a 'dark bare-chested man' with a 'great white-toothed, rich-lipped smile': 'His eyelids shone like satin, his lashes cast long slanting shadows on his cheek-bones', and 'he put his strong male-smelling arm under me and helped me to my feet' after the rub-down. With another masseur in Badrapur, 'It felt pleasant...to feel Akbar's strong hands limbering up my calves and my buttocks.' In Central Asia he picks up a guide – 'the long lashes and the curling hairs on his temples looked like those of a whore, deliberate and enticing' – who soon offers to be his servant for life (for a price): 'I will do everything....I will love you always.' When the narrator tries to shake him off, Ahmed wonders if he is not pretty enough. Rejected, he attacks the hero, who awakes to find Ahmed 'squatting nakedly above me, staring at me, wildly', wielding a knife. The narrator pins him to the ground, and the youth begins to cry: 'I could feel his warm brown chest rise and fall with sobbing.'[35] He apologises, and they fall asleep with the boy's head buried in his lap.

At the next stop, in Baluchistan, men are described as 'dark magnificent animals', one of whom returns the compliment, telling the hero that he looks 'strong and passionate and shy'. In Peshawar, among the 'soft-lipped boys with enormous turbans', one hangs around to watch the American undress. In a marketplace, 'two slender Arab youths meandered past...closely side by side, hips touching and hands clasped'; 'consciously graceful and elaborate, their eyes were sensuous but melancholy'. A café is 'full of smoke, full of men, full of rich masculine smells', a place where dancing boys perform, 'limber as snakes and nastily drunk....The place was rapidly becoming bawdy.' Kashmiris are 'built like gods' with 'lean brown legs...tense with strain and bright with sweat'. Sinhalese youths walk 'gracefully as panthers, smelling vaguely of cinnamon'.[36] On it goes, every stage of the colonial pilgrim's progress revealing more fetching youths and creating more compromising situations. Prokosch never actually says that his hero has sex with men along the way, but the descriptions leave little to an alert reader's imagination.

If the narrator of *The Asiatics* is excited by men in Central and Southern Asia – he is less interested in Eastern Asians – his greatest love is for a Frenchman. Towards the start of his epic journey, he meets Antoine Samazeuilh in the French-mandated territory of Syria, a 'wonderfully handsome man' from Rouen,

> strong as an ox, with rich blonde curls....He needed a shave badly. But he would have looked well under any condition....He had a clear strong body, a regular Apollo, hard as a statue, and flowing metallic muscles....The hero, the survivor, the true male.

He sees more of the hairy-chested, amply muscled Samazeuilh when they swim naked together. Soon the hero is, to all but the dimmest reader, in love with the Frenchman. Samazeuilh spouts philosophy, struts around in macho fashion and tells the narrator that, though he needs women, he despises them – the narrator soon has sex with the same woman whose services his friend has just enjoyed. The narrator and Samazeuilh separate only a few chapters into the novel, yet meet up later in Vietnam, where again, 'I was overcome with joy. The great hearty voice, the great powerful body, the great indiscriminate face: they warmed my heart; my voice grew hoarse; tears came to my eyes.' The two pal around, engaging in affectionate horseplay, then Samazeuilh has sex with a woman who was one of the narrator's bedmates at an earlier stop in Iran – swapping partners reinforces their ties. Samazeuilh cannot be pinned down by man or woman, for he is an elusive beast:

> He was very handsome. I could see the pock-marks, the large pores, the hairs in his nostrils and his ears, but all of them added to the strong manlike look about him. Yes, he was a fine animal, he was fit, he'd survive. I looked at his heavy cruel lips glowing in the sunlight and wondered why I still liked him so well.

The narrator asks Samazeuilh not to abandon him: 'Don't be afraid, little boy,' he replies as he runs his fingers through the American's hair.[37] But soon Samazeuilh does disappear, leaving the narrator pensive.

In Prokosch's novel, Europeans take the rewards of imperialism, but European control is not necessarily admirable, nor is it secure. Europeans are all on the make, interested in money, sex and adventure. In Central Asia and India, the hero makes fun of expatriate ladies in pearls and Worth frocks, those whose wealth and leisure let them move from one resort to another. Miss Bariton and other English women in Kandy are insufferably pompous and condescending. In French Indo-China, the narrator walks among shops patronised by 'brownish Chinamen and a few shabby Frenchmen'. In Phnom-Penh, 'A French flag hung greyly over the walk, and behind the pillars, under the balcony, sat the white-clad Frenchmen reading *Le Matin* and drinking rum punches.' Life for colonials remains tedious. In Saigon, 'The coolies looked stupid with opium, the Frenchmen stupid with conceit.' The Indian rajah, educated at Oxford, spouting Milton and Tennyson (as well as Whitman and Wilde), is a caricature of an Anglicised native in his palace complete with billiards room, bridge tables and stables of racehorses; his son, on the Varsity XI at Balliol, has already smashed three cars. Guests at the rajah's ball include a bishop, an authoress and assorted colonial public servants who chatter about croquet and cricket; 'two or three pretty rajahs from the neighbourhood' do liven up the party.

Politics regularly troubles colonial life. In Vietnam, the narrator hears about a Communist conspiracy, the arrest of forty rebels, the execution of thirty-three others and prisoners tortured by the police. He notes that a French officer appeared quite placid about such a bloody outcome: '"Well, they'll get us sooner or later," he said whimsically. "But in the meantime we shall be forced to make it uncomfortable for them."' At the other end of Asia, a man had told him:

> how the Turks hated the English for the treaty they had made after the war [of 1914–18]; and the French for the Senegambians they had stationed in Asia Minor; and the Greeks for their invasion and dishonesty; and the Armenians on general principles of decency; and the Jews for their exploitations. And how they still suspected Mussolini of trying to annex Anatolia, and the Germans of trying to monopolize the factories and the aeroplane service, and the Belgians of trying to control the railways, and the Americans of trying to govern the whole world.

In Malaya, Dr Aigner – a European doctor ruined by tropical conditions, alcohol, drugs and *anomie* (and who proves a real cad) – rails:

> Everything that's nasty here....it's recent, you'll observe and it's Western. Don't you agree? Everything that's old is going. The temples are being deserted, the fields are rotting, the forests are falling, the old quarters in the cities are growing vile. And why? Because we won't keep our dirty panic-stricken paws off the East! We insist on giving them our stinking progress. Away with the Vedas and the Peace Everlasting. Bring in the Fords and the factories. What's a bit of faith compared to a fresh oil-well or a new road? Civilization. Rot. All it means is making money and making things easier for those who've made it and killing the spirit in themselves as well as in everybody else. Kill everything that's brought them peace. Well, we'll see who wins in the end. I'm not so sure, myself. Asia has one or two weapons we never thought of.

Prokosch's novel pictures a homosexual teetering between sublimation and lust 'on the road' from Beirut to Haiphong. The picture of swarthy tribesmen and delicate princes differs little from other sexualised stereotypes of the period, but for Prokosch they are exciting and appealing types rather than unnatural and repellent ones. Asia is fearsome, mysterious, maddeningly vague, yet the place where secret desires can be satisfied, whether with fellow expatriates or natives, macho adventurers or gentle houseboys. 'Solitude can be very sad for a young man,' the narrator remarks, and in the world of busy markets and caravans, populous cities and well-endowed courts, for a European whose 'skin is smooth' (as a masseur tells him), and who has a bit of money and a stroke of luck, loneliness need not be a problem. Whether more is possible in this great transcontinental quest – 'Life's a degrading and nightmarish affair, and there's only one thing that gives it any meaning, and that's the existence of love,' one lady advises the narrator – remains uncertain.[38] The cynical planter in *The Soul of Malaya*, Torral in *Les Civilisés*, Addy in *The Hidden Force* and Alberto in *Gioco d'infanzia* would not disagree.

In the Pacific islands

The South Seas provided a congenial domain for sexual adventurers, as explorers, artists and writers from Captain Cook to Paul Gauguin discovered. Instead of the old civilisation, 'degenerate' people, complex religions, spices and opium of Asia, the South Seas offered primitivism. Early visitors described the physical beauties of Polynesians (though less often did they enthuse over Melanesians), and either enjoyed or bemoaned their loose morals. Through the nineteenth century, myths continued to surround Oceania, though by the end of the 1800s, the imperial powers had scrambled for, and divided, the distant isles of the Pacific.

Among the authors who created the legend of the South Pacific was the American Herman Melville (1819–88); though better known for his later *Moby Dick*, Melville's first major works were set in the Pacific, *Typee* (1846) and the sequel *Omoo* (1847). Published as factual travelogues, the books are better considered as novels or as fictionalised autobiographical accounts.[39]

In *Typee*, set in the Marquesas Islands, only recently annexed by France when Melville visited, the author remarks on the physical attractions of women and, particularly, of men. As his boat sails to the shore, 'Their appearance perfectly amazed me; their extreme youth, the light clear brown of their complexions, their delicate features, and inexpressibly graceful figures, their softly moulded limbs, and free unstudied action, seemed as strange as beautiful.' The novel's hero, Tom, is accidentally injured but cared for by Marquesans, his recovery turning into a sort of captivity. Despite the injury and fear that escape will be difficult, Tom takes pleasure in the sights. One Polynesian especially strikes his fancy, Marnoo:

> The stranger could not have been more than twenty-five years of age, and was a little above the ordinary height; had he been a single hair's breadth taller, the matchless symmetry of his form would have been destroyed. His unclad limbs were beautifully formed, whilst the elegant outline of his figure, together with his beardless cheeks, might have entitled him to the distinction of standing for the statue of the Polynesian Apollo; and indeed

the oval of his countenance and the regularity of every feature reminded me of an antique bust. But the marble repose of art was supplied by a warmth and liveliness of expression only to be seen in the South Sea Islander under the most favourable condition. His cheek was of a feminine softness, and his face was free from the least blemish of tattooing, although the rest of his body was drawn all over with fanciful figures.

Marnoo, to Tom's despair, takes no notice of his persistent attentions, but later plays a role in the European's escape.

The portrait of Marnoo is emblematic of Europeans' descriptions of Polynesian 'natives'. The comeliest have no parallel in the gallery of contemporary human beauty, but many are crude savages. The best are inevitably compared with European icons of beauty, yet their copper skin colour and curious hairstyles form part of their attraction. Body ornamentation, such as tattooing, is generally loathsome, but occasionally reaches the heights of art. Polynesian men are macho, yet 'feminine' features shade in ambiguity. A lingering gaze on their bodies, often fixed on specific details (the tree tattooed along Marnoo's spine, for instance), slides into voyeuristic homoeroticism. Either implicit or, frequently, explicit is the contrast between 'children of nature' in their muscular nudity and European men, who never quite measure up:

> When I remembered that these islanders derived no advantage from dress, but appeared in all the naked simplicity of nature, I could not avoid comparing them with the fine gentlemen and dandies who promenade such unexceptionable figures in our frequented thoroughfares. Stripped of the cunning artifices of the tailor, and standing forth in the garb of Eden – what a sorry set of round-shouldered, spindle-shanked, crane-necked varlets would civilized men appear! Stuffed calves, padded breasts, and scientifically cut pantaloons would then avail them nothing, and the effect would be truly deplorable.[40]

Melville shared the Rousseauist 'good savage' view of Polynesians, though always mixed with the contrary impression of primitive savagery. He was scathing about French takeover of the islands. One of his first sights is the handsome natives and lush bay of Nuku-Hiva:

> No description can do justice to its beauty; but that beauty was lost to me then, and I saw nothing but the tri-coloured flag of France trailing over the stern of six vessels, whose black hulls and bristling broadsides proclaimed their warlike character.[41]

The French had disembarked five hundred troops, whom Melville watched carrying out drills on the beach. The Marquesans 'cordially hated them' and feared the invaders. The 1842 French conquest constituted a 'signal infraction of the rights of humanity'; French conduct was 'iniquitous'. Colonists engaged in 'shameless subterfuges' 'to defend whatever cruelties they may hereafter think fit to commit in bringing the Marquesan natives into subjection....The enormities perpetrated in the South Seas upon some of the inoffensive islanders will nigh pass belief'. Melville's verdict on colonisation was uncompromising: 'Were civilization itself to be estimated by some of its results, it would seem perhaps better for what we call the barbarous part of the world to remain unchanged.'

The encounter between islanders and foreigners – at least as personified by the French, since authors such as Melville considered themselves exempt from reprobate behaviours – was a 'fatal embrace' that would eventually destroy island culture.[42] A particular feature of Polynesian life that, Melville implied, would be endangered was the practice of a man taking a *tayo*, a bosom friend or mate (who might be a foreigner):

> The really curious way in which the Polynesians are in the habit of making bosom friends at the shortest possible notice is deserving of remark. Although, among a people like the Tahitians, vitiated as they are by sophisticating influences, this custom has in most cases degenerated into a mere mercenary relation, it nevertheless had its origin in a fine, and in some circumstances, heroic sentiment, formerly entertained by their fathers. In the annals of the island are many examples of extravagant friendships; unsurpassed by the story of Damon and Pythias; in truth, much more wonderful; for, notwithstanding the devotion – even of life in some cases – to which they led, they were frequently entertained at first sight for some stranger from another island.

In *Typee*, Tom's *tayo* is Kory-Kory, 'though the most devoted and best natured serving-man in the world, he was, alas! a hideous object to look upon'. A strapping six-foot 25-year-old, his shaven head, plucked beard and full-body tattoo appear revolting to the narrator. If he physically could not compete with beautiful Marnoo, Kory-Kory impresses with eloquence and devotion. A later *tayo* seems better to combine various virtues: 'Among the simple-hearted natives, we had a friend all round. Mine was Poky, a handsome youth, who never could do enough for me.' He gives the American fruits and shells, and is:

> of course, my companion and guide....Gallanting me about, every one was stopped and ceremoniously introduced to Poky's 'tayo karhowree nuee', or his particular white friend....Though there was no end to Poky's attentions, not a syllable did he ever breathe of reward; but sometimes he looked very knowing.[43]

Another island, another book, another friend, and, in *Omoo*,

> Kooloo was a candidate for my friendship; and being a comely youth, quite a buck in his way, I accepted his overtures. By this, I escaped the

importunities of the rest; for be it known, that, though little inclined to jealousy in love matters, the Tahitian will hear of no rivals in his friendship.

All is well for a while, despite Kooloo's demands, and his ministrations provide comfort. Then:

> after sponging me well, he one morning played the part of a retrograde lover; informing me that his affections had undergone a change; he had fallen in love at first sight with a smart sailor....It was a touching interview, and with it our connection dissolved. But the sadness which ensued would soon have been dissipated, had not my sensibilities been wounded by his indelicately sporting some of my gifts very soon after this transfer of his affections.[44]

The narrator of *Typee* is ostensibly heterosexual, presented by a chief with an attractive female companion, but the language in that book, and *Omoo*, suggest other interests. Melville's own sexuality was ambivalent, and Robert Martin has presented a convincing case for his homosexual inclinations. In *Typee*, even before landing in Polynesia, Tom has an intimate friend in a mysterious shipmate, Toby, with whom he jumps ship. Homoerotic descriptions of Polynesian buddies, his series of 'particular friends', the account of the break with Kooloo in words befitting a jilted lover – all suggest homosexual interests. Martin further suggests that the Pacific islands formed a 'golden land', a 'paradise of male friendship' that Melville experienced with his shipmate and, in a different way, with Polynesians.[45] Yet the very ease of such liaisons, the mores that permitted them, also brings them to an end. Shipmates leave, islanders expect money for companionship, Polynesians shift their affections and the traveller must return to civilisation. The story is common in homoerotic travel literature.

These same themes appear in higher relief in the works of one of the most blatantly homoerotic writers of the nineteenth century, Charles Warren Stoddard. Born in Rochester, New York, into a middle-class Protestant family, in 1843, Stoddard grew up in San Francisco. In 1864, after an apparent nervous breakdown, he went to Hawaii for six months, and fell in with Kane-Aloha, a Polynesian later to figure in his stories. Four years later, he again went to Hawaii, to visit his sister, the wife of a plantation owner. Again he experienced the seduction of the tropics; another young friend, Joe of Lahaina, became the hero of a story. In 1870, Stoddard undertook his third journey to Oceania, this time to Tahiti, enjoying shipboard camaraderie but falling on such hard times on the island, where he had no relatives or work, that he soon returned to the United States. Two years later, Stoddard headed for Samoa, but circumstances keep him from travelling further than Hawaii.

In 1873, Stoddard published *South-Sea Idyls*, a book of largely autobiographical stories that is his most enduring work.[46] Stoddard was struck by the natural beauty of the islands, the melancholy lethargy of local life and the physical attractions of a people living amidst tropical bounty. Swimming or strolling around dressed only in a pareo, muscular bronzed men quickly seduced the American. Almost every story in *South-Sea Idyls* is suffused with homoeroticism, couched in the ornate and overwrought prose Stoddard favoured – a style that now appears camp indeed. The narrator watches in lustful awe as 'naked and superbly built fellows' shinny up trees in 'Taboo – A Fete Day in Tahiti'; in 'Under a Grass Roof', at the end of a trek with a local guide, 'a moon-faced youth, whose spotless garments appealed to me', undresses for the night: 'In a moment the fine linen of mine host is hung upon the peg, and a good study of the Nude returns to me for further orders.' In 'A Canoe-Cruise in the Coral Sea', the oarsman is a veritable study in exotic beauty: 'He sat with his back to me – a brown back, that glistened in the sun, and arched itself, from time to time, cat-like, as though it was very good to be brown and bare and shiny.' Stoddard was not just a voyeur. In 'Kahele', youths:

> came out of the sea like so many mermen and mermaids. They were refreshingly innocent of etiquette…and, with a freedom that was amusing as well as a little embarrassing, I was deliberately fingered, fondled, and fussed with by nearly every dusky soul in turn. 'At last,' thought I, 'fate has led me beyond the pale of civilization.'[47]

Stoddard's tales are peopled by pairs of men bound by circumstance and affection – the narrator with his Polynesian companions (or, in one story, a French sailor), two priests in 'Chapel of Palms', a ship-captain and his 'mahogany-tinted East-Indian steward' in 'Love-Life in a Lanai', and another seaman who was 'the happy possessor of a tight little African, known as Nero….as handsome a specimen of tangible darkness as you will sight in a summer's cruise' in 'In a Transport'.[48] Plots almost invariably turn on possibilities for intimate encounters. Some stories, however, become more than erotic and tropical *tableaux vivants*. 'Joe of Lahaina', based on Stoddard's memories of his Molokai boyfriend, sees the narrator setting up housekeeping with a Polynesian youth (later destined to die in a leper colony). In 'Pearl-Hunting', the narrator and a Polynesian are wrecked on a pearling expedition; Hua Manu saves the visitor, though having to pierce his own vein, in a Leda-like act of self-sacrifice, to give him a sustaining drink. The European survives, but the Polynesian perishes.

Nowhere is engagement between a European and a Polynesian clearer than in 'Chumming with a Savage' – a title pregnant with meaning. This is the recounting of a meeting that left Stoddard with 'all that I ever knew of genuine, spontaneous, and unfettered love'.[49] Actually a fifty-page novella, 'Chumming' has three sections. In the first, Stoddard (the narrator is patently the author) meets and falls in love with Kána-aná, a fetching 16-year-old whom he seduces away from his former mentor, a doctor. Kána-aná takes him through the jungle and takes him to bed. In (to present-day readers) the most clearly homosexual scene, hardly disguised by its prose, Stoddard says that when he became solemn, then Kána-aná would think of some fresh appetizer or other, and try to make me merry with good feeling. Again and again he would come with a delicious banana to the bed where I was lying, and insist upon my gorging myself, when I had but barely recovered from a late orgie of fruit, flesh, or fowl. He would mesmerize me into a most refreshing sleep with a prolonged and pleasing manipulation.[50]

The import of that scene is reinforced elsewhere, as Kána-aná crawls into the narrator's bed naked, they pet each other, and lie in the heat for hours. Yet along with fun and games, Stoddard falls deeply in love, and returns home with great reluctance. In the second part of the novella, Stoddard, back in the United States, sends for Kána-aná; the Polynesian is intrigued by the United States, but uncomfortable in Western clothes, cold, lonely and bored. The visit proves less than a success, and he hurries home to Oceania. In the third and final section, Stoddard goes to the islands to search for Kána-aná, but discovers, to his grief, that the boy has died.

'Chumming with a Savage' is melodramatic and maudlin, but says a great deal about attractions between men of two cultures, about the desire of the American (or European) to escape the confines of his own society, and the difficulty in surmounting the divides between different worlds. Travel to the Pacific is discovery of one's inner self. The narrator's Polynesian companion brings comfort to his body and release to his soul: 'I felt myself at the mercy of one whose calm analysis was questioning every motive of my soul.' He desperately wants to 'go native': 'I renounced all the follies of the world, actually hating civilisation....I resolved on the spot to become a barbarian.' He apostrophises 'my dear barbarians, who hate civilisation almost as much as I do, and are certainly quite as idolatrous and indolent as I ever aspire to be'. The second part of the novella is entitled 'How I Converted my Cannibal', yet the narrator concludes: 'I think that, perhaps, instead of my having converted the little cannibal, he may have converted me.' [51] The buttoned-up American, however, can never truly be part of the naked island and give up 'civilisation' – he frets about his worn boots, for instance, and ultimately decides to leave. Kána-aná can never fit into the United States; he drops to his knees and brings offerings to a tobacconist's statue of an Indian, thinking it a Pacific *tiki*. Stoddard is eventually struck with guilt for having ripped Kána-aná out of his world, and worries that the youth's disorientation may have caused his death, perhaps provoking suicide.

'Chumming with a Savage' is a love story, but also an exploration of the gaps between cultures and the effects, both good and bad, of one on the other. Imperialism lies everywhere in the background. Stoddard, who converted to Catholicism, lauds the dedication and friendship of two priests in 'Chapel of Palms', but in 'A Tropical Sequence' is not so sure about islanders' real commitment to Christianity, or its benefits for them. The narrator visits a pastor in Tahiti, only to discover that the minister's daughter has abandoned her faith and family, and married a heathen Polynesian. 'South-Sea Show' is a horrifying portrait of a showman who returns to Europe with Pacific children whom he parades before a paying public. In 'Kahele's Foreordination', as in the chronicle of Kána-aná, an islander goes to the United States with his friend, but steals stock certificates and flees to an uncertain future in Mexico. French gendarmes, shop-keepers and sailors move about the Tahitian stories, transforming island life; the French ship in 'In a Transport' fights a mock battle with Prussians. Expatriates do not impress the narrator, as 'The Prodigal in Tahiti' realises when he considers returning home:

> I said as much to a couple of Frenchmen, brothers, who are living a dream-life over yonder, and whose wildest species of dissipation for the last seven years has been to rise at intervals from their settees in the arbor, go deliberately to the farther end of the garden, and eat several mangoes in cold blood.

This is a tropical *dolce far niente* that had tempted Stoddard.[52] Those who try a permanent metamorphosis become objects of amused scorn (such as the lieutenant in 'Love-Life in a Lanai').

Stoddard's second volume of Pacific stories, *The Island of Tranquil Delights* (1905), continues in the same vein: homoerotic tales mixed with reminiscences about island life (and a couple of ghost stories). In the title story, the narrator is warned about misbehaviour by a consul in Tahiti. Wandering around the island, the hero is borne down a ravine 'by a young giant, sleek and supple as a bronzed Greek god, who held me captive till I surfeited on bread-fruits and cocoanut [sic] milk'. 'I was a child of nature again,' he cries, a 'new Adam, in the beauty of the Eden of his infantile innocence.' Later, travelling home, he is propositioned on board ship by the consul. He shows the diplomat the keepsakes in his trunk, and 'we unmasked the mystery of my nature'. 'He embraced me madly....[and] filled my palm with the creamy seeds [pearls] such as are found in the fisheries of the South Pacific'. (The language needs no comment.) The narrator, nevertheless, declines an invitation to live with the consul in tropical paradise.[53]

In 'On the Reef', a visitor to Hawaii disembarks to see 'a dark object stretched motionless....The prize was mine, and I hastened forward. It was a youth just out of his teens, a slim, sleek creature, unconscious, unclad, sprawled inartistically.' Kane-Pihi goes wrong when he converts to Christianity, providing another opportunity for Stoddard to lambast the missionary enterprise:

> Having sped the gentlest of savages out of the sea for the purpose of teaching them how to die, the American Missionary calmly folds his hands over the grave of the nation and turns his attention to affairs more private and peculiar.

The narrator visits Kane-Pihi in prison, and later learns that he dies of smallpox, a metaphor for the impact of colonisation. In a happier tale, the love story 'Kane-Aloha', a visitor pals up with a swimmer. 'Naked beauty' and 'Arcadian landscape' combine: friendship ripens quickly in the tropical sunshine. At the end of the day,

> we slept the sleep of the just made perfect by the realization of our wildest dream.…We had certainly transgressed the unwritten law but we were not in the least sorry for it.

When fate decrees that the narrator return home, he presents his horse to Kane-Aloha as a memento of their summer romance.[54]

Stoddard, after his trips to the South Seas, lived a restless life. He made friends with Robert Louis Stevenson (who credited Stoddard with bringing him under the spell of the islands) and Mark Twain (who unkindly referred to Stoddard, who worked briefly as his secretary, as 'such a nice girl'). He lived for four years in Europe, largely in London but with travels to Germany, Italy and the Middle East, writing articles for American newspapers. He had sexual liaisons, some chance meetings, others longer lasting – particularly important was a three-year relationship with a teenage street tough. From 1889 to 1902, Stoddard was professor of literature at the Catholic University of America. He published a number of works on the leper colony in Molokai, St Anthony of Padua, his conversion to Catholicism and his travels. Homoeroticism appears in many of them. In *Exits and Entrances*, a portrait of 'The Pasha of Jerusalem' dwells on the charms of a young interpreter; in 'An Arabian Night', a traveller quits his tour group to spend a night with a male friend on an island in the Nile, and has visions of 'my slaves legions [sic] of Berbers girded with gold, shining with oil, musky and shapely fellaheen'. 'A Fair Anonymous' recounts an encounter with a dark-eyed blond cavalier in Egypt, whom the narrator sees again in Jerusalem, then in Istanbul and finally in Naples, where the alluring but enigmatic creature is improbably revealed to be an Englishwoman in disguise.[55] In the novel *For the Pleasure of His Company* (1903), lovers dream of going to the South Seas and, at the end, the hero cruises off and beckons to islanders rowing out to his ship – a suitable valediction for the writer, who died in 1909.[56]

Stoddard's works, never wildly popular with reviewers, gained readers who enjoyed overly ripe prose and romantic situations. Many undoubtedly over-looked the sexual aspects, which now seem inescapable, and Stoddard's style often veils sex as Platonic friendship in the acceptable climate of sensuality and luxuriance excused by the tropical setting. His writing was in some ways deeply colonialist. His view that Polynesians formed 'a race that has positively nothing to do but to be indolently picturesque'[57] would be castigated by modern critics, as would such unremitting statements as, 'The crowning luxury of savage life is the multitudinous bondman who anticipates your every wish, and makes you blush at your own poverty of invention by his suggestions of unimagined joys.'[58] Stoddard shared the nineteenth-century view that the people of Oceania were a doomed race, fated to extinction by natural evolution or Westernisation. 'Natives' are portrayed as fun-loving, lazy, mischievous and sometimes dishonest. Stoddard's vocabulary in describing islanders as savages, cannibals or 'innocent children of nature' reflected contemporary imperialist attitudes.

But Stoddard also saw the heathenism and savagery of the South Seas in a positive light, for – as in *South Sea Idyls* – only they make it possible for him to find physical and emotional pleasure. He wrote in *Exits and Entrances*: 'I have known that [thorny] hedge [of Presbyterianism] to shed its thorns and miraculously blossom, under the sweet influences of the Torrid Zone. After all is said, your tropic is the truest test of a man's moral integrity.' This integrity, Stoddard hoped, would not, at least in traditional Christian terms, and despite his Catholicism, weather the tropics: 'Cold indeed is the heart in which the dulcet beguilements of the South Sea siren finds no responsive echo.'[59]

Stoddard also voiced strong critiques of Westernisation. He remarked that Polynesians had been unfortunately unaware that 'one of the Thirty-nine Articles of Civilization [is] to bully one's way through the world'.[60] In an essay on Stevenson, he thundered about detritus littering the Pacific:

> the filth that has been industriously shipped into the South Seas ever since the days of that insalubrious old marauder, Captain Cook, and his infectious crew – the filth that gathers in all the seams of well-dressed civilisation and is easily, far too easily, hidden – the filth that is sometimes nourished by the very men who are swift to despatch the enthusiast to the ends of the earth that the nations may be brought to the knowledge of some missionary society or other. It is the ill-advised assiduity of these Protestant missionaries that has driven the children of nature into red flannels and the fear of hell, and has engrafted upon the most ingenuous of races hypocrisy and other distinguishing characteristics of the Children of Light'.[61]

By the time *Exits and Entrances* was published, Stoddard referred to Hawaiians – whose islands now formed an American colony – as 'the worst abused people that were ever betrayed by the representatives of enlightened politics and piety'.[62] He also praised Stevenson for 'his admirable defence of the ill-governed Samoans, fretting under the tyranny of German misrule'.[63]

Just as many other late nineteenth-century writers, Stoddard remained ambivalent about Oceania. Like other Europeans, he was lured to the islands to shed the mores of Western society, but realised that the very presence of foreigners and inevitable Westernisation was forever changing the people to whom he was emotionally and sexually attracted. He was a Catholic, his sister's husband owned a plantation and he spent, in total, less than two years in the islands. Yet the mixture of travel, sex and political observation in his work makes him representative of those who went overseas to find adventure and to find themselves.[64]

Colonialist novelists: Buchan and Loti

Colonialist homoeroticism was apparent, in attenuated form in African and Middle Eastern settings, in writers better known than Stoddard. Two of the most popular novelists in the early twentieth century whose careers were linked to imperial governance were John Buchan and Pierre Loti. Buchan, married and a father, was to the public eye entirely heterosexual. Loti was incontrovertibly bisexual, although much of his writing concerns the sexual attractions of women. In works by each novelist, however, a homoeroticised portrayal of characters and either an austere masculine camaraderie (in the case of Buchan) or a feverish but ambivalent exoticism (for Loti) point to contrary sexual tension.

John Buchan was a Scot, born in 1875 in Perth, the son of a Free Church minister. Educated at the University of Glasgow, he took a second degree at Oxford, where he began publishing articles. By the time he left Brasenose College, he was the author of five books. He was called to the bar, then spent the years from 1901 to 1903 at the British High Commission in South Africa. Afterwards he worked for a London publishing house, then for the government during the First World War, becoming Director of Information. (A duodenal ulcer kept him off the battlefield.) Buchan subsequently worked as assistant director of Reuters, but won election to parliament as a Conservative member representing the Scottish universities from 1927 to 1935. Raised to the peerage as Baron Tweedsmuir, he became Governor-General of Canada, where he died in 1940. He published dozens of volumes, including biographies, novels and political works.

Buchan was possibly bisexual. Some biographers predictably avoid the issue, while others go to great lengths to reject such allegations. David Daniell, writing in 1975, disingenuously develops a psychobiographical hypothesis that Buchan was homosexual, only to disavow both the conclusion and the approach. Buchan's works include one-dimensional portraits of women, yet finely drawn profiles of men who often are reluctant to consummate their relationships with women. *The Half-Hearted* displays considerable 'male articulate emotionalism [which] at such a point reveals possibly too great an interest in men for our comfort'. Buchan's heroes show a particular interest in mortification of the body (although Daniell fails to show why this trait should be connected with homosexuality).

> If we are not careful, we shall simply take some of the elements that seem to us odd, not to say queer, and then come up with yet another simplified label about Buchan. His heroes, we might argue, as we warm to our theory, like punishing their bodies in cold waters on bleak moors, and perform unbelievable feats far from civilisation preferably in the company of other men: women are kept away, and several heroes shy away from possible closer contact with them; the woman is transformed into an insubstantial romantic ideal, and any sort of physical consummation is shudderingly avoided. The woman's place as sharer of deeper emotions is taken by special male friends.

Strong 'homosexual' feelings are all the more exciting through being forbidden.

Daniell concludes: 'Evidence can be piled up, until with a thick Viennese accent and a certificate hanging on the wall we can pronounce on Buchan's "sickness".'[65] Quite so, it would be possible to comment – without the diagnosis of homosexuality as 'sickness'. Daniell does concede that the title of one of Buchan's works, *Ordeal by Marriage*, is rather suggestive about his view of matrimony, and that 'two of his best books, *Prester John* and *The Thirty-Nine Steps*, have no women in them at all'. Another commentator, Andrew Lownie, extracts quotations from Buchan's novels to show the discomfort of male characters with women – 'Women had never come much my way, and I knew about as much of their ways as I knew about the Chinese language,' says a British mining engineer in Africa, who adds, 'All my life I had lived with men only, and a rather rough crowd at that.' Lownie sees this as a product of 'the public school system and a life in the empire'. He denies that 'Buchan's heroes display signs of homosexuality, but merely that they fit into the tradition of Victorian and Edwardian popular fiction.' He thus conveniently ignores the homoerotic tradition in that genre. Nevertheless, many of Buchan's women appear mannish; several male characters seem curiously girlish.[66] Emotional links in his works are often between men, rather than between men and women; as one character remarks, 'Women, bless their hearts! can never know what long comradeship means to men.'[67]

Sexual ambivalence is evident in Buchan's most famous African novel, *Prester John* (1910). Originally published in a boys' magazine, the novel tells the story of a 19-year-old Scotsman, the rugby-playing son of a Presbyterian minister, who interrupts university studies in Edinburgh when his father dies. He takes a position as shop-keeper in a remote Transvaal outpost. David Crawfurd moves into a man's world – a girl housekeeper, in whom he shows no interest, is the only female on the colonial frontier – and his closest companion is a quiet school-teacher. The other Europeans are Crawfurd's alcoholic boss and a sleazy Portuguese profiteer. Crawfurd soon becomes embroiled in combating the efforts of the Reverend John Laputa (an African clergyman whom he had coincidentally seen in Scotland before going to Africa) to foment an uprising, establish a Christian kingdom based on the notion of 'Africa for the Africans' and assume the mantle, or, rather, the priceless and seemingly long-lost ruby necklace, of the legendary Christian Abyssinian emperor, Prester John.

The novel is full of high dangers and narrow escapes, mysterious ceremonies and great adventure. Despite imperialist sentiments and the inevitable defeat of the rebellion by Crawfurd's sheer courage, the book portrays Laputa as a noble and worthy man. Laputa is Crawfurd's obsession. From his first sight of Laputa, tracing an enigmatic circle on a Scottish beach, the face of the African would 'haunt my sleep and disturb my waking hours' (as Crawfurd says in the first paragraph of the book, and he repeats the sentiment about 'the face [that] stamped itself indelibly upon my mind' a few pages later). Laputa's resonant voice and distinguished bearing also stick in Crawfurd's mind, 'for he is a fine figure of a man'. When Laputa comes to Crawfurd's shop at Blauwildebeestefontein,

> As my eye fell on his splendid proportions I forget all else in my admiration of the man. In his minister's clothes [in Scotland] he had looked only a heavily built native, but now in his savage dress [of linen tunic and a leopard-skin kilt] I saw how noble a figure he made. He must have been at least six feet and a half, but his chest was so deep and his shoulders so massive that one did not remark his height.

Buchan immediately tempers this masculine portrayal: 'He put a hand on my saddle, and I remember noting how slim and fine it was, more like a high-bred woman's than a man's.'[68]

Although Crawfurd initially fears that Laputa may cut his throat, he is irresistibly attracted to the African.

> First I made him sit on a chair opposite me, a thing no white man in the country would have done. Then I told him affectionately that I liked natives, that they were fine fellows and better men than the dirty whites round about.

Crawfurd is, of course, engaging in hypocritical subterfuge, at least on the surface, as he tries to divine Laputa's plot. But he cannot help following Laputa, even at great risk, and over the next few chapters gazes admiringly as Laputa, assuming leadership of the rebels, on two occasions strips off his clothes.

> By rights, I suppose, my blood should have been boiling at this treason. I am ashamed to confess that it did nothing of the sort. My mind was mesmerized by this amazing man....Indeed I was a convert, if there can be conversion when the emotions are dominant and there is no assent from the brain. I had a mad desire to be of Laputa's party. Or rather, I longed for a leader who should master me and make my soul his own, as this man mastered his followers.

The plot thickens, and Crawfurd manages to wrest the ruby necklace from Laputa, draping it around his neck to ford a stream, then stripping naked to dry – re-enacting Laputa's undressing while sporting the African's jewels. Laputa discovers the theft and captures Crawfurd, who offers to show him where he has by now hidden the necklace in return for his life. The bargain struck, the two men climb to the cave where Crawfurd had witnessed Laputa's consecration as leader. As Crawfurd plots the defeat of Laputa, he again confesses, 'I was hypnotized by the man.' Outwitted by the British, Laputa admits defeat. He once again strips naked, with Crawfurd as sole witness, dons the ruby necklace and jumps to his death in a chasm.[69]

Civilisation – that is, colonialism – triumphs, and savagery – 'Africa for the Africans' – is vanquished. The 'natural' imperial order is restored. Crawfurd emerges a hero, and immensely wealthy as well, thanks to the diamonds that Laputa gave him just before his death. *Prester John* proves the victory of the whites, but presents in a surprisingly articulate and detailed fashion the grievances of the blacks. The novel could hardly be called a homosexual story, and yet a current of sexual and emotional tension runs through the book. Women are banished. Laputa and Crawfurd are manly men, yet both have a touch of passivity, Crawfurd describes himself as 'a well-set-up lad, long in the arms and deep in the chest', but admits that 'I remember feeling a puny weakling compared with those lusty natives who could make such good going on steep mountains.' In his transcendental experience of Laputa in the sacred cave, he says that he would happily be a 'subaltern soldier' to Laputa's 'general'.[70] The stripping away of clothing, the passing back and forth of the necklace, the obsession with which Crawfurd follows the African, and the refusal of each to kill the other, bespeak a curiously profound and complex relationship. Perhaps most telling is the implication that such a bonding, fatal though it be, can solely be contracted outside the bounds of European society, when the Scot goes to Africa and the African, literally, sheds his European presbyter's garb. Only defeat of Laputa and everything he represents – including possible sexual temptation – can restore the imperial and moral order.

Pierre Loti, whose real name was Julien Viaud, was born in Rochefort in 1850. When he was eight, his beloved brother, Gustave, fourteen years his senior and a doctor in the French navy, left for a tour of duty in Tahiti, which whetted the boy's interest in travel, but Gustave's death at sea in 1865 left a permanent scar on Julien. He decided to follow Gustave into the navy and seems thereafter continuously to have sought a replacement for the handsome, virile and adored elder brother. After completing studies at the French naval academy, he sailed in the Mediterranean and Atlantic, and then, in 1872, went to Polynesia. He searched for traces of his brother and, like him, had an encounter with a Tahitian woman; his account, *Le Mariage de Loti* (1880), became a best-seller. Viaud also left Tahiti with the *nom de plume* of Loti. He spent the rest of his career in the navy, serving for forty-two years, and his tours to Turkey, Africa, Iceland and Japan provided material for colourful and melodramatic novels. Sometimes at odds with the military establishment because of his eccentricities, and particularly when he voiced criticism of French incursions into Tonkin in the 1880s, Loti remained an immensely popular author. He received a state funeral on his death in 1923.

Highly emotional liaisons with men marked the first decades of Loti's adult life. When Joseph Bernard, a fellow cadet from whom he was inseparable, was posted to Senegal, Loti pulled strings to get himself transferred to Western Africa; Loti's experiences there were transformed into one of his most successful novels, *Le Roman d'un spahi*. Bernard broke with Loti in the mid-1870s, after about four years of intense intimacy. Lesley Blanch suggests that 'the rift was caused by Joseph wishing to extricate himself from his former perfervid emotional ties with Loti'.[71] The two men never met again, and Loti's letter to Bernard asking if he could attend his friend's wedding was returned unopened. After a trip to Turkey, Loti, now a rising officer, took up with a Breton sailor named Pierre Le Cor. Again there was inseparable companion-ship, especially since the two shared a house in Lorient – unusual between men of different ranks – and happy visits to each other's families. Again his friend became the hero of a novel, Yves Kermadec in *Mon Frère Yves*. Loti remained loyal to Le Cor (who, like the fictional character, became an alcoholic) until they separated around 1886; they remained in friendly contact for another five years.

One probable reason for the parting of ways was Loti's fascination with yet another young sailor, Léo Thémèze, with whom he kept company from 1887 to 1894. According to Clive Wake, 'Loti's friendship with Léo Thémèze was, from his point of view, the most perfect expression of the fraternal relationship he ever achieved.' Loti described their partnership in intense and moving fashion:

> He is indeed the one whose soul I feel closest and most similar to my own, the true brother, who understands [me] even unto the depths, and who I would like to have near me at the hour of my death.

Never had he felt, he recalled, 'such a complete fraternal affection and commu-nion of spirit'.[72] In a repetition of earlier friendships, Loti made Thémèze a character in a novel, *Matelot*.

For a quarter century, from the moment he met Bernard to the time he and Thémèze drifted apart, Loti was seldom without a steady male companion. From voyages overseas and affairs with women, Loti returned to men friends (when he was not accompanied on his travels by them). Loti's preferred 'type', personified by Bernard, Le Cor and Thémèze, was a tall, robust European, which may explain why he rebuffed the overtures of an exotic young man whom he met in the Levant.

In 1876, Loti made the acquaintance of a boatman when his ship docked in Salonika, still part of the Turkish empire.

> Among a group of Macedonians, I noticed a young man with a curious kind of beard – separated in small curls, like the antique Greek statues. He was observing me with lively curiosity. He had something of the manner of a big angora cat, and when he yawned, he showed a double row of very small teeth, white as pearls. He was in rags, barefooted and barelegged, his chemise in tatters, but he was meticulously clean, like a cat. This person was Samuel.

Loti also espied a young woman hidden behind a veil and the iron window-bars of her house. Enchanted by Aziyadé, he recruited Samuel to help him make contact with the woman. Samuel was much taken with Loti, and ferried him around as boatman, acted as tour guide, introduced him to kif-smoking in cafés and went along with his whims to dress in Turkish clothing.

Blanch says that 'while desiring Aziyadé madly, he [Loti] does not appear to have made very convincing efforts to discourage Samuel'. Loti recorded their adventures in his diaries, referring to Samuel as 'Daniel':

> My evenings are spent with Daniel. With Daniel I have seen strange things: strange practices and prostitutions in the cellars where they are completely drunk on raki or mastic. That is how things are in Turkey: women are for the rich, who can have many: for the poor, there are boys.

He confessed:

> The sins of Sodom flower everywhere in this ancient city of the Orient....Though I do not share the unavowed physical desires of this man [Samuel], chance has brought us together....Am I destined always to wear this mask of extreme youth? The fascination which I can exercise over a man plunges me into troubled thoughts, a vague uneasiness and even mysterious horrors....Yet how can I repulse some humble creature who loves me without reserve when it costs me nothing to spare him that sort of rebuff – the most bitter of all? Everything is relative. Is there a God – a moral?

Disingenuous in his diary confessions, genuinely troubled by contrary sexual feelings or too transfixed by Aziyadé to give in to other temptations, Loti may or may not have spared Samuel the 'rebuff'. Blanch notes that Loti gave different versions of the episode in his diaries and in *Aziyadé*. In the diaries, he says:

> 'But what do you want of me? Che volete mi?' [asked Samuel in ungrammatical Italian]...His hand trembled in mine, and I lifted his head....There was a strange light in his eyes, and his whole body trembled....'What do you want from me?' he repeated, his voice sombre, troubled. And then he took me in his arms, and holding me close, pressed his lips on mine ardently. I had achieved my ends....indeed I had gone terribly beyond them: I should have foreseen this dénouement.

In the book, however, Loti rejects Samuel's advances, telling him that the love he proposes is forbidden in Loti's country:

> 'Never think of it again, or I shall have to send you away from me.'...Samuel buried his face in his arms and remained silent. But from that night, he had been at my service body and soul....his being is, as it were, absorbed in mine. Wherever I go, whatever the costume I have chosen, he is my shadow, ready to defend my life at the risk of his own.[73]

Samuel did not give up his pursuit, and turned jealous when Loti took on another domestic and confidant, Achmet. In 1877, when Loti prepared to leave Turkey, Samuel remained disconsolate at his unreciprocated affections. 'He cannot understand that there is a great gulf between *his* love', Loti wrote, 'and the uncomplicated, brotherly affection of Achmet....Samuel is an exotic plant, impossible to transplant to my orderly home.' He declined to take Samuel (or Achmet) with him to France, but sent him back to Salonika from Istanbul, noting somewhat ambiguously, 'Nevertheless I loved him, and something in his tears broke a corner of my heart.' On his next visit to the Ottoman Empire, Loti found that Samuel had vanished, and Achmet had died in the Russo-Turkish War.[74]

In 1892, when Loti was elected to the French Academy, the critic Edmond de Goncourt wrote about 'this author, whose love, in his first book, was a man'. Aziyadé was, however, a woman – after her death, Loti brought back her funerary monument and erected it in the 'mosque' of his house in Rochefort. He had a series of romances with women – a gypsy who provided sexual initiation as an adolescent, a young woman he met in a Paris restaurant, a Tahitian *vahiné*, a Basque mistress by whom he fathered several children – and he was married. His private writings nevertheless hint at sexual uncertainty, though Blanch argues that 'Loti was heterosexual, loving women passionately.'[75] It might be better to label Loti, at least emotionally, bisexual.

Friendships with Bernard, Le Cor and Thémèze, and confused relationships with Samuel and Achmet, point to diverse desires. Loti's diaries allude to unclarified sexual longings. A drawing of his shipmates shows macho bearded sailors, several bare-chested (and one, curiously, in a harlequin's outfit). (Loti presented a nude drawing of Le Cor to Sarah Bernhardt, who had admired the muscular sailor.) Loti's novels also display homoerotic insistence on the beauty of male characters.

In *Le Roman d'un spahi*, the tall, well-set up Jean Peyral is a dashing figure in red vest and fez – 'extremely handsome, with a masculine and severe beauty and his large bright eyes'; after three years in Africa, Peyral 'had tanned, but his strength had developed, his features were refined and accentuated in all of their fineness and beauty'. Peyral has an affair with a mixed-race Creole woman, and then takes an African mistress, who bears him a child; she kills the child and commits suicide after Peyral's death in the climax. Yet *Le Roman d'un spahi* contains intimations of ambivalence in this heterosexual man's man. On his arrival in Africa, Peyral befriends another soldier, repeatedly described as 'the handsome Müller', and an African, 'a fine statue of black marble'. He avoids prostitutes and 'strolls along alone, with such a grave and severe air that he intrigued the people of Saint-Louis'. After he meets the *métisse*, he takes to wearing perfume and carefully combing his moustache and hair. The man who displaces him in her bed remarks, with a patronising tone, that 'he is very handsome, this boy'. After his first adventure, Peyral is offered various experiences – he finds himself in a cabaret-cum-brothel with 'little twelve-year old Negresses and also young boys!' – but remains chaste until he meets the black woman who becomes his lover. Later in the story he is said to be 'not warlike enough, not enough of a soldier'.[76] One critic suggests that 'sensuality is forced on the Spahi from the outside. He is a passive lover, seduced by [the Creole] Cora and later driven by nature to take [the African] Fatou-gaye as his mistress'; at one point, Peyral refuses physical contact with Fatou-gaye and, 'when he will not sleep with her, she provokes him to beat her'. Clive Wake hypothesises that through female characters like Fatou-gaye, 'Loti is representing his own sexual attraction towards the handsome sailor.'[77]

Such characters as Peyral embody the characteristics of the sailors Loti frequented, the strong men who represented ideal companions and perhaps who he wished to be. According to Wake, 'The figure of a handsome sailor is the central figure of Loti's novels when it is not the author himself.'[78] The seductive seaman appears in much colonial literature and in the many writings with a homoerotic cast – in Melville, Conrad and Loti (and, later, Genet): the foot-loose sailor, visiting distant ports, haunting the dives of harbour towns, filled with pent-up sexual energy and keen for new experiences, a man tanned by the sun and salt of the ocean. From Melville's Billy Budd to Genet's Querrelle, the sailor is a figure of sexual ambivalence and homosexual desire, venturing to exotic lands where Europeans traded their goods and raised their flags. Viaud, the navy officer, and Loti, the dramatist of sailors' lives, recapture the ambiance of shipboard mateship and sexual voracity on shore.

Furthermore, *Aziyadé* testifies to interest in homosexuality, the writer as voyeur if not participant. The minarets of Salonika stand over 'a dirty and dark city where the vices of Sodom flourish'. With Samuel, Loti sees 'strange things…cases of morals that few people' have known, like dancing boys in a café. A watchman accosts him at night, manifestly wanting sex. An old man tells him that women are expensive, but other distractions are less costly, and the narrator suggests they can discuss his handsome son. Meanwhile, Loti corresponds with an Englishman, Plunkett, who repeatedly pledges his 'affection and unlimited devotion', the troth of a would-be lover. Loti remarks that 'in the old Orient anything is possible', and in mysterious Istanbul rejects Christianity, Western obligations and moral conventions.[79] The East thus becomes an escape route, a pleasure garden and a warren of temptations, with Loti the archetypal sexual and moral expatriate, the consummate hedonist.

Loti personified the *fin de siècle* aesthete with traits often identified with homosexual inclinations. Nattily attired in his military uniform, he also loved having himself photographed wearing foreign costumes. He decorated his house in Rochefort with Turkish carpets, furniture and foreign accoutrements. He was obsessively fit, training as an acrobat and posing nude to show off his taut body. He cultivated effete decadence that may have discomforted friends such as Bernard – the product of a wealthy and piously Catholic family – and caused raised eyebrows among navy colleagues. Despite a respectable marriage, he was always attracted to exotic women, whether gypsy, Tahitian or Turk.

Blanch sees Loti as an 'escapist', fleeing conventions of his Protestant and provincial background for the life of a sailor and writer, donning masks and dabbling in foreign cultures, living and writing romance (in every sense of the word). For Wake, Loti wrote himself into the characters of women enamoured of robust sailors and soldiers.[80] For Alec Hargreaves, imperialism and lyricism combine in sometimes muddled and hallucinatory fashion. Homosexuality – as erotic portrayal, intense comradeship and what might now be termed camp performance of sexuality – fills his works. The world overseas – Africa, the Ottoman Empire, Tahiti, Japan – provides a theatre of sensual delights for Loti, a stage on which the diminutive, shy figure could revel in tropical luxuriance and Oriental voluptuousness. His career afforded opportunities to fraternise with hunky sailors, court foreign women and dally with men like Samuel. His novels, the very model of colonialist literature, indulge in lavish descriptions of ship and harem, Polynesian village and Japanese court. Indeed the vision of the exotic and erotic Orient so important in the late nineteenth century, and so much a part of colonialist imagery, owes much to Loti's ambivalent nature and *œuvre*.

Some of Loti's sexual ambivalence is reflected in his attitudes towards colonialism.[81] Loti took part in an 1883 expedition to impose a French protectorate on Tonkin (which bombarded the Vietnamese imperial capital of Hué in a textbook episode of gunboat diplomacy). Seventeen years later, he sailed aboard one of the ships sent to quell the Boxer Rebellion and secure France's commercial and political influence in China. Loti sometimes took issue with this strategy, and was less than enthusiastic about France's penetration of Indo-China in particular. However, he never condemned imperialism, and indeed defended the colonial mission. He immersed himself in the exoticism of places he visited, but showed little real interest in their cultures. Even the interest in his beloved Turkey was more a question of robes and carpets, the architecture of mosques and marketplaces, his fling with Aziyadé and flirtation with Samuel, than engagement with Ottoman civilisation. Loti disliked South-East Asians and black Africans, about whom he wrote in undisguised racist terms. (In *Le Roman d'un spahi*, African canoeists were 'great slender Hercules, admirable in their figures and muscles, and with the faces of gorillas'.)[82] In *Le Mariage de Loti*, he shed tears over the destruction of Tahitian culture, the end of the noble savage, a process in which he and fellow Europeans took part. This ambivalence – or hypocrisy – is visible throughout his life. For example,

> Loti loved North Africa, and in his private journal in 1880 he bemoaned the effects of colonisation on the indigenous inhabitants of Algeria. Yet the following year he regretted having missed the chance to participate in the military operations by which Jules Ferry was busy imposing a protectorate on neighbouring Tunisia.[83]

A similar lyricism, confusion and literary imperialism – to note the three themes through which Hargreaves analyses Loti's works – appear in many other writers with mixed feelings about both sexuality and the world outside Europe.

Colonial homosexuality and literature

Homosexuality appears in various forms in a number of significant novels about the overseas world. What unifies these works is that the foreign situations and imperialist background – chance meetings with fellow Europeans or natives, the heated sensual atmosphere of the tropics or desert, the sexual ambivalence of Asians, Africans or islanders, the liberation from Western conventions felt by Europeans abroad – prove congenial to liaisons. Polynesians, Sri Lankans, North Africans and Indo-Chinese are available, proffering charms and affections. In return, they pocket coins, gain a foreign mentor or perhaps are invited overseas. Different countries provide varied pleasures, and reflect differing stereotypes. The primitive innocence of the Pacific islands allows intimate male bonding, while the sophisticated decadence of Asian societies offers refined pleasures. Rough nomads in Central Asia or North Africa, and gentle Vietnamese or Ceylonese, promise diverse delights. What the Europeans thought about these arrangements can be read into the stories: deep yearnings (but sometimes troubled desires), fascination with (and occasionally repulsion by) different physiques, timid overtures or brazen approaches, the bliss of tropical romances and the disappointment of separation from inviting climates and partners. In their overseas sojourns, these writers participated in, benefited from, but also criticised European imperialism. They experienced pleasures difficult to find at home because of law, social mores, religion and their own inhibitions. Their writings often perpetuated colonialist images, but also (in veiled or revealed fashion) recounted acceptance and enjoyment of reprobate sexual and romantic desires, and described or fantasised about sexual paradises that would welcome those with contrary inclinations: colonies as potential homosexual utopias.

Notes

1 This chapter looks only at fictional (or fictionalised) works. Several fiction writers, however, such as E.M. Forster, G.F. Green, and French writers on North Africa, are discussed in other chapters.

2 See several other examples in Alistair Sutherland and Patrick Anderson (eds), *Eros: An Anthology of Friendship* (New York, 1975), Ch. 9.

3 See Joseph Bristow, *Empire Boys: Adventures in a Man's World* (London, 1991), esp. pp. 80–90, and Richard Phillips, *Mapping Men and Empire: A Geography of Adventure* (London, 1997), pp. 61–2 and 115–16.

4 Peter J. Hugill, 'Imperialism and manliness in Edwardian boys' novels', *Ecumene*, Vol. 6, No. 3 (1999), p. 326.

5 Robert R. Hodges, 'Deep fellowship: Homosexuality and male bonding in the life and fiction of Joseph Conrad', *Journal of Homosexuality*, Vol. 4, No. 4 (summer 1979), pp. 379–93.

6 Gregory Woods, 'Fantasy islands: Popular topographies of marooned masculinity', in David Bell and Gill Valentine, *Mapping Desire: Geographies of Sexualities* (London, 1995), pp. 126–48.

7 Ronald Firbank, *Valmouth* (London, 1919), pp. 5, 22, 112, 83.

8 Ronald Firbank, *Prancing Nigger* (London, 1977 [1925]); quotations from pp. 36, 61, 37, 50–1, 72.

9 See Joseph Bristow, *Effeminate England: Homoerotic Writing after 1885* (Buckingham, 1995), Ch. 3.

10 Annemarie Schwarzenbach, *Orient exils*, trans Dominique Miermont (Paris, 1994).

11 After falling out with Erika Mann and trying to commit suicide, Schwarzenbach married a French diplomat and joined him in Persia, where she met a real-life Yalé. Annemarie Schwarzenbach, *La Mort en Perse*, trans Dominique Miermont (Paris, 1997).

12   William Beckford, *The Episodes of Vathek*, trans Frank Marzials (Sawtry, Cambridgeshire, 1994), and *Histoire du Prince Ahmed* (Paris, 1993).
13   Thomas Mann, 'The Transposed Heads', in *Mario and the Magician and Other Stories*, trans H.T. Lowes-Porter (London, 1996).
14   Jacques d'Adelswärd-Fersen, *Hei Hsiang: Le Parfum noir* (Paris, 1921).
15   *Le Livre des Beaux* (Paris, 1996), pp. 41, 42, 26, 24, 30, 33, 36, 38, 47, 55, 63, 64, 69, 72, 65, 86.
16   Mark Seymour, 'Comisso, Giovanni', in Robert Aldrich and Garry Wotherspoon (eds), *Who's Who in Gay and Lesbian History: From World War II to the Present Day* (London, 2001), pp. 88–90.
17   Giovanni Comisso, *Jeux d'enfance*, trans Soula Aghion (Paris, 1989); translations from the French are my own.
18   *Ibid.*, pp. 36–7.
19   Giovanni Comisso, *Loves of the Orient* (New York, 1954), pp. 7, 9–11, 14.
20   *Ibid.*, pp. 23–6.
21   Alain Quella-Villéger, *Le Cas Farrère: Du Goncourt à la disgrâce* (Paris, 1989), p. 26.
22   Claude Farrère, *Les Civilisés*(Paris, 1997), pp. 25, 31, 82.
23   Henri Fauconnier, *The Soul of Malaya*, trans Eric Sutton (Kuala Lumpur, 1965), pp. 9, 163, 162.
24   *Ibid.*, p. 142
25   Ian Buruma, 'Louis Couperus: The Eurasians of the Dutch East Indies', in *The Missionary and the Libertine: Love and War in East and West* (London, 1996), pp. 70–1.
26   Louis Couperus, *Eastward* (London, 1924), p. 160.
27   Buruma, p. 65.
28   Louis Couperus, *The Hidden Force* (Harmondsworth, 1990), pp. 103–4, 107, 205.
29   *Ibid.*, p. 117.
30   *Ibid.*, p. 122.
31   Radcliffe Squires, *Frederic Prokosch* (New York, 1964) provides biographical information. Prokosch's own memoir, *Voices* (New York, 1983), a tedious, name-dropping ramble, provides little of interest.
32   Frederic Prokosch, *The Asiatics* (New York, 1935).
33   Quoted in Squires, p. 34.
34   Prokosch, pp. 67, 109, 335, 288.
35   *Ibid.*, pp. 170, 187, 193, 271.
36   *Ibid.*, pp. 17–18, 345, 372, 375.
37   *Ibid.*, pp. 341, 351.
38   *Ibid.*, pp. 24, 323.
39   The following editions have been used: Herman Melville, *Typee* (Harmondsworth, 1938) and *Omoo* (London, 1893).
40   Melville, *Typee*, p. 248.
41   *Ibid.*, pp. 46, 51–3, 63.
42   *Ibid.*, p. 63.
43   *Ibid.*, p. 160.
44   Melville, *Omoo*, p. 162.
45   Robert K. Martin, *Hero, Captain, and Stranger: Male Friendship, Social Critique, and Literary Form in the Sea Novels of Herman Melville* (Chapel Hill, 1986), esp. Ch. 1; quotation from p. 38.
46   The quotations below are taken from the second edition, Charles Warren Stoddard, *South-Sea Idyls* (New York, 1903).
47   *Ibid.*, pp. 64, 173, 241.
48   *Ibid.*, pp. 266–7.
49   *Ibid.*, p. 46.
50   *Ibid.*, p. 32.
51   *Ibid.*, pp. 21, 47, 66.

52 *Ibid.*, p. 323.
53 Charles Warren Stoddard, *The Island of Tranquil Delights* (London, 1905), p. 34.
54 *Ibid.*, pp. 34, 161 ('On the Reef') and 259, 161, 269, 271 ('Kane-Aloha').
55 Charles Warren Stoddard, *Exits and Entrances* (Boston, 1903).
56 Roger Austen, *Genteel Pagan: The Double Life of Charles Warren Stoddard*, ed. John W. Crowley (Amherst, MA, 1991).
57 *Ibid.*, p. 31.
58 *Ibid.*, p. 280.
59 Stoddard, *South-Sea Idyls*, pp. 20–1.
60 *Ibid.*, p. 55.
61 Stoddard, *Exits and Entrances*, p. 29.
62 *Ibid.*, p. 34.
63 *Ibid.*, p. 35.
64 In another example of South Seas romance, 'L'Oiseau des îles', by Louis-Charles Royer, the French hero notices a young Polynesian man sashaying around town with a flower in his hair and asks a friend if the islander is a homosexual. He answers that decorating hair with flowers is common among Tahitian men, but adds that there are 'several Englishmen who are known in Papeete for their preference for a companion of the same sex' (Louis-Charles Royer, *Amours bizarres* (Paris, 1961), p. 118).
65 David Daniell, *The Interpreter's House: A Critical Assessment of John Buchan* (London, 1975), pp. 14, 84.
66 Andrew Lownie, *John Buchan, The Presbyterian Cavalier* (London, 1995), p. 199.
67 Quoted in Lownie, p. 200.
68 John Buchan, *Prester John* (London, 1956), pp. 9, 16, 76, 85–6.
69 *Ibid.*, p. 86.
70 *Ibid.*, pp. 145, 135, 108.
71 Lesley Blanch, *Pierre Loti: Portrait of an Escapist* (London, 1983), p. 99.
72 On these friendships, see Clive Wake, *The Novels of Pierre Loti* (The Hague, 1974), Ch. 2 ('The handsome sailor') and further information in Blanch, *op. cit.*
73 Quoted in Blanch, pp. 107, 109–10, 115.
74 Blanch, p. 125.
75 *Ibid.*, p. 128
76 Pierre Loti, *Le Roman d'un spahi* (Paris, 1881); quotations from Folio edition (Paris, 1992), pp. 68, 69, 88–9, 119.
77 Wake, pp. 85–6.
78 *Ibid.*, p. 32.
79 Pierre Loti, *Aziyadé* (Paris, 1991), pp. 40, 44, 46.
80 Wake's analysis of Loti's sexuality betrays a rather old-fashioned perspective on homosexuality. Speaking about the alcoholism of Pierre Le Cor/Yves Kermadec, he remarks:

> In Yves' alcoholism Loti sees reflected his own psychological weakness. If this weakness was in fact a homosexual tendency, it is not difficult to see the similarity with Yves' alcoholism, since both of them cause a deep-seated inability to adapt to the responsibilities of adult life which can only be overcome by a superhuman act of will.

(p. 99)

81 Alec G. Hargreaves, *The Colonial Experience in French Fiction: A Study of Pierre Loti, Ernest Psichari and Pierre Mille* (London, 1981), which, however, does not discuss Loti's sexual ambivalence.
82 Loti, *Spahi*, p. 46.
83 Hargreaves, p. 75.

5   Artists and homoerotic 'Orientalism'

Visual images form important testimony to Europe's encounter with the rest of the world, and imperialism provided a great opportunity for artists and, later, photographers and film-makers to record impressions of the world overseas. Artists accompanying explorers sketched the new flora and fauna – and people – they discovered. A school of 'Orientalist' art emerged with scenes of battles and bazaars, harems and temples, deserts and tropical jungles, picturesque landscapes and no less picturesque 'natives', and the invention of photography in the mid-1800s provided a new medium to capture 'scenes and types'. This chapter looks at artists associated with the colonial world who used homoerotic themes and, more generally, examines connections between homosexuality and colonialism in painting and photography, and, more briefly, music, dance and design.

Visual images served a variety of purposes. Tourists sent postcards as souvenirs of travel and holidays. Anthropologists made films as an archive of vanishing customs and ceremonies. Colonial promoters and administrators used photographs and film documentaries to champion the benefits of European control and the riches of the overseas domains (while anti-colonialists used pictures to campaign against imperialism). Painters experimented with new techniques in the sunny and colourful countries of the colonial world. Advertisers designed posters to sell commodities imported from the empire. Writers illustrated books with sketches, photos and paintings.

Visual imagery was seldom neutral. Some representations were intentionally conceived for propagandistic value, and almost all, perhaps not surprisingly, stressed the exoticism of the colonies, the strangeness of local architecture, the decorativeness of costumes, the mysticism of mosques and stupas, and the dangers of ferocious beasts and raging rivers. Obsession with the picturesqueness of the non-European world itself embodied cultural and political imperatives. Some pictures are nothing more than stereotypes with crude racist and ethnocentric perspectives. Yet many paintings and photographs are splendid works of art, rendering scenes and people with great dignity, technical finesse and a clearly evident respect for local cultures.[1]

Eroticised images were stock-in-trade for painters and photographers – Ingres's painting of naked women in a Moorish bath (a scene that he had never actually witnessed) is only one of a number of pictures of bare-breasted, alluring women disporting themselves in harem or hammam. Much has been written on representations of women, the way that models were posed suggestively, and how the pictures created and perpetuated European notions of the sexual attributes of Ouled-Naïl entertainers in North Africa, nautch-dancers in India or *vahinés* in Polynesia. Many such representations served as soft-core (and sometimes hard-core) pornography pandering to European men's voyeuristic fantasies about foreign women.[2]

Eroticised pictures of colonised men are less common (or less often preserved in public collections and published works), though there existed an iconographic tradition of powerfully masculine warriors, whether Arab horsemen in battle garb or semi-nude tattooed Polynesians in a 'state of nature'. Part of the explanation for the rarity of such materials is that most painters and photographers were probably heterosexual men, composing works that presumably reflected their own tastes and those of their patrons and the majority of their public. However, showing 'native' men as too potently sexualised might have proved unsettling in an age much concerned with perceived sexual threats to 'white women', possible rebellion against Europeans and the implicit challenge to colonial authority that 'native' virility posed.[3] Furthermore, European notions of male beauty, more persistently than images of female beauty, remained indebted to classical Greek paradigms that provided the main historical legitimation for homoerotic desires in the nineteenth and early twentieth centuries.[4]

Nevertheless, painters and photographers trained in 'figure studies' could not but be attracted by the physiques of men from Africa to the Pacific, whom physical labours, diets and climates often turned into fine 'specimens' of humanity. Models in 'life-drawing' classes in European art academies seemed pale in comparison. The boundary between exoticism and homoeroticism in many images is almost impossible to trace. The sexual orientation of numerous painters, poster artists and photographers remains unknown, and portrayal of a handsome naked man does not necessarily indicate homoerotic intention. Yet appreciation of art lies in the eye of the beholder – pictures focusing on attractive male physiques may well have been appreciated for their homoerotic value regardless of their purpose.

The ambiguous nature of paintings, and painters' lives, can be illustrated by an amateur, one of many artists who produced works for his own enjoyment. André Ragot was born in 1894, took a degree in medicine in Bordeaux and spent his life as a doctor in the French Navy. He served in various overseas postings, notably in Indo-China in the 1930s and 1940s, working as director of navy medical services there. The holder of prestigious French and colonial decorations, Ragot's hobbies included biology, natural sciences, archaeology, the history of religions and Orientalism; he was also a member of the Association des Amis de Pierre Loti.[5] In his travels, Ragot painted over a dozen watercolour portraits of men whom he met (often inscribing their names on the reverse of the pictures). These included sailors, a Legionnaire, soldiers and young men from the colonies: a man posed for Ragot in every port. The works, except for a bare male torso, are discreet, finely drawn and coloured images, several of which capture a particular mood or attitude. The Legionnaire, wearing *saharienne* and *képi*, is a bronzed, tousled-haired example of French derring-do. A Martinican sailor, clad in a T-shirt, looks angelic, while a New Hebridean, captioned 'The one who ate the tax-collector', appears more mischievous. While not avoiding racial stereotypes, such as the supposed anthropophagy of Melanesians, Ragot's portraits represent his acquaintances with dignity and affection. It is improbable that the unmarried artist did not experience an emotional or sexual attraction to the men whose pictures he painted.[6]

Africans, Arabs and European colonials in Orientalist art

Africans are often visible in Western art. Richly dressed servants appear in the backgrounds of early modern paintings; taking centre-stage are powerful 'savages', elegant concubines or 'civilised' Christians, or conversely wretched slaves. Portraits of African men, often undressed, as was usual with academic studies, appeared with increasing frequency in modern art and sculpture, sometimes as metaphorical representations of the African continent. (Asian and North African men are generally clothed.) By the Romantic era, blacks had become a regular theme, as seen with the black man dying in agony in Géricault's *The Raft of the Medusa* in 1819. Certain artists made depiction of blacks a speciality, often using as models Africans who lived in Europe. A black American named Wilson, working as a sailor, travelled to England in 1810 and, according to Hugh Honour, 'caused quite a stir in the artistic circles of London'. A professor of anatomy at the Royal Academy brought him to the attention of painters, who lauded his beauty. Thomas Lawrence compared Wilson to Antinous, 'the finest figure he had ever seen'. Benjamin Robert Haydon described Wilson as 'a perfect model of beauty and activity'. The adulation continued for several pages in Haydon's diary: 'Pushed to enthusiasm by the beauty of this man's form, I cast him, drew him and painted him till I had mastered every part.' Haydon made a plaster cast of Wilson's body (which almost suffocated the model) and took precise measures of his torso and limbs.[7] This may have been just anthropometric and academic interest, but the sentiments expressed about Wilson bespeak an emotional response to black beauty.

Several works by the Victorian William Etty (1787–1849) show at least a passing interest in both exotic men and naked men. Etty, a life-long bachelor of Methodist and artisan stock, studied at the Royal Academy, travelled in Italy and met Delacroix, who influenced the young painter. He did history paintings, portraits and landscapes, but specialised in the nude. Etty indeed was 'the only major British painter before the twentieth century to have devoted his career to the nude'.[8] A subject from a far-away place shows up in *The Missionary Boy*, an early painting of a swarthy foreigner, perhaps a Christian convert or a child preacher, dressed in a scarlet cap, lilac tunic and mustard waistcoat. *The Persian* is a woolly-bearded patriarch, and, in *The Corsair*, a dangerously dark brigand carries off his captives. Etty painted many male nudes: a half-naked *Prodigal Son*, a *Good Samaritan* tending an unclothed wayfarer, a shapely Prometheus. Nude males appear standing and reclining, alone or in couples. The sensual delights of a *Youth at the Prow and Pleasure at the Helm* are not entirely stifled by a figure of morality pursuing him in the clouds. Another young man lounges with spread legs on a leopard-skin in *Reclining Male Nude (Bacchanal)*. *The Wrestlers*, from around 1840, is unusual in nineteenth-century art in showing an unclad white man and black man intertwined. The bearded white man, facing the viewer, stands wearing only a loincloth, while a strong black man, bent with one knee on a red cushion or drapery and with his back to the viewer, is completely naked. The black man is shown as more than a physical match for his competitor. The lustrous black skin, and powerful physique, of the black man contrast with the pale body of his partner. The wrestlers' 'hold' is almost an embrace, though they look away from each other, and the intimacy of white and black male flesh is remarkable. How erotic the image seems may well depend on the perspective of the viewer.

Other artists painted blacks in a way that best emphasised their physical strength – George Dawe's *A Negro Overpowering a Buffalo* (1811) depicts a naked and very muscular black man wrestling a buffalo to the ground, his skin shining in the light, the muscles of his back, arms and legs highlighted with careful draughtsmanship.[9] Other works dwelling on physical beauty include Delacroix's elegant *Head of a Black Wearing a Turban*, a striking figure study of a nude black man by the Orientalist painter Théodore Chassériau (1819–56) and William Henry Hunt's black model wearing only drawers (c. 1830). More directly alluding to colonialism were Victor van Hove's statues of strongly muscled but supine slaves (from the 1850s), bare-chested African men (and women) in a bronze relief on the Livingstone Monument in Glasgow (1877) and a shapely tribesman, clad only in a belt of leaves, on the Albert Memorial in London (1864–70).[10]

The heyday of imperialism provided many opportunities for artists to picture native peoples. Alexandre Iacovleff, who took part in the Croisière Noire automobile rally in Africa in the 1920s, in *Chief Mazinga* (1925) shows an African chieftain with finely chiselled features, a short beard and moustache, hairy chest and broad shoulders; with a head-dress of green and white feathers and a raffia waistband, he is a noble-looking African 'type'. To some viewers, he might have looked simply curious, to others a bit fearsome or savage, but to still others (whether male or female) he might have exuded sexual allure. Evariste Jonchère's bronze sculpture *Le Rhythme africain*, a young African beating a drum, plays on the stereotype of African musicality, but a powerful chest and arm muscles, and a prominent crotch bulge covered by a rudimentary strap, also emphasise sexual attributes. Bas-reliefs sculpted by Alfred Janniot for the museum constructed for the Paris Exposition Coloniale of 1931 (now the Museum of the Arts of Africa and Oceania) illustrate the peoples of the colonies and the benefits of agriculture, industry and trade for France. Comely 'natives' gather crops, build houses and otherwise display themselves. Statues of athletic Africans by Arthur Dupagne – *The Rower*, for instance, an African wearing only a loincloth – decorate the Belgian colonial museum (now the Royal Museum for Central Africa in Tervuren). New media, such as advertising posters, provided further chances to dwell on statuesque black men. One printed around 1950 for the Aéromaritime airline service in French West Africa takes up the image of the handsome stripped-down, shapely African shooting an arrow with an aeroplane speeding through the background.[11]

An even more blatant representation of black virility, from an earlier period, is a portrait of Jean-Baptiste Belley. Born in 1747 on the island of Gorée, in Senegal, and sold into slavery in Saint-Domingue, Belley became a republican, an officer in the revolutionary armies and a *député* to the French Convention. His portrait was painted in 1797 by Anne-Louis Girodet to honour the (temporary) abolition of slavery by the Convention. Girodet was almost certainly homosexual. Though his artistic tastes usually ran towards mythological figures, he was often seen in the company of non-Europeans, whose beauty much impressed him. In this work, the black parliamentarian, dressed in frock coat and cravat, a tricolour sash around his waist, and a plumed hat in his hand, stands propped against the plinth of a statue. Belley – whom one contemporary called 'this good-looking Negro whom everyone admires' – flaunts an almost obscene bulge in his trousers, its dimensions highlighted by his pointing finger.[12]

Even in rigorously heterosexual scenes, many pictures of black men emphasise the sexual potency of their subjects, for instance, the black man holding a knife at the throat of a horse in Delacroix's *The Death of Sardanapalus* (1827–8). Similarly, Georges Clairin's *Palace Guard* pictures a strong, elegantly outfitted black man in a Levantine setting suggestive of the secret pleasures of the seraglio.[13]

Images of explicit male homosexuality, however, seem taboo. According to Donald A. Rosenthal,

> Male homosexuality…was a theme that dared not speak its name in the Orientalist painting of the Salons. Many of the great French writer-travelers to the Near East…commented on the practice of pederasty in Turkey, Egypt, and North Africa….Visual representations of the subject, however, were not considered acceptable even for private contemplation.[14]

An exception, perhaps, is one particularly splendid Orientalist painting, *The Snake Charmer*, by Jean-Léon Gérôme (*c.* 1880). Against a backdrop of elaborate Ottoman architecture, a group of largely elderly men watch a naked young boy with a long snake coiled around his waist and shoulder. For one commentator,

> The magic-weaving spell of the charmer or the storyteller is the quintessential stuff of an *Arabian Nights* fantasy. There is a touch of taboo, too, as well as mystery, in the anticipatory atmosphere of this all-male scene, hinted at by the phallic snake coiled around the naked, muscled body of the young

boy-performer. This sublimated homoeroticism creates a more subtle sexual display than that found in Gérôme's comparable scenes of exotic entertainments featuring women, where the body is in full frontal view.[15]

Few other paintings by the masters contain even such restrained suggestions of homosexual inclinations, though private collections may hide more blatant examples. An anonymous work called *Les Prisonniers* (c. 1930) shows three nubile men, one of whom rather elegantly wears wrist-irons and a chain, otherwise naked except for their head-coverings – a cap on one, a headband on the second, a turban on the third – and flowing robes that cover their genitals (though with a glimpse of the pubic hair of one man). Their effeminate poses and hand gestures – one fingers a necklace, another bends his arm behind his head – underline the ambiguity of the scene. An arrangement of seashells in the foreground adds an aesthetic (and aphrodisiac) touch, while on the rear wall hangs a placard with an Arabic inscription.[16] The artist and the story are not known, but the tableau may imply that the men have been captured as catamites by some sodomitical ruler, that they have been arrested for misbehaviour, or that imprisonment opens the way to homosexual practices, whether through 'situational' relations or by rape.

One of the best examples of an Orientalist painting that appears homoerotic, at least to a modern viewer, is *The Barber of Suez*, painted by Léon Bonnat in 1876, a few years after his trip to Egypt. Otherwise known for Italian landscapes, religious scenes and society portraits, Bonnat produced a work that contemporaries hailed as a *tour de force*, and a modern expert on Orientalist art praises it for 'betray[ing] a personal vision far removed from the ethnographic tendencies that determined the choice of subject'.[17] A comely young man sits cross-legged on a rug, his robe open at his neck, while another well-muscled man, wearing only a loincloth, stands behind him, leaning over to shave his chin. The sitting man, with a look of plenitude, nestles his head into the barber's crotch. Hugh Honour remarks on the photographic nature of the picture in which 'these two motionless figures [are] completely absorbed in one another, sealed off in their own world, observed but unobserving'.[18] The contact between head and genitals, the tenderness and intimacy of the barber's gesture, as he spreads the fingers of his free hand over the side of his client's face, and the blissful look of the man being shaved, combined with the general portrayal of handsome partially unclothed black men, might well have struck responsive chords in homosexual viewers. Ironically, a coded meaning might have been more apparent to Arabs than to Westerners because of (in the words of the anthropologist Malek Chebel) 'the homosociality that every man must have experienced in going to the barber', exemplified by a tenth-century poem about a barber by Al-Sariy al-Mawçouli: 'He has a palm whose caress is relaxing. / It passes over the head like a breeze, / When the razor shines in his hand, / It spreads on the head the water of well-being'.[19]

Whereas erotically portrayed women are omnipresent in Orientalist art, blatantly eroticised men are thus far less common, although homosocial scenes

– lion hunts, warfare, men drinking in cafés or bathing in the hammam – abound.[20] Other works hint at sexual ambiguity. Henri Regnault's *Hassan and Namouna* is described by Théophile Gautier:

> On a divan laden with brocade, silk and leather is seated or, rather, reclines, a young man, nude to the waist, tanned almost like a mulatto, with his arm pressed against his knees in a bold and artful movement. He is a strange figure – a loosely rolled turban covers his brows, and projects a mysterious shadow over his eyes. One might say he was an Oriental Manfred or Don Juan who perhaps has known another civilisation and is looking for new diversions.

At his feet sits a woman, her gown open to reveal neck and chest, playing a guzla. The painting thus appears a heterosexual *mise-en-scène*, though Gautier notes: 'Nothing is more separate than these two beings, young and beautiful both, yet placed at either ends of a divan.' Gautier adds that the work suggests 'boredom with luxury, the desire for the unknown, the weariness of "artificial paradises", as Baudelaire calls them'. [21] However, a viewer so inclined might see the lack of interest between Hassan and Namouna as opening up new possibilities, and the moody, almost cruel beauty of Hassan could serve as an invitation to a sensual experience unknown and unpaintable.

'Native' men were not the only ones to attract the attention of artists overseas.[22] Portrayals of French soldiers underline their fit physiques, masculine valour and heroic stance. Bernard Boutet de Monvel's *Portrait of Georges-Marie Haardt* pictures a lean French officer dressed in pith helmet, open-collared shirt, khaki trousers and long boots – the stereotypical presentation of the manly soldier.[23] A French recruiting poster for colonial troops has a similarly dressed young soldier standing at dockside, with a bare-chested African paddling a canoe in the background, while other Europeans sit with newly unloaded gear: masculine prowess at the conquest of the empire, an all-male world of adventure and bravery. Almost all recruiting posters for colonial forces portray 'men's men' willing to go forth and rule the empire. Bulging muscles, a frank look and intimation of proud and perhaps brutal bravado provide essential attributes. If images of 'natives' and Frenchmen are not pornographic, they are inevitably sexually charged. They are not homosexual, but reinforce notions of colonial masculinity: a machismo that to many homosexuals was (and is) sexually exciting, reinforced in iconic fashion by well-cut uniforms and sturdy boots.

Occasionally, paintings of Frenchmen abroad do seem *risqué* in focusing on sexual characteristics. Gérôme's *Napoleon in Egypt*, painted in 1863 to represent Bonaparte's expedition to the land of the pharaohs, shows the general standing in the desert in front of mosques with two horses and an Arab horseman in attendance. One striking element of this heroic portrait is Napoleon's enormously protuberant crotch, a scarcely subtle hint of the fusion of the general's military and sexual vigour.[24]

One of Napoleon's companions on his Egyptian expedition was Dominique-Vivant Denon, savant, author, future director of the Louvre Museum and an accomplished artist. Among other drawings that Denon amused himself in doing were twenty erotic sketches, 'priapic' works as he called them, including *Le Phallus phénoménal*. (Denon's penchant for erotic drawing had helped get him expelled from Venice in 1797, the year before Napoleon's voyage to Egypt.) Armand-Philippe-Joseph Béra in 1804 painted *Dominique-Vivant Denon en Egypte* to illustrate an episode in his *Voyage dans la Basse et la Haute Egypte*. Denon described how:

> in a ceremony (it was the first *prise de possession* of Rosetta) a young Greek came over to me, kissed me on the shoulder and, with his finger on his lips, without a word, mysteriously slipped me a bouquet that he had brought to me: this demonstration was a full expression of his sensations, his political position, his fears and his hopes.

This was presumably a gesture of solidarity at a meeting between two European Christians in the land of the infidels, as well as a sign of the Greeks' hopes for the success of the French venture. Nevertheless, the painting visually suggests other possibilities in the encounter, as Denon, nattily done up in frock coat and riding boots, turns away from the tree stump on which he is writing to smile benignly at the handsome young Greek, whose muscular shoulders and legs are left bare by his brown toga-like garment, as he daintily lays flowers on Denon's thigh.[25]

The examples of Orientalist paintings, ostensibly heterosexual portraits and scenes by heterosexual artists, show that representations of African and Arabic men underlined stereotypes of native sexual potency, as well as the homosocial camaraderie enjoyed by both natives and colonials. This formed a minor theme in European art compared to portrayal of exotic women, but nevertheless hinted at unbridled foreign sexuality, opportunities for diverse forms of sexual pleasure overseas, and the allure, to both European women and men, of potent foreign partners. Orientalist painting invited viewers to fantasise about the *volupté* of distant places, but not all visitors to picture galleries (or all artists) focused their gaze on the women.

Homosexual artists and exotic painting

It is impossible to know – and pointless to ask – how many homosexual artists lived in or visited the colonies, and there is no reason to assume that homosexuals necessarily painted works revealing their proclivities.[26] The paintings of Etienne Dinet (1861–1929), a French Orientalist, do not contain explicitly sexualised male images; pictures of boys frolicking are the only ambiguous ones, and all of Dinet's nudes are women. Dinet lived for many years with an Algerian man, his Arabic teacher and closest friend. Dinet and Sliman ben Ibrahim met in Algeria in 1889, when the unmarried Dinet was twenty-nine years old. In 1896, Sliman accompanied Dinet to Paris, where he organised a dinner of the Société des Peintres Orientalistes Français (of which Dinet had been a founder). A newspaper referred to him as a 'superb Arab' (and congratulated him on the couscous that he had prepared): 'Sliman has been brought from Algeria by the painter Dinet, whose life he had saved during an ambush led by Algerian Jews. It goes without saying that they feted this brave son of the desert.' A portrait by Dinet captures Sliman walking across the Place de la Concorde; another shows a bearded young man wearing a turban and cloak, his breast sporting three decorations. In 1899, *Antar*, a poem by Sliman, was published with illustrations by Dinet, and the two collaborated, in 1902, on *Rabia El Kouloub, ou le Printemps des coeurs*, three Saharan legends retold by Sliman.[27] They visited Egypt together in 1897, and shared living quarters in Algeria. Dinet converted to Islam and, with Sliman and Sliman's wife, made a pilgrimage to Mecca in 1929, just before his death. Sliman (who lived until 1953) established a small museum in Dinet's memory.

Dinet's most recent biographer denies that their relationship was homosexual, yet admits close emotional attachment and affection.[28] The president of the Orientalist painters' society, Léonce Bénédicte, had commented: 'Sliman was the link between the Arab race and Etienne Dinet.' Dinet himself described his life's project: 'Not to die before seeing the complete union of the hearts of the Mother Country and Algeria.'[29] The political programme in that wish – a naïve but progressive view of imperialism – was fated not to be realised, but Dinet and Sliman crossed the breach between France and Algeria through friendship and cultural collaboration.

Another possibly homosexual artist was the symbolist Gustave Moreau; according to James Saslow, 'His panoply of favorite subjects – eroticized male androgynes and menacing femmes fatales like Salome – constantly hint at what his carefully covered tracks never quite confirm.' In *The Angels of Sodom*, 'with the poignant ambivalence of a repressed homosexual who destroyed personal papers and forbade any biography, he paints the avenging spirits as a pair of androgynes hovering arm in arm'.[30] Moreau possibly had an intimate relationship with the Orientalist painter Eugène Fromentin, a long-time friend.[31] Moreau's paintings take up mythological and Biblical motifs, but he was also fascinated by the Orient, particularly India. When young, Moreau had studied Mughal miniatures, and was enthused by visits to colonial exhibitions and trips to the zoo in the Jardin des Plantes. Reading Etienne Burnouf's *Inde française* – an account of France's attempt to carve out an empire in the sub-continent – further excited his imagination, and led to paintings inspired by India. The Oriental king in *Les Rois Mages*, in Moreau's words, evoked 'the golden, indolent race, the voluptuous race, the race of dreams'.[32] A picture of a dancing Salome introduces an explicitly erotic note into his painting, while a tableau of *Le Triomphe d'Alexandre le Grand* pictures the Macedonian conqueror at the doors of India, mounted on his throne amidst local women, elephants and a statue of Buddha. *Un Chanteur Indien* (1884) is a fetching portrait of a finely dressed, rather androgynous Indian musician.[33]

Henry Scott Tuke, another ambivalent artist, was mostly attracted to young bathing boys, but painted a portrait of the Indian cricketer Ranjitsinhji dressed in full robes and jewels. Tuke also painted a young cadet, *Picture of 'Gray'* (1922), generally considered to be a portrait of Lawrence of Arabia (and which hung in Lawrence's collection). In 1923, Tuke travelled to the West Indies with an author and explorer called Arthur Mitchell-Hedges. In Jamaica, he headed for the beach to bathe with sailors from his ship, and then recruited local boys as models, including one who 'looks like a fierce savage and is gentle as a dove'. Several watercolours – *Sunny Hours in Jamaica* (1924), picturing a youth dozing on the seashore, and *On the Fringe of the Caribbean* (1924), in which two young boys shelter under a tree – present languidly attractive black boys whom he met.[34]

Connections between art, empire and homosexuality were more evident in the life and work of Duncan Grant. Born in India, where his father served as a military officer, Grant spent much of his childhood travelling around the subcontinent. Many of his Bloomsbury friends had colonial connections, but Grant was little attracted to Orientalism, though he enjoyed several holidays in Morocco. Grant did display an occasional penchant for black men and had an affair with a Jamaican model, Patrick Nelson, the son of a well-known wicket keeper. During the Second World War, Nelson was taken prisoner in Germany, and Grant sent him supply parcels. (Broken by three years of imprisonment, however, Nelson developed mental illness and died penniless in the early 1960s.)[35] Grant had other black sexual partners and models, and did over thirty drawings, only published posthumously, explicitly portraying a range of sexual activities, including oral and anal sex, masturbation and mild sadomasochism, between black and white men.[36]

Yet another early twentieth-century artist fascinated with colonial black men is Glyn Philpot. Born in 1884, Philpot was the son of a prosperous surveyor bankrupted when his partner fled to Australia with the firm's money. Philpot studied at the Lambeth Art School in London and the Académie Julian in Paris, during which time he converted to Catholicism. His first recognised paintings illustrate Christian themes, and he helped establish a Guild of Catholic Artists. Philpot was also interested in Eastern themes, and in 1907 painted *The Moorish Betrothal*: 'I have no very definite explanation of the subject....It was an expression of the feeling I had on hearing or reading stories of the East.' The next year, he travelled to Spain, Portugal and Morocco. Back in England, society portraits followed, and brought handsome commissions and fame; among his subjects were the Marquis of Salisbury, the Bishop of Oxford, the Headmaster of Winchester College, the Speaker of the House of Commons, Prime Minister Stanley Baldwin and Dame Nellie Melba. Art awards and election to the Royal Academy recompensed his efforts. A picture of a shirtless worker won a prize in Pittsburgh; Philpot collected it during a trip to the United States with Robert Allerton, an American ten years his senior, whom Philpot described as 'everything that is beautiful and true'. During the First World War, Philpot served as an officer, then as a war artist and had an affair with Vivian Forbes-Carter, a fellow soldier in the Royal Fusiliers.[37]

Philpot subsequently made regular trips, sometimes with Forbes-Carter, to France, Italy, the United States and North Africa. In Tunisia he acquired a North African servant and model,

> Ali ben Amor ben M'rad, a tall, muscular man with a powerful neck and shoulders and light-coloured skin. He was working on the road when he was first seen by Glyn, who was so taken with him that he arranged for Ali to come to England.

Philpot and Forbes-Carter went to Paris to fetch Ali, who had made his own way to France from Tunisia. They put him in a servant's room at their hotel and outfitted him in new clothes; Philpot wrote to his sister that Ali 'at once conducted himself with great ease, intelligence and dignity. Even V. was quite won over.' Ali posed for various works and, dressed in Arab robes, worked in London as Philpot's servant, though Philpot found him passive and unsophisticated, and was annoyed at his off-handed treatment of such famous visitors as Lawrence of Arabia. He became involved in some shady deal that got him into trouble with the police, and Philpot sent him back to Tunisia.[38]

The years passed with more society portraits, travel, a twelve-year homosexual partnership, and friendship with famous people, including such other homosexuals as the writer Marc-André Raffalovich and the designer Oliver Messel. Philpot's paintings were appreciated, though *The Great Pan* (1933), which depicted the naked god with an erection not convincingly hidden by a transparent fig leaf, was rejected for a Royal Academy exhibition. (Philpot then destroyed the work.) Encounters with the colonial world occasionally occurred. Philpot was engaged to paint a *Creation of Man* for the vice-regal lodge in New Delhi, and did a plaster statue of *Primitive Man* for his friend Allerton's garden. Several works featured black men, generally modelled on Henry Thomas. Messel had encountered the Jamaican wandering around the National Gallery and introduced him to Philpot, who soon adopted him. According to J.G.P. Delaney, Thomas was 'simple, guileless, unsophisticated', but was 'good-looking, and had an ideal male body, with strong calves, narrow hips and broad shoulders.…Glyn preferred him to wear an Afro haircut, but Henry had it cut when West African friends made fun of him.' Thomas appears in Philpot's painting *Baltazar* and a bronze, *Negro Walking*, among other works, sometimes in the nude. He also worked around Philpot's house, more efficiently than Ali, but developed a drinking problem. Delaney says that Thomas was not Philpot's lover, but the artist retained an abiding and solicitous affection for him, as he did for many other young male friends who were never lovers.[39]

Philpot painted his first black man in 1912–13, and black men continued to be favourite subjects; he sent seven depictions of blacks to the 1934 Royal Academy show. Besides Thomas, black models included a Martinican cabaret performer named Julien Zaire, whom he painted while living in Paris in the 1930s, and other black men recruited by Zaire. According to Delaney, 'Glyn's tendency to paint black men was no doubt partly sexual, but it was never principally that.' During an American train trip, he wrote to his sister that there were 'nigger porters & conductors so of course I was very happy'; for Delaney, this 'suggests more than sexual attraction, but an enjoyment of their presence and company'. Black men in Britain, mostly from the West Indian colonies, 'appealed to Glyn's love of the exotic and the same protective side as did the ne'er-do-wells. They may also have been an antidote to the highly sophisticated circles that Glyn frequented, and in which he was never really at home.'[40]

North Africa also attracted Philpot, and, during visits in the 1920s and 1930s, he completed paintings of an Arab wedding, street scenes, café patrons and Marrakesh women. (Philpot went to Egypt to do a commissioned portrait of King Fouad.) Only one work, however, is suggestive; 'hints of a homosexual flirtation', in Delaney's words,[41] are signalled in a painting of two clothed men sitting in an alcove. The older, bearded man expostulates on some subject, while his young companion reclines, leaning back invitingly, his shapely leg stretched towards his companion, an arm raised behind him in a debonair fashion, a flower charmingly placed behind his ear.

Philpot did do erotic paintings, and many of his works that portray men reveal a catholic appreciation of masculine beauty – acrobats in singlets and shorts, a dashing Spanish circus boy, an Italian soldier, fresh-faced English boyfriends and African protégés, a St Sebastian, mythological figures. Philpot seems to have enjoyed a full and uncomplicated sexual life. When he died in 1937, Thomas attended the funeral, leaving a wreath with a card reading: 'For memory to my dear master as well as my Father and brother to me. God blessed him and forgive him for his kind heart and human nature from his poor servant Henry.'[42]

Philpot's circle included the rich and famous, but also poor and simple black men who had moved from Britain's Caribbean colonies to the imperial metropolis. Several of his friends, notably Messel and Grant, also enjoyed the company of black men met in London, who modelled for them and sometimes became bed-fellows. In his journeys to North Africa, Philpot joined a great procession of writers, artists and composers attracted to Morocco and Moroccans. The contrast between London and Marrakesh would have been particularly great, just as Thomas or Ali made different companions from the titled personages or the tousled-haired Englishmen in Philpot's circle. The context of imperialism facilitated such encounters – the migration of West Indians to Europe, the travels of Europeans to North Africa.

A final case of an artist with the travel bug, and an interest in men from Africa and Asia, was the Australian Donald Friend (1914–89). From a prosperous family with interests in both Sydney and the bush, Friend in 1931 ran away to tropical Queensland to search (in vain) for a half-Thai man who had spent several nights in his bed, and who 'had much to do with that interest in orientals and orientalism which spread to include the whole coloured races of the world and has always been the strongest factor and influence in everything I've done'.[43] In the frontier town of Cairns, he took up with, and painted,

Aborigines, Malay migrants and Melanesians from the Torres Strait islands: 'When I got out of the plane in Cairns I was immediately in a different world. The air was like warm treacle and scented with a number of half-familiar odours. Molasses, frangipani, mango and other things hard to recognise.'[44] The atmosphere entranced Friend, and a Torres Strait island family befriended him.

Like many other aspiring Australian artists, Friend in the 1930s spent time in London. There he met a Nigerian who became his model and lover, 'the wonderful delightful African Ladipo, whose companionship was certainly the most profound of my European experiences'.[45] In 1938, inspired by that relationship, Friend journeyed to the land of the Yoruba, where he lived in the remote town of Ikerre until the outbreak of the Second World War. He worked for the indigenous ruler (the ogoga), collected African sculptures and painted local scenes and people. Returning to Australia at the start of the war, Friend went to Labuan and Borneo as an official war artist. His pictures show Australian soldiers working, showering or lounging in their camps, as well as Malays in villages. The chance to share the homosocial life of Australian troopers, and observe the indigenous inhabitants of the British colony, provided the only agreeable benefit of Friend's military life. War and colonialism appalled him, and he wrote in his diary how Malays had suffered under both British and Japanese imperialists.

After a stay in Australia, wanderlust again hit Friend, and he travelled in Italy, where he kept company with another young black man and met an Italian with whom he had a decades-long, though sometimes stormy, relationship. For a while, he again lived in London, where he met several other black men, including Omu, 'the model I have longed for. The superb exquisite little figure, black as ebony.'[46] For long periods, Friend was an expatriate. He lived in Sri Lanka for five years from 1957 and in Bali from 1967 to 1980. Neither, by that time, was a colony, but many of the old colonial structures remained in place. With his wealth, Friend could live a privileged life, and his artistic talents adapted to local circumstances. He surrounded himself with a bevy of houseboys and other young companions, though as he aged, he admitted that his sex drive slowed. He accepted commissions for artworks – a large mural painting of Galle, executed for a shipping firm in Colombo, represents a documentary on turn-of-the-century colonialism with nicely dressed settlers surveying a busy port with Arab prows and British steamships at anchor. He entertained visitors, though he avoiding old colonials who had stayed on, 'a few mildewed white exiles in an Asia populated by Asians', whose pretensions he ridiculed. Of an Englishman reminiscing about colonial days in Borneo, Friend imagined:

> him sitting down for luncheon at a folding card-table in his jungle Kingdom. It is furnished with products suggesting nostalgia for an England he remembers without a trace of homesickness yet carries with him in symbolic shapes – the bottle of Holbrooke's Worcestershire sauce. The cruet with Keen's Mustard. Bonox – *A Bull in a Teacup*.[47]

Meanwhile, Friend painted. Paintings or drawings of young tropical men, sometimes in the nude, became a speciality. Lovers, employees and village adolescents posed for portraits. Indigenous designs or landscapes form backdrops for *Bathers by the Road*, *Boy with Screen Background* or *The Lagoon*, works focusing on the physical beauty of Balinese youth. Occasionally Friend juxtaposed ancient sculptures and real-life men, as in a *Sleeper, Ceylon*, a slender youth dozing, guarded by carved owls borrowed from traditional Sri Lankan art. Some works suggest allegories of love and lust; in *Youth, Death and the Maiden*, contact between two males is barred by a skeleton interposed between them, while an outdone young lady watches. Other paintings – landscapes, naïve historical scenes, still lives, near abstractions – bear no sexual allusions.

While overseas, and back in Australia, Friend also wrote novels, accounts of his overseas sojourns and over thirty volumes of diaries. A decade before his death, he published a large-format and limited-edition work called *Bumbooziana*, 'Sundry Notes & Papers: being the recently discovered notes and documents of the Natural & Instinctive Bestiality Research Expedition'. Joyfully pornographic in text and numerous images, it sent up imperialism, travel writing and autobiography. Characters include the author himself, a photographer, a mannish woman explorer, the manager of a transvestite cabaret, an officious German doctor and a lady who carries out research in epigraphy, palaeontology and lepidoptery. Sturdy African men are usually clad in red tarbooshes or checked keffiehs, and little else. Sex, of various sorts and in countless occurrences, is enjoyed by all in a comedy of manners combined with a mock nineteenth-century exploration saga.[48]

In *Bumbooziana*, Friend recapitulated many of the stereotypes of sex overseas. He did not spare himself in the caricature of men whose social status, money and race allowed them to enjoy the pleasures of colonial and post-colonial life, yet some of whom – among whom Friend counted himself – developed deep interest and empathy for foreign cultures and peoples. Painting his Melanesian friends in Australia, African friends in England or Nigeria, and the Asians he knew in Ceylon and Bali, Friend once called himself the 'Gauguin of Warialda' (taking the name of his family property in New South Wales). More than any other artist of his age, Friend was the gay Gauguin who, he confessed, had always desired 'a wild, tropical, exotic life among dark-skinned native people'. The last entry of his diary read: 'Goodbye world of lovely colours and amicable nudes.'[49] His ashes were buried in Bali, where he had lived and painted, and where he followed in the footsteps of earlier homosexual cultural figures seduced by the East Indies.

Walter Spies and Bali

For many Europeans, possibly the most exotic spot in the world during the inter-war years was Bali, a luxuriantly green island with a Hindu-based culture in the Netherlands East Indies (now Indonesia). Dutch colonists had long appreciated the hospitality of the Balinese, the pageantry of temple ceremonies and ritual cremations, the sensuality of bare-breasted women dressed in batik sarongs, and the smell of spices and incense in the tropical heat. Such, at least, was the vision of Bali put forward in the 1930s, as the island was 'discovered' by tourists and popularised by foreign writers, such as Miguel Covarrubias, whose travelogue became a best-seller, and Margaret Mead, the world's leading anthropologist.[50] Not surprisingly artists and photographers were drawn to Bali to record their idyllic impressions of daily life.

One of the most famous expatriates in Bali was Walter Spies, painter, composer, musicologist, curator and prisoner. Spies was born in 1895, in Moscow, to a prominent and wealthy German family that had lived in Russia for several generations; his father and grandfather had been German consuls, and his mother's family included artists, scholars and public servants. Spies grew up in the family's city mansion and country estate, until he was sent, at the age of fifteen, to study music in Dresden. There he frequented the avant-garde and beau monde, but returned to Russia at the start of the First World War. In 1914, Spies's father was interned as an enemy foreigner, and the family turned their house into a military hospital. The following year, when Spies reached military age, he was taken into custody, and sent to the Ural mountains. He spent three years in Central Asia in a not too uncomfortable detention, living with a Tatar family, and learning the Kirghiz language, painting and composing; much influenced by local art and music, he remembered this period as a stimulating and happy time.

Near the end of the war, Spies made his way back to Moscow and, clandestinely, on to Germany, where he rejoined his family (who had escaped from Russia). Back in Dresden, he met modern artists such as Oskar Kokoschka and Otto Dix, and, in 1919, mounted his first exhibition. He contracted intimate friendships, too – 'Happiness beyond joy!' he described his friendship with one male partner. Spies also met the film director Friedrich Murnau, who provided him with a studio and almost certainly became his lover. Spies worked with Murnau designing film sets, and, on a visit with Murnau to the Black Forest, he made the acquaintance of a Dutch couple. They organised an exhibition of his works in Amsterdam, where Spies enjoyed a visit to the Dutch Colonial Institute (now the Tropenmuseum), a treasure-trove of art and artefacts from the East Indies. Increasingly distressed by his deteriorating relationship with Murnau, Spies announced that 'it is no longer going to be possible to feel at home in Europe'.[51]

In 1923, Spies took off for the East, never again to set foot in Europe. His first stop in the East Indies was Bandung, in Java, where he found jobs playing the piano to accompany silent films and giving concerts at the Dutch colonial club. Soon he encountered Sultan Djojodipuro, heir to the Jogjakarta sultanate, the centre of Javanese culture. The sultan, who noticed Spies's interest in the traditional Javanese orchestra, the gamelan, hired him as Master of the Sultan's Music in 1924. Living in the sultan's palace compound with an orchestra of thirty musicians under his direction, and waited on by a bevy of servants, Spies studied gamelan music, then little known in the West. The xylophones, cymbals and other percussion instruments fascinated him; he became an accomplished player and developed a system of notation for gamelan music, transposing pieces for piano and composing for both piano and Indonesian instruments. Spies also painted and took part in an exhibition in Surabaya in 1925.

Spies greatly appreciated the beauty of the Indonesians. 'The people, the Sundanese and Javanese, are so incredibly beautiful, so delicately built, brown and aristocratic'; the sultan's courtiers were 'slim and delicate, beautiful as gods in their costumes defying the imagination' (unlike European colonial ladies dressed 'in the most ghastly Parisian fashion'). Servants ministered to his every need – 'My dinner has just been brought in,' he wrote back to Germany one day, 'by my delicate, lotus-eyed, barefoot boy, whom I have as good as adopted.'[52]

In 1925, Spies made his first visit to Bali, which so enchanted him that he moved there permanently two years later. He stayed on a rajah's estate, and then built a house at Campuan, on land given him by the local ruler. For the next years, Spies lived happily, painting, composing, taking photographs and assisting in a film about *The Island of Demons*, helped financially by a large legacy he received from Murnau on the director's death in 1931. He associated with Balinese and other expatriates, such as Rudolf Bonnet, another homosexual artist. Visitors included Mead and her husband Gregory Bateson, Covarrubias and his wife, Barbara Hutton (who gave him a Leica camera), Charlie Chaplin and Noel Coward. Another visitor was the German sexologist and homosexual emancipationist Magnus Hirschfeld, who recorded that Spies 'is an enthusiast on the subject of Bali and has built himself a house in pure Balinese style'; Hirschfeld observed that Bali was 'full of strikingly beautiful women, men and children'.[53] With Beryl de Zoete, a British woman loosely connected with Bloomsbury, Spies took photographs and wrote *Dance and Drama in Bali*, published in 1938. With Colin McPhee, a homosexual Canadian composer, he pursued studies of Indonesian music.

Spies was now a celebrity, a resident much honoured by both the Balinese and the Dutch colonial authorities. He became curator of the Bali Museum in Denpasar, planned a cultural programme for a tour by the Dutch viceroy and organised the Balinese display and performances for the East Indies pavilion at the Paris Colonial Exhibition of 1931. With Bonnet, he founded an association of local artists whose 150 members were encouraged to experiment with new media and techniques. Indeed, Spies was so busy and so often solicited by visitors that he found a mountain retreat for himself, leaving his house in the hands of a German baron, who rented out rooms and whose bad reputation and arrogant deportment attracted unfavourable attention from Dutch officials.

In this happy environment, a homosexual scandal broke in Indonesia in the mid-1930s, producing numerous arrests and dismissals, and several suicides.[54] Heretofore, homosexuals had lived contentedly in Bali since many Balinese regarded homosexuality as a harmless pastime to be enjoyed by unmarried men.[55] With Spies's known homosexuality and association with some of those indicted, it was inevitable that he would eventually become a target, and he was arrested on 31 December 1938. Not only his sexual behaviour, but the better relations he had with the Balinese than did many Dutch colonial figures, contributed to his downfall.[56] Spies was charged with having sex with a minor. (Mead, noting that it was difficult to tell the age of Balinese men, remembered his 'light involvement with a Balinese male youth'; she defended Spies and attacked Western prudery.) The youth's father told the court that Spies was much respected, and that, if his son and Spies were having a consensual relationship, he could see nothing wrong with it. The judges nevertheless convicted Spies, and he was kept in prison until 1 September 1939. Life resumed, more or less normally, when Spies was released, and he turned his attention to collecting insects, but he enjoyed only six months of liberty. After Germany invaded the Netherlands, colonial officials interned German nationals in the East Indies. The Dutch held Spies in Java, then in Sumatra, before putting him onto a ship bound for the Netherlands. A Japanese aeroplane bombed the ship in the sea between Indonesia and Ceylon, and Spies, along with the rest of the passengers, was killed on 18 January 1942.

Spies's Balinese paintings are not overtly homoerotic (though he did do an engaging portrait of his servant Hamid). Influenced by Chagall, 'Le Douanier' Rousseau and German Expressionists, he painted magico-realist landscapes of fishermen in boats, hunters stalking deer or, in his most often used theme, a peasant leading an ox, dwarfed by rice paddies, palm trees and mountains. In some works, such as one of a deer running in a forest, then shot with an arrow and finally resurrected, different scenes merged into one canvas as a 'multiple exposure'. His works convey the overpowering presence of tropical nature, the quiet gestures of everyday work, but communion between man and nature in Bali. Spies's photographs record the complex Balinese dances and provide a visual ethnographic perspective on local culture. Several photo portraits of young Balinese, or snapshots of youths bathing, are the major hints of his sexual interests.

Sexual affinity contributed to Spies's attraction to Bali, and his liaisons did not trouble the Balinese or Spies's sophisticated visitors. Young artists who gathered around him found encouragement for their work. Bali's reputation, which attracted so many visitors, owed much to Spies's promotion of the island. Friends remembered Spies fondly, and commented on his contribution to Bali. Rose Covarrubias reminisced that:

> he knew every village and all the people in it, the days of their temple feasts, the names of their dancers, musicians, actors, artists....The best part of Walter's life was his friendship with the Balinese people. He loved them and their island and was rewarded with their love and respect.

The author of *Island of Bali* continued, 'He created the modern schools of painting and sculpture....[Local] artists were so impressed and influenced by Walter's painting that they all began to imitate his style, combining it with their own traditional temple painting.'[57] For Wim Pijbes,

> Spies supplied the young, talented Balinese artists with better materials and with alternatives to traditional Hindu themes like the 'Ramayana' legends. As a result, they began to portray their immediate surrounds – nature, hunting and daily village life. It was Spies, especially, who infused the Balinese artists with the dramatic and magical possibilities of painting and drawing. Freed for the first time from the constraints of convention, Balinese artists explored their own imagination and creativity, myth, magic, and realities resulting in a transition from applied art to Modern Art.[58]

The anthropologist Jane Belo remembered Spies as 'a very blond young man, handsome in an ethereal sort of way, with blue eyes', who was 'a painter and a musician, an authority on all the Balinese arts from the shadow-play to the most recent developments in the plastic arts'. For Mead, 'Walter Spies' choice of Bali...seemed part of his repudiation of the kind of dominance and submission, authority and dependence, which he associated with European culture, and which could be revived in him when he encountered officialdom or rank.'[59] Cultural interests, sexual attractions and the seduction of an Asian location linked Spies to Bali, while the attitudes and actions of conservative, puritanical and vengeful colonial authorities brought about his death.

If Spies did not concentrate on pictures of young men, several fellow artists did so. Rudolf Bonnet often portrayed slender Balinese wearing ceremonial head-cloths and sarongs, lounging on the ground, lying in the tropical heat or crouching before the artist's sketch-book. Bonnet, a good friend of Spies, arrived in Bali in 1929, at the age of thirty-four, after spending his early life in Amsterdam and living for a time in Italy. He became involved in setting up a museum in Ubud and worked in health-care and education projects. Interned by the Japanese during the Second World War, he remained in Indonesia until 1958 and visited Bali several times afterwards before his death in 1978. Like Spies, he had a great impact on local artists. Another painter of Balinese land-scapes and youth is Arie Smit, now over eighty years old. Smit arrived in 1938 in the East Indies, where he completed his Dutch military duty in the army's topographical service. He remained in the country, becoming a citizen of Indonesia and moving to Bali. A latter-day Spies, he has promoted Balinese artists and exhibited his own paintings widely (a museum in Ubud devotes a gallery to his work). Among his paintings are a number of brightly coloured portraits of attractive young men against a somewhat stylised tropical back-ground.[60]

Bali, the 'island of love', as it was sometimes labelled, thus was – for a time – an island of homosexual love, where men such as Spies and Bonnet could paint, photograph and compose outside the constraints of a Europe plunged into Depression and Fascism. They benefited from colonial conditions, but their interest in Balinese culture hardly earns them a 'colonialist' judgement. Indeed, the recrudescence of colonial puritanism in the 1930s, instigated by right-wing newspapers, reactionary parliamentarians and self-appointed moral authorities, brought to an end their dream of Bali.

Hubert Stowitts and India

A contemporary homosexual artist to Spies and Bonnet, whose greatest successes came from paintings of India, was Hubert Julian ('Jay') Stowitts. Born in the American Midwest, in the state of Nebraska, in 1892, his father was a shop assistant and his mother, a teacher. The family moved to South Dakota several years later, then to California, and in 1911 Stowitts enrolled at the University of California in Berkeley. He won both academic and athletic awards. After attending a ballet performance in San Francisco in 1913, he began private lessons, and was soon dancing at the parties of prominent and socially ambitious hostesses and in university productions at the Greek Theatre. In his last year at university, he was 'discovered' by the great Anna Pavlova, who invited him to join her dance company. Stowitts abandoned the postgraduate business studies that he had been scheduled to undertake at Harvard to become the first American to partner Pavlova.

Stowitts and Pavlova toured North and South America for several years, during which time Stowitts began to paint. They continued on to Europe, where Stowitts danced in Madrid, Paris and London, and set up an art studio in Montmartre. Though well received as a dancer, Stowitts decided to leave Pavlova's company and strike out on his own. Following a season at the *Folies Bergère*, he began to paint a series called *The Fall of Angels*. Among his models was Serge Lifar, the new favourite of Serge Diaghilev, impresario of the Ballets Russes; Stowitts portrayed Lifar in full-frontal nudity. The painting, 'near life-sized with a relatively "quiet" colour palette, terribly romantic...[but] infused with eroticism', according to Anne Holliday,[61] has survived only in photographs. In 1926, Stowitts completed designs for a ballet set in China, *Fay-Yen-Fah*, and appeared in a movie, *The Magician*, adapted from a Somerset Maugham novel. The next year he lived in Venice, painting portraits of Ezra Pound, Principessa Anna-Maria Pignatelli and Benito Mussolini.

Orientalism and primitivism appeared throughout Stowitts's life. American Indian dances in South Dakota, then Chinese opera in San Francisco, were early influences. While a student, he performed a 'Buddhist Pantomine', followed by an 'Indo-Chinese' solo and later a Syrian ballet for Pavlova's company. Subsequent dance performances included the Persian-inspired 'La Péri', 'The Peddler' (in which Stowitts danced as Krishna in a Balinese décor to a score by Darius Milhaud), a 'Brigand's Dance' staged in London, an Inca ballet in South America, a 'Chinese Porcelain Dance' and 'Congo' in New York, and an 'Egypt' in Paris. Stowitts based his elaborate paintings for *Fay-Yen-Fah* on Asian works that he saw in the British Museum and the Musée Guimet in Paris, although the short production time available before the première (in Monte Carlo) did not make it possible to use his designs.[62] A book of his paintings for the opera was nevertheless published in 1927; the bright colours and sinuous lines of a princess, a court lady and a sage suggest a fascination with an alluring, exotic China. The design for a *Marathon Man* reveals a strongly muscled, animated dancer in bejewelled loincloth, and hints at homoerotic interest. Continuing the Orientalist mood, Stowitts's paintings of the Ballets Russes featured Vaslav Nijinsky in many of his exotic roles in *Schéhérazade, Les Orientales* and *Le Dieu Bleu*.[63]

By the late 1920s, Stowitts had achieved success. He boasted an impressive circle of friends, including leading cultural figures as well as openly homosexual men. By this period, after living in Paris for six years, Stowitts had achieved celebrity as a dancer, and found the courage to retire at his prime and launch himself as an artist in an entirely new medium. He had also come to terms with his homosexuality. Now he decided to travel, 'eager to leave European culture which he found decadent and dull'.[64] Asia attracted him for its dance and art, as well as its philosophy. According to Holliday, 'Stowitts considered Asia to be the origin of all civilization....Stowitts sensed that Westerners were destroying Asia, and that cultures, craftsmen and artists were disappearing.'[65] He wanted to see and record mythical Asia before it vanished.

In Java Stowitts studied Indonesian dance and painted. Moving on, he exhibited seventy-five life-sized portraits of Indonesian dancers at the National Museum in Calcutta. Stowitts did 150 paintings of India, which attracted much attention when shown in Europe and America in the 1930s; Queen Mary attended the opening of his exhibition at the Imperial Institute in London. On returning to the United States after a decade overseas, Stowitts starred as Prometheus in a stage production in Hollywood and made the film *The Painted Veil* with Greta Garbo and another with Spencer Tracy. He also began a series of portraits of American athletes. The works were displayed in Berlin during the Olympic Games in 1936 until Nazi authorities closed the show because of the portrayal of black and Jewish athletes. The photographer and film-maker Leni Riefenstahl, whom he had met in Paris in 1924, nevertheless befriended Stowitts, and he helped edit her *Olympia* film. He meanwhile made an appearance in the film *Fanny Elssler*, the first feature film depicting the world of classical ballet. Stowitts choreographed, and designed costumes, for the dance sequences. According to Holliday, he ended up creating a wonderful, albeit bizarre, Javanese ceremony complete with a huge corps of scantily clad 'Javanese' men, whom he choreographed to gamelan music, and created a role for himself as the Javanese prince who captures the swooning Lilian Harvey in the title role, and a *pas de deux* complete with waterfalls, lagoons and Germany's idea of Javanese orchestrations.

Stowitts finally saved enough money to return to the United States in 1937. He finished a book manuscript on dance, did a number of paintings on *The Golden Age of the Ballets Russes* and lectured on Indian and Javanese culture. He remained poor, earning extra money as a caretaker at a holiday house. In 1940, in a case of police entrapment, he was busted by the vice squad for allegedly soliciting a man for sex in Los Angeles's Griffith Park, an incident that humiliated the artist. From the mid-1940s, his health declined. Becoming increasingly mystical, he composed cosmic-style and esoteric geometrical designs,[66] and paintings on the labours of Hercules. He died in 1953, largely forgotten.[67]

Stowitts's most ambitious paintings were his *Vanishing India* series, brilliantly coloured works executed in tempera. William Rothenstein, of the Royal

Academy, wrote: 'Nowhere have I seen a truer, a more forceful and convincing rendering of the faces, figures, dress, ornaments of Prince and peasant, ascetic and fakir, Rajput warrior and Bengali youth, craftsmen and gypsies, musician, merchant, mendicant and mummer.'[68] Through what he called ethnographic works, Stowitts had wanted to record traditional India, both the elite, including maharajahs who hosted him, and the common people. (He also painted Nehru and Gandhi.) The Maharajahs of Kolhapur and Udaipur are splendidly portrayed in court finery, while common artisans (men and women) are shown at daily tasks. Some are fully clothed, others clad only in dhotis. *Printing Cloth with Gold Leaf* shows a handsome artisan working at a table, and *Hunting Lynx of the Ruler of Jaipur* is a dual portrait of an animal and his fetching handler. *Kanikar Aboriginals* pictures a couple representing the original inhabitants of India; the woman is bare-breasted but demure; the man, powerfully muscled and scantily dressed. *Hanuman Beggar* shows another strong man dressed as a hero of the *Ramayana* epic. *Travancore Potters* depicts a shapely Brahmin and his apprentice.[69]

The pictures are softly erotic in their portrayal of the muscled, gleaming and semi-naked male bodies, though they suggest no homosexual activity. *The Tiller of the Soil*, painted in Jaipur in 1930, is the most powerful of the physique pictorials, a handsome young man sitting with legs spread, his hand propped on the floor to emphasise the muscles of his chest and shoulders. Other paintings show groups of men interlaced. In *Water Carriers Dispute*, six Muslims bicker about their work, their bodies intertwined to provide a good view of athletic torsos and crotches covered by loincloths. The most sexually charged picture in the series, *Bengali Darhwan or Watchman*, is a slender young Indian lounging on a wall. He wears only a necklace and a long white dhoti that hangs open to reveal a bare leg and thigh, and clearly outlines his genitals. The pose, with spread limbs and languorous sensuality, is one of erotic invitation. Stowitts's text for the illustration in the original *Vanishing India* catalogue read:

> Throughout all of India one encounters thousands of watchmen who really do no watching at all....In some parts of the country there are castes of thieves who are engaged by householders to keep their fellows away from the property, and the saying goes that no house has ever been robbed which was guarded by a thief.[70]

Such works, as well as pictures of nude dancers and athletes, leave little doubt about Stowitts's aesthetic and erotic attraction to his subjects.

Stowitts's interest in male physiques is underlined by the contemporary description of a *Bihar Wrestler* in a catalogue prepared by the Dutch Colonial Institute for an exhibition in Amsterdam: 'Krishna Ram was a famous wrestler in the United Provinces, and noted as having perfect proportions according to the old Indian poem which sang of men with waists like lions and shoulders like elephants.' The catalogue preface speaks of the way in which Stowitts:

brought together the brilliant sunlight, the vivid array of court ceremony and costume, the warm color of the Hindu skin, the ripple of muscles and the dexterity of fingers at work, the sharp flash of jewels and the burnt-out eyes of the ascetic, incorporating the beauty of the painter's vision and the truth of the scientific point-of-view into a living panorama of India.[71]

Stowitts probably did not have sexual liaisons in the East. According to Holliday, in Bali, Java and India, he 'found freedoms and opportunities unthinkable in his native US or Europe' and 'experienced personal freedoms that clearly transcended those he experienced in New York, Paris and even Buenos Aires'. However, Holliday adds, 'My sense of Stowitts' sexuality is that he learned early on – in a boyhood spent in...South Dakota as a child of educated, yet puritanical parents – to sublimate his homosexual identity.' Furthermore,

> Stowitts also adhered to a core belief that the body is an instrument of God....He was a near fanatic about diet, fitness and health. He railed against the excesses of peers such as Cocteau who indulged in drug use, which Stowitts believed resulted in a squandering of talents. He also feared venereal disease, which had taken no small toll on so many within his immediate artistic and cultural circles in those pre-penicillin years.[72]

The trend towards modernism, the dislocation to the art world created by the Second World War and the disappearance of many of Stowitts's most important paintings into a private collection between the 1950s and 1981 reduced his audience. For those who knew of him, Stowitts incarnated early twentieth-century homosexual sensibilities linking athleticism, Orientalism and the aestheticism of the avant-garde.

Ethnographic and documentary photographs

In colonial photography, as in painting, homoerotic images testify to men's attraction to foreign places and exotic partners. The colonial era saw a great vogue for what the French term *scènes et types* images, often reproduced on postcards, of traditional life and people. Photographers sometimes took unposed shots but, especially in the early years of complicated equipment and long exposure times, photographs were often carefully arranged and choreographed, and indigenous people were frequently photographed in studios against 'appropriate' backgrounds. The presence of a comely man or woman in the picture provided an added attraction. Before Western clothing styles replaced the often more rudimentary outfits worn in hot climates, pictures of half-naked 'typical' people proliferated. For instance, one collection of official French photographs from 1930 to 1960 reveals a bare-chested adolescent after his ceremonial circumcision in Congo bushland, a group of highly decorated, and again bare-chested, dancers at an initiation ceremony in Togo and an engagingly friendly-looking servant in Algeria.[73] A photograph of Tahitian men, from 1870, displays nine muscular Polynesians, naked to the waist, posed in the triangular form common for group portraits of the period – two standing at the back, a row of sitting men, three squatting figures, with another man reclining in the foreground. The rather 'campy' pose of the reclining figure, with the hand of the man behind him resting on his shoulder, and the spread legs of one of the squatting figures, are probably just happenstance or conventions of Victorian studio photography, but the image underlines the physicality of 'natives' lauded for masculine beauty.[74]

The aestheticisation of native men is particularly evident in five booklets of photographs by E. Troubat, published in Paris in 1931–2, with an introduction by the director of France's Ecole Coloniale. Issued during and just after the international colonial exhibition meant to foment French colonial pride, the pictures, said Georges Hardy, represented an 'aesthetic rehabilitation' of non-Europeans: 'Look at these slender nomads with their compact and vigorous muscles, or these blacks whose torsos show the grace of a beautiful vase.' Many Europeans could not match such standards of beauty, and natives, living almost naked, physically active and supple from work and dancing, were often admirable: 'All "savages" are not marvels of physical beauty – far from it – but in the most wretched races are to be found at least honourable specimens.' Photographs of men and women indeed show handsome subjects living under French rule: a striking Tahitian lad wearing a wreath of frangipani flowers ('a gracious ornament which the Tahitian man, and woman, would not go without'), another shapely Polynesian, a boatman photographed in a landscape of sea and palms ('the silhouette of a man, whom no clothing imprisons, stands out in this paradisiacal scene'), two boatmen from Niger ('the labour of their muscles, far from lacking grace, on the contrary places in relief the pure lines of their flanks'), another West African throwing a spear ('his natural pose betrays no physical effort but shows off the male beauty of his naked torso, both muscled and sinewy'), and a Martinican ('This Martinican negro incarnates male beauty as we understand it: muscled and sinewy arms, shoulders suggesting a strong back, a broad and elegant chest').[75]

Aesthetic sentiments mixed with colonial ones in appreciation of these photographs. Immediately after the comment about 'honourable specimens' of foreign races, Hardy added:

> In order for the Beautiful finally to win out over the ugly, it is necessary for us, the civilised people, to save [these races] from hunger, from discomfort and from barbarian practices. Colonisation with an eye to aesthetics is only in appearance a paradox, and it is good that once again, as the author [photographer] has discovered, Art can serve Humanity.

The *mission civilisatrice* thus included an aesthetic mandate to safeguard the beauty of the colonial world and its people. Not surprisingly, captions to some of Troubat's photographs reminded readers of savagery as well as beauty – men from Dahomey, 'colossuses with powerful muscles are really big children'. A

man from Haute-Volta 'seems peaceful and not very courageous despite the
hatchet that he refuses to put down, and that his robust arms must wield
without great effort'. Nevertheless, underlining one of the paradoxes of
colonialism, an occasional caption pointed to the effects of 'civilisation' in
destroying photogenic customs: in Oceania, 'unfortunately, with European
influences, these costumes [pareos], which are perfectly adapted to the
picturesqueness of the place, are destined to disappear'.[76]

Troubat's photos are not, as such, erotic or homoerotic, but might well have
appeared so to viewers. Indeed, any representation of a handsome man – from
an anthropological picture of naked figures shown in standard front, side and
rear views to a romantic portrait of a beautiful young man labelled 'Algérie –
'Type Nègre du Sud' – might possibly have been the work of a homosexual
photographer and exuded sexual or romantic attraction for some viewers.[77] It is
unnecessary to assume a photographer (or viewer) was *not* homosexual. In any
case, many of these depictions matched ideas about the sexual potency of
'savages', the endowments of non-Europeans, and the sensual *frissons* to be
experienced overseas.[78]

Some pictures taken for commercial sale are nevertheless presented in a way
that appeals to the prurient imagination – iconographic emphasis on the masculine attributes of the figure, posing of subjects intentionally to reveal bare chests
or limbs (when nudity would not be essential in the activities pictured), choice
of a particularly attractive model. Photographs made privately, or intended for
private viewing, could be more open. Snapshots of naked adolescents
photographed by a French official in Tunisia in the 1950s, for instance, betoken
more clearly homosexual desires.[79] Undoubtedly many similar collections have
been lost or destroyed.

A number of publicly presented photographs are homoerotically charged,
notably in the works of Rudolf Lehnert (1878–1948) and Ernst Landrock
(1878–1966), the leading photographers of North Africa in the early twentieth
century. The Bohemian-born Lehnert and the German Landrock met in
Switzerland in 1904, when both were twenty-six years old, and later that year
travelled to Tunis, where they opened a photographic studio and worked until the
outbreak of the First World War. During the war, their studio was closed and the
men briefly interned – Lehnert in Algeria and then Corsica – but they then
managed to get back to Switzerland. In 1920, they opened a new Oriental
photography business, with headquarters in Leipzig. In 1923, Lehnert journeyed
to Egypt, Palestine and Lebanon, and two years later the pair established a studio
and postcard business in Cairo. They separated in 1930, when Lehnert married a
Frenchwoman and set up a studio in Tunis; Landrock returned to Germany in
1938. Throughout their partnership, Landrock ran the business, and Lehnert
(who had trained as an artist) produced images for reproduction on postcards.[80]

One speciality was desert scenes, showing the photographer's mastery of light
and formal composition. Views of oases, arcades, fountains and sunsets
portrayed a traditional culture seemingly little touched by colonialism, though
shots of busy urban centres – and a picture of the forlorn border-marker

standing in the otherwise undivided desert between Tunisia and Algeria – were reminders of the impact of Western rule. Pictures of hat-makers, money-changers, calligraphers, card-players, *habitués* of cafés and rabbis illustrated 'typical' figures of North Africa and the Middle East. Lehnert and Landrock's postcards proved immensely popular, promoting Oriental beauty and exoticism with an erotic tingle. Pictures of naked or semi-naked women, often labelled (not always truthfully) as Ouled-Naïl dancers, were outrightly pornographic with an emphasis on bare breasts, slender torsos and suggestive poses.

In their soft-core porn, Lehnert and Landrock mostly focused on nude women, but they also shot young men. A photograph of a Tunisian from around 1910 poses a sweetly pretty youth in a neo-classical setting; he is naked except for a scarf around about his head and a cloth draped across his loins.[81] The pensive mood and slender unclothed body suggest both vulnerability and avail-ability. Other photographic postcards hint at the sexual allure of boys (though some of adolescents, such as an Arab potter, are straightforwardly ethnographic, even if an off-the-shoulder robe adds a seductive touch). One postcard, simply entitled 'Arab Type', shows a beautiful boy, his head turned in profile to reveal classical features, with a flower tucked behind his ear and a scarf arranged artfully about his head; his open robe reveals a smooth chest and nipple. A tinted photograph of a 'Young Arab' shows a boy affecting a similarly seductive pose that now seems campily gay. 'The Little Porter' is even more suggestive: a youth sits at the base of a column, his head tilted backward, with an inviting smile and 'bedroom eyes'. His short jellaba falls open to show a nipple, and he rests one hand between his legs. (Alain Fleig remarks that the porter's 'attitude, equivocal at the very least, violates the usual good taste' of the photographer.)[82] This leaves little doubt about the sexual intentions behind the image – and the broader implication of the sexual delights to be had in Arab lands, and perhaps already enjoyed by someone who mailed the postcard.

A final category of erotic photograph of non-Western men current in the colonial era was pictures of muscle-men in physique magazines. Charles Atlas developed a vogue for heavily muscled physical fitness; the models who achieved Herculean proportions and won contests, such as the Mr Universe pageant, featured in a host of magazines which flourished from the 1930s to the 1950s. Hunky semi-naked bodybuilders appealed to many homosexuals, and the (generally brief) texts, emphasising physical prowess, the camaraderie of the gym and the outdoors, and the oiled narcissism of weight-lifters, could hardly avoid homosocial and homoerotic innuendos.

Most physique models were white men, although black men participated in and won bodybuilding championships. However, black men were often marginalised in muscle magazines, and in other exhibitions of male flesh, including movies starring bodybuilders (such as toga films, sagas of ancient gladi-ators and warriors). Indeed, some black bodybuilders were excluded because of race – Serge Nubret, a handsome bodybuilder of African ancestry from the French West Indian territory of Guadeloupe, won a Mr Universe competition in 1960 but, unusually for someone holding the title, never starred in such a film.[83]

Non-European men did occasionally show up in muscle publications. For example, a two-page spread in a book published by Atlas in 1931 featured men from Thailand, China, the Dutch East Indies and India (as well as the United States), each displaying rock-hard biceps and washboard-flat stomach.[84] The Indian pictured was K.V. Iyer, who appeared in various other publications as well. Said to be from Bangalore or Bombay, depending on the publication (perhaps indicative of disregard for geography among publishers of physique magazines), he was described in one, pictured preparing to throw a discus, as 'regarded by Hindu sculptors and painters as an ideal type'.[85] With slicked-back hair, regular features and the requisite powerful muscles – and a leg carefully turned or a fig leaf-like pouch meticulously positioned to hide his genitals – Iyer seems a match for the blond-haired, blue-eyed bodybuilders. Iyer's photos are printed in magazines exalting health and fitness; his photo as discus-thrower appears on a page with short articles on '"Pigeon chest" corrected by physical culture' and 'Appendicitis cured through diet', and advertisements for a trouser-garter designed to hide bow legs and a cure for pyorrhoea. For those wishing for a thrill, bodybuilding snapshots provided a shiver in an age before hard-core porn (particularly of the homosexual variety) became widely available. Photographs of Iyer, and of a Thai, Indonesian and Chinese, whether intentionally or not, also suggested that Asians were not necessarily the weak, passive and effeminate men often portrayed in colonial books or movies.

Von Gloeden and the Arcadian Circle

One of the best-known photographers of explicitly homoerotic works in the late nineteenth and early twentieth centuries was Wilhelm von Gloeden. Born in Germany in 1856, he spent much of his life in Taormina, Sicily, where he died in 1931. Photography turned from a hobby into a profession for Gloeden, and he achieved considerable renown for images of Italian peasants, many printed as postcards and used as magazine illustrations. Gloeden gained fame among homosexuals for thousands of pictures of naked ephebes that combined erotic voyeurism with a romanticised view of the attractiveness of Mediterranean youth and allusions to the pederasty of the classical world. Gloeden, homosexual himself, apparently enjoyed both an active sex life and widespread respect in Sicily.[86]

In the 1890s, Gloeden visited Tunis, and took pictures of local sights; he later seems to have used some North African models in studio photographs, though he preferred Italian scenes and *ragazzi*. Gloeden was interested enough in North Africa, however, once to photograph himself attired as an Arab. Most of his Tunisian scenes were landscapes, such as two figures on a roof-top with a minaret in the background, or three figures wearing harem pants and turbans, posed on a belvedere with elegant tilework and stucco filigree. Other photographs, not unlike the work of Lehnert and Landrock, show the robed figures common in European images of the Maghreb. A portrait of a Berber (looking somewhat sternly at the camera) renders the exoticism of face and costume, but accords the sitter considerable dignity. Pictures of 'Arabs' (a caption applied to Maghrebins and black Africans) lie on the borderline between *scènes et types* and individualised portraits. An elaborate 'Arabic Pasha' shows a handsome young man sitting on a leather chair with a finely worked wooden table and ceramic pitcher at his side; an ornamented curtain reinforces the dramatic tone, though the man's crossed legs give an informal note. An 'Arabic Child' and a Tripolitanian girl – from a region that Italy would conquer in 1911 – provide winsome images of innocent youth.[87] Such views avoid eroticism and differ little from other images guaranteed to intrigue Europeans with foreign costumes and models.

A few images are more sexualised. In 'Achmed' (or 'Asrah'), a model with long eyelashes and pretty face poses with his robe open on a smoothly burnished chest, a romantic photograph of Oriental male beauty. An especially handsome, darker-skinned man poses with bent arm raised to highlight well-muscled biceps and shoulders, and his naked armpit, the oblique turn of his head emphasising his fine features. Another photograph features a swarthy, lean adolescent brandishing a sword, his head covered in a Pharaonic turban.[88] Such photographs would have caused no offence even to sensitive viewers, and no more *risqué* Arabic pictures taken by Gloeden survive. Perhaps his stay in Tunisia was too short, or he lacked the privacy of a studio to take daring photographs. North Africans might have been less willing than Sicilians to pose nude or assume sexually suggestive positions. Gloeden may simply not have been sufficiently taken with North Africans to attempt such *mises-en-scène*. His North African pictures remain more aesthetic than erotic, though a homosexual viewer could hardly be immune to the beauty of several youths, or the possibility, lightly implied, of sexual adventure in Tunisia.

Contemporaries of Gloeden also took sexualised photographs of Africans, though they too generally concentrated on Italian youths reminiscent of classical beauty and the homosexual behaviours condoned in Antiquity. Guglielo Plüschow, for instance, photographed an Ethiopian or Somali youth with a plaid loincloth pulled down to reveal belly and hips (though not genitals); with one hand dramatically raised and his chest thrust out, the model's position looks contrived, but the shot emphasises what nineteenth-century viewers called 'ebony' skin.[89] Another Italian photographer, V. Mattarese, did a picture of a shapely black African with hair close-cropped in 'native' style, sitting on a folding chair, somewhat oddly holding a Japanese fan.[90]

A later photographer who shared an interest in men, though his work is in a decidedly more modernist style that that of Gloeden, was another homosexual German, Herbert List (1903–75). Still-lives, landscapes of Italy and Greece, portraits of celebrities, shots of young men on the Baltic or Mediterranean coast, juxtapositions of classical statues and southern *ragazzi*, and pictures of war-devastated Germany all feature in his work, but there is also an occasional photographic flirtation with lands outside Europe. List, the son of a wealthy coffee merchant, travelled on family business in Central and South America in the 1920s and again visited Latin America and the Caribbean in the 1950s.

Among his photographs from the latter period are attractive Haitian coffee-pickers. In 1934, List had gone to Tunisia, where he visited George Hoyningen-Huene – a Russian *émigré*, and fellow photographer and homosexual. Of the few photographs from his visit to Hammamet are several of Amor, Hoyningen-Huene's houseboy. In one shot, the black man stands naked on the beach, his back to the viewer, and, in another, his torso and face are covered with soap lather. More aesthetic than erotic, the pictures nevertheless pay tribute to the beauty of Amor (a name of suggestive, if coincidental *double entendre*), and the photographer's chance to enjoy his nudity. In 1955, List again went to North Africa, where he unwittingly got caught in a riot in Rabat – and was forced by rioters to take photographs of dead and mutilated corpses – then went on to Tangier to photograph Paul Bowles, already the centre of a cultural and homosexual set in the port city.[91]

The aesthetics of black masculinity: R. Holland Day

Except for anthropological shots, photographs of non-European male nudes were uncommon in the nineteenth and early twentieth centuries. Among the first to pioneer art photographs of nude black men was F. Holland Day (1864–1933). Born in Massachusetts the son of a wealthy leather merchant, he spent part of his life as a publisher, and his firm issued the American edition of Oscar Wilde's 'Salomé'. Day was much interested in the work of the Decadents, and he also met and photographed the homosexual emancipationist Edward Carpenter. While in Britain in the 1890s, Day became involved with the Linked Ring, a group promoting photography (still considered only a craft in some quarters) as art. His works were exhibited in London in 1900 and in Paris the following year. Day produced pictorialist and symbolist works with classical or religious themes, and, from 1896, homoerotic poses of nude or near-naked young men.

According to Estelle Jussim, Day 'never documented his homosexual activities in terms of physical relationships',[92] and Verna Posever Curtis is dubious about reading a too strongly homosexual interpretation into his art.[93] Nevertheless, many details of Day's life point to a homosexual orientation. He befriended Greek, Syrian, Italian and Portuguese immigrant youths in Boston. One handsome protégé and model was Nicola Giancola, one of three Italian boys of whom he was particularly fond.[94] For his young friends and other needy boys, Day organised summer trips to his country house. Another companion was Kahlil Gibran, a young Syrian introduced to Day when the boy was thirteen. With dark skin, big brown eyes and black hair, Gibran immediately attracted Day, who took photographs of him posed either in folkloric Syrian costumes or Western suits. Day, interested in mysticism, Rosicrucian beliefs and theosophy, convinced Gibran to abandon the Christianity in which he had been reared for the Eastern ideas that Gibran turned into a cult classic, *The Prophet*. Day and Gibran stayed in contact for many years, though Day's friends felt that he never showed Day sufficient gratitude for his assistance.

Day travelled to Algeria with a young male friend in 1901, fulfilling a long-held ambition to visit North Africa. Photographs of 'A Sacred Tree', 'A Moorish Archway' and 'An Algerian' record his sojourn, although little else is known about his stay except that he may have hoped to meet André Gide there. On his return, he photographed a 'Youth in North African Costume'. The lily-skinned boy appears in different disguises in other photos, but here his head is bound in a turban and a richly patterned robe leaves his chest bare. Day got himself up in Arab robes to visit the British photographer Frederick Evans, who took photographs of him in the outfit.

Day was much attracted to the exotic, and collected Chinese silks, Japanese lacquer and Persian brass, all accoutrements for photographs – in 'The Vigil', an adolescent wearing a kimono holds a sword over his head, and, in 'The Lacquer Box', a boy in a similarly exotic gown rubs a box, which (Day implies) might reveal ancient secrets or release a genie. Among other models were several East Asians.

Arguably the most interesting of Day's photographs, and the ones in which he introduced artistic images of the black male nude, is his 'Nubian Series'. The model was J. Alexandre Skeete, an aspiring artist, whom Day photographed both nattily attired in suit and hat, and wearing 'native' African garments.[95] In 'An Ethiopian Chief' (1897), Day posed the athletic Skeete holding a staff, wearing a head-band of pigeon wings and a Moorish robe open to the waist. In 'African Chief', he seated the black man on a chair draped with a leopard skin. The model holds a staff or spear in each hand, and wears a metal head-piece and a curious metal belly ornament. In the more informal 'The Smoker', he again sits against a leopard-skin backdrop, with an immaculately white robe thrown over one shoulder but otherwise totally naked (though shadows hide his genitalia), holding a long narrow pipe. 'Ebony and Ivory', one of Day's most accomplished photographs, pictures his black model, viewed in profile, sitting naked on the leopard-skin, holding a blindingly white small statue of a classical Greek athlete. In 'Armageddon', a black warrior is set in a central medallion; a worried sinner sits on the left, a happily sleeping, righteous fellow lies on the right in this representation of the final battle between Good and Evil.[96]

Day's photographs of black men challenged the late nineteenth-century public, and Jussim credits him as one of the first to ennoble black men in photography. With striking light and shadow, and the juxtaposition of Skeete's dark skin and a white robe or a Greek statue, Day's pictures pay homage to the aesthetic beauty of the African American. The black man with the Greek statue implies, rather heretically at the time, that black beauty could be classically beautiful. Day's works do not constitute colonialist images as such. However, it is indicative of contemporary views that Day found it appealing to pose a black American as an African chieftain – play-acting meant to resonate with popular views although with images of a proud and dignified African ruler rather than a degraded, heathen savage. Day's labelling of one work as 'An Ethiopian Chief' (or 'Menelik') was not coincidental. Just a year before the photograph was published, Ethiopian armies dealt an ignominious defeat to the invading troops of an Italian imperialist army. Ethiopia, a largely Christian country said to be the home of the Biblical Queen of Sheba or the legendary Prester John, seemed a model of good and heroic Africa. Yet the choice of an African American rather than an Ethiopian, and the use of robes and head-gear that bear no resemblance to the real ceremonial vestments of Emperor Menelik, reveal a not uncommon vagueness about African culture, and make Day's works an aesthethic appreciation of black men rather than an explicit commentary on imperialism. His sensitive portraits of African Americans (and Asians) never-theless both widened the homoerotic visual repertoire and tapped into the vogue for erotic exoticism current in the *fin de siècle* and *belle époque*.

Homosexuality and Orientalism in music, dance and design

Affinity between European homosexual men and the colonies, or traces of homoerotic Orientalism, can be identified in other areas of culture besides painting and photography, for instance, music. Georges Bizet's *Les Pêcheurs de Perles* (1863) uses the setting of Ceylon for one of opera's most beautiful duets between two men, who sing of their abiding love and affection. Although both the composer and the plot of his opera were heterosexual, the aria has neverthe-less become an iconic musical representation of friendship between men. The song cycle *Schéhérazade* by Maurice Ravel, who probably was homosexual, is replete with images of Oriental seduction. It includes the setting of a poem in which a soprano bemoans that an alluring but effeminate stranger is immune to her charms, a hint that he might not be inclined to heterosexual dalliance. Camille Saint-Saëns was sexually ambivalent, rumoured to enjoy the company of young Algerians on trips to North Africa; in his compositions, 'he showed in the works where he had a choice of subjects a strong attraction towards themes with homosexual connotations'.[97] *Suite algérienne* (1880) evokes the arrival of a visitor in North Africa, the bustle of the French military, Arabic street dancing and a sunset reverie. Another composer drawn to North Africa and Orientalism was Karol Szymanowski (who also wrote an unpublished, and now lost, homo-sexual novel). He found Biskra 'divine'. A visit to Tunisia 'renewed and intensified his interest in exotic cultures':

> It is possible that, like Gide before him, these journeys into exotic lands where forbidden fruit was freely to be had (especially by well-to-do foreigners) enabled him to realise the true direction of his sexual impulses, and that this affected in no small way the blossoming of his creative personality.[98]

Szymanowski composed eleven *Love Songs of Hafiz*, inspired by a fourteenth-century Persian poet who celebrated the love of young men, as well as *Songs of the Infatuated Muezzin*. His opera *King Roger* (1926), set in Sicily, introduced a Dionysian shepherd, come from the Ganges, who troubles the monarch and awakens his unsatisfied longings.[99] The Canadian composer Colin McPhee was a denizen of 1930s Bali, about which he wrote a book, and was much influenced (like his friend Walter Spies) by gamelan music, incorporating Indonesian rhythms into an orchestral piece, *Tabu-Tabuhan* (1936). Although accompanied to the East Indies by his wife (whom he later divorced), he confessed to being in love with a Balinese man; McPhee escaped Bali just as a homosexual witch-hunt erupted.[100] Another homosexual friend of McPhee was Benjamin Britten, similarly influenced by Oriental music, which featured in his ballet, *The Prince of the Pagodas* (1956); 'Orientalism in its sexual mode' also appears in *The Midsummer Night's Dream*.[101] Although Francis Poulenc did not venture to the East, the gamelan music he heard at the Paris Colonial Exhibition in 1931 was reflected in a concerto for two pianos.[102] Meanwhile, North Africa continued to attract homosexual composers, including Paul Bowles and Brion Gysin (and Bowles's friend Ned Rorem, who had an affair with a French medical doctor in North Africa), and they collected traditional North African music.[103]

Homoerotic Orientalism also showed up in dance, as already seen in the case of Hubert Stowitts. Orientalism was indeed a staple for the famous Ballets Russes in the early twentieth century; one ballet, *Le Dieu Bleu*, set in India, counted homosexuals as leading dancer (Vaslav Nijinsky), librettist (Jean Cocteau), composer (Reynaldo Hahn) and producer (Serge Diaghilev). *Cléopâtre*, *Schéhérazade* and *Les Orientales* were among productions with Orientalist themes, and Nijinsky's roles regularly combined the physical attraction of an erotic (and, in his case, bisexual) dancer with exoticism. Nijinsky won fame for a new sort of dancing *élan*, based on a powerful but ambivalent male sexuality, and the Orientalist plots and costumes allowed him to challenge notions of conventional masculinity. Nijinsky's roles included such characters as a black slave and an Eastern god, conventional images of exoticism during the colonial era. Pieces like a 'Danse siamoise' reminded spectators of Eastern sexuality, and the occasional work – such as *Petroushka*, where Petroushka is in love with a woman, but also attracted to a Moor – hint a bit more openly at taboo homosexuality.[104]

Even in interior design, certain homosexuals' mania for Orientalism can be detected. King Ludwig of Bavaria, attracted to Wagnerian music, Gothic grandeur and handsome German officers, fitted out several of his palaces with Oriental rooms.[105] The turn-of-the-century French aesthete Robert de Montesquiou indulged a taste for Oriental collectibles.[106] Marshal Lyautey's château at Thorey had Moroccan and Malagasy rooms with booty from his imperial conquests. Pierre Loti's house in Rochefort was turned into an Oriental palace, including a pretend mosque; his servants sometimes dressed in Turkish outfits, and a factotum called the 'faithful' to prayer at his soirées.[107] Lord Frederick Leighton, friend and portraitist of Richard Burton and traveller in North Africa, created an elaborate 'Arab Hall' in his London mansion, which, like Loti's house, was furnished with tiles, carpets and divans.[108]

Orientalism was fashionable in the late 1800s and early 1900s, a taste not restricted to those with homosexual inclinations, or limited to those with palaces or mansions. Furthermore, by no means were all homosexuals attracted to foreign countries. However, for some, North Africa or South-East Asia beckoned, and there they found licence for expression of their sexual desires, and inspiration for their paintings, photographs, compositions or interior decoration. European imperialism facilitated sojourns, and the images they imported back into Europe reinforced notions of the sexually sublime and scandalous world of tropical jungles and labyrinthine kasbahs.

The homoerotic culture of colonialism

The figures surveyed in this chapter fall into several groups. For a few, the colonies provided a career. The photographers Lehnert and Landrock fall into this category. Spies's and Bonnet's most significant paintings were done in Bali, and McPhee's signature score dates from his Balinese period. A second group is composed of those with more episodic, but still significant, contact with the colonies, often during visits of longer or shorter duration. Stowitts went to India; Gloeden, Saint-Saëns and Szymanowski journeyed to North Africa. In ease case, homoerotic colonial images reappear in their *œuvre*, the Algerian motifs in Saint-Saëns's compositions, the 'Eastern' and Dionysian themes in Szymanowski's opera, the music of xylophones and cymbals in McPhee's *Tabu-Tabuhan*, and Stowitts's portraits of Indian rajahs and artisans. Others travelled to the colonies, but the exotic influences in their works more often came from encounters with colonial men at home – Philpot's picture of a Martinican, Grant's drawing of black men encountered in London, and Day's photographs of Gibran and the African American he dressed up as an Ethiopian emperor. A final group are those who, with little or no direct contact with the colonial world, nevertheless took on board the general Orientalist mode pervading Europe, as seen in productions by the Ballets Russes, paintings by Moreau and Arabic décors in the houses of King Ludwig or Lord Leighton

Several of these men had companions from distant places – Grant's Jamaican lover, Philpot's Tunisian protégé and Day's Syrian friend. Spies was arrested because of amorous liaisons in Bali, and McPhee had a relationship with a Balinese lad. Whether some of the others had sex with African, Asian or Arabic men, in Europe or overseas, will never be known. However, encounters with the colonial world and with men from the colonies had a direct impact. The colonies gave them a refuge, for a holiday or a longer period, away from the climate (literally and figuratively so) of Europe. The colonies fertilised their works with the sounds of the gamelan, the colours of the tropics, the *scènes et types* of the marketplace. Commonly held views – the luxuriance of colonial life, the new and illicit experiences on offer in the hammam, the availability of youthful partners, the sexual proclivities of men from the Maghreb, black Africa or South-East Asia – find reflection in their work. Racial presuppositions appear with regularity in images of ephebes displayed to a voyeuristic gaze, or in a vagueness of time and place in pictures where accoutrements seem interchangeable in order to turn an American into an Ethiopian, or Oriental motifs are borrowed eclectically to add colour to art, music or dance.

These figures form a complement to the heterosexual experience of colonialism and the ways in which it affected European culture. The absence of larger numbers of 'known homosexuals' amongst Orientalist painters shows that even with the broad margin of sexual manœuvre permitted in the colonies, tolerance had limits. Collectors would buy, galleries would hang and art magazines would publish countless pictures of luscious women. There was less of a market for homoerotic images, and more dangers to be faced (as the Indonesian scandal of the 1930s showed) by those whose sexual trespasses became too public. In art, music and dance, just as in literature, colonial homoeroticism expressed itself through suggestion. Initiates picked up on a reference to Ganymede or Antinous, and they saw what they wanted in snapshots of muscle-bound athletes or naughty-looking street-boys, Indonesian peasants in a paradisiacal island, or a barber sensually shaving a client. Perhaps unbeknownst to the creators of these images themselves, the signals they sent out could be felt by a receptive audience, creating a homoerotic artistic tradition of the seduction of the exotic foreigner.

Notes

1   John McKenzie, *Orientalism: History, Theory and the Arts* (Manchester, 1995).
2   Malek Alloula, *The Colonial Harem* (Manchester, 1986).
3   See, e.g., Mrinalini Sinha, *Colonial Masculinity; The 'Manly Englishman' and the 'Effeminate Bengali' in the Nineteenth Century* (Manchester, 1995).
4   See Robert Aldrich, *The Seduction of the Mediterranean: Writing, Art and Homosexual Fantasy* (London, 1993).
5   *Who's Who in France, 1963–1964* (Paris, 1964), p. 2,012.
6   Ragot's works were displayed in an exhibition at the Au Bonheur du Jour gallery, Paris, November 2000–January 2001.
7   Hugh Honour, *The Image of the Black in Western Art*, Vol. IV: *From the American Revolution to World War I*, Part I: *Slaves and Liberators* and Part II: *Black Models and White Myths* (Cambridge, Mass., 1989), Part I, pp. 23–4.
8   Richard Green, 'William Etty', in Jane Turner, *Grove Dictionary of Art*, Vol. 10 (London, 1996), p. 645. See also Dennis Farr, *William Etty* (London, 1958).
9   Reproduced in Honour, p. 25.
10 These examples are taken from Honour's two-volume study, *op. cit.* Mention should also be made of the American Winslow Homer's paintings of West Indians. See Patti Hannaway, *Winslow Homer in the Tropics* (Richmond, 1973).
11 Caroline Haardt de la Baume, *Alexandre Iacovleff* (Paris, 2000). Jonchère's sculpture and the advertising poster are reproduced in Nicholas Bancel, Pascal Blanchard and Armelle Chatelier, *Images et colonies (1880–1962)* (Paris, 1993), pp. 146 and 281, respectively.
12 Helen Weston, 'Girodet's portrait of C. Belley, ex-representative of the colonies: In remembrance of "things sublime"', in Adrian Forty and Susanne Küchler (eds), *The Art of Forgetting* (Oxford, 1999), pp. 75–86. Weston, while acknowledging the 'explicit and graceful sexuality' of the work, advances a contrary interpretation. The painting contains many allegorical details and classical references, and one possible source for representation of the change in status for slaves is classical boundary herms: 'These might also offer a different explanation for the prominent genitals usually regarded as signifying excessive sexual appetites in eighteenth-century stereotypical theories of blacks.' The bust of the Abbé Raynal, a prominent

emancipationist, placed next to Belley, with a decorative egg-and-dart motif, Weston argues, might be an adaptation of a herm (meant to invite worship and give protection to travellers) and generally surrounded with the head of Hermes and with an erect phallus protruding from the stone:

> It is entirely in keeping with Girodet's practice of visual punning and witty but erudite referencing that, instead of an erect phallus on the pedestal beneath Raynal…he should have placed an adaptation of an egg and dart motif to resemble a penis and testicles.

(pp. 85–6)

13 These pictures are reproduced in Lynn Thornton, *Les Orientalistes: Peintres voyageurs* (Paris, 1993), pp. 68, 50, 148.

14 Donald A. Rosenthal, *Orientalism: The Near East in French Painting, 1800–1880* (Rochester, NY), p. 99.

15 Caroline Jordan, caption to illustration, in Roger Benjamin, *Orientalism: Declacroix to Klee* (Sydney, 1997), p. 99. Malek Chebel, *Encylopédie de l'amour en Islam* (Paris, 1998), p. 478, remarks on the way the audience 'savour the lascivious swaying of the ephebe'.

16 Reproduced in C. Beurdeley, *Beau Petit Ami* (Fribourg, 1979), p. 244.

17 Christine Peltre, *Orientalism in Art* (New York, 1997), p. 162.

18 Honour, Part 2, p. 112.

19 Chebel, p. 313.

20 Examples include Horace Vernet's lion hunts, which show bare-chested, handsome men (reproduced in Honour's work) – Auguste-Xavier Leprince did a similar painting of a lion hunt, this one with naked black hunters – and Gérôme's portrayal of the all-male sociability of a Cairo café (reproduced in Peltre).

21 The painting is reproduced, and Gauthier quoted, in Benjamin, pp. 120–1.

22 Not only in Africa did French artists portray sexually ambivalent scenes involving local men. Gauguin's paintings of Polynesia focused on handsome 'native' men (as well as the women for which he is better known), sometimes with a homoerotic gaze. (See Daniel Guérin, 'Gaugin et les jeunes Maoris', *Arcadie*, Vol. 20, No. 230 (February 1973), pp. 57–65.)

23 Boutet, married and the father of several children, specialised in society portraits; see Stéphane-Jacques Addade, *Bernard Boutet de Monvel* (Paris, 2001).

24 Reprduced in Rosenthal, p. 118.

25 Denon is quoted, and the painting reproduced, in [Marie-Anne Dupuy], *Dominique-Vivant Denon: L'Oeil de Napoléon* (Paris, 1999), pp. 26–7.

26 John Singer Sargent, an American artist who spent most of his career in Europe, and who was probably homosexual, visited Morocco and Tunisia in 1879 and 1880. He sketched young men of the Tangier quay, and noted that 'the aspect of the place is striking, the costumes grand and the Arabs often magnificent'. In America, Sargent did homoerotic paintings of black men (John Esten, *John Singer Sargent: The Male Nudes* (New York, 1999), pp. 6, 56–61, 68–71).

27 Denise Brahimi, *La Vie et l'oeuvre de Etienne Dinet* (Paris, 1991), pp. 36–8.

28 François Pouillon, *Les Deux Vies d'Etienne Dinet, peintre en Islam. L'Algérie et l'héritage colonial* (Paris, 1997).

29 Quoted in Brahimi, pp. 36–8.

30 James M. Saslow, *Pictures and Passions: A History of Homosexuality in the Visual Arts* (New York, 1999), p. 189.

31 Michel Larivière, *Homosexuels et bisexuels célèbres: Le Dictionnaire* (Paris, 1997), pp. 254–5.

32 Description panel in exhibition on Moreau and India, Moreau Museum, Paris.

33 Reproduced in Jean Selz, *Gustave Moreau* (Paris, 1978), p. 54.
34 David Wainwright and Catherine Dinn, *Henry Scott Tuke, 1858–1929: Under Canvas* (London, 1989), pp. 100–1 (Ranjitsinhji), 128–94, 134 (Lawrence), 137–41 (West Indies). See also Emmanuel Cooper, *The Life and Work of Henry Scott Tuke* (London, 1987).
35 Frances Spalding, *Duncan Grant: A Biography* (London, 1997), pp. 371–2, 382.
36 Douglas Blair Turnbaugh (ed.), *Private: The Erotic Art of Duncan Grant, 1885–1978* (London, 1989).
37 This section is based on J.G.P. Delaney, *Glyn Philpot: His Life and Art* (Aldershot, 1999); I am grateful to Professor Delaney for answering several questions about Philpot in an email of 26 September 2000.
38 Delaney, pp. 52–3.
39 *Ibid.*, pp. 95–7. Philpot and his sister continued to look after Thomas, trying to find some steady job for him – one plan was to enrol him in the French Foreign Legion. He continued to sit for Philpot through the 1930s, and died of alcohol poisoning around 1957 (*Ibid.*, pp. 148–50).
40 *Ibid.*, pp. 97–8.
41 Caption to illustration C11, *Après-midi tunisien* (1922), in *ibid.*
42 Quoted in *ibid.*, p. 154.
43 The anecdote is from Gwen Friend, *My Brother Donald: A Memoir of Australian Artist Donald Friend* (Sydney, 1994), pp. 58–61, and the quotation from Gavin Wilson, *Escape Artists: Modernists in the Tropics* (Cairns, 1998), p. 19.
44 Quoted in Wilson, p. 64.
45 Quoted in Barry Pearce, *Donald Friend 1915–1989: Retrospective* (Sydney, 1990).
46 Quoted in *ibid.*, p. 146.
47 Donald Friend, *The Cosmic Turtle* (Sanur, 1976), p. 43.
48 Donald Friend, *Bumbooziana* (Melbourne, 1979).
49 Quoted in the *Sydney Morning Herald*, 18 August 1989.
50 See Adrian Vickers, *Bali: A Paradise Created* (Melbourne, 1989).
51 Hans Rhodius and John Darling, *Walter Spies and Balinese Art* (Zutphen, 1980), p. 19; most of my biographical information on Spies comes from this work.
52 Quoted in *ibid.*, pp. 19 and 21.
53 Magnus Hirschfeld, *Men and Women: The World Journey of a Sexologist* (New York, 1935), pp. 120, 115.
54 See Chapter 6.
55 Michael Hitchcock and Lucy Norris, *Bali – The Imaginary Museum: The Photographs of Walter Spies and Beryl de Zoete* (Kuala Lumpur, 1995), p. 29.
56 *Ibid.*, p. 30.
57 Quoted in Hans Rhodius, *Walter Spies (Maler und Musiker auf Bali 1895–1942)* (The Hague, 1964), pp. 278–9.
58 Wim Pijbes, 'The artists of the tropics: The artists of the future', *IIAS* [International Institute for Asian Studies] *Newsletter*, No. 23 (October 2000), p. 37.
59 Quoted in Rhodius, pp. 318, 359.
60 Ruud Spruit, *Kunstenaars op Bali* (Amsterdam, 1996), which contains reproductions of the paintings by Spies, Bonnet and Smit.
61 Anne Holliday, chief curator of the Stowitts Museum, personal communication, 28 August 2000.
62 Renée Renouf, '"The greatest Bohemian of all": Joseph D. Redding', *The Californians*, Vol. 12, No. 3 (no date), pp. 10–22.
63 *Nijinsky Dancing: From the Golden Age of the Ballets Russes* (exhibition catalogue, Stowitts Museum and Library, Pacific Grove, CA, 1996).
64 Anne Holliday, personal communication, 28 August 2000.
65 Quoted in *Alta Vista Gallery*, supplement to the *Monterey County Herald*, 2 March 1997, p. 6.

66 See J. Joseph Dunaway, *Mandalas of the Hidden Wisdom: The Cosmos According to Stowitts* (Pacific Grove, CA, 2000).

67 Biographical information from Anne Holliday, on the Stowitts Museum's website (www.stowitts.org) and her essay, 'Stowitts: His life and art', in Dunaway, pp. 12–45.

68 Quoted by Pratapaditya Pal, 'An American artist in India', www.stowitts.org.

69 Exhibition catalogue, *The Heritage of India* (Carmel-by-the-Sea, 1986).

70 My thanks to Anne Holliday for this quotation.

71 Royal Colonial Institute Amsterdam, 'Vanishing India: One hundred and fifty paintings of Indian types, arts and crafts and portraits of princes by Stowitts' (1931–2 exhibition).

72 Holliday, personal communication.

73 Nicolas Bancel, Pascal Blanchard and Francis Delabarre, *Images d'empire, 1930–1960: Trente Ans de photographies officielles sur l'Afrique française* (Paris, 1997), pp. 21, 67, 123.

74 The photograph is reproduced in Charles-Henri Ravrod, *Etranges Etrangers: Photographie et exotisme, 1850/1910* (Paris, 1989).

75 E. Troubat, *Toutes les races. La Beauté du corps humains* (Paris, 5 booklets, 1931–2); the captions are presumably by Troubat.

76 *Ibid.*

77 These two examples of photographs are taken from Pascal Blanchard, *et al.*, *L'Autre et nous. "Scènes et Types"* (Paris, 1995), pp. 98, 24.

78 For some comments on the eroticisation of the savage, see Edward Lucie-Smith, *Adam: The Male Figure in Art* (London, 1998), 'The noble savage', pp. 94–111.

79 This collection was offered for sale by a Paris gallery, Le Bonheur du Jour, in 2000.

80 See Charles-Henri Favrod and André Rouvinez, *Lehnert & Landrock: Orient, 1904–1930* (Heidelberg, 1998), and Philippe Cardinal, *L'Orient d'un photographe: Lehnert et Landrock* (Paris, 1987).

81 Reproduced in Peter Weiermair,*The Hidden Image: Photographs of the Male Nude in the Nineteenth and Twentieth Centuries* (Cambridge, MA, 1988), p. 73.

82 Alain Fleig, *Rêves de papier: La Photographie Orientaliste, 1860–1914* (Neuchâtel, 1997), p. 35.

83 Richard Dyer, 'The white man's muscles', in Harry Stecopoulos and Michael Uebel (eds), *Race and the Subject of Masculinities* (Durham, NC, 1997), pp. 286–314.

84 Charles Atlas, *Everlasting Health and Strength* (New York, 1931), pp. 36–7. I am grateful to Alan Miller for this and the references in the following note.

85 *Physical Culture*, July 1929, p. 20; see also *The Strong Man*, Vol. 1, No. 2 (July 1931), p. 16.

86 See Aldrich, esp. pp. 143–52.

87 Ulrich Pohlmann, *Wilhelm von Gloeden – Sehnsucht nach Arkadian* (Berlin, 1987), pp. 114 ('In Tunis'), 115 ('Arabischer Pavillon', 'Belevedere'), 117 ('Berber'), 116 ('Arabischer Pascha'), 120 ('Arabisches Kind'), 122 ('Tripolitana'), 118 ('Araber') and 119 ('Junger Araber').

88 *Ibid.*, pp. 110 ('Achmed') and 109 ('Araber'). Several of these photographs also appear in Peter Weiermair, *Wilhelm von Gloeden* (Cologne, 1994), pp. 9, 61 and 78.

89 The photograph is reproduced in Peter Weiermair, *Guglielo Plüschow* (Cologne, 1993), p. 43.

90 Reproduced in Weiermair, *Hidden Image*, p.72.

91 Max Scheler and Matthias Harder (eds), *Herbert List: The Monograph* (New York, 2000), pp. 184–5 (Amor), 274–5 (The Massacre) and 228 (Bowles).

92 Estelle Jussim, *Slave to Beauty: The Eccentric Life and Controversial Career of F. Holland Day, Photographer, Publisher, Aesthete* (Boston, 1981).

93 Verna Posever Curtis, 'Actors and adolescents – The idealised eye of F.H. Day', in Pam Roberts, Edwin Becker, Verna Posever Curtis and Anne E. Havinga, *F. Holland*

Day (Amsterdam, 2000), p. 48. Most of the photographs discussed in this section are reproduced in this book.

94 Pam Roberts, 'Fred Holland Day (1864–1933)', in *ibid.*, p. 26.

95 The model is often, incorrectly, said to be Alfred Tanneyhill, Day's chauffeur and man-servant (Curtis, p. 46).

96 Interpretation of 'Armageddon' from Edwin Becker, 'F. Holland Day and symbolism', in Roberts, p. 61.

97 Brian Rees, *Camille Saint-Saëns*(London, 1999), p. 192.

98 Christopher Palmer, *Szymanowski* (London, 1983), pp. 13, 23.

99 Teresa Chylinska, 'Szymanowski', in Stanley Sadie (ed.), *The New Grove Dictionary of Music and Musicians* (London, 1980), Vol. 18, pp. 501–2.

100 Carol J. Oja, *Colin McPhee: Composer in Two Worlds* (Washington, 1990), and Colin McPhee, *A House in Bali* (Singapore, 2000 [1947]).

101 Philip Brett, 'Eros and Orientalism in Britten's operas', in Philip Brett, Elizabeth Wood and Gary C. Thomas, *Queering the Pitch: The New Gay and Lesbian Musicology* (London, 1994), pp. 235–56.

102 *Ibid.*, p. 239.

103 Michelle Green, *The Dream at the End of the World: Paul Bowles and the Literary Renegades in Tangier* (New York, 1991), pp. 208–11; Ned Rorem, *Knowing When to Stop: A Memoir* (New York, 1994).

104 Tirza True Latimer, 'Balletomania: A sexual disorder?', *GLQ*, Vol. 5, No. 2 (1999), pp. 173–97; Lynn Garafola, *Diaghilev's Ballets Russes* (New York, 1989), and 'Reconfiguring the sexes', in Lynn Garafola and Nancy Van Norman Baer, *The Ballets Russes and Its World* (New Haven, 1999); Richard Buckle, *Nijinsky* (London, 1971); Kevin Kopelson, *The Queer Afterlife of Vaslav Nijinsky* (Stanford, 1997).

105 Michael Peltzet, 'Ludwig and the arts', in Wilfred Blunt, *The Dream King: Ludwig II of Bavaria* (London, 1970).

106 See P. Jullian, *Robert de Montesquiou* (London, 1967).

107 Bruno Vercier, Jean-Pierre Melot and Gaby Scaon, *La Maison de Pierre Loti* (Paris, 1999).

108 Leonée and Richard Ormond, *Lord Leighton* (New Haven, 1975).

6   Scandals and tragedies

Homosexuality was often scandalous, as the trials of Oscar Wilde and others proved. Conviction in Europe – or fear of arrest – propelled many homosexuals to flight. Wilde himself had been advised to escape from Britain rather than face trial; he refused, and was convicted, but left for France after release from prison. The colonies, and other exotic places, beckoned as refuges from criminal prosecution and social persecution, as was the case with another of the great homosexual scandals of the late nineteenth century. The Cleveland Street affair centred on Lord Arthur Somerset, the Eton-educated son of the Duke of Beaufort. Somerset was posted with a regiment in Africa, took part in the shelling of Alexandria in 1882, and then three years later was wounded and decorated for service in the expedition to rescue General Gordon in Khartoum. He became the main figure in the 'Cleveland Street scandal' of 1888, when police learned of a male brothel in London where many of the prostitutes were 'telegraph boys' from the nearby post office, and many of the clients were aristo-crats, including Lord Arthur. ('Prince Eddy', heir to the throne, had also visited the establishment.) The scandal excited public opinion and led to the arrest of the brothel's owner and several 'telegraph boys', but the noble gentlemen escaped. Somerset hurried to the continent when he learned that a warrant for his arrest would be issued, but considered more distant destinations, remarking, 'I want to get either to Russia or ever further East.' In Vienna, he thought of Lake Garda: 'It is between that and Africa or Asia to my mind'; he rejected Cape Town 'as I know a lot of people out there'. Somerset tried Turkey, where he hoped his sexual proclivities would be accommodated, but left when he discovered that treaties between Britain and the Ottoman Empire would allow his extradition. A woman friend suggested that a maharajah acquaintance might help him set up in India, but nothing came of the idea. In the event, Somerset remained in Europe, to die and be buried in France, but far-away lands had loomed as real options.[1]

Colonies were themselves sites of homosexual scandal. One that rocked Britain just before the Cleveland Street affair was the 'Dublin Castle scandal' in Britain's closest colony. The incident took on overtones of English immorality versus Irish morality. The homosexual activities of several British officials in Dublin were revealed in 1884 by William O'Brien and Tim Healy, both Irish

Nationalist members of Parliament and promoters of Home Rule; O'Brien was editor of *United Ireland*, and Healy would become the first Governor-General of the Irish Free State. A District Inspector of the Royal Irish Constabulary in County Cork had told Healy about the homosexual practices of James Ellis French, head of the Criminal Investigation Department at Dublin Castle, seat of the British government. O'Brien published an article saying that the 'life and adventures, and what is known as the "private character" of various Crown Employees in Ireland' ought to be exposed, naming French, who sued him for libel. O'Brien's informants refused to testify, so, through a London solicitor, he hired a private detective, who found evidence of 'a criminal confederacy, which for its extent and atrocity, almost staggered belief', a homosexual fellowship ranging from aristocrats to 'outcasts in the most loathsome dens'. The chief suspect was Gustavus Charles Cornwall, 62-year-old Secretary of the General Post Office and, after forty years of work, a much respected civil servant. Four younger men – one of independent means, two employees in a bank and a shipping company, and an army officer – agreed to give evidence against both Cornwall and Major Martin Kirwan of the Royal Dublin Fusiliers. O'Brien spoke in Parliament of the supposed vice network – he stood accused of hiring 'a scoundrel to go over to Dublin and trump up infamous charges against innocent men' – and in his newspaper, and was subsequently sued for libel by Cornwall and George Bolton, French's superior officer, also named as one of the 'precious trio' of perverts. O'Brien, however, was only fined for contempt for discussing *sub judice* cases in the press.

In the midst of the libel trial, O'Brien's barrister discovered that several of his witnesses hesitated to appear (and the army officer had fled to France), presumably fearing self-incrimination. Feverish efforts finally persuaded them to give testimony. One swore that Cornwall had 'showed great familiarity' with him and engaged in 'very reprehensible conduct', testimony substantiated by other witnesses. The jury found O'Brien not guilty of libel. As Montgomery Hyde says, 'This verdict naturally caused great jubilation in the Irish Nationalist camp.' The joy continued when Bolton also lost his libel action against O'Brien. Cornwall, French, Kirwan and others were arrested. Their trial was held *in camera*, and the court records were destroyed during the Irish Civil War, but apparently they revealed the existence of a male brothel in central Dublin. The jury could not agree on a verdict in the cases of Cornwall, Kirwan and French (though another man was convicted after pleading guilty), and at a retrial they were acquitted on the basis of insufficient evidence. French, who had meanwhile suffered a mental breakdown, was nevertheless tried a third time, convicted and sentenced to two years' imprisonment.[2]

Hyde argues that the scandal, and belief that homosexuality was rampant in official circles in Ireland, did much to discredit the British government of the day. Irish Nationalists, especially conservative Catholics, would have been left with the image of British officials, regarded as imperialist occupiers of their island, as immoral and dissolute perverts, sexually preying on young men in Dublin.

Homosexual scandals, great and small, punctuate imperial history, especially in societies – notably, Britain and its colonies – where homosexual acts were made illegal. Scandal often linked, however, to political considerations, with pursuit of alleged or known sodomites a means to rid countries of men whose political behaviour, or very presence, was awkward or dangerous. Homosexual fraternisation with natives also provided justification for action, as shown by the twentieth-century cases examined here: two British imperial heroes, Sir Hector Macdonald and Sir Roger Casement, supposed homosexual vice networks in British Malaya and the Dutch East Indies, and the example (in fact and his fictional writings) of G.F. Green in Ceylon.[3]

Hector Macdonald – from Scotland to Ceylon

Sir Hector Archibald Macdonald was a paragon of military courage and imperial loyalty, a self-made man who rose to become military commander of a colony, but whose life ended in suicide after accusations of sexual misconduct. Macdonald came from Britain's Celtic periphery, born in 1853, the son of a crofter in Scotland. He worked as an apprentice draper before enlisting in the Gordon Highlanders at the age of seventeen, in 1870. Serving in India, he advanced to the rank of colour-sergeant and took part in the durbar celebrating the proclamation of Queen Victoria as Empress of India in 1876. In the late 1870s, he saw battle on the Afghan frontier, was mentioned in dispatches and received an officer's commission – an unusual step upwards for a 'ranker'. In 1881, the army sent Macdonald to South Africa, where he distinguished himself in the Battle of Majuba Hill.[4]

During subsequent postings in Britain and Ireland, Macdonald secretly contracted a common-law marriage with a 15-year-old Scots girl (whom he saw only four times during the next nineteen years). He again left for Africa in 1884 with the ill-fated expedition to relieve Gordon, after which he was seconded to the Egyptian gendarmerie. Service with the Egyptian army, and command of a Sudanese battalion, followed. Macdonald was awarded a DSO in 1890, and promotions came regularly. He helped conquer the Sudan in 1898, the real hero at Omdurman. With the rank of colonel and appointment as ADC to the queen, Macdonald received the thanks of Parliament and a cash award. Fellow Scots greeted him as conquering hero, though some felt that too much credit for the Sudan victory had been taken by the expedition commander, Lord Kitchener.

In 1900 Macdonald went to South Africa during the Anglo-Boer War, again to serve under Kitchener. A wound kept him from seeing much action, leaving Macdonald frustrated. He nevertheless criticised his commander's strategy and, unpopularly, promoted conscription of soldiers. In 1901, although Kitchener disbanded the Highlanders regiment that Macdonald commanded, he received a knighthood for service in South Africa. Command of the South District army in India followed, but Macdonald had barely taken up the posting when he was transferred to command the British army in Ceylon in 1902.

Only a year later, superiors recalled Macdonald to London on suspicion of sexual misconduct with boys in a train carriage in Ceylon, informing him that he would be court-martialled on his return to the colony. Field-Marshal Lord Roberts informed Macdonald that he could remain in the army only if he cleared his name. Setting out on the journey back to Ceylon, Macdonald stopped in Paris and shot himself in a hotel room.

The exact circumstances of Macdonald's misbehaviour are unknown, and the relevant archival documents have disappeared. According to one report, Macdonald 'tampered with' four boys in a train in Kandy; another account suggested that he exposed himself to seventy school-boys in the train. The governor of Ceylon wrote that 'he is charged with the habitual crime of misbehaviour with several schoolboys'. Macdonald's sexuality had been a source of quiet concern for several years. In 1900, Roberts and Kitchener had repeated rumours that, while guarding British concentration camps in South Africa, Macdonald was alleged to have homosexual relations with a Boer prisoner. Two years later, Kitchener mentioned 'grave suspicions' about his behaviour during his short posting as army commander in Belgaum, India. His marriage, and the existence of a son, remained unknown to officer colleagues.

Macdonald had ruffled feathers in Ceylon when he told the unkempt and undisciplined British militia, formed mostly of planters' sons, to show more spit and polish. The governor, Sir Joseph West Ridgeway, son of an Anglican cleric, did not take to Macdonald, and let it be known that he would prefer a Commander-in-Chief with better 'antecedents'. The British expatriate community disliked the rough-hewn Scottish commander, especially when he declined their social invitations but became friendly with mixed-race Burgher families. He socialised in particular with the De Saram family, headed by a bank employee who had once been charged with larceny; De Saram had two sons. A resident of Ceylon later told Ian MacLeod that:

> Sir Hector had given these boys such tangible items as tokens of his fond-ness for them as bicycles [and] further stated that it was 'well-known' in Ceylon that these two Burgher lads were Sir Hector's 'catamites'....But again all of this is hearsay, without any tangible proof or support.[5]

Macdonald's relationships with fellow officers, especially Kitchener, remained stormy, and Kitchener may have harboured resentment at Macdonald's upstaging him at Omdurman. Kitchener himself was also rumoured to be homosexual and this may have been an issue – fear of expo-sure of his own proclivities. Had Macdonald been more favoured, perhaps alternatives to court-martial would have been found; one clergyman commented: 'I venture to say with all due respect of the nobility, that had he been the son of a duke, an easier way of escape would have been made for him.'[6] Kenneth MacLeod, a defender of Macdonald's reputation, implies that there may have been a plot against him in Colombo and London. Ridgeway telegraphed the Colonial Office, after Macdonald's death, that the editors of an English-language newspaper in Ceylon, *The Native Observer*, whom he characterised as 'both ex-convicts' in the employ of a Scottish association in London, were campaigning for the case to be re-examined. He complained that the paper was 'accusing me of driving Macdonald to suicide by treachery and spite', and wanted to prosecute the editors; the Colonial Office told him not to do so, as London did not wish the case reopened. (Ridgeway left Ceylon soon afterwards.)[7] Indeed, *The Native Observer* had written that Ridgeway's life and conduct had 'demoralised the public service' and dismissed the governor's pronouncements as the 'speech of a Padre's son'. The newspaper wrote of Macdonald that 'the late General, after he came to Ceylon, had interested himself in many a native movement conducing to the advancement and progress of the natives'.[8]

Response to Macdonald's suicide, and the circumstances surrounding it, was mixed. All hailed the hero that he had been, but expressed outrage at what he might have become; some expressed relief that he had acted 'honourably' at the end. *The Ceylon Times*, mouthpiece of British residents, reported his death with sententious words:

> Terrible as is the news published in the world today, it is not so terrible as Sir Hector Macdonald's return to Ceylon would have been....It is better so, for witnesses are spared a greater ordeal than they previously had to face, and the piteous anticlimax of a splendid career is not prolonged.

His defenders argued that not misconduct, but simply being brought under suspicion, had led Macdonald to take his own life. His brother affirmed: 'The thought that anyone could believe him capable of the most abominable charges alleged against him was more than he could bear.'[9] But even if Macdonald had cleared himself of the charges, his reputation would perhaps have been so tarnished that he would forever be disgraced; knowledge of this inevitable fate drove him to suicide.[10] An unofficial commission set up after his death nevertheless seems to have cleared Macdonald of any impropriety.

Authors differ on whether or not Macdonald was homosexual, and no incontrovertible evidence proves that he was so – the Scottish verdict of 'not proven' may be appropriate. Conviction for the offences on which he would have been charged could have led to dismissal, imprisonment and execution. Yet, for one such as Macdonald, the very rumour of homosexuality was enough to drive a man to suicide. Allegations of sexual misbehaviour, particularly in such a manifestation as relations between a senior officer and native youths (or an enemy prisoner), whether true or false, provided a way to discredit a figure who was perhaps not quite of the 'right sort', someone who had rankled superiors and criticised expatriate Englishmen, who had become too intimate with local people and seemed too sympathetic to indigenous movements.

The life and death of Roger Casement

On hearing of Macdonald's suicide, Roger Casement wrote in his diary, 'Pitiably sad. The most distressing case this, surely, of its kind.'[11] Casement did not know that thirteen years later, he would go to the scaffold, an appeal for his conviction for treason rejected largely because of revelations about his homosexuality. In 1903, Casement was investigating mistreatment of workers on rubber plantations in the Congo Free State – Africans press-ganged into back-breaking labour on estates in King Leopold's private colony, tortured, mutilated and killed when they did not produce their quota of rubber, a modern form of slavery that outraged even die-hard imperialists in Britain. Publication the following year of Casement's report on the Congo, and the efforts of an association that he formed with E.D. Morel to combat the brutalities, brought acclaim to Casement and ultimately forced Leopold to transfer control of the Congo to the Belgian state and to undertake reforms in the colony.

Casement was born into a middle-class family in County Dublin in 1864. He was publicly baptised an Anglican, according to the religion of his father, but secretly baptised into his mother's Roman Catholic faith three years later. Both parents died while he was a child, and he was reared by an uncle, a director of the Elder Dempster Shipping Company. In 1881 Casement found employment with the company, first in Liverpool, and then as purser on one of their ships trading in Western Africa. In 1884, he began working for the International Association, organised to explore and develop the resources of the Congo region; ironically, in view of Casement's later denunciation of labour conditions there, the Belgian king headed the association. Casement helped survey the Congo basin, and then directed construction of a railway from Matadi to Stanley Pool. He afterwards accepted appointment with the British Consular service to a post in the Oil Rivers Protectorate (present-day Nigeria). Positions followed as assistant director of Customs at Old Calabar, and consul in Lourenço Marques in Portuguese Mozambique, Luanda in Angola and Boma in the Congo. Consular work was interrupted by the Anglo-Boer War, when Casement was sent to South Africa to take part in a planned but aborted commando raid.

While a consul, Casement looked into labour conditions in the Congo. The British government rewarded him with a knighthood for his exposé. He was then appointed consul in São Paulo, Brazil, in 1905, and soon transferred to Rio de Janeiro. In 1910, Casement again investigated labour exploitation, this time of rubber plantation workers in the Putumayo region of Brazil. (The involvement of a British-registered company, and use of labourers from the British colony of Barbados, justified London's commissioning an inquiry.) What Casement found was, if anything, worse than what he had witnessed in colonial Africa: 'slavery without law'.[12] Casement saw labourers, mostly American Indians, shackled in chains, pre-adolescent children forced to carry thirty or more kilograms of rubber through dense jungle, women stripped naked working on the plantations, workers whose backs and buttocks bore permanent scars from being beaten. He concluded:

This thing we find here is carrion – a pestilence – a crime against humanity, and the man who defends it, is consciously or unconsciously putting himself on the side of the lowest scale of humanity, and propagating a moral disease that religion and conscience and all that is upright in us should uncompromisingly denounce.[13]

Casement's report on the Putumayo, published in 1912, earned applause from humanitarians.

In 1913 Casement retired from the consular service, fatigued by the mental and physical effects of life in tropical Africa and Brazil. Now he took up another cause, Irish nationalism. Always interested in the history and culture of his native land, Casement had gradually converted, through the influence of friends, into a nationalist, and favoured separation of Ireland from Britain. Increasingly he took a more radical position on an issue that divided the British elite, and inflamed passions in Ireland, like no other. In 1914 he journeyed to the United States to promote the cause. After the First World War began, Casement and fellow nationalists saw an opportunity to intensify their efforts, despite the dangers such action entailed. In April 1916, a rebellion at the Post Office in Dublin, the famous 'Easter Rising', was swiftly put down by British troops, but showed the strength of nationalist sentiments and the sensitivity of British authorities, particularly in the midst of war.

Meanwhile in October 1914, Casement had travelled to Germany to enlist support for the Irish cause, behaviour considered as treason. The mission, to recruit Irish prisoners-of-war held in Germany to take part in an insurrection, proved not particularly successful, and Casement imprudently returned to Ireland in a German U-boat. Police quickly captured him in Kerry and took him to the Tower of London. Committed to trial for high treason, Casement's defence provided an eloquent statement of Irish nationalism, denunciation of British imperialism in Ireland and a rejection of the court's right to sit in judgment of him. 'The Government of Ireland by England rests on restraint and not on law; and since it demands no love it can evoke no loyalty,' Casement argued, characterising the Irish struggle for self-government as 'the noblest cause men ever strove for, ever lived for, ever died for.'[14] The court convicted Casement and sentenced him to death by hanging.

Prominent Britons protested the sentence and called for clemency, citing Casement's service to the British government and his humanitarian work. However, prosecutors at the time of the trial, and during the period when pleas for a reprieve were being made, had showed Casement's private diaries, the 'Black Diaries', to King George V, a representative of the Archbishop of Canterbury, MPs and the American ambassador. The diaries recorded, in graphic detail, Casement's prolific homosexual activities in Britain and overseas. The diary of 1910, for instance, covering a trip to Brazil, provided shocking admissions. Casement listed his sexual encounters, recorded the measurements of his partners' penises and noted the amounts of money he paid for their services. Precise anecdotes – such as, concerning a stop in the Portuguese colony of Madeira,

> 18, Thursday… Splendid testemunhos [testicles] – soft as silk & big & full of life…Carlos Augusto Costa – 189 Rua dos Ferreiros, Funchal 7/6 Very fine one – big, long, thick. Wants awfully & likes very much. João – Big £1.12.6. International Hotel. Bella Vista

followed by '29, Friday. Hotel 1.0.0 Carlos Augusto Costa 1.10.0. Total £2.10/-. Last time Carlos. 9 to 11. Huge Extension' – were, to many, almost unbelievable accounts of perversion and vice.[15] Diaries of 1903, 1904, 1910 and 1911 recorded Casement's enjoyment of anal sex, a fetish for well-endowed men, willingness to pay for sex and an ability to pick up partners easily in England, Ireland, Madeira and South America.

The diaries sealed Casement's fate, despite his defenders' suggestions that they had been forged. As Roger Sawyer points out, 'the parties involved in the diary controversy at this time were united in one respect only: all found homosexual activity to be at least as damning as an act of high treason'.[16] The British were determined to execute a traitor – thus warning the public of the price of collusion with the enemy and support for insurrection – while the Irish, embarrassed by revelations of the 'unnatural vice' of one of their best-known sympathisers, put pressure on the British to suppress the diaries. In the circumstances, a successful appeal or commutation of Casement's sentence was unthinkable, and, after being received into the Roman Catholic Church, he was hanged on 3 August 1916.

The British government forbade publication of the *Black Diaries* in 1925, a partial version only appeared in 1959, and not until 1995 did the full diaries become accessible. Several scholars continue to maintain that they were forged in order to discredit Casement. They question the lack of corroborating evidence about Casement's sexuality, wonder why a man with such a large appetite for sexual pleasures was never caught *in flagrante delicto* and express concern that the *Black Diaries* exist only for the years covered by the *White Diaries* (recording his non-sexual activities), which would have provided contextual information needed by a forger. It has been suggested that a homosexual in British employ – Sir Basil Thomson, later arrested for gross indecency – might have been responsible for the forgery. Experts on handwriting and 'word frequency comparisons' differ. Indeed, editors of two versions of the Amazon diaries, published in 1997, come to opposite conclusions about whether the *Black Diaries* are Casement's own work.[17] Reservations, however, do not explain why the government would have gone to such expense and effort to produce them, since Casement was duly convicted for treason, not sexual misconduct. The diaries seem realistic, if unusual in the explicitness of their detail. Whether genuine or not, they played a crucial role in Casement's fate.

Certain writers have been manifestly uncomfortable with Casement's sexual exploits, as were contemporaries. For the Irish nationalist Eamon Duggan, allowed to examine the *Black Diaries* along with Michael Collins in 1921, they 'repeat[ed] ad nauseum details of sex perversion….It was disgusting.'[18] Casement referred to homosexuality as a 'disease' in his diary entry on

Macdonald's death, but probably considered it no worse than illnesses such as diabetes. He sought sexual encounters at every opportunity, finding men on street corners and public squares, having sex in hotels and parks, enjoying swarthy Portuguese in Madeira, an exotic Algerian he met at London's Oxford Circus, fair-haired boys in Belfast, mestizos on board ship. He evoked the physical charms of men he met – 'a young half Indian moço of 18 or 19 – *beautiful face & figure – a perfect dusky Antinous*'[19] – and he described exactly the anal intercourse ('up to the hilt') in which he engaged. The explicit details suggested to some that he was mentally off-balanced, and his barristers considered a plea of treason because of insanity caused by sexual promiscuity and the strains of tropical life. By the lights of the first decades of the twentieth century, Casement's behaviour (and recounting of it) was indescribably scandalous, though his renditions now seem almost quaint, and his appetite not particularly gargantuan.

Casement's sex life did not interfere with his professional work; he apparently never used his consular status to gain sexual favours. In the Congo and Brazil, he remained celibate, taking pleasure from associating with natives, watching Amerindians bathe and attend to their daily chores in a state of undress. He occasionally made foreign friends – he took two Indians to London for a visit, though there is no indication that he had sex with them. Casement's sexual interests may have sensitised him to the plight of plantation-workers, as he took pity on the scarred and starved men reduced to servile labour. 'Perhaps it was his very homosexuality,' suggests the Irish novelist Colm Tóibín, 'and his deep interest in "a certain portion of their anatomy", to quote Eamon Duggan, which made him into the humanitarian he was, made him so appalled.'[20] That Casement found so many sexual partners is evidence of the easy availability of homosexual sex in his time. That he had to hide his sex life (and did so with care) underlines the rigid moral standards he felt obliged to honour publicly, even when he was fearless in denouncing colonial exploitation in Africa and South America, and British overlordship in Ireland. His execution shows the way in which authorities could use accusations of homosexual behaviour for political ends.

From West Africa to South-East Asia

Discretion was the wiser part of sexual relationships, but scandal could and did erupt unless incidents were hushed up by authorities. This was not true just of such *affaires* as those involving Macdonald and Casement. In British Africa, for instance, bachelors or husbands whose wives remained in Europe looked for sexual expedients, with alternatives to women prostitutes: 'Some turned to sleeping with youths as more easy to conceal from suspicious and bored European women's eyes; others did so from inclination.'[21] Europeans travelled, shared quarters and otherwise consorted with African men more openly than with women without raising eyebrows, and by choice or need might find sexual relief from them. One incident is particularly revealing about homosexuality and official attitudes. The episode is related by Stanhope White, a British colonial servant in Nigeria:

> Amongst the old files that I found in Kano was one of some interest in view of the allegations of homosexuality which are levelled at Roger Casement. This file – which my Resident and I destroyed – recorded the trial for sodomy of one of the first European traders to arrive in Kano in the early days of this century. The evidence, recorded in sickening detail, was conclusive; there was no defence but the accused tried to excuse his actions by alleging that such activities were common amongst Government Officers, and were condoned as he well knew from his many years spent in the Oil Rivers [region] before coming to Kano. The Court was unimpressed and he was sentenced to a term of imprisonment; he then asked for the facts of the case to be placed before the acting Governor, Temple, and he elaborated on his allegations. Temple was unmoved by the plea and was indeed highly indignant at the accusations against the members of the Government Service in the neighbouring Territory. Pending his removal to some prison in the south where a European could serve his sentence, the prisoner was confined in the small European hospital – consisting of a couple of rooms only – and the morning after he had been told that Temple refused to intervene, he was found dead alongside a broken poison cupboard. It appears incredible that this possibility had not been foreseen; someone, perhaps the Medical Orderly, had had compassion on his shame. Was there some truth in the allegations? Was sodomy a common failing amongst Europeans in the Oil Rivers Protectorate at the end of the last century?[22]

White does not answer his own questions.

Much in White's account is worth underlining. Though he pronounced himself and the Resident sickened by the accounts of homosexuality, neither denied the defendant's argument that 'such activities were common amongst Government Officers'. A term in gaol – in a prison suitable for European offenders, not one for Africans – seemed the appropriate punishment. However, extraordinarily, authorities allowed the convicted man access to drugs, and White implies that this was intentional. He thus did the 'honourable' thing and took his life, as had Macdonald. White expresses no shock at the outcome. Perhaps the most remarkable aspect of the episode, however, is that he and the Resident blithely destroyed the report concerning the case.

A homosexual scandal in British Malaya in the 1930s was less successfully covered up, although, as almost always, details remain sketchy. The memoirs of a retired colonial official refer to

> the social upheaval of the Thirties when the diary of a professional Chinese catamite fell into the hands of the police, resulting in an official inquiry, the disgrace of several prominent persons, and the suicide of two of those who were implicated in the matter.[23]

No details are recorded in published works, but homosexual practices appear far from unknown in the colony. One informant told the author of a book on the British in Malaya, somewhat off-handedly,

> that in the 1930s two-thirds of European men at some time had homosexual relations with Asians. Others, however, claimed that such relations were not common. It would seem that the intensity with which homosexuality was condemned must have discouraged such relations from being common.

John G. Butcher notes that 'it is unfortunate that because of a lack of information homosexual relations between European men and Asian boys' could not be discussed in detail in his own work, testimony to the success of contemporaries in hiding traces of illicit activities.[24] An author writing about the late 1800s remarks on the great imbalance between the number of European men and women, but the extensive availability of native female prostitutes in Malaya; most colonials, according to his informants, considered gratification of sexual appetites natural by whatever means lay at their disposal. Indeed one cleric, the Reverend W.G. Shellabear, confessed that homosexuality was a lesser sin to adultery and prostitution: 'It seems to me more horrible for wicked men to ruin innocent young girls than that wicked men should ruin each other.' In the late nineteenth century, transmission of venereal disease between men, as between men and women, was not uncommon in Malaya, and 'there was an increase in the incidence of anal syphilis among servants' after the repeal of the Contagious Disease Ordinance in 1888 (which mandated regular medical examination of prostitutes).[25] Such circumstantial evidence suggests that a 'professional Chinese catamite' who allegedly consorted with Europeans, and recorded their names in a diary, might not have been an oddity.

A former official in Malaya, Jim Allen, responding to a historian's request for details about homosexuality in Malaya, has commented:

> As far as homosexuality in the M.C.S. [Malayan Civil Service] is concerned: yes, I agree, people do tend to raise it, and I think there may have been a few contexts – in the post-1945 period – where suspicions of it (e.g., the Chinese thinking that all Malays were homosexual, the Malays thinking that all British were etc.) may actually have flavoured race relations. But by and large I doubt if this was much more or less prevalent than in any colonial situation – or than in many other situations for that matter – and I agree that the incidence of it was probably not of the slightest importance at all.

Allen admitted, however, that two incidents had troubled the colony.

One case in the 1930s involved succession to the sultanate of Selangor. The ruling sultan agreed with the colonial governor, according to Robert Heussler, 'that his eldest son was not suitable, being extravagant, in debt to the government, and generally irresponsible'. The sultan preferred his second son, but the British resident, Theodore Adams, disagreed, judging that 'the youth was even less worthy than his older brother', and promoted the third son. Adams, the son of a clergyman, educated at King's School, Canterbury, and Oxford, had entered colonial service in Malaya when he finished his studies:

> he was already, at thirty-six, a well-known and somewhat awe-inspiring figure. Highly intelligent, hard working, a fanatic cricketer, he was notoriously the most pro-Malay officer of his generation. He was a lifelong bachelor, 'very courteous to ladies in company but seldom willingly seeking this' [in the words of one contemporary].

According to Allen,

> The Heir Apparent had long hair and waggled his hips and Adams, who but for an English Public School might have been much the same (I knew him in old age – and shared his public school!) got very uptight about it and wouldn't have him.

The third son, whom Adams considered a fit candidate for the throne, 'was a clean-limbed KK [Malay College, Kuala Kangsar, an elite school] boy who knew how to hold a knife and call a Resident "Sir"'. He commented that 'Adams' patent pre-occupation with an issue which he would have done well not to underline embittered the controversy a great deal'. Allen added that he was not implying that, if Adams had not been to a British public school, he might have affected long hair and long nails:

> I don't mean that he wasn't [sic] homosexual or that homosexuality is not often a bye-product of the English public school system – far from it – but that the system often (especially before 1945) produced fairly violently suppressed homosexuals, some of whom wrote letters to *The Times* from time to time saying 'Castrate the buggers!' and others of whom, like Adams, got very worked up when they encountered someone who flaunted his homosexuality (as they saw it: as a matter of fact such people were often, especially in Southeast Asia, entirely bi-sexual).

In the event, Adams's stand, says Heussler, led to 'a minor *cause célèbre* that eventually brought in the King, the cabinet, the C.O. [Colonial Office] and [Sir Frank] Swettenham', the former senior British officer in Malaya, who retained considerable influence in colonial policy. The upshot was that Adams's candidate was made heir to the sultanate, the other sons were appropriately satisfied by remuneration and, in order to pacify the ruling sultan, Adams was transferred to northern Nigeria, where he was made Chief Commissioner and given a knighthood.[26]

A postscript on what is presumably the same scandal comes from an old Malaysia hand interviewed by Charles Allen. It led, he said, to a:

> purge on homosexuals...who were ruthlessly banished from the country...provoking a number of scabrous jokes in the process. Ipoh [on the west coast of Malaya] was said to be a centre of homosexual vice where the Volunteers were not prepared to fall in the front rank...and the Blue Funnel Line steamer taking the victims of the purge back to England was said to have entered Penang harbour stern first.[27]

Jim Allen knew little about the second scandal to which he referred:

> There was some incident in – I think – Kelantan after 1945 when the topic was really stirred up, in a way that must have affected the MCS' morale and attitudes to each other and other races. I never learnt the details but there was a police round-up of quite a number of European 'deviant cases' including several civil servants. This must have been shattering in an isolated state and, I would guess, was one more nail in the coffin of MCS' faith in themselves and in the myth of their own cohesiveness and superiority – a myth which really helped them a good deal for a long time.[28]

Allen implied that the primary concern with 'deviance' was that it might compromise the white man's reputation and the solidarity of the colonial service, and any 'outbreaks' ought to be expedited as quickly and quietly as possible.

Allen's views about homosexuality merit consideration, as they constitute a rare and straightforward discussion by a former colonial official. He wrote to an American scholar that he

> entirely agree[s] with you about what happens in tropical countries (and probably not just tropical ones – N. China, Japan etc., as well, no doubt), that is, men who are somewhere on Kinsey's bi-sexual scale go to bed with local men as well as/instead of women, which they would not dream of doing at home, simply because (a) it is more tolerated (b) white women are not available and possibly (c) memsahibs in backwoods district [*sic*] are often such a bloody nuisance. (I know: we still have a few in Lamu [Kenya, where Allen was then working] and they would turn anyone misogynist!).

He did not believe, however, that homosexuality as such provided a motivation for going to the colonies: 'I doubt if the possibilities for homosexuality in the Empire were a reason for more than a tiny minority of colonial civil servants joining the service'; 'on the other hand there is, of course, an undoubted hook-up with race of some sort, though I'm not exactly sure what sort'. Allen did speculate on the links:

Many homosexuals I know would not dream of bedding down with one of their own race. Some (but not all) of them would also have a bit of trouble bedding down with someone of another race but their own intellectual/educational level. This isn't necessarily race domination – many white homosexuals who only like other whites (e.g., E.M. Forster) also have trouble going to bed with their intellectual/social equals. It's certainly not 'white domination' *per se* but I think you'll have to work out a delicate formula showing that colonial homosexuality, if we may call it that, did in many cases have racial overtones of various sorts.

Allen felt that homosexuals held more open-minded views than heterosexual colleagues:

> I would say that the homosexual administrators were more often the liberals on race questions (though often paternalistically inclined). I doubt, from my own experience, if the same could be said of homosexual white businessmen, policemen, PWD [Public Works Department officials], planters etc in colonial contexts.[29]

The statement implies that homosexuals (or bisexuals) were not a rare species in the colonial service. Their proclivities – perhaps exacerbated in tropical postings – might be indulged if sufficiently discreet. Moreover, sexual orientation could inflect the policies they executed, though homosexuality did not breed liberalism in every colonial mind.

Scandal in the Dutch East Indies

If scandals in Malaya were more or less hushed up, one in the Dutch East Indies was not.[30] On 13 October 1936, a small-circulation local newspaper in the Dutch East Indies sensationally reported incidents of homosexuality in several cities in Java and identified homosexual meeting places in the colonial capital, Batavia (now Jakarta); highly placed civil servants were said to be involved in homosexual vice. Although homosexuality itself was not illegal in the Dutch East Indies or in the Netherlands, since the early twentieth century metropolitan and colonial law forbade sexual relations between an adult and a male partner under the age of twenty-one. The maximum sentence for a person convicted of the crime was five years in gaol (a more severe penalty than the four years prescribed by law in the Netherlands). Homosexuality was in the news in the Netherlands following the arrest of the nation's Chief Treasurer, one of the highest-ranking officials, L.A. Ries, for having sex with a minor in May 1936.[31] That scandal now echoed in the East Indies, where the European population was feeling ill at ease because of the Depression, the menace of an expanding Japan and the rise of Indonesian nationalism. A Christian political party (which had contacts with the extreme right in Europe) requested the Governor-General, A.W.L. Tjarda van Starkenborgh

Stachouwer, to order a police investigation and take measures against the 'spreading sin of homosexuality'.

In January 1937, P. Dekker, the Police Commissioner of Batavia, advised that the police were aware of a number of persons thought to be homosexual. (Indeed, the police maintained a list.) He denied that homosexuality was spreading, and commented that the muck-raking of the yellow press was more harmful to the government's prestige than homosexuality. The Resident of Batavia, H. Fievez de Malines van Ginkel, supported the investigator's conclusion, as did the Governor-General. Meanwhile, a question had been asked in the Dutch parliament about pederasty in the East Indies, a member suggesting that several senior civil servants – he named one of the government physicians and a retired Resident – ought to be examined. The Dutch Minister-President (prime minister), Hendryk Colijn, who also held the colonial portfolio, replied that he doubted any fall in standards of morality among officials, but promised to bring the issue to the attention of the Governor-General. Nothing further happened immediately, and, a year later, another Minister of the Colonies repeated the Governor-General's assurances that moral corruption in Java had not spread – any seeming growth was simply due to wider reporting of the activities of a minority.

The Resident of Batavia by now had received letters of concern about possible persecution of homosexuals from several figures prominent in the cause of homosexual emancipation, notably Jonkheer Jacob Schorer, head of the Dutch homosexual movement, and the Scientific-Humanitarian Committee, an affiliate of the worldwide movement started in the 1890s by the German sexologist Magnus Hirschfeld (whose research centre and archives were destroyed by Nazis). The Resident said that the editor of *De Ochtendpost*, which had published the reports of homosexuality in 1936, had agreed to restrain its coverage. However, in early 1938, *De Ochtendpost* and another sensationalistic colonial newspaper, the *Java-Bode*, published new allegations, including charges that three senior officials in Surabaya had been recalled because of homosexual offences. The *Java-Bode* linked the scandal with the activities of Schorer's group (although it had no local branch). Schorer soon sent a letter of protest, but police began observations of one of Schorer's correspondents in the East Indies. He was arrested in November 1938 after he had received men under the age of twenty-one in his hotel room. The police also found an extensive correspondence between 'Van E.' and homosexuals in the Netherlands and throughout the East Indies, letters that showed that a number had indeed engaged in sexual relations with minors. The scandal became public and large-scale. From December 1938 through January 1939, 223 Europeans as well as local *katjangs* (street-boys) were arrested in Batavia, Bandung, Surabaya, Palembang, Medan and Bali. An unknown number took flight, and three men committed suicide after the *Java-Bode* published the names and professions of the suspects.

Among those arrested in Java and on other islands were European doctors, dentists, journalists, businessmen, public servants, soldiers, police inspectors, a school-master, planters, a tailor, artisans and several retired men – a roll-call of colonial society. The most prominent official arrested was Fievez de Malines van Ginkel, the Resident who had earlier stated that there was no reason to be alarmed about homosexual vice. He had cruised for boys in native *kampongs* and taken partners to his country home. The Attorney-General had advised Fievez to resign when he came under suspicion, since he was known to frequent homosexual meeting places; officials agreed that he could then quietly slip away to America. The Police Commissioner admitted that he had not released complete information about some suspects, as he feared the reaction of senior officials if their activities were publicly revealed. He also remarked that his understanding of the law was that only sexual relations between an adult and a *European* under the age of twenty-one were illegal.

The Attorney-General had ordered house searches, and the Governor-General directed that officials suspected of homosexuality were to be dismissed or transferred, although he also cautioned against a full-scale witch-hunt. If their sexual contacts were shown to be illegal, they were dishonourably discharged from the colonial service and declared ineligible for pensions. The possible homosexual activities of future applicants would be investigated before they were posted to the colony. It is unclear how many civil servants were arrested; one was 'Van E.', convicted in 1939 and sentenced to a year in prison, but released after an amnesty; he remained in the East Indies, served as a translator during the Second World War, and returned to the Netherlands in 1946.

The scandal received significant coverage, both in the East Indies and in the Netherlands (though a few quality newspapers discreetly ignored the *affaire*). Journalists speculated on the psychological basis of homosexuality and the influence of native morals on Europeans (or vice versa). Some feared that Dutch prestige would suffer because of revelations of homosexuality (though others said that the arrests, rather than the sex, would lead to loss of prestige). Foreigners like the artist Walter Spies, who was among those arrested, were occasionally accused of promoting opposition to Dutch rule, and editorialists predicted that the Netherlands' international position would be compromised by such vice.

The East Indies scandal victimised colonial homosexuals in a campaign carried out by sensationalistic newspapers intent on besmirching the reputation of the liberal government officials who had first refused to undertake a 'witch-hunt'. Pieter Koenders, who has reconstructed the *affaire*, says that H.C. Zentgraaff, editor of the *Java-Bode*, made no attempt to hide his sympathies for the National Socialist movement, a portrait of whose leader hung in his study. If neither he nor the Attorney-General, Marcella, joined the Dutch Nazi party, Marcella's wife was a member. The Attorney-General also appears to have enjoyed the support of the public prosecutor, De la Parra, who was known to dislike homosexuals and displayed great assiduity in travelling around Java searching for witnesses and suspects. Personal hatred for homosexuals thus combined with archconservative political sentiments and an attack on the principles of liberal democracy.

The scandal in the East Indies affected Indonesians, Dutchmen and foreigners. It animated debates and remained alive in local memory and through the accounts of overseas visitors. Beryl de Zoete, the English photographer friend of Spies, talked about the scandal to André Gide when she encountered him in Egypt in 1938. Leif Rovsing, a Danish tennis champion who had been barred from participating in tournaments because of his homosexuality, had earlier lived for a time in Bali. On a return visit in 1939, he found that most of his friends had disappeared because of the scandal. Rovsing blamed the *affaire* on harassment of homosexuals by petty-minded colonials with a 'diseased soul', who flourished in a gossipy intolerant milieu:

> Those who did not thrive wanted revenge on those who did thrive, at least over the weakest of them. Somebody had to pay for their suffering in this horrible land of tropical islands, in faraway places where loneliness racked the nerves, where longing for home, the hot climate, and the unmerciful sun destroyed body and soul – where spite and malice became the external expression of sickness and suffering.

Many who did thrive were men who 'found in the brown boys what Zeus in his day found in Ganymede'. As the years passed, and more and more men enjoyed these pleasures, 'the quiet stream [of indignation] became a river, and when the forces of the church in Holland, in favour of preserving decency, added themselves to the river in order to save men from a deluge, the dikes of reason broke'. Rovsing, in a rambling commentary, continued: 'Their motto – which instigated the persecution – must have been: Why should anybody feel good, when we suffer? Or was it in order to save the Muslim boys from sin? But for them it was not sin, but pleasure!'[32]

Homosexuals provided scapegoats, in Europe and elsewhere, Rovsing added, just as in other situations people of a different skin colour or creed suffered persecution. Some, like Rovsing himself, had fled Europe:

> Many cultured and talented men had discovered [in the East Indies] the tolerance and freedom which democratic Holland through its church denied. Those who, like the Emperor Hadrian, preferred a beautiful boy to an empress could be found in the undemocratically ruled East Indies. They went there and found a land to live in, honoured and esteemed by the Javanese and the Balinese. These men fell in love, first with the population, then with the country.

Such men, said Rovsing, thanks to close contact with the East Indians, had become intermediaries between the 'natives' and the Dutch colonialists. They proved useful to the authorities, so long as the Governor-General was able to resist moralistic calls for a witch-hunt. But the irresistible pressure on him by 'holy people in Holland' forced the Governor-General to institute an 'inquisition', which, Rovsing hypothesised, dangerously divided the white population

of the colony at a time of great international danger, and also stirred up nationalist sentiment among Indonesians who had made the 'cultured whites'
welcome. Men such as the Resident of Batavia, a Catholic bishop, the chief
consultant at the largest hospital in Java, a district attorney's son, 'all the great
artists living in the East Indies' and journalists were sacrificed to appease the
moralists. Not homosexuality but the reaction against it weakened Dutch rule:

> The sex affair was a great loss of prestige to the Dutch government. The
> [native] population did not understand why their friends had suddenly
> become dangerous criminals; it was an arbitrariness that made many believe
> that the idea was to subject them to Christian morality and the Christian
> faith, which they abhor. The sex affair, which naïve minds probably saw as
> strengthening the Dutch rule over the East Indies, became a disaster that
> took away from Holland its dearest [colonial] ornament.[33]

Rovsing's thesis, that the homosexual inquisition weakened Dutch authority
by destroying the very men who provided the most amicable link between the
Indonesians and the colonials, is intriguing. It demonstrates how the sexual
became political, and how political imperatives led to sexual repression in the
colonial world. It also suggests that, at a different time, the colonial administration had been tolerant of homosexuals, even willingly complicit with them,
including homosexuals who served in its midst.

The scandal involved a surprising number of officials implicated in homosexual activities, often liaisons with native youths or men (but also Dutch
soldiers and sailors who willingly had sex with men for pay). There existed an
identifiable network of homosexual contacts – including meeting places and
correspondence – and colonial homosexuals maintained links with the organised homosexual emancipation movement in Europe. In the colonial context,
and with a government that prided itself on its liberal policies, such goings-on
caused little problem. When they were brought to unwelcome public attention,
the first response was to hush up the incidents, minimise their import or arrange
for those in trouble to depart quietly. Only when right-wing editors and ambitious prosecutors began a campaign against homosexuals, armed with
accusations that the government had failed to act properly and promptly against
illegal activity, did the scandal blow up, and homosexuals paid the price to the
detriment of both Europeans and East Indians.

Scandal, tragedy and literature: the life and work of G.F. Green

Elsewhere in Asia, homosexual scandal and tragedy came together poignantly
in the life and work of G.F. Green. George Frederick Green was born in 1910
near Chesterfield, Derbyshire, third son of the owner of an iron foundry; one
brother became a literary agent, the other ran a tea plantation in Ceylon before
opening a pub in Wiltshire. After studying at Repton in Derbyshire (which he

did not enjoy), Green went to Magdalene College, Cambridge. He was happy at university, making friends with literary and artistic fellow students. Among his closest friends was the actor Sir Michael Redgrave – Green was later godfather to Redgrave's daughter, Vanessa. After obtaining an English degree in 1932, Green briefly tutored the son of the director of the Jonathan Cape publishing house, but lived, according to his sister-in-law, as 'a sort of nomad', staying here and there with various people, meanwhile publishing his first stories in small magazines.

The outbreak of the Second World War brought Green's conscription to the army. An anti-militarist, even pacifist, Green did not become a conscientious objector because of unwillingness to upset his beloved mother. After training in England, he was commissioned as a second lieutenant and posted to Ceylon. In Colombo, attached to the Public Relations Office of the British Commander-in-Chief, Green edited Sinhalese- and Tamil-language periodicals (though he spoke neither language) destined for the native population. During two years of duty, he travelled extensively around the island, coming to love the country and its people, just as had earlier Englishmen such as Edward Carpenter and Hector Macdonald; the colony offered many pleasures, including plentiful alcohol and sexual companionship. Green was easily able to make contacts with handsome young Ceylonese. His sexual behaviour, however, grew increasingly indiscreet, while his drinking became heavier – sexual dalliances and drinking sessions on the porch of his house he referred to as 'verandahism'. In 1944, Green was caught *in flagrante delicto* with a rickshaw-puller, arrested by military police and court-martialled for 'conduct unbecoming an officer'.

Green's behaviour certainly contravened military law, but his superior officers may have been looking out for an incident with which they could 'get' someone who apparently was more open than appropriate in criticism of the army. A military tribunal sentenced Green to prison, part of the sentence to be served in Ceylon, the remainder in Wakefield in York. After his release, Green had a quiet life. He recovered entirely from alcoholism by stopping 'cold turkey'. With an inheritance from an uncle in 1957, he bought a property in Somerset, and lived there for the rest of his life. Chloë Green and A.D. Maclean remember his happy, outgoing personality. He made no attempt to hide his homosexuality, but never had a long-term sexual relationship. In the quiet of the countryside, Green pursued his writing and kept company with neighbours and relatives. He never returned to Sri Lanka, though he sometimes thought of going for a visit; he did go on holiday to Morocco around 1975. Suffering from lung cancer, Green took his own life two years later.

Green's literary production was small, as he was a meticulous craftsman who continually revised his works. His first book, *Land without Heroes*, appeared in 1948; two years later, he edited a collection entitled *First View: Stories of Children* (reissued in 1954 as *Tales of Innocence*). *In the Making: The Story of a Childhood* followed in 1952. His next work, *The Power of Sergeant Streater*, was not published until 1972. Green's other writings were collected with reminiscences by friends as *A Skilled Hand* in 1980.[34] His literary influences included Flaubert, Lawrence and Proust; and Alan Sillitoe, a friend, compared him to Hardy. Though not major commercial successes, his books were well regarded by E.M. Forster, Stephen Spender and Christopher Isherwood.[35]

Green attracted attention for stories about working-class Derbyshire during the Depression. *Land without Heroes* paints a realistic picture of the poor conditions of miners; few can hope to escape their situation, and an undercurrent of loss and violence marks their lives. Significantly, many of the characters are misfits, unable to find love or happiness. However, several of the stories portray 18- or 19-year-old workmen in homoerotic tones, describing bonds of camaraderie and intimacy, and hinting at homosexual relationships.

Green first explicitly tackled homosexuality in *In the Making*. The novel is again set in the English moors, but the hero, Randal, is a dreamy 7-year-old with an overheated imagination who sits in front of the fireplace imagining an Indian prince and his tiger, or fantasising about himself as Ivanhoe. Several years later, at boarding school, he finds a soul mate, and this love, though unreciprocated, will eventually allow him to come to terms with himself – the making of a self-accepting homosexual and a dedicated writer.

The Power of Sergeant Streater and Green's four posthumously published short stories are set in Britain and the colonies. They form perhaps the most searing portrait of homosexuality in a colonial environment in English literature, reflecting the author's own experiences, but are tales that belie the contentment Green ultimately found in his own life.[36] *Streater* comprises three intertwined novellas, the first with the same title as the collection. A story of open and repressed homosexual desires, and of British imperialism and nascent nationalism in Ceylon, it is set in a military police station at Mategala. The main characters are Sergeant Streater, a 24-year-old former carpenter, strong and compact of body, punctiliously neat, an anti-intellectual hearty, emotionally 'up-tight'; Peter Lusaka, a smooth and seductive 23-year-old Eurasian, son of a government agent, a university graduate; Dharmasena (or Dharma), Lusaka's companion, 'as beautiful as an idol' and a student; and Rama, a 17-year-old Sinhalese, a friend of Dharma and a budding nationalist. From its opening the story posits a complex interplay between the political and the sexual. Lusaka and Dharma are sitting on the veranda when Rama arrives and tries to recruit the flirtatious Lusaka into his political movement; when he leaves, Dharma warns Lusaka about Rama's temper. Going for a walk, Lusaka encounters Streater, who hints darkly that Lusaka or Dharma might be implicated in a fire at a flying school. Meanwhile, reports arrive that Rama, hired to ferry soldiers on a reconnaissance mission, may not have tried hard to save them when the boats capsized; Lusaka fears a set-up. The quarrel becomes personal as Lusaka hurls at Streater: 'You've never touched anybody in your life, have you?...The only security you're interested in is your beautiful, pure, clean, stupid body. Why don't you...go to bed with someone for a change.'[37] Streater shoots back, asking Lusaka if he pays Rama for sex; when Lusaka hits him, Streater retorts that he is simply trying to warn Lusaka.

Lusaka soon again encounters Rama, who claims that he is no longer a nationalist; they sleep together, and Rama pledges loyalty to him. When Streater also meets Rama, he appears attracted to the Sinalese; to recruit him to the British side or just to tease him, he confides that he does not believe Rama was the culprit in the drowning of the soldiers, but that he does know who was responsible. Streater gets a fetching Malay, Mahmoud, to write and take a message to Dharma, Rama and Lusaka when the three are next gathered. Rama has cooked dinner, and Dharma is encouraging Lusaka to take him to bed when Mahmoud arrives. When Rama reads the message, he attacks and stabs Dharma – the message says that Dharma had betrayed Rama and implicates the young man in the soldiers' deaths. After the commotion has settled, Streater tells Lusaka that he has arranged for Rama to be acquitted. Lusaka asks Streater to sleep with him, which he does. The following day, Streater tells Lusaka that Rama has been tortured and will be imprisoned for life. Soon Streater reports to a colleague that Lusaka has drowned, though in what circumstances remains unclear.

In the second section of *Streater*, 'The Last of the Snow', set in northern England in 1929, the interplay of race and desire is replaced by a comparable interplay of class and desire. The adolescent David Sheldon, son of a wealthy family, befriends Leonard Williams, a poor miner's son. A few years later, when they meet again, Sheldon develops a crush on Williams. They go to the cinema and a fair, and then enjoy an idyllic excursion to a farmhouse. But Sheldon feels no qualms about returning to the pleasures of a bourgeois circle from which Williams is excluded. When the two eventually go out together again on a skating date, winter is drawing to a close, and skating is dangerous on the thawing ice. Before Sheldon's eyes, Williams falls into the icy water and drowns.

For the third story, 'The Man Who Could Do No Harm', the scene shifts back to Ceylon, where an adult Sheldon is acting Assistant Government Agent in Kalawa. He has made friends with 23-year-old Lakemba, a strong, slim, hirsute Malay with whom he is manifestly obsessed, but who may be a thief. Lakemba remarks that Sheldon, however, will not sleep with him because he is 'too real', and offers to find him another boy. A new police officer arrives in Kalawa: Sergeant Streater, now twenty-six, accompanied by his servant, Mahmoud. As Streater snoops around, Sheldon feels uncomfortable, yet flirts with the muscular officer. The town's residents – especially Vas, owner of the hotel at which all the men congregate – are suspicious of Streater, knowing about his past. Vas tries to keep on Sheldon's good side, praising Lakemba as 'our treasure' and 'beautiful beyond comparison'. Streater, finding Sheldon's manuscript of 'The Last of the Snow', now discovers the government agent's own past. While drinking at the hotel, Sheldon remarks to Streater that his watch has been stolen, speculating that the thief is Perez, the youth whom Lakemba recruited as Sheldon's sexual partner. A few days later, Sheldon and Lakemba drive into the jungle to buy back the watch that Perez had stolen (or was given), and sold to an elderly villager. In a fit of anger, Sheldon refuses to pay the old man; when Lakemba protests, Sheldon throws him from the jeep. Later Lakemba publicly hurls abuse at Sheldon. Vas says he must compensate the old villager and warns him about Lakemba. Sheldon and Streater subsequently find themselves together in a bungalow, when Lakemba arrives and an argument ensues between him and Sheldon: Streater threatens to have Lakemba arrested. Lakemba shouts that Streater is incapable of human contact and marches off; Sheldon follows and calms him.

A few days later, Lakemba is discovered dead after a fall from a cliff. Rumours circulate that Sheldon pushed Lakemba to his death. Streater defends Sheldon, to whom he seems increasingly close, and an acquaintance, a lawyer and gem merchant, De Soyza, promises to sort out the affair if given a free hand. After Lakemba's funeral, Streater confesses to Mahmoud that he had struck Lakemba, who fell over the cliff; he fears that Sheldon will have him arrested. Streater kisses Mahmoud and professes his love. Mahmoud signs an obviously untruthful affidavit affirming that Streater did not strike Lakemba, and De Soyza mean-while has Mahmoud himself arrested for the attack. Streater tells De Soyza that Sheldon drove Lakemba to his death, but De Soyza is persuaded that Lakemba fell accidentally. He promises his good offices to secure Mahmoud's release, provided that Streater goes to live with Sheldon, who does not want Streater to see Mahmoud again. At the end of the novel, Streater's belongings have been shifted to Sheldon's bungalow, and Mahmoud's possessions have been removed from Streater's affairs. Sheldon tells Streater that he can arrange for transfer to another town, presumably so that they can live together. The plot ends, enig-matically, as they walk towards the perilous path from which Lakemba fell.

Streater is a dark and complicated story. Sheldon relives his past obsession for Williams with Streater, though he seems unable to express normal human affec-tions. Streater, having destroyed the lives of three youths in Mategala in fighting his homosexual inclinations, has found a lover in Mahmoud, but Sheldon is willing to destroy Streater's happiness to obtain Streater for himself. The extraordinary psychological cruelty of both men – using sex as weapon and reward – implies the impossibility of Englishmen to work out their sexual prob-lems satisfactorily. Time and again, Streater and Sheldon are told that they are emotionally stunted. By contrast, natives engage in easy and uncomplicated sexual liaisons – Lusaka and Dharma are lovers, yet Lusaka has a fling with Rama, Mahmoud becomes Streater's lover, Perez is available for love or money and other boys can be had at the local hotel. The natives, especially Rama and Lakemba, are godlike: strikingly beautiful, exotically seductive, but also powerful and dangerous. Far from innocent, they use Europeans for political or personal ends, jousting with each other in rivalry. Yet the locals bear the cost of involvement with Europeans: Dharma and Lusaka are killed, Lakemba dies by suicide or murder, Rama and Mahmoud are imprisoned.

The violent and fatal shadows in the picture of sexual adventures on palm-lined beaches and in cinnamon-scented forests return in Green's posthumously published stories. 'Brigade Headquarters' nevertheless holds a promise of contentment. Xan befriends Captain Nick Farley, who has been arrested for stealing money to buy jewels for a mixed-race girlfriend, but he can do nothing to save him. Xan himself takes refuge in the hut of Johnny, a Sinhalese, suggesting that he may have a better chance of finding happiness with a local man. The other stories have a more sombre conclusion.

'The Sad Festivities' illustrates the possibilities for pleasure presented by the tropics, and the dangers involved. Adam Marsh, son of an English barrister, complains that he has not seen the 'real' Sri Lanka, and goes looking for an abused, branded slave boy. The patron of a sleazy bar approaches him:

> Perhaps I should offer you my help. I have something for everyone, girls and boys and women and men capable of every kind of performance. I can show you interesting sights or, if you accept that everything takes place in the mind, I have weeds which I can put at your disposal.

They proceed to an even more louche bar; a pickpocket, Amaradasa, steals Marsh's wallet but is discovered. Marsh decides not to press charges, and offers the boy money ('What do you want me to do?' the boy asks) before learning that he is a prostitute. Marsh looks him up a few days later, takes him to a cheap restaurant, and plies him with more food and brandy than the boy wants. When they return to the boy's lodgings and begin to undress, the boy vomits from overeating. Marsh notices the welts on his back where the boy's pimp has beaten him. The Englishman pushes the boy onto the bed, but Amaradasa tries to reject him, saying that he thought Marsh did not expect sex for the money he gave him. Marsh says he wants to help the boy, but Amaradasa asks Marsh to leave, which he does.

Two other stories of homosexual entanglements end tragically. In 'The Rock Paintings at Annuwariya', Robert Lane, the governor of a prison, declines an opportunity to return to Britain because he wants to remain with his boyfriend, Shariff (a Malay), whom he has taught to read and write, and has set up making batik. They take an excursion to see paintings at the Annuwariya caves, which inspire Shariff's work. Back in the city, Shariff is arrested for not paying his rent and sent to Lane's prison. The youth's landlord offers to drop the charges in return for a job as a warder, a proposition Lane angrily refuses. But he allows Shariff, now suffering from malaria, to escape from gaol; indeed, they head off together in a dhow. Lane reveals that he has changed his mind and will return to Britain; of course, he cannot take Shariff with him. He promises, however, that, if the youth is apprehended, he will only be imprisoned for a short time, and then can make a living from his batik. Shariff, distraught, commits suicide by throwing himself into the sea.

'The Mission' is the most powerful of the Ceylon stories. Roderick, a young Englishman with few prospects at home, is sent by his father to manage a mission school. He enjoys the company of a beautiful university student, Channa, who shares his lodgings. They flirt but go no further – Roderick confesses that at twenty-six he is still a virgin – and Roderick gives the Ceylonese the gold watch he received as a twenty-first birthday present. Meanwhile, Roderick becomes obsessed with his gardener, Ananda (whom he fears, with no evidence, is stealing from him). He watches longingly as the bare-chested youth labours, chats with him and invites him into the house to shower after work. While Channa is away, Roderick toys with asking Ananda to stay. One day, after Ananda has showered, Roderick notices that the gold watch is missing; he rushes into the garden with a cricket stump and violently attacks Ananda, seriously wounding him. Channa returns, wearing the watch. They later discover that Ananda has permanent brain damage. Roderick nevertheless writes to his father saying that all is well and that he has taken into his care a young man who had an 'accident', but reflects privately on Ananda's fate and their wasted lives.

The final story in *A Skilled Hand*, 'A Visitor to Tekaouen', is set in Morocco, but the plot again reveals the difficulties of overseas liaisons. A former platoon officer, James Ashton, holidaying near Tetuan, remembers an incident when he was young and another soldier had touched his shoulder and buttoned his epaulet – 'Could a single moment be all of life?' he asks himself, thinking that this one gesture meant more to him that the 'physical union of two bodies' championed as 'the height of experience'. Now he is travelling in North Africa, and a young Moroccan shows him the sights, and offers for '50 dirhams you do things with me', a proposal Ashton declines. He encounters several others who also proffer their services. When Ashton must leave, one youth who had partic-ularly caught his attention, Rifi, offers to accompany him for part of the way. They climb into the bus: 'He [Rifi] reached up to put the case on the rack. Ashton felt the edge of the shirt touch his face and beyond the pale brown body, warm and alive and secure.' When the bus breaks down, they shake hands and part. Ashton remains in a café, thinking of that instant:

> A sensation of power and of unimaginable beauty and kindness overcame him. He saw the mountains stretching under the blue sky and people with goats and small houses and he heard the voices in broken English and he knew this was part of the aeons of time and space and must last forever and was part of him.[38]

In Green's stories, colonial encounters provide catalysts for sexual self-discovery and resolution of sexual problems (or the failure to do so). His characters are troubled, ill at ease in Britain, and search overseas for new experi-ences, and romantic and sexual gratification. They represent the range of colonial professions, a teacher, bureaucrats, soldiers. They arrive in the baffling colonial world eager but innocent, unsure of themselves but wanting to prove their mettle. Tropical sensations inebriate them, yet crises ensue. Sex provides the arena for combats with their own psyches, and battles with both local men and fellow expatriates. The repressed Sergeant Streater, carrying large chips on his shoulder, and the uncertain David Sheldon, weighted down with guilt for the death of a childhood friend, come 'out of the closet', though with destruc-tive results. Roderick, the mission teacher, can only act on his unaccepted homosexuality first through awkward approaches to a housemate, and then through murderous violence on a servant. Adam Marsh, the barrister's son, descends into the *bas-fonds* of the colonial city to search for sex and affection. Sexual pleasures, however, are transitory. Imprisonment and death destroy Sheldon's and the diabolical Streater's circles of acquaintances. Robert Lane, the prison governor, enjoys a good tour of duty before abandoning his boyfriend to suicide. Scandals and tragedies are the price of dangerous liaisons. Happy endings seldom occur, though Xan might find happiness with his new Sinhalese companion, and Ashton treasures the memory of a magic moment on a Moroccan bus.

The luxuriance of Ceylon (and the no less stimulating landscape of Morocco) provides the environment for what seem to be easy sexual encounters. Gentle students, obedient subalterns, friendly houseboys and rough village beauties propose sexual services; suspect bars and accommodating hotels provide brokerage for sexual meetings. Hindus, Sinhalese, Malays (and Moroccans) parade exotic beauty. A playful and guilt-free native sexuality promises pleasures troubled only by occasional bickering between favourites or sometimes too insistent demands for monetary benefits. Yet Green's portrayal turns bleak, and tragedy generally awaits. The fault, however, lies with the Europeans, not the natives; the British are unable to accept their sexuality, too fearful to take the last step into desired but unknown sexual territory, unwilling to settle into the easy relations on offer, bound up with concerns about defeating nationalists, shouldering the white man's burden, returning home, maintaining respectability. (Even Streater and Sheldon, two blood-brothers abroad, cannot get together satisfactorily.) This, Green implies, is the paradox of colonialism, and his works illustrate the obstacles men face trying to breach gaps between races and social backgrounds, whether at home or overseas.

'The wages of sin'

Green's stories show the dangers inherent in taking advantage of the sexual opportunities provided in the colonies. No matter how congenial the tropics to those with homosexual inclinations, homosexual practices – at least in the British Empire – remained illegal; moral standard-bearers still regarded homosexuality, most generously, as a psychological aberration. Personal rivals, or political leaders seeking to buttress their authority, could use charges of homosexuality to shoot down opponents. Colonial leaders considered it essential to uphold morality, at least in public, or otherwise see their position threatened. Losing the moral high ground against 'heathen' beliefs and immoral practices, and having European civilisation undermined by the renegade behaviour of expatriates, weakened the very foundations of colonialism.

In these circumstances, homosexuals always needed to be wary; indiscretion was the first sin. Superiors might turn a blind eye towards indiscretions, but only so long as they did not become too blatant, and so long as those activities did not directly challenge the authorities' personal and institutional power or menace the colonial project. In the cases discussed in this chapter, and several others explored elsewhere, men transgressed too far, and paid the cost for sins against the colonial order. They were indiscreet – Macdonald may have acted improperly in a whole train carriage of school-boys, Casement recorded assignations in unguarded detail in his diaries. Another diary, in Malaya, compromised homosexuals there. Expatriates in Malaya and the Dutch East Indies perhaps became too confident in flaunting their liaisons, and Green entertained companions in full view of other officers (just as his fictional characters played out their sexual conflicts too openly). In each case, reprisals followed.

The second mistake that ruined careers was to fraternise too closely with the 'natives'. Inter-racial liaisons were common in the colonies, though the unequal relationship of 'coloniser' and 'colonised' often extended to the bedchamber. Yet many of those whom misfortune struck had dared to go beyond acceptable bounds in their private friendships. Green was too chummy with men who visited his veranda. Homosexuals in Indonesia seemed too *indigénophile*, too pronative with their manifest interest in local culture and life. Macdonald consorted too closely with the Ceylonese to please a puritanical governor and an exclusivist settler elite. Casement, honoured for a campaign against labour exploitation in South America and sub-Saharan Africa, might have been considered, in some circles, too sympathetic to the 'native' side.

Finally, these men overstepped the boundaries in their implicit or explicit criticisms of superiors. Green chafed at army discipline, and did not always bite his tongue. Macdonald, the upwardly mobile ranker, rubbed Kitchener the wrong way at Khartoum and in South Africa, and then in Ceylon criticised settlers, disparaged their militia and shunned their company. Casement, most boldly and heinously, condemned British imperialism in Ireland and joined nationalist 'traitors'. In the Netherlands in the 1930s, as the right wing gained influence, an allegation that colonial authorities had gone soft on immorality, sheltering a homosexual community (including bureaucrats who had participated in the damnable practices), served as a wholesale indictment of liberal society and democratic institutions.

Homosexuality, in such cases, did not remain a matter of private life. No longer were homosexual relationships a variant on regular colonial misalliances, nor a question of behaviour that, at other times and places, colonial society might tolerate. Political exigencies (in the broad sense) intervened. Misbehaviour – or, rather, public knowledge of it – provided an excuse to settle quarrels with officers who had come too close to subordination, such as Macdonald or Green, to promote a suitable boy to a sultan's throne, as happened in Malaya, to rid colonies of 'undesirables', as occurred there and in the Dutch East Indies, and to attack Irish nationalism by executing its spokesman.

A political reading of these events must not exaggerate. Neither Green nor Macdonald was a placard-waving critic of the 'establishment', and Macdonald remained a staunch imperialist to the end. Homosexuals in Malaya and the Netherlands East Indies did not form a 'fifth column' intent on sabotaging imperialism. (And the British men in Green's stories, though often troubled misfits whose colonial careers come undone because of sexual contrariness, never disavow the colonial enterprise.) Nevertheless, sexual behaviour had a political side, as was the case, too, with Stanley, Lyautey, Lawrence of Arabia and other colonial figures with homosexual proclivities. Moreover, political considerations, as well as heterosexual outrage, provoked the crackdown on sexual dissidents. The sexual, in Europe and in the colonies, was political, and imperial *raison d'état* sometimes demanded the sacrifice of individual lives.

Notes

1 H. Montgomery Hyde, *The Cleveland Street Scandal* (London, 1976), pp. 28–9, 99, 103, 119–20, 125, 131.
2 H. Montgomery Hyde, *The Love That Dared Not Speak Its Name* (Boston, 1970), pp. 127–57.
3 There were a number of other scandals and tragedies, the most notorious of which involved the killing of a hundred Ugandan youths by forces of the Kabaka of Buganda from 1885 to 1887. Under pressure from Protestant missionaries and converts, they refused to have homosexual relations with the Kabaka and other members of his court. See Ronald Hyam, *Empire and Sexuality* (Manchester, 1990), pp. 186–9.
4 This account is based on John Montgomery, *Toll for the Brave: The Tragedy of Major-General Sir Hector Macdonald K.C.B., D.S.O., A.D.C.* (London, 1963), Trevor Royle, *Death before Dishonour: The True Story of Fighting Mac* (Edinburgh, 1982), and Kenneth I.E. MacLeod, *The Ranker: The Story of Sir Hector Macdonald's Death* (Cortland, NY., 1976) and *A Victim of Fate* (Cortland, NY., 1978).
5 MacLeod, *The Ranker*, p. 37.
6 Quoted in MacLeod, *The Ranker*, p. 4.
7 Quoted in MacLeod, *A Victim of Fate*, p. 23.
8 Quoted in *ibid.*, pp. 10–11.
9 Quoted in MacLeod, *The Ranker*, pp. 18, 7.
10 This is the interpretation of MacLeod, *op. cit.*, who underlines the difficulties the peasant-boy turned commander had with his superiors, British expatriates and the governor of Ceylon.
11 Quoted in Brian Inglis, *Roger Casement* (London, 1973), p. 65.
12 Roger Sawyer (ed.), *Roger Casement's Diaries – 1910: The Black and the White* (London, 1997), p. 159.
13 *Ibid.*, p. 156.
14 Quoted in Inglis, pp. 406–7.
15 Sawyer, p. 63.
16 *Ibid.*, p. 11.
17 Sawyer, *ibid.*, argues that the *Black Diaries* are genuine; his edition contains the whole 1910 *Black Diary* and an abridged transcription of the *White Diary* of 1910. Angus Mitchell (ed.), *The Amazon Journal of Roger Casement* (London, 1997), argues that the *Black Diaries* are not genuine. His book includes the full version of the *White Diaries* (with annotations), but not the *Black Diaries*. The introductions of both books discuss the issue of authenticity. See also the review by Colm Tóibín in *The London Review of Books*, 2 October 1997, pp. 24–7. Peter Singleton-Gates and Maurice Girodias, *The Black Diaries: An Account of Roger Casement's Life and Times with a Collection of His Diaries and Public Writings* (Paris, 1959), includes excerpted materials from the 1903, 1904 and 1911 diaries as well, but Sawyer points out errors in the transcription.
18 Quoted Tóibín, *ibid.*, p. 24.

19 *Ibid.*, p. 114.
20 *Ibid.*, p. 26.
21 Michael Crowder, *West Africa under Colonial Rule* (London, 1968), p. 395.
22 Stanhope White, *Dan Bana: The Memoirs of a Nigerian Official* (London, 1966), pp. 166–7.
23 Victor Purcell, *The Memoirs of a Malayan Official* (London, 1965), p. 250.
24 John G. Butcher, *The British in Malaya, 1880–1941: The Social History of a European Community in Colonial South-East Asia* (Kuala Lumpur, 1979), p. 194.
25 Leonore Manderson, *Sickness and the State: Health and Illness in Colonial Malaya, 1870–1940* (Cambridge, 1996), pp. 166–7, 179.
26 Robert Heussler, *British Rule in Malaya: The Malayan Civil Service and Its Predecessors, 1867–1942* (Westport, CT, 1981), pp. 253 and 294. Jim Allen to Robert Heussler, letters of 16 April 1975 and 18 May 1975, MSS Brit. Emp. 480/8/2, Rhodes House Library, Oxford University. I am grateful to Dr Ronald Hyam for providing me with this reference. Incidentally, Allen, replying to a Heussler question about the 1930s scandal, said, 'I have to admit this is the first I've heard of it.'
27 Charles Allen (ed.), *Tales from the South China Seas: Images of the British in South-East Asia in the Twentieth Century* (London, 1983), p. 134.
28 Allen letters, *op. cit.*
29 Allen letters, *op. cit.*
30 Information on the East Indies scandal has been taken directly from Pieter Koenders, *Tussen christelijk reveil en seksuele revolutie. Bestrijding van de zedeloosheid met de nadruk op repressie van homoseksualiteit* (Amsterdam, 1996), with extra details from Gosse Kerkhof, 'Het Indische Zedenschandaal, een koloniaal incident' (Doctoral thesis, University of Amsterdam, 1982). I am very grateful to Paul Snijders for bringing this case to my attention and for translating and paraphrasing relevant pages in Koenders's book for me.
31 Paul Snijders, 'Ries, Leopold Abraham', in Robert Aldrich and Garry Wotherspoon (eds), *Who's Who in Gay and Lesbian History: From Antiquity to World War II* (London, 2001), pp. 371–2.
32 Wilhelm von Rosen, 'Rovsing, (Ludvig) Leif (Sadi)', in Aldrich and Wotherspoon (eds), *Who's Who in Contemporary Gay and Lesbian History*, pp. 383–4.
33 Leif Rovsing, *I tropesol og måneskin* (Copenhagen, 1959), pp. 169–72. I am very grateful to Wilhelm von Rosen for translating the relevant pages from Danish.
34 G.F. Green, *A Skilled Hand: A Collection of Stories and Writing*, eds. Chloë Green and A.D. Maclean (London, 1980).
35 I am very grateful to Chloë Green (the author's sister-in-law) and A.D. Maclean for discussing Green with me in December 1998 and for commenting on this section.
36 G.F. Green, *The Power of Sergeant Streater* (London, 1972); the stories are collected in *A Skilled Hand*.
37 Green, *Streater*, p. 27
38 Green, *A Skilled Hand*, pp. 217–18

Plate 1 'The Wrestlers' (c. 1840) by William Etty, the foremost painter of Victorian nudes, a rare representation of a black and a white man caught in an embrace.

Source: York City Art Gallery.

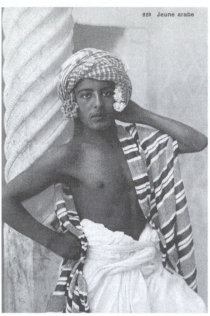
869 Jeune arabe

Plate 2 A postcard produced by Lehnert and Landrock, the premier producer of *scènes et types* postcards and soft-core Orientalist porn.

Plate 3 Another example of Lehnert and Landrock's work, seen as ethnographic by some, as erotic by others.

Plate 4 Early twentieth-century postcard by Lehnert and Landrock; emphasis is placed on the craftmanship of the artisan, but the lighting, pose and handsomeness of the model create an aestheticised erotic image.

Plate 5 Lehnert and Landrock use the *décolleté* jellabah, the suggestive placement of the boy's hand and his inviting smile to imply that porterage is not the only service 'le petit porteur' is willing to provide.
(*All from author's collection.*)

Les Cynghalais de l'Exposition Coloniale de Paris, 1906

Plate 6 A postcard sent from the 1906 Colonial Exhibition in Paris, at which a group of dancers from Sri Lanka performed. The young men embodied European perceptions of the alluring East, and the sender of the card has marked with an 'x' one particularly 'nice' performer.

Source: Collection of the author.

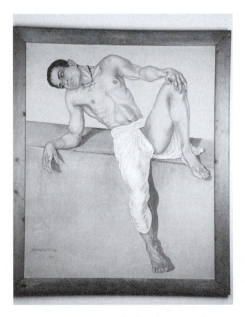

Plate 7 Hubert Jay Stowitts was an American ballet dancer and painter. In the early 1930s he travelled to the East Indies and India, where he did a large number of 'ethnographic' portraits of 'vanishing India'. This one portrays a comely guard.

Source: The Stowitts Museum, Pacific Grove, California.

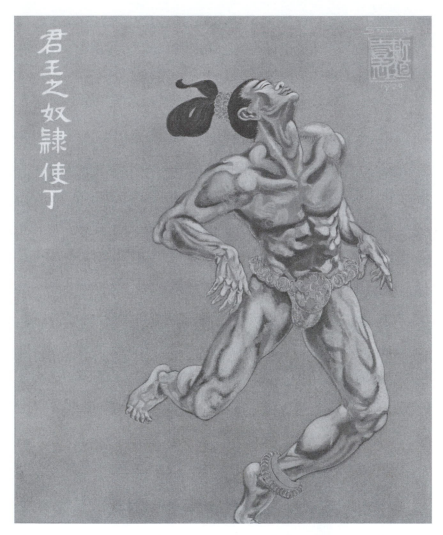

Plate 8   Hubert Jay Stowitts, 'Marathon Runner', an eroticised image of an Asian man, comes from a set of designs for a Chinese-inspired ballet.

Source: The Stowitts Museum, Pacific Grove, California.

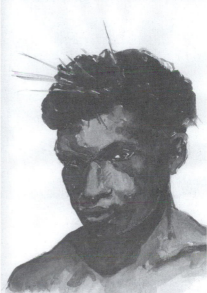

Plates 9 and 10 André Ragot was a French Navy doctor who painted a boy in every port, including Paraclet, an angelic Martinican sailor, and a mischievous New Hebridean the latter is captioned, 'He ate the tax-collector'.

Source: Collection of the author.

Plate 11 A naughty drawing of sex between a European soldier and an African man. In another card in the same series, the positions are reversed

Source: Collection of the author.

Plate 12 Esprit de corps takes on new meaning in this drawing of sex among soldiers at a colonial cantonment, one of a series circulated in Tunisia in the 1950s.

Source: Collection of the author.

Plate 13 James Brooke journeyed east and became the Rajah of Sarawak, a region of Borneo that his family ruled for a hundred years. He had a number of intimate friendships with European men (and a Malay). A nephew inherited his throne, since Brooke produced no children.

Source: National Portrait Gallery, London.

Plate 14 In India, Sir Richard Burton carried out an investigation into male brothels. He also developed a theory about the 'Sotadic zone', where homosexuality supposedly flourished. Many believed Burton engaged in homosexual practice as well as theorising.

Source: National Portrait Gallery, London.

Plate 15 Another iconic figure of British imperialism, Cecil Rhodes was caricatured for his expanionist policies in southern Africa. But certain comments seem to fore-shadow the 'don't ask, don't tell' policy of later years.

Source: National Portrait Gallery, London.

Plate 16 Marshal Hubert Lyautey, who fought in Indochina, governed part of Madagascar, presided over the French protectorate of Morocco and organised the 1931 Paris Colonial Exhibition, was the pre-eminent French colonialist. His writings include enraptured descriptions of both French subalterns and foreign men.

Source: L'Illustration (Paris), special edition on Paris International Colonial Exhibition, 1931.

Plate 17 T. E. Lawrence ('Lawrence of Arabia') wrote about the sexual play of Arab youths and dedicated *The Seven Pillars of Wisdom* to Dahoum, a young man with whom he had fallen in love. He also claimed to have been raped by Turkish soldiers during the First World War.

Source: National Portrait Gallery, London.

Plate 18 E. M. Forster and Syed Ross Masood. The British novelist and the Indian student (at Cambridge) with whom he fell in love. Masood could not physically reciprocate his affections, but the two became almost life-long friends.

Source: King's College, Cambridge.

Plate 19 Alexandria. E. M. Forster met Mohammed el-Adl, a tram conductor, on this line connecting central Alexandria with the beach.

Source: Collection of the author.

Plate 20 Mohammed el-Adl is shown in this studio photograph attired in a Western suit complemented with a Levantine fez and fly-whisk.

Source: Alexandria Collection, King's College, Cambridge.

Plate 21 Captain Moonlite, a late nineteenth-century Australian bush-ranger, an Antipodean Robin Hood, who wrote passionate letters to James Nesbit and wished to be buried alongside him after his execution.

Source: Police Museum, Melbourne.

Plate 22 James Nesbit, the young partner-in-crime and comrade-in-arms of the bush-ranger Captain Moonlite

Source: Australian Sketcher, 22 November, 1879.

Plate 23 Edward Carpenter, a British radical who defended homosexuality, criticised imperialism and promoted socialism, here looking a dapper English gentleman.

Source: National Portrait Gallery, London.

Plate 24 Kalua, the Indian who accompanied Carpenter during part of his travels in the sub-continent, and who is fondly described, and pictured, in Carpenter's travelogue.

Source: Edward Carpenter, *From Adam's Peak to Elephanta: Sketches in Ceylon and India* (London, 1892).

Plate 25 Henry Morton Stanley, and his two bearers, the Palestinian Selim and the African Kalulu, after their trek through 'darkest Africa', here in a studio photograph taken in the Seychelles.

Source: Musée Royal de l'Afrique Centrale, Tervuren, Belgium.

Plate 26 A sketch of one of the heroes of Stanley's novel My *Kalulu*, older, more robust and rather more erotic than the real-life Kalulu.

Source: Henry Morton Stanley, My *Kalulu; Prince, King and Slave: A Story of Central Africa* (London, 1873).

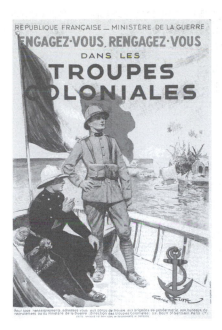

Plate 27 This recruiting poster for the French colonial army shows handsome young officers, upstanding models of European masculinity – the homosociality of military service allied with temptations and pleasures that await in the tropics.

Source: Collection of author.

Plate 28 The homosexual *pied-noir* poet Jean Sénac, who defended the cause of Algerian nationalists against the French, pictured with friends at the Algiers beach after his return to independent Algeria in 1962.

Source: Poésie au Sud: Jean Sénac et la nouvelle poésie algérienne d'expression française (Marseille, 1983).

Part II

Sites of colonial homosexuality

7 Sex in settler societies
The case of Australia

All sorts and conditions of European men – explorers, soldiers, civilians, writers, artists – appreciated the homosexual seduction of the colonies. Some were content to gaze, while others tried transforming fantasy into reality, with either felicitous or tragic results. Few Europeans with homophile tendencies enthused about arctic regions, and a relatively small number were attracted by black Africa. By contrast, Bali – for a time – beckoned as a homosexual Eden. Several other sites served as magnets for homosexual voyagers, while residents of settler societies constructed homosexual cultures in their new homelands. Not surprisingly, homosexuals migrated to colonies where their mother countries had political interests, the Dutch to the East Indies, the British to South Asia, the French to North Africa and Australians, to a lesser extent, to nearby Oceania. This tour of sites of colonial homosexuality begins in the Pacific, with Australia and Melanesia.

Colonisation in its strict sense is the establishment of settler societies, associated initially with overseas expansion from the fifteenth century onwards by the Spanish, Portuguese, French and British in the Americas, and the Dutch in South Africa. One of the most important, and successful, later attempts at colonisation was the European conquest and settlement of Australia after 1788. This chapter examines the evolution of various types of homosexual behaviour (and the reaction to it) in Australia as a case study of homosexuality in a settler society.

For the British, the Australian colonies – federated into a commonwealth in 1901 – provided penitentiaries for the transport and rehabilitation of convicts, and a possibility for free settlers to develop the continent's agricultural, pastoral and mining potential. Grand ambitions meant the brutal dispossession of the country's indigenous inhabitants, and attempts to recreate Britain in the antipodes. The establishment of British law and institutions, commercial and political ties with the mother country, and the sense of belonging to the empire knit together Australia with Canada and New Zealand into a family of Anglo-Celtic nations that still saw Britain as 'home'. Administration might be devolved to responsible governments, but the British monarch continued to reign, and the colonies gave the fruits of their soil and, when necessary, the blood of their soldiers to defend sovereign and country. The practice of British rituals – from afternoon tea and cricket matches to evensong and loyal toasts – reproduced the ceremonies of the old country. Most of the white settlers, at least in the elite, shared the vision of a happy imperial family.

Yet settler societies, no matter how strong their ties to mother England, refused to be clones of Britannia. The 'tyranny of distance', in the famous words of an Australian historian, necessarily distended ties; the exigencies of the frontier created new social and economic conditions. Settlers battling hostile 'natives', carving out homesteads or sheep and cattle stations from the vast outback, developed new ways of living. Convicts, gold-miners, selectors and coastal traders did not always obey, or even believe in, the precepts of the established Church and Victorian respectability. Indigenous populations – despite the racism with which they were treated – maintained different attitudes and behaviours, as did migrants from continental European countries, Asia and the South Pacific islands. New cities emerged, from 'marvellous Melbourne' to bustling Sydney and tropical Brisbane, presenting opportunities for high living and low.

Discussion of homosexuality and colonialism in Australia encounters the problem of when Australia ceased to be colonial. The confederation of different colonies marked neither political independence nor a major change in social structures and morals, and British influence endured for decades afterwards. Indeed, finding an independence day for Australia has provoked historiographical and legal controversy. The Statute of Westminster of 1931, which recognised the equality of all the dominions with Britain in international affairs, is taken as a convenient date, though severance of constitutional links between Australia and Britain was far from complete. However, Australia did not immediately ratify the act, either seeing such action as unnecessary in a still triumphantly imperial age or fearing the dangers of going adrift in the midst of the Great Depression and increasing international conflict. Somewhat ironically ratification came only after a homosexual scandal in the Australian Navy.

At the beginning of the Second World War, the Australian Prime Minister, Robert Menzies, an ardent supporter of Britain and empire, placed the Australian armed forces under British command, which meant that British laws would apply in courts-martial. That occurred when, on the evening of 12 March 1942, a sailor on the *Australia*, Stoker J.J. Riley, was stabbed fourteen times in the stomach, liver and lungs. Before passing out, he told a surgeon that he had been attacked by a fellow sailor, Acting Leading Stoker A.R. Gordon, 'because I found out he was a poufter' – 'poofter' (in the usual spelling) is Australian slang for a homosexual. Gordon and Stoker E.J. Elias, both covered with blood – which they said came from trying to aid Riley – were arrested. The next morning, Riley again identified Gordon and Elias as his assailants. When asked by the ship's second-in-command, 'Did you accuse them of being bugger-boys?,' Riley replied, 'Yes.' Surgeon Lieutenant N. Larkins inquired, 'Have you ever seen them at it?' 'No, but I have certain proof,' Riley replied. 'Did you try and get money from them at any time?,' Larkins continued, to which the answer was 'No.' By evening Riley was dead.

A court-martial was convened with two officers from the *Australia* and two from a New Zealand ship as judges. A Melbourne lawyer represented the accused, and the commander of the *Australia*, Harold Farncomb (later an admiral), prosecuted. Arguments revolved around a motive for the attack, which was implied in Riley's statement that he knew that Gordon and Elias engaged in homosexual acts, which were illegal. He had claimed to have proof, but was now dead. According to Evan Whitton, a legal writer, his statement could not be admitted as evidence because it was only hearsay; a statement by a dying person is exempted from the prohibition on hearsay, but only if that person is aware that he is dying. The surgeon, however, had not told Riley that he was in imminent danger of death when he made the accusation and, on this technicality, the court could not accept his statement. Perhaps to the relief of all concerned, this avoided the need for discussing homosexuality involving Gordon, Elias or Riley – or considering, in more general fashion, sodomy in the Australian Navy. However, circumstantial evidence proved strong enough for Gordon and Elias to be found guilty of murder.

The sentence created a problem. According to the Australian Defence Act of 1903, sailors could be hanged only for mutiny, desertion or treason, but since Australian ships were now formally under British law, the obligatory penalty for the murder, according to an 1866 British act, was execution. The prosecutor pleaded on humanitarian grounds, but in vain, for the capital sentence not to be pronounced. The 24-year-old Gordon, he explained, was an orphan, and Elias, one year younger, had a widowed mother. The two had been at sea for over two years, and 'they were not in possession of their faculties'. The case was turned over to the Australian Attorney-General, E.V. Evatt, who supported Gordon and Elias in an appeal against the death sentence to the High Court. A full bench 'were unanimous in rejecting the possibility that a miscarriage of justice had taken place'. King George VI commuted the sentences to life imprisonment on the advice of the Australian Governor-General. Evatt stated that the problem with sentencing had arisen only because Australia 'has not adopted the Statute of Westminster', and proceeded to push ratification through Parliament, despite concern that the move would appear unfriendly to Britain during wartime. Ratification of the Statute of Westminster duly took place on 29 September 1942, just over six months after Riley's murder, but eleven years after the statute had been proclaimed by Britain.[1]

The Riley case shows an interesting incident of alleged homosexuality on board ship – a liaison between two sailors (or even a triangular affair), the possibility of blackmail, murder, and the desire of officers to muffle discussion of homosexuality in the navy. It also underlines enduring ties between Britain and its settler societies, and the difficulties of finding a simple endpoint to the colonial period in the dominions. It is reasonable, therefore, to examine homosexuality in Australia through the nineteenth century and down to the inter-war years. In the 1920s and 1930s, the traits that marked Australian society as 'conventional, moralistic, respectable' remained little changed from those of the Victorian colonial heyday.[2] Indeed, the years of the Second World

War – with the questioning and flouting of accepted morals that ever-present danger induced, the rambunctious social life of port cities where local soldiers and American GIs on 'rest and recreation' leave sought all manners of pleasure, and the economic and social changes that the war set in train – mark the genesis of a new sort of homosexual sub-culture in metropolitan Australia.[3]

The history of homosexuality in Australia involves attitudes and behaviours of diverse cultures, both indigenous and migrant. Explorers and early visitors noticed, often to their horror, same-sex practices in Australia. Ethnologists and anthropologists now reject the argument that homosexual practices represent a 'white man's disease' unknown to Australian Aboriginals before European arrival. Evidence exists of 'boy-wives' kept by older men in continuing arrangements resembling marriage, as well as casual homosexual practices between adolescents and older men. Masturbation, interfemoral, subincisional and anal intercourse all appeared among indigenous groups. Simulation of same-sex intercourse featured in rituals, and oral literature contains references to homosexual acts. Traditional anthropologists proved taciturn or condemnatory in discussing 'sexual abnormality' or 'perversion' among indigenous people, and missionaries and public authorities in Australia, as elsewhere, attempted to eradicate 'immoral' practices. Many contemporary Aboriginal Australians remain reticent in discussing same-sex practices in traditional societies, and those who consider themselves gay still face double discrimination because of ethnicity and sexual orientation, encouraging reticence.[4]

Convicts and settlers

Europeans in colonial Australia also engaged in homosexual activities. Especially among convicts, homosexual practices became so widespread as to provoke parliamentary questioning, and colonial Sydney was branded the 'Sodom' of the South Seas.

The transported prisoners, soldiers and administrators who disembarked from the First Fleet in Sydney in 1788 left a country where the penalty for sodomy was death, and where civil and religious authorities tried to extirpate the unnameable sin, but where a sodomitical culture flourished in the 'molly-houses' of London. Most early migrants did not come from the aristocratic classes rumoured to engage in the libertine pleasures of Georgian England, but many belonged to milieux – the military and the prison population – where homosexual practices were considered endemic.[5] Perhaps fearing immorality in his new domain, the first governor of New South Wales remarked before leaving Britain that the death penalty should be reserved for only two crimes, murder and sodomy, adding, with a curious mixture of humour, racism and vitriol against sodomites,

> For either of these crimes I would wish to confine the criminal until an opportunity offered of delivering him to the natives of New Zealand, and let them eat him. The dread of this will operate much stronger than the fear of death.[6]

Indeed, the first 'executions' for sodomy had taken place in Australia more than sixty years before Governor Phillip and the British planted their flag in Sydney. In 1727, a Dutch ship bound for the East Indies ran aground off what is now Geraldton in Western Australia. The survivors spent nine months building a boat, but two young sailors were accused and convicted of sodomy, sentenced to death and confined to separate tiny islands, without food or water, there to await their inevitable fate.[7]

Not until publication of Robert Hughes's *The Fatal Shore* in 1987 did historians of convict Australia show interest in sodomy. Hughes suggested that homosexual practices were widespread in New South Wales and the other prison colonies, Van Dieman's Land (Tasmania), Norfolk Island and Moreton Bay (which became Brisbane in Queensland). He explained such activities by absence of European women, promiscuous conditions in gaols, use of force by older and stronger convicts to coerce sexual favours from other prisoners, and the natural inclinations of some men to search for companionship and sexual satisfaction with the same sex. He stressed, however, that sex was often a weapon, with rape and humiliation serving as potential punishment for malefactors, a tool as well in the warders' arsenal used to maintain control and spread terror in the penal colony.[8]

The first recorded court case involving homosexuality in British Australia occurred in 1796, when Francis Wilkinson was charged and acquitted of sodomising a 60-year-old settler called Joseph Pierce. By the 1820s and 1830s, sodomy seemed more common. From 1829 to 1835, twenty-four men were tried for sodomy or sexual assault on men, of whom twelve were convicted. Four were sentenced to hang, but only one was executed. Hughes logically associates increased public attention to sodomy with the campaign in Britain against transportation. Those opposed to sending prisoners to the antipodes argued that the colonies were hotbeds of vice and breeding grounds for depravity. The Benthamite prison would regenerate wrongdoers, while transportation to Australia could only further pervert morals. By the third decade of the nineteenth century, free settlers in Australia were also concerned that continued transport of convicts, and the vice it allegedly created, tarnished the reputation of colonies where honest yeomen were building a new life and where the merino sheep was set to build a booming economy.

The British Parliament, in 1837, convened a Select Committee on transportation chaired by Sir William Molesworth, an avowed opponent to transportation, which took testimony about evil in the Australian colonies. William Ullathorne, the Roman Catholic Vicar-General in Sydney (and, later, a bishop), in particular, alluded to 'crimes that, dare I describe them, would make your blood to freeze, and your hair to rise erect in horror upon the pale flesh'. (Ullathorne had already sent a report to the Sacred Congregation for the Propagation of the Faith in Rome which alleged that two-thirds of prisoners on Norfolk Island engaged in sodomy.) On-the-scene commentators also wrote about the incidence of homosexuality. In *The Exile's Lamentation*, a diatribe against transportation written by a Shropshire man sent to the colonies because of participation in the Captain Swing movement of rural rebels, Thomas Cook described (though without what he termed the 'nauseous details') the life of 'wretched men in depravity'. Unmentionable acts occurred in crowded lodgings, roundly ignored by authorities, and convicts castigated their fellow prisoners who denounced such acts. Stockmen in the bush gave themselves over to reprobate passions. Among all overseers on road gangs, Cook revealed, only two did not engage in sodomy with workmen. From Norfolk Island came further reports of sodomy, though calculations varied widely. One observer counted a single episode in a decade, but another tallied up fifty to sixty episodes a day during a visit in 1832, a total that, for a population of some 600 people, Hughes says, testified to 'an impressive priapic energy on the prisoners' part'. More than a decade later, in 1846, Robert Pringle Stuart remarked that sodomy was still prevalent on the island:

> How can anything else be expected? Here are 800 men immured from 6 o'clock in the evening until sunrise....Atrocities of the most shocking, odious character are there perpetrated, and that unnatural crime is indulged in to excess; the young have no chance of escaping from abuse, and even forcible violation is resorted to.

Similar scenes took place in penal settlements in Van Dieman's Land, where Bishop Francis Russell Nixon warned that sodomy was so common that 'unless sternly arrested in its growth, [it] must not only ensure the moral degradation of the colony, but draw down divine vengeance upon it'. Convicts disappeared into the bush to commit their foul acts or even did so in the chapel itself.[9]

Such accounts must be placed in the context both of the general disapprobation of sodomy held by most observers and the increasingly powerful movement against transportation. The abolitionists, partly because of portrayals of the brutality, misery and vice that infected penal settlements, finally secured cessation of transportation – in 1840 in New South Wales, but in Western Australia not until 1868 – after more than 160,000 prisoners had been shipped to the Australian colonies. Termination of convict migration, however, did not end homosexual activities, as court cases throughout the nineteenth century evidenced.

Crime and punishment

Robert French has calculated that from the start of British colonisation of Australia, 153 men were convicted of 'unnatural offences' in New South Wales (to 1839), 110 in Tasmania (to 1821), 15 in Victoria (to 1925), 42 in Queensland (to 1907), 13 in South Australia (to 1877) and 16 in Western Australia (to 1905); of these, more than twenty were executed for their crimes, at least six in New South Wales and fourteen in Tasmania.[10] The figures correlate between sodomy cases and those colonies – particularly New South Wales and Tasmania – that hosted the greatest number of transported convicts.

Colonial law codes on morals offences and other crimes followed British law, which in the early 1800s prescribed death for sodomy (as well as forfeiture of property by the convicted offender), but demanded proof of anal penetration and seminal emission – difficult and delicate evidence to procure. In 1828, the Peel Amendment modified the law to permit conviction 'complete upon Proof of Penetration only'. (It also ended property confiscation.) In 1861, the Offences Against the Person Act abolished the death penalty for sodomy; henceforth those convicted could be sentenced to gaol for terms ranging from ten years to life. Although penalties were reduced, the law added new crimes of attempted sodomy and indecent assault upon a male person, taken to include kissing and caressing, masturbation and oral sex. These provisions were generally adopted into colonial codes, although not immediately – New South Wales, by the Criminal Law Consolidation Bill of 1883, took twenty-two years to adopt the provisions concerning attempted sodomy and assault despite ten earlier attempts to amend the law. (Homosexuals could also be prosecuted on various other charges, including indecent exposure.)

In New South Wales, 439 cases involving homosexual offences were prosecuted by colonial courts from 1796 to 1901. The first trial resulted in acquittal, and, in the next forty years, only sixteen cases followed. The first offender convicted of sodomy, in 1808, received a death sentence, commuted to life imprisonment. Alexander Browne, in 1828, became the first man in the colony executed for sodomy, although his accomplice was reprieved. A spate of trials occurred during the 1830s, when debate about transportation raged, but arrests then diminished. Another upturn came in the 1860s, when eighteen trials achieved a particularly high conviction rate, half resulting in death sentences. By the end of the nineteenth century, after the change in law allowed arrest for any sort of 'indecent assault' whether in public or private, prosecutors found conviction easier to secure. An average of thirteen cases a year reached the courts from 1885 to the turn of the century: a rise in homosexual prosecutions, while the total number of sex-related crimes in New South Wales declined. According to Walter Fogarty, this accompanied a developing notion of homosexuality, and, by the last decades of the century, colonial society, or at least the judiciary, had constructed homosexual identity as a sexual orientation (rather than simply viewing sodomy as an aberrant act). Only one case of conviction, involving a captain (who was acquitted), concerned a prominent member of society; others convicted came from the 'lower orders'. Despite arguments early in the nineteenth century that scarcity of European women had been responsible for 'situational' homosexuality, the arrival of more women produced no dramatic fall in the incidence of homosexual arrests. Abolition of transportation, judging by court statistics, had manifestly failed, too, in reducing the number of unnatural acts.[11] Homosexual behaviour thus appeared less 'situational' than earlier commentators argued (and hoped).

In Victoria, 356 men were arrested for 'unnatural offences' from 1871 to 1900, an average of one per month. Though the numbers of arrests decreased as the years passed, the rate of conviction rose. In Queensland, with a particularly unbalanced sex ratio in the early nineteenth century – fewer than a quarter of non-Aboriginal inhabitants were women in 1846 – only three court cases involving male-to-male sexual assault have been identified in the 1850s. From 1860 to 1900, however, thirty-eight clearly homosexual offences appeared in court depositions; sentences ranged from ten months with hard labour to twenty years in prison. Eighteen cases were discharged. Half of all cases involved only adults, the others concerning men and youths (generally between thirteen and sixteen). A substantial number involved Asian and Melanesian migrants, a larger proportion of the population in Queensland than in other colonies. In Western Australia, to which twenty-four men had been transported from Britain for the crime of sodomy, twelve men were tried from 1872 to 1905; half were former convicts. Seven had engaged in consensual sex, while five had been incriminated in episodes involving the use of force. Those brought to trial were generally repeat offenders or had been involved in disorderly behaviour. Trials from 1911 to 1915 in Western Australia focused on Muslims in Perth and Filipinos in the pearling town of Broome; one case from the earlier period involved a Chinese and an Indian man.[12]

Though the number of cases is relatively small, making generalisations about regional and chronological variations hazardous, several patterns emerge. Victorian courts seemed somewhat more lenient than those in other colonies, and convictions occurred almost always when force was used or one of the males involved was a minor. In Western Australia, given the high number of emancipists convicted, it appears that the justice system was particularly concerned with controlling former convicts, considered a suspect and dangerous social group. In over twenty years, not one defendant was acquitted of sodomy. Asians and Islanders may well have been over-represented, suggesting particular vigilance against poor, transient and non-European men.[13] The intensity of arrests in the last decades of the nineteenth century could have related to increased awareness of homosexual practices, particularly in New South Wales, where jurists would have been cognisant about the debate in Europe on what was increasingly called 'homosexuality'. Revision of law codes also made it possible for police to arrest men for acts falling short of anal intercourse.[14]

Trial records allow historians to draw a profile of offenders, map a geography of encounters and chart the emergence of a homosexual culture in colonial Australia. A necessary caveat is that trial records concern only men who were caught, often because they committed sexual acts in public or semi-public places, generally with casual partners, or because their advances to other men were unwelcome. A large proportion of cases also concerned sex with legal minors. Those more discreet – or, perhaps, just luckier – escaped detection and prosecution. Their stories are less well known, and court cases are skewed towards men of briefer education, lesser means and lower status, working-class men who socialised in pubs, lodged in boarding-houses and sought recreation in city streets.

Despite scanty details, records reveal the human stories behind arrest and imprisonment. They show a variety of men arrested for homosexuality, and many different situations in which homosexual connections happened. One example provides an illustration. William Williams arrived in Sydney in 1818, sentenced to seven years' transportation after theft of furniture and furnishings from the London house where he worked as caretaker. A cook by profession, he arrived in New South Wales at the age of forty-one and, three years later, received a ticket-of-leave, allowing him to work for a private employer. Soon afterwards, however, he was convicted of an 'unnatural offence' and sent to Newcastle, a prison settlement reserved for transported prisoners who had reoffended in New South Wales. In 1824, he was freed and found work with the Colonial Treasurer, but soon was convicted for stealing rice and meal. By 1828, again released, Williams proved upwardly mobile, as he was Head Cook at Government House in Sydney. The 51-year-old chef was then arrested, along with a 29-year-old sentry, for 'Indecently and Unnaturally exposing their persons to each other in or by a Privy'. A gift of beer had enticed the sentry, who confessed that Williams had asked him 'to take hold of his thing'. Insufficient evidence caused the charge to be dropped, but Williams made another appearance in court only fourteen months later. He and an Indian sailor, out from Bombay, were convicted of sodomy. Policemen had spied Williams and John Solomon striking up a conversation in a pub and followed them to a paddock, where Solomon sodomised Williams. The judge imposed the death sentence, but both men were reprieved for transport to Van Dieman's Land, Solomon sent straight away and Williams first kept in a Sydney gaol for two years. Williams died at Port Arthur in 1846.[15]

Such extensive details are available on few other cases, but even sketchy indications confirm the diversity of homosexual practices and liaisons. In Western Australia, for example, in 1898, a 13-year-old boy was raped by two 20-year-old brothers with whom he worked in a vinegar factory, even though he tried to resist their sexual advances. The victim suffered considerable physical and psychological pain, while the perpetrators, as in many rape cases, seemed interested in exercising power and violence more than gaining sexual satisfaction. (The brothers were sentenced to seven and ten years in prison.) By contrast, three years earlier, an adult arrested for homosexual practice told police, 'I can't help it, it's a disease. I prefer a man or a boy any time to a woman.'[16] Of the three Queensland cases in the 1850s, one involved a quarreyman who claimed that his bedmate tried to violate him after a night's drinking. Another took place on a ship moored in the port of Gladstone. Witnesses testified to oral and anal intercourse between a European and two Aboriginals, who agreed to sex in return for promises of blankets and money. The third occurred in the Brisbane gaol, when a group of men assaulted a 16-year-old boy.[17] Assault, 'congenital' homosexuality and a kind of barter or prostitution all appear among sexual arrangements.

The court cases call for some reflection. Despite the horrific nature of potential punishments, the total number of men convicted was not remarkably large, nor was the severity of punishments actually meted out particularly harsh. Although the death penalty remained permissible for sodomy during much of the nineteenth century, only several dozen men were executed for the crime in all of Australia. In Queensland, Clive Moore remarks that 'most sentences were well below the possible maximum'. All-male juries were not so horrified by homosexuality as might be expected.[18] Adam Carr judges Victorian courts lenient. This may represent idiosyncratic responses by different courts, or regional variations, especially since courts in New South Wales and Western Australia – where the convict heritage was more marked and, in the case of New South Wales, with a much larger population – were more aggressive in sentencing sodomites. In Tasmania, with a particularly weighty convict legacy, at least fourteen men were executed (compared to twenty-odd in far more populous New South Wales), which confirms perceived links between prosecution, penal settlements and transportation.[19]

By the late nineteenth century, the incidence of indictment shows the new arsenal of laws that made it easier for colonial authorities to prosecute homosexual acts, whether consensual or not, in public or private, involving anal or oral intercourse or masturbation, but also kissing, caressing or 'touching up'. Legislators, police officers and judges clearly intended to establish a moralistic society after decades of convictism and somewhat lax morals, and they used judicial weapons to enforce heterosexuality.

Evidence exists of specific attempts to discover and harass sodomites, even in 'victimless' crimes. Police officers testified to watching suspicious men drinking in pubs, and then carefully following them to their assignations. Constables kept an eye on men who had once been arrested or convicted to see if they might reoffend. Officers identified notorious beats and patrolled them assiduously. Later cases in Australia attest to police entrapment, which may also have occurred in the nineteenth century. Trial records give explicit details of homosexual activities, as was necessary for conviction, especially when penetration had to be proven, but there is an almost voyeuristic fascination with what men did, mixed with embarrassment at recounting the specifics. Some policemen watched what was going on perhaps a bit longer than necessary, and carried out their duties with particular vigilance, for instance, by thrusting their hands into the private parts of men to see if 'connection' had occurred.

The cases suggest rather unromantic sexual arrangements between men. Danger, fear of being apprehended and a need to 'do the deed' as quickly as possible afforded little time for foreplay. Kissing and caressing appear less often in court records than genital sex, and anal intercourse figures largely in accounts. Even in incidents of boarding-house sex, fornication was often consummated with a minimum of fuss and bother. (In a few trials, however, men were clearly regular partners sharing a great measure of affection – they appear, in short, to have been in love.)[20] Some level of violence appears frequently, though it must be remembered that a defence of lack of consent or unwilling participation in sex provided one of the few mitigating circumstances for which judges might reduce sentences. A number of men, conveniently or not, claimed that they were asleep or dead drunk when they were 'tampered with' by other men. Rape, evidenced by recollections of physical pain, appears not infrequently, especially for younger men.

The age difference between many partners brought to trial is also remarkable. This points, however, to two specific considerations about nineteenth-century colonial life. Disparities in age were not unusual between sexual partners; heterosexual men often married much younger women. Moreover, in a society where very few youths finished school but where most worked from a young age, what would now be called teenagers were probably socially mature and not unacquainted with the 'ways of the world'. Crowded housing in cities, and familiarity with the breeding of farm animals in the bush, brought young men to sexual awareness, and gave them sexual experience, at an early age. Cases of child abuse did exist, and were viewed with disapprobation. However, the social context of sexual encounters, whether heterosexual or homosexual, promoted early, quick and often clandestine encounters for all who lived outside the bonds of holy wedlock.

The majority of men arrested for homosexual behaviour in early and mid-nineteenth-century Australia were ordinary blokes, common men, many of whom – convicts, emancipists, labourers and sailors, Aboriginals and Asians – lived on the fringes of respectable society. Men of higher social standing were nevertheless occasionally arrested, such as a pastor convicted for homosexual relations, 'to the great scandal of all humankind and against the peace of our Lady the Queen her Crown and Dignity', with a pupil in an Adelaide school in 1854.[21] When a respected man, a pillar of society, a standard bearer for British civilisation, became involved in a homosexual offence, however, the ranks could close and the affair would be hushed up, the offender hustled off into obscurity. The example of William Yate proves the point.

Colonial scandal: the Yate affair

Conversion of 'benighted heathens' formed one of the major imperatives of imperialism, and few organisations proved so active in the campaign as the Church Missionary Society. From headquarters in London, it despatched missionaries around the world, seeing the Pacific Islands – the preserve of naked savages given to lewd and lascivious conduct, but possessing a child-like innocence – as a particularly necessitous realm. Samuel Marsden, a leading Church of England cleric in the Australian colonies in the early 1800s, promoted evangelisation of Aborigines, with little success, but had great expectations for mission stations in New Zealand. Yet the first head of the Church Missionary Society outpost in New Zealand was dismissed by Marsden for adultery, the second for drunkenness. He thus vested high hopes in the Reverend William Yate, who arrived in the Bay of Islands in 1828. Yate threw himself into his work, taking consummate interest in the Maoris, learning their language and translating scripture, catechisms and hymns, and lugging a printing press to New Zealand after a visit to Sydney in 1830 so that he could distribute his translations. He also travelled to Tonga in the course of his work, collecting botanical specimens and becoming a scholar of Maori culture and Pacific science. In 1834, Yate returned to Britain to oversee publication of his *An*

Account of New Zealand; the public greeted the work with enthusiasm, and King William IV received Yate at Brighton. In 1836, Yate left Britain, in the company of his sister, and headed back to New Zealand. Stopping in Sydney, however, he agreed to take up a post at the fashionable St James' Church, where his sermons soon attracted a large congregation.[22]

Within a short time, Bishop William Broughton told Yate of reports about his immoral conduct on board the *Prince Regent* during the journey to Sydney; Yate denied the accusations, but the bishop suspended him from clerical duties. Yate demanded an inquiry to clear his name, and there was talk of setting up a consistorial court. Though some circumstances of the affair remain unclear, the court was never convened and, after a number of delays, Yate returned to Britain in late 1836, accompanied by his sister and a friend, Edwin Denison, still publicly protesting his innocence. The Church Missionary Society refused to reopen the case, but Yate's reputation had been tarnished. When a workhouse offered him a chaplaincy in 1843, the Bishop of London refused to approve the appointment. Three years later, Yate finally found a parish, a mariners' church in Dover, where he lived in apparently happy obscurity until his death at an advanced age.

The accusations that brought about Yate's fall were that he had engaged in immoral behaviour with the third mate of the *Prince Regent*, none other than Edwin Denison, and had misbehaved with other young sailors, including one bearing the remarkable name of Dick Deck. Hand-clasping, tickling and sharing of hammocks were said to have taken place. Yate had moved into lodgings with Denison when he landed in Sydney, and neighbours had complained about their behaviour. Deck had also been a visitor, joining Yate and Denison in bed but, as Deck later said, 'There had been so much tickling that I was obliged to get out of bed and sleep on a sofa in the next room in order to obtain any rest.'[23] Yate had corresponded with Denison and indeed showed his letters to the bishop, hoping that they would prove his innocence; ironically, they confirmed questions about his relationship. The letters testified to close affection – 'My dear Father,' wrote Denison, 'Once more I indulge myself with a few moments of melancholy pleasure, imagining myself sitting by your side whilst lying on the sofa preparing your Manuscript before the afternoon service.' A poem Yate had written to Denison was, in Judith Binney's phrase, 'couched in language of erotic piety' not uncommon to Evangelicals but with suggestive metaphors. The narrator imagined the consolation of a Christian death and afterlife, 'A bed where you and I shall sleep / Locked in the arms of mutual love / Nor aught shall e'er our slumbers break / Till waked by thunders from above'.[24]

The Sydney bishop and the New South Wales Crown Prosecutor also learned more about Yate's activities in New Zealand through the British Resident in the Bay of Islands, who took depositions from several converted Maoris and reported other rumours. Yate, they said, had engaged in mutual masturbation and oral sex with as many as one hundred Polynesian men in New Zealand and Tonga. According to Samuel Kohi,

He said to me, Pull off your clothes. I said to him, For what purpose? He said to me, That we may copulate. I replied, I do not understand what you are going to do. He said to me, All Europeans act thus while they are single men. Then because they sleep with their wives this practice is left off. But as for me my wife is this, a hand.

Kohi added that on another occasion, after divine service, Yate said,

Let us go (you and I) to my store and there we will *titoitoi* [mutually masturbate]. We went there. He said to me, Take hold of my penis, *titoitoi* with your hand. He said to me, Undo the buttons of your trouser. I undid them, he took hold with his hand and I with my hand took hold of his penis, and *titoitoi*. He gave me six pipes and six figs of tobacco on the Sabbath days, as payment.

These were not isolated occurrences: 'I went to him three times before my baptism, and since my baptism I have been many times, more than I can count.'[25]

Such accounts scandalised Sydney, and left Marsden so upset with his erstwhile protégé that he sailed to New Zealand to get personal confirmation of the reports. Since there was no evidence of anal intercourse, Yate had not committed a crime, and prosecutors could not lay charges. Yate himself refused to play the martyr, proclaimed his innocence and resisted efforts to force him to leave Sydney immediately. Sydney opinion divided into supporters and opponents of the priest, and, subsequently, some historians have suggested a conspiracy against Yate. His relatively positive view of the Maoris did not go down well with settlers. His attempts independently to raise money for his parish, outside the normal channels of the Church Missionary Society, provoked hostility, as did the way in which he preened in the acclaim his book won in Britain.

The Yate affair offers several interesting insights. If the depositions about his behaviour were valid (and they seem so), he was engaging in a gross abuse of authority by seducing parishioners, misleading them about 'all' Europeans engaging in mutual masturbation, and rewarding them with tobacco and pipes for sexual favours. Yate was clearly hypocritical because his sermons and writings never missed an opportunity to damn sin (and letters from Maoris recalled how he had instilled a Christian notion of sin in them), yet he was obviously not practising what he preached. But there is also something of the 'coming-out' story in Yate as well – the conservative English missionary who dared to frolic with sailors on board ship, shack up with a seaman in Sydney and consort with 'natives' in New Zealand and Tonga. Shipboard licence and the discovery of a society with tolerant sexual mores led him to engage in behaviour anathema to his creed. He refused to flagellate himself for moral failings and beg cravenly for forgiveness.

Yate's behaviour represented what would now be seen as sexual exploitation, yet the Maoris might have been less outraged than imagined. None of them (and there may have been dozens) reported his activities during his six years in New Zealand. Kohi seemed more puzzled than offended by Yate's overtures and agreed to participate in his sexual games 'more [times] than I can count'. Yate would have exercised great authority over the young men, of course, making it difficult to refuse his advances or denounce his behaviour, yet pre-Christian attitudes towards sexual activity, still alive despite evangelisation, may not have been condemnatory of the practices in which Yate and his partners engaged. Indeed, the sexual latitudes of Maori society may have created an opening for Yate's sexual explorations. As Binney puts it, 'Did he fall because he was exposed to the fearful test of another society unburdened by the Calvinist belief in the immediacy of temptation and the actuality of guilt?'[26]

The Yate affair, moreover, shows the ambiguity of moral laws and their enforcement. Without evidence of anal penetration and seminal emission, Yate could not be prosecuted for sodomy. Undoubtedly statutes existed under which he could have been charged, but religious and secular authorities decided not to pursue the case against him. Perhaps they felt that there was already too much discussion about sodomy in the Australian colonies, or feared that missionaries had not effectively stamped out immorality among 'natives'. The spectacle of a man of the cloth, an internationally known writer, a priest received by the King, a friend of Governor Darling and the protégé of a famous bishop, being hauled before the courts would hardly have been appealing. Yate's sexual commerce with men was but part of his offence – he had dared to cross the boundaries of race and class, he had shown that reprobate sexual leanings did not occur just among sex-starved convicts or ne'er-do-well denizens of the back streets of port cities. In Sydney, it was far better to hush up the affair, bustle Yate out of the colony and redouble efforts to stamp out the unmentionable vice. Back in the Bay of Islands, the missionaries and their converts burned Yate's possessions, shot his horse and mounted an attack on the scholarship of his *An Account of New Zealand*.

The Yate case illustrates the temptations of situations where respectable men came into contact with sailors, soldiers or 'natives'. Authority and money could procure favours, but at the expense of possible exposure and ruin. Indiscretion might lead to downfall, but the colonial elite preferred silence to spectacle. Disgrace and obscurity provided fitting punishments when the proof of a hanging offence was difficult to obtain, and efforts to do so would have embarrassed colonial compatriots.

Just friends?

Testimony about convicts and cases brought to criminal courts in the Australian colonies emphasise both the physical side of homosexuality and the fleeting nature of many contacts. The Yate *affaire* also presents rather episodic encounters, even if more is known about the priest's partners. Several variants of homosexual behaviour and persona – neither men cruising the beats and doing the deed in cheap rooming-houses or dimly-lit parks, or spiriting parishioners into their vestry – can be identified in colonial Australia. A few individuals have left traces of a rather 'campy' life unsanctioned by the law. George Francis Alexander Seymour, future Marquess of Hertford, born in 1871 and educated at Eton, later a lieutenant in the Warwickshire regiment, moved to Queensland, bearing the courtesy title of the Earl of Yarmouth, in 1895. He became a successful farmer, but scandalised local people by donning a sequined outfit to perform dances and hosting male-only parties. William Lygon, later Earl of Beauchamp, was born the year after Seymour and also educated at Eton (and Oxford). He arrived in Sydney in 1899 to become Governor of New South Wales, and carried out his duties efficiently. He meanwhile frequented Bohemian circles and admiringly wrote of Australian men, 'splendid athletes, like the old Greek statues....The life-savers at the bathing beaches are wonderful.' His term as governor ended, Beauchamp returned to Britain (and married), though he regularly visited Australia afterwards. In 1931 his wife petitioned for divorce, threatening to reveal his homosexuality. King George V, upon hearing about the matter, made a remark destined to become famous, 'I thought men like that shot themselves.' Beauchamp resigned as Liberal leader in the House of Lords and died in New York in 1938. Hertford died in London two years later.[27]

Other men lived in ways that, without the usual pattern of matrimony and fatherhood, hint at homosexual orientation. The Mayne family became one of the wealthiest and most prominent in early twentieth-century Brisbane, bene-factors of the University of Queensland, to which in the 1930s they gave land for a new campus, endowed chairs of medicine and provided a bequest (that by the 1990s returned an income of over a million dollars annually). The family, however, was touched with scandal and tragedy. The patriarch, who had migrated from Ireland and became a successful butcher, confessed on his deathbed in 1865 that he had obtained the capital with which he had started his rise to fortune from a man whom he had robbed, then murdered, and whose corpse he had dismembered. Shame continued to taint the family, and Mayne's six children all vowed that they would never marry. Several of the men had little inclination to do so, and possibly all three sons were homosexually inclined – Isaac, a solicitor who became a rogue, William, who after earning a BA and MA at the University of Sydney seldom worked, and James, who took out a medical degree and spent six years doing postgraduate medical study in London. James returned to Queensland to a post at the Brisbane General Hospital, of which he served as superintendent from 1898 to 1904. Isaac, who enjoyed gambling parties on a boat that housed a floating sugar mill, kept company with several young men, one of whom, a 24-year-old Japanese, was killed in 1904; public opinion held Isaac responsible and judged the death a *crime de moeurs*. Isaac, known to have mental problems, was bustled away to an asylum; after his release, he was implicated in the suicide of another young man, and then committed suicide himself.

James Mayne bore his family problems with resignation and was an honoured member of the Brisbane professional community. A dapper gentleman, he dressed in formal coats with gloves, a bowler hat, diamond tie-pin and boutonnière. He was known to enjoy the company of the robust lads of the Toowong Rowing Club, of which he served as president. In 1918, he met 21-year-old Frederick Whitehouse, a University of Queensland geology student, his regular companion until Mayne's death in 1939.[28] Whitehouse, who held a doctorate from Cambridge, was by that time an associate professor at Queensland, but was dismissed from his post in 1955 after conviction for a homosexual offence. No stains on the sheet prove that the Mayne brothers were homosexual, but none fits the mould of the happily married heterosexual. It is easy to characterise James Mayne as a sad and repressed homosexual, but perhaps the companion-ship of Whitehouse and other young friends, whether or not they had sexual relations, provided consolation, pleasure and fulfilment to a man whose life was haunted by family misfortune.

Australian history provides other examples of intimate male friendships from which sentiments and behaviours that would now be termed homosexual cannot be excluded. Often the conditions of the frontier, such as explorations of the outback, proved particularly propitious to such bonding.

One early explorer of Australia was Edmund Kennedy, born in 1818 into a prosperous family on Guernsey, in the Channel Islands. Kennedy arrived in Australia in 1840 and, at the very young age of twenty-two, became assistant surveyor of New South Wales. He worked in western Victoria (then administered from Sydney), but created commotion because of protests against a particular magistrate and because of a liaison with an Irish girl, by whom he fathered a child. Recalled to Sydney, Kennedy established himself, in the words of Edgar Beale, 'as a popular and charming member of society, with a rowdy, boyish sense of fun. His gifts included a pleasant singing voice and considerable skill in sketching.' In 1845, Kennedy was appointed second-in-command of an expedition to seek an overland route to the Gulf of Carpentaria. After successful completion of the trip, he agreed to lead a further expedition in 1847 – composed of eight men and an Aboriginal boy – to ascertain if the Victoria River (later renamed the Barcoo) drained into the gulf. Another expedition followed in 1848, when Kennedy set out to cross the Cape York Peninsula to its most northerly point whence, after replenishing his supplies, he was meant to return southwards to Sydney.

Among his companions on the expedition to Cape York, Kennedy took an Aboriginal man named Galmahra, generally known (as were many other Aborigines) as Jackey Jackey. 'Probably little more than a boy,' according to Beale, he came from a tribe near Muswellbrook, and 'soon acquired a reputation for hard work, sagacity and superb bushcraft; as privation and disaster gradually overcame the party he steadily emerged as one of its strongest members.' Mangrove swamps, shrinking supplies and illness placed obstacles in the expedition's path, and Kennedy decided to leave some of his men at an intermediate stop, in Weymouth, while along with four others, including Galmahra, he tried to reach a supply ship on the coast. Two of the men at the camp died from starvation, and one of Kennedy's party accidentally shot himself and had to be left behind with two others to care for him. Kennedy, now accompanied only by Jackey Jackey, pressed on. Twenty miles from their goal, they encountered crocodile-infested swamps, and then were attacked by Aborigines. Kennedy suffered a spear wound and, recounts Beale, 'soon afterwards died in the arms of the devoted Jackey Jackey', who buried him and managed to escape. Jackey finally reached the supply ship, but 'though completely exhausted, he could not rest the first night of his return, but grieved for his dead master'. The following year Jackey Jackey served as guide on an expedition that went looking, unsuccessfully, for survivors among the men Kennedy had left. The expedition's leader 'praised Jackey's skill, modesty, respectful manner and touching devotion to Kennedy's memory'. Jackey was later honoured with presents, and returned to his tribe, but drifted and took to drink. He died when he fell into a campfire in 1854. Beale refers to 'the deep *rapport* between Kennedy and Jackey', neither of whom ever married. The exact nature of that *rapport* is left unstated, and will never be known.[29]

Another famous explorer of Australia was Ludwig Leichhardt, born in 1813 in Prussia. Leichhardt studied philosophy and languages at several universities, and at Göttingen made friends with a fellow student, called John Nicholson, who studied medicine and sparked Leichhardt's interest in natural sciences. Leichhardt also studied with Nicholson's younger brother, William, and went to . Gloucestershire with William when the Englishman returned home in 1837. The two lived and worked together over the next four years and travelled to London, France, Italy and Switzerland to continue their research. In 1841, Nicholson provided the money for Leichhardt to go to Australia, paying for his ticket and supplies, and giving him the considerable sum of £200. Arriving in Sydney, Leichhardt surveyed the local region and, without success, campaigned for official appointment. The 29-year-old also became friends with a 42-year-old unmarried lieutenant, Robert Lynd.

In 1844 Leichhardt raised enough money by private subscription to mount an expedition to Port Essington in the far north, reaching his destination in December 1845 after a journey of over 5,000 kilometres (and the loss of one of his men in a skirmish with Aboriginals). A rapturous reception, as well as a generous government subvention, awaited him back in Sydney. Leichhardt published an account of his journey, delivered lectures to large audiences and organised a further expedition. His very ambitious plan was to traverse Australia from Darling Downs (in present-day Queensland) to the western coast of the continent, on the Indian Ocean, and then follow the coast down to the settlement at the mouth of the Swan River (now Perth). The first attempt failed, despite six months of travel, but Leichhardt remained undaunted and took encouragement from Kennedy's exploits in northern Australia. Leichhardt left the Condamine River in March 1848 and called at a sheep station on the Darling Downs on 3 April. He was never seen again, and no trace of his expedition has been found. Scientists bemoaned his loss, but valued his observations and the collections he preserved from his earlier expeditions.[30]

Leichhardt had a complicated personality. The *Australian Dictionary of Biography* quotes one of his hosts saying that he was 'the most amiable of men', but that he was also considered 'jealous, selfish, suspicious, reticent, careless, slovenly, wholly unfitted for leadership and "very lax in his religious opinion"'.[31] Not surprisingly, he has attracted much attention from writers, and was made into the character Voss in the novel of the same name by the Nobel Prize-winning author Patrick White. Voss is a sexually ambivalent character, and the novel strongly hints at his homosexuality. (White himself was openly homosexual.)[32] There has been speculation on the real-life Leichhardt, partly because of his homoerotic descriptions of Aboriginal men and because of his friendship with Nicholson and Lynd. One biographer, Alec Chisholm, emphasises the privations Nicholson suffered to support Leichhardt, and quotes a letter from Leichhardt to his father about this friendship that was 'transformed into the loving care which affected us mutually'. Chisholm remarks on the 'motherly' affection of Nicholson, 'his lonely and generous nature' and the 'queer alliance' of the two men. Chisholm notes further that, in Sydney, Leichhardt and Lynd 'met by chance and kindred interests caused the acquaintance to ripen. Possibly, too, Lynd felt compassion for the waif from Europe.' Leichhardt himself reported in a letter: 'He is a like a father and brother combined to me; and his home is always mine.' Later he referred to Lynd as a substitute for Nicholson. Dino Hodge argues that Chisholm's own attitude towards sexuality was little enlightened, and quotes Manning Clark, the dean of Australian historians in his day, who, writing forty years later, 'reflects an attitude more understanding of sexuality'. Clark refers to Nicholson straightforwardly as 'the man he [Leichhardt] loved' and surmises that one of his goals in Australia was 'an "heroic friendship" with another man;...he spoke much of that love between man and man which surpassed that of woman, as though it were a love between souls, but was much given to "brotherly kissing"'. Leichhardt's account of his voyage to Port Essington, adds Hodge, was dedicated to the people of New South Wales, and to Nicholson and Lynd.[33]

Two other cases showing close male-bonding that may have been sexual come from opposite ends of the social spectrum in colonial Australia – high-ranking bureaucrats and bushrangers.

Bushrangers were outlaws, active mostly from 1860 to 1890, feared as criminals by respectable people, regarded as heroes by the poor for their robberies of the rich, and famed as Robin Hoods in Australian legend. The archetypal bushranger was Ned Kelly, killed in a shoot-out with policemen. He became an Australian icon, subject of paintings by Sidney Nolan, one of the earliest Australian films and a Booker Prize-winning novel by Peter Carey. Several historians have suggested that homosexual relations helped bind together the men in Kelly's gang, especially Joe Byrne and Aaron Sherritt. (Another member of his gang, Steve Hart, gained notoriety for galloping around the countryside dressed in a frock, ostensibly as a disguise.) Special friendships are even more evident in the lives of Andrew George Scott and James Nesbit. Scott was born in Ireland in 1842, son of an Anglican vicar; at the age of fourteen, he went to London, where he lived with a guardian, whose membership of the council of the British Museum gave him access to the museum's rich library. Scott met the great engineer Isambard Kingdom Brunel, which confirmed his own ambition to become an engineer. First, however, he travelled to Italy, where his biography begins to read more like a novel (and indeed some details remain unsubstantiated). In 1860, he served with Garibaldi's redshirted volunteers who conquered Naples. After a brief return to Ireland, Scott took passage to New Zealand, where he fought for the British in the Maori wars. Then he moved on to the United States, journeying overland from San Francisco to Washington and joining General Sherman's Union Army. At the end of the Civil War, in 1865, he set up as an engineer in San Francisco, but two years later sailed to Sydney. There, and then in Melbourne, he moved in elite circles, dining with the Governor of New South Wales and staying as a house guest with the Bishop of Melbourne. The former soldier and engineer eventually became a lay-reader in an Anglican parish in the Victorian goldfields.

Scott's copybook already contained blotches – he was discharged from the colonial army in New Zealand for malingering, and he had made a lot of money in a suspicious manner while serving with the American Union army. In 1869, Scott, who became known as Captain Moonlite, was implicated in a bank robbery in Egerton, Victoria. He fled to Sydney, where he was arrested for trying to steal a yacht to sail to Fiji. Imprisoned and then released in 1872, he was soon rearrested for the Victorian robbery and extradited to Victoria; while awaiting trial, he escaped, was recaptured and sentenced to gaol. In Pentridge Prison, he met James Nesbit, a 'currency lad' (native-born Anglo-Australian), a poorly educated juvenile delinquent – then in his late teens – convicted for assault and robbery. The two men became fast friends, and when they were released set up house together in Melbourne. Scott, amazingly, earned a living lecturing on prison reform, though he was occasionally taken into custody when Captain Moonlite was supposedly sighted at the scene of a crime. Apparently tired of the harassment, Scott and Nesbit decided to move to New South Wales. On the way, they formed a gang with other men and took over a sheep station near Wagga Wagga. The police laid siege, and the inevitable shoot-out followed. Nesbit was killed, and a contemporary writer noted of Scott, 'his leader wept over him like a child, laid his head upon his breast, and kissed him passionately'. The other men, including Moonlite, escaped but were apprehended. Scott was sentenced to death.

In the weeks before his execution, Scott wrote numerous letters to friends and benefactors, messages that prison authorities confiscated. In them, he spoke in detail about Nesbit, 'my own dearest Jim'. 'Jim was a brave true man as good a friend as ever lived,' said Scott; 'I am proud that my own dearest friend, despised bushranger though he be, had a heart as kind as it was brave.' In even more emotional words, he lamented, 'We were one in heart and soul, he died in my arms and I long to join him where there shall be no more parting.' 'Well have we loved' read part of a poem he penned to his dead friend, and Scott designed a tombstone for the grave where he wished to be buried with Nesbit: 'This stone covers the remains of two friends James P.N. Born 27/8/1858, Andrew G.S. Born 8/1/1845, Separated 17/11/1879, United 20/1/1880'. Scott was hanged on 20 January 1880, but buried in Sydney far from his friend's grave near the place he had been shot.

The relationship between Scott and Nesbit – an odd couple separated by background, education and thirteen years of age – may have been the sort of feverish friendship dear to Victorians and often described by them in poetic language. It may have been a particularly intense embodiment of mateship, the particular sort of Australian male bonding that developed in the nineteenth century. However, Garry Wotherspoon, who has examined Captain Moonlite's prison writings, remarks, in a careful but felicitous formulation, 'clearly, if these letters had been written about a person of the opposite sex, we would be in no doubt as to what sort of relationship it was, and indeed would probably even presume a physical side to it'.[34]

A final case of special friendship concerns Robert Herbert and John Bramston. Herbert was born in 1831, son of a barrister and grandson of the Earl of Carnarvon. He was educated at Eton and at Balliol College, Oxford, taking a BA in 1854, after which he became private secretary to the Chancellor of the Exchequer, William Gladstone. Soon he was appointed private secretary to the governor and colonial secretary of Queensland; in 1859, at the age of twenty-eight, he became the premier of Queensland, a post he held until 1866. Bramston, born the year after Herbert, studied at Winchester and Balliol, where he met Herbert. After graduation, they shared rooms in London, where both studied law and were called to the bar. Bramston left London for Brisbane with Herbert; he became clerk of the Executive Council, then entered parliament in 1863 and served as minister without portfolio under Herbert. Herbert and Bramston shared a house together, joining their names to call it 'Herston'. The two had complementary personalities, with Herbert bookish and Bramston more interested in 'manly' sports.

In 1866, Herbert and Bramston returned to London together. Herbert worked at the Board of Trade and then the Colonial Office, of which he was permanent undersecretary from 1871 to 1892, and again from 1899 until his retirement in 1900. He never married, and died five years later. Bramston took posts in Devon and Cornwall, and then became Queensland's Agent-General in London. In 1872, he married the niece of the new Queensland governor. He briefly worked again in Queensland as a judge, but in 1876 joined Herbert at the Colonial Office, remaining for twenty-one years. He died in 1921. For almost half a century, Herbert and Bramston's lives had been joined – studying together, sharing houses, moving to the colonies then returning home, and working as colleagues in Brisbane and London.[35]

In none of these cases – Kennedy and Jackey, Leichhardt and his friends Nicholson and Lynd, Moonlite and Nesbit, Herbert and Bramston – is there proof positive of sexual relations. The word 'homosexual' would have been unknown to all but the last pair, and the practice of sodomy might have been abhorrent to all of them. Yet each is a case of conjoined lives, benefaction and affection. All of the couples shared lodgings and most shared careers, whether in exploration, colonial governance or outback outlawry. Jackey and Moonlite grieved over their dead mates. With the exception of Bramston's marriage, ties with their male partners formed their strongest adult attachments. In each case, too, historians have intimated relationships that went beyond the norms for nineteenth-century men. These were not criminals hauled before the law courts for intercourse in the dark lanes of Sydney or Brisbane, assault in boarding-houses or drunken misconduct in pubs. Their relations, whatever the exact nature, were consensual, enduring and marked by what it would be uncharitable not to call love.

Homosexual cultures

By the end of the nineteenth century and the first decades of the twentieth, Australia's cities boasted a vibrant and identifiable homosexual culture, complete with a rich slang vocabulary to identify sexual poses and performances.[36] In Sydney, men who wanted to have sex with men could find encounters in Hyde Park or Boomerang Street, while in Melbourne men could promenade along George Street and Collins Street, or visit the Botanic Gardens. In Adelaide, they might cruise the parkland near the Torrens River. In Brisbane, parks and the riverside also afforded opportunities. Certain hotels, such as the Australia Hotel in Sydney, were known to be congenial to men with special tastes, as were public baths. Public lavatories, despite surveillance by the police and the insalubrious conditions they offered, became virtual social centres for homosexual men. Boarding-houses provided beds, a modicum of privacy and an assembly of often footloose and fancy-free young men. A hard night at the pub might lead to a furtive dalliance in a back lane or in a boarding-house bedroom, with drink lubricating morals and lowering inhibitions.[37]

Those engaging in homosexual activities spanned the social spectrum, and included several prominent citizens. In 1930, for instance, a prominent Adelaide man was arrested; Bert Edwards, hotel owner, philanthropist and member of the South Australian parliament, was found guilty of an unnatural offence and received a sentence of five years' hard labour.[38] Articles in the Melbourne *Truth* from 1913 to 1945, generally based on sensationalistic reporting of court cases, recorded arrests of a labourer, an Indian hawker, a police sergeant, a schoolmaster and a headmaster, a gardener, a cook, a musician, a clergyman, an art dealer, a sailor, a chemist, a doctor, 'a wealthy recluse' and a baronet. The ages of partners who willingly engaged in homosexual activities ranged from seventeen to seventy-five, with a concentration of men in their twenties and thirties. Victims of homosexual rape were as young as eleven and twelve. Many men were arrested after being discovered in casual encounters, but other homosexual goings-on were more institutionalised. Sir Sidarthur Affleck, a 32-year old baronet, along with his brother and a third accomplice, were arrested (in Brisbane) in 1937 as organisers of 'a club of jaded businessmen who like to play around in the nude', after they had abducted a youth, knocked him unconscious and taken photographs of him naked. (They then tried to blackmail him, and the young man went to the police.) Several convicted homosexuals were repeat offenders. Dr Robert Storer, author of a 1932 book on sexuality, sued *Truth* in 1938 for accusing him of sexual dealings with teenage boys whom he had contacted through newspaper job ads and then taken sailing. Storer was awarded one farthing damage for libel. But the next year, Storer, then thirty-nine, was arrested for indecent behaviour and indecent assault on a man in a public park. The judge sentenced Storer to twelve months in prison and remarked, 'You have a bisexual tendency. By your writings, it would appear to me that you yourself realised this tendency.' Four years later, Storer, now director of a clinical laboratory, was again arrested for gross indecency.[39]

Newspaper exposure, trial, conviction and imprisonment did not deter Storer, but the humiliation of court appearances and sentences had a deleterious effect on many lives. Some men got off lightly if their case came before a sympathetic judge. In 1942, a Melbourne judge heard the case of two men who pleaded guilty to a charge of committing an unnatural act. After evidence from a psychiatrist, the judge remarked that the men had been doing something that to them was clearly natural. He had no choice but to find them guilty according to the letter of the law, but sentenced them to a half-hour of 'imprisonment' in the courtroom itself. The Melbourne *Truth* headlined, 'Judge Says Law Should Catch Up With Science – Homily on Homosexuality'. Other judges did not prove so enlightened, and some men could not even face the shame of a trial. In 1937, a 'high caste Indian mystery man', a 37-year-old art dealer and artist, was arrested for sexual commerce with youths; he took poison, and his dead body was found on a beach. Court cases, and newspaper articles, revealed tormented figures unable to accept their sexuality or confronting personal problems in a desperate fashion – in 1936, a 27-year-old shot his 18-year-old boyfriend after the partner starting dating a girl, and then committed suicide himself.[40]

Yet it is worthwhile to remember that men whose homosexual relationships did not bring them to the attention of the law lived happier lives and created conditions in which their sexual and emotional preferences could be satisfied. Those with the money, leisure and willingness to find regular partners, those who avoided blackmail or police entrapment, and those who did not seek out sex in 'public places' went through life uncharged. However, few men, searching for partners and engaging in acts that (even in private) remained illegal, could avoid ever-present dangers. Even those who were successful in the face of social opprobrium usually remained securely locked 'in the closet'. At their most generous, said law-makers, policemen, judges and clerics, it was all right to be homosexual – so long as one did not have sex.

Despite interdictions on homosexual activity, a sense of homosexual identity emerged. Men clearly felt themselves drawn primarily or exclusively to other men for sexual comfort, they developed social networks and scouted out places for locating partners, and they sometimes even publicly confessed to their orientations. Exactly when this identity was born is a subject of conjecture that has preoccupied historians and fuelled much of the debate between 'essentialists', who argue for innate homosexuality, and 'constructionists', who counter that the 'homosexual', as name, category and personal and collective identity, was created only in the last three decades of the nineteenth century. Whatever the resolution of a sometimes sterile debate, in the Australian case, by the turn of the twentieth century, homosexuals were so identified by others and by themselves.

Settler homosexuality

Lack of works on homosexuality in the other British dominions makes an extensive comparison of Australia with different settler societies impossible. What evidence has been excavated from the archives does suggest that Australia was not unusual. In Canada, for instance, homosexuality was also illegal, and courts heard cases involving men arrested in compromising situations in public parks and boarding-houses, but a homosexual culture and identity seem to have developed by the early twentieth century, just as in Australia.[41]

What were the connections between homosexuality and imperialism in a settler society such as Australia? At one level, the Australian colonies reproduced British society – such were the intentions of the colonialists who established and administered the antipodean domains. Homosexual acts remained criminalised, in the separate colonies, and then the Commonwealth, until well after the Second World War, just as in Britain. Nevertheless, a homosexual culture that would not have been foreign to the 'mother country' emerged and flourished in Australia. Men met in pubs and parks, and they enjoyed casual encounters or contracted long-term liaisons. Certain venues became notorious for being frequented by homosexuals looking for partners, 'beats' in Australian parlance. Men fell victim to blackmail, coercion and violence in procuring sexual favours. Some were cross-dressers, others dandies, still others effected macho stances. None of this was unknown back 'at home' in Britain: both normative and 'deviant' patterns of behaviour had been exported.

Closer examination shows that Australia provided a somewhat distorted mirror of British society. The timing of legal changes, for instance, did not always coincide with new acts of the British parliament. It took New South Wales legislators twenty-two years to amend local law to criminalise attempted sodomy, as a British statute had done in 1861. Not until 1919 did the state parliament of Victoria adopt legislation similar to the 1885 British Labouchere amendment. By contrast, a man was executed in Tasmania for sodomy in 1863, two years after capital punishment for the crime was ended in Britain. Colonial legislators had different priorities, and responded to varying social and political imperatives, from their counterparts at Westminster.

It is impossible to know if incidence of homosexual activities was greater in Australia than in Britain. Critics of convict transport implied that it was, one saying that sodomy was one hundred times greater, a clearly unsubstantiated and likely risible claim. Confinement of so many men to penal establishments, however, quite possibly did lead to greater frequency of 'situational' homosexuality than would have otherwise existed. Moreover, great disparities in the sex ratios between men and women, particularly during early decades of colonisation and in rural Australia, might have prompted some men to engage in acts that they would otherwise have foresworn. The presence of Aborigines and the arrival in the Australian colonies, particularly Queensland, of Asians and Pacific Islanders meant that inter-racial sexual encounters were relatively common.[42] Court records suggest that the incidence of inter-generational sex was also especially high in colonial Australia, and a disconcerting number of cases involved violence, rape or what would now be termed child abuse.

Judges and political authorities tried to combat homosexuality, moves seconded by clergymen and campaigners for moral purity. Hundreds of men were convicted of homosexual acts from the early 1800s to the early 1900s, and more than thirty were executed. Prison terms were harsh, aggravated by hard labour, flogging and solitary confinement. Nevertheless, those numbers do not give evidence of a particularly vicious campaign against homosexuals, despite police harassment and entrapment, and the generally outraged sentiments expressed from the bench. Convictions in Victoria in the last three decades of the nineteenth century show judicial insistence on convicting men only where minors or violence were involved. Throughout the nineteenth century, only in the 1830s, at the time of the Molesworth Commission and mounting opposition to transportation and the moral degradation it supposedly produced, was there anti-sodomitical hysteria in Australia. Scandal-mongering newspapers such as the Melbourne *Truth* might well headline cases of perversion, but such was the nature of yellow journalism.

These caveats minimise the horrific penalties imposed by the law, and the necessity for homosexuals to deny their sexuality and live in dangerous clandestinity. Ruin came to many men when they were arrested for 'unnatural' acts. Colonial Australia was certainly no paradise for sodomites.

The persistence and strength of homophobia in Australia can also be connected with the country's colonial past. In the 1950s, a New South Wales police chief proclaimed that homosexuality was the greatest danger facing Australia, and the campaign for decriminalisation of homosexual acts proved long and arduous. Male homosexual acts only became legal in New South Wales in 1984, and in Tasmania, last of the states to decriminalise homosexuality, in 1997. Right-minded Australians were eager to live down the convict past and erase the stain of transportation. The high incidence of sodomy revealed at the Molesworth inquiry was hardly something of which respectable Australians could be proud, especially when many carried a chip on their shoulders about early Australian settlements as refuse heaps for the undesirables of Britain. Fears that bushmen or Diggers might sometimes have been too intimate, that burgeoning cities housed dens of iniquity, that migrants from outside England brought suspect morals, or that artists and intellectuals were not 'real men' all animated anti-homosexual hostility. Such a climate caused some Australian homosexuals, such as the artist Donald Friend, to spend much of their life overseas, and instilled an ambivalent attitude towards his native land in the author Patrick White.[43]

Nevertheless the colonial world had the latitude to accommodate a variety of sexual and affectional relationships to at least as great a degree as, and probably to a greater extent than, Britain. Australian contemporary views of the trial and conviction of Oscar Wilde hint that, at least in certain milieux, a 'don't ask, don't tell' policy prevailed. One of Wilde's plays enjoyed its first Sydney production the week of his arrest in London. The author's name disappeared from the publicity but the show went on, allowing *The Bulletin* to remark acidly on the compromise 'between conscience and pocket by suppressing the author's name on the playbills, while continuing to pouch the profits of his talents'. *The Bulletin* also criticised the *Sydney Morning Herald* for failing to mention Wilde's name in an otherwise enthusiastic review of *An Ideal Husband*. 'Australia's response to Wilde was more generous than London's,' remarks David Marr. 'While Wilde's works closed in London's West End, they played on in Sydney and Melbourne. The Governor of Victoria attended the opening night of *The Importance of Being Earnest*, for example, by which time Wilde was already in gaol.' For Marr,

> the coyness of the local press might explain the difference. In London Wilde's disgrace provoked passionate editorials every step of the way and detailed – but not very detailed – reports of the trials....But so discreet was the quality press in Australia that respectable readers had only the bare bones of the story....Readers of *The Sydney Morning Herald* were spared even reports of the charges Wilde faced.[44]

Whether silence bespoke relative lack of outrage, a moral horror so great that certain crimes could not even be mentioned, or perhaps concern about parallels to Wilde's activities in colonial Sydney might be debated.

The homosexual cultures that emerged in colonial Australia did have some lacunae in comparison with Britain. Early colonial Sydney did not sport the 'molly-houses' common in Georgian London. A century later, at the *fin de siècle*, colonial societies remained too preoccupied with taming the continent to provide a hospitable environment for a dandified coterie of aesthetes. Commentators gossiped about the Wildes of Sydney, and men such as Earl Beauchamp fit the profile, but the lily-carrying, aphorism-spouting man-about-town of the Wilde type was a rarity.[45] Similarly, the hothouse circles of intellectual men reading the classics and looking to Antiquity for sexual titillation and legitimation – common in Oxbridge colleges – was not well developed in Australia's nineteenth-century institutions of higher learning. Distance made it difficult for those schooled in the classics to slip over to Italy to enjoy the delights of the antique and modern Mediterranean. Australia, as many interested in culture bemoaned, remained an un-intellectual, even anti-intellectual, society at the time. Only John Le Gay Brereton, in Sydney, and Bernard O'Dowd, in Melbourne (and, perhaps, Henry Lawson),[46] were antipodean Walt Whitmans singing the manly love of comrades; nineteenth- and early twentieth-century Australia produced no Edward Carpenter or André Gide to write apologias for homosexuality, no Karl Ulrichs or Magnus Hirschfeld to campaign for decriminalisation of homosexual acts. Nor did it give birth to a Tardieu or a Krafft-Ebing researching the origins, or possible cure, for homosexuality.[47] Such cultural figures would emerge – sexologists, novelists with homosexual themes, theorists of gay liberation – but not before the mid-twentieth century.

What did arise in Australia was mateship. This archetypal male bonding, the stuff of Australian legend, has been widely discussed, its origin linked to English male camaraderie, but also to the lack of extended families among migrant communities, which prompted particularly close ties between men without local relatives. Mateship has been connected, in particular, to working-class solidarity, in the bush, on sheep-stations, in gold mines and the city, a sense of egalitarian and corporate loyalty that contributed to the strength of the Australian trade union movement. Service in the military, especially the defining experience of Anzacs at Gallipoli, has been credited with solidifying the ties of mateship. Mateship has been linked, too, to the sociability of exclusively (or dominantly) male gathering places, from the pub to the cricket pitch and rugby oval. Feminist historians have pointed out an inherent misogyny in Australian mateship. Racism was also a component, since Aboriginals, Asians and Pacific Islanders (or even Mediterranean migrants) were rarely admitted to the confraternity of Anglo-Celtic mates. Others have emphasised how it standardised and enforced social mores, cutting down 'tall poppies' and shirking those whose race, political beliefs, aspirations – or sexual proclivities – did not or could not bow to peer pressure.[48]

Historians have pointed to the homosocial aspects of mateship, though such comments remain anathema to traditionally minded Australians. Russel Ward, in *The Australian Legend*, published in 1958 – hardly a propitious time, in the conservative Menzies era, to talk about sex – intimated that a bushman in colonial Australia appeased his 'spiritual hunger by a sublimated homosexual relationship with a mate, or a number of mates, of his own sex'. Some homosexual authors have not been entirely convinced by the notion of sublimated (or not so sublimated) homosexuality as hypothesised by Ward. Dennis Altman, Australia's premier gay theorist, is 'increasingly sceptical of the usefulness of defining friendship/mateship in terms of sexual repression/sublimation. There may, of course, be many occasions where sexual desire expresses itself through friendship, but this does not mean the latter necessarily stems from the former.' Altman notes that many personal accounts of 'coming out' (such as those in Garry Wotherspoon's edited collection, *Being Different*) speak of the isolation of homosexuals in the early and mid-twentieth century. These Australian homosexual men felt excluded from the cult of mateship precisely because of their contrary sexual urges.[49]

Other observers continue to see connections. Robert Hughes, writing on the convict period, says that conditions:

> promoted the pair-bonding, the feeling of reliance on one's 'mate', that would lie forever at the heart of masculine social behaviour in Australia.

Because there were no white women in the bush, it meant – as some authorities grudgingly acknowledged, by the end of the 1830s – that 'mateship' found its expression in homosexuality.[50]

For Bob Hay, rather than mateship giving rise to homosexuality, homosexual practices in penal establishments might have contributed to the formation of mateship:

It is tempting to speculate, for example, that the experience, perforce, in the early days by large numbers of Australian men of satisfying and intimate sexual relations with other men laid the foundations for later day 'Aussie mateship' and contributed significantly to our traditional male egalitarianism.[51]

Libby Connors underlines the homosociality of much Australian male popular culture, which provided a conducive environment for men who sought sexual partners, not just drinking and yarning companions, in pubs and other venues.[52] Clive Moore emphasises the signficance of male friendships on the frontier; even if such 'romantic friendships' did not extend to sexual intercourse, the emotional ties bonding men often provided the most significant ones in their lives.[53]

Contemporary gay Australia retains traces of its homosexual colonial past. Men still congregate in pubs, and sometimes engage in immoderate drinking, before pursuing sexual encounters, much as in the Victorian age. Certain areas where gay men now socialise, notably Sydney's Oxford Street, already in the nineteenth century bustled with blokes drinking at pubs, young soldiers wandering out of the Victoria Barracks, former inmates of the Darlinghurst Gaol (the place of incarceration for several convicted sodomites), clients attending Mr Wigzel's sex-segregated Turkish Baths and fashionable shop assistants from the street's department stores. These were all near to 'that part of College Street from Boomerang Street to Park Street [which] is a parade for them'.[54] One of the major drinking spots for 1990s gay men in Oxford Street, by chance, was the Beauchamp Hotel, named after the former governor who appreciated handsome swimmers and wild parties. In nearby Surry Hills, Bourke Street, which now plays home to a concentration of gay residents, boasted a gay 'haunt' in 1895.[55]

'Beats' – areas where men cruise for (often anonymous) sexual encounters, frequently parks, beaches and public lavatories – have a long history as sites of male conviviality and, in the words of Clive Moore, 'are at the core of male homosexuality in Australia in both its pre- and postliberation forms'. Some beats have been gathering places for men seeking sex with men for decades, and Moore has identified one stretch of beach in Townsville, a coastal city in tropical Queensland, where men were arrested for homosexual activities in 1870; local newspapers wrote about The Strand as a much-frequented gay beat in 1980 and it remains so today. The popularity of such outdoor venues is linked both with Australia's warm and sunny climate, which permits a range of alfresco activities, and the historical need of men to seek out secluded places where casual lingering might go unnoticed and sexual contacts could be easily made.[56]

Furthermore, sexual relationships and partnerships between men of different ethnic backgrounds are not uncommon in Australia, where groups of gay 'ethnics', particularly Mediterraneans and Asians, have been organised. The large-scale migration of Southern Europeans after the 1940s, and of Asians from the 1970s onwards, has created in Australian cities one of the world's most diversified societies. Yet colonial Australia was already an extremely cosmopolitan place – Chinese miners in the goldfields of Victoria, Italian cane-cutters and indentured 'blackbird' labourers from Melanesia in Queensland, Malay pearlers in Western Australia, Indian and Ceylonese seamen, and migrants from other parts of the world. Social observers often feared that such foreigners were bringing dishonourable customs into the colonies, and there is indeed evidence of homosexual practices among, for instance, Melanesian labourers in Queensland.[57] The presence of homosexuals of varied ethnic backgrounds, and the incidence of cross-cultural liaisons, thus has a history stretching back to colonial days. The first apparent sodomy trial involving an Asian in New South Wales, for instance, dates to 1853, and a trial involving Aboriginals took place in Queensland in 1855.

Other characteristics of contemporary gay life may also have colonial roots. The irreverence of Sydney's annual gay and lesbian Mardi Gras parade echoes the rebelliousness and non-conformity of larrikins and bushrangers. A certain hedonism in gay urban life may not be unrelated to the promiscuity (in various senses of the word) of nineteenth-century port-cities and frontier towns. The pin-up of Australian masculinity, the 'spunky' lifesaver with blond hair and bulging muscles, desired by both homosexual men and heterosexual women, emerged from the sun-drenched beaches and rolling surf of Australia's coastline. This is an image profoundly different, physically and metaphorically, from the tousled-headed, rosy-cheeked British lad or the swarthy Italian *ragazzo*. If colonial Australia was created in the image of its British maker, the evolution of colonial society produced a type of homosexual who had moved far away from his British forefathers.

Notes

1 Evan Whitton, 'Sub plot', *The Weekend Australian*, 31 January–1 February 1998, p. 27, based largely on James Goldrick, 'The "Australia" court martial of 1942' (MLitt thesis, 1983); Robert French, *Camping by a Billabong: Gay and Lesbian Stories from Australian History* (Sydney, 1993), pp. 79–83.

2 Garry Wotherspoon, *City of the Plain: History of a Gay Sub-culture* (Sydney, 1991), p. 37.

3 Wotherspoon, Ch. 2; cf. Clive Moore, *Sunshine and Rainbows* (St Lucia, Queensland, 2001), Ch. 7. See Robert French, '"Where the action was": Archival sources for gay history in Australia', in Robert Aldrich and Garry Wotherspoon, *Gay Perspectives: Essays in Australian Gay Culture* (Sydney, 1992), pp. 181–95. For an overview, see Craig Johnston and Robert Johnson, 'The making of homosexual men', in Verity

Burgmann and Jenny Lee (eds), *Staining the Wattle: A People's History of Australia since 1788* (Melbourne, 1988), pp. 86–99.

4 Gays and Lesbians Aboriginal Alliance, 'Peopling the empty mirror: The prospects for lesbian and gay aboriginal history', in Robert Aldrich (ed.), *Gay Perspectives II: More Essays in Australian Gay Culture* (Sydney, 1994), pp. 1–62.

5 Garry Wotherspoon, 'Sodom in the South Pacific: Male homosexuality in Sydney, 1788–1809', in Graeme Aplin (ed.), *A Difficult Infant: Sydney before Macquarie* (Sydney, 1988), pp. 91–101. See also Bob Hay, 'The sodomites' guide to colonial Sydney, being a guide to the principle places of shirt-lifting in Sydney town during the convict Era (1788–1843)', website (www.lemon.rainbow.net.au/fabfanny/bhay/).

6 Quoted in Robert Hughes, *The Fatal Shore: A History of Transportation of Convicts to Australia, 1787–1868* (London, 1987), p. 264.

7 French, *Camping by a Billabong*, p. 6.

8 Hughes, esp. pp. 264–72.

9 Hughes, pp. 265, 271, 530–1.

10 French, 'Where the action was', p. 185.

11 Walter J. Fogarty, '"Certain habits": The development of a concept of the male homosexual in New South Wales Law, 1788–1900', in Aldrich and Wortherspoon, *Gay Perspectives*, pp. 59–76, and 'Indecent connection: Notions of the development of the homosexual in New South Wales law, 1788–1900' (BA Honours thesis, University of New South Wales, 1989), which provides a full list of trials involving homosexual offences.

12 Adam Carr, 'Policing the "abominable crime" in nineteenth century Victoria', in David L. Phillips and Graham Willett, *Australia's Homosexual Histories: Gay and Lesbian Perspectives V* (Sydney, 2000), pp. 27–40; Libby Connors, 'Two opposed traditions: Male popular culture and the criminal justice system in early Queensland', and Clive Moore, 'That abominable crime; First steps towards a social history of male homosexuals in colonial Queensland, 1859–1900', in Aldrich (ed.), pp. 83–114 and 115–48, respectively. And Jill Bavin-Mizzi, '"An unnatural offence": Sodomy in Western Australia from 1880 to 1900', in Charlie Fox (ed.), *Historical Refractions (Studies in Western Australian History XIV)* (Perth, 1993), pp. 102–20; Bruce Baskerville, '"Agreed to without debate": Silencing sodomy in "colonial" Western Australia, 1870–1905', in Robert Aldrich and Garry Wotherspoon (eds), *Gay and Lesbian Perspectives IV: Studies in Australian Culture* (Sydney, 1998), pp. 95–115.

13 Fogarty underlines the racist overtones, for instance, in the trial of the first Asian prosecuted for sodomy in New South Wales, in 1853. Fogarty, 'Unnatural connection', p. 68.

14 *Ibid.*

15 Bob Hay, 'A charge of something unnatural: A brief history from the records of Australia's earliest known "homosexual" convict', in Aldrich, *Gay Perspectives II*, pp. 63–72.

16 Bavin-Mizzi, p. 106.

17 Connors, op. cit.

18 Moore, *Sunshine and Rainbows*, p. 43.

19 Unfortunately, historians have not yet tabulated statistics for South Australia, to which no prisoners were transported.

20 See, for example, the case of love-letter exchanges between two mates on a ship, in Fogarty, 'Unnatural connection', p. 80.

21 French, *Billabong*, p. 21.

22 This account is taken from Bill Wannan, *Early Colonial Scandals: The Turbulent Times of Samuel Marsden* (Melbourne, 1972), pp. 163–9; Judith Binney, 'Whatever happened to poor Mr Yate? An exercise in voyeurism', *The New Zealand Journal of History*, Vol. 9, No. 2 (1975), pp. 111–25; French, *Billabong*, pp. 21–5.

23 Quoted in French, *Billabong*, p. 22.
24 Binney, p. 116.
25 Quoted in French, *Billabong*, p. 24.
26 Binney, p. 113.
27 Clive Moore, 'Seymour, George Francis Alexander', and 'Beauchamp, William Lygon, 7th Earl', in Aldrich and Wotherspoon (eds), *Who's Who in Gay and Lesbian History*, pp. 403 and 43–4, respectively. (On reaction to the Beauchamp scandal in Sydney, see Wotherspoon, *City of the Plain*, pp. 42–4.)
28 Rosamond Siemon, *The Mayne Inheritance* (St Lucia, Queensland, 1997), and Moore, *Sunshine and Rainbows*, pp. 83–4.
29 Edgar Beale, 'Jackey Jackey' and 'Kennedy, Edmund Besley Court', in A.G.L. Shaw and C.M.H. Clark (eds), *Australian Dictionary of Biography*, Vol. 2 (Melbourne, 1967), pp. 7 and 43–4, respectively.
30 'Leichhardt, Friedrich Wilhelm Ludwig', unsigned entry in Shaw and Clark, pp. 102–4.
31 *Ibid.*, p. 104.
32 Valerie Beattie, '*Voss*: A "queer courtship"', in Aldrich and Wotherspoon (eds), *Gay and Lesbian Perspectives IV*, pp. 41–70.
33 Dino Hodge, *Did You Meet Any Malagas? A Homosexual History of Australia's Tropical Capital* (Darwin, 1993), pp. 2–3, quoting A.H. Chisholm, *Strange Journey: The Adventures of Ludwig Leichhardt and John Gilbert* (Sydney, 3rd edn, 1973), pp. 59–69, 280–1, and C.M.H. Clark, *A History of Australia*, Vol. III (Melbourne, 2nd edn, 1987), pp. 338–40.
34 Garry Wotherspoon, 'Moonlight and…romance? The death-cell letters of Captain Moonlight and some of their implications', *Journal of the Royal Australian Historical Society*, Vol. 78, No. 3–4, 1992, pp. 76–91, from which this account is taken.
35 French, *Billabong*, pp. 27–30 ('More than just friends?', written with Garry Wotherspoon); Moore, 'That abominable crime', pp. 116–19, and *Sunshine and Rainbows*, pp. 43–5.
36 Gary Simes, 'The language of homosexuality in Australia', in Aldrich and Wotherspoon, *Gay Perspectives*, pp. 31–58.
37 On Sydney, see Wotherspoon, *City of the Plain*; for other cities, Graham Carbery, 'Some Melbourne beats: A "map" of a subculture from the 1930s to the 1950s', John Lee, 'Male homosexual identity and subculture in Adelaide before World War II', in Aldrich and Wotherspoon, *Gay Perspectives*, pp. 95–112 and 131–46, respectively, and Clive Moore, 'Poofs in the park: Documenting gay "beats" in Queensland, Australia, *GLQ*, Vol. 2 (1995), pp. 319–39, and *Sunshine and Rainbows*, especially Ch. 4.
38 David Hilliard, 'Edwards, Albert Augustine', in Aldrich and Wotherspoon (eds), *Who's Who in Gay and Lesbian History*, pp. 142–3.
39 Wayne Murdoch, 'Homosexuality and the Melbourne *Truth*: An annotated listing', in Phillips and Willett (eds), pp. 177–221.
40 *Ibid.*, pp. 214, 199, 203.
41 Steven Maynard, 'Through a hole in the lavatory wall: Homosexual subcultures, police surveillance, and the dialectics of discovery, Toronto, 1890–1930', *Journal of the History of Sexuality*, Vol. 5, No. 2 (1994), pp. 207–42, and '"Horrible temptations": Sex, men, and working-class male youth in Urban Ontario, 1890–1935', *The Canadian Historical Review*, Vol. 78, No. 2 (June 1997), pp. 191–235.
42 On inter-racial homosexual activities, see in particular Clive Moore, *Sunshine and Rainbows*, Ch. 3, which details instances of encounters between Europeans and Aboriginals, Melanesians, Chinese, Sinhalese and Papuans in colonial Queensland.
43 On White, see David Marr, *Patrick White: A Life* (Sydney, 1991).
44 David Marr, 'After the fall', *Sydney Morning Herald*, 25 November 2000, p. 4.
45 For reactions to the Wilde trial, see Fogarty, 'Unnatural connection', pp. 89–90.

46 One biographer has suggested that Lawson, the 'bush balladeer', leading intellectual figure and major contributor to a distinctive Australian identity in the late 1800s, was a repressed homosexual. See Xavier Pons, *Out of Eden: Henry Lawson's Life and Works – A Psychoanalytic View* (Sydney, 1984).

47 However, Richard Storer, the man repeatedly arrested for his homosexual activities, in 1932 published a *Survey of Sexual Life in Adolescence and Marriage*, which argued that humans were bisexual (Johnston and Johnson, p. 92).

48 For an historiographical overview, see Ken Inglis, 'Mateship', in Graeme Davison, John Hirst and Stuart Macintyre (eds), *The Oxford Companion to Australian History* (Melbourne, 1998), pp. 416–18. On homoerotic aspects of military traditions, see Fiona Nicoll, *From Diggers to Drag Queens: Configurations of Australian National Identity* (Annandale, NSW, 2001).

49 Dennis Altman, 'The myth of mateship', *Meanjin*, No. 2 (1987), pp. 163–72; see Garry Wotherspoon (ed.), *Being Different* (Sydney, 1986). On Australian masculinity, see Clive Moore and Kay Saunders (eds), *Australian Masculinities: Men and Their Histories*, special issue of the *Journal of Australian Studies*, No. 56 (1998).

50 Hughes, p. 320.

51 Hay, p. 76.

52 Connors, p. 91.

53 Clive Moore, 'The Frontier makes strange bedfellows: Masculinity, mateship and homosexuality in colonial Queensland', in Garry Wotherspoon (ed.), *Gay and Lesbian Perspectives III: Essays in Australian Culture* (Sydney, 1996), p. 26.

54 Clive Faro with Garry Wotherspoon, *Street Seen: A History of Oxford Street* (Melbourne, 2000), p. 103.

55 French, *Billabong*, p. 43.

56 Moore, 'Poofs in the park', *op. cit.*

57 Moore, *Sunshine and Rainbows*, Ch. 3.

8 Sex in the South Seas
Melanesia

The islands of Polynesia, thanks to images drawn from the early explorers, and later writers such as Melville, Loti and Stoddard, gained a reputation as sexual paradises. Further west, the islands of Melanesia did not enjoy the same mythic status. Europeans generally found dark-skinned Melanesians less attractive than the Polynesians, though they often remarked on the muscular build of the men. The islands themselves, Europeans proclaimed, were the preserve of Stone-Age cannibals and head-hunters engaging in bizarre rites of initiation. Here was 'primitive' life at its most stereotypical, an object of both fear and fascination.

The 'scramble' for Oceania did not exempt the Melanesian islands, as the British, Australians, Germans, Dutch and French divided the south-western Pacific. Traders in sandalwood, copra and other tropical products moved in; colonialist governments set up garrisons, created administrative outposts and encouraged settlement. Adventurers scouted remote islands and forbidding highlands. Anthropologists – such as Bronislaw Malinowski – investigated the mores of 'primitive' people. Missionaries preached the Gospel. Gradually, a veneer of colonial order emerged. The islands of Melanesia remained some of the last possessions to be decolonised – Indonesia took over Dutch New Guinea in the 1960s, Papua New Guinea (PNG) gained independence from Australia in 1975, the Solomon Islands separated from Britain three years later, and the Franco-British condominium of the New Hebrides became independent as Vanuatu in 1980; New Caledonia remains a French overseas territory.

PNG and the Solomon Islands provide case studies of colonial homosexuality in the South Pacific. Homosexual acts played an important role in rites of initiation in the highlands of New Guinea, as the ingesting of semen by young men (orally or anally) marked a requisite step towards acquisition of adult male virtues and power.[1] Europeans recruited Melanesian labourers, assigned to exclusively male barracks on plantations, a condition that favoured situational homosexuality. Europeans found willing sexual partners among men on plantations or in growing towns, sometimes taking advantage of their status and wealth to procure sexual services from 'natives' eager for colonial money and other benefits.

Homosexuality and colonialism in Papua New Guinea

Britain, under pressure from Australia, had taken over the south-eastern quadrant of the island of New Guinea in the 1880s. London passed control of this colony, along with the north-eastern part of the island (colonised by Germany and then captured during the First World War), to Australia. PNG formed one of the most intriguing of all imperial possessions – islands with a myriad of tribal groups and over 800 languages, highlands not explored by white men until the 1930s, a population reputed to engage in acts of the basest savagery, yet a country that lured foreigners for its very mystery and 'primitivism', as well as spectacular landscapes and dramatic art. By the 1970s, over 40,000 Europeans, primarily Australians, lived in PNG as mine-owners, planters, traders, missionaries and administrators.

Europeans realised that homosexual acts were part of initiation rituals in some regions. Missionaries and government authorities were eager to stamp out such practices, as well as other immoral behaviour that they regarded as inherent in the barbarity of Melanesia. Yet European practices, such as confining labourers to plantations, ironically may have encouraged same-sex intercourse. According to one writer in the 1940s: 'Some plantations are situated close to native villages, and in such cases the boys may resort to surreptitious prostitutes. Ordinarily, however, homosexual practices are the easiest adjustment; all Europeans agree that they are very common and are increasing.' Stephen Windsor Reed, a sociologist, continued: 'The natives have a growing awareness of the extreme revulsion with which Europeans view such behavior.' Under Australian administration, penalties for homosexual offences were harsh. According to Reed, sodomy fell into the class of 'crimes of native against native which endanger the peace and are repugnant to European morals. These include warfare, homicide, headhunting, cannibalism, immolation of widows, sorcery, rape, incest, and sodomy. These crimes are punishable by fines, imprisonment, penal servitude, and death.' In traditional cultures, 'there existed no such severe sanctions on this form of conduct, and thus the native will try to get away with it when he can'. Reed was sceptical about changing local behaviour:

> Enlightened Europeans, in private life as well as in governmental service, realize that there is a problem of the white man's own making. The only sanctioned 'solution' offered to the natives so far is the sublimation preached by the missionary. It simply does not work.[2]

As late as 1970, Australian authorities were still expressing anxiety about sexual irregularities in PNG. One board of inquiry into labour conditions wrote about young men who engaged in fighting, gambling and fornication:

> It was hardly to be expected that men in their late teens and early twenties would be able to subdue their sexual impulses. Few of the compounds were located near a village, however, and a still smaller number had a resident prostitute. Precautions had therefore to be taken to avoid the rape of white

women. A native found in the European section of the towns after a certain hour was imprisoned, and all bedrooms were protected by bolts and strong wire netting, 'boy-proofing' as it was called.

The threat to white women – a regular feature of colonial paranoia – was accompanied by concern about homosexuality:

> In the circumstances, homosexuality was inevitable, and the men of more mature years made a practice of taking a youth of sixteen or seventeen as a lover. He was first attracted by gifts of tobacco, sweets and gaily coloured clothing and then seduced. Resistance was countered with the threat of sorcery, of which many are still in deadly fear. Bitter rivalries developed if young lads were in short supply or if one of them attempted to transfer his allegiance. Blows were struck, and there have been occasions when the men, mad with jealousy, have resorted to knives. The most popular dance by far was the Bagana, in which each main performer paraded openly with his sleeping partner of the moment. Certain of the movements, which were carried out by separate couples, were unmistakably indicative of sexual congress.

The report continued that '"unnatural vice" – which in this instance was "natural" enough' – was severely punished. Sex could also become an employment weapon:

> Those who were without a paramour, either through inclination or temporary loss, were thus able to levy blackmail on their more fortunate companions, an advantage which they were not slow to seize upon. I have heard of native foremen, themselves married and with a wife on the spot, who made a habit of threatening exposure to anyone who refused to renew his contract of indenture. Each recruit earned the foreman a bonus.[3]

A few Australians seemed to accept this situation. One colonial public servant noted without shock and horror that a young Manus islander had given the football jersey which the Australian had lent him to his male Sepik island lover: 'Kalil enjoyed the pleasures of sodomy, a common practice in the Aitape villages.'[4] Some seemed content to let the islanders follow their own traditions. According to Lloyd Rhys, whose anthropological observations remain those of an amateur:

> that form of misbehaviour which the law regards as an unnatural offence is ordinarily a fairly common practice amongst natives, and in many tribes it forms part of the initiation ceremony. There is little doubt that in spite of religious teaching it is allowed to increase, and is even condoned by some missionaries and Government officials. It is estimated on good authority that ninety per cent of recruited male natives, or natives in contact with 'civilization', practice sodomy. In the more settled areas this takes place at regularly

organized sing-sings to which the participants come gaily dressed, and adorned with beads and other ornaments. At the outlying villages the gatherings are more open and of more frequent occurrence, and are regarded by the scattered white settlers as just another unpleasant feature of native life.[5]

Others, both Australians and Melanesians converted to Western religion and attitudes, proved less tolerant. In 1939, the Wau Progress Association lobbied the administration to act against homosexuality among islanders, one of a number of calls by those outraged at such practices. The demand of the Wau Association that sing-sings be investigated encountered a major obstacle – the Melanesian policemen who would carry out the inquiry were themselves regular participants in the sing-sings. An investigation was nevertheless undertaken, and 'on one occasion seventy boys up to the age of fourteen years were arrested'. Little else was done, and Rhys reported that:

> it became obvious to members of the Progress Association that Administration officials did not want to face the problem. Pressure was brought to bear and the matter carried to [colonial] headquarters, with the result that the Federal Government called for a report. But rather a dead end was reached when it became known that a missionary had said that 'sodomy was better than immorality' [presumably, adultery or heterosexual pre-marital sexual relations]. Official correspondence recorded that it was 'merely a harmless emotional outlet'.[6]

A few years later, a priest raised a cry against sing-sings and sodomy. Monsignor Van Baar, Superior of the Divine Word Missionaries in New Guinea, wrote to the Australian Minister for External Territories about the immorality of sing-sings, in which, he claimed, a man sometimes would take a boy, 'using him as a girl in a rough native way'. Such practices continued 'night after night'; the islanders' enjoyment of the festivities, he argued, produced detrimental economic effects as 'the boys were too tired or lazy or stubborn' to work on the plantations afterwards.

> But apart from that there is a more serious aspect of that sing-sing Bagina [or Bagana]. The small boy has to be the 'girl' of the sing-sing. He is held by the big boy and they 'kiss' him in their rude way, (pardon me to say it) it is a licking off of the boy-girl, manipulating him as they like. The boy-girl gets paid for that.

The 'boy-girl' was passed around among the men, then:

> goes back to her 'owner' and they sleep together. If that is not the worst inducement to sodomy, then I don't know. To 'prove' sodomy from case to case is impossible; but I reckon it is the government that must step in and forbid it.

The administration duly ordered an inquiry, which concluded that the outlawed dances took place. Despite concluding that sodomy was not part of the celebrations authorities again banned sing-sings.[7] The administration evidently wished to eradicate local cultural practices, especially if they might give rise to lewd behaviour, but 'native' culture rather than sodomy was the real target.

Writers thus commented regularly, with greater or lesser tolerance, on same-sex practices among islanders, and admitted the failure of admonitions to Christian-style sublimation. If they gave much thought to homosexuality among expatriates, they would have said that civilised and Christian Europeans would control their desires. This was not always the case. A young New Guinean employed as a hotel barman in the 1920s fondly remembered his job and the access to alcohol it provided:

> His only complaint was about the amorous advances of some of the male Europeans in the hotel to himself and other natives of his own age. Even so, he was not particularly upset and seems to have shrugged the matter off as a puzzling, if annoying, hazard of service with white men. It certainly did not warp or embitter his subsequent relations with them.[8]

In 1925, a Resident Magistrate in PNG reported information justifying court actions against two Europeans, one for sodomy with a native boy, the other for rape of a woman. Amirah Inglis comments on the lack of a trial in the sodomy indictment: 'The members of the Executive Council had argued that...the man should not be prosecuted provided he gave an undertaking to leave the country, an argument based on compassion for his respected wife and her children.' (Authorities finally decided to let the accused man in the rape case go free as well.)[9] Silence was preferred to scandal, departure of an offender favoured rather than unpleasant revelations. Failure to enforce colonial statutes, at least when white men had contravened the law, was not viewed as hypocritical, and no concern was expressed for a raped woman or a possibly unwilling male sexual partner so long as the sanctity of the white European family was preserved.

Given widespread reports of 'native' homosexuality, and the possibility that Europeans might engage in immoral activities, Australian officials occasionally expressed concern about their compatriots. During the Second World War, the United States Army began a crackdown on homosexuals among GIs, and passed on the names of reputedly homosexual Australian soldiers in PNG to their Australian superiors. The Commander of the Australian New Guinea Force sought advice from Canberra on what action to take about 'homosexual males'. Those who were 'addicted', he was instructed, should be sent to a psychiatrist and, after examination, discharged from the military. The commander then remarked that faked claims of homosexuality might be used by 'weak-minded' individuals to secure transfer from the war front or discharge. In the event, no action appears to have been taken.[10]

Australian colonial law in PNG made homosexual acts illegal, and prescribed punishments included fines, imprisonment and, until the 1940s, whipping.[11] Courts regularly heard cases involving homosexual offences, though it is difficult to tabulate the incidence of arrests and convictions. Jurisdiction fell to courts of petty sessions, the Central Court, Supreme Court and courts of native affairs. Statistical records do not always make it clear which cases were referred to higher jurisdictions or indeed came to trial. They furthermore report offences under a variety of rubrics (sometimes in such portmanteau categories as 'indecent, offensive, riotous and threatening behaviour'). The list comprised sodomy, attempted sodomy, permitting sodomy, gross indecency between males, attempted gross indecency, carnal knowledge against the order of nature, indecently dealing with a boy under fourteen years of age, unnatural offences, indecent assault and indecent practices.

In the first year of operation of the New Guinea Central Court, in 1921–2, judges heard eight sodomy trials, 11.5 per cent of all cases (compared to three rape cases, eight manslaughter cases, twenty-five murder trials and twenty-five breaches of various local ordinances). In 1924–5, three sodomy cases accounted for 12 per cent of total court cases (and 37 per cent of all cases involving sex offences). From 1921 through 1939, the Supreme Court heard 150 cases concerning homosexual activity, the number ranging from no cases in a couple of years to two dozen cases in 1934–5. The number of cases, therefore, was far from insignificant. Most men brought before the court were indigenous New Guineans, though statistics do not always indicate the race of those charged. At least three Europeans (and one Asian) were charged with gross indecency from 1930 to 1937. The conviction rate was high for both New Guineans and foreigners.[12]

Post-Second World War statistics show a continuing series of trials and convictions, particularly in the courts judging native affairs. From 1946 to 1955, twenty-five men (including three Europeans) were tried for homosexual offences in the district courts, compared to just under 180 in the courts for native affairs. In most years, charges of homosexual offences counted for about half of 1 per cent of charges laid against indigenous New Guineans, who could be prosecuted for a very broad range of offences. Yet the numbers charged with homosexual offences are not inconsequential. In 1950–1, for example, the Supreme Court heard eight cases involving homosexuality, one case of incest, ten offences connected with the White Women's Protection Ordinance, one case of a native convicted of 'an offence of an indecent nature against a white woman', one case of a man charged with coming within the boundaries of a town from which he had been barred, and two of unlawful carnal knowledge of girls under the age of fourteen. Homosexual offences seem to be well represented among morals cases, suggesting both the opportunities for 'unnatural' sex in PNG, and the particular vigilance of courts at this time in cracking down on such 'vice'. Penalties ranged from three months' imprisonment for gross indecency between males to one year with hard labour for sodomy. From the mid-1950s onwards, charges against Europeans increased, perhaps linked to the growing expatriate population of New Guinea – in 1955–6, for instance, five Europeans and four New Guineans were tried for unnatural offences, with five Europeans and only one indigenous person brought to court on the same charges during the following year. From the early 1960s until 1970, the Supreme Court heard fifty-six charges of unnatural and indecent offences, an average of seven per year. These resulted in thirty-nine convictions, with sentences from six months' to four years' imprisonment; thirteen men were discharged, and charges in four cases were dropped.[13] Courts in Papua (a separate judicial district) heard trials concerning a similar variety and incidence of offences.[14]

Charges for homosexual offences thus formed far from a trivial number of court cases, and the conviction rate was high. Penalties ranged from a fine ($40 and £50 are mentioned) to imprisonment with hard labour, including one sentence of seven years in gaol. The variety of offences with which men could be brought to court allowed the police to lay charges (such as attempted sodomy or unnatural offences, which included fellatio or masturbation rather than anal penetration) liable to gain conviction. Whether the practices for which men were indicted were traditional tribal sexual acts cannot be discerned; the police and courts might well have been attempting to stamp out homosexual acts in initiations. Many cases probably fell outside the bounds of traditional tribal behaviour since Europeans would have been unlikely to witness rituals largely performed in secret. Relatively few Europeans were brought to trial, but authorities preferred not to bring whites to public attention for sexual improprieties unless their behaviour – such as that of a European arrested for interfering with a boy under the age of fourteen – was particularly shocking.

The figures provide some indication of the frequency of homosexual offences, the types of acts performed and the punishments meted out. Details flesh out the picture of homosexual life in the colony and indicate the issues surrounding homosexuality in PNG. A number of incidents provoked general concern about the effects sexual irregularities might have on colonial rule. In 1959, for instance, the Chief Justice of PNG, A.H. Mann, warned about the dangers of immorality after some ten cases of 'gross indecency' involving European men and natives had been reported within a year. He revealed, though without providing further details, 'There has been more of a suggestion of the existence of a form of conduct amounting to male prostitution.' The explanation, the chief justice was quoted as saying, was that 'the social conditions applicable to large numbers of unmarried men of both races in Port Moresby [the capital] create a special danger of conduct of this kind developing into a grave situation'. Mann added that 'the Police Force is to be congratulated for their efforts in preventing such a situation from arising'. He specified the court's attitude:

> I want it to be clearly understood that although first offences of this kind require very special consideration, I take the view that in cases of repeated offences of this nature, the protection of the public, and especially the native public from this form of corruption becomes a paramount consideration.

The *South Pacific Post* quoted 'an authority' as remarking that 'there have been a number of Europeans involved in this type of offence who have been asked to catch the first aircraft out of town'. The newspaper also noted that 'in some cases substantial payment had been made to the natives'.[15]

That sketchy report is pregnant with interpretation about homosexuality in PNG, implying that the incidence of illicit inter-racial contact was frequent enough to require vigilance, that the imbalance in the sex ratio in the capital was at least partly to blame for 'situational' homosexuality, and that Europeans bore some responsibility for corrupting 'natives'. The appropriate treatment for those involved, it appeared, was to make certain that the white man left the territory speedily, and to pay off the 'native'. This would keep scandals from erupting and presumably remove the problem, leaving white prestige intact. A desire to hush up morals cases was clear, as the *South Pacific Post* noted that it had been approached by a man who asked the paper not to report on an 'indecency offence' being heard before the Supreme Court. The editor responded that the newspaper 'did not normally report cases of this kind'.[16] The paper nevertheless continued to report offences involving white men indecently assaulting both European and islander women. Homosexual offences had become too sensitive for the press to touch by the late 1950s. Since reports of homosexual incidents had reached the pages of the *South Pacific Post* in the past, the editorial decision not to report them may have been connected with rising proto-nationalism and concern about the future of Australian colonial control, or a more intense climate of moral censorship during the Cold War.

Editors had been less reserved in the early 1950s, when they reported on a small spate of trials. One illustrative incident in 1952 hints at a developed circle of homosexuals (or bisexuals) and some orgiastic activity. William Mervyn Creighton, a single 32-year-old medical assistant, was charged in Wewak with raping a native woman and 'with having wilfully committed an indecent act with intent to insult or offend Kurandumm, a male native, at Ambunti'. Meanwhile, John Pearce Cahill, a patrol officer, and Geoffrey Bernard Gilbert, described as a minor, 'appeared in Wewak Court on the same day. Both pleaded not guilty and reserved their defence when charged with having wilfully committed an indecent act with intent to insult or offend Kurandumm.' The police testified that the offence had taken place in Cahill's home, with Creighton, Gilbert and Cahill all present. Both Cahill and Gilbert were committed to trial. Cahill and Gilbert were also committed for assaulting Lance Corporal Nopari, on the same day, and Cahill was committed for assaulting Kaviam, 'a male native', three days later; both New Guineans claimed that they had been punched.[17] Cahill and Gilbert may then also have been charged with the rape of a woman, as they were acquitted of such an offence in September. Creighton, however, despite avowing that the rape charge was 'a pack of lies' and a 'frame-up', was found guilty of the rape of a woman and sentenced to four and a half years in gaol. The High Court in December 1952 upheld his appeal and ordered a retrial; he was found not guilty at the second trial.[18] The

European men (including a patrol officer and a legal minor) seem to have led an active, and varied, sex life, perhaps working together to procure male and female partners.

In another case, in 1952, George Francis Toohey, an officer in the colonial education department, was charged with an act of gross indecency against a native male soldier; whether he was convicted was not reported.[19] In 1953 the Port Moresby newspaper noted that a 45-year-old Australian storeman, also employed by the Department of Education, admitted to 'indecency towards a Chimbu [male] native'.[20] In the case of Knut Wessel-Brown, a Norwegian national charged with having 'attempted to procure a male person to commit an act of gross indecency' in 1955, the verdict was guilty with a sentence of nine months in gaol.[21]

The casebooks of Justice R.T. Gore of the Port Moresby Criminal Court, covering the period from 1948 to 1953, provide good examples of situations in which men were arrested, the arguments made in their defence and the penalties imposed.[22] Gore's notes record twenty-two cases connected with homosexual practices. Most involve PNG men, many police constables or prisoners from the Sepik region, where homosexual initiations were practiced.[23] The sexual activity recorded is usually anal intercourse, and Gore's handwritten notes provide explicit details. In 1948, Sapundua, from Wewak, was arrested for carnal knowledge of a fellow policeman in a Port Moresby barracks. He admitted: 'Yes I pick arse bilong him this fashion bilong New Guinea.' He and another man slept on the same mat;

> after I had been asleep for some time I woke up and me like pick arse bilong Waukagu. His lap lap was loose so I push my cock into his arse. After a little while water come out my cock and Waukagu woke up. He was very cross and said he would report me to Sgt. Major Ingita. We went together to the Sgt. Major's house but could not wake him up. We then went back to bed and went to sleep again.

Waukagu had told Sapundua that they should not have sex together because they were policemen.

In a case from 1952, where allegations were not denied, a difference in sexual tastes between the men is implied (and a set-up involved). Iranu Wate was discovered sodomising a fellow prisoner, Iubu Lea, at midnight. The prosecutor asked Lea, 'Did you make any humbug [a common phrase in New Guinea for sexual intercourse] on the night of 14 January?' Lea replied that Wate 'had fucked him two or three times'. This was 'not my fashion', he said, and so he alerted two other men in the cell to keep a look-out one evening when he thought Wate would come to his bed. When that happened, they called the guard. All gave graphic details of the intercourse, and Wate confessed, saying simply of such a sexual act, 'It is my fashion.' Gore sentenced him to nine months in gaol, to be served cumulatively with his first sentence (for theft), while Lea was given six months for allowing himself to be sodomised.

Another man, Paimuru-Ove, denied allegations of sodomy when a sergeant testified that he had caught him in the act:

> I see some water on the blanket on the bed...like milk. I spoke to Paimuru and said 'you drop white water'. He got up from under the bed and he told me....'Just now I make tea and spill some tea water'. I said 'that is not tea'.

Paimuru was sentenced to nine months of imprisonment with hard labour. In cases involving two other men, money had changed hands – one Ranu had said to Karakeri-Bominji that if he gave him some money 'he would let me fuck him'. (A twelve-month sentence was imposed.) An islander testified that he had been sodomised when he leaned over to cut bamboo; the accused countered that his partner had told him 'that is very sweet' during the act and asked him to 'push it strong'. (The accused was found not guilty.) In the case of a man claiming that he was an unwilling sexual partner, a witness said that he had seen the same man acting amorously with another man on a different occasion. One accused man was clearly a repeat offender, previously convicted for sodomy.

Two cases Gore heard involved Europeans. Philip James Guise, nineteen-years old, was brought to court for unlawfully assaulting a white man, identified as a Mr Craven, by hitting him on the head with a piece of wood. Guise had asked Craven, an unmarried motor mechanic, to drive him home, but the Australian had taken him to his own house instead. Craven had told him: 'Philip there is nothing wrong with you. You are a handsome boy and a pretty boy and there is nothing wrong.' (The case notes do not say what Guise thought was wrong with him.) Another European, present before Craven and Guise set off (and whom Craven had kissed on the cheek), had warned Guise to be careful of Craven. At his house, Craven told Guise, 'You are sleeping with me tonight.' In order to escape, Guise had attacked Craven. Despite the seeming 'self-defence' (though he admitted that no direct sexual advance had occurred), Gore found Guise guilty of assault and sentenced him to eleven months in gaol. In another case involving indecent assault, Michael O'Hara was arrested after he approached an islander and asked if he wanted a cigarette. When he accepted, O'Hara proposed a walk, and he then put his hand down the islander's rami (a kilt-type garment, generally known as a lap-lap) and felt his genitals. The New Guinean pushed him away, and O'Hara gave him four shillings. O'Hara admitted his actions, saying, 'I don't know what came over me,' explaining that he had grabbed the Melanesian's penis because he wanted to see what, if anything, islanders wore under their rami – 'Yes, I wanted to see if he was like a Scotsman.' The money was an attempt to keep the islander quiet, but the man who had been fondled, unfortunately for O'Hara, turned out to be a policeman. O'Hara was arrested, convicted and given a six-month suspended sentence.[24]

Reports from the Port Moresby press, and a colonial judge's casebook, show some of the contexts in which sexual activity between men took place in the late 1940s and early 1950s. Accounts coming from the end of the colonial period, when the Port Moresby newspaper again began publishing details of homosexual morals offences, provide further information. In May 1968, a 40-year-old company secretary in Madang was found not guilty on a charge of gross indecency brought by a 21-year-old Melanesian trainee at the local Teachers' College, after an incident in an automobile. The judge dismissed an application for the case to be heard *in camera*: 'He said it was necessary that these cases be heard publicly.' The prosecution lost because the plaintiff's testimony was uncorroborated and, according to a newspaper, 'by his own evidence' the Melanesian 'had proven that he had been an accomplice if an act of indecency had occurred'.[25] Four months later, an unemployed Melanesian man received four months in gaol for indecent behaviour at Ela Beach in Port Moresby, having pleaded guilty to an offence one evening five minutes before midnight. The judge was told that two men were seen behaving indecently in a dark corner near a swimming pool on the beach; both men were chased and caught, but the police inspector stated that the other man escaped as they neared the Central Police Station: '"I believe he was a European," Inspector Anderton said.'[26]

In these two cases, middle-class white men went scot-free, while an unemployed islander was sent to gaol, and an up-and-coming Melanesian saw an accusation of what might later be called sexual harassment (that is, if he was not a willing accomplice) come to nought. The actual dynamics of the encounters – did the policeman allow the white man to escape arrest in the beach incident? – cannot be discerned, but it is clear that certain situations and venues existed for men to take part in 'indecent acts', including meeting late at night at a swimming pool or in a car on a beach road.

A case in December 1968 involved two Europeans. Dennis Bradney, a 33-year-old architect-draughtsman, a suburban Sydney man who had been in PNG for four years, appeared in the Boroko district court on two morals charges, 'having carnal knowledge against the order of nature on or about December 4' and 'committing an act of gross indecency on or about December 6'. He was allowed bail of $400 and remanded for trial. At the committal hearing, the magistrate wondered why no charges had been laid against Simon Alban, the 21-year old theatre projectionist and cleaner with whom Bradney was alleged to have had 'carnal knowledge' (in Alban's car). A request by Bradney's counsel for hearings to be closed to the press and public, on the grounds that he would suffer adversely from the publicity even if he were discharged, was denied. By the time the case came to trial in January, police had brought morals charges against Alban, who (like Bradney) pleaded not guilty. A witness testified that he had seen Bradney behaving indecently towards Alban, but Bradney maintained that he had 'just been talking in the dark'. He denied interfering with Alban, pointing out that both of them had been fully dressed. A crown witness, Muret Tavnaia, said that 'when he looked into the car Alban covered himself with a newspaper', but admitted that he had not actually seen the alleged offence take place. The judge, according to the newspaper report, 'said he would like to know whether it was normal for Bradney to meet a man on Wednesday, see him again on Friday and arrange for a further meeting on Sunday'. In a surprise development, Alban changed his plea to guilty and gave evidence for the crown against Bradney. Bradney was found guilty of gross indecency and given a two-year good-behaviour bond, urged by the judge 'to take the opportunity to re-establish himself'. He escaped from a harsher penalty because of lack of aggravating circumstances and 'corruption of youth' (in the judge's words), and was aided by several character references, including one from John Gunther, the Vice-Chancellor of the University of PNG. Alban, despite turning crown witness, was convicted and given a similar two-year good-behaviour bond.[27]

In July 1969, John Douglas Flavell, forty-one years old, employed by the Administration stores and supply branch at Badili, Port Moresby, was committed on three counts, charged 'with having carnal knowledge against the order of nature with Sine Malena, of Weleksema village, Simbu District, with having intimidated and threatened Sine Malena and with having unlawfully and indecently assaulted Sine Malena'. (The triple accusation seems designed to secure a conviction.) The episode was said to have occurred in Flavell's house. While under arrest, Flavell was examined by a medical officer, who proved unable to determine whether or not he had engaged in intercourse. The magistrate dismissed the charge of intimidation and threatening, but said Flavell had a case to answer on the other two charges. Malena was also arrested, and charged with permitting Flavell to 'have carnal knowledge with him and to have permitted an act of gross indecency'. Malena's counsel told the court that Flavell had made indecent advances towards his client, speaking in a domineering manner, threatening him with a knife and forcefully preventing him from calling out. The prosecutor argued that Malena made no attempt to run away and permitted Flavell to make advances. However, the judge dismissed the charge against Malena because he was 'frightened and threatened into allowing another man to indecently assault him'. The Port Moresby newspaper did not record the outcome of Flavell's trial.[28]

Only ten days after Flavell's arrest, the *South Pacific Post* reported that Koiko Opute, twenty-seven, of Orumba village, had been gaoled for four years after pleading guilty to indecent acts against a boy aged between twelve and fourteen. The judge commented that this was a most serious crime, as the convicted man performed the act on 'a young boy and you did this against his will....You have put him in danger of corruption.' (That statement implies that the youth might be 'made' homosexual because of the incident.) A week later in Rabaul, a policeman told a district court that Nuboi Apilan of Sanon village, in the Morobe District, had committed sodomy with a boy on a beach one night. Apilan had given the boy $1.20 after twice having intercourse with him, and the policeman called the youth 'a male prostitute'. Apilan pleaded guilty and was fined $2 in default of one week in gaol; the magistrate warned him, 'If you do this thing again, I will not hesitate to gaol you for six months.'[29]

The following month brought to the pages of the twice-weekly Port Moresby newspaper a letter from a writer who signed himself only 'Priest', with an address at Milne Bay, about a recent Rabaul incident. A Melanesian man who had been charged with homosexual acts 'may perhaps be sympathised with, as much condemned if my own pastoral experience is anything to go on'. The colonial administration 'is directly responsible for this sorry state of affairs [homosexual practices], which is prevalent in all the main towns, Rabaul being no exception, save that it was there that a man was (accidentally) caught'. The reason was the administration's practice of employing only unmarried men for subaltern jobs: 'An ordinary labourer employed by the Administration is literally condemned to a life of celibacy, or else forfeit his job and return to the village to marry and live....The alternative is female prostitutes or sodomy.' Unlike manual labourers, Melanesians higher up in the Cadet Patrol Office, he noted, were given a promotion, along with an allowance for their wife and housing, when they married. If a labourer married, he was dismissed, so he could only 'go looking for prostitutes or "freelancers", thus increasing the illegitimacy rate – or (if only for safety) try sodomy'.[30]

These reports show a range of homosexual arrangements and behaviours in PNG: sex conceded after intimidation and sex given for money, sex between New Guineans and between Europeans and New Guineans, as well as between Europeans, sex on the beach, in a car and in a house, sex that may have been 'situational' among labourers without women companions, but also sex that fell into a regular pattern of cruising to find partners and continuing links between homosexuals, sex between men conscious of their homosexual desires or considered repeat offenders by the authorities and between men who said homosexuality was their 'fashion'. And away from European eyes occurred homosexual practices as part of initiation rites. Colonial law banned homosexual acts, while administrators and clerics worried about vice and tried to combat 'native' savagery and European immorality, but, in the tropical shadows, 'sodomy' flourished.

Homosexuality entered into public discussion in PNG through scandals and trials. Records occasionally suggest that sexual misbehaviour and renegade political attitudes went hand in hand, or at least that accusations of perversion could be used against those who aroused suspicion. In 1957, the Reverend H. Irving of Port Moresby wrote to the Australian Minister for Territories, Paul Hasluck, that an Australian company had sacked a local boy on the sole grounds that he had drunk cold water from a European's glass. Irving said that the manager responsible for dismissing the youth was 'anti-Papuan'. He asked the government minister to intervene, and criticised the way in which the colonial administration handled the issue of local employees' conditions of work. He concluded: 'The paper up here [*South Pacific Post*] is so full of complaints against native behaviour but so much could be said of the other side too.' The minister in Canberra forwarded the letter to the Papua New Guinea Administrator, Donald Cleland, who responded with what Hasluck termed a 'defensive' memorandum, questioning Irving's right to use the title of 'reverend' and casting doubt on his knowledge of indigenous affairs. Hasluck, considered relatively 'pro-native', wrote to the secretary of his department that he was 'more disturbed by Mr. Irving's letter now than I originally was because of the manner in which the Administrator has dealt with it'. When the secretary mentioned the problem to Cleland, he admitted that some branches of his administration did react defensively in such situations. Meanwhile, Hasluck wrote to Irving, thanking him for his letter and taking note of the issues he had raised. Irving replied, again detailing poor treatment of local labourers, particularly housing conditions. This again put Cleland on the defensive and, faced with a persistent trouble-maker, he argued in a lengthy and legalistically punctilious letter that the islanders had not been mistreated or disadvantaged. He then fired a blow below the belt at Irving:

> The Acting Commissioner of Police, Port Moresby, has advised that the Revd. Irving is known to the Police as a convicted sexual pervert. In New Zealand on the 25th February 1946, he was convicted of Indecent Assault (Male) on five (5) counts and sentenced to two years imprisonment with hard labour.

He added that Irving had left PNG for Australia early in 1957; one can only conjecture whether Cleland or the police had harassed Irving into leaving the territory. The report of his sexual activity – 'dirt' dragged up by the police – was meant to sully Irving's reputation and discredit his comments on native policy. With Irving gone, Cleland was rid of the critic and the aspersions cast on his administration, and Hasluck dropped the affair, though wondering whether Irving's criminal record was known when he had been given permission to live in PNG.[31]

Accusations of homosexuality could also be levelled at political leaders. In 1965, Frank Martin, a white member of the House of Assembly from the Sepik province, alleged that a committee of ten leaders set up by the New Guinea United National Party included, among other miscreants, two homosexuals. He thundered:

> Two of the party's working committee are active communist people, two of them are people that normal males do not like to associate with and one is a drunk. I do not think that it is fair go for the Administration to allow this sort of thing to go on.

However, he did not provide proof for his allegations.[32] Tarring and feathering nationalists as communists or perverts was intended to compromise the forces pushing for greater self-rule and, ultimately, independence. The Administrator of PNG later denied that there were any active Communists associated with the New Guinea United National Party, though he said nothing about possible homosexuals or an alcoholic.[33]

Europeans in New Guinea, though somewhat isolated from international developments, would have been aware of the increasing public debates on sexual issues that occurred in Australia in the post-war years – the homophobia of the 1950s, the 'sexual revolution' of the 1960s, the gay rights demonstrations of the 1970s. They sometimes became too aware for comfort of changing mores. In 1963, for instance, the film *Victim* was screened in Port Moresby. Starring Dirk Bogarde, it was, according to a local review, 'the story of a homosexual...who is trying to overcome his problem'. The sympathetic writer said that 'it shows a cross-section of homosexuals living in every other respect, normal lives without giving sanction for complete licence. Young people must be protected, and the film scores this point.'[34] Though it had only a short run, the film would have made viewers aware of the issue of homosexuality, and may have made some curious about homosexuals in their midst.

Even in remote Melanesia, colonials could thus not avoid confrontation with homosexuality. In 1968, right-minded residents of Port Moresby expressed outrage on learning that cadet patrol officers had been set an examination question in a law course dealing with a hypothetical sex orgy involving a group of nurses and patrol officers. James Griffin, a senior lecturer in history at the University of Papua New Guinea, responded that 'the law courts in this country deal with a considerable number of "sex cases" as do the courts in any other country', and argued that it was realistic for candidate officers to study such matters. 'It would be delightful if we could all successfully delude ourselves that "sex crimes" do not take place,' he continued, 'but a law lecturer suffering from such a delusion would be as much use to a group of law students as an illiterate teacher trying to teach primary school students how to read.'[35]

Through the late colonial period, and despite scandals and trials, discreet sodomitical fun could nevertheless be excused for both natives and Europeans. One Australian in PNG told a historian that homosexuals were left alone 'as long as they didn't race around the landscape obviously trying to seduce the natives' or parade as 'an obvious trissy queen'. One Australian who had lived in the territory reminisced:

> The boundaries were that the person concerned [as a sexual partner] had to be recognisably an adult, much more so than would be true in Australian or European society. The relationship could exist between a European and, say, his domestic servant. That was fairly common, and acceptable. It was seen as one of the solaces for the white man's burden.

He also spoke about another 'model' of homosexual relationship:

> between Europeans and Papua New Guineans where the son of some adult known to the European would be brought up by the European and given many advantages. The relationship between the European and the young man was tacitly recognised by the parents, and by society in general, but nobody said anything because the advantages were seen to be all for the

young guy who was being educated, housed, clothed, fed, whatever. There was little reaction on the part of Papua New Guineans against this kind of relationship. If anything it led to humour rather than to condemnation. It was thought to be mildly amusing that the big white master would dally with a young gentleman rather than many of the available young ladies who'd cheerfully have gone to bed with him at any time. It was just thought to be yet another of the quaint peculiarities of the European.

Most of the native young men later 'grew out' of their liaisons, 'but the benefits to these young men who were involved in relationships of this kind were very real'.[36]

In this context, some Australians could live and love without hindrance. One example is Harold William Rogers, an Anglo-Catholic Anglican priest from Sydney. Rogers served in PNG as a lance corporal and medical orderly in the Australian Army in 1944–5, and then worked at the Mukawa Mission station from 1951 to 1953. A posting to a Sarawak church followed from 1956 to 1960, and Rogers again returned to New Guinea, to live in Mt Hagen from 1966 to 1970. During his first stay, Rogers enjoyed a 'busy love live [*sic*] in the tropics, with the lads behind the mess huts in the moonlight'. Much later, Rogers also recollected a memorable sexual encounter with a passing German captain. He reviewed his position in the colony in the 1950s:

> I was part-time nurse, full-time teacher and priest to my lovely people. My role represented, complemented, the slowly vanishing Australian Raj up there. We weren't as pukka as the British version in India and elsewhere. We were more benevolent, not conquerors and Empire-builders but supporters and advisors to our native people. Pervasive cultural destroyers nevertheless.

Rogers – in his advanced years, a campy and alcoholic minor celebrity – presumably kept his political and sexual proclivities discreet while in the colony.[37]

Reminiscences of Australians who lived in PNG in the last years of colonisation confirm that homosexual encounters were easy. Venues such as the General Post Office in Port Moresby were known as hang-outs for young men eager to be picked up. Those interested in finding partners generally cruised in the evening, often from their cars, and simply motioned to youths who caught their fancy to accompany them home. The young men were occasionally city boys but often rural migrants, or constables or soldiers – the forces, large concentrations of unmarried males, generally proved a good source of sexual partners. With little to occupy their time (especially before the advent of television) and with few reservations about sexual activities, they were willing bedmates. Expatriates knew that, depending on their region of origin, men were likely to prefer oral or anal intercourse, or be active or passive, or more versatile, partners – they found Tolai men both particularly attractive and sexually enthusiastic. Conversation and a few beers facilitated the move from veranda or sitting-room to bedroom, and the Europeans usually drove the young men home afterwards, perhaps giving them a bit of money (although with beer and 'gratuity' included, the encounter seldom cost more than several dollars). Most local men saw these meetings as pleasurable physical encounters that gave them 'something to do', but did not engage their emotions or imply long-term commitment. Almost all eventually married and fathered children, though marriage did not necessarily bring their homosexual adventures to an end. Interested Europeans could find a stream of comely partners for casual sex (even for group sexual activities), though sometimes they suffered misadventures such as petty theft. Europeans and Melanesians with more pronounced and public homosexual identities meanwhile frequented 'artistic' circles, such as the theatre, in Port Moresby.[38]

The case of the Solomon Islands

Papua New Guinea's neighbour, the Solomon Islands Protectorate, to foreigners a little-known set of islands inhabited mostly by Melanesians, was arbitrarily divided from PNG by the vagaries of colonial conquest. Given the name of the Biblical king by Spanish explorers who hoped (in vain) that the islands would reveal a treasure-trove of precious metals, the archipelago remained a backwater of the British Empire. A few European planters and missionaries formed the bulk of the expatriate community, but there were only 400 whites, to 93,000 Melanesians, by the 1950s. Copra provided the major export; many islanders found employment – sometimes pressured into contract labour – in the sugar-cane fields of Queensland and elsewhere in the South Pacific. The plight of 'blackbird' labourers provoked much criticism in the late 1800s, leading to the banning of what many considered a new slave trade. The Solomons again gained world attention during the Second World War (particularly with the Battle of Guadalcanal), but there was little incentive for independence until the 1970s.

Europeans knew some men in the Solomons practised same-sex intercourse, such activities being seen as further proof of the heathenism and barbarity of the Melanesian islands. Europeans also realised that homosexual practices on large copra plantations, with all-male labour forces of recruits from different islands of the archipelago, were not uncommon in the Solomons, as in PNG. New arrivals often formed special friendships with 'old hands'; sexual contacts, along with mentoring and companionship, provided the benefits of these relationships (though they could also provoke jealousy and violence), to which Europeans generally turned a blind eye.[39] Europeans noted a rise in what one book called 'sexual maladjustment', which even 'savage punishments' – such as sentencing a youth of seventeen to seven years in gaol for 'unnatural behaviour' – failed to curb.[40]

Incidents of homosexuality involving Europeans were not unknown, though administrators and clerics predictably condemned homosexual practices. In the 1870s Henry Townsend, previously tried on homosexual charges in Samoa and Fiji, set up as a trader in the Solomons, accompanied by a young Melanesian man who served as his companion and presumably lover. Townsend was killed only a few days after his arrival, though there is no reason to presume that his death was related to any sexual offense.[41] Homosexuality also appeared in the respectable ranks of missionaries. The Melanesian Mission saw the Solomon Islands as prime territory for evangelisation, though islanders proved resistant to the Gospel throughout the nineteenth century. Many missionaries were young men from England, inspired by religious revivalism and the Oxford Movement, dreaming of winning souls for Christ in pagan islands. Some were led into temptation in the Solomons. A missionary named Brooke eagerly embarked for his adventure in the 1870s: 'There was I, the only white man on the Island, without so much as a pop-gun to defend myself with, dwelling amidst that crowd of eager bloodthirsty savages....The romance of the life appealed to me strongly.' However, 'part of the romance for Brooke lay in the emotional relationships that he established with his male pupils. In 1874, when overt homosexuality was discovered, he was abruptly dismissed from the Mission.'[42] A.E.C. Forrest, a lay teacher associated with the Melanesian Mission, set up a school at Nendo on Santa Cruz island. He worked there from 1887 to 1896, when it was revealed that he had engaged in sexual relations with his male students. One observer wrote:

> He has led some of our best boys into indecent offences with himself, & has gone on doing so for more than 2 years at least. The headteacher at [Santa Cruz], & many others I fear have been led into beastliness, & it would almost seem as though all was ruined [for the mission station] for a time.

Forrest was dismissed, but remained on the island as a trader, earning a reputation for drinking, swearing and anti-clericalism. In 1901 he was arrested on a charge of gross indecency and shipped to Sydney, where he escaped custody. He moved to the Torres islands, in present-day Vanuatu, where he committed suicide in 1908, afterwards 'to become the subject of colourful traders' tales of the fallen gentleman of "artistic temperament" who had been hounded to death by vindictive Christians'.[43]

Several decades later, sexual misconduct again troubled the Melanesian Mission. In 1928, Frederick Merivale Molyneux was appointed Assistant Bishop in charge of the Solomon Islands, with high hopes that his arrival would improve the fortunes – both evangelical and monetary – of the mission, which had been inefficiently running a costly steamship. The missionaries proved loath to abandon the old ship, and the Depression, precipitating a drop in both copra prices and donations from the faithful, further compromised the mission's parlous position. Financial strain was cited as the ostensible reason for Molyneux's surprise resignation in 1931, although accusations of homosexuality provided the real cause of his discreet departure.[44]

Europeans occasionally became embroiled in court cases because of sexual improprieties; not all scandals could be hushed up. In 1911, L.W. Keppel, a temporary assistant district officer on Malaita Island, was charged with having criminally assaulted a young male worker recruited on Rendova Island. Keppel, the plaintiff stated, had called him to his bedroom, caught hold of him by the arm and pushed him onto his bed. With one arm, Keppel held Ganga down, while with the other he turned off the light. Keppel took off Ganga's trousers and 'criminally assaulted' him. Keppel's superior did question how such an uninvited sexual overture was possible with a European colleague in a room nearby, how Keppel had managed to hold down and disrobe Ganga while turning down the wick of a kerosene lamp, why the young man had not cried out and why there was no reaction from the sentry stationed at the house. The sentry testified that he had indeed heard a cry, but Keppel claimed that Ganga had called out when he hit the Melanesian for not cleaning the lamp. After the incident, Ganga ran away and reported the assault. He was allowed to return to his home island, and Keppel left the Solomons. Such rudimentary archival details suggest that some Europeans did not hesitate to use force to get sex, and that authorities preferred that a guilty European slip quietly away rather than provoke a trial and possible conviction.[45]

That episode paled in comparison with an affair that hit the pages of the press forty-five years afterwards. In February 1956, Reginald Poole was put on trial for the murder of a 10- or 12-year-old Melanesian, the episode made more scandalous because of Poole's homosexuality. Poole was a 24-year-old Englishman from Stoke, who had decided to become a missionary after completing national service in the Royal Air Force. Learning that the Melanesian Mission in the Solomon Islands was desperately seeking lay missionaries, he signed up in 1954. After travelling to Sydney, he took a ship bound for the Solomons, via the New Hebrides. In a brief account published in the mission's journal, he recalled the unpleasantly rough sea voyage, but expressed enthusiasm for stations he visited *en route* to his posting in Pawa. In rather naïve style, he enthused over Father Jim's coffee at one outpost, and marvelled at the ducks and hens roaming about another mission. Pawa, he wrote, 'commands an elevated view of the Pacific Ocean, and is surrounded by spacious gardens'. He characterised the church building as a 'work of art' and found the layout of the school 'impressive': 'The behaviour and discipline of the boys were particularly striking. The horse-play which is so prevalent in English schools is completely absent from Melanesian schools.' The students had 'a remarkably versatile capacity for both manual and book work'. Poole found the tropical climate to have 'rather an enervating effect', but looked forward to his tasks: 'Everywhere the beautiful Spirit of the Master inspires the work that is being accomplished here in his name.'[46] Within a few months of arrival at Pawa in February, however, Poole was surprisingly transferred to the Maravovo Mission Station, on the island of Guadalcanal. This occurred in July 1955, according to a later report in the *Pacific Islands Monthly*, after 'two Solomon Islands boys at the school told the headmaster...that Poole was a homosexual'.[47]

Missionaries at Maravovo had been busily developing their station – clearing land for a copra plantation and a cattle paddock, harvesting copra for export, erecting new dormitories for students and a storehouse on the beach, and building a bridge over a river that divided their property. Describing the bustling station and the students who lived there, missionaries paid tribute to the 'lads' keenness' in undertaking the work, yet underlined the challenging efforts – for example, to treat and prevent tuberculosis – that remained.[48]

Murder soon broke the spell of optimism and happiness at this promising outpost of Christianity in the South Seas. *Pacific Islands Monthly* recounted the events of 17 November 1955, following Poole's lunch with the Reverend D. Hoey:

> After the meal was finished, Poole went to his own house, called 'One Boy' (this or 'one fella boy 'e come', is the usual summons in Melanesian Pidgin when a boy is wanted) and a few minutes later rushed to Hoey to tell him that he had killed the boy.

Hoey found the schoolboy, Henry Kwakwaoa, with a pick-axe sticking out of his arm-pit; he was bleeding from three wounds, including a blow that had fractured his skull. The boy died within half an hour. Poole was sedated, and then taken to the protectorate capital, Honiara. He initially wanted to plead guilty with no defence to the charge of murder, though his barrister persuaded him to plead not guilty by virtue of insanity. Poole admitted that he had killed Kwakwaoa, a boy whom he claimed not to know (but who in fact had entered the small school three weeks before his death), because he was concerned over debts and family affairs, and 'he had been worried because of his homosexual tendencies'. He had attempted on several occasions to commit suicide, and thought that the murder would result in his execution, a death he seemingly desired. The doctor who treated Poole in December, John McGeorge, the official New South Wales government psychiatrist, hypothesised that an 'early neurosis had developed into early schizophrenia'. According to *Pacific Islands Monthly*,

> the doctor said that Poole had admitted to him that he had indulged in unnatural practices and that he had murdered the boy to avoid temptation. He (Poole) had tried to commit suicide but that the 'murder would achieve the same result'.

Such a diagnosis accorded with a view – progressive for the time – for which McGeorge was well known, that homosexuality was an illness to be treated, but not an evil or necessarily a crime in itself.[49]

The Judicial Commissioner and three Assessors (including one islander) constituted a court (since there was no trial by jury in the protectorate). Various witnesses testified, and from the dock Poole confessed, 'I am sorry I killed the boy. I did not know what I was doing. I had been worried for a long time about my father, money and things I had done.' The court found Poole guilty on 1 February 1956, deciding that he did indeed know the victim and that he was cognisant of the wrongfulness of his act. Based on the doctor's expert views, they rejected the defence of insanity. Poole was sentenced to death by hanging. The British High Commissioner for the Western Pacific had authority to commute the sentence, and Poole's family – his mother had flown out from England to attend the trial – were reported to be considering a plea for clemency to the Colonial Office.[50]

Poole did file an appeal, and a court in Suva, Fiji, headquarters of the British High Commission, overturned the verdict of the Honiara court, finding Poole insane. The defence convincingly argued that the first trial had been improperly conducted, since McGeorge was not fully cross-examined and did not make his report on Poole's condition available to the accused man's legal counsel prior to the trial. The judges ruled that McGeorge's evidence that Poole was not clinically insane thus ought not to have been admitted, as it was prejudicial to the defence. The appeal judges decided that Poole was legally insane (even if not medically so) based on the frenzied way in which he had killed the boy and because of his strange behaviour in the Honiara court (the details of which are not provided in press accounts). With his acquittal, Poole returned to England, via Sydney – where newspapers noted the transit of the by now notorious murderer – to enter a psychiatric hospital; his fate is unknown.[51]

Did Poole make a sexual overture to his unfortunate victim before he murdered him, and, if so, was that gesture welcomed or rebuffed? Did Poole have sexual relations with other young men at the Marovovo station and, beforehand, at the Pawa mission? What had caused the schoolboys to report him to his superiors at Pawa? Had he come to the Solomon Islands in the hope of sublimating or curing his homosexual desires, might he have regarded work in the Pacific as providing sexual opportunities unavailable at home, or did he discover his orientation only after he moved to the tropics? Deep in Poole's psyche were there scars from 'horseplay' at school in England? What sort of sex life had he experienced in the past? Was Poole clinically insane or not? Answers to these questions would be speculative.

Reaction to the gruesome incident is interesting. Some newspapers, such as the organ of the Sydney Anglican archdiocese, avoided the case – a single article, containing no mention of the homosexual aspect, noted that the Primate had allotted £500 for Poole's defence.[52] Other newspapers published contradictory reports about the attitude of the Melanesians. Sydney tabloids initially shied away from sex as well, though the *Daily Mirror*, keen not to miss a good headline, titled one story 'Perversion claim in island trial'. The *Sun-Herald*, another Sunday tabloid, titled a front-page story: 'Drums beat for hanging – White killer drama', and breathlessly reported that Poole's 'trial was the queerest and most fantastic of the century in a British Court of law'. Reports remarked on the water-filled gin bottles on the Bench, the judge sweating in tropical heat in gown and wig, the purple-robed bishop pacing back and forth outside the courtroom, the masses of Melanesians held back behind rope barriers. A sub-head proclaimed 'fear of murder, arson, stealing', and pictured Poole's grief-stricken mother and the 'Death scene: The huts at Maravovo Mission on Guadalcanal where Poole killed the boy'. Another Sydney news-paper quoted the Bishop of Melanesia, A.T. Hill: 'I would gladly sacrifice myself to the natives to prevent a bad outbreak of violence if Reginald Poole is not hanged.' He foreshadowed 'reprisal killings' and feared that he himself might be a target. Hill thought that 'if Poole is not hanged, the natives will lose confi-dence in whites'. The *Daily Telegraph* reported that 'white men sitting in Poole's trial got more than a cold shiver down their spine'. With a proto-nationalist cargo cult, Marching Rule, already active – leading natives to 'lapse into mass frenzies and wild carousals of drink and sex to prelude the end of the white man's rule' (in the words of the *Sunday Telegraph*) – Europeans faced 'the threat of a fearsome Mau-Mau like rebellion against colonial rule'. A report sent to *Pacific Islands Monthly*, however, testified to:

> the small number of natives attending the trial and the calmness almost amounting to apathy of Solomon Islanders in Honiara. Although the murder aroused deep feeling in the dead boy's district of North Malaita, there were no disturbances and the proceedings both inside and outside the court-house were characterised by an almost church-like quiet.[53]

Discrepancy in the views reveals the extent to which expatriate fears, and media desire for a 'good story', influenced perspectives.

The killing of a Melanesian boy by a white man, even without the homo-sexual motive, could well have inflamed passions. Indeed, the Australian government dispatched a Navy tug with forty officers and sailors to prevent or control possible rioting and to protect Europeans from any reprisals. The ship was told to sail past the islands, but shore parties (according to instructions from the Australian Prime Minister's office) were to be provided only at the request of British authorities and 'only for the preservation of life and property and nothing more' – an indication of Canberra's fears that trouble might eventuate, and an expression of imperial solidarity between Australia and Britain. HMAS *Sprightly* toured the islands uneventfully for a month.[54]

Worries expressed by missionaries, journalists and bureaucrats about blood-thirsty revenge attacks on individual whites, or an uprising against colonial rule, proved unwarranted. The daily press had reacted to the event with what a calmer *Pacific Islands Monthly* termed 'hysteria' and 'sensationalism'. The maga-zine meanwhile wondered if Poole had got justice in the Honiara trial, pointing out that the death sentence would have routinely been commuted in Australia; it seemed relieved when the Suva court did overturn the verdict.

The various publications, and those concerned by the trial, engaged in much discussion about responsibility for the circumstances leading to the murder. The Melanesian Mission had retained legal counsel, briefed Poole's barrister, hired a doctor to examine him and paid for Mrs Ruth Poole's journey to the Solomon

Islands, though she publicly asked whether 'my son has been left to rot in an island jail, friendless and deserted by the missionaries he yearned to join and help?' The *Sun-Herald* quoted her as saying, in tears, 'Why didn't they send Reggie home from Pawa for treatment? Then the tragedy would never have happened.' *Pacific Islands Monthly* was also critical of the mission:

> No one in their right senses – and the PIM least of all – can understand why the Mission, when it found Poole to have homosexual tendencies as long ago as July, 1955, did not pack him off to England instead of waiting for a far bigger tragedy to overtake them all.

The reporter continued in a sceptical vein:

> In its Christian unwisdom [*sic*], it may have imagined that Poole could overcome his unfortunate weakness by prayer. But missionaries these days are not expected to be sheltered dreamers. They are expected to understand the darker side of human weakness and cope realistically – and most of them do. The Mission's first duty, as a mission and as European, was the protection of the young natives entrusted to it. There is also, still, the remnants of the almost outmoded business of keeping up European prestige. The Mission failed in both these duties.

In the *Sydney Morning Herald*, one letter writer, Anne P. Nettleship, did not mince words:

> The tragedy of Reginald Poole should make the Anglican Mission in the Solomon Islands think twice before sending young men, full of hope and enthusiasm for the work they are about to undertake, to a country with a frightful climate, loneliness, and with starvation rates of pay.

She remembered meeting Poole, 'a normal British boy, fun-loving, with a good sense of humour and a great interest in his work', when he stopped in Sydney on the way to the Solomons. He had told her that when he first learned his salary, £5 a week, he thought such a paltry sum was only his pocket money, and she was not surprised that he suffered financial worries. Mrs Nettleship felt that Poole had been corrupted by the natives and echoed his mother's words:

> Why did the Board of Missions allow a boy – he was no more than that – to go to a place where homosexual relations are the order of the day among the natives, see him succumb to these practices, and yet keep him there to finish out his term of two years? Why was he not transferred away from the country? Why was he not sent home to England and given the help he so desperately needed?

She concluded in convinced tones:

Sent somewhere else, not New Guinea or the Solomons, he in all proba-
bility would have become a worthy member of society. I know the native
habits, having lived in New Guinea for some years prior to World War II,
and they have not changed.[55]

Such reports pointed the finger at the mission for failure to exercise its
pastoral duty with regard to Poole. The missionaries responded in a reserved but
defensive way, skirting discussion of homosexuality. The head of the Australian
Board of Missions reported to his colleagues about the 'appalling tragedy', 'as far
as I know...the first murder of a Melanesian by a European since law and order
were established in the protectorate'. His personal diagnosis, which made no
mention of Poole's alleged homosexual activities or feelings, was that 'undoubtedly Poole must have had a temporary brainstorm as he had given no
indications of abnormality....But looking back I realise how very immature he
is.'[56] The Melanesian Mission's journal, the *Southern Cross Log*, reported briefly
on the 'terrible tragedy', though with no hint of the reasons for Poole's murder
of the islander or his homosexuality. Mission authorities clearly wished to avoid
the question, and the implication that they either welcomed a known homosexual into their midst or made no efforts to convert him away from his awful
urges. In somewhat self-serving fashion, the missionary newspaper's anonymous
writer stressed that the English Committee of the Mission had paid for Poole's
mother's trip, that 'everything possible' was done to comfort the dead boy's
family, and that 'the Bishop and others regularly visited the accused during the
long weeks of waiting for the trial and the appeal'. It concluded, stoically and
self-righteously: 'The Church in Melanesia has had to bear many bitter experiences in the past hundred years, but no war against evil in any of its many forms
can be fought without casualties, hard though they be to endure.'[57]

Supporters of the mission and some armchair experts on Melanesia denied
that homosexuality was widespread in the region (though they did not defend
the mission against charges of neglecting its duties by not repatriating Poole
after the Pawa allegations). Replying to Mrs Nettleship in the letters column of
the *Sydney Morning Herald*, Canon M.A. Warren of the Australian Board of
Missions said that her claim of homosexuality being rife among New Guineans
'is unwarranted and contrary to the experience of those who have lived for years
among the natives'. He had lived in PNG for seven years and maintained close
contact with the islands for three decades, the priest said, and 'not a single case
has ever come under my notice'. For good measure, Warren added:

Recently I conferred with one of our men who has lived for almost 40 years
in close contact with the lives and minds of the native people and has an
intimate knowledge of their habits: 'As a native weakness it [homosexu-
ality] does not exist.'[58]

However, a writer in *Pacific Islands Monthly*, 'Tolala' (the *nom de plume* of
Gordon Thomas, ex-editor of the *Rabaul Times*), refuted such observations:

To say that homosexuality does not exist there is just so much poppycock. It is a well known fact that in most parts of the Sepik and Aitape districts many native men would not recruit for work on plantations unless they were accompanied by their "monkeys" (young boys). Homosexuality was an accepted practice in those districts and there was nothing anti-social in such activity. In some areas of NG [sic] it existed; in others it did not. Just the same as cannibalism, head-hunting and the immolation of widows. Different tribes, different customs.

Tolala quoted Stephen Reed's *The Making of Modern New Guinea* in support of his observations.[59]

Pacific Islands Monthly spoke of homosexuality as an illness that might be brought on or made worse by tropical fraternisation with young men:

It is difficult for normal people to understand a homosexual's urges. They have to take the medical profession's word for it that it is a disease needing treatment. But even the naivest person should know that to isolate Poole in a community far from people of his own age and class and to place him in daily contact with young native boys was the worst possible treatment for his trouble.

(Among other unstated assumptions in that nevertheless relatively tolerant generalisation is that homosexuals were predatory paedophiles.) Interestingly, the magazine, and other writers, seemed little concerned to denounce vice and stamp out sin, and rather more concerned about too open a discussion on the frequency of homosexuality in PNG and the Solomon Islands. Tolala worried about the attention given to the Poole case by the Sydney press: 'I confess I had some fears of homosexual skeletons being tumbled out of cupboards.' Another writer in *Pacific Islands Monthly* admitted straightforwardly: 'Although opinion on the Poole murder case is divided, most residents of long standing in the SW Pacific are unanimous about one thing – homosexuality always has existed there, if not in one district, then in another.' One unidentified member of the administration had written to the magazine to disagree with Canon Warren's assertation that there was no endemic homosexuality in the region: 'I have dealt with dozens of cases – and the least said about the Europeans, the better.' Somewhat coyly, the journalist added:

He then mentions a few of the Europeans – one of which would surprise a number of people. Few people with any length of residence in this part of the Pacific have to think long before recollecting natives who practiced the vice, or recalling one European known or suspected. These observations should not give the impression that the vice is rampant amongst Europeans. It isn't. But for anyone afflicted in that manner the opportunities are greater and, because of isolation, so is the compulsion. However, in a native community 'keeping it dark' is virtually impossible and discovery is inevitable...[*sic*] whereupon the European involved was, in the past, usually persuaded to fade silently from the scene and no scandal resulted. Like our reader, we think that the less said by Missions and everyone else about homosexuality in the SW Pacific the better. The mere mention of the word must produce the sound of rattling skeletons from many cupboards.[60]

The headline of the article – 'Homosexuality – Skeletons in many cupboards' – intriguingly emphasised the hint, despite denials, that homosexuality was frequently practised by both islanders and Europeans (including some easily recognisable if their names were published), but that discussion of the matter remained inappropriate.

Pacific Islands Monthly did not argue the necessity of mounting an attack on homosexuality in order to 'civilise' natives (though it did place homosexuality alongside such barbarous practices as cannibalism). Nor did it imply that homosexual dalliances would inevitably weaken white rule. Talk about homosexuality, by implication, was more dangerous than homosexual acts themselves. The best way of dealing with homosexuals who had got into trouble was to ship them home as soon and as quietly as possible, as had been done in several earlier instances (and ought to have been done with Poole). But even if a European had committed murder, as a result of a homosexual 'brainstorm', it would be preferable for him to be declared insane and discreetly repatriated rather than have the spectacle of a white man hanged. This represented a disconcerting admission about the double standards of colonial justice – the likelihood of a native going free after killing a white man or woman was improbable. The father of Poole's victim well understood this anomaly: 'Malaita man angry – white man unchanged.' The boy's uncle added, 'It is no good having one law for the white man and another for the native Malaita man.'[61]

The more considerable attention given in the press to Poole's fate and the responsibility of the mission than to the effects on the island boy's family and community speaks for itself. That the letters and commentary on the Poole affair concentrated on the question of homosexuality (not crime) underlines social concerns about sexual irregularity, whether among islanders or Europeans, including fear of homosexual skeletons tumbling out of European closets. Lack of debate on other questions raised by the affair – Europeans' easy access to possible weapons, failure of the mission to supervise its charges, recruitment of inappropriate staff, inadequate preparation of missionaries, the penurious wages they received, any reparation to the dead boy's family, the system of colonial justice, the freeing of a confessed murderer – indicates, not surprisingly, the continuing focus of European concern.

In 'diagnosing' homosexuality, commentators judged it an illness; tropical conditions could bring about mental and sexual disorientation, and a fragile European with a predisposition could be conducted to vice by 'natives', among whom homosexuality was said to be endemic. Yet, reports also suggested that 'natives' could be corrupted by immoral Europeans. In Melanesia, as in other tropical and colonial regions, the dangers of sexual misadventure were constantly present, and sublimation difficult. Europeans gave in to temptation often enough that full and frank discussions about their behaviour might bring unpleasant revelations about colonial society.

The Poole *affaire* is an extreme example of personal psychosis and collective fears and recriminations, the case of a man whose inability to assume his homosexuality drove him to murderous violence, and of a public debate (on a small scale, to be sure) about the causes, incidence and treatment of homosexuality. It reveals colonial European preoccupations; the desire to 'civilise' a primitive world by dispatching priests, soldiers and administrators, instituting European law, converting local morals and assuring white rule. In the Solomons and in PNG, Europeans faced a sexual and moral universe different from their own, and they found – to their horror – that some of their compatriots succumbed to the sexual lure of the tropics. Efforts by religious and legal authorities to wipe out homosexuality, whether traditional rites in native villages, homosexual liaisons among uprooted labourers, or inter-racial rendezvous in growing cities or European stations, had not surprisingly failed.

The contours of colonial homosexuality in Melanesia are different from other parts of the world that fell under European dominion. Records have not yet revealed a Melanesian equivalent of Lawrence and Dahoum. Sexual engagements have not left traces of long and intellectually charged friendships. There appears no conqueror of Melanesia such as Stanley or Lyautey motivated by an erotic appreciation of fellow colonialists or exotic local men. There is little intentionally eroticised European imagery of Melanesian men. Homosexual men of letters of the colonial era were not drawn across the Pacific as they were drawn across the Mediterranean. Europeans did not fantasise about Melanesian islands as they did about North African souks or hammams. Unlike Arabs or Indians, Melanesians did not enter European homosexual mythology, perhaps because they were too unfamiliar and too distant, both literally and metaphorically, from the centre of European life and fantasy, too different and unknown to fit into European erotic categories. Yet these little outposts of European colonialism could provide homosexual opportunities and sometimes provoke sexual crises. Even there European colonialists instituted regulations making homosexual practices and attitudes into crimes, sins and illnesses. There, too, they worried about the effects of the tropics, and native practices, on errant Europeans.

Notes

1 See Gilbert Herdt, *Guardians of the Flutes: Idioms of Masculinity* (New York, 1981), and for a participant-observer account, Tobias Schneebaum, *Where the Spirits Dwell: An Odyssey in the Jungle of New Guinea* (New York, 1988).
2 Stephen Windsor Reed, *The Making of Modern New Guinea* (Philadelphia, 1943), pp. 175, 220–1.
3 Rodney Magwich (Industrial Advocate, Public Service Association of PNG), 'A submission on plantation wages to Rural Wages Board of Industry', 13 May 1970, National Archives of Australia, Canberra (uncatalogued).

4 Ian Downs, *The Last Mountain: A Life in Papua New Guinea* (St Lucia, Qld, 1986). Such general statements, sometimes made on the basis of casual observations, might be questioned.

5 Lloyd Rhys, *High Lights and Flights in New Guinea* (London, 1942), pp. 238–9; other observers said sexual practices were limited to mutual masturbation.

6 *Ibid.*

7 Divine Word missionaries, National Archives of Australia A518/1, Item R838/1 Part 2.

8 Peter Lawrence, *Road Belong Cargo: A Study of the Cargo Movement in the South Madang District New Guinea* (Melbourne, 1964), p. 118.

9 A. Inglis, *Not a White Woman Safe: Sexual Anxiety and Politics in Port Moresby, 1920–1934* (Canberra, 1974), pp. 79–80.

10 Robert French, *Camping by a Billabong: Gay and Lesbian Stories from Australian History* (Sydney, 1993).

11 In 1950, the United Nations General Assembly called upon administering colonial powers to abolish corporal punishment, and the Australian minister recommended that whipping be abolished for unnatural offences and sexual offences involving males only, and certain acts of violence, e.g. murder and attempted murder, but retained for offences by juveniles, sexual offences against females, certain acts of violence (such as garroting and sabotage) and mutiny (National Archives of Australia A518/1 Item A846/6/148).

12 Information compiled from the Australian *Annual Reports* on Papua.

13 Information compiled from the Commonwealth of Australia's *Report to the General Assembly of the United Nations on the Administration of the Territory of New Guinea.*

14 From 1947 through 1955, twelve men were charged with sodomy, five with permitting sodomy and four with attempted sodomy, six with carnal knowledge against the order of nature, six with indecently dealing with a boy under the age of fourteen, two with committing acts of gross indecency with a male person and one each with permitting carnal knowledge against the order of nature and procuring a male person to commit gross indecency. Twenty-nine of thirty-seven charges resulted in convictions. From 1955 through 1967, when statistical tables used only the rubric of 'unnatural offences', the number of charges rose, but the conviction rate fell, from over three-quarters to just over half; thirty-seven of sixty-three charges in the twelve years after 1955 resulted in convictions.

15 *South Pacific Post*, 17 July 1959, p. 3.

16 *South Pacific Post*, 2 June 1959, p. 3.

17 *South Pacific Post*, 4 July 1952, p. 3.

18 *South Pacific Post*, 5 September 1952, 24 December 1952, 13 February 1953.

19 *South Pacific Post*, 20 August 1952, p. 1.

20 *South Pacific Post*, 1 July 1953, p. 3.

21 *South Pacific Post*, 14 September 1955, p. 3.

22 The following cases are taken from casebooks contained in the papers of Justice R.T. Gore, MS 2819, National Library of Australia, Canberra.

23 Several examples of homosexuality among PNG police are recounted in August Ibrum Kituai, *My Gun, My Brother: The World of the Papua New Guinea Colonial Police, 1920–1960* (Honolulu, 1998), pp. 257–9.

24 Australian-enforced fashions for islanders, curiously, seemed designed to emphasise their sexuality. Most Melanesians preferred long ramis (also called lap-laps or lavalavas) reaching to their ankles, yet 'there was an irrational belief among Europeans in Rabaul that long lavalavas were an expression of insolence and worn by persons of insubordinate or even subversive nature'. Authorities required Melanesians in the public service, such as constables and court officers, to wear short wrap-arounds: 'Judge Phillips' staff were apparently obliged to wear cloth so short that their physical appendages were in jeopardy' (Downs, pp. 52–3).

25 *South Pacific Post*, 13 May 1968, p. 3.

26 *South Pacific Post*, 20 September 1968, p. 3.

27 *South Pacific Post*, 9 December 1968, p. 1; 11 December 1968, p. 1; 6 January 1969, p. 1; 8 January 1969, p. 8; 26 February 1969, p. 1; 14 March 1969, p. 1; 17 March 1969, p. 6.

28 *South Pacific Post*, 1 July 1969, p. 1; 5 August 1969, p. 10; 6 August 1969, p. 1.

29 *South Pacific Post*, 10 July 1969, p. 16.

30 *South Pacific Post*, 4 August 1969, p. 1.

31 National Archives of Australia, A452/1 Item 57/183.

32 *South Pacific Post*, 6 September 1965, p. 3.

33 *South Pacific Post*, 10 September 1965, p. 3.

34 *South Pacific Post*, 3 December 1963, p. 26.

35 *South Pacific Post*, 27 September 1968, p. 1; 14 October 1968, p. 18.

36 Hank Nelson, *Taim Bilong Masta: The Australian Involvement with Papua New Guinea* (Sydney, 1982), pp. 181–2.

37 Brian Cartledge, 'The Biography-in-Progress of Harold William Rogers, Anglican Priest [1922–1988]', in Robert Aldrich and Garry Wotherspoon, *Gay Perspectives: Essays in Australian Gay Culture* (Sydney, 1992), pp. 113–29; quotations from pp. 122 and 125.

38 Personal communication for a former Australian resident of Port Moresby. Two fictional works that contain homosexual characters portray similar relationships in the colonial period. See Nigel Krauth, *JF was Here* (Sydney, 1990), and Trevor Shearston, *A Straight Young Back* (Pymble, NSW, 2000).

39 Judith A. Bennett, *Wealth of the Solomons: A History of a Pacific Archipelago, 1800–1978* (Honolulu, 1987), p. 174.

40 H. Ian Hogbin and C. Wedgwood, *Development and Welfare in the Western Pacific* (Canberra, 1943), p. 9.

41 Bennett, pp. 58–9.

42 David Hilliard, *God's Gentlemen: A History of the Melanesian Mission, 1849–1942* (St Lucia, Qld, 1978), p. 184.

43 *Ibid.*, pp. 185–6.

44 *Ibid.*, pp. 249–51.

45 British Solomon Islands Protectorate archives 14/6 and 14/40. I am grateful to Clive Moore for bringing this incident to my attention and allowing me to use his notes.

46 Reginald Poole, 'Introductions', *Southern Cross Log*, Vol. 62, No. 2 (May 1955), p. 52.

47 *Pacific Islands Monthly*, February 1956, p. 20.

48 D. and I.H. [*sic*], 'Maravovo regained', *Southern Cross Log*, Vol. 62, No. 2 (May 1955), pp. 41–4.

49 *Pacific Islands Monthly*, February 1956, pp. 20–1, and April 1956, p. 25.

50 *Pacific Islands Monthly*, February 1956, pp. 20–1, and April 1956, p. 25; *British Solomon Islands Protectorate News Sheet*, No. 5 (1 January–15 March 1956); *Fiji Times and Herald*, 31 January 1956.

51 Reports in the *Daily Telegraph* (Sydney), 1, 3 and 4 February 1956, *Sunday Telegraph*, 5 and 12 February 1956, *Daily Mirror* (Sydney), 31 January, 1, 2 and 3 February 1956.

52 *Anglican*, 9 March 1956, p. 5.

53 *Sun-Herald*, 14 February 1956, p. 2; *Daily Telegraph*, 12 February 1956, p. 19.

54 *South Pacific Post*, 21 March 1956, p. 1.

55 *Sydney Morning Herald*, 14 February 1956; *Sun-Herald*, 14 February 1956, p. 3; *Pacific Islands Monthly*, March 1956, p. 28.

56 Agenda, Australian Board of Missions Meeting, 7–9 February 1956, ABM Collection Box 45 (69), ABM Board Meeting Minute Books, ML MSS 4503, Mitchell Library, Sydney.
57 *Southern Cross Log*, Vol. 63, No. 2 (June 1956), pp. 33–4.
58 *Sydney Morning Herald*, 20 February 1956, p. 2.
59 *Pacific Islands Monthly*, March 1956, p. 28.
60 *Pacific Islands Monthly*, April 1956, p. 20.
61 *Daily Mirror*, 3 February 1956, p. 1.

9 The British (and others) in South Asia

India exercised an irresistible attraction to Britons in search of cultural *dépaysement*, adventure, spiritual enlightenment or the social advancement that colonial service could provide.[1] Imperial authorities were much troubled about immorality among expatriates, and such after-effects of sexual encounters as venereal disease and illegitimate births. These concerns gave rise to legislation concerning brothels, and medical policies to treat disease. Officials nevertheless accepted that young soldiers' and administrators' desires would motivate them to seek sexual relationships. They thus tolerated female prostitution, including the establishment of camp brothels to cater to the military.[2] Homosexuality, however, was a different question, and British law codes made homosexual acts illegal in India, though they did not forbid the close intimacy between men that might have a homosocial component.[3] Colonial rulers also reacted against homosexuality among the Indian elite. Lord Curzon drew up a list of princes with homosexual tastes, which he blamed on early marriage: 'A boy gets tired of his wife, or of women, at an early age, and wants the stimulus of some more novel or exciting sensation.' Curzon sent one homosexual prince to the Cadet Corps to learn self-discipline, but then fretted that his influence might corrupt other young men.[4] Despite such efforts, homosexuality did not disappear among either Indians or British expatriates.

Travellers, too, followed the lead of Richard Burton and enjoyed the pleasures India offered. In 1912, E.M. Forster and his friend Goldsworthy Lowes Dickinson travelled to India. At Chhatarpur, they found that the maharajah shared their sexual orientation; according to Dickinson, 'It soon turned out that he was homosexual, in a curious (or not curious) way which combined what would be called perverted sexuality with philosophic and religious curiosity and yearning.' Dickinson, meanwhile, found the British in India insufferable; he memorably described society life in one cantonment as 'twaddle and tea, after tennis'. Hinduism inspired some interest in him, but the stronger pull was to Hellenism and the West. Indian scenery and people were engaging: 'The gait and dress (or nudity) of the people is the great beauty – such reds and greens and blues in the landscape; and primitive goats and cows; and the lovely brown skins. But it is really distressing to feel the gulf – everyone salaaming to the white man, cringing and begging'.

Dickinson's own intellectual attraction outside Europe lay in China, and his sexual tastes ran to a life-long boot fetish.[5]

Dickinson resisted the lure of the Raj, but India conquered Forster. He had already fallen in love with an Indian student in England, and the trip with Dickinson further developed an interest that would manifest itself in *A Passage to India* and other works. Forster will be the subject of a separate chapter, while the present one will look at several very different men with varying reactions to South Asia: Forster's friend J.R. Ackerley; their contemporary, a soldier called Kenneth Searight; two Westerners drawn to India religion, Charles Leadbeater and Alain Daniélou; and a procession of visitors to Sri Lanka, centring on Edward Carpenter.

J.R. Ackerley at a maharajah's court

Forster met J.R. Ackerley (1896–1967) the year after he graduated at Cambridge in 1921, and the two remained life-long friends. Ackerley was destined to serve as the much respected literary editor of *The Listener* from 1935 to 1959 and to publish several well-received books, including a biography of his beloved Alsatian, *My Dog Tulip*, and a posthumous autobiographical volume, *My Father and Myself*, in which he talked about his own homosexuality, and the bigamy and bisexuality (and early homosexual prostitution) of his father. During his lifetime, Ackerley's most popular book was *Hindoo Holiday*, originally published in 1932, reissued two decades later in an edition that restored the 'naughty' bits. The memoir chronicled the four-month sojourn that Forster had arranged for Ackerley at the court of his acquaintance the Maharajah of the central Indian state of Chhatarpur (which he mischievously called Chhokrapur, or 'city of boys') in 1923 and 1924. Chhatarpur was a nondescript state, but its diminutive 57-year-old ruler was an alert and endearing prince. Ackerley had very vague duties as secretary, but the maharajah really wanted a companion: 'He wanted some one to love him....He wanted a friend. He wanted under-standing, and sympathy, and philosophic comfort.' The maharajah was interested in philosophy and his broad, if eclectic, reading prompted questions about God, sin, truth and the nature of life, queries the young Ackerley found challenging to answer.[6]

The maharajah, though married, was basically homosexual, his proclivities known to members of his court and to his British overlords (who perhaps denied him a knighthood because of his penchants). He enjoyed the company of a troupe of handsome young dancers, 'the Gods'. The ruler also had a strik-ingly attractive 20-year-old 'valet', Raghunandi ('Sharma' in Ackerley's memoir), who regularly had sex with him, and Ackerley revealed that sodomising the maharajah (and having intercourse with the maharani) was among his courtly duties, and he was beaten if he did not perform properly.[7]

The maharajah also courted another young man, Mahadeo ('Narayan' in the book), a guest-house clerk, although his firm rebuffs antagonised the prince. The maharajah longed for other comely men as well, and Ackerley recounted his efforts to bring to his palace a village boy whom he referred to as Napoleon the Third.

The maharajah's homosexuality did not limit itself to sex with courtiers and pining after subjects. He fondly remembered the visit of Forster and Dickinson, with whom he acknowledged affinities. He was familiar with the writings of Edward Carpenter and the life of Oscar Wilde, and was particularly attracted to the Ancients. The maharajah confessed to owning a toga, devised a plan to build a Grecian temple on his estate and said that he wanted to turn his state into a Greek kingdom. The Hellenophilia was an attempt to build a land fit for a man such as himself: 'Goodness, wisdom, and beauty – that is what the Greeks worshipped and that is what I want…a good, wise, and beautiful friend.'[8]

Ackerley's position in the maharajah's scheme was ambiguous. India intrigued him, though he was baffled by many customs and annoyed by some of the Indians with whom he associated. He ridiculed the maharajah in his letters, but presented a more sympathetic portrait in the memoir. He played along with the maharajah's talk of the classics, joking that, if he stayed in Chhatarpur, he would help the ruler resurrect Antiquity, and he gossiped cheerily with the maharajah about the attractions of various boys. Ackerley made friends with Sharma and Narayan, admiring the beauty of both, and developed an infatuation with Narayan. The Indian lads, good friends but rivals, spent much time with Ackerley, and (to a limit) reciprocated his affections. Ackerley put his arms around them and tried to steal kisses. Sharma at first resisted (but told Narayan about the attempt), and Narayan gave in, although, as a Brahmin, he regarded kissing a Western meat-eater as sinful. Ackerley did not understand that, in the words of the Dewan (Prime Minister), 'a kiss on the mouth is a very big thing; it is a completed sexual act'. The maharajah gently chided Ackerley for trying to kiss Sharma, but Ackerley replied, 'I must kiss *somebody*.' 'I want to love you very much,' Ackerley declared to Narayan. Narayan said that he never 'lay with' men, yet grew extremely fond of Ackerley, his gestures to the Englishman 'full of love'. Sharma's sexuality was even less clear, an indication of the different sexual patterns that existed in India. Narayan told Ackerley enigmatically that Sharma was only 'half-made' and would not say whether he had sex with his wife. Narayan apparently did not love his own wife, though he had sex with her frequently.[9]

Ackerley described Sharma, Narayan and other Indian youths in homoerotic fashion, dwelling on their lithe brown bodies, the way in which the muslin dhotis shaped their figures, and their gentle manners. The maharajah himself developed an extended metaphorical description of ideal male beauty. Even the Dewan remarked that friendship must contain passion, 'though not necessarily sexual', and added that 'only boys were capable of that passion and enthusiasm'.[10] The sensual world of India – the maharajah's silk and brocaded robes, sultry heat, the fun of the Holi festival – contrasted with the unbearable attitude of the British colonials. One English lady warned Ackerley, 'Don't go Indian', but Ackerley was almost seduced.[11] He pulled back, aware no doubt that both Indians and British would be *au courant* of every move. He shied away from pressing his attentions on Sharma and Narayan, staying celibate although opportunities for sex occurred, returning to Britain although the maharajah and his companions urged him to stay on.

Hindoo Holiday presents the curious scenario of an Indian maharajah who conceives of his own sexual yearnings in Greek style, and the classically educated middle-class Englishman who happily flirts and keeps company with Hindu youths in a fairy-tale India. Ancient culture and sexual interest in men formed a bond between the maharajah and Ackerley. The Englishman enthused that 'Napoleon the Third' was a 'bronze Ganymede', at which the bemused maharajah asked, 'Then where is the eagle?' 'Who should know better than you, O Zeus?,' Ackerley responded appropriately. High-minded allusions occasionally came back to earth, as when Ackerley asked the maharajah where his 'Gods' came from: 'Did they fall off Olympus, or were they a Christmas present?' The Indian answered, '"No…", shaking with laughter; "I bought them. They were not very expensive".'[12] Eastern and Western views of love and sex, after all, did not really meet, and India remained a country of poor village boys and wealthy rajahs. Ackerley visited Narayan's poor hut, and the boy offered to become his servant; before leaving, Ackerley could only recommend him to the maharajah for preferment. Ackerley went back to Britain, seeking for affection from fair compatriots not dark foreigners, and the maharajah continued his search for truth and youthful beauty.

Captain Searight and his friends

One of the most intriguing of homosexual visitors to India – someone about whom little is known – was Kenneth Searight (1883–1957).[13] Dickinson and Forster had encountered him on their journey east on board a ship in the Red Sea. Dickinson noted, briefly: 'We discovered one interesting figure – a young officer called Searight, of a romantic Byronic temperament; homosexual and perpetually in love with some boy or other, with a passion for literature.'[14] Searight was an officer in the Indian Army. After schooling at Charterhouse, he trained at the Royal Military College in Sandhurst. In 1904 (or 1907), he won his first command, serving in the Queen's Own Royal West Kent Regiment in Calcutta, and he was in Peshawar by 1912. He then explored the Punjab and Rajasthan, and, after 1914, worked as a railway transport officer in Karachi, Lahore, Cherat, Simla and Bombay. There are traces of him later in Bangalore, and in 1918 he took part in the Mesopotamia Expeditionary Force in Iraq. He qualified at an intelligence course and earned the grade of first-class interpreter, working in Arabic, Baluchi, Persian and Pushtu. In 1923, he also qualified as a rifle- and machine-gun-shooter. He held the rank of captain by the early 1920s and last appears in the Indian Army List in 1925. He apparently then left the army, and in 1926 settled in Rome. Searight maintained his interest in languages, and invented an 'auxiliary neutral language', which he called 'Sona', more suitable to be an international language than Esperanto, since it was not based solely on Western languages.[15]

Searight's manuscript on his sexual adventures was never published and has disappeared. In 1966, Toby Hammond, a London author writing in the *International Journal of Greek Love*, a small-circulation periodical devoted to man–boy love, stated that he had seen the manuscript 'now in a private collection in London, the owner having purchased it for a considerable sum of money from a bookseller who, it is rumored, paid half-a-crown for it in the Charing Cross Road'. What became of the manuscript afterwards is unknown.[16]

According to Hammond, Searight's manuscript bore the title 'Paidikion/Vol. I An Anthology or the Book of Hyakinthos and Narkissos with thirteen full-page photographs from life'. The manuscript contained a list of 129 youths with whom Searight had sexual relations, indicating the date and place of each encounter (from 1897 to 1917), the name, age and race of each partner, the nature of the sexual acts performed, the number of orgasms he had and various other information. (Searight had sex in Britain, the table revealed, as well as in Italy, Egypt and India.) The frontispiece was a youth in toga and thonged sandals, photographed by Vincenzo Galdi. Other photographs portrayed nude youths sitting in armchairs, reclining on couches and standing in suggestive poses, clearly in the manner of Wilhelm von Gloeden and others who specialised in artistic soft-porn photographs of adolescents. (Indeed, one of the photographs in the manuscript was a Sicilian picture taken by Gloeden.) The manuscript was the omnium gatherum of an amateur – translations of the word 'boy' into twenty-four languages, a verse essay on 'The Thirty-Three Joys of Paiderasty and their Symbols', an account of the first sexual experience of a young man with a soldier from the Horse Guards, a translation of a work by the Roman Petronius Arbiter, a tale of liaisons between a schoolmaster and his students, and doggerel verse entitled 'Ten Little Bugger Boys'. In one story, a shipwrecked man forced a 17-year-old to submit to his desires; the boy then suicided, and the man committed necrophilia and cut off the youth's genitals. In a less gruesome story, the hero was seduced by an attendant in a Turkish bath in Naples. Yet another erotic tale was set at Eton, and a final one took place in a boy brothel. A 2,706-line poem was called *The Furnace: An Autobiography in which is Set Forth the Secret Diversions of a Paiderast*, and, says Hammond, 'there can be nothing similar to this achievement in any erotic work'.

Searight preferred British boys to foreigners as sexual partners, although the manuscript recorded numerous trysts in most of the places he worked or travelled. Hammond says that the youngest partners in the chart of sexual conquests were from overseas: 'The youngest boys are aged seven, one being a Muslim boy named Rahimbu whom the author merely handled, the other an Arab named Mohammed Ali with whom he practised mutual masturbation, fellation and anal intercourse.' One of Searight's stories was a nine-page work set in the British Indian summer retreat: '"Simla: the Tale of a Secret Society" was a long story concerning the hero's encounter with Eric, a 13-year-old schoolboy. He introduces two other boys, Foster, 17, and Fred, 16. Every possible sexual act is performed.' Another section of the manuscript was 'Two Pathan Love Songs to his Boy'. Sexual contact with the Pathans, it seems, was particularly easy for Searight. Ronald Hyam, who saw the Searight manuscript before it disappeared, notes that it recalled one meeting thus: 'I groaned: the [Pathan] boy's untamed ferocity / So different to the young Bengali's love, / Filled me with anguish'.[17]

Searight's manuscript is consistent with stereotypes of sexuality in India and Britain – the susceptibility of boarding-school boys to homosexuality, the reputation of bath-houses as venues of homosexual encounters and the supposed homosexual proclivities of northern Indian warriors (which Burton had also mentioned). It was not unlike other soft- or hard-core pornography circulating in late nineteenth- and early twentieth-century Europe, and the interest in adolescents was hardly uncommon. Searight's care in recording his encounters parallels the meticulous way in which Roger Casement listed his partners and their endowments in the *Black Diaries*. Searight appears a voracious, and rapacious, homosexual, open enough for Forster and Dickinson to know of his penchants. Keeping a diary indicates lack of embarrassment at sexual identity, and the poems and stories show a desire to translate personal experiences into literary endeavours. Searight did not share Ackerley's timidity, though similar allusions to Greek love present in *Hindoo Holiday* and the maharajah's conversations reappear in Searight's *carnet*. Nothing suggests that Searight encountered difficulties in his military life because of his sexual nature and prolific activities. For a man of discretion, even with a great appetite, often for young boys, ample sexual opportunities presented themselves in India and other places in Europe and overseas.

Religion and sex

Chances for sexual dalliance and cultural exploration sometimes came together, as evidenced in the case of Charles Webster Leadbeater. With Annie Beasant, Leadbeater was one of the leaders of the Theosophical Society, the well-known and highly syncretic religion started by Madame Blavatsky. Theosophy claimed to discover the secret wisdom of Eastern religion, mixing it with various other spiritual beliefs, ceremonies and miracles. At the turn of the century, Theosophy gained a surprisingly large audience among Europeans in search of spiritual renewal and tempted by the mysteries of the East. Leadbeater became one of the main proponents of the new religion, and a personality of some note in British India.

Leadbeater made a practice of sharing his bed with boys and bathing with them in the morning. He advocated massage, which he taught and practised with select boys in Britain and India; massage, he argued, could elevate a person to ecstasy and provided a psychic propulsion towards 'Logos'. ('The closest man can come to a sublime spiritual experience is orgasm,' Leadbeater also philosophised.) Leadbeater kept company with an Indian whom the Theosophists proclaimed a god, Jiddu Krishnamurti. When Leadbeater discovered him in 1909,

Krishnamurti was a scrawny and sickly 14-year-old on the estate of the Theosophy school at Adyar. Leadbeater told an associate (who thought the boy dim-witted) that he was impressed with the size of Krishnamurti's 'aura', and predicted that he would become a great spiritual teacher. Whether Leadbeater had sex with the handsome Krishnamurti is uncertain, though his habit of undressing and washing the boy led to protests from the Indian's father. Beasant also took an interest in the youth, and sent him to England for training; in 1925 she proclaimed him the Messiah, sent to lead the World Order of the Star in the East. Krishnamurti later renounced his divine status and left the Theosophists, although he remained a popular promoter and teacher of Indian religions in the West until his death in 1986. He had long outlived Leadbeater, whom many suspected of irregular morals and fake philosophy; Leadbeater ended up in Australia as Presiding Bishop of the Liberal Catholic Church, and died in 1934. His sexual tastes were as eclectic and non-traditional as his religion, and India provided inspiration and satisfaction for both body and the soul, or at least a place where philosophical aspirations could justify worldly passions.[18]

A near contemporary to Leadbeater, a Frenchman drawn to Indian religion and culture, was Alain Daniélou, openly homosexual and one of the leading European Indianists of his generation.[19] Daniélou was born in 1907, his father of Breton origin, a Radical politician and several times minister under the Third Republic. His mother boasted an aristocratic background, and her grandfather, a general who died in Indo-China, was a favourite protégé of Marshal Lyautey. Known for her piety, she founded a Catholic teaching order. Daniélou's brother Jean entered the priesthood, became a cardinal and was elected to the Académie Française. Early in life, Alain Daniélou rebelled against the religiosity of his mother, who burned his copies of Gide and Proust when he was an adolescent and remarked that she would rather a child of hers die than commit a mortal sin. He had little contact with his father, often absent on government business. Daniélou did have the benefits of life in a privileged milieu of bourgeois apartments in Paris and country manors. After secondary school, he spent a year at an American university (where he had his first sexual experience with a man), and then a brief period as apprentice to an architect. He subsequently followed his artistic inclinations and became a dancer, achieving some recognition (though his mother expelled him from the family house because of his profession and loose social life). He also exercised his talents at painting and music. In 1931, while on a visit to the Côte-d'Azur, Daniélou met Raymond Burnier, a handsome blond Swiss, a budding photographer from a wealthy family – his grandfather had invented the condensed milk commercialised under the brand name Nestlé. Burnier had spent most of his childhood on a farm in Algeria. They quickly became lovers and remained partners, though not monogamously so, for almost forty years, until Burnier's death in the late 1960s.

In 1932, Daniélou and Burnier took a trip to visit the son of the king of Afghanistan, after the prince had stayed with Daniélou's parents for a summer.

They did not find Kabul to their liking, despite the royal welcome, but enjoyed a trip into the remote and dangerous hinterland of Afghanistan. The two men then drove southwards into India, their first contact with the country where they would later live. Daniélou and Burnier returned to India in 1934 and 1936 (the latter stop part of a world tour), and then settled there in 1939.[20] They rented from the Maharajah of Rewa an enormous palace on the banks of the sacred Ganges in Benares (Varanasi) and lived there until the 1950s.

Daniéliou immersed himself in Indian life (as did Burnier, though to a lesser degree). He learned Hindu, Sanskrit and Tamil, and for several years refused to read books in Western languages. He studied philosophy and cosmology with a Hindu sage, Swami Karpatri, and both he and Burnier converted to Hinduism, shaving their heads, taking Hindu names and completing other initiation rituals. Daniélou's brand of Hinduism was an orthodox and philosophical stream of the religion, and he remained unsympathetic to modern Hindu reformist movements: 'What appeared dangerous to the representatives of tradition was the false Hinduism of the Anglicised Indians, who claimed to adapt traditional doctrines to Christian concepts which were considered more compatible with the realities of the modern world.'[21]

While Burnier took photographs (later published in several albums, including a much lauded series of photographs of the Khajuraho temples), Daniélou began translating classical Hindu works and nurturing an interest in Indian music. Their house formed a social centre for visitors, and the men developed friendships with various colonial figures, including British public servants, and particularly Indian intellectuals. The poet Rabindranath Tagore became a close friend, and offered Daniélou the directorship of the music department in the school that he had established at Shantiniketan. Jawaharlal Nehru's sister was another dear friend. The composer and musician Ravi Shankhar (and his brother, Uday, a choreographer) counted among Daniélou's closest associates. Diplomats, scholars and titled European gentlefolk called on Daniélou and Burnier in Benares, and Daniélou became an eminent foreign specialist on Indian culture, as well as a celebrity.

During his time in Benares, Daniélou worked as associate director of the school of music at the city's university. In 1954, after fourteen years in Benares, he left to take up a post as director of the Sanskrit studies centre at Adyar, the Theosophy headquarters near Madras, although he professed disdain for Theosophy's watered-down and mixed-up concoction of Eastern religions. (The bisexual Burnier had married the daughter of an official, and later director, of the Theosophical Society.) After three years, Daniélou moved on to become head of a new Indological Institute in the French colony of Pondicherry.

In the late 1950s, Daniélou and Burnier (by now divorced) finally returned to France, where Daniélou was attached to the Ecole Française d'Extrême-Orient. He also directed a UNESCO project recording traditional music from around the world, which saw the compilation of almost 140 records and took Daniélou to South-Eastern Asia, Western Africa, Iran and the Soviet Union. From 1963 to 1968, Daniélou headed the International Institute of

Comparative Musical Studies in Berlin; afterwards, he mostly lived in Italy. He wrote many books, including a study of Indian polytheism, a history of India, a book on yoga, translations of two Tamil literary classics, several translations from Sanskrit (including the *Kama Sutra*), volumes on Indian music and a comparative study of ancient religions in the West and East, *Shiva and Dionysus*. Although certain academics regarded Daniélou's works as amateur, he remained widely respected and honoured. He was decorated by the French government, praised by Indian politicians such as Indira Gandhi – 'You have done more than anyone to make Indian music known in the West,' she wrote – and elected as the only foreign member of the Indian Academy of Music. Daniélou's musical setting of a Tagore poem was even adopted as India's national anthem. He was still researching and writing at the time of his death in 1994. He never returned to India after his departure in the 1950s.

Daniélou enjoyed the benefits of wealth and social position. He and Burnier employed an entourage of retainers and travelled around the world in style. To tour India, they imported a caravan from California; Daniélou claimed that it was the first on the sub-continent. He belonged to the last generation for whom travel could be considered adventure and exploration, and, when he and Burnier determined to drive from Lebanon to India, nothing stopped them, even the shock of their friends. The happy voyagers managed to arrive safely, having barely escaped an earthquake, and having enjoyed the hospitality of a warrior bandit whom the Indian colonial government branded a dangerous criminal. Throughout his life, Daniélou adopted aristocratic disdain for the bourgeoisie and middle class, and their mores. He expressed utter contempt for most Westerners attracted to India and Hinduism, whose interest, he charged, was slight and whose understanding of the complexities of Hindu philosophy came close to nil. The famous ashram of Sri Aurobindo and Mirra Richard in Pondicherry, a pilgrim destination for many foreigners, he characterised as 'one of the principal enterprises utilised to deform the message of India and to exploit the goodwill of many sincere people searching for a "different" truth'. 'Ashram', indeed, ought to be defined as 'a pseudo-spiritual gathering-place for unbalanced Westerners looking for a little exoticism'. He aimed similar charges of betraying Hindu thought against Indian leaders, calling Nehru (despite their acquaintance) an imitator of the English and a misguided socialist idealist. He lambasted Gandhi, who filled him with 'revulsion', as a silly idealist and little less than a fake: 'This scrawny little man, puritanical and neurotic, seemed the very embodiment of the revolutionary – people who have created an idealism which can attract crowds, but who identify their ideal with themselves and their secret taste for absolute power.' (Daniélou accused the anti-colonial Indo-Chinese nationalists of the same aggressive and single-minded revolutionary zeal.) Indian swamis, gurus and other would-be sages who tried to seduce Westerners came in for harsher, if more legitimate, denunciation.[22]

Daniélou considered himself a true devotee of Hinduism, one of the few in the West to understand Indian religion. He spoke highly of the subtlety of

Hindu thought, the way in which the various gods embodied cosmological forces, and the tolerance of a religion that accommodated multiple deities and rituals. By contrast, the Christianity of his mother and brother he called a 'totalitarian ideology', and he accused all monotheistic religions of subjecting believers to a single-minded version of the truth. Opposition to Christianity and other monotheistic beliefs was both personal and philosophical:

> From the perspective of the Hindu religion, which accepted me into its midst, there is nothing in my way of living and thinking that is reprehensible. This is not the case from the Christian point of view, for which I am a heretic, a pervert, an immoral person: a strange contrast between two worlds which claim to help man to approach the divine.[23]

Religion and sexuality intertwined in India, and in life in general, Daniélou thought, in a way not understood by Christians. 'I had been conscious of this since my childhood and never had the slightest anxiety or the least doubt about the value of this particularity of my nature,' he stated of his sexuality. He continued:

> All of my life was surrounded by youth, by tender friendships. I have always venerated physical beauty. The gods, say the Hindus, are perpetual adolescents. The cult of love has always been mixed with the sentiment of the divine for me.

Mind and body came together, and homosexuality provided his entrée into religion: 'My destiny would have been impossible if I had not had the advantage of preferring masculine love.'[24]

Daniélou professed little interest in politics, whether in Europe or India, and wrote infrequently about the poverty, illiteracy and disease that disabled most Indians. Philosophers, not paupers, attracted Daniélou, and his creed looked towards the attainment of the end of suffering and the cycle of rebirth rather than social amelioration in the contemporary world. The Second World War passed him by almost unawares, and he took relatively little note of India's struggle for independence, though he always pronounced himself an anti-imperialist. Visiting the French colony of Djibouti, he damned public servants who:

> because of higher salaries than in France, leave for 'the colonies' and for the most part are mediocre men, racists, men filled with arrogance, ignorant of the history and the culture of the countries that they are going to administer and to which they bring the supposed benefits of the 'civilisation' from which they themselves appear not to have profited greatly.

He judged that British rule was responsible for the 'aggressive puritanism of modern Indians'.[25] He later accused the Soviets of being fundamentally colonialist in their treatment of minority peoples in the USSR.

Daniélou moved in worldly circles in Europe; among his friends were the poet Max Jacob, Jean Cocteau, Jean Marais, Igor Stravinsky, the celebrity hairdresser Gaylord Hauser – many of the 'jet set' homosexual celebrities of his day. A notorious homosexual whom he much admired was Jean Genet, also a rebel against Western culture. Yet on his return to Europe from India (after almost ten years away), Daniélou declared,

> I felt myself completely foreign to the world in which I had been born. In my way of thinking, feeling, living, I now belonged to another civilisation. Europe was for me a land of exile which could be pleasant and interesting, but which was no longer my homeland.

In the 1940s, he had thought himself as Indian: 'Indeed I was totally integrated into Hindu life.' Daniélou later admitted, however, that he could not be truly Indian:

> because the evolution of India and its modernising government made it impossible for me to continue to live in this archaic and millennia-old civilisation, in this golden age of humanity which I had discovered and which was now slipping away from me.[26]

Sexual matters remained uncomplicated for Daniélou. He denounced sexual prudery: 'Chastity, when it is not a disguise, is a form of masochism. It is obvious that it leads to a sort of sadism and to a perverse disorientation in values.' His partner Burnier had a series of affairs with Indian men, and Daniélou was untroubled by these relationships or by Burnier's marriage. Daniélou's autobiography is nevertheless reticent about his own sexual experiences on the sub-continent, though he confesses to later liaisons with Italians, generally young larrikins. He clearly linked sexual experiences with his philosophical outlook: 'My romantic relationships allowed me to perceive the finesse, the little taboos, the nuances of behaviour and sentiments that differentiate civilisations.' In a general sense, he affirmed: 'I had learned from India that the primary duty of every man is to understand his own nature.'[27]

In his interest in Indian religion and culture, and disdain for those who did not share the depth or seriousness of his commitment, Daniélou went far beyond the 'Indianophilia' of many other Europeans. He tried to be Indian, though without abandoning links with the West or forfeiting eventual return to Europe. His homosexuality clearly played a role in Daniélou's attraction to India, and its philosophy, which seemed congenial to his sexual desires. He admitted to physical and intellectual flight from Europe and Christianity. He was more interested in Indian sexual philosophy, such as the *Kama Sutra*, than to the search for Indian sexual partners; his long-lasting emotional attachment was to a Swiss man not an Indian, and sexual liaisons with Indians left few specific traces in his works.[28]

Highly critical of British and French imperialism, Daniéliou's personal contacts and financial wherewithal made it possible for him, as for other expatriates, to live well in colonial India. He defended social inequalities and the notion of race that he borrowed from Indian philosophy, even denouncing egalitarianism and damning an 'anti-intellectual, anti-noble, anti-commoner racism'[29] – sentiments ironically not far from the ideas of many colonialists (and such contemporaries as Wilfred Thesiger). Daniélou's residence in India was almost evenly divided between the colonial and post-colonial periods, but neither the administrators of the Raj nor those of independent India won his favour. Along with a number of other Europeans attracted to colonies, Daniélou lauded the traditional and abhorred the modern, bemoaning the Westernisation of 'his' natives and posing as the real, if self-appointed, last guardian of values being undermined by political and cultural change. He felt nostalgia for the 'golden age' of Indian civilisation that he felt he had discovered, avoiding the countless problems of Indian life from which he had insulated himself, including the real sexual constraints of indigenous Indian society. Such were the paradoxes of life for a Westerner in the East.

Daniélou sought, and seemingly found, nirvana in the East, but in a romanticised East already much remodelled by colonialism, modernisation and Westernisation. Already he remarked in the 1930s on the contrast between ancient and contemporary, the survival of natural beauty amidst ugly foreign incursion. He noted at one stop on his grand tour that 'the Ceylonese countryside is splendid with its rich forests and its rubber plantations'. Yet,

> unfortunately, tourism and the indifference of public authorities in Ceylon have left a marvelous art and civilisation to die….Everything is dead here: the soiled temples have been abandoned by the faithful; Time and the jungle, always voracious, have quickly turned them into ruins. But the tourist agencies are not put off. In front of the ancient frescoes, they have painted lurid hoardings and thrown up cardboard idols and make-believe colonnades. In such a Luna Park, and for a certain price, the enthusiastic traveller is guided around this 'primitive art', to see these strange customs and savage people.[30]

The elegy for Ceylon, Daniélou's indictment of tourism, illustrated his antipathy to the changes he witnessed, but also provided a dissident view to earlier visitors' enchantment with the Indian Ocean island.

Serendipity in Ceylon

Sri Lanka, colonial Ceylon, with its beaches and tropical vegetation, Buddhist and Hindu temples, and other delights, was as inviting to foreigners as was India. Many European men found the Ceylonese, both Sinhalese and Tamils, particularly attractive. Perhaps the most expansive evocation of the beauty of men in Ceylon comes from a work by Ernst Haeckel, published in 1883. The very model of a nineteenth-century scientist and traveller, a medical doctor and zoologist, professor at the University of Jena, Haeckel was forty-eight years old when he went to Ceylon. He had already worked in Italy, the Canary Islands and Egypt, was the author of a book on coral reefs in the Persian Gulf and boasted an acquaintance with Charles Darwin. Being married and a father did not keep him from admiring and forming close links with men in places he visited. Arriving in Ceylon in 1881 with sixteen cases of luggage, he was immediately seduced by 'that evergreen island of marvels, where I was about to spend the most instructive and delightful months of my life', and which became, for a time, his 'idyllic home'. Handsome boatmen caught his attention straight away. Everywhere he went he was entranced by Sinhalese with their 'singularly slender and feminine character of limbs', and Tamils, 'tall and graceful; the general proportions of [their] frame corresponding so nearly with the artistic standard of beauty…many specimens come remarkably near to the Greek ideal'.[31]

Haeckel developed a special relationship with one young man. His words express appreciation of the ephebe's beauty and the way in which Haeckel approached him, as well as providing details on the youth's background and the sort of friendship they established. Haeckel met his protégé in a rest-house operated by a man whom he called Socrates (a well-chosen name). As he entered the inn, Haeckel spied a young man,

> with uplifted arms in an attitude of prayer, a beautiful naked, brown figure, which could be nothing else than the famous statue of 'Youth Adoring'. How surprised I was when the graceful bronze statue suddenly came to life, and dropping his arms fell on his knees, and after raising his black eyes imploringly to my face bowed his handsome face so low at my feet that his long black hair fell on the floor!

Haeckel learned that the youth was a pariah, a member of the Rodhiya caste who generally performed menial chores, such as washing. The boy was also an orphan, taken in by 'Socrates' and now assigned to serve Haeckel. The German learned that his name was Gamameda:

> Of course, I immediately thought of Ganymede, for the favourite of Jove himself could not have been more finely made, or have had limbs more beautifully proportioned and moulded. As Gamameda also displayed a peculiar talent as butler, and never allowed anyone else to open me a cocoa-nut or offer me a glass of palm-wine, it was no more than right that I should dub him Ganymede.

The youth left a lasting impression:

> Among the many beautiful figures which move in the foreground of my memories of the paradise of Ceylon, Gamameda remains one of my dearest favourites. Not only did he fulfil his duties with the greatest attention and conscientiousness, but he developed a personal attachment and devotion to me which touched me deeply.[32]

The boy had been an object of contempt as an outcaste, and 'no one perhaps had ever cared for him any way'. Now Gamameda had a solicitous patron, his devotion strengthened when Haeckel removed a thorn from his foot: 'After this the grateful Gamameda followed me like a shadow, and tried to read my wishes in my eyes.' He brought coconuts as soon as Haeckel awakened in the morning. He cleaned the scientist's dissecting equipment and microscope. He accompanied him on expeditions to collect specimens, shoot or fish, basking in the tasks with which he was entrusted, while higher-caste Sinhalese wondered how a pariah could have been adopted by the distinguished foreigner. Indeed, Haeckel's interpreter 'was especially jealous and indignant; he took every opportunity of blackening Gamameda's character, but soon arrived at the conclusion that I would allow my favourite to come to no harm'. Gamameda became almost a research assistant to Haeckel, who paid tribute to him:

> I owe many beautiful and valuable contributions to my museum to Gamameda's unfailing zeal and dexterity. With the keen eye, neat hand, and supple agility of Cinghalese youth, he could catch a fluttering moth or a gliding fish with equal promptitude.[33]

Inevitably the time came for Haeckel to leave, and, of all his farewells, the 'hardest of all was parting from my faithful Gamameda'. The youth 'wept bitterly', clung to Haeckel's knees and begged to return to Europe with him. 'In vain I assured him many times before that it was impossible, and told him of our dull climate and dull skies,' Haeckel recalled.

> I was at last almost obliged to use force to free myself from his embrace. I got into the carriage which was waiting, and as I waved a last farewell to my good brown friends, I almost felt as if I had been expelled from paradise. Adieu, Bella Gemma.[34]

Haeckel admits to no sexual relationship with Gamameda. Yet an educated German of his age was hardly unfamiliar with the view that Ganymede had been Jove's lover as well as cup-bearer. Haeckel dwelt on the beauty of his friend and others in the Rodhiya caste, whose comeliness he felt gave compensation for their lowly status, since Nature had 'bestowed on him the attractive grace of beauty of form and limb, and as he wears the smallest possible amount of raiment there is ample opportunity for seeing and admiring it'.[35] As his servant, Gamameda would have had access to Haeckel's room and no doubt helped him with bathing and dressing, as well as carrying out scientific work. That he provided other comforts cannot be excluded.

Haeckel's portrayal of Gamameda and other men in Ceylon says much about late nineteenth-century attitudes, despite the obvious affection that he held for the youth. The Sinhalese appear somewhat effeminate, and Gamameda's 'features were even softer and more girlish, reminding me of Mignon' (perhaps, incidentally, another homosexual allusion). Gamameda's servile manners –

going down on his knees when he met Haeckel – and his loyalty and efficiency pleased the visitor. Beauty, however, was often skin-deep: 'The boys particularly are remarkable for a poetical beauty of expression in their fine Aryan features. This is conspicuous in a finely cut mouth and very dark, inspired-looking eyes, promising much more than the brain within fulfills.' Noble in body, the natives were inferior in civilisation:

> Like all primitive races, the Cinghalese are in many respects mere grown-up children, and will perhaps remain so, for under the easy conditions prevailing in this Eden-like island the struggle for existence is a very easy one, and hard labour is unknown. Harmless play and incessant chatter are their principle amusements.

A Rousseauist view of 'good savages', and avoidance of problems of poverty, excruciating plantation work and the ill effects of outcaste status felt by someone such as Gamameda, speak for themselves. Occasional reference to local men or women as 'specimens' reduces humans to the level of plants or animals collected by the good zoologist. One of the most interesting aspects of Haeckel's portrayal – a perspective repeated by other writers of the period – is insistence on viewing local beauty through classically tinted glasses. Seeing the handsome Sinhalese and Tamils, 'often it would be easy to fancy that a Greek statue had come to life'. Again, 'many specimens come remarkably near to the Greek ideal'. Haeckel saw youths such as Gamameda largely in aesthetic terms and, taking a swipe at Europeans and the state of culture at home, he suggested:

> How much better might a sculptor here study the true beauty and proportion of the human form among these naturally developed models, than in the life-school of European academies, where some model, found with difficulty among the degenerate sons of civilisation and forced into some unwonted attitudes, is but a poor substitute for the genuine child of nature.[36]

Edward Carpenter and Ponnambalam Arunachalam

One of the finest examples of combined homosexual and cultural interest in South Asia, and Ceylon in particular, is Edward Carpenter. Among the best-known and most influential British radicals of the late nineteenth and early twentieth centuries, Carpenter's origins fitted him for a conventional life. He was born in Brighton in 1844, the son of a former navy officer and barrister, wealthy enough to live from his rent revenues, and a prudish Scots mother. Carpenter was educated at Trinity Hall, Cambridge, where he took holy orders and won a fellowship. His temperament, disenchantment with Christian doctrines, an encounter with the work of the American poet Walt Whitman in 1869 and travels on the Continent, especially a visit to Rome in 1873 (where he marvelled at the ruins of Antiquity, among other sights), moved him away from predictable belief and behaviour. Soon Carpenter became a rebel. He left the priesthood, and gave up his fellowship in 1874 to work as a university extension lecturer. He lived a 'simple life', in the company of his working-class lover, in Millthorpe, in the Yorkshire countryside. As teacher, journalist and writer, he espoused and popularised socialism and such other causes as equality for women, vegetarianism, anti-vivisection and the campaign against urban pollution. In *Sex-Love and Its Place in a Free Society, Woman, and Her Place in a Free Society* and *Marriage in a Free Society*, pamphlets published in 1894, Carpenter focused attention on gender issues; the same year, he circulated privately a work on *Homogenic Love, and Its Place in a Free Society*, one of the first overt defences of homosexuality in modern literature. *Iolaüs, an Anthology of Friendship* (1902) collected excerpts from Plato, Michelangelo, Whitman and other authors who extolled love between men. *The Intermediate Sex* (1908) further developed Carpenter's ideas about homosexuality, while *Intermediate Types among Primitive Folk* (1914) continued his historical and anthropological researches by looking at the religious and military roles of the 'third sex'. Coming only a few years after the trial of Oscar Wilde, these works, complementing Carpenter's refusal to hide his own sexuality, represented courageous pronouncements in favour of homosexual emancipation. By the time of his death in 1929, he stood as an almost mythical figure for the British left and for such homosexuals as E.M. Forster, who paid visits to him and hailed his pioneering writings.[37]

Carpenter's family and friends had many colonial connections. His grandfather served in the Royal Navy during the American War of Independence, and fought in the West Indies during the Anglo-French wars of the Revolution and Napoleonic era. His father retired from the navy because of damage done to his health by service in the Indian Ocean. One brother, also in the navy, took charge of the Marine Survey of India and, in 1885, led British warships up the Irrawaddy River in conquest of lower Burma. Another brother joined the Indian Civil Service and worked in the North-West Provinces and Nagpore before being been killed in a steeplechase accident in India in 1876. One of Carpenter's fellow students was Charles Dilke, later to coin the phrase 'greater Britain' and become a major promoter of British expansion. A close friend was the South African novelist Olive Schreiner, who inspired him to write about the Boers.[38] Carpenter met the Bengali poet and Indian nationalist Rabindranath Tagore in London. He also knew Annie Besant and other Theosophist leaders.

Carpenter's closest personal contact with the empire, however, came from friendship with Ponnambalam Arunachalam. Arunachalam was born in 1853 into a prosperous and distinguished Tamil family in Ceylon and came to Christ's College in Cambridge in the early 1870s, when Carpenter still held his fellowship at Trinity Hall. Handsome, urbane and an excellent student, Arunachalam counted among the small number of 'colonials' who studied in Britain and, authorities hoped, would return to their countries as valued and loyal collaborators in British rule. According to Carpenter's autobiography:

I first came across Arunachalam at a meeting of the *Chitchat* or some such
society at Cambridge... As in the case of other Hindus his extraordinary
quickness and receptiveness of mind had very quickly rendered him *au fait*
in all our British ways and institutions. With engagingly good and natural
manners, humorous and with some of the Tamil archness and bedevilment
about him, he was already a favorite in his own college – and at that time
these early comers to the Universities from India were certainly received
by our students with more friendliness and sense of equality than they are
to-day. His father having been a wealthy man and occupying a good position in Ceylon, Arunachalam had received a good education and was
fairly well up in Greek and Latin, French and German, and their litera-
tures, besides his own Eastern languages, like Tamil and Sanskrit.
Altogether he was a very taking, all-round sort of fellow, capable of talking
on most subjects, and full of interested inquiry about all. Many were the
afternoons or evenings we spent together – walking or boating or sitting by
the fireside in College rooms – and I learned much from him about the
literature of India and the manners and customs of the mainland and
Ceylon.[39]

Thus began a long and fertile friendship – 'my almost life-long friend', as
Carpenter referred to Arunachalam in his memoirs.[40]

After taking his degree at Cambridge, Arunachalam studied law in London,
and then returned to Ceylon. He joined the Civil Service, working first as a
magistrate, and then rising to become the colony's Registrar-General and the
highest-ranking native bureaucrat. Arunachalam scored high praise for his
direction of the 1901 census, and was elected a member of the Legislative
Council. He afterwards drew criticism from the Colonial Secretary, however, for
the stance he took as a member of a Railway Commission. His sympathies for
the plight of workers, and recommendations for higher wages and better conditions, seemed to excuse a railway strike in 1912 and smack of a dangerously
leftist perspective. Arunachalam retired from the Civil Service in 1913 and was
rewarded with a knighthood. Already known for reformist positions, he spent
the remaining years of his life – he died in 1924 – in nationalist causes and
social work. In 1915 he established the Ceylonese Social Service League, which
started night schools and first-aid classes for the poor, set up credit unions and
undertook food relief. In a major speech in 1917, Arunachalam called for self-
government for Ceylon and founded the Ceylonese Reform League. Two years
later, he became the first president of the Ceylonese National Congress.
Arunachalam's denunciation of colonial government and his adoption of
Gandhi's philosophy of *swaraj* placed him in the forefront of the nationalist
movement. Arunachalam strongly supported Hindu revivalism in Ceylon,
though, with open-minded interest in all religions, he gave aid to the Buddhist
movement as well. Arunachalam was also sympathetic to Western interest in
Indian philosophy, receiving the Theosophists Colonel Olcott and Madame
Blavatsky when they visited Ceylon.[41]

Nothing suggests a physical relationship between Carpenter and Arunachalam. Their friendship began during the *crise de conscience* that resulted in Carpenter's leaving Cambridge, after his reading of Whitman reconciled him with his sexual proclivities. Carpenter's sexual interests ran towards working-class Englishmen – 'my ideal love is a powerful, strongly built man, of my own age or rather younger – preferably of the working class' – not wealthy, foreign intellectuals. Arunachalam married and fathered several children. Ties of respect and tenderness, indicated by Arunachalam's signing his letters 'Your affectionate friend', bound the two men. In their correspondence, Carpenter asked after Arunachalam's children, and Arunachalam sent greetings to Carpenter's lover; he called on Carpenter and George Merrill at Millthorpe when he visited Britain. Carpenter's homosexuality clearly was not a bar to their intimacy. After Arunachalam's death, and with the aid of his widow, Carpenter edited a collection of extracts from their letters, to which he added essays, including 'The lingam and sensual desire', 'Birth control and bisexuality' and 'The endeavour to control desire', which suggest that the two might have discussed sexual issues in the context of Indian philosophy. Carpenter himself tended to downplay the physical expression of sexuality in 'homogenic love':

We may yet say that it would be a great error to suppose that the homogenic love takes as a rule the extreme form vulgarly supposed; and that it would also be a great error to overlook the fact that in a large number of instances the relation is not distinctively sexual at all, though it may be said to be physical in the sense of embrace and endearment.[42]

In Carpenter's own terms, his relationship with Arunachalam was one of 'homogenic love'.

What is interesting in the friendship between Carpenter and Arunachalam is not a possible sexual liaison, though there is no reason to exclude either mutual or unreciprocated attraction, but the way in which that friendship breached the gulf between the Europeans and the Asians, and, also, contributed to the enrichment of each man's philosophy. Arunachalam's writings and speeches mirror Carpenter's brand of undoctrinaire and somewhat utopian socialism, his critique of capitalism, his vaunting of a simple life and his interest in spiritual issues. Arunachalam, like Carpenter, was a syncretic thinker. His works quoted from the Tamil classic, the *Tiruvalluvar*, but also from Chamberlain, Macaulay and Carlyle, as well as Marcus Aurelius and Pericles; Arunachalam also praised the Japanese model of Asian economic and political development. Both Carpenter and Arunachalam quoted Mazzini, the Italian patriot much admired in Victorian Britain. In speeches after his retirement from the colonial service, Arunachalam voiced increasingly strident criticism of colonialism. He castigated 'government despotism' (and, more gently, 'grandmotherly government'), demanded reform of the civil service to promote indigenous Ceylonese to positions of higher authority, called regularly for the establishment of a Ceylonese university, denounced indentured labour and advocated prison reform. He bemoaned lack of spiritual interest among his fellow Hindus and, in a frequently repeated catchphrase, asked for 'our youth to spiritualise public life'.[43] Such sentiments were hardly foreign to Carpenter.

Carpenter's interest in the East and in Indian thought owed much to Arunachalam. 'I feel that I owe a great debt to him,' Carpenter said in his autobiography,

> because long ago, in '80 perhaps or '81 he gave me a translation of a book, then little known in England, the *Bhagavat Gita* – the reading of which...curiously liberated and set in movement the mass of material which had already formed within me, and which was then waiting to take shape as *Towards Democracy*....It gave me the needed cue, and concatenated my work to the Eastern tradition.[44]

Carpenter became so interested in Indian spirituality that when Arunachalam invited him to South Asia to meet the guru with whom he had studied, and whose teachings they had already discussed in letters, Carpenter eagerly accepted. He journeyed to Ceylon and India in 1890, met with the guru daily for several weeks and claimed to have learned much from him thanks to Arunachalam's introduction and translations. On his return, Carpenter wrote *From Adam's Peak to Elephanta* (1892), a travelogue that contained a lengthy section (also published separately) about his meeting with the *gñani*. Carpenter did not convert to Hinduism (or become a Theosophist); indeed he expressed fear that a life of contemplative renunciation could lead to 'over-quiescence, and even torpor', and worried about the lack of attention to the subject of love in Indian philosophy.[45] Yet he was much taken with the dedication and asceticism of Indian mystics, and with the idea of the unity of creation and the merging of individual souls into a common whole.

From Adam's Peak to Elephanta, which several times mentions Arunachalam,[46] is a typically Victorian portmanteau work with descriptions of places Carpenter visited, people whom he met and the atmosphere of the still exotic East. In unsurprising language for the time, he refers to the Sinhalese as 'though a long-civilised race' now 'as primitive as savages in their dress, cabins, etc.' He characterised Ceylonese as 'diabolical' (an adjective, however, that was not entirely negative in his use), curiously nicknaming them 'oysters' – because they contained pearls of wisdom or beauty? – and also alluding to them as 'darkies'. As did many tourists, he complained about heat, mosquitoes, dirt and crowds, but Carpenter took keen notice of Ceylonese and Indian culture and monuments, and gazed with interest on the local population. Everything interested Carpenter, and he commented frequently on personal relationships and, also, on sexual issues. He remarked in passing on the 'bachelors' household' of a European doctor who lived with two young men, a Eurasian and a Sinhalese. He recorded the Ceylonese view of sex. He mentioned the famous nautch girls, entertainers-cum-prostitutes. Perhaps with Arunachalam as a model, he took particular note of Tamils, describing their physical attributes in generally complimentary fashion, fascinated by their semi-nakedness but evoking them with European references: 'Some of them of course are thick and muscular, but mostly they excel in a kind of unconscious grace and fleetness of form as of the bronze Mercury of Herculaneum, of which they often remind me.'[47]

Carpenter's attention was attracted by several young men who became temporary companions. Kalua, 'a Cinghalese peasant whose acquaintance I had lately made', showed him around Colombo and took him to visit a neighbouring village, where he introduced Carpenter to his family and served him palm beer. Carpenter wrote:

> Kalua is remarkably well-made, and active and powerful. He is about twenty-eight, with the soft giraffe-like eyes of the Cinghalese, and the gentle, somewhat diffident manner which they affect; his black hair is generally coiled in a knot behind his head, and, with an ornamental belt sustaining his colored skirt, and a shawl thrown over his shoulder, he looks quite handsome.

This impression is borne out by a studio portrait of Kalua in his book. Kalua had worked as a dancer and, recruited by a German circus company, had performed in Europe; 'since that time the old peasant life has palled upon our friend, and it is evident that he lives in dreams of civilisation and the West'.[48] Carpenter remarked on Kalua's obsession with Europe:

> All the modern facilities and inventions are sorts of wonderful toys to this child of nature; and though I think he is attached to me, and is no doubt of an affectionate disposition, still it is partly that I am mixed up in his mind with all these things.[49]

Carpenter spent New Year's Day with Kalua and his brother, 'and I kept being reminded of Herman Melville and his Marquesas Island experiences – so beautiful the scene, the moon rising about ten, woods and valleys all around – the primitive little hut'. On an excursion up-country, Kalua took Carpenter's hand to help him up a steep path, and later lay beside him as they rested. A river voyage 'suits his lazy social temperament', and 'his savage strength and *insouciance* are splendid'.[50]

Carpenter found another companion for his visit to Calcutta, a young man also photographed for *From Adam's Peak to Elephanta*. Panna Lal, brother of a schoolmaster, 'is a bright-mannered youth of about twenty, of a modest, affectionate disposition, and with a certain grace and dignity of bearing'. Though not much interested in books, Lal was:

> quite an athlete, and interested in anything in that line. He took me one day to a little bit of ground where he and some friends have their horizontal bars, etc.; they did some good tumbling and tight-rope walking, and with their golden-brown skins and muscular bodies looked well when stripped.[51]

Lal accompanied him to Benares, where Carpenter watched as Lal bathed in the Ganges; Carpenter chatted with other visitors until 'I had satisfied the curiosity of one or two bystanders who wanted to know whether I had come with him all the way on this pilgrimage out of friendship.'[52] Moving on, in Delhi, Carpenter admired 'some handsome faces, verging a little towards the Greek or Italian types – but looking fine with their dark skins'.[53] At Agra 'the men in the streets...are very handsome, many of them, with their large eyes and well-formed noses'.[54] There is no intimation that Carpenter had sexual experiences while in the East, but his descriptions of men (and occasionally women) reveal fascination with dark-skinned beauty and the charms of what he considered the natural paradise of Ceylon. (He was somewhat less enamoured of India.)

If Carpenter's tone in speaking about the Ceylonese now seems patronising, his views of the British in the East are far harsher. Carpenter was not an out-and-out anti-colonialist: his target was British economic and political misrule, and the philistinism and racism of British expatriates, more than overlordship itself. Indeed, he admitted that the bringing of so many regions and groups under British control, administration of the country by a 'mere handful of foreigners' and the 'liberal spirit of administration with less of rapine than perhaps ever known in such a case...makes one feel how wonderful an achievement the thing has been'.[55] Some members of the Indian Civil Service, he said (perhaps with his brother in mind), proved competent and humane administrators, but he accused most expatriates of arrogance and 'insularity', charging them with forming a closed 'class' within the imperial structure. He mocked their inability to leave off British customs, continuing for instance to dress in heavy European clothing in tropical weather. He condemned the colonial economy for creating artificial needs among local people and for favouring production of tea for export rather than rice for subsistence. He saw Indian philosophy and culture being undermined by Westernisation: 'Anything more antagonistic to the genius of ancient India – the Wisdom-land – than this cheap-and-nasty, puffing, profit-mongering, enterprising, energetic, individualistic, "business", can hardly be imagined.'[56]

Carpenter's romantic view of the East combined with radical political opinions to leaven his critique. He saw a parallel between the plight of the European working class and colonised people overseas, and his manifest for change in Europe and the colonies embodied a moral vision as much as a political programme:

> The evils of a commercial class-government which we are beginning to realise so acutely at home – the want of touch between the rulers and the ruled, the testing of all politics by the touchstone of commercial profits and dividends, the consequent enrichment of the few at the expense of the many, the growth of slum and factory life, and the impoverishment of the peasant and the farm, are curiously paralleled by what is taking place in India; and in many respects it is becoming necessary to realise that some of our difficulties in India are not merely such as belong to the country itself,

but are part and parcel of the same problem which is beginning to vex us at home – the social problem, namely.[57]

The issues, thus, at home and abroad, were economic and political domination, but also the 'want of touch', of human understanding.

Without demanding British withdrawal from the colonies, Carpenter did hope for a more humane administration, based on greater respect for local cultures, rejection of capitalist greed and more personal empathy. Referring to the Indian National Congress, formed five years before his visit, Carpenter supported demands for Indian self-government, the only way to avert violence and civil war, he warned. Political will was needed, as well as personal commitment: 'there is no real touch, no real sympathy, between them [the British] and the native races', 'how much a few unpretending and friendly Englishmen might do to endear our country to this people'.[58] (In words that echo Carpenter, Arunachalam avowed: 'The relation between England and us requires the magic touch of sympathy and the alchemy of imagination.')[59] Personal links were needed, the sort of intimacy Carpenter enjoyed with Arunachalam, whose 'charming frankness and grace....established at once the *human* relation as the paramount thing'.[60] He quoted with approval the view of one Mr Beck on how to 'bridge the fatal gulf':

> Incredible though it may appear, all degrees of friendship are possible between the Anglo-Indian and his Eastern fellow-subject....To know the people, and to be so trusted by them that they will open out to us the inmost recesses of their hearts; to see them daily; to come to love them as those who have in their nature but an average share of affection cannot help loving them when they know them well – this is our ideal for the Indian civilian.

Yet Carpenter did not disagree with Beck on the aim of such bonding: 'If it become the normal thing the Indian Empire will be built upon a rock so that nothing can shake it.'[61]

Carpenter did not work out a theory of imperialism; his writings on empire were episodic, though his comments were perceptive, his criticisms biting and his phrases often memorable. The 1892 travelogue recounted his initiation into non-Western societies and his first-hand view of colonialism. In 1900, Carpenter published an article on 'Boer and Briton', full of sympathy for the Boers then engaged in war with the British in South Africa. The same year came a prose poem, 'Empire' (later reprinted in the fourth part of *Towards Democracy*); empire, he trumpeted, was a fake utopia for Britain: 'Blind, fooled, and staggering from her throne, I saw her fall, / Clutching at the gaud of Empire'. Empire diverted attention from dire social conditions at home, profiting those who enjoyed 'the club and drawing-room life', hoodwinking the masses: 'This thing from all her smoky cities and slums, her idiot clubs and drawing-rooms, and her brokers' dens / Cries out to give her blessings to the world! / And even while she cries / Stand Ireland and India at her door / In rags and famine'. Colonialism bled India of sterling: 'Taken to feed the luxury of Britain, / Taken, without return – While Britain wonders with a pious pretence of innocence / Why famine follows the flag'.[62]

At the turn of the century, Carpenter published several articles on overseas issues, such as 'India, China, and ourselves' in the *Independent Labour Party News* in 1900. After a trip to North Africa in 1903, he published ten articles on Morocco in 1906 and 1907.[63] All the while, he retained interest in Indian culture, and returned, at least in literature, to the East to edit Arunachalam's letters just two years before his own death.

The East therefore resonates through the work of Carpenter, sensitised by his visit to India and Ceylon, enlightened by Indian philosophy, loyal to a life-long friendship with an educated and powerful Tamil civil servant and nationalist, and not immune to the charms of simple lads such as Kalua and Panna Lal.[64] More than any other influence, Arunachalam opened Carpenter to the ideas of the East. Carpenter's idea of democracy owed much to the *Baghavad Gita*, to which he had been introduced by Arunachalam, and its portrayal of the divine self in the body and soul of every creature.[65] The political and economic situation he witnessed in India and Ceylon stimulated his consideration of imperialism. Indian philosophy provided an alternative spirituality to the Christianity he had abandoned. Hindu reverence for the lingam, and other sexual views which appeared disturbing to Westerners, contributed to his reflections on the 'intermediate sex', 'homogenic love' and bisexuality. For Carpenter (as, later, for Daniélou), taking inspiration from Hinduism, sex and religion were linked. Like Leadbeater, Carpenter compared religious enlightenment at its extreme form with orgasm:

> its burning, withering intensity – the fixed almost rigid condition which precedes its culmination, the threads like lightning streaming from all parts of the organism to their fulfilment, and the ecstatic deliverance. The man becomes God! No wonder that this condition has from farthest back times been glorified as holy!'[66]

Just as Carpenter tried to combine Eastern and Western thought into a personal philosophy of life, so Arunachalam mixed English political philosophy with Hindu religion and Ceylonese history to arrive at nationalism. Arunachalam's efforts proved effective, though after his death, in achieving independence for Sri Lanka. Carpenter's ideas passed down into movements embodying the concepts of socialism and 'simple living' with sometimes even vaguer notions of Eastern thought, from the era of gay liberation and the hippies to the vogue for New Age beliefs and 'queer theory'. That the genesis of both men's ideas owed much to the friendship between an Englishman and a Tamil, one homosexual, the other opening his friend to the erotic and philosophical culture of the East, represents a special episode of cross-cultural relations in the age of empire.

The Indian pilgrimage

Westerners went to India seeking enlightenment, and Carpenter, Leadbeater and Daniélou all had religious experiences and appropriated Eastern philosophies – Ackerley and Dickinson appeared somewhat disappointed that they had not felt a great mystical awakening, and Searight and Haeckel were too busy with other activities to be bothered by higher thoughts. All felt untethered in India, where Western categories and verities seemed not to apply, but all wished (literally or metaphorically) to bathe in the Ganges, burn incense in temples and sit at the feet of the renowned philosophers. None could avoid the sensuality of the subcontinent, whether the squalor of cities or the luxuriance of jungles. Men proffered their services as guides, hotel attendants, disciples or courtiers, companions whose beauty, and in some cases, sexual favours were available as one of the pleasures of the Indian sojourn. Romances between European gentlemen and Indian or Ceylonese peasants were brief and circumstantial. Longer-lasting friendships, such as that of Carpenter and Arunachalam, were reserved for those of similar social standing.

Travellers benefited from their European advantages; Searight the soldier, Haeckel the scientist, Carpenter the social critic, Daniélou the wealthy scholar – all could visit colonial India in comfort and with the assurance of their colonial position, and Daniélou pronounced disdain for a new tourism that allowed those less fortunate to visit the sub-continent. The men (except for Searight, whose opinions are unknown) remained ambivalent about India and its future. Carpenter lambasted colonialism, yet Daniélou found much in independent India to criticise. Daniélou, in particular, was self-righteous about *his* understanding of India, versus the vulgar dabblings in Indian life and thought ventured by other visitors, such as Leadbeater. The men went home after a few weeks or a few years, Haeckel's farewell wave to his young friend symbolic of inevitable separation between Europeans and Indians. Yet India left an indelible imprint, seen in Searight's lost sexual travelogue and Haekel's memoir, Daniélou's philosophical and musical studies, and Carpenter's writings about India and his friendship with Arunachalam.

Notes

1 See Jeffery Paine, *Father India: Westerners under the Spell of an Ancient Culture* (New York, 1998).

2 Kenneth Ballhatchet, *Race, Sex and Class under the Raj: Imperial Attitudes and Policies and their Critics, 1793–1905* (London, 1980).

3 H. Edwardes and J. Nicholson, British officers in India in the 1850s, are among those bound in particularly close friendship, as suggested by the letters from Nicholson to Edwardes in the Oriental and India Office Collections of the British Library (MM Eur E.211/3).

4 Ballhatchet, pp. 120–1.

5 G. Lowes Dickinson, *Appearances, being Notes of Travel* (London, n.d.), pp. 179, 16, 35; see also G. Lowes Dickinson *The Autobiography of G. Lowes Dickinson*, ed. Dennis Proctor (London, 1973).

6   J.R. Ackerley, *Hindoo Holiday* (London, 1952), p. ix; quotations from 1983 Penguin edition. See also Peter Parker, *Ackerley: The Life of J.R. Ackerley* (London, 1989), especially Ch. 5.

7   That particular detail was revealed only in a letter to Forster, 23 April 1924, reprinted in Neville Braybrooke (ed.), *The Letters of J.R. Ackerley* (London, 1975), pp. 11–12.

8   Ackerley, *Hindoo Holiday*, p. 27.

9   *Ibid.*, pp. 221, 251, 243, 82, 217.

10   *Ibid.*, p. 207

11   *Ibid.*, p. 66.

12   *Ibid.*, p. 131.

13   Ronald Hyam, *Empire and Sexuality: The British Experience* (Manchester, 1990), pp. 128–31, unearthed the Searight saga, and I have drawn on his account.

14   Dickinson, *Autobiography*, p. 178

15   Kenneth Searight, *Sona: An Auxiliary Neutral Language* (London, 1935).

16   Toby Hammond, 'Paidikion: A paiderastic manuscript', *International Journal of Greek Love*, Vol. 1, No. 2 (1966), pp. 28–37, from which the following details are taken.

17   Quoted in Hyam, *op. cit.*

18   Gregory Tillett, *The Elder Brother: A Biography of Charles Webster Leadbeater* (London, 1982).

19   The following account is based on the second edition of Daniélou's autobiography, *Le Chemin du labyrinthe. Souvenirs d'Orient et d'Occident* (Monaco, 1993).

20   Daniélou also remarked on the bath-houses in Shanghai (where encounters would be easy, 'but we did not want to visit these famous bathing establishments bearing these signs [in English]: "Massage by girls or boys very expert". All that is too sophisticated for us'). (Alain Daniélou, *Le Tour du monde en 1936* (Paris, 1987), pp. 113–14.

21   Daniélou, *Le Chemin du labyrinthe*, p. 151.

22   *Ibid.*, pp. 224, 226, 193.

23   *Ibid.*, p. 30.

24   *Ibid.*, p. 54.

25   *Ibid.*, pp. 123, 333.

26   *Ibid.*, pp. 231, 103, 231.

27   *Ibid.*, pp. 22, 335, 336.

28   Another Westerner attracted to Indian religion and philosophy was the British homosexual writer Christopher Isherwood.

29   *Ibid.*, p. 330.

30   Daniélou, *Le Tour du monde*, pp. 117–18.

31   Ernst Haeckel, *A Visit to Ceylon*, trans Clara Bell (London, 1883), pp. 73, 265, 284.

32   *Ibid.*, p. 265.

33   *Ibid.*, p. 200.

34   *Ibid.*, p. 273.

35   *Ibid.*, p. 202.

36   *Ibid.*, p. 284.

37   Chushichi Tsuzuki, *Edward Carpenter, 1844–1929: Prophet of Human Fellowship* (Cambridge, 1980); Dilip Kumar Barua, *Edward Carpenter, 1844–1929: An Apostle of Freedom* (Burdwan, 1991). See also the interesting article by Parminder Kaur Bakshi, 'Homosexuality and Orientalism: Edward Carpenter's journey to the East', in Tony Brown (ed.), *Edward Carpenter and Late Victorian Radicalism* (London, 1990), pp. 151–77.

38   Carpenter was also influential on Schreiner; Havelock Ellis lent the author of *The Story of an African Farm* a copy of Carpenter's *Towards Democracy*.

39   Edward Carpenter, *My Days and Dreams* (London, 1916), p. 251.

40   *Ibid.*, p. 48.

41 See James T. Rutnam, *Sir Ponnambalam Arunachalam, 1853–1924* (Colombo, 1988), and Visakha Kumari Jayawardena, *The Rise of the Labor Movement in Ceylon* (Durham, NC, 1972).

42 Quoted in Tsuzuki, p. 131.

43 Ponnambalam Arunachalam, *Speeches and Writings* (Colombo, n.d.), p. 7.

44 Carpenter, *My Days and Dreams*, p. 251.

45 *Ibid.*, p. 144.

46 He is referred to only as 'A.', presumably so that Carpenter's views would not in any way compromise Arunachalam, then a civil servant.

47 Edward Carpenter, *From Adam's Peak to Elephanta* (London, 1892), p. 14.

48 *Ibid.*, p. 27.

49 *Ibid.*, p. 74.

50 *Ibid.*

51 *Ibid.*, p. 240.

52 *Ibid.*, p. 262.

53 *Ibid.*, pp. 277–8.

54 *Ibid.*, p. 290.

55 *Ibid.*, p. 267.

56 *Ibid.*, p. 355.

57 *Ibid.*, p. 350.

58 *Ibid.*, p. 317.

59 Arunachalam, p. 83.

60 Carpenter, *My Days and Dreams*, p. 252.

61 Quoted in Carpenter, *From Adam's Peak*, p. 351.

62 *Towards Democracy*, Part IV, in Edward Carpenter, *Selected Writings* (London, 1984), p. 374.

63 On Carpenter's views of imperialism, see Tzuzuki, pp. 152–5.

64 See Barua, chapter on 'The impact of Indian thought', pp. 127–50.

65 Tzuzuki, p. 46.

66 Carpenter, *Light from the East*, pp. 103–4.

10 Forster, Masood, Mohammed and the maharajah

The previous chapter looked at homosexual Britons in South Asia, and the following one examines Frenchmen in North Africa. E.M. Forster provides a link between the two regions, a key figure whose life and writings engaged with the Raj and the Arab world. Both a canonical British novelist and an iconic personality in the history of twentieth-century homosexuality, Forster is an excellent example of the seduction of overseas places, and the way homoerotic experiences enjoyed with foreigners transformed into literature and influenced political attitudes. This is apparent in Forster's almost life-long friendship with Syed Ross Masood, his experiences in India in the 1920s and his encounter with Mohammed el-Adl in Alexandria during the First World War.

A vast amount of critical literature has been published on Forster, including two books specifically on homosexuality in his work. Parminder Kaur Bakshi's *Distant Desire* argues that homoerotic love rather than a political critique forms the major theme of *A Passage to India*. The attraction between the English bachelor Fielding and the Indian widower Aziz is complemented by 'references from Indian religion and mythology to convey intimacy between men'. Though ultimately thwarted by social and political circumstances, and psychological reticence, Fielding and Aziz manage moments of intimacy and essay a fraternal bonding that makes their friendship the failed model of an ideal homoerotic love. Contributors to a volume on *Queer Forster* emphasise how Forster's homosexual desire was generally conjugated in the form of liaisons with men of other classes or races, and how his experiences in India shaped his writing, combining a utopian vision of male love and friendship with fetishisation of the 'other'. Sara Suleri, decoding Forster's 'imperial erotic', suggests that *A Passage to India* 'explores mythologies of colonial friendship', but also is 'resolutely critical of an "only connect" rhetoric that would allow for the fiction of any transcultural male bonding', while Joseph Bristow focuses on the 'painful tension between homoerotic experience and imperial domination' in Forster's work. Arthur Martland shows how Forster nevertheless 'explored the reality of those "rare" individuals who had surmounted the barriers between the races'.[1]

The focus here will be on historical details of Forster's encounters, the biographies of the two foreign men most important in his life, Masood and Mohammed, and the socio-historical situations in which he experienced homosexuality overseas.[2]

Forster and Masood

The relationship between Forster and Masood, according to Peter Stansky, 'was the most influential friendship in Forster's life'. Moreover, 'largely thanks to Masood, he would develop a life-long interest in India'.[3] When he met the 17-year-old Masood in late 1906, Forster was a 27-year-old Cambridge graduate who had just published his first novel, *Where Angels Fear to Tread*. Although financially comfortable, increasingly associated with the literary avant-garde in Bloomsbury and a gentleman of culture, Forster had not come to terms with his homosexuality. He met Masood through Sir Theodore Morison, a neighbour in Surrey, former principal of the Muslim Anglo-Oriental College in Aligarh (now in Pakistan). Masood had come to England to study at Oxford, and Morison recruited Forster to coach him in Latin for the entrance examination. Masood, a handsome six-footer, bright, sportsmanly and outgoing, hailed from a prominent and prosperous Indian background – a paragon of the Indian deemed valuable to the British empire.[4]

Masood was the grandson of Sir Syed Ahmed Khan, founder of the Muslim-Oriental College (which became Aligarh Muslim University in 1920). Khan, an aristocrat with Mughal titles, had briefly worked for the East India Company. He supported the British during the Mutiny of 1857 although, in *Causes of the Indian Revolt*, he analysed the rebellion as the result not of inherent tendencies of disloyalty among Indians, but because the British government failed to appreciate the political and social conditions of Indians, and to treat them justly. Khan lauded the British in terms that echoed the ideas of Edward Carpenter and Ponnambalam Arunachalam: 'The English are here as friends and not as enemies. I want the creation of real sympathy between Englishmen and Indians...friendly and brotherly feelings between the two.' But he also told his countrymen, 'Once sound and true education has been acquired, you will become conscious of your political rights that eventually you will get.' (The Aligarh college indeed became the incubator of Muslim nationalism in British India.)[5] Khan published a book on *The Loyal Mahommedans of India* in 1872, and a pamphlet on the shortcomings of the Indian educational system. He established several schools and a scientific society for translating English books into Urdu. In 1875, he founded the Anglo-Oriental College, a residential English-style institution; most, though not all, students were Muslim. Khan's school practised British pedagogy and concentrated on arts subjects, while upholding Muslim precepts; the school's board preferred Englishmen, such as Morison, as headmasters of the 'Muslim Eton'. A British observer called the Aligarh school the 'first modernist institution in Islam', and an Indian noted that an Aligarh boy can always be recognised in any Society.…His characteristics are (1) his good manners, (2) neatness and cleanliness, (3) the inward feeling of honour and manliness, (4) his abhorrence of everything that is mean and ungentlemanly.[6]

The description perfectly fits the founder's grandson. Later commentators, however, criticised Khan for confining education to the Muslim feudal elite, over-emphasising higher education (at the expense of general schooling for the masses) and producing public servants for the colonial state.[7]

Khan's son, Syed Mahmud, continued the Anglo-Indian tradition with a Cambridge education and studies in law, and was destined to take over the college. He became a justice on the Indian High Court, but the Chief Justice accused him of delays, lack of co-operation and intemperance on the bench; he also drank heavily, argued with his father and behaved oddly (ordering servants to carry him around his house lying on a bier). Syed Mahmud died in 1903, leaving an adolescent son, Syed Ross. Masood thus arrived in England the scion of one of India's most notable Muslim families, but with the memories of a sometimes unsettled family life.

Masood proved a great success in Britain, where he read history at New College and played tennis. The historian H.A.L. Fisher, his tutor, reminisced: 'I cannot recall the name of any young Indian who entered more thoroughly into the life of Oxford or obtained more of the best which Oxford has to give.'[8] In 1910, Morison, Masood's legal guardian, gave a progress report:

> You will be glad to hear how well Ross Masood has been doing in England. He has worked steadily and well at the Oxford University. He has made excellent friends in England. Masood is a person of weight in the College Society.…[sic] has grown into a very fine muscular young man.[9]

With such credentials, it is not surprising that Masood attracted Forster's attention. His exuberance, charm and dynamism added to the fascination, though Forster also realised that Masood could be light-headed, extravagant, pompous and full of himself.[10]

Forster and Masood saw each other regularly and exchanged correspondence frequently during Masood's stay in Britain.[11] Tones of jocularity, affection and increasingly fast friendship mark their letters. Forster, from Weybridge in 1907, thanked Masood for a pair of shoes and joked whether he could smoke raspberry jam in his hookah, another gift. The formal 'Dear Masood' gave way to 'Dearest Boy', and Forster felt comfortable enough to sign off, 'from Forster, member of the Ruling Race to Masood, a nigger'. (Masood referred to himself, playfully, as Forster's 'slave' or 'a poor heathen oriental'.) He sent regards from his mother and aunt, whom Masood had met, and chatted about mutual acquaintances (such as the Morisons, and Goldsworthy Lowes Dickinson, as well as other Indian students, whom Masood had presented to Forster), travel, parties and Masood's studies. Masood's influence becomes apparent, as Forster wrote of reading the Koran and various books on India, including a biography of Masood's grandfather. He chided Masood for not writing even more assiduously, and offered to lend him money if he fell short. Masood visited Forster in Weybridge, Forster visited Masood in Oxford and they saw each other in London. They went to Paris together while Masood was an undergraduate – Masood scolded Forster for the undemonstrative way he said good-bye at the Gare du Nord – and took a holiday in Switzerland. Forster confessed that, whenever they parted, he missed Masood and looked forward to their next meetings. 'Why cannot life be like this for ever?,' he wrote after one visit in 1910.[12]

Masood's messages were sometimes even more exuberant as he recounted his activities and spoke of his friendship for Forster. A letter from November 1910 is a case in point: 'What a dear fellow you are, and your letter shows me that you love me as much as I love you.' Speaking of a planned trip together to Constantinople, Masood added,

> if you knew how much I loved you and how I long to be alone with you in that romantic part of the world....Let us get far away from the conventional crowd, and let us wander aimless if we can, like two pieces of wood on the ocean....I love you more than any other man friend of mine and so kiss you *au revoir*.

A letter of 20 December suggested that Forster write a book on India, 'for I feel convinced from what I know of you,' wrote Masood,

> that it will be a great book. I do not wish to flatter you in any way but the fact is that you are about the only Englishman in whom I have come across true sentiment & that, too, real sentiment even from the oriental point of view. So you know what it is that makes me love you so much, it is the fact that in you I see an oriental with an oriental view of life *on most things*.

Masood went on to encourage the shy Forster to develop his imagination and physical senses: 'Our senses both intellectual & physical are to use a Western simile like a marconigram always ready *to receive* & quivering to receive some impression.'[13]

By this time, Forster was in love with Masood, desirous of a sexual relationship and probably emboldened by the sentiments in Masood's letters. On 28 December 1910, after a performance of Strauss's *Salomé* in London, Forster declared his sexual passion for Masood. Masood responded calmly, 'I know', but made Forster aware that a sexual relationship was not possible. For several days, without a letter from Masood, Forster worried that their friendship might have been ruined, but was relieved to receive a letter on 2 January 1911. The letter does not survive, but Forster soon replied, 'everything is understood'.[14]

Forster's declaration manifestly did not harm the friendship. Correspondence and visits continued, and in the summer of 1911 Forster and Masood went on holiday to the Italian Alps. Forster then (and perhaps once again later) reiterated his declaration of sexual love, but realised that friendship was more important than sex. His avowal of sexual interest, though in vain, seems to have cleared the air; if anything, reciprocal feelings of friendship deepened, and Forster and Masood become even greater confidants, confessing their troubles and yearning for each other's presence. Forster could write to Masood in 1913, for instance, that 'your damned self has become part of my life'.[15] Only a few months later, from India, Masood wrote to Forster about his own surging sexual desires for women – they had discussed several of his previous encounters – and forthcoming marriage. He pleaded with Forster to visit or even to live in India, saying that he had kept aside land for him:

> We will build our houses together and live together and if possible die together....If you come I promise never to leave you. You can write beautiful books and I rotten ones, always spending the long evenings together with Zorah [his future wife] inspiring both of us....Dearest Morgan you don't know how sincerely and earnestly I long for it.[16]

In 1912, after studying law in London, Masood had returned to India, not very happily. From his ship he wrote to an Indian friend (in French) that 'I have said adieu to the charming country called Europe, where my beloved lives' – the masculine form of '*le bien aimé*' can only be a reference to Forster.[17] Masood practised law for a short time, then became headmaster of a school in Patna and afterwards accepted a post as history professor at a college in Cuttack. In 1918, he was appointed to a covenanted Indian Civil Service position as Director of Public Instruction for Hyderabad; during his tenure, the number of public schools quadrupled, with a tripling in pupils, and he oversaw the establishment of Osmania University. In his official capacity, he visited Japan, developing great admiration (like Arunachalam) for its educational progress, commercial success, religious tolerance and sense of national purpose. He subsequently published a study of the Japanese educational system, championing Japan as a model for other Asian countries.[18]

Things went badly for Masood in the late 1920s, as he left his Hyderabad job, his marriage broke down and he fell ill during a trip to Europe (and then lost money in the Depression). He and his wife finally divorced in 1928, and five years later Masood married a much younger woman. His two sons were sent to Britain for education and placed under Forster's guardianship. In 1929, Masood returned to Aligarh to become Vice-Chancellor of the university founded by his grandfather, a position he held until 1934. Disagreements with the university governing body on personnel matters precipitated his resignation, but he had also faced personal and professional enemies at Aligarh – and earned the antipathy of the British (despite being awarded a knighthood) for inviting Gandhi and Nehru to speak at the school. His final post was as Minister of Education in Bhopal.[19]

Forster, in the company of Dickinson, went to India in 1912, largely to see Masood, and to explore the country that he had discovered through him. He visited Masood in Aligarh and Patna, and they travelled to Delhi together. On his return home, after more than five months in India, Forster began writing *A Passage to India* – fulfilling Masood's hopes – but the novel, dedicated to Masood (who read and commented on the manuscript), was only published in 1924. (In the meantime, Forster wrote his homosexual novel *Maurice*.) Forster had seen Masood in England in 1919, and visited him several times in India in 1921, when Forster worked for the Maharajah of Dewas Senior. Other visits, in England, took place in 1928 and 1934. Their correspondence during the last fifteen years of Masood's life was less regular than earlier, but still had intense moments. In 1922, Forster, in a moment of depression, wrote: 'I seem to need you more than usual today....You are the only person to whom I can open my heart and feel occasionally that I am understood.' Masood responded with similar affection.[20]

Masood died suddenly, at the age of forty-eight, in 1937, and Forster delivered a moving obituary for an Urdu journal. He spoke of Masood's artistic temperament, his appreciation of Musset and Tolstoy, his work in India and his wry judgement of Englishmen in the Raj:

> 'As for your damned countrymen, I pity the poor fellows from the bottom of my heart, and give them all the help I can.' He was irritated by the English, he was sometimes bitter about them, but he realized that they were awkwardly placed in India.

Forster expressed gratitude for Masood's influence: 'My own debt to him is incalculable. He woke me up out of my suburban and academic life, showed me new horizons and a new civilization, and helped me towards the understanding of a continent.'[21] In 1945, again in India, Forster paid a tearful visit to Masood's grave.[22] Fifteen years later, he gave £1,000 towards construction of the Urdu Hall in Hyderabad in memory of Masood. Masood's sons continued to call on him in Cambridge through his later years.

Forster and Masood never had sexual relations, to Forster's disappointment. Masood was tolerant of homosexuality, and fond enough of Forster to take his declarations of sexual love in his stride – there is no 'homosexual panic' in his writings or actions. The Pakistani editor of Masood and Forster's letters, in a long footnote, mounts an attack on 'the unnatural and unethical practice of buggery, sodomy or homosexuality – call a gutter by any name, it will stink in your nostrils all the same'. He quotes Koranic condemnations of homosexuality and, not surprisingly, but gratuitously, denies that Masood was guilty of any such 'heinous act'.[23] Masood might have been aware of the tradition of homoerotic friendship in Indian history (such as the Emperor Babur's infatuation with an 18-year-old), as well as Persian and Arabic literature extolling boy-love. He no doubt realised that a number of Forster's friends – Carpenter, Ackerley, Dickinson, Lytton Strachey, Duncan Grant, John Maynard Keynes – were also that way inclined. Was Masood tempted to engage in homosexuality? It seems unlikely. Was he sexually teasing Forster? It is possible, especially at the start of their friendship, but perhaps unawares, given the banter and effusion in his letters. Masood's expressions of love and affection were less unusual between men in the first decades of the twentieth century than now, yet indicate a profound and sincere intimacy with Forster.

Forster's sexual interest in Masood dissipated as time passed, but friendship remained strong, while Masood continued to hold what he called, in a letter of 1908, the 'great affection, real love and sincerest admiration I have for you'.[24] A thirty-year friendship across two continents, and two cultures, had provided a mooring for Masood in Britain, and had opened the world of India to Forster. Forster's famous maxim of 'only connect' seemed to be put into practice in their platonic but sexually charged friendship. As for Masood's influence, Forster summed it up in the journal he kept during his trip to India in 1945. Enjoying meeting students who asked for his autograph (but scolding himself for his eternal reticence when he failed to express more enthusiasm for a charming young man who wanted to show him his poems), Forster remarked that 'the present emptiness is not a deception for India if she views my life for the past 30 years as a whole. I have always "loved her", since Masood arrived at Weybridge.'[25]

Forster and Mohammed el-Adl

During the First World War, with Masood in India, Forster volunteered to do non-combatant war service for the Red Cross, and was sent to Alexandria, where his job, as a 'searcher', was to trace missing soldiers and keep records on the wounded. Arriving in the autumn of 1915, he remained until January 1919. Forster's efficient performance of his duties earned praise, and he learned touching stories from soldiers injured in battle. Forster used his leisure time to good advantage, researching the city for *Alexandria: A History and a Guide*, published in 1922, and a small book of essays, *Pharos and Pharillon*, published the following year. He contributed a number of pieces to an Alexandrian English-language newspaper, writing on 'Shakespeare and Egypt', 'A musician in Egypt', 'Handel in Egypt', 'Gippo English' and other occasional subjects.[26] He made friends with various Europeans, particularly Constantine Cavafy, the leading Greek-language poet of his day, with whom Forster shared an intellectual interest in history and a sexual attraction to men.[27]

Alexandria was a cosmopolitan metropolis of Egyptian, Armenian, Turkish, Greek, Jewish, British and French residents, a city with a history stretching back thousands of years and one of the most bustling ports in the Mediterranean. The Egyptian khedive had nominally been a vassal of the Ottoman sultan, but, after Egypt went bankrupt, British ships bombarded Alexandria in 1882, and the British Agent and Consul-General became virtual ruler of the country. At the beginning of the First World War, Britain established a formal protectorate over Egypt, and 25,000 Allied troops were stationed there.

Alexandria's layers of Pharaonic, Arabic and modern history provided a rich culture, although many traces of the ancient past had been effaced. A Turkish fort stood over the site of the famous Pharos, Alexandria's lighthouse, and a mosque had been built over the supposed tomb of Alexander the Great. Eclectic architecture and rundown suburbs were balanced by gardens and beaches. Forster did not particularly like present-day Alexandria when he arrived: 'The "sights" of Alexandria are in themselves not interesting, but they fascinate when we approach them through the past.'[28]

Forster was sexually frustrated and lonely during his first months in Alexandria. He did enjoy the company of invalid soldiers, and wrote enthusiastically to Edward Carpenter about the agreeable sight of bronzed troopers bathing and frolicking in the surf. He added that some Egyptians could no doubt relieve his loneliness, but they were unaware of his situation, and he did not know what to do.[29] In October 1916, Forster nevertheless had a sexual experience – perhaps his first 'complete' sexual encounter, the loss of his 'respectability', as he wrote to one correspondent – with a soldier at Montazah beach. But he declined sexual offers from young Arabs who frequented a hashish den that he visited.[30] Sexual opportunities abounded in a city of foreign soldiers and poor peasants, labourers and office-workers; Cavafy's poems recounted his own multiple meetings, generally brief encounters, with clerks or waiters.[31] Expatriates such as the long-time Egyptian resident 'Bimbashi' McPherson found ample homoerotic possibilities in the international city.[32]

Forster ultimately had one of the most significant homoerotic relationships in his life – second only to his friendship with Masood – with an Egyptian.[33] Thanks to his preservation of Mohammed's letters, and Forster's own correspondence, particularly with Florence Barger, it is possible to reconstruct their affair and friendship in a way rarely possible for homosexual colonial romances.[34]

In the spring of 1916, Forster came across Mohammed el-Adl, a handsome conductor, about sixteen years old and dressed smartly in khaki uniform and a red tarboosh, on the tram that he regularly took to a suburban Red Cross hospital. A studio photograph of Mohammed from several years later shows a dandified young man in bowtie and three-piece suit, wearing a fez and with spats on his shoes, sitting at a table with a fly-whisk in his hand, staring resolutely and rather aristocratically at the camera. Carpenter, who saw the picture after the relationship between Forster and Mohammed had taken an erotic turn, remarked:

> What a pleasure to see a real face after the milk-and-water, mongrelly things one sees here [in England]! It was a literal refreshment to me. Those eyes – I know so well what they mean, and I think you do too, *now*![35]

Mohammed seemed to Forster the only conductor who did not step on passengers' feet as he walked through the carriage. Forster also noticed that Mohammed once playfully fingered the buttons of an English officer when he alighted. One winter night, some months after Forster had first seen him,

Mohammed spoke to Forster – he had learned English at the American Mission School – to ask him to stand up so that he could retrieve his overcoat beneath Forster's seat. Forster's courtesy surprised the conductor, accustomed to brusquer treatment from foreigners. (A drunken English officer had once punched him in the jaw, and another had hit him with his cane when Mohammed interrupted a conversation with a nurse to ask whether they intended to board the tram.) In March 1917, Mohammed told Forster that he would not have to pay for his tram journeys because of his courtesy. By the next month, after Forster had repeatedly waited at the tram station hoping to see Mohammed, sometimes in vain, the Egyptian told him his schedule. Soon, when an inspector asked Forster for his ticket, Mohammed answered that he had a dispensation or a pass (Forster did not understand the Arabic). The inspector determined that Forster had no such exemption (although he was entitled to pay half-fare), and threatened Mohammed with a fine; as a foreigner in uniform, Forster was above censure. Mohammed remarked simply that he had done a good deed in allowing Forster to travel free. Forster asked a friend, owed a favour by the station manager, to intervene. A grateful Mohammed agreed to meet Forster after work.

At their first private meeting, Forster made a *faux pas* when he brought along a box of cakes; Mohammed said he did not like sweets, and implied that he feared they might be poisoned. In fact, he was uncomfortable with the obligation of reciprocal gift-giving, and perhaps did not welcome what he considered Forster's proffering of bakshish. Forster learned that Mohammed had arrived in Alexandria, from Mansourah, a town in the Nile delta, around the same time as he did. His parents still lived there, but Mohammed's mother was ill. He did not get along well with his father, who kept a second wife. After their initial talk, Forster visited Mohammed's modest room in what Mohammed called the 'Home of Misery'; Mohammed emptied out a box of his little treasures for Forster to see. At their third meeting, in Forster's lodgings, they settled onto the bed and began to stroke each other's hair. Forster noticed that Mohammed had an erection (as did Forster) and began to unbutton his flies. Forster groped Mohammed too aggressively, however, and a minor scuffle ensued in which Forster grazed his hand and Mohammed hurt his eye. The misunderstanding was transitory and laughed off the next day, and soon Forster and Mohammed were seeing each other several times a week, though for only a few hours at a time. They also began having sex. Conditions necessitated discretion, partly because of the evident disparity in age, race and status between them; as Mohammed was dark-complexioned, Forster said they made a particularly noticeable couple. Neither Forster nor Mohammed wore uniforms when they met after work, and they did not travel together to their rendezvous. Forster's Greek landlady at first was suspicious of his bringing the Egyptian home, and the arrival of Mohammed's half-brother in Alexandria made it difficult for them to meet in the 'Home of Misery'. A friend of Mohammed occasionally lent a flat, but they generally met in a public garden. Moments of intimacy had to be stolen as often as possible.

By July 1917, Forster wrote of his great happiness, describing his new relationship most lengthily to Florence Barger. The affair might 'seem odd', he admitted, but he assured her that he and Mohammed had a 'very perfect understanding'. Barger, delighted, asked for details. He sent her one of Mohammed's own letters, and enclosed a photograph of the youth, recording the origin and evolution of their relationship, and his intention to commit the story to paper, if only privately so.

To Carpenter, Forster spoke of the young man's frankness, charm and independence. By October 1917, he reported, 'We are now wholly devoted to one another', adding that he was 'freed forever from the burden of loneliness and failure'. Forster wrote to Dickinson about his 'adventures', charting the friendship as it developed from an encounter 'like Searight's affair' (a reference to the sexually voracious officer he and Dickinson had met on board ship to India in 1912) – 'this will convey to you age, race, rank, though not precisely relationship'. He wrote more circumspectly to Masood, telling him that he had 'got to know an Egyptian whom I greatly like and who sometimes reminds me of you'. A note to Cavafy spoke of his joy, and in guarded terms Forster even mentioned his friend to his mother.[36]

Forster and Mohammed chatted, smoked, played chess and generally enjoyed each other's company as the months passed. The death of Mohammed's mother, in July 1917, took him away to Mansourah, and Forster's sympathy cemented the friendship. Mohammed, however, was unsatisfied with his job, which paid only two shillings a day and afforded little leisure, and he asked Forster to help him find other employment. Forster contacted friends in the Suez Canal Zone and secured a job for Mohammed doing low-level intelligence work for the British in Kantara, at several times his previous wages. Mohammed began work in October 1917, and did not see Forster for several months. The relationship was secure enough, however, for them to write to each other frequently, which alleviated Forster's renewed solitude.

Mohammed's letters are cheerful and chatty, though once slightly testy at Forster's request for a photograph and for asking him to meet a friend travelling in the Canal Zone. In one letter, he turned philosophical to comment about Forster's and his respect for each other's religion. Mohammed thanked Forster for presents of a hat, a uniform and a tie-pin. He told Forster that he was working hard, and enjoying bathing in the canal. Mohammed said that his English was improving thanks to fraternising with English soldiers, although he did not really enjoy drinking with them and could down 'only' two bottles of stout.[37] He did not recount in the letters, but told Forster in person, about a sexual encounter with an English soldier.[38]

For unknown reasons, Mohammed grew unhappy with the Canal Zone job and resigned early in 1918. He saw Forster again in Alexandria, but, in June, had to return to Mansourah when his father died; with tragic coincidence, his brother drowned in a swimming accident at almost the same time. Forster sent a telegram of condolence and followed with a visit. The brief stay went off exceptionally well, and Forster adapted to Mohammed's simple house – a few rooms, crowded conditions, rudimentary sanitation – in an almost slum; he enjoyed the 'lavish' food served by a 'semi-slave'. Mohammed gave Forster a tour of Mansourah's esplanade and cafés, they took a boat ride on the Nile and Forster met some of his friends.[39]

Mohammed enjoyed Forster's visit, thanking him for shoes he had brought and joking that he had found a pair of Forster's socks near the latrine. The Egyptian used his time at home to sort out family affairs, and tried to learn some shorthand. He considered marrying his brother's widow, as custom would have sanctioned, but decided against her in favour of another young lady, whom he described to Forster as a 'vergin [sic] and very beautiful indeed'. In August, Mohammed went to Alexandria to see Forster.[40]

Mohammed inherited the family house, and a small sum of money from his father, and decided to become a cotton-trader, buying cotton from peasant producers and selling it in Cairo.[41] He found a business partner, and used his legacy, plus a £70 loan from Forster, to get started; the business began promisingly. Mohammed described his dealings in letters, and confided personal details as well, for instance, a visit with a friend to a brothel, and his fear of having caught 'sifless' from the (female) prostitute. He mused about visiting Forster in England or India once Forster left Egypt, and hoped Forster would come again to Mansourah. He thanked Forster for sending him some buttons, which he would wear only 'in case of smartation'. In October 1918, Mohammed married and enthused about his wedded happiness. There was, however, worrying news of illness, as Mohammed began to spit up blood; a doctor told him that he was not consumptive, but must look after himself. Health problems nevertheless continued, and Mohammed carefully noted the fluctuations in his weight. Financial worries were a preoccupation; the cotton business was not earning sufficient revenue to cover expenses, and he had narrowly avoided arrest when bales of cotton that he procured from a farmer and sold turned out to be rotten. He asked if Forster could help him to find another job. While giving news of himself in regular letters, Mohammed always enquired about Forster, sympathising with his concerns, wondering how his book on Alexandria was going and sending regards to Forster's mother in England.[42]

In November 1918, Forster again visited Mansourah, staying with Mohammed and his wife (a violation of local custom, since Forster was an unmarried man and not a family member). The first day of the visit was 'as perfect as I have known'. Forster found Gamila sweet, simple, 'intelligent in a country way', though shy, and praised her skills as a excellent cook. He wrote to Barger that Mohammed thought of her as a comfort but also as something of a financial burden; Forster had been giving Mohammed a shilling a day for food, and he resolved that Mohammed should not repay the loan.[43]

As the time for Forster's departure from Egypt drew closer, Mohammed had become ever more become solicitous. 'Can't you stay in Egypt for ever a good life it will be,' he wrote in October. He had obtained some whistles, at Forster's request, as presents for Barger's children, and added that he was searching for a memento of Egypt for Forster. In January 1919, before leaving, Forster paid a final visit to Mansourah, and delighted Gamila with an Indian box – Mohammed playfully astounded his wife by greatly over-estimating what Forster had paid for the gift. Mohammed wrote: 'I am thankful to you and never forget your kindness.' 'I leave him on his feet and don't deny myself the satisfaction of thinking that I helped to place him on them,' Forster wrote to Barger. Mohammed, however, judged his perspectives bleak: 'I am not looking forward to my future nor to my career.'[44]

In his first surviving letter after Forster's arrival in Britain (which also thanked Forster for a further gift of £10), Mohammed sent greetings from his wife and noted that, exceptionally, he was observing the Ramadan fast 'owing that my wife is very simple and very poious [sic]'. In hopes of finding some better employment, perhaps as a shop-keeper, he had begun studying book-keeping and commercial arithmetic, and he had learned to type.[45]

Meanwhile, the year 1919 saw great political troubles in Egypt, fuelled by the simmering campaign for independence. A nationalist, Saad Zaghlul, a former Minister of Education and Justice, then Vice-President of the Egyptian assembly, after the First World War promoted independence for Egypt. British authorities refused him permission to go to London to negotiate the country's status and exiled him to Malta, provoking riots in Alexandria, and elsewhere, and the deaths of several Englishmen. The events, coupled with the uncertain future of Egypt and the old Ottoman states following the war, made for a tense climate, especially while thousands of foreign troops remained in Egypt. Fears of further insurrection troubled colonial authorities, yet the situation also provided the chance for some profit-making. Mohammed, out of a job but entrepreneurial as ever, bought beans in the countryside, selling them to urban consumers at a handsome profit.

In the midst of the political turmoil, however, Mohammed was arrested by military police. A friend alerted Forster (who promptly sent money to cover Mohammed's fine). The details, which Forster later learned from Mohammed, were that he had one day come across a friend, to whom Australian soldiers were trying to sell an army revolver. Mohammed intervened, telling him not to buy the gun, thereby angering the soldiers, who reported to the police that the Egyptians had been trying to purchase a firearm. Both were arrested, held in custody for seven days and then tried by a tribunal of four officers. Mohammed was convicted and sentenced to six months in gaol and a fine of £10 (or a further three months of imprisonment if the fine was not paid), and his friend received a lesser sentence. In the context of nationalist stirrings, and British fear of armed Egyptian attacks, the word of Allied soldiers carried more weight than the defence of a simple Egyptian.[46]

Mohammed's incarceration was difficult, and he described to Forster the appalling prison conditions. Without paying bakshish to guards, and a further 800 PT bribe for transfer to hospital (the soldiers had offered their revolver for 300 PT), Mohammed said that he would have died. Imprisonment left him with anti-English feelings – 'I found in my dictionary that English means cruel' – but did not change his warm feelings for Forster. When a son was born, he named him Morgan in Forster's honour; unfortunately, the baby fell ill and died in April 1920.[47] Mohammed, himself now increasingly ill, admitted that, since the infant died, he did not have to worry about its unpromising fate. One letter contained a sentence of suicidal thoughts, but Mohammed, reconsidering, had crossed out the lines.[48]

Forster was happy to see Mohammed for four hours in Port Said when his ship stopped there on the way to India in early 1921. Mohammed was in a buoyant mood, though he had lost weight and had no job. Bringing Forster a box of cigarettes (minus several he had given as bakshish), Mohammed came aboard ship; Forster recorded that he and Mohammed had sex. On a quick tour of the town, they walked to the statue of de Lesseps on the waterfront, and stopped in cafés; the brief visit was, in Forster's word, 'dreamlike'.[49] Forster continued to write to Mohammed while working for the Maharajah, a position that awed Mohammed,[50] and the Egyptian seemed bemused by Indian customs. A letter to 'dear silly Morgan' implies that Forster intimated a sexual encounter with an Indian barber. Mohammed reported that he had a job (although the sort of employment went unspecified); he complained about his father-in-law and told Forster of the birth of a daughter. Political sentiments also come out in his letters. Mohammed admitted to being pro-nationalist, a supporter of Zaghlul and unimpressed by a visiting delegation of English parliamentarians. He reassured Forster, however, 'that there are many good Englishmen'.[51]

Mohammed's health was now seriously deteriorating, and, when Forster saw him on his return journey home to Britain in 1922, he was alarmed at Mohammed's state. Mohammed, who had collapsed a fortnight beforehand, was unable to meet the ship. Forster arranged for Mohammed to consult a doctor in Helouan, who confirmed that he had consumption and was beyond cure. Forster paid for Mohammed's wife and daughter, and Mohammed's sister Farida, to join them in Helouan; his letters again speak highly and fondly of Gamila. Mohammed rallied while Forster was in Egypt, and they went on several excursions – Forster remembered Mohammed riding on a donkey with the pyramids in the background. Forster wrote to his friends about Mohammed, and both Barger and Masood (who, of course, had never met him) sent letters to the Egyptian, gestures Forster found touching. Masood also offered to give money to Forster to ensure that Mohammed was looked after, but Forster replied that he had sufficient funds for six months or a year. Having made appropriate provisions, Forster returned to Britain, seen off in Cairo by Mohammed, certain that he would not see his friend again.[52]

In February 1922, Mohammed wrote to say how much he had enjoyed Forster's visit, but that he remained unwell, and that his daughter was in hospital. (She would soon die.) Three weeks later, he wrote gloomily from Helouan hoping that he and Forster 'will meet again or in heaven'. 'My love to you,' he closed the letter. Around 6 May, he sent Forster a photograph; staccato comments in a weakened hand read, 'the family are good', but 'I am very bad'. Courteous as ever, Mohammed sent 'compliments to [Forster's] mother', and ended 'My love to you / My love to you / My love to you / do not forget your ever friend'. On 8 May, he acknowledged money Forster had sent and said that he was too weak to stand. Clearly with great difficulty, he scribbled, 'My love to you / My love to you'.[53] He died soon afterwards, aged approximately twenty-three; a friend confirmed his death to Forster.

Mohammed left his ring to Forster, and his sister, Farida, arranged to have it sent to England – in memory of his friend, Forster put on the ring once a day for months afterwards. Forster sent money to Farida, who complained that her brother's death would cause financial problems for her. In an unpleasant postscript, Gamila wrote to Forster saying that Farida had stolen her jewellery and other possessions, and asked him not to write to the sister or send her further presents.[54]

Over the past months, realising that Mohammed was dying, Forster had waited for the inevitable to happen: 'I want him to tell me that he is dead, and so set me free to make an image of him,' he confessed to his *Locked Diary* the day before Mohammed's last letter to him was posted. Several days later, he confessed that Mohammed's death would cause him no pain, and he began to worry that, in retrospect, Mohammed's warmth towards him seemed to come from politeness or pity. Forster admitted that Mohammed had often been 'cold' to him: 'Determined my life should contain one success I have concealed from myself and others Mohammed's frequent coldness toward me.'[55] When his death occurred, however, Forster was much saddened. He began dreaming of Mohammed almost every night, and, apostrophising his dead friend, bewailed that he was 'oppressed with you'.[56] He wrote to tell Masood, thanking him for his understanding and support during his affair with Mohammed, and no doubt hoping for comfort.[57] Looking through Mohammed's letters upset Forster and inspired him to record his thoughts in a small brown notebook, possibly purchased in Egypt.

Writing about Mohammed was meant to be cathartic for Forster, a way to make peace with his dead friend and himself: 'I write for my own comfort and to recall the past, but also because I am professionally a writer and want to pay you this last honour.' The first and longest entry, dated 5 August 1922, remembers Mohammed fondly, but tries to exorcise him by dwelling on his death and the 'putrescence' of his body in an Egyptian cemetery. One day soon afterwards, Forster added extra paragraphs recounting their meeting, and then several pages about the 'sensual' side of their relationship. Written months later, another paragraph noted that Mohammed's memory had become 'dimmer'. Seven years later, he wrote a final paragraph to consign Mohammed to his past.[58] In his *Locked Diary*, which contained Forster's most private thoughts, he also chronicled the fading of memories. Some time in 1923, he confided that he was now forgetting Mohammed, going for days without thinking of him. On 31 December 1923, he realised that this was the final day on which he could say that 'last year' he had kissed Mohammed. By New Year,

> I shall be in bed…with your ring ['my ring' is crossed out] on my finger, your whistle under my garment and your first and last letters to me under

my pillow. I will not do this again, but the end of our daily lives together has come. Tomorrow I shall feel you have gone from me in the form I remember....Good-bye Mohammed el-Adl.[59]

Three weeks later, when he finished *A Passage to India*, Forster marked the end of the manuscript with Mohammed's pencil.[60]

Forster put away the notebook about Mohammed, but took it out again in 1960, neatly copying out Mohammed's letters, and then writing several pages of quotations from Mohammed, culled from his memory and his letters from almost half a century before. Three years later, at the age of almost eighty-five, he wrote to William Plomer that Mohammed was the 'greatest thing in my life' except for one other.[61] That one other was surely Masood.

Mohammed emerges from Forster's letters and reminiscences, and his own letters, as an interesting and dynamic young man. His background was modest, although his brother was a tailor, and his father wealthy enough to support a second wife, employ a 'semi-slave' to do housework and leave a not inconsequential estate. Mohammed was well educated enough to speak and write good English – his letters sometimes show a deft turn of phrase – and the *bons mots* that Forster recorded indicate lively thought. He took pride in himself, and was a natty dresser; indeed, he nagged Forster about his own shabby clothes. Forster spoke about his independence of mind. This manifested itself in willingness to give Forster free passage on the tram, and his occasionally brusque reactions (as when Forster first gave him cakes), but also the determined way in which he took hold of affairs after his father's death. He remained loyal to his family, and had a loving and respectful relationship with his wife. He observed Muslim customs – arranging for prayers for his dead father, agreeing to observe the Ramadan fast with his wife – yet was willing to drink alcohol and to allow Forster, an unmarried man, to meet his wife. Although not particularly religious himself, he questioned Forster as to why foreigners did not respect Islam. He told Forster that if he had great wealth, he would first of all build an eye-hospital (Mohammed sometimes wore spectacles), and then a mosque. He was ambitious in changing jobs, and had an entrepreneurial spirit, trying to improve his English, studying book-keeping, commercial arithmetic, shorthand and typing, and setting up as a cotton-trader (although that venture proved ill-fated). He bore his illness with courage, and the deaths of family members with stoicism.

Mohammed suffered abuse from foreigners. Expatriates had insulted him on the tram, and, as he developed more of a political consciousness, he opposed British rule in Egypt and expressed dislike for many Englishmen. His experiences in 1919 – arrest by military police after false accusations by Allied officers – not surprisingly played a part in his anti-imperialist sentiments. Yet Mohammed had enjoyed benefits from foreigners as well, such as employment in the Canal Zone. From Forster he received a substantial amount of money (probably well in excess of £100 in cash and provisions for medical care), as well as clothing and other presents, for which he expressed sincere thanks. Forster provided an opening to the outside world, companionship for the young migrant to Alexandria, sympathy as he suffered the loss of his mother, father and brother within the space of a year (and, later, the deaths of his infant children), and support during his financial troubles and the beginnings of an illness that proved fatal.

Forster and Mohammed's sexual relationship was perhaps not dissimilar from other colonial liaisons. Forster was exclusively homosexual, though he had not yet had sexual relations (beyond some kissing and cuddling) before he arrived in Egypt. Mohammed was not bound by the Western dichotomy between homosexual and heterosexual behaviour. He recounted a visit to a brothel, married and fathered two children. But his caressing of a soldier's buttons on a tram ride might have indicated an early homosexual contact, and he admitted to a liaison in Kantara. Mohammed willingly let Forster touch his knee, run his fingers through his hair and kiss him on their third 'date', and his manifest erection led Forster to ask how fond Mohammed was of him (a question he appeared not to understand), and then to grope him. Mohammed responded roughly, but the incident quickly passed. Forster puzzled over Mohammed's reaction, but accepted his explanation: 'My damned prick always stands up whoever it is, it means nothing.'[62]

Forster wrote to Barger about his efforts to break down Mohammed's resistance to sex. In July 1917, Forster said he wanted to part with 'Respectability', his code word for lack of sex, even though Mohammed was not keen:

> It indeed seems right to me that we should, and I thought his objections trivial, and beat against them. He has made me see that I must not do this – they are profound if mistaken – but he has made me see it with so much tenderness and affection that I feel our friendship is only now beginning.

In September, Forster reported on Mohammed's continued recalcitrance:

> Completely to part with R[espectability] he refuses 'Never! Never!' – then with an indescribable mixture of detachment and tenderness turned my head away and said 'I want to ask you a question. Do you never consider that your wish has led you to know a T= C= [tram conductor]? And do you not think that a pity for you and a disgrace? – While answering my questions you are not to look at me.'…Once before, with proud [Forster crossed out the word 'infinite'] sadness, he feared he was only externals for me.

On 8 October, Forster reported to Barger that at the 'Home of Misery', three days before, 'R has been parted with, and in the simplest most inevitable way'. When visiting Mohammed in Mansourah in July 1918,

> I theorised to him, by the way, rather deeply against R[espectability] – how afterwards I found its absence even more important than at the time. He said very gently 'I quite understand' – so I have the happiness of knowing that things are sound even on an intellectual basis.[63]

Forster proved remarkably persistent in seeking sex from Mohammed. Whether Mohammed's resistance was deeply moralistic, showing disapproval of homosexuality, or personal, because he did not fancy sex with Forster, is debatable. He clearly thought, for a while, that Forster was only interested in his body, and afterwards seems to have acquiesced to sex with a certain amused reluctance. Exactly what they did, and how many times they did it, is unclear. Because of the difficulties in arranging assignations, the two may have only spent some twelve nights together.[64] Forster wrote in his memoir that 'my carnal ecstasies with you have never been supreme'. However that was not central, for:

> I remember more the caress to my hair....the firm caress of your arm round my body in your sleep, a kiss, sudden and hard on the lips when I asked for one, and the times I have fondled your thighs. You would always let me do this after a gruff demur, would untie the linen drawers and lean back a little.[65]

Forster and Mohammed had sex during his lay-over in Port Said in 1921:

> I hadn't seen you for two years and took joy in touching your stiffened flesh again. You said 'Foolish'. I: – 'All have their foolishness and this is mine.' While in India, 'I thought of this side of you (but it has always been a small part of the sum of my thoughts) and I promised myself that on my return I would get you to penetrate me behind, however much it hurt and although it must decrease your respect for me.

(The statement implies that they had not earlier had anal intercourse.) Mohammed's illness made sex impossible, but 'I used to massage you a little in your bed at Helouan while you thought of women'.[66]

The nature of Forster and Mohammed's sexual relationship is important only because Forster himself was adamant in discussing it in letters with Barger and in several pages in his notebook. Mohammed's own letters do not mention their sexual relationship. He was hardly an enthusiastic lover with men, and both his desire and his experience – Forster, a soldier in the Canal Zone and perhaps a soldier in Alexandria are the only examples – may have been limited. For an unmarried young man, there were no real alternatives for sexual activity except prostitutes and homosexual encounters, however, and Mohammed's initial opposition to sex with Forster seems to be more a question of readiness and particular interest than religious or moral rejection of 'vice'. He agreed to have sex with Forster in 1921 after he was married, and Forster presumed that he would be willing to do so again the following year. For Mohammed, homosexual behaviour, in sum, appears to have been a not unnatural part, when the occasion warranted, of more general social relations. Forster had written to Barger that Mohammed 'differs from the northerner in being unsentimental, and in keeping his senses apart from his mind'.[67] Somewhat ironically, Forster himself came to share the view, embedding his sex life with Mohammed in a wider context of friendship with the Egyptian, a companionship that survived separation and illness, and stayed with Forster long after Mohammed's death.

Mohammed had enormous influence on Forster. Their affair was the first full sexual relationship Forster had, the first time that his desire for someone had been so indulged. He told Barger that he would have written *Maurice* differently if he had already had the experience he obtained with Mohammed.[68] Forster also discovered a new type of sexual and emotional attachment not fraught with unrequited longing, tormented guilt or great sentimentality. The lightness with which Mohammed attached himself to Forster occasionally led him to wonder how great his affection really was, but also showed an ease in personal relationships new to Forster: 'At present I am all for Orientalism. To get rid of sentimentality yet retain Romance – that's what he has done,' Forster wrote to Carpenter.[69]

Companionship with Mohammed also changed Forster's stay in Alexandria from a dull sojourn in a city he found uninteresting into one of the most memorable periods of his life. It relieved the distress and dislocation of the war years; almost guiltily, Forster said that 'the war has jerked me off a branch on to a bed of leaves'.[70] Furthermore, it changed his notion of Egypt; at the beginning of his stay, he did not like the country, but, when he passed through in the 1920s, his opinion had altered. Forster's attitudes towards 'natives' changed, thanks to Mohammed, who forced him to abandon imperialist stereotypes. He remarked to Barger:

> Natives, especially of the lower city class, are dirty in body and mind, incapable of fineness, and only out for what they can get. That is the theory to which, after some reluctance, I had fully subscribed, and like all theories it has broken down.[71]

This political *prise de conscience* expressed itself in Forster's contribution, a historical section, to a Fabian Society pamphlet, published in 1920, which called for the British to renounce the 1914 protectorate and allow Egyptians freely to choose affiliation with the British Empire or independence. Forster's chapter discussed the press censorship, martial law, compulsory labour and racist attitudes that had fomented the anti-British sentiment which he had already witnessed in his last year in Alexandria. Although the foreign population 'contain[s] men of character and culture whom it is a privilege to have known', the expatriates were 'aliens in Egypt and have come to exploit it; they despise Oriental ways, they are agnostics or Christians who have no sympathy for Islam, and they feel for the natives a fear that too often proceeds from a bad conscience'. Immune from prosecution by native courts and exempt from customs and land tax, they lived happily from the profits of the Suez Canal that, paradoxically, brought limited benefits to Egyptians. Not surprisingly, 'every Egyptian sympathised openly or secretly' with Zaghlul and the nationalists.[72] The tram conductor had thus led Forster to both a sexual and a political awakening.

Forster in India

Egypt was an interlude, although a most significant one, whereas India occupied Forster's attentions for decades; Egypt never excited Forster's sympathies as did India. During his first visit to India in 1912, thanks to Forster's friend Sir Malcolm Darling, he had met the Maharajah of Dewas Senior. In 1916, while Forster was in Egypt, the Maharajah had invited him to work as his Private Secretary. The proposal was scuppered by a British official, who intimated in a letter that Forster was 'a decadent coward and apparently a sexual pervert'.[73] In 1921, the Maharajah successfully renewed the offer. The state of Dewas Senior, as Forster wrote in his recollections about the sojourn, *The Hill of Devi*, 'can have no parallel, except in a Gilbert and Sullivan opera'.[74] Because of an obscure family conflict, the Dewas dynasty and realm were divided into two branches, Senior and Junior – territorially, one side of a street might belong to Senior, the other to Junior. Dewas Senior comprised 446 square miles with a population of 80,000, and it exported grains, oil-seeds, cotton and opium. Darling, who tutored the young ruler of Dewas, found it picturesque:

> With its tiled houses, shadowing eaves and purely Indian atmosphere, Dewas by day was always a pleasant sight. But at night, and as now under a half moon, with scattered lamps throwing an uncertain light upon the houses and upon the turbanned heads passing to and fro, its charm was irresistible.[75]

Other visitors did not find it particularly memorable.

The ruler of Dewas was Maharajah Sir Tukoji Rao Puar III; born in 1888, he succeeded his uncle to the throne eleven years later. Darling described him in 1907 as 'short and slim…but a thick black moustache makes him look much older than he is.…He is certainly high-spirited and alert. He has, too, a most engaging manner.' (Darling's mother enthused, 'I quite fell in love with him.') His manners were simple and unorthodox; he broke precedent (and 'had narrowly escaped the Hindu equivalent of excommunication') for dining with Europeans, and even drank from the same cup as Darling at a tennis club: 'With him friendship brushed away all petty scruples.' He had a reputation, confirmed by Forster, for playing practical jokes.[76] Following a thorough Anglo-Indian education, he became a faithful ally of the British, who awarded him a knighthood, raised his title from rajah to maharajah and accorded him a fifteen-gun salute.[77] He intoned in one speech:

> It was after the establishment of the Pax Britannica that the doors of modern education and liberty were thrown open to Indians…the modern advance Indians were and are making towards their being turned out useful and loyal colleagues, citizens and servants not only in helping them in all the various problems of this country, but also in that splendid and great British Mission of Civilization and Empire.[78]

The Maharajah attempted modernising policies – opening schools, ending 'untouchability' in places of worship, adopting a constitution with provisions for a representative assembly and pursuing land reforms. He was of a mystic temperament, but also spent lavishly on entertainments and an ambitious building programme, spendthriftiness that caused his downfall. Tukoji Rao had married the daughter of the enormously wealthy Maharajah of Kolhapur, but she left him in 1916 to return home.

Forster – just as his friend Ackerley during a stint as Private Secretary to the Maharajah of Chhatarpur – had vague administrative duties, but his major brief seemed to be providing companionship for the Maharajah. Forster and the Maharajah got on famously. He accompanied the ruler on a 'royal progress', dressed in Indian garments to take part in court life and participated in the Holi celebrations and Gokul Ashtami, the festival celebrating the birth of Krishna. The sounds of cymbals and trumpets, the colours of saris and the bright powders thrown around at festivals, the smell of incense, the ceremonial of the court and the amiability of the Maharajah enchanted Forster. He nevertheless quickly became aware of the complexities of Indian life, and of the British Raj. A minor incident occurred when a British Assistant Political Agent offended the Maharajah by not behaving correctly towards Forster, underlining the awkward position of Englishmen in the employ of Indian rulers, themselves vassals of the British Viceroy. The contrast between old and new India, and differences between Hindu and Muslim India, became apparent when Masood visited Dewas. Masood was taken aback by the ramshackle state of Dewas; embarrassingly for Forster, he heralded the wealth and efficiency of the ruler for whom he worked, the Nizam of Hyderabad, and politely remonstrated Tukoji Rao for his backwardness.

Although Forster did not think much of Dewas Senior ('an untidy ant-hill'), he developed an abiding fondness for its Maharajah. Fifteen years after his stay, Forster wrote to Tukoji Rao of 'the eternal affection which binds us together', acknowledging a cable as 'one more proof that our hearts beat together and they will not cease to beat thus until they are stilled'. 'I love you very much,' said Forster in another letter.[79] Although his writings give no hint of sexual attraction to the Maharajah, a not unattractive man, Forster displaced some of his emotional longing for companionship with Indians onto Tukoji Rao, as indicated in the similar language he used to both Masood and the Maharajah. Coming after his renewed but brief contact with Mohammed *en route* to India, the Maharajah's comradeship filled his need for a friend and confidant. In later editions of *A Passage to India*, Forster added the name of the Maharajah to that of Masood in the dedication. By that time the Majarajah had quarrelled with his son and heir, suffered bankruptcy brought on by mismanagement and the Depression, and faced British determination to set up a commission of enquiry into Dewas's finances. The problems had prompted him, in 1933, to flee to the French colony of Pondicherry, where he died in 1937 (the same year as Masood). Disgrace did not affect Forster's loyalties, and in *The Hill of Devi*, published in 1953, Forster concluded, 'He was certainly a genius and possibly a saint, and he had to be a king.'[80]

Unlike some other works written by British homosexuals travelling in India (notably Carpenter's *From Adam's Peak to Elephanta*), *The Hill of Devi* almost conspicuously avoids eroticisation of Indians, Forster only noting that several well-built wrestlers resembled Greek statues. Sexual improprieties and misbehaviour by a previous Private Secretary, who had served the Maharajah for only a matter of days, perhaps steered Forster away from descriptions that might be misinterpreted. Still publicly reticent about his own homosexuality, Forster's erotic experiences were confided to writings published posthumously. 'Kanaya' records his sexual experiences in Dewas Senior; the narrative also provides insight into sexual attitudes in princely India.[81]

Forster was tormented by sexual desires in Dewas, not so much from the sight of the young men around him at court ('nearly every hanger-on was so ugly') but because of the heat: 'The climate soon impaired my will; I did not suffer from the heat in other ways, but it provoked me sexually.'[82] Attempts to take his mind off sex, and masturbation (three times during one siesta), failed to give relief, and he began to notice the attentions of a Muslim coachman who made his availability clear, but whom Forster found unattractive. Forster then flirted with a Hindu servant, who responded seductively. Finally, Forster screwed up his courage to arrange an assignation, but was horrified to hear the youth tell other servants about the rendezvous. Filled with guilt, and terror at possible repercussions, especially since the Maharajah had spoken badly of homosexuals, Forster did not show up to meet the 'coolie'. Persuaded that the Maharajah's attitude towards him had changed the next time he saw the ruler, Forster confessed all; the Maharajah remarked calmly that he had heard nothing and reassured Forster that his desires were perfectly natural, for him if not for others.

The Maharajah was relieved that Forster had not attended his meeting with the youth, and proposed to find his Private Secretary a suitable sexual partner, settling on the barber who shaved Forster. If the youth was agreeable, said the Maharajah, Forster should discreetly have sex with him, and the Maharajah would send money to the young man. On his second subsequent meeting with Kanaya, Forster began a sexual relationship, one that had to be conducted clandestinely (and consummated rapidly) because of lack of privacy in the palace. The arrangement was satisfactory if not ideal: 'I couldn't get from Kanaya the emotional response of an Egyptian, because he had the body and soul of a slave, but he was always merry and he improved my health.'[83] Things went well enough until, while Forster was away visiting Masood in Hyderabad, Kanaya boasted of their relationship to an official; Forster returned to find that gossip had spread throughout the court and beyond. The Maharajah once again reassured him, and Kanaya was repentant. When Kanaya later used his sexual relationship with Forster to solicit employment from the Maharajah, even implying that the Maharajah shared homosexual proclivities, both Tukoji Rao and Forster were outraged. Forster boxed Kanaya's ears and admitted that, when they resumed having sex, 'it was now mixed with the desire to inflict pain'.[84] Forster gave Kanaya money when he left Dewas – the boy did not seem to think it enough – and continued to enjoy the Maharajah's good graces. Forster regretted that 'had K. [sic] not been a chatterbox, I should have avoided feeling trivial and being brutal'.[85]

The experience juxtaposes Forster's reticence, guilt and fear of 'outing' with the Maharajah's understanding and generous willingness, despite seeming disapproval of homosexuality, to make appropriate provisions for his protégé. When Forster confessed to the Maharajah, the Indian immediately replied that Forster should have told him earlier and relied on him for comprehension and assistance. Never did he castigate Forster or express shock at his homosexual orientation, but did counsel him to be discreet and not to play the passive role in sex. The Maharajah considered that a youth would be Forster's desired partner, rejecting one 28-year-old as too old. That he would be a subaltern, who would be monetarily compensated for his services and silence, was taken for granted. That such a man would use his new position to secure advancement at court, however, was inadmissible. The Maharajah himself was not especially interested in sex, and his court was hardly a hotbed of sexual intrigues (even if songs at the ruler's soirées, to Forster's discomfort, were often bawdy).

For his part, Forster displayed customary timidity and nervousness about sex, and the kindness shown by Tukoji Rao deepened his friendship for the Maharajah. He had ignored manifest possibilities for sex before almost compromising himself with the 'coolie'. Forster was then frustrated that he could not spark an emotional response from Kanaya, though he enjoyed their physical relations. Forster's profound respect for the Maharajah was not matched by his feelings for Kanaya, a 'silly little soul'.[86] He did not hesitate to slap Kanaya around the head, and admitted, 'I just felt he was a slave, without rights, and I a despot whom no one could call to account' – sentiments that contrast with the deference he displayed to the Maharajah, his fraternal love for Masood and his solicitousness about Mohammed. The Englishman silenced all mention of his liaison in *The Hill of Devi*, though 'Kanaya' suggests that his desire for sexual companionship, the relationship with the barber and the troubles sex caused formed major preoccupations during his stay in Dewas. Forster's warm feelings for Tukoji Rao, even in exile and humiliation, were not unconnected with the Maharajah's response to his homosexual fumbling: 'In no essential did he ever fail me.'[87]

As for Kanaya and the other court youths with whom Forster might have had sex, their attitudes are more difficult to judge. The Indians were puzzled at why a man of Forster's age, forty-two, was unmarried, and some realised that he may have been looking for a male partner. A coachman, a 'coolie' and a barber were willing to engage in homosexual activities, though not averse to gossiping about doing so, and hoping for money or preferment in return. Despite his duplicity, Kanaya was a pliable partner, whose status (and undoubted financial needs) left him little choice but to acquiesce to the requirements of his lords and masters.

Friendship, sex and empire

In Forster's life and writings, many obstacles stood in the way of happy long-term relationships with foreign men, especially partnerships where satisfaction of physical desires and of emotional and intellectual needs could combine. The beloved Masood could not physically respond in the way Forster hoped, and he returned to India. Mohammed gave Forster sexual comfort and companionship, but he too married, Forster went home and Mohammed died at a young age. In *A Passage to India*, circumstances thwart Aziz and Fielding's friendship, and the expression of any other sentiments.

In the two pieces of erotic fiction that Forster set in the colonies, published only posthumously, the scenario is even more tragic. In 'The Life to Come', a European missionary, sent to evangelise the heathen, has sex with a chief, who responds by conversion to Christianity and hope for profane love from the minister. The missionary guiltily suppresses his own sexual inclinations, refuses the chief's overtures and collaborates in the ruin of his realm by foreign interests. Struck with a mortal illness, years later, the chief extracts a last act of tenderness from the missionary, then kills the pastor and flings himself off a parapet. 'The Other Boat', vaguely inspired by Captain Searight, was the last short story Forster wrote – a reminder of how earlier experiences continued to haunt him into the 1950s. A handsome, young and hearty English officer, Lionel, must share a ship cabin with a seductive *métis*, Cocoanut, whom he had once met in childhood. While playing up to the odious image of the English colonial on deck, Lionel ecstatically enjoys sex with Cocoanut below deck – 'the Nordic warrior and subtle supple boy'. When the paradox becomes untenable, Lionel strangles Cocoanut and throws himself into the ocean.[88]

The stories (not unlike those of G.F. Green) provide subtle portraits of the dangerous stakes in inter-racial affairs in the colonial world and the great gaps between different cultures. Chief Vithobai cannot see why the Christian love of which Mr Pinmay speaks cannot include sexual love, either in this life or the life hereafter. Cocoanut sees no wrong in an erotic liaison with an Englishman to while away a long voyage. Yet the Englishmen, upholding the Gospel and fighting for the Crown, do not see things in that way. They have trouble resisting temptation as they enter the Sotadic Zone, and inhibitions slip further away as the boat passes from the Mediterranean to the Red Sea to the Indian Ocean, or men penetrate further into the jungle. Finally they crack, but pleasure leads to guilt, fear of social disapproval and concern at the loss of the principles for which they have set out to the colonies. They can only react with cruelty directed at others and at themselves. The Englishmen are revealed as duplicitous, hypocritical, incapable of love, embarrassed and guilty about sex. The brutality of their colonialist attitudes – the missionary establishing a theocracy, the officer killing natives and imposing an exploitative foreign order – is linked with the unresolved, barely repressed homosexual desires that ultimately destroy them and their partners.

The stories may seem proof of the impossibility of homosexual romances, particularly with those who come from different horizons, and Forster's vision in the works is particularly bleak. They are a warning about the hazard of seeking sex rather than friendship, of connecting carnally rather than emotionally and spiritually. His personal experiences were gentler, and he did find companionship, pleasure and friendship with an Indian and an Egyptian. 'The Other Boat' and 'The Life to Come' are thus nightmares contrasting with Forster's dreamlike memories of Masood and Mohammed. But the pieces, showing his most erotic and most anti-colonialist sides, also represent indictments of ideologies that dominated Britain during his life, both social constraints on the expression of homosexual desires and an imperialist imperative to rule the world. In an oblique way, they form Forster's strongest statements of support for personal sexual emancipation and his strongest denunciation of imperialism.

Forster has been taken to task by many present-day commentators for imperialist views, misogyny and fetishisation of working-class and foreign men, as well as for the 'closeted' discomfort with his homosexuality that led him to censure his writings and often only guiltily to seek sexual satisfaction. Forster's 'exotic' liaisons, in a post-gay liberation era, may seem a pathetic commentary on the difficulty of accepting a contrary sexual orientation and effecting sexual connections. He yearned in vain for the unobtainable young Masood, had his first sexual relationship tardily at the age of almost thirty with Mohammed and embarrassedly slept with Kanaya. His letters to Masood, and the Mohammed notebook, may now seem obsessive and maudlin, cloying in language and agonising in sentiment.

Forster's accounts of his decades-long friendship with Masood and the shorter-lived but crucial affair with Mohammed nevertheless remain moving revelations about early twentieth-century emotional and sexual attitudes, as well as illustrations of the sexual paradoxes of imperialism. Forster met Masood barely a decade after Wilde's imprisonment, and several years after Macdonald's suicide. The British government only decriminalised homosexual acts in the last years of Forster's very long life. The milieu in which he lived, especially in his early years, despite the homosexual inclinations of many Bloomsbury and Oxbridge friends, placed limits on public expression of 'unnatural' sexuality. Going abroad provided sexual emancipation.

Forster went overseas, metaphorically – with an Indian in England – or literally, for sexual awakening (the word he used in his tribute to Masood), and his adventures left him with haunting dreams (as he experienced after Mohammed's death). These experiences, crossing the boundary of race (just as Forster crossed the class divide), left indelible traces. They brought him to a full realisation of his sexual orientation, teaching him about both romance and coition, and provided the *éducation sentimentale* that he had not received from compatriots. The paradox, for Forster as for others, was that the imperial enterprise, complete with the idea of bringing civilisation to the wider world, provided opportunities for a sexual emancipation that countermanded the moral order at home.

The experiences contributed importantly to Forster's philosophy of life. 'Only connect' was his motto, even when that was not possible, 'not there', 'not now' (as *A Passage to India* concludes) or 'not yet' (as 'Kanaya' has it). Sex might not be possible, and would always be transitory, but friendship endured. For Forster, and for others in his circle, friendship was foremost, and Forster's own experiences showed how friendship and sexual attraction constituted not contradictory but complementary impulses. Forster's friendships with Masood, Mohammed and the Maharajah were permutations of a similar urge, one with a homoerotic denominator, to befriend others and to be befriended by them.

Liaisons with exotic 'others', individuals and cultures, transformed themselves into literature. They also introduced Forster to Hindu and Muslim civilisation, and sensitised him to the effects of European imperialism. Writing letters to newspapers about the Egyptian riots and the Amritsar massacre in 1919, Forster could not but think of Mohammed and Masood. Imperialism had provided sexual opportunities for Forster, but sexual experiences with men from the colonies inspired his critical stance on imperialism.

Notes

1 Parminder Kaur Bakshi, *Distant Desire: Homoerotic Codes and the Subversion of the English Novel in E.M. Forster's Fiction* (New York, 1996), p. 209; Robert K. Martin and George Piggford (eds), *Queer Forster* (Chicago, 1997), especially chapters by Charu Malik and Yonatan Touval; Sara Suleri, *The Rhetoric of English India* (Chicago, 1992), pp. 132–3; Joseph Bristow, 'Passage to E.M. Forster: Race, homosexuality, and the "unmanageable streams" of empire', in Chris Gittings (ed.), *Imperialism and Gender* (Hebden Bridge, 1996), p. 140; Arthur Martland, *E.M. Forster: Passion and Prose* (London, 2000), p. 194. See also Elaine Freedgood, 'E.M. Forster's queer nation: Taking the closet to the colony in *A Passage to India*', in T. Foster, C. Siegel and E. Verry (eds), *Bodies of Writing, Bodies in Performance* (New York, 1996), and Christopher Lane, 'Volatile desire: Ambivalence and distress in Forster's colonial narratives', in Bart Moore-Gilbert (ed.), *Writing India, 1757–1990* (Manchester, 1996).
2 This account is based primarily on Forster's own writings, and on the authoritative biography by P.N. Furbank, *E.M. Forster: A Life* (London, two vols, 1977 and 1978).
3 Peter Stansky, *On or about December 1910: Early Bloomsbury and Its Intimate World* (Cambridge, MA, 1996), p. 129.
4 The most detailed account of the friendship is R.W. Noble '"Dearest Forster" – "Dearest Masood": An East-West friendship', *Encounter*, June 1981, pp. 61–72.
5 Furbank, Vol. I, p. 227.
6 S.K. Bhatnagar, *History of the Muslim-Anglo-Oriental College, Aligarh* (Aligarh, 1969), quotations from pp. 10, 16, 336.
7 M.S. Jain, *The Aligarh Movement: Its Origins and Development, 1858–1906* (Agra, 1965), pp. 57–9.
8 Quoted in Jalil A. Kidwai (ed.), *Khayaban-e-Masood* (Karachi, n.d.), p. 21.
9 Quoted in Bhatnagan, p. 309.
10 See Furbank, Vol. I, esp. pp. 142–6 and 167–8.
11 The correspondence is published in Jalil Ahmad Kidwai (ed.), *Forster-Masood Letters* (Karachi, 1984); quotations from p. 58 (letter of 14 January 1910) and p. 59 (undated 1910 letter). This is the most comprehensive collection of the Masood–Forster correspondence, although some letters are also published in E.M. Forster, *Only Connect: Letters to Indian Friends*, ed. Syed Hamid Husain (New Delhi, 1979). Many of Forster's letters to Masood, and to other correspondents, have been published in Mary Lago and P.N. Furbank (eds), *Selected Letters of E.M. Forster* (London, two vols, 1983). I have used all of these, as well as the originals held at the

Modern Archive Centre of King's College, Cambridge (hereafter KCC), but have indicated letters simply by the date of writing and addressee.

12 Forster to Masood, 1910 (undated).
13 Forster to Masood, November and 20 December, quoted in Furbank, Vol. I, pp. 193–4.
14 Forster's reference to his declaration of love and subsequent concern about the friendship, and lack of a letter from Masood, were recorded in his *Locked Diary*, in KCC. See entries of 29, 30, 31 December 1910 and 1 and 2 January 1911.
15 Forster to Masood, 15 August 1913.
16 Masood to Forster, 15 March 1914.
17 Quoted in Furbank, Vol. I, p. 263, who does not specify the '*bien aimé*'.
18 Syed Ross Masood, *Japan and Its Educational System* (Hyderabad-Deccan, 1923).
19 See Furbank, Vol. II, pp. 156–7 and 218.
20 Forster to Masood, 28 December 1922, KCC.
21 E.M. Forster, 'Syed Ross Masood', in *Two Cheers for Democracy* (London, 1951), quotations from pages 286 and 285.
22 See his unpublished 'Indian Journal', 4 November 1945, KCC, in which he bemoaned the state both of the Aligarh University and Masood's grave.
23 Kidwai, *Letters*, pp. 167–8, note 26.
24 Letter of 22 November 1908, Kidwai, *Letters*, p. 97.
25 'India Journal', 4 November and, on the student, 23 November 1945.
26 See Hilda D. Spear and Abdel-Moneim Aly (eds), *The Uncollected Egyptian Essays of E.M. Forster* (n.p., 1988).
27 See Jane Lagoudis Pinchin, *Alexandria Still: Forster, Durrell, and Cavafy* (Princeton, 1977).
28 E.M. Forster, *Alexandria: A History and a Guide* (London, 1982), p. xx.
29 Forster to Dickinson, 12 April 1916.
30 Forster to Dickinson, 18 May 1916. In an example of self-censorship, Forster did not mention the homosexual possibilities of the drug parlour in 'The den', published in *Pharos and Pharillon* (London, 1923), pp. 79–81.
31 See Robert Liddell, *Cavafy: A Critical Biography* (London, 1974).
32 Barry Carman and John McPherson, *Bimbashi McPherson: A Life in Egypt* (London, 1983).
33 Furbank, Vol. II, pp. 36–41, 49–51, 103–4, 107–8, recounts the friendship and, with Forster's own unpublished memoir, is the basis of this account, although interpretations are my own.
34 Forster's correspondence with Barger from this period has been published in Lago and Furbank, Vol. I, pp. 236–59, from which I have taken quotations.
35 Quoted in Francis King, *E.M. Forster* (London, 1978), p. 64.
36 Forster to Carpenter, 22 July and October 1917 (undated); Forster to Dickinson, 25 June, 14 and 31 August 1917, Forster to Masood, 8 September 1917, Forster to Cavafy, 1 September 1917.
37 Mohammed to Forster, 31 August, 10 November, 5 December 1917, 19 January, 15 February 1918.
38 Mohammed notebook, KCC.
39 Forster to Barger, 16 July 1918.
40 Mohammed to Forster, June 1918 (undated), 26 June 1918, July (undated), 23 July, 10 August 1918.
41 Not coincidentally, Forster wrote an essay on 'Cotton from the outside', published in *Pharos and Pharillon*, pp. 73–9.
42 Mohammed to Forster, 22, 27, 30 August, 2 October 1918.
43 Forster to Barger, November 1918 and January 1919.
44 Mohammed to Forster, 15, 20 October, 2, 6, 21 December 1918, 24 January 1919, March 1919 (undated).

45 Mohammed to Forster, March 1919 (undated).
46 Mohammed Gouda to Forster, 31 August 1919, Mohammed (el-Adl) to Forster, 23 September 1919.
47 Forster, disappointed that Masood had not named his first-born after him, was particularly pleased with Mohammed's gesture.
48 Mohammed to Forster, 26 September, 10 October, 4 November 1919, 15 April 1920.
49 Forster to Barger, 17 and 20 March 1921, but the admission of sex during the stopover appears only in the KCC Mohammed notebook.
50 See Forster to Dickinson, 31 May 1921.
51 Mohammed to Forster, 24 April, 26 August, 21 December 1921.
52 Forster to Barger, 28 January, 11 and 25 February 1922; Forster to Dickinson, 28 January and 25 February 1922; Forster to Masood, 25 January, 8, 18 and 23 February 1922.
53 Mohammed to Forster, 22 February, 10 March, 6 (?) and 8 May 1922.
54 Mohamed Abdul Rahman to Forster, 23 October 1922; Madam [*sic*] Gamila to Forster, 11 June 1922.
55 *Locked Diary*, 11 May 1922.
56 *Locked Diary*, 7 and 11 May, 27 June 1922.
57 Forster to Masood, 30 May 1922.
58 Mohammed notebook, KCC.
59 *Locked Diary*, 31 December 1923.
60 *Locked Diary*, 21 January 1924.
61 Forster to Plomer, 20 November 1963.
62 Mohammed notebook, KCC.
63 Forster to Barger, 31 July, 30 September and 8 October 1917, 16 July 1918.
64 This is the calculation of Nicola Beauman, *Morgan: A Biography of E.M. Forster* (London, 1996), p. 129.
65 *Ibid.*, p. 316.
66 Mohammed notebook, KCC.
67 Quoted in Furbank, Vol. I, p. 51.
68 Forster to Barger, 8 October 1917.
69 Forster to Carpenter, October 1917 (undated).
70 Forster to Dickinson, 24 March 1917.
71 Forster to Barger, 25 August 1917.
72 *The Government of Egypt: Recommendations by a Committee of the International Section of the Labour Research Department, with Notes on Egypt by E.M. Forster* (London, 1920); quotation from p. 9.
73 Letter quoted in Furbank, pp. 27–9.
74 E.M. Forster, *The Hill of Devi* (London, 1965 [1953]), p. 15.
75 Malcolm Darling, *Apprentice to Power: India, 1904–1908* (London, 1966), pp. 146–7.
76 *Ibid.*, pp. 137, 138, 146.
77 Manohar Malgonkar, *The Puars of Dewas Senior* (Calcutta, 1963).
78 Quoted in *Review on the Administration of the Dewas State (Senior), 1913–1914* (New Delhi, 1915), pp. ii–iii.
79 Forster to Tukoji Rao, 24 January 1936, 20 October 1937 and 3 January 1937.
80 Forster, *The Hill of Devi*, p. 45.
81 E.M. Forster, 'Kanaya', *Indian Journals and Essays* (London, 1983), pp. 194–208.
82 *Ibid.*, p. 195.
83 *Ibid.*, p. 203.
84 *Ibid.*, p. 208.
85 *Locked Diary*, 31 December 1921.
86 'Kanaya', *op. cit.*
87 *Ibid.*, p. 57.
88 E.M. Forster, 'The Life to Come' and 'The Other Boat', in *The Life to Come and Other Stories* (London, 1972), pp. 65–82 and 166–97; quotation from p. 170.

11 The French in North Africa

North Africa was the most prized possession in France's colonial empire. Napoleon's expedition to Egypt in 1798 whetted desire to spread French influence in the southern Mediterranean. The conquest of Algiers in 1830, and subsequent expansion throughout Algeria, was followed by establishment of protectorates in Tunisia in 1881 and Morocco in 1912. Algeria became France's major settler society, by the early 1960s counting one million migrants and their descendants (settlers from Italy, Spain and Malta, as well as France). With its large European community, prosperous wine-growing and pastoralism, and French-style cities, Algeria appeared to colonialists an extension of France itself. Tunisia and Morocco attracted far fewer settlers, but provided important strategic and commercial advantages to France, as well as the powerful lure of the desert and the kasbah. Morocco, in particular, seduced generations of visitors with the bustling and colourful markets of Marrakesh and Tangier, the picturesque seafront of Essaouira and the dunes of the Sahara.[1]

Frenchmen in the Maghreb

Nineteenth-century Frenchmen fantasised about the sensuality of the harem and hammam in North Africa and the Middle East, and encounters with Ouled-Naïl dancers – troupes of performers available for sexual services as well – and prostitutes brought fantasies to life. The French knew that irregular pleasures also awaited in North Africa, and widely believed that all Arabs enjoyed homosexual contacts, both with each other and with foreigners. As seen in a previous chapter, French military authorities worried about the pernicious effects of service in North Africa, and fraternisation with Arabs, on French morals, admitting that during campaigns some soldiers indulged in sodomy.

Not all Frenchmen were horrified by such sexual misbehaviour. The novelist Gustave Flaubert took sodomy in his stride. During a trip to Egypt in 1850, he wrote to a friend about 'berdaches':

> Here it's quite well accepted. One admits one's sodomy and talks about it at the dinner table. Sometimes one denies it a bit, then everyone yells at you and it ends up getting admitted. Traveling for our learning experience and

charged with a mission by the government, we see it as our duty to give in to this mode of ejaculation. The opportunity hasn't presented itself yet: nonetheless, we are looking for it. It's practiced in the baths. One reserves the bath for oneself…and one takes one's boy into one of the rooms. By the way, you should know that all the bath-boys are berdaches.

A few months later, he wrote again:

You ask me whether I have consummated the bath project. Yes, and on a young, pockmarked lad with an enormous, white turban. It made me laugh, that's all. *But* I'll do it again. For an experience to be done well, it must be repeated.[2]

When in Egypt, have sex as do the locals, Flaubert seemed to think, though ultimately he did not find sodomy to his liking.

Not only writers of Flaubert's stature described homosexual situations in North Africa, as shown in two *fin de siècle* stories by A. Desbiefs. In 'Le Vice en Algérie', Théodule Vendeur is a rich middle-aged Algiers jeweller with a penchant for 20-year-old Arab men. Each night, he whistles from the window to summon Ahmed, or Ali or Kaddour for a couple of hours of pleasure. However, Vendeur begins to fear that his Arab companions are gossiping about him and may be leaguing against him, so he replaces them with Italians, Spaniards and a Belgian. The Arabs are jealous of his new partners (despite having been paid off), and Vendeur misses his swarthy bedfellows. One evening, he goes 'cruising' near his apartment and, when he has assumed a compromising position with a suitable partner, a group of Arabs set upon him and throw him down an embankment. His proclivities well known, Vendeur decides it is prudent to move to a country house, where he continues to enjoy the attentions of young 'friends'. In another tale, 'Inséparables', two Europeans known as Orestes and Pylades live together in Hamam-Ville, going about their daily life, making catty comments on the women of the town and conversing about Oscar Wilde, until one of them, in a propitious deal, makes a fortune and abandons the other.[3]

The stories are low-brow literature, probably written to caricature the foibles of colonials. They picture North Africa as a place of vice, and repeat racial stereotypes about Arabs as handsome and virile young men who appeal to rather effete European homosexuals. They are all available, though for a price. They must be taught acceptable habits – Vendeur demands that Ahmed bathe each evening before visiting so that he will not catch 'vermin'. They are prone to theft – Vendeur's friend Ahmed has been arrested four times – and rivalry, willing to blackmail partners and commit violence on them.

A number of distinguished Frenchmen from the colonial period who were homosexual (or rumoured to be so) had an interest in North Africa. As already discussed, Marshal Lyautey enthused over the Maghreb and the subalterns who accompanied him on his conquests. Charles de Foucauld, an aristocratic army officer before he became a priest and set up a hermitage at Tamanrasset in the Algerian Sahara, where he was killed by Tuaregs in 1916, was also thought to be homosexual.[4] The homosexual authors Henry de Montherlant (1896–1972) and Roger Martin du Gard (1881–1958) both wrote about North Africa. The plot of Montherlant's *La Rose de sable*, an unfinished anti-colonial novel set in Morocco, includes a friendship between a French lieutenant and an adolescent shop assistant (though the book protests, perhaps too much, that their relationship is not sexual). In the posthumously published *Moustique*, he wrote about travels in North Africa with an Arab companion. His journeys in the late 1920s and early 1930s served Montherlant for 'Poèmes d'inspiration africaine' (in *Encore un instant de bonheur*), which give voice to pederastic sentiments.[5] Martin du Gard's *Le Lieutenant-Colonel de Maumort*, another posthumously published novel, again features a French colonial officer with ambivalent sexual identity, a portrait probably modelled on Lyautey.[6]

However, three other French metropolitan writers, two of them canonical figures in twentieth-century literature, best exemplify French homosexual, political and cultural engagement with North Africa. The travels in the Arab world of André Gide, François Augiéras and Jean Genet span much of the twentieth century, and the writings in which homosexual encounters with North Africans appear encompass novels, plays, travelogues and autobiographies.[7]

André Gide

The key French example of homosexual colonial experience is found in the life and work of André Gide (1869–1951), the most significant figure in French homosexual writing in the early decades of the twentieth century. Gide's novels placed homosexual figures and situations in a more prominent position than did works of any of his contemporaries. Gide was openly homosexual, and a series of Socratic dialogues, *Corydon*, publicly published in 1924, provided an apologia for homosexuality. Winner of the Nobel Prize for Literature in 1947, Gide was an acclaimed and popular man of letters, whose life charted many of the politi cal and literary developments of his age. Not only the question of homosexuality, but also the issues of colonialism (Gide wrote on both North Africa and sub-Saharan Africa), political commitment to (and subsequent disenchantment with) Marxism and the role of the intellectual in public life are illustrated in his career. Not surprisingly, a great deal has been written on Gide. Biographers and specialists of literature show endless fascination with the life of the affluent Protestant who managed to be both bourgeois and rebel.[8]

Perhaps the text that best testifies to the lasting importance of inter-racial sexual pleasure in Gide's life is a relatively little-known travel diary. In 1939, the 70-year-old Gide took a seven-week trip to Egypt, recording his impressions in a notebook that he began writing, he admitted metaphorically, to get the rust out of his pen, and continued to keep conscientiously if unenthusiastically until the end of his journey. The *Carnets d'Egypte* – twenty-eight pages in the version published after Gide's death – chronicle a not entirely surprising tour. Staying in Luxor, Gide visited the temples of the Valley of the Kings, took an excursion to Cairo to view the pyramids and, at the invitation of one of his literary fans, spent several days on a sugar plantation. Expatriates guided him around – he toured the Cairo museum with one of its directors, and inspected the Luxor archaeological site with the chief of the dig. The headmaster of the French *lycée* guided him around Alexandria. An old school friend, a genteel Russian *émigré*, a Swiss archaeologist, a French architect and a baroness provided companionship, and Gide enjoyed a long and intimate conversation with Louis Massignon, a leading French specialist on the Islamic world. The English head of the National Bank gave him a novel by Agatha Christie, which Gide liked more than Thomas Mann's *Joseph in Egypt*, a work he read, along with a tome on *Le Nil et la civilisation égyptienne*, to immerse himself in local culture. He also read some of La Fontaine's fables, an anthology of British poetry, a collection of Chekhov's stories and Renan's study of Averroës. And he went to the cinema.

Gide worked, as well, correcting proofs of his *Journal* sent from France and writing a play. He bought a few souvenirs, including a couple of typical dolls and, by necessity, a fly-whisk. As did many other tourists, he complained about heat, high prices and uncomfortable trains, and was annoyed at constantly being importuned for bakshish. Recurring fever disrupted his sleep, despite a variety of medications, but he manfully refused to remain idle.[9]

For the first few days, Gide (like Forster a quarter-century earlier) did not like Egypt, largely because he did not feel himself in sympathy with the Egyptians and, more particularly, as he did not find local people attractive. A nice-looking face, he remarked on the first day of his diary writing, would relieve the boredom. A visit to the Cairo museum two days later awakened him to the aesthetic attraction of the locals as, 'overwhelmed', he made the connection between Egypt and his own European culture. Then in the dining room of the famous Shepheard's Hotel, he 'realise[d] that the swarthy hotel servants, similar to those of the time of the Pharaohs, much less ugly than they first seemed, have kept an unchanging appearance through the centuries'. The discovery sparked Gide's erotic interest, though in a guarded fashion he noted the following day:

> No, I do not have a great desire to fornicate; at least this is not a need as in the good old days of my youth. But I do need to know whether, if I wanted, I could; do you understand that? What I mean is that a country only pleases me if multiple opportunities to fornicate present themselves. The most beautiful monuments in the world cannot replace it – why not confess it frankly?[10]

The insight followed an encounter with a comely lad whom Gide had met while walking to Karnak. Fourteen- or 15-year-old Ali, and his less attractive (and nameless) companion, had crossed paths with Gide, followed him and offered him a few carefully selected leaves of a lettuce to munch. The other boy disappeared, and Ali drew Gide into the native town and inside a house. Locking the door behind him, without ceremony, Ali pulled up his tunic and lowered his pants, revealing his 'charming body' and offering his backside to Gide. The Frenchman, fretting that he was carrying all his money on him and worried that the companion might return (Ali having had a shouted conversation with someone through the closed door), declined the offer, but nevertheless playfully petted Ali and gave him two piastres.

A couple of days afterwards, Gide sought out Ali. They sat for a while among the ruins on the banks of the Nile, but Gide did not reveal in his diary any further intimacy. By now Gide was noticing the seductive looks of other lads, and becoming aware that sexual opportunities abounded. The young gardeners at the Winter Palace Hotel – twenty to thirty boys, he counted – all made rude gestures and propositions as he walked around at nightfall, one even removing his clothes to show himself off. A hotel waiter brought a handsome youth to Gide's table, introducing him and implying that the Frenchman might appreciate his services. A black boatman smiled invitingly, a donkey-boy offered sex more straightforwardly and the hotel mechanic took him for a visit to his family house. Indeed 'the surfeit of offers took away my appetite', Gide commented, adding that by the end of his stay he was 'satiated' with propositions. He had nevertheless distributed coins to each of the garden boys 'in order not to discourage them'.[11] He caressed one or two young men, and finally had a fuller experience just before his departure. Gide noticed an Englishman chatting intently with a particularly handsome youth and realised that it was Ali. Gide signalled, and Ali joined him. A boatman rowed them to the middle of the Nile:

> Ali and I lay down in the bottom of the barque, intertwined under the complacent gaze of the boatman and the searing sun. Rarely such a reciprocity of caresses, such a cheerful languour. Not a single defect in his young body, already muscled like an athlete, supple, elastic and hard, or in this still beardless face with its full cheeks and thick lips which his smile opens to reveal strikingly white teeth, in his tender, affectionate, joking – and amused – looks.[12]

Gide's experiences in Luxor parallel those of many other homosexuals overseas. Disparities of age – here an older European and adolescent Egyptians – and wealth are patent. He and his European friends are reminded of their foreignness, and privileges, as they watch Arabs processing to a cemetery bearing a corpse and the roughly hewn planks for a coffin, while they themselves picnic pleasantly with provisions from their smart hotels. Gide records shock at the misery of the Egyptian peasants, a boy with no legs dragging himself down the street on his hands, the rags in which the garden-boys and donkey-drivers are dressed, the busy streets full of wretched people he must cross to take tea at the elite Savoy. Yet his erotic contacts took place with these poor street youths, willing to provide companionship and sex for a paltry consideration. At his first meeting with Ali, Gide gave him two piastres (about five pence at the time), a sum almost equal to the daily wage of a fellah and not much more than the price of a newspaper. (He paid twenty piastres to a donkey-driver to take him to Thebes.) Everywhere youths were ready to provide sexual favours of various sorts, Gide noting that, unlike Tunisians, Egyptians would agree to play the passive role in relations, and the youths clearly judged that a single European man such as Gide was in the market for sexual services. Yet demands for money and the danger of theft, violence or blackmail lurked, in Egypt as in other countries. A reminder came when Gide met Beryl de Zoete, who recounted the witch-hunt of homosexuals by Dutch authorities in the East Indies.[13]

The *carnets* dwell more on erotic encounters than on the splendours of ancient sites. Gide learned to like Egypt through a visit to a museum and flirtations with youths – culture and sex mediated his appraisal of the country – and, in a fashion typical of the European littérateur, he consigned his experiences to a notebook. Even if Gide had not gone to Egypt for sex, and initially abjured fornication, his rendezvous provided much pleasure. The idyllic encounter with Ali in the barque rounded off his stay and proved to Gide that he was not too old for such carnal delights.

> The mortal remains that I will soon owe to the tomb, I hope, will not be too chilled. I do not think it to be wisdom to extinguish the last embers of desire but rather to rekindle them. Let death do its own work – why aid it in its task?[14]

Gide's trip to Egypt, and the dalliances of an older man, form the complement to the homosexual initiation through which he had passed almost four decades earlier, while in his twenties, and famously recounted in the novel *L'Immoraliste* and his autobiography, *Si le grain ne meurt*. In *L'Immoraliste*, published in 1901, Michel, a 25-year-old graduate of the prestigious Ecole des Chartes, bourgeois and Protestant, journeys to North Africa with his new wife Marceline, who nurses him when he contracts tuberculosis. However, Michel is more attracted to the Arab boys than his French wife. Their 'golden nudity', their 'bronzed skins saturated by the sun' seduce him, and he enjoys a 'light-hearted friendship which costs only half a franc a day'. Michel recovers under the Saharan sky, and gives in to the sensuality of the Maghreb, for the first time realising his sexual desires, yet finally declining to act fully on them: 'I seemed to be abandoning the abstract for real life.' His near loss of virginity is suggested at an encounter with a young Arab in the Biskra oasis. Returning to France, Michel attempts a model life as husband, professor and landowner, but remains haunted by his sexuality and recollections of North Africa: 'The memory and the desire of the South obsessed me.' When Marceline falls ill (also with tuberculosis), they travel through Switzerland, Sicily, Tunisia and Algeria, where Marceline dies while her negligent and immoral husband is having sex with a female prostitute, 'but each time that I encountered her, she laughed and joked that I preferred her younger brother. She claimed that he was the one who kept me here. Perhaps she was just about right.'[15]

To the casual reader, the homosexual attraction in *L'Immoraliste* was embedded in the story of a husband lacking integrity, but, to those who examined the work more closely, it formed the key to Michel's *prise de conscience*. Homosexuality hovers in the background throughout the book, and everywhere the inexperienced Michel ventures in North Africa. Tunis produces 'new sensations' that move 'slumbering faculties' in his inner being, and that crystallise in erotic desire as he makes the 'palpitating discovery' of life itself. Marceline, manifestly aware of his desires (and his incapacities as husband), introduces into his bedchamber a young Arab named Bachir, who sits on the floor and carves a phallic-shaped flute while Michel admires his ankles and shoulder, which a threadbare gandoura leaves bare: 'I needed to touch him. I leaned over; he turned and smiled at me. I made a sign for him to pass me his flute, which I took and pretended to admire.' The following day, again carving, Bachir cuts his finger, and Michel looks on as he licks away the blood. Bachir brings marbles and insists that an increasingly troubled Michel play with him. Soon he visits almost every morning.[16]

Rejuvenated, Michel leaves his sickroom and goes into the garden, hoping for 'the chance of a happy encounter'. He meets Ashour, and wants to invite him home, but fears Marceline's opinion. Later, though he no longer needs a shawl, he nevertheless takes it with him in the hope that some young man will offer to carry it. The sight of a young shepherd, Lassif, 'almost naked', creates a mood of 'lightness' and 'exaltation'. His agile and golden-brown brother Lachmi is even more tempting. Moktir, a protégé of Marceline, also provides alluring company, and, when Moktir steals Marceline's scissors, Michel sees but ignores the theft. In short, *L'Immoraliste* is a story of would-be sexual consummation. Michel tries to come to terms with his homosexuality in a country where homosexual acts seem not to be forbidden, and there is a panoply of seductive potential partners, but he never takes the final step. His friend, Ménalque, with more colonial experience, is not so timid.

Ménalque, in Paris, offers Michel glasses of Shiraz wine, 'the wine about which Hafiz sang' – mentioning the Persian poet who sang the praise of boys – and shows him expensive fabrics from far-off Nepal. Ménalque has returned from Biskra, and tells Michel about the reputation he has earned there, recounting his meeting with Moktir. Then Ménalque disappears on another mission for the Colonial Ministry, joking about his own suspect morals. The lesson he teaches Michel is that a man must search for what he really wants, 'rejecting culture, decency and morality', a shocking lesson for conventional readers, but a mandate of emancipation for those with reprobate desires. Ultimately, Michel goes back to Italy, then further south to North Africa, and locates Moktir, recently released from prison and still the handsomest of his companions. 'Oh, God, let me meet new races, unsuspected types of beauty,' Michel intones as he plunges deeper into the Sahara.[17] For Michel – as for Gide – sexual initiation and homosexual liberation could take place only among the irresistible youths of the classical Mediterranean or exotic North Africa, although conventional Northern Europeans sometimes found the effort too hard, even in those inviting climes.

In 1921, twenty years after *L'Immoraliste*, Gide published an autobiographical account of his trips to North Africa in *Si le grain ne meurt*. The account confirms details of Michel's adventures as Gide's own, but with the revelation that Gide gave in to his desires in the dunes. This second volume thus reinforces the canonical impression of sexual escape to the 'Orient'. He recounts that, from his arrival in 1894, he began to notice handsome young men, such as the Arab who half-undressed in front of him and robust Maltese guides on the road to Biskra. There he stayed in a hotel suite that had been prepared for Cardinal Lavigerie, archbishop and founder of the Pères Blancs missionaries. In poor health (like the fictional Michel), Gide strolled around carrying a coat and shawl, and one day a fetching youth called Ali offered to help him. The two wandered to a:

> sort of funnel or crater, from the edges of which one could keep a look out over the countryside. As soon as we arrived, Ali threw down the shawl and the coat on the sandy slope, then he threw himself down and lay on his back, his arms stretched out, and began to look at me and laugh. I was not so stupid as not to understand his invitation, yet I did not immediately respond. I sat down, not far from him, but not too close, and stared at him fixedly, waiting, curious to see what he would do.

As Gide waited, Ali's smile faded and he stood up, bidding Gide farewell. Gide took hold of the hand he extended and rolled him back onto the ground, provoking a new smile. Ali drew out a knife to cut the knots of his belt, then cast away his jacket. The two coupled: 'His body was perhaps hot, but felt in my hands as refreshing as shade. How beautiful was the sand! In the awesome splendor of the evening, what beams clothed my joy'.[18]

Gide portrays his sexual initiation as both longed-for and fortuitous, a complicity between the seductive Arab boy and the timid, but yearning European. During the remainder of his trip, Gide dabbled in heterosexuality. With his travelling companion, the artist Paul-Albert Laurens, he went to see the Ouled-Naïl prostitutes, one of whom, Mériem, returned to their hotel with the men. Laurens and Gide took turns with her, but Gide admitted that while he had sex with the woman, he could think only of a handsome young drummer-boy he had spied (the experience turned into the last scene of *L'Immoraliste*). Word of Gide's bad health reached his mother in France, and the formidable Madame Gide hurriedly arrived, cutting short the games, but not before she had spied Mériem leaving the hotel. Gide, reducing his mother to tears, told her about his trysts with the woman, though apparently not about Ali. She did, however, meet another Arab destined to play an important role in Gide's life, for it was during the trip that Gide and Laurens made the acquaintance of Athmann, a sturdy 14-year-old working in the hotel where they were staying. Athmann guided them around, served their meals, shined their shoes, carried Laurens's painting equipment and officiated as general factotum.

Home in Europe, Gide (like Michel) was miserable, corresponding with Athmann and feeling growing nostalgia for the voluptuous idyll that Algeria represented. The following year he returned and, while checking out of a hotel in Blidah, discovered that Oscar Wilde and Lord Alfred Douglas were fellow guests. Embarrassed at fleeing without greeting his old friend, Gide turned around and spent an evening with Wilde, who told him about Douglas's difficulties in courting a café waiter. Gide and Wilde met up again in Biskra, while Douglas remained behind in Blidah. Wilde took him to a louche café, where Gide was enchanted with a ravishing flute player. Full of mischief, Wilde arranged a rendezvous and, after leading Gide from café to café, took him to an apartment where Wilde spent the night with a waiter, and Gide spent the night with Mohammed, the flautist. Gide experienced transports of joy – and apparently five ejaculations – 'holding in my naked arms this perfect little body, savage, ardent, lascivious and tenebrous'. He added: 'Every time since then when I have searched for pleasure, it has been to chase after the memory of that night.'[19] He admitted, however, that love did not play a part in such sensual pleasures, and he felt no jealousy when his friend Daniel later had sex with Mohammed. Meanwhile, Douglas arrived with his waiter, whom Gide was surprised to see dressed sumptuously and acting the part of a grand seigneur (if a bit effeminately). Gide increasingly found Douglas annoying with his constant chatter about sex, and was not displeased when Wilde and his party left. This, among other benefits, allowed Gide to monopolise the attentions of Athmann and to hatch the idea of taking Athmann back to Paris with him.

Commentators have written much on Gide's North African books and his experiences in the Maghreb. Jonathan Fryer reconstructs the meeting between Gide and Wilde, and their adventures in Blidah and Biskra, where the pleasures of boys, hashish and exoticism openly beckoned both British and French visitors. Jonathan Dollimore, who also focuses on the encounter, emphasises the importance of Gide's sexual experience, 'the event which was to change Gide's life and radically influence his subsequent work', suggesting that 'Gide's experience in Africa is one of the most significant modern narratives of homosexual liberation'. Lawrence R. Schehr concurs, but notes pertinently that 'even when Gide is telling the truth about a sexual encounter in the blazing sands of North Africa, this truth is the truth of capitalism and imperialism', and adds that the very notion of sexual liberation 'is a Eurocentric argument that is a simulacrum of the dominance of white male heterosexuality', in which the foreign tourist, in a play of 'power dynamics', gave vent to his own desires at the expense of the Maghrebins. Schehr posits a certain displacement of sexuality for Gide: from Europe to Africa, from homosexuality to pederasty, and from sexuality to erotics. Michael Lucey, using a psychological approach, analyses Gide's trip to North Africa as not only a sexual rite of passage, but also an escape from his mother's sexual universe and the Oedipal constraints imposed by family life.[20]

From a socio-historical perspective, several points are worth underlining. One is indeed the emblematic flight from the religious and social demands of Europe (even tolerant and naughty *fin de siècle* Paris) to search overseas for health, warm climates, enchanting landscapes and cultures, and some sort of self-realisation. Colonialism manifestly aided such journeys. France had ruled Algiers for almost seventy years by the time Gide first visited, and he found the agreeable hotels and restaurants, and the cultivated, international company, that made the exotic hospitable. Imperialism, and Gide's status as a moneyed Frenchman, gave him a position and privileges that enhanced his visit. He was acutely aware of being in a colonised region; as he points out in another work on North Africa, *Amyntas*, imperialism had taken its toll. He travels in the midst of a 'vanquished people', a 'people in rags'. He characterises one neighbourhood of Algiers as a 'rubbish tip'; he cannot help but notice the 'monumental quays' and the 'hideous warehouses', the stupid tourists, the sound of cannon from warships in the harbour, all reminders of the French presence.[21] In *Le Renoncement au voyage*, written after his sixth trip to North Africa in 1903, Gide describes in heartfelt terms the famished children he saw camped around a port, his little friend Bachir who smoked kif to forget his troubles and hunger, and three generations of a family crowded into a shack, the ugly side of a country that nevertheless had brought him joy, pleasure and emancipation.[22] Insistent evocations of the poor in *L'Immoraliste* and *Si le grain ne meurt* show that Gide was indeed cognisant of social conditions.

A second important aspect of Gide's sojourns is the existence of a homo-sexual culture in North African cities. Wilde and Douglas were even more attuned to its existence than, at first, was Gide. The visitors from the British Isles (and, soon, the Frenchman) knew that café waiters, flute players and other young men were willing to provide sexual favours. A little money went a long way, and youths were abundant. Whether this was prostitution in the strict sense, a context for establishment of patron–client relationships or the expres-sion of sexual behaviour unshackled by Western mores did not overly concern visitors. By the time Gide arrived, local ephebes had a well-developed practice of offering themselves for sex; their gestures and propositions were well-rehearsed, and they proved expert at seducing European men by approaching them, offering food, a tour or some small service. There was also a geography of homosexual encounters – hotels where foreigners gathered, gardens where men and boys strolled at twilight, the riverside where youths bathed and rowed. Far from disapproving of sexual encounters, adults proved complicit, as shown by the waiter introducing a youth to Gide, café owners opening their establish-ments to suspect outsiders and hotel-keepers cheerfully making rooms available to foreign gentlemen and their native companions.

Third, the importance of North Africa in Gide's writing merits emphasis. His North African experiences appeared in *L'Immoraliste*, *Si le grain ne meurt*, *Amyntas*, *Les Nourritures terrestres*, *Oscar Wilde*, *Le Renoncement au voyage* and (to a lesser degree) *Corydon*, with echoes in *Les Faux-Monnayeurs* and *Les Caves du Vatican*, a literary œuvre spanning a quarter of a century and several genres. These received consecration as classical French texts, holding a special place for homosexual readers searching for literary reflection of their desires, including some who followed in Gide's footsteps to North Africa. Unwittingly or not, Gide became a promoter of homosexual tourism to generations of readers. Moreover, Gide's life and work contributed mightily to the general phenomenon of eroticisation of North Africa.

Not just youths he encountered, but also the erotic luxuriance of the 'Orient' itself, attracted Gide to North Africa. *Les Nourritures terrestres*, an early volume in which he spoke about North Africa, only mentioned Athmann and other adolescents in passing (though with fond nostalgia), and the only references to sex in the Maghreb are with women prostitutes. That book was published in 1897, before both *L'Immoraliste* and *Si le grain ne meurt*, and its silence might be interpreted as Gide's reticence to speak of homosexuality – the work of a 'closet case' before he openly identified as homosexual. However, the book may also be the most expansive expression of his sexual desire, for sex is subsumed to a general 'sensualisation' of North Africa with lyrical descriptions of gardens and oases, evocations of brilliant sunrises and perfumed springtime, the smell of tea or absinthe in a café, or spices and resins in a street market, the bustle of cara-vans and the solemn tranquillity of the desert. Longing and its possible satisfaction fill the landscape. A garden is 'peopled only with desires', Gide hears the sound of a flute from the door of a café (Mohammed's flute?), dreams of desire replace restful sleep and he proclaims that Athmann need wait for him no longer for he has returned. The earthly needs are all awakened, and North Africa (or, at least, his romantic image of it) becomes the very object of desire.[23]

Commentators have focused more on Gide and his works than on his sexual partners and friends in North Africa. To be sure, most North Africans pass into and out of his writings with few details. However, one figure has a special place, Athmann ben Salah. Surviving information on Athmann reveals much about cross-cultural encounters in North Africa, the genuine interest some Europeans and Maghrebins felt for each other, the mutual benefits that could result from sexual partnerships and longer-lasting friendships. Athmann met Gide in 1894 in Biskra, an oasis much favoured by visitors, 'a little Eden', as Laurens called it. Gide described Athmann as good-natured, amusing, honest and tall for his age. Athmann quickly charmed the visitors, showing them around, and taking them to his home, where his mother offered them dates and other little presents. While Laurens painted, Gide wandered around villages making the acquain-tance of Arabs, telling stories, clowning around in Arab clothing and otherwise playing tourist, his guidebooks in hand and Athmann his regular companion.[24]

Before Gide saw Athmann again, they exchanged letters, and Athmann also worked as guide for Gide's friend Pierre Louÿs. Gide introduced him to Wilde and Douglas in 1895, and decided to invite Athmann to Paris. This project encountered opposition from his entourage, despite his vaunting of Athmann's merits – his family worried about the financial expenses involved, his mother expressed her 'moral scruples' and his wife 'absolutely condemned' the plan, arguing that Athmann would be 'uprooted' in France, adding (in good colo-nialist fashion) that his merits, 'a bit negative in Biskra, will be transformed into positive defects in our civilised world'. Most influentially, Gide's mother's long-time and much loved servant Marie threatened to resign if Gide brought his 'Negro' into the house. Gide abandoned the idea, but saw Athmann again in 1896. On this trip, he introduced Athmann to the poet Francis Jammes; the meeting proved a revelation, and Athmann soon began writing poetry himself. Gide and Athmann met again in Algeria in 1899, this time with Gide's wife, Madeleine, who was charmed by Athmann and abandoned her opposition to his visit to France. The following year, Gide brought Athmann to Paris for the Exposition Universelle; Jacques-Emile Blanche painted a portrait of Athmann (dressed in princely garb) with Gide and several friends in a '*café maure*' at the fair. Athmann came to France under his own steam for a brief stay in 1902, and he and Gide saw each other in Algeria several years later. In 1905, Athmann married, living for the rest of his life in his native Biskra, though as a tour guide he frequently travelled around Algeria.[25]

Letters that Athmann wrote to Gide between 1897 and 1914 testify to deep affection between the two men. The formal *vous* soon gave way to the familiar *tu*, and Athmann addressed Gide as his 'dear friend'. He enquired carefully about Gide, his wife, his mother and aunts, sending especially solicitous messages – and a poem hoping for speedy recovery – when Gide's wife ('La Gide', as he called her) fell ill, and chatting about friends of Gide whom he had met in Algeria or France. He also expressed concern when too long a period passed without news from Gide. Athmann wrote, as well, about his own family, sending greetings from his mother, talking about his brother and hoping that Gide would come to Biskra for his marriage. Descriptions of the ripening of dates and watermelons reminded Gide of the beauty of North Africa, and Athmann promised to have his mother's couscous and crêpes ready for Gide when he returned. After the visit to Paris in 1900, Athmann posted letters to Gide as he travelled homewards, joking that he managed to steal a couple of kisses from a young woman in the compartment of his train, and confessing that he had enjoyed the company of a prostitute, 'clean and well-built', in a 'house of Ouled-Naïls' in Lyon. He could not stomach the famous Lyonnais pork sausages, though he enjoyed a night at the theatre. In provincial France, Athmann noticed that some people pointed and made fun of him: these 'savages' or 'Eskimos', as he playfully called them, 'because they found me a little dark, coming from a hot country'. But, on one occasion, when he was nattily attired and stopped for a beer in a brasserie, 'everybody took me for a prince', and workers coming out of a factory in Saint-Etienne thought him a 'minister'. In Aix-les-Bains, he remarked on pretty gardens and a drunken priest. On the ship back to North Africa, he made other passengers laugh with his stories – one woman told him that only his presence made the journey bearable – but confessed that he cried like 'a poor man in love' at his separation from Gide and France.[26]

Athmann's letters, not unlike those Forster received from Mohammed, were simple but thoughtful and filled with good humour. They also commented on the social situation in North Africa. Athmann mentioned being glad for rain, scarce in Biskra, because the poor often became sick with 'fevers' from the stale water they drank. He opined that 'modern equality is a dream, perhaps in France, yes. But it is rare in Africa. No one listens to the poor person, no one sees the poor person, and people make fun of the poor.' Athmann accepted his own varying fortunes with equanimity, though admitting 'my health is good, my wallet is not so good'. He invoked the name of God (and noted that he was keeping the Ramadan fast, though once previously he had not done so). He occasionally philosophised, and mentioned the poet Abu Nuwas.

Athmann eagerly awaited Gide's return and meanwhile worked for tourists, including acquaintances of Gide. He learned some English, enabling him to attract other clients, and in 1908 could write to Gide, 'I am so well known among the English and the Americans that people naturally think of me as the most famous guide, but also poet, interpreter and travelling companion.' Athmann seemed happy, prosperous and busy. His letters to Gide then became less frequent, making it difficult to follow his life. By 1914, however, things had taken a bad turn. One or two earlier letters revealed a certain melancholy, despite Athmann's generally optimistic spirits. The last surviving letter from Athmann to Gide, written in far less coherent French than his normal style, cried that 'for the last month I am wandering about bare-foot, my clothes torn to pieces by wear, scorn covering the sky…your friend is dying of hunger and you must not forget Athmann ben Salah'.[27] The reason for the change in Athmann's fortunes remains unknown. When Gide returned to Algeria in 1943, long after losing contact with Athmann, he learned that, some ten years previously, Athmann had one evening wandered off alone into the desert, a seeming suicide.

We do not know if Gide and Athmann had sexual relations or, if so, how long a physical relationship lasted. A friendship marked by regular visits and correspondence endured for twenty years. The relationship was, in many ways, typically colonial, and the social and cultural gap between the distinguished French author and the Algerian guide was great. Yet both received benefits. Athmann got work as guide and interpreter for Gide and other visitors. He was given a trip to Paris in 1900. Gide encouraged him to write poetry and gave him access to European culture that might otherwise have been lacking. At Athmann's request, Gide sent him copies of Molière and Lamartine, among other books. His letters show affection for Gide, 'my truly dear friend', 'my help', 'my protector'; Gide referred to Athmann as 'his sole key' to North Africa and his 'open sesame', his 'black pearl'. Athmann's letters never ask for money or other favours, but only that Gide not forget him. They show a young man of intelligence and spirit, thoughtful and tenacious, someone who knew his own mind and was aware of his actions.[28] In return, Gide and his friends (such as Laurens and Louÿs) got help in their travels, insights into the Maghreb and inspiration for their work; the pleasures of the company of a handsome and friendly young Algerian cannot be discounted. The question of whether Gide attempted to go to the aid of his young companion in his time of distress (or considered doing so) remains unanswered, but his poignant attempts to trace him in 1943 evidence lasting memories of a friendship that it is wrong to reduce to a balance sheet of benefits.

Was Gide in love with Athmann? Were his feelings towards the young man fraternel, avuncular, paternal, amicable or erotic? It is hard to know, and perhaps pointless to ask. Athmann was certainly attractive, and Gide enjoyed sexual encounters with other Arabs. He did not pursue the relationship with Athmann solely for sexual fulfilment, since they continued to write to each other long after they had seen one another. Gide's phrases about Athmann sometimes bespeak unsurprising condescension, lauding the merits of fidelity and conscientious work, and expressing a desire to bring Athmann to France initially 'to create a servant of perfect loyalty' (an excuse that might have been advanced, however, to convince his dubious family).[29] However, the friendship between Gide and Athmann provides – just as that between Forster and Mohammed – an example of the way in which the gulf between colonising foreigners and colonised indigenes could be breached, at least partially. Such a joining of two individuals, and two cultures, was relatively rare in the colonial world. Gide might be castigated for perpetuating a kind of sexual colonialism, but he was also one of the singular Europeans who tried to reach across the great cultural and political divide.

Writing on North Africa, Gide seldom mentioned politics explicitly, which has led some commentators to charge complicity with the colonial enterprise or suggest that he was so enamoured of North African youths that he was unconcerned with imperialism. Yet, as Eric Marty argues, Gide experienced North Africa as a personal and spiritual liberation from both sexual and social shackles, and felt that he could learn much from the civilisation to which he was attracted. The *déracinement* and transcendence he felt constituted an acknowledgement of indigenous North African culture, and with Athmann he tried to shuck off his 'Occidentality'. Gide noted that he might well have talked about the Gafsa phosphate mines or Lavigerie's priests, the sales of absinthe or the expropriation of Arabs by banks, but such was not his mission in North Africa.[30]

In tropical Africa, Gide turned his attention away from affairs of the soul and body to considerations of politics, but without cutting the links that always existed between the two domains in his life and *œuvre*. In 1926–7, Gide made his one and only trip to sub-Saharan Africa, not as a tourist but as an investigator into labour conditions in French Equatorial Africa, one of the darkest corners of the French Empire. The French Congo for many years had been left to administration and exploitation by concessionary companies that exported local products. The use of Africans as porters, rubber gatherers and construction workers on the railway linking Brazzaville to the coast became a scandal. Chad, in the Sahel, was an arid and poor colony that France had taken over largely to preclude annexation by other powers; it returned few profits but provided labourers. Although, by the time of Gide's visit, Paris had curtailed the rapacious concessionary companies, given widespread outrage at conditions in tropical Africa, what remained was still an ugly sight.

Gide's reaction to sub-Saharan Africa was cultural curiosity and political anger rather than sexual desire, even if he spoke in the first pages of *Voyage au Congo* about 'joy in being among the Negros', and added that 'everything here seems to promise happiness, pleasure and oblivion'. Some of his reactions were stereotypically racialist: 'Naked Negros shout, laugh and argue, showing their cannibal teeth.' Here and there he commented on the attractive physical attributes of 'three superb blacks', a chieftain's son, 'particularly handsome, svelte, elegant', 'a superb child of fifteen or sixteen', a 12-year-old 'of a surprising robustness and admirable proportions'. He remarked on 'the beauty in the gaze of these indigenes, the moving intonation of their voices, the reserve and dignity in their deportment, the noble elegance of their gestures'.[31] Only rarely did he experience the erotic feelings, and the cultural empathy, however, that were constants of his contacts with North Africa.

Gide's tenderest words concerned Adoum, a guide recruited in Brazzaville: 'I didn't have the heart to leave this good fellow', who, said Gide, was ready to follow his party to the end of their trip and even back to France, because nothing was 'dearer to him than our trust, this friendship which we had shown him, the depth of which I measured to my distress'. Adoum typified the good native for Gide, showing 'so much devotion, humble nobility, a childlike desire to do good'. His reaction avoided eroticism, for Adoum represented the whole continent of Africans that had won Gide's sympathy: 'Through him, I felt for all of this suffering humanity, this poor oppressed race, whose beauty we have so little understood.' Gide and Adoum both had tears in their eyes as they parted, Adoum first kneeling 'the better to show his deference', and Gide placing his hand on the youth's shoulder. A companion told Gide that Adoum would soon forget him, and Gide hoped that this was so. Gide's assessment of Adoum typifies the paradox – or hypocrisy – of colonial relations. He was fond of the boy, and eloquently critical of French colonialism, yet Gide could not cast off the received notions of colonialists. On one occasion Gide gave Adoum fifty-five rather than fifty francs, ostensibly by mistake, to test whether Adoum would tell him of the error and return the extra five francs (which he did). Gide gave reading lessons to Adoum, who copied out phrases and memorised them, 'so strong was his desire to educate himself and thereby to draw closer to us'. He was touched that Adoum would not sit on a chair, or even a crate, when Gide instructed him, but insisted, because of his 'deference', on kneeling or sitting on the ground. Despite his critique of colonialism, only dimly did Gide admit that the *mission civilisatrice* in which he was engaged, and the deference inculcated into Adoum, formed part of the ideology of colonialism, however noble the sentiments and close the links between teacher and student. Furthermore, Gide could not avoid idealising and romanticising the African, borrowing images current in colonialist language:

> I see only in him what is childlike, noble, pure and honest. The whites who find a way to make these beings into rascals are worse rascals themselves, or very pitiful blunderers. I do not doubt that in order to protect me Adoum would have thrown himself under a blow, even if it were mortal. I never doubted him – from that comes my gratitude.

Others speak about the stupidity of blacks, Gide added, but what would whites know about this?

> I do not want to make the black out to be more intelligent than he is, but his stupidity, when it is evident, could only be that of an animal, and natural. That of the white in relation to him...shows something monstrous.[32]

Such comments, no matter Gide's discomfort with colonialism, point up abiding differences between European reactions to North and sub-Saharan Africa, the dissonance between political and sensual sentiments, and the difficulty of jettisoning colonialist attitudes.

The years from the 1890s, when Gide had first visited the Maghreb, through the 1920s, when he journeyed to black Africa, and the 1930s, the time of his trip to Egypt, encompassed the heyday of European colonialism and imperialism. In the last years of Gide's life, the colonial project came unstuck. At the time of his death, the Algerian war of independence, episodically flaring up since the 1940s, was becoming bloodier (and France was fighting for its colonial life in Indo-China). This provided the context for another author, François Augiéras – a man who worshipped Gide and shared certain affinities with him, even though their literary styles and outlooks differed – to 'discover' North Africa.

François Augiéras

François Augiéras was born in Rochester, New York, in 1925, the son of a French father, a concert pianist who had moved to the United States, and a Polish mother – Augiéras often claimed that 'wild' Slavic blood coursed through his veins. Augiéras's father died several months before the child's birth, and as soon as possible his mother took him to France, where they spent eight years in Paris, and then moved to Périgueux. While his mother earned a living decorating Limoges porcelain, Augiéras continued his schooling (though he did not finish the *lycée*), and then enrolled at a drawing academy. His introduction to North Africa came during childhood: a priest lent him an edifying book, his memoirs of a trip to *Immortelle Carthage*, and Augiéras also learned of a mysterious uncle who lived in the Sahara, but about whom the family did not care to speak. For five years, the talented young man painted and took part in Pétainist youth groups in a France occupied by German forces. To earn money, he toured with a theatre company, worked on a farm and was briefly employed as a social worker with troubled children. In 1944, Augiéras joined the French Navy and was sent to Toulon, where (as he recalled) the sight of black American soldiers dancing in the night excited his desires. From there, he was posted to Algiers. His short military career was not successful, punctuated by bouts of illness (and psychiatric treatment) and repeated periods of leave before he was demobilised. Augiéras then decided to visit his uncle, who lived in the oasis of El Goléa.[33]

Marcel Augiéras had won acclaim as an African explorer. In 1921, *Le Petit Journal Illustré* published on its front page a drawing of Augiéras, wearing a pith helmet and sitting atop his camel, after a four-and-a-half-month and 4,500 kilometre trek from Algiers to Dakar, the first such expedition from North to West Africa.[34] A contemporary photograph shows a dapper if severe man in military uniform, sporting a neat moustache and beard, and a pince-nez. In the late 1920s, he took part, along with W.P. Draper, an ethnologist, Vladimir Besnard, a geologist, and the young Thédore Monod, a zoologist and botanist (later to become France's most respected authority on the Sahara), in an expedition supported by the prestigious Société de Géographie. From Algiers, the group traced a route southwards to Laghouat and on to Ghardaia, and then deeper into the Sahara, to El Goléa, In-Salah and Tamanrasset. On his return, promotion in the army and the Legion of Honour rewarded Augiéras's exploits.[35] He wrote books about the expeditions, corresponded with geographical societies and meanwhile carried out his military duties. After the German defeat of France in 1940, Augiéras, then in French Equatorial Africa, rallied to de Gaulle's Free French. On retirement, he acquired a *bordj* (a small fortress) in El Goléa and turned it into a Saharan museum, filled with weapons, artworks and other artefacts collected on his travels. The museum was well enough known to appear in tourist guides, and Augiéras printed postcards of it. In El Goléa he indulged his passions for collecting, hunting and astronomy, living alone except for African servants. His nephew later recalled: 'He preferred soldiers to women and supposed that peace, beauty and earthly silence were to be found in the desert.'[36]

The 20-year-old François Augiéras, handsome and sturdily built, met his uncle Marcel, then over 60 years old, in El Goléa in 1945. Augiéras subsequently wrote about his relationship with the uncle, and his desert experiences, in several works, beginning with *Le Vieillard et l'enfant*, his first publication. The book, which recounted, with explicit details, an incestuous and sadomasochistic sexual relationship between a youth and an old man, became a minor *succès de scandale*. Augiéras privately published the book in 1949 under the *nom de plume* of Abdallah Chaamba, and sent copies to a number of well-known writers. The book impressed André Gide (to whom Albert Camus had shown it), who wrote asking the real identity of the author. Within months of receiving the letter, Augiéras sought out Gide, who was holidaying in Taormina. When he approached the grand old author, Gide reacted brusquely. Later Gide sent him a second letter, excusing himself for his lack of warmth in Sicily, and Augiéras searched him out again in Nice. They conversed, and Augiéras let Gide caress his neck and shoulders; Gide held Augiéras's arm so tightly (according to Augiéras's account) that he pierced his skin with his nails, and then lifted the young man's bloody wrist to his lips. Augiéras fantasised that he could have become Gide's last lover and new literary protégé.

Le Vieillard et l'enfant was commercially published in 1954, and Marcel Augiéras wrote indignantly to his nephew's publisher to denounce the book, deny the relationship it portrayed and demand that copies be withdrawn from sale. (François Augiéras wrote further versions of the book, though without changing details of the story.) The portrayal of the youth and the old man evidences the writer's literary interests, psychological needs and avowed alienation from Western cultural and moral norms. The extent to which the book is fact or fabulation is difficult to discern. Augiéras admitted that he was intensely searching for the father that he never had – his uncle and Gide both served as father figures – yet for his entire life was emotionally and sexually fascinated by adolescents. The plot of the novel is clearly based on real experiences, although the boy in *Le Vieillard et l'enfant* is about seven years younger than Augiéras himself at the time of his stay in El Goléa.

In *Le Vieillard et l'enfant*, the old man welcomes his nephew, a 13-year-old, to his *bordj* with a meal, but afterwards makes him solve mathematical problems and do a dictation test. The boy is curious but put off by the man, whom he describes as repulsively effeminate with soft lips and a podgy white belly. He is also intrigued by the fossilised bones, skulls, bird skeletons, elephant jaws, stuffed monkeys and other curiosities cluttering the explorer's museum. The old man gets him to dust his precious objects and proudly shows off the medal presented to him by the Paris geographical society. He warns the boy: 'I want to make a soldier of you, to harden you so that you will not fear either dying or killing.' Then he whips the youth, who asks him to continue the punishment. The boy nevertheless soon runs away to the mountains, where 'I cry out my hatred without cease', but fear and hunger force him to return. The old man remarks that making love if you do not love someone is sad, but adds that the boy loves him, and then fellates the adolescent. Further beatings – the old man flogs him with a belt, leaving wounds that must be covered with a jacket so that the servant does not see them – and sexual encounters follow: 'His mind always invented some new sort of infamy.' There is more work in the museum and conversations about Africa, and the old man shows him a picture of another youth (presumably also a lover) who lived at the *bordj* for five years. He buys a bicycle for the boy, but he thinks of escape, despite his great, still unfulfilled, desire to find a father: 'I am not satisfied in this house. I will leave tomorrow. The old man is not my Father,' he concludes as the novel ends.[37]

In *Une Adolescence au temps du Maréchal*, which purports to be more factually biographical, Augiéras admitted that his uncle attracted him to Algeria in the first place: 'I signed up [with the Navy] only in order to hurry to him, to reach this desert and this man.' After an initial visit, he decided to walk from El Goléa to Algiers (a distance of several hundred kilometres), but turned back to his uncle's house, where 'he almost reduced me to slavery'. Every night the old man called him to his bed, set up under the stars on the roof. His uncle was 'abominable', but Augiéras speaks of his 'more or less declared admiration for the old man'. The uncle cut him off from others, and cut him down to size,

> repeating to me that I am a delinquent, living away from other men, with this old man, in the desert, writing by candle-light, often on the rocks, hopeless under the stars, I am becoming an artist who looks at the sky, who ENCOUNTERS THE ETERNAL [sic] in this region of the oasis.

Some time later, Augiéras made another visit to El Goléa, inescapably drawn by the 'strange love which I have for this evil old man'. This time the uncle initially refused to receive him, but finally agreed to let him spend one night. The next morning Augiéras obeyed an order to leave, after bathing provocatively in a fountain in full view of his livid uncle and sneaking back into the house to steal food. The uncle then put an envelope outside with money for his nephew, but Augiéras crept into the house again to take a blanket, bargained for more food with the servant and left prickly palm leaves in his uncle's bed. Once more, he entered the house surreptitiously, startling his uncle with his bare-chested appearance, to spend a night 'so dazzling that I thought I would die'. When he subsequently struck his uncle, the old man chased him away with a gun. Escaping, the young Augiéras tried to stop two men from hunting gazelles, but was beaten to the point of unconsciousness by the men, whom he guessed were thugs hired by his uncle to rough him up. Augiéras nevertheless returned straight away to his uncle's house for a final visit before moving on to Gardaia.[38]

Whether an accurate description, or literary embroidering, the account provides a troubling scenario of a violent relationship, and a young man's desperate search for some figure to whom to anchor himself. The encounter at El Goléa was more than just a disturbing sexual contact. Augiéras's relationship with his uncle provided sexual initiation, but was also a literary apprenticeship and a transcendental awakening to the mysticism of the desert. El Goléa marked the début of his vocation as artist and writer, and provided an experience that haunted him and his work until his death.

In various genres, which inevitably return to the same themes and episodes, Augiéras detailed the places and situations of his omnivorous sexual encounters. His uncle sodomised him. An elderly Arab tried to seduce him. When he was ambushed in a deserted house on the road from El Goléa to Algiers, Arab workers locked him up and pulled out their penises and knives (but Augiéras escaped through a window). In *Le Voyage des morts*, Augiéras recorded his travels in North Africa in the 1950s, including easy sexual contacts with Maghrebins, shepherds in the Atlas mountains and city youths in Agadir. Some were 'one-night stands', furtive pleasures in bushes or at the beach, often in a climate of extreme danger, which added a *frisson* to Augiéras's enjoyment, in the years leading up to Morocco's independence and in the midst of the Algerian war. (During one sexual encounter, he heard not so distant gunfire.) Other relationships were longer lived, as when Augiéras fell in love with an Arab named Alec, whom he met outside a cinema and for whom he attempted to find employment on the same ship where Augiéras himself had a job. Other partners included Arab men and fellow Frenchmen, as well as the numerous women whose services he procured in brothels.

After the stay with his uncle, Augiéras journeyed through Algeria and Morocco from 1946 to 1949. In 1955, Augiéras was for a short time a student in a veterinary school at Tadmit, Algeria, and the following year he travelled in Senegal. During the Algerian war, he served briefly with the Compagnie Saharienne, a French unit stationed in Zirzara. He also accompanied his friend

Paul Placet on a hunting and ethnographic expedition to sub-Saharan Africa. The various stages of his trips metamorphosed into the five sections – on Tadmit, Gardaia, El Goléa, Agadir and Senegal – in *Le Voyage des morts*, published in 1957. In the meantime, just after signing up with the army, he had inherited his uncle's property at El Goléa; Augiéras paid a visit to the site and painted frescoes on the inside of an abandoned blockhouse. The property proved unsellable, and the war made it impossible for Augiéras to remain there. (After the independence of Algeria in 1962, the *bordj* and museum were ransacked.) In 1961, Augiéras prepared an application for a post as a drawing instructor in Morocco, but nothing came of the project. In the 1960s, increasingly attracted to an esoteric but idiosyncratic mysticism, he turned his attention to Greece (which he had already visited in 1956), travelling in Mount Athos in 1964 to study icon painting, and writing a book about the all-male Orthodox monastery. He also spent much time as a recluse in the Périgord, painting and writing about a region that he imbued with mysterious natural powers.

During the last year of his life, Augiéras returned to North Africa after an absence of over a decade. In May 1971, he went to Tunis to organise an exhibition of his paintings, staying in Tunisia until August. Mixed with the satisfaction of seeing his art well received were contradictory personal impressions of the country. 'North Africa is cruel, dangerous and hard; the Arabs, disquieting,' he wrote to a friend. He encountered a Frenchman whose house was the scene of 'sordid and refined debaucheries' with adolescents whom the owner picked up in the streets, young Arabs whom his acquaintance, 'a pervert, a refined sadist', treated as 'slaves'. Augiéras himself met:

> a marvellous boy…a young savage lost in Tunis.…Between the two of us there was an immediate and deep friendship: the recognition…that we were of the same blood, similar.…He gave me his heart without reserve! And I gave him mine!

During a stay on the Kerkennah islands near Sfax, he took as houseboy a 14-year-old named Hermès Mourad, the son of a Greek shipper and a Tunisian prostitute, so brutally mistreated that he had fled alone to the islands, 'a divine creature, and who seemed…to be waiting to become for me more than a son'. Augiéras bought him a pair of tennis shoes, and 'I was soon for him a God, a Father. For my part, I gave the full tenderness of my soul to this wild child, who asked only to love me with an absolute adoration, unreserved devotion.' They went sailing, and Augiéras experienced 'divine days', but the idyll came to an abrupt end when Mourad's half-brothers appeared and dragged the youth away.[39]

Returning to France, Augiéras, now seriously ill, wrote his last work, *Dromme, ou essai de l'occupation*, which he characterised as his first work of philosophy. His young Tunisian friend (or perhaps another incarnation of the eternal youth) appears as a kindly boy whom the fatherly Augiéras sees every day as he sits in the sun drinking tea and reading, and the boy cuts grass for his rabbits. With brown skin and dark eyes, he does not seem European, but a foreigner, or a god – 'it is difficult to be so beautiful, so simple, so pure' – sent to offer friendship to the lonely and troubled writer.[40] The mysterious youth gives him flowers, and then water, which the narrator accepts as divine gifts. Soon after finishing the book, Augiéras died, at the age of forty-six, after spending his last weeks in a hostel for indigents.

Homosexuality appears in various guises in Augiéras's work: scenes of sadism and masochism, episodic sexual trysts, passages of yearning and love, non-sexual meetings between innocent children and troubled father figures. Augiéras's views on homosexuality were most clearly stated in *Le Voyage des morts*. He theorised about 'two types of pederasty, one derived from a superabundance of vitality, the other from decadence'. His own proclivities belonged to the first category, which included the sexual urges of 'the boys of Greece, healthy, robust, noble, useful to society, with unlimited desire irrigated by a too powerful current of liberty'. In landscape, and in sexual practices, North Africa recalled ancient Greece: 'Arcadia must resemble the environs of Médéa.' He added: 'For me, relations with youths are the source of an extreme joy and emotional equilibrium.' His sexual encounters with shepherds or peasants represented purified physical and emotional pleasure: 'Nothing is more beautiful than love…that of one's companions in adventure, love born around the campfire.' Partners, even in hurried encounters, assumed mythical status, as Augiéras joined visions of past and present in a landscape that itself belonged to the sexual experience. About one young man with whom he had sex in the desert, he wrote: 'He was waiting for me in the sand. It seemed as if I had always known him, he was my soul come from the far past, he had an odour of myrtle and thyme, his lips were cool.' (The attraction of another partner grew because 'his clothes had the smell of the desert close by'.) In Agadir, Alec was 'the companion for whom I had always longed and hoped to keep for eternity': 'Our morals dated back to the first nights of the world.' Away from Europe, France, Paris ('an ugly, dirty and sad city'), a new civilisation could come into being: 'It is possible that a new definition of man will appear more clearly on the frontiers of Europe than in Europe itself.' Africa could be 'the last terrain for experimentation in the Occident', and 'in 1950, when endless wars appeared in history, a style of voluptuousness and solitude was about to be born'.[41] Ancient Greece and modern Africa, sex and philosophy, attraction to the desert and desire for male partners thus fused.

Augiéras experienced, and expressed, a sense of physical and mental exhilaration in North Africa. 'The desert exercised an irresistible attraction on me', it had an 'invincible appeal', 'everything pleased me in these steppes, the light, the silence, the rays of the sun', 'the desert was beautiful: peace, the immensity of the Saharan solitudes'. He found 'what I had long desired: the azure and the night of the sea'. A voyage on a boat constituted 'my days in Paradise'. African 'fetishes' 'for me were calls to which I responded passionately, calls which spoke of love and seduction'.[42] The landscape became sensualised, part of eroticised experience. Augiéras not only wanted to be part of this landscape, but to become an Arab. 'Lost in the Sahara, I fraternised instinctively with the indigenes. My behaviour, my lovers were not those of a racist. I found in them savages on my own level.' The writer who had written his first work under an Arab name affirmed, 'I am an Arab in my heart, and profoundly so.'[43] The impossible desire to assume another identity represented both the dream of a misfit expatriate and a quest to achieve sexual and cultural union in the foreign land.

Augiéras carried rejection of the contemporary West, and adoption of the Arab world, to a greater length than other colonial homosexual writers: 'I am becoming an Arab...[sic] and I detest the French.' The world overseas – sometimes, it seems, any part of the world away from Europe – furnished a counterpoise to home: 'What a temptation to refer to India, to Egypt, to Sumer, when one hates to death, as I do, the art of Paris, the prestige of Paris, the sensibility of Paris, and why not say it outright, France?'[44]

Yet Augiéras's Algeria (like the other countries to which he referred) was, even more than the Algeria of Gide's time, a profoundly colonised country. *Une Adolescence au temps du Maréchal* describes the strong imprint of a century of colonisation around Médéa, for instance, 'little towns that wanted to be French, *monuments aux morts* [monuments to the First World War dead], churches with pointed spires, squares and bandstands dating from the time of Louis-Philippe'.[45] In El Goléa, at his uncle's house, Augiéras lived, literally, in a museum of colonisation, dusting hunting trophies and exploration medals, listening to stories of military deeds and expeditions. Colonel Augiéras gave him an old military uniform, and François served in the navy and bore arms during the French war against Algerian nationalists.

Augiéras's political views, however, remained simple. He shunned his French compatriots, but in a flight to the desert rather than as a considered rejection of colonialism. Empathy with Muslim Algerians arose more from pity than political commitment to the legitimacy of the independence struggle. The psychological and physical distress he suffered when down and out in Algiers:

> was nothing compared with that of the Algerian children, hungrier than I was, nourishing themselves on rotten oranges thrown into the gutter, and scraps dug out of rubbish bins, barefoot, clothed in rags. The misery and the health of the Algerian people are awful....Children sleep rough, on doorsteps; they take all sorts of appalling little jobs shining shoes, selling greasy fried foods and brochettes. The dirtiness tops it all off; the kasbah is filthy...they cough, spit and shiver with cold, the children are kicked about by hard and hateful policemen.

The sight of such wretchedness stunned Augiéras, touching an emotional chord:

> I like them [the Algerians]...they are simple, human, passionately human, searching for a gesture or a fraternal smile that will bring them out of their loneliness, ready to accept a hand sincerely extended, shaking it with tears in their eyes.[46]

The Arabs who attracted Augiéras, the ones he painted and about whom he wrote, were the 'pure' shepherds and peasants of the Sahara or the Atlas, the fetching but wretched adolescents of Algiers, not the nationalist leaders with their revolutionary manifesto. Even the fellaghas who appear in his paintings are often atemporal figures silhouetted in beauty and solitude against the sky or the sands, not emblems of a war of independence. In 1958, he stated: 'I am not against France, but I think unceasingly of the FLN [Algerian National Liberation Front].'[47] Such sentiments did not inspire Augiéras publicly to criticise French colonialism during the Algerian War or to refuse military service.

Augiéras's contradictions sum up the colonialist dilemma of attraction and repulsion to foreign places, a desire both to integrate and to dominate, the idealisation and simplification of different cultures. He wanted to be an Arab, to transform himself into a foreigner – a colonialist fantasy carried to the ultimate limit – yet yearned for literary recognition by the great men of French letters. He wanted to be one of the shepherds whom he romanced and romanticised. He longed to live in the desert that provided inspiration, but roundly ignored the Islam that provided the strict religion of the nomads whom he admired. He treated any Arab man as a potential sexual partner and hired prostitutes like the most banal of sexual tourists, but posited a utopian vision of a new life in North Africa and repeated a colonialist myth of a new pan-Mediterranean race. He called himself a 'savage' and a 'barbarian' like Maghrebins (or his imagined Slavic ancestors), perpetuating notions of primitivism on the outskirts of Europe. North Africa was the destination for his escape from the West, the place for discovery of his body and soul, a transcendental opportunity unavailable elsewhere. But after Morocco and Algeria became independent, he no longer went to North Africa, except for that last trip which left mixed impressions, and in Kerkennah in 1971 he confessed that he was tired of being only with 'indigenes', the only foreigner on the islands.[48]

Augiéras seemed unaware of how close his dreams came to the classical French imperialist project. Since the conquest of Algiers, colonialists had described the Maghreb, dotted with classical ruins, as a kind of Arcadia, or its opposite. Imagists of North Africa, from policy makers to postcard vendors, focused on the picturesque – portraits of rugged shepherds, hard-working boatmen or endearing children, incarnations of supposedly untainted and traditional Berber civilisation. Alternatively, Arabs were portrayed as pitiful creatures, mired in filth and poverty, lost in the warren of the kasbah. Promoters of colonialism vaunted the regenerative powers of Africa contrasted with the decadence and flaccidity of contemporary Europe, and pictured the colonies as a laboratory for the creation of a new, purified man – some of Augiéras's phrases could have come straight from the pen of Marshal Lyautey. He, too – as well as Gide – was no stranger to the passionate exhilaration Augiéras felt in the Sahara, the mystical appreciation of the sand and sea of North Africa. And many colonials imbued sexual encounters, however casual, with the aura of philosophical and cultural enlightenment as well as carnal pleasure. Augiéras's desire to escape from the West recalled other flights from Europe, from the earliest colonial adventurers to later back-packing tourists.

Without avoiding attitudes of the most rampantly colonialist variety, powerful passages in Augiéras's works eloquently describe communion with the North African landscape and people. They also provide sociological clues to late colonial sexuality in North Africa: the omnipresence of brothels for French soldiers and settlers, the willingness of young Maghrebin men to engage in sex with casual partners, the possibilities for an old homosexual such as Colonel Augiéras to take refuge in the desert with pliant servants, the sensuality of the Mediterranean that inflamed the passions of northern visitors. *Le Voyage des morts*, in particular, maps meeting places in the bushes behind the beach, or in streets outside cinemas, where men met men for sex. It points, as well, to the dangers – what would now be called 'gay-bashing', including the murder of homosexuals – faced by men as they sought for partners and coupled in the undergrowth. It suggests a sexuality that remained largely 'untheorised' by the participants, men and youths not concerned with limiting their desires to one gender, identifying with a homophile community, or 'setting up house' with long-term partners – a ludic and very physical sexuality untrammelled (for better or worse) by questions of psychology, identity or politics.

North Africa obsessed Augiéras. References to the Maghreb, black Africa and other foreign lands continuously reappeared. He even evoked Mount Athos as an enclave of:

> bearded men, dirty, as savage as Arabs; this was no longer Greece, but a marvellous country, without women, like certain regions of India where hermits live....I beg for bread along the pathways, I work for four days for a hermit, in short, I live the life that Kipling's Kim lived in India.[49]

Back in provincial France, the narrator of *Les Noces avec l'Occident* slept in a bedroom decorated by North African soldiers with crescents and Arabic calligraphy, and then met an Algerian prostitute who 'had seen, without surprise, several garrisons, both French and foreign, pass through her bed'.[50] The further he got from 'civilisation', the happier Augiéras became. After several agreeable weeks in a monastery in the Atlas mountains in 1945, he pressed onwards:

> My future is there, deep in the Algerian South in the Sahara, everything has led me to this path in my life, everything has prepared me for this. Every turn of the wheel which brings me closer makes my joy and my exaltation grow stronger.[51]

The African landscape and the foreign partner are inextricably entwined in *Les Noces avec l'Occident*. The handsome, pure young man – generally a real foreigner, otherwise an otherworldly figure symbolising renewal and perfection – moves through Augiéras's novels. On a visit to Mali, he meets a youth who draws him out of his solitude; the narrator builds a house and sets up a bed for the boy, takes him fishing, gives him books, though the youth sneaks out at night for sexual encounters by the riverside.[52] In a French village, after his return from North Africa, Augiéras's images of the Maghreb and the adolescent come together in a poem: 'In other times, I galloped across the plains of the Orient; / tomorrow where will I pitch my tent?' He experiences, or remembers or imagines an encounter: 'I have rediscovered my brother Abd Allah. / How beautiful were his cheeks and his body suffused with odours [of the desert]'. 'Exiled' back to France, he considers North Africa his spiritual home: 'My eternal motherland has sent me an ambassador / Abd Allah, I know when you come / You are beautiful when you stand in the rising sun / I have no other god than my friend Abd Allah'.[53] One story tells of a Dionysian youth, come from somewhere else, wandering around France, looking, eating and drinking, and having sex, another incarnation of the dark stranger bringing pleasure and salvation.

Augiéras's sexual and emotional engagement with men in North Africa exploded in all directions. His accounts of voracious sexual desire discomfort readers for the taboos of homosexuality, incest, sado-masochism and paedophilia that they break, or because of the 'politically incorrect' context in which they take place. Many of Augiéras's fantasies were directed to ephebes, and his encounters generally occurred with adolescents, sexual behaviour that would now see him castigated as a paedophile, even a child abuser. Nomadic sexual conquests would now see him labelled a sexual tourist. Sexual liberation, but a certain sexual unease, appears in his life and work. The image of the brash but naive Frenchman – sailor, soldier, painter, writer, hunter – swaggering his way around Algeria, sleeping with all and sundry, as the country passed through the throes of independence, is not altogether edifying. Augiéras's picture of a cruel and brutish uncle – locked in his fort, obsessively rearranging his 'curiosities' and reliving his days as a heroic explorer, beating and sodomising young men who came within his reach – is even less noble. The letter from Tunis in 1971 sets up an unconvincing and self-righteous dichotomy between his own pure relationships and the perversions of other French homosexuals.

Augiéras's psychology was complex; extreme elation alternated with deep depression, anger and bitterness mixed with lyrical transcendence. The word '*solitude*' (meaning both solitude and loneliness) appears regularly in his writings, which betray enormous distress, alienation and desperation. A frenzied physical and spiritual itinerancy marks his life and books. Though he hardly believed in a traditional notion of original sin, he seemed constantly to search for innocence and purity, even in the landscape, in 'sands pure from all soiling, as at the dawn of the world'.[54]

Augiéras was an accomplished artist, as well as writer, and his paintings reflect his sexual and emotional preoccupations, and fascination with foreign places and youths. Showing the influences of Antonello da Messina, Di Chirico, prehistoric Lascaux cave paintings, the ancient frescoes of Fayoum and Byzantine gold-leaf icons, Augiéras's works, painted on board, cardboard or cloth (though seldom on canvas), often appear illustrations of his works. *The*

Master and the Child, a magico-realistic portrayal of a man lying on a roof-top beckoning to a boy under a starry sky, is clearly inspired by *Le Vieillard et l'enfant*. A *Shepherd-Fellagha*, a shepherd boy clad in the battle-dress of a freedom fighter, and a soldier mounted on a horse, draw on experiences in war-torn North Africa. More pictures of soldiers and Arabs (*On the Red Rocks*, *In the Desert*, *Guerrilla*) depict encounters, whether of pleasure or violence, between Frenchmen and Arabs – the Arab and Frenchman in the desert are complementary figures, two halves of a dilemma about sex, war and the clash of civilisations. One painting, *The Algerian War* (1962), shows a young Arab crucified between two standing figures, one a nomad, another a more Westernised figure wearing singlet and jeans. In another picture, a soldier standing near a multi-coloured hut could be Augiéras himself guarding the blockhouse in El Goléa that he so carefully painted. Pictures of armed children are reminders of the effects of war on youth. An adolescent with a sickle prefigures the young man about whom Augiéras wrote in *Dromme*. A splendid *Abdallah*, around 1960, showing a wide-eyed North African whose robes hang open to reveal the handle of a dagger or a camel-driver's whip stuck into his belt, is a portrait of 'my desert brother', the youth evoked in *Les Noces*.

Figures appear, frequently alone, in the desert, on a precipice, looking upwards at the sky or outwards towards the horizon, emblems of both homo-erotic desire and solitude. *An Arcadian Shepherd*, a *Nomad with a White Head-dress* and other paintings from the late 1950s and early 1960s reveal the continuing influence of Augiéras's wanderings in North Africa and his testimony to the Algerian war. A series of *Paintings of an Unknown Civilisation*, completed in the last years of his life, mostly representing a young man and a boy in a stylised North African setting, relive the irrepressible memories of the traumatic experiences with his uncle of a quarter of a century earlier.[55]

Augiéras's paintings have the oniric, mystical quality of his writings, in which the desert of North Africa, and the cohabitation of Frenchmen and Arabs in the 1950s, provided opportunities for self-revelation and discovery. The iconic style gives them a religious value. A mood of serenity, as Paul Placet remarks, combines with danger. The innocence of young boys is placed against the menace of armed soldiers. Pictures of a crucifixion bespeak suffering, an *Angel of the Revolution* might bring hope and a *Passer of Souls* hints at a mythical figure who will transport men to another world. The deracinated, mystical style of figures so closely related to Augiéras's trajectory through North Africa, his experiences of the colonies in the 1940s and 1950s, and his idealisation of the emancipatory and sensual effect of the Sahara sum up the psychological and historical paradoxes of the colonial 'barbarian', another version of Gide's 'immoralist'.

Jean Genet

A third example of homosexual fascination with North Africa and the Arab world, and the same coalescence of sexual and literary life as evident with Gide and Augiéras, is Jean Genet (1910–86). Genet's links with Arabs spanned his life and appear in many of his writings. An introduction to the Islamic world came in 1930, when, as a young soldier, he was sent to Damascus, Syria, then ruled by France under a mandate from the League of Nations. In the months he spent in the Middle East, Genet experienced the 'exoticism, freedom, [and] army [life which] defined Damascus', and he fell in love with a 16-year-old hair-dresser. The next year, Genet was posted to Morocco, where he fell for a Legionnaire, who let Genet have sex with him but would not or could not reciprocate his affections.[56]

By the early 1950s, now a famous if controversial writer, Genet became involved in political affairs, taking part in protests against the Algerian war in 1955, a move that led to his being attacked in the press as a 'professional pederast'. The same year, he met Abdallah Bentaga, with whom he formed one of the most significant relationships in his life, and who Edmund White says, of all Genet's lovers, 'would leave the deepest mark (one might say scar)' on him.[57] Genet was forty-five, and Bentaga eighteen, when they met; Bentaga was the son of an Algerian man and a German woman, and he followed his father into the circus to become a high-wire walker (his lessons paid for by Genet). In 1957, Genet dedicated to Bentaga 'Le Funambule', a meditation on the danger and possible accidental death faced by a high-wire walker. Genet encouraged Bentaga to desert from the French Army after he was called up to serve in Algeria; since Bentaga faced arrest for doing so, the two spent several years trav-elling around Europe. Genet pushed Bentaga to pursue his performing career, becoming – in White's phrase – the Pygmalion for the half-literate young acrobat, then coming to his aid when he fell and injured himself, but still hoping that Bentaga would return to the high-wire. By the early 1960s, Genet's affections turned towards another man. Bentaga became increasingly depressed because of both Genet's waning interests and his own physical inability, after injuries, to continue an acrobatic career. He committed suicide in 1964, leaving Genet distraught.

A few years later, Genet began visiting Morocco, where he had an affair with a barber (whom he invited for a visit to Paris). In 1970, he took his first trip to Palestinian camps in Jordan, and made the acquaintance of a man called Hamza; although Genet saw Hamza for only twenty-four hours, the young Palestinian haunted him afterwards. In 1974, in Tangier, Genet met Mohammed El Katrani, a Moroccan whose father had served in the French Army; El Katrani became his final companion. They lived together in Tangier and Paris; Genet built houses for El Katrani and his wife and son, and for Genet himself, in Larache, Morocco. Genet was buried there.[58]

Somewhat curiously, Genet engaged little in homoeroticisation of Arabs and other non-Europeans in his early works, though he occasionally addresses the high-wire walker in 'Le Funambule' in blatantly sexual language: 'Get hard. Your body will have the arrogant vigour of a tumescent, irritated phallus. That is why I tell you to dance before your image, and to fall in love with you....It is Narcissus who dances.'[59] In one scene of *Querelle de Brest*, a black barman sodomises the French soldier, an implication of black virility and the submission of the white man – a reversal of the typical colonial social relationship – but the book does not insist on the point. Eroticisation of the black man also appears in *Les Nègres*, where the white Queen cries: 'I die – I must confess – choked by my desire for a Big Black Buck. Black nakedness, thou hast conquered me.'[60]

Sexualised representations of non-European characters are more pronounced in Genet's film *Chant d'amour* (1950). A dancer in a prison cell, played by a professional Paris dancer who worked under the stage name 'Coco le Martiniquais', is portrayed erotically (as are the other prisoners), his large penis again alluding to racial stereotypes. The two main characters are involved in an inter-racial homosexual relationship, both in the prison, where they symbolically make love by blowing smoke through a hole in the wall between their cells and masturbating, and in an idyll in which they gambol around a forest and embrace on the grass (a fantasy in either their own minds or the mind of the voyeuristic warder). The younger, a strikingly handsome European, was played by Genet's lover of the time, Lucien Sénémaud. The older prisoner, a masculine, hairy-chested figure, was identified as 'a North African [Tunisian] pimp who also worked as a barber in Montmartre'.[61] The sensual, and consensual, relationship between them contrasts with the violent intentions of the homosexual guard, who bursts into the Arab's cell and cruelly thrashes him with his leather belt, and then inserts the barrel of his gun into the prisoner's mouth: a scene of sado-masochistic rape. The different episodes suggest two types of sexual and romantic contact, and might be interpreted as a metaphor for the violence of colonial relations and Genet's competing vision of the utopian sexual congress between an older and a younger man, a European and a foreigner.

The play *Les Paravents*, written in 1957 during the Algerian War and Genet's affair with Bentaga, focuses most clearly and critically on French colonialism. Not staged in Paris until 1966, the first performances provoked an uproar in the theatre and virulent criticism outside from those who said Genet had dishonoured the memory of the French war dead and betrayed France.[62] The main character, downtrodden Saïd, is hardly a sex symbol, but sexuality suffuses the play: Saïd's unhappiness at having to marry an ugly wife because he is too poor to afford a more beautiful one, constant visits by Arabs and Legionnaires to brothels, badinage about virility and more serious comments on whether the Arabs have the 'balls' to defeat their colonial oppressors. Homosexuality appears in various forms, though never as the major theme. Genet portrays (and caricatures) soldiers as handsome macho men – the Mother remarks of one man that 'he is so handsome he could have been a *goumier* or a Legionnaire'. (Nevertheless a hint of uncertainty about French behaviour intrudes, as an Arab remarks that, if Saïd and his unlovely spouse went to France, 'they'd jump on Saïd not his wife'.) The character of the lieutenant can be read as homosexual. 'A soldier must be hairy...and handsome....Good warriors, brave warriors, of course, but first of all handsome warriors,' demands the lieutenant, who insists that his men be neatly shaved even if they must use spit to moisten shaving-brushes. He talks about the pleasures of a massage and, uncharacteristically for a hardened soldier, confesses that he would have liked to learn the violin. A sergeant remarks that the lieutenant often looks deeply into his eyes, whereupon the lieutenant wipes his subaltern's baldric clean with his handkerchief. The lieutenant tells a Legionnaire that he must look straight into the eyes of his fellow soldier, and then counsels that each man must be a 'mirror' for his comrades:

> Two legs must look and see each other in the two legs in front of him, a torso in the torso in front of him, a mouth in another mouth, eyes in eyes....Looking at and seeing a perfect beauty...total seduction.

Such beauty, he adds enigmatically, will be irresistible to opponents, who can be vanquished through moral victory. The soldiers themselves feel obliged to live up to the legendary reputation: 'Virile beauty, that's us,' one soldier cracks, but then disarmingly adds, 'That's what I've read.'[63]

The play also points, with theatrical and political caricature, to European eroticisation of Arabs. A member of the French Academy – who, along with military officers, settlers and missionaries, represents the colonial population and metropolitan supporters – confides, 'Ah, General, the young fifteen- to seventeen-year old Muslim', and licks his lips lasciviously. However, Genet again provides a disarming parry in the words a soldier addresses to the general: 'Be careful. You start by developing a taste for the fifteen-year old Muslim. Three months later you understand him. Then you accept his political grievances. And finally, you become a traitor to your race.' Fraternisation with Arabs, Genet hints – no doubt with autobiographical insight – might lead to political conversion to their cause. Most of the French, however, even those who enjoyed sexual commerce with the natives, did not espouse the nationalists' aims, and Genet comes close to a psychosexual suggestion about their hatred of Arabs. In stage directions for one scene, he writes about the cruelty of the sergeant (the same officer who takes the fancy of the lieutenant):

> What is the origin of the sergeant's brutality? To be honest, I have no idea, but I'll invent a reason: the Arabs who people the night on the hillsides have a reputation for monstrous virility, but that of the sergeant is threatened. Around it he elaborates a pomp....of muscle and trappings right down to his swearing and his attitudes in order to dissimulate what is a concern that obsesses him so much as to give him the desire to kill.

A soldier whose manliness is endangered by Arab virility turns into a 'hunter of Moorish penises', just as Amerindian warriors became collectors of scalps.[64]

Genet therefore not only points to erotic fantasies about both French soldiers and Arab natives, but also suggests that sexual ambiguity can, on the one hand, create empathy for the colonised or, on the other, combined with gender insecurity, promote militarism and colonialism, and lead to murderous campaigns to castrate the enemy through assassination. The first alternative, manifestly, was Genet's own choice. The other option was bloodily exemplified by the practice of fighters cutting off the genitals of men whom they slaughtered and stuffing them into their victims' mouths.

Genet was nevertheless reticent or perhaps simply uninterested during the Algerian War in writing about his sexual liaisons with Arabs, or in eroticising non-European figures more overtly. He could hardly go too far in satirising the lieutenant's or *académicien's* sexual interests without raising questions about his own motivations. Later, however, he wrote more openly about attraction to Arabs and, in a self-reflective way, examined the mixture of sexual and political engagement that he had experienced. *Le Captif amoureux* appeared in the year of Genet's death and recounted his association with Palestinians and American Black Panthers, whom he regarded as heroic fighters against Western imperialism. Genet lived in Palestinian camps in Tunisia and Jordan on and off for several years in the late 1960s and early 1970s, enjoying the male camaraderie of the Palestinian nationalist struggle. He confessed to the erotic tingle he felt bedding down next to young soldiers, his enjoyment in seeing them bathe and dance. His homosexuality was no secret to most Palestinians; some, he admitted, found it 'repugnant', others – such as a soldier who ostentatiously urinated in front of him or another who joked about his own shapely legs – seemed to take delight in parading their attributes. He marvelled at their preening machismo, but noted how their carefully arranged hairstyles, whether long or short, straight or curly, oiled or windblown, offset muscular virility with a grace note of ambivalent elegance. Genet evoked the charm and physical beauty of the Palestinian guerrillas, such as comely Ferraj or hunky Moubarak, a black Sudanese who had cast his lot with the Palestinians, a colossus who treated Genet in a coquettish fashion. Others were so handsome that they even robbed the old man of his lust, he said, yet 'each appeared not only as the transfiguration of my fantasies but their materialisation waiting there, before me, as if they were offered to me'. Genet's favourite was Hamza, a 20-year-old whose 'smile, gaiety, a voice so sweet that it was almost dangerous, with a sort of lightness and sudden gravity' captivated Genet's affections. He spent only one night in Hamza's mother's house in Irbid, sleeping in the young man's bed while he was on guard duty, but Hamza left an indelible impression. Fourteen years after meeting him, and then losing contact, Genet returned to the Middle East and searched for the companion with whom he had enjoyed a chaste fellowship, but found that Hamza had married and moved to Germany. *Le Captif amoureux* closes with a personal reminiscence:

> I had done all that I could to understand how this revolution was so unlike others and, in a certain sense I had understood, but what remained was this little house in Irbid where one night I slept, and for fourteen years I endeavoured to find out if this night had really taken place. This last page of my book is transparent.[65]

Hamza and his comrades-in-arms provided a reason for Genet's interest in the Palestinian struggle but, equally importantly, Genet's political commitment to the Palestinian cause provided a chance for enjoyment of the soldiers' companionship. 'Haven't you ever thought that revolution and friendship go together?,' one Palestinian, on the point of journeying to meet his close friend at another camp, asked Genet. 'And the friendship that you are talking about, would you dare speak of it as love?,' Genet asked, to which the young man responded,

> Yes, it is love. Right now, at this minute, do you think I am afraid of words? Friendship, love? One thing is clear: if he died tonight there would always be a hole next to me, a hole into which I must never fall.

The sentiments about friendship, love and revolution expressed Genet's own feelings, he admitted straightforwardly, 'how vulgar desires and dreams of orgies metamorphosed into sublime devotion'.[66]

In other writings about the feddayin, notably an essay on the Chatila massacre, Genet in an often surprising and controversial, but always self-examining, way insisted on the link between eroticism and revolution, sex and the liberation struggle.

> Affirmation of a beauty that is particular to revolutionaries poses a number of questions. We know – we suppose – that young children or adolescents living in old and severe milieux have a beauty in their faces, their bodies, their movements, their gazes, which is rather close to that of the feddayin. The explanation is perhaps the following: shucking off old constraints, a new liberty emerges from dead skins, and the fathers and grandfathers will find it difficult to put out the fires in their eyes, the voltage of their temples, the lightness of the blood in their veins.

Theorising about the beauty of independence fighters, Genet moved from reflection on Palestinians in the 1980s to Algerians in the 1950s:

> Before the Algerian war, the Arabs were not attractive, they carried themselves with a heavy-footed and dawdling gait, their looks were odd, but almost at once, victory beautified them, although already, a little before it became so blinding, when more than half a million French soldiers were breaking their necks and dying in the Aurès and all over Algeria, a curious phenomenon had become perceptible, at work on the faces and in the bodies of Arab workers: something like an advent, a foreshadowing of a still fragile beauty that would astound us when the scales finally fell from their skin and our eyes. We had to accept the evidence: they had liberated themselves politically to appear as we had to see them: very beautiful.[67]

The connections Genet makes between the nobility of the struggle for freedom, whether of Algerians colonised by France or Palestinians colonised by

Israel, and the beauty of their people, both physical and moral, is evident. By taking part in their struggle, by accepting their cause, we can see their beauty, Genet says, but the very struggle of these people, their ultimate victory, transforms the colonised from brow-beaten, shameful ugliness to radiant, glorious beauty.

> Is a revolution really a revolution when it does not make the faces and bodies shed the dead skin which enervates them? I am not speaking about an academic beauty, but about the impalpable – unnameable – beauty of bodies, of faces, of cries, of words which are not dismal, I mean a sensual joy which is so strong that it tries to banish eroticism.[68]

Abjuring sexual lust for a higher appreciation of physical beauty, in an almost Socratic fashion,[69] Genet thereby makes the revolution itself – even more than the revolutionaries – the object of desire and commitment, and thereby, from his engagement with the Algerians and the Palestinians, develops a theory fusing the personal and the political: the ultimate seduction.

The seduction of oasis, desert and feddayin camp

Though their lives all intertwined with the colonial history of North Africa, Gide, Genet and Augiéras are not clones. Gide, who first visited North Africa in the 1890s, belonged to the generation of colonial conquest and the apogee of imperial rule. Augiéras arrived almost half a century later, and experienced Algeria in the 1950s as colonial control was disintegrating. Genet's interaction with the Arab world lasted from his posting in Syria in the 1930s through commitment to the Palestinians in the 1980s. Gide had no links with the military, Genet completed military service in the colonies but encouraged his lover to refuse conscription and Augiéras was, briefly, a volunteer in France's anti-colonial war. Gide was the elegant, learned and wealthy Parisian gentleman; Genet the self-declared thief and autodidact who roamed France and the world; Augiéras the self-styled 'barbarian' who pronounced his hatred for Paris and France. Gide's sexual initiation occurred in North Africa, but liaisons in later life occurred with protégés in the bourgeois and artistic circles of Paris. Genet's sexual world was manned by sailors, acrobats and prisoners, but then the Moroccan with whom he ended his life in a father–son relationship. Augiéras, after an incestuous affair as a young man, and multiple encounters with women, sought the company of North African shepherds and fishermen, but ultimately retreated into mystical solitude.

Despite their differences, for Gide, Augiéras and Genet, North Africa (or the Middle East) was a refuge for those who did not fit in at home, or who chose to reject Europe and its conformity – Gide's 'immoralist', Augiéras's 'barbarian' and Genet's revolutionary and 'prisoner of love'. At the outer limit, it represented outright hatred for France, as Augiéras admitted, and as Genet explained in speaking of identification with the oppressed of the world: 'Hating France, that's not enough, you've got to do more than hate it, you must vomit it up....I could only feel at home among oppressed people of colour or the oppressed in revolt against whites.'[70] (Gide, however, would have disowned such a sentiment, although professing loathing for specific institutions, notably the conventional family.) Identification as a foreigner, with 'the other' – which accompanied sexual attraction to him – allowed these men fully to assume their homosexual condition. Those whom Western moralities had rejected established an emotional bond with other reprobates, those colonised by conquerors championing the morals of European civilisation. All experienced colonialism at first hand, and all, to differing extents, took the side of the colonised – Gide in denunciation of labour trade in French West Africa, Genet in *prises de position* on behalf of Algerians and Palestinians, Augiéras in less focused fashion in rejection of European values and mores.

Gide, Augiéras and Genet had flesh-and-blood relationships with North Africans that illustrate the diversity of homosexual liaisons the colonies afforded. These ranged from casual sexual encounters to long-lived attachments with partners who were not, in a European sense, homosexual. Gide had sex with Ali in the sand dunes of Algeria and with another Ali in a boat on the Nile, Augiéras slept with innumerable men in the Atlas mountains and Agadir, Genet had passing rendezvous in Syria and elsewhere. They found willing partners in hotel gardens, at the beach, in busy colonial cities and, for Genet, among North Africans in France. Not all relationships were brief and anonymous. Augiéras fell in love with an Arab called Alec, even if he could not take him back to France, while Gide maintained a twenty-year friendship with Athmann, and Genet found in Bentaga and El Katrani long-term companions. Gide invited Athmann to France, and Genet went to live near El Katrani in Morocco; Augiéras searched, unsuccessfully, for the home away from Europe for which he yearned.

North Africa (and North Africans) provided sexual passion that often eluded these men in France. But theirs was not just an erotic encounter to be enjoyed with individual foreigners, for their writings treated the whole of the North African world (although a romanticised, mythified one) as a sensuous experience. For Gide, sexual encounters formed a part, a crucial one, of the colourful, fragrant, sonorous luxuriance that the Maghreb offered, and which produced his 'exaltation'. For Augiéras, the experience of mountains and deserts in North Africa, sensual as well as mystical, brought on a transcendental ecstasy. For Genet – of a less romantic and spiritual turn than the other Frenchmen – it was not so much the Arabic landscape that was eroticised as the nationalist struggle of the Palestinians, the sexiness of the revolution.

Notes

1 See Daniel Rondeau (ed.), *L'Appel du Maroc* (Paris, 1999).
2 Quoted (and translated) in Jarrod Hayes, *Queer Nations: Marginal Sexualities in the Maghreb* (Chicago, 2000), p. 30.
3 A. Desbiefs, *Le Vice en Algérie* (Paris, 1899).

4 Jean-Edern Hallier's novel *L'Evangile du fou* (Paris, 1986), makes much of Foucauld's homosexuality.
5 Henry de Montherlant, *Encore un instant de bonheur* (Paris, 1934), *La Rose de sable* (Paris, 1968) and *Moustique* (Paris, 1986).
6 Roger Martin du Gard, *Le Lieutenant-Colonel de Maumort* (Paris, 1983); see Christian Gury, *Lyautey–Charlus* (Paris, 1998), Ch. XXVII, 'Lyautey–Maumort'.
7 A homosexual *pied-noir* poet and activist, Jean Sénac, will be discussed in Chapter 12.
8 The standard biography is Alan Sheridan, *André Gide: A Life in the Present* (London, 1998). See also Christopher Robinson, *Scandal in the Ink: Male and Female Homosexuality in Twentieth-Century French Literature* (London, 1995).
9 André Gide, *Carnets d'Egypte*, in *Journal d'André Gide, 1939–1949, Souvenirs* [Pléiade edition] (Paris, 1954), pp. 1,049–77.
10 *Ibid.*, p. 1052.
11 *Ibid.*, p. 1070.
12 *Ibid.*, p. 1073.
13 Gide wrongly deciphered Beryl de Zoete's name (as Zoebe) on her letter. On the Balinese scandal, see Chapter 6 above.
14 *Ibid.*, p. 1,062.
15 André Gide, *L'Immoraliste* (Paris, 1902), pp. 52, 66, 57, 169, 182 (Folio edition).
16 *Ibid.*, pp. 24, 31, 33 (Folio edition).
17 *Ibid.*, p. 174.
18 André Gide, *Si le grain ne meurt*, in *Journal d'André Gide* [Pléiade edition], pp. 560–1.
19 *Ibid.*, pp. 593–4.
20 Jonathan Fryer, *André & Oscar: Gide, Wilde and the Gay Art of Living* (London, 1997), Ch. 7; Jonathan Dollimore, *Sexual Dissidence: Augustine to Wilde, Freud to Foucault* (Oxford, 1991), pp. 3, 12; Lawrence R. Schehr, *Alcibiades at the Door: Gay Discourses in French Literature* (Stanford, 1995), pp. 118, 119, 124; Michael Lucey, *Gide's Bent: Sexuality, Politics, Writing* (New York, 1995).
21 André Gide, *Amyntas* (Paris, 1925), pp. 142, 97–8 (Folio edition).
22 See Martine Sagaert, 'Exotisme, métissage et écriture', in *Bulletin des amis d'André Gide*, Vol. XXII, No. 102 (1994), pp. 184–7, a special issue on Gide and Algeria.
23 André Gide, *Les Nourritures terrestres* (Paris, 1897).
24 See Sagaert, pp. 173–89.
25 Guy Dugas, 'André Gide et Athmannn: Le Roman d'une amitié rare', *Cahiers de Tunisie*, Vol. 30, No. 119–20 (1992), pp. 247–65.
26 Pierre Masson, 'Sur quelques lettres d'Athmann', *Bulletin des Amis d'André Gide*, *op. cit.*, pp. 269–86.
27 *Ibid.*
28 See Dugas, *op. cit.*, who counters the notion that Athmann was stupid and manipulative.
29 Quoted in Dugas, p. 256.
30 Eric Marty, 'Le Poète sans livre', in *Bulletin des Amis d'André Gide*, *op. cit.*, pp. 218–26; on the meaning of Gide's trips, see also Pierre Masson, 'L'Algérie d'André Gide, de l'indicible à l'ineffable', pp. 191–202.
31 André Gide, *Voyage au Congo* (Paris, 1928), pp. 15, 17, 184, 172, 212, 233, 244.
32 André Gide, *Retour du Tchad* (Paris, 1928), pp. 357–60.
33 Augiéras described his childhood, and later experiences, in *Une Adolescence au temps du Maréchal et de multiples aventures* (Paris, 1968). Paul Placet, *François Augiéras: Un Barbare en Occident* (Périgueux, 1988), and Philippe Berthier, *François Augiéras: L'Apprenti sorcier* (Seyssel, 1994), are biographies. See also Paul Placet and Pascal Sigoda, *Augiéras, une trajectoire rimbaldienne* (Charleville, 1996); Annick Lontin, *Pour François Augiéras* (Lyon, 1990), and Association des Amis de François Augiéras, *Ecrivain-Peintre: 'Une Aventure de l'esprit' 1925–1971* (Périgueux, 1985). Gert

Hekma, 'François Augiéras (1925–1971)', *Paidika*, Vol. 10, No. 1 (1991), pp. 57–64, examines in particular the theme of inter-generational sexuality in Augiéras's work. A dossier on Augiéras in *Masques*, No. 13 (Printemps 1982), pp. 26–49, explores aspects of homosexuality in his life and work.

34 *Le Petit Journal Illustré*, 24 April 1921.
35 See *D'Alger au Sénégal – Mission Augiéras–Draper, 1927–1928* (Paris, 1931).
36 François Augiéras, *Le Voyage des morts*, (Paris, 1979), p. 102.
37 Abdallah Chaamba [François Augiéras], *Le Vieillard et l'enfant* (Paris, 1949), quotations from pp. 34, 73.
38 François Augiéras, *Adolescence*, quotation from 1980 edition, pp. 185, 218, 250.
39 Letter to Bruno and Marie-Jo Roy, 19 September 1971, published in *Masques*, p. 61; further details in Placet, pp. 222–3.
40 The passage is printed in *Masques*; quotation from p. 64.
41 Augiéras, *Le Voyage des morts*, pp. 45, 37, 75, 79, 185, 186, 125, 101.
42 *Ibid.*, pp. 58, 188, 141, 153, 212, 137.
43 Quoted in Placet, pp. 62, 95.
44 Augiéras, *Adolescence*, pp. 208, 219–20.
45 Augiéras, *ibid.*, p. 191.
46 *Ibid.*, pp. 202–3.
47 *Ibid.*, p. 360.
48 Quoted in Placet, p. 223.
49 François Augiéras, *Lettres du Mont Athos* (Paris, 1994), pp. 15–16.
50 François Augiéras, *Les Noces avec l'Occident* (Paris, 1981), p. 55.
51 Augiéras, *Adolescence*, p. 213.
52 François Augiéras and Paul Placet, *La Chasse fantastique* (n.p., 1996), p. 75.
53 Augiéras, *Noces*, pp. 34–6.
54 Augiéras, *Le Vieillard et l'enfant*, p. 21.
55 Claude Michel Cluny and Paul Placet (eds), *Augiéras peintre* (Paris, 2001). Augiéras's work also includes geometrical paintings and landscapes.
56 Edmund White, *Genet* (New York, 1993), p. 102.
57 *Ibid.*, p. 509.
58 Details of Genet's involvement with the Arab world are taken from White, *op. cit.*
59 Jean Genet, 'Le Funambule', in *Oeuvres complètes* (Paris, 1979), p. 19.
60 Jean Genet, *Les Nègres* (Paris, 1958).
61 Jane Giles, *The Cinema of Jean Genet: Un Chant d'amour* (London, 1991), p. 20.
62 See Lynda Bellity Peskine and Albert Dichy, *La Bataille des Paravents* (Paris, 1991).
63 Jean Genet, *Les Paravents* (Paris, 1961), pp. 50, 175, 123, 182 (Folio edition).
64 *Ibid.*, pp. 147, 140–1.
65 Jean Genet, *Le Captif amoureux* (Paris, 1986), pp. 244, 172.
66 *Ibid.*, pp. 121, 172.
67 Jean Genet, 'Quatre heures à Chatila', reprinted in *Jean Genet et la Palestine*, special issue of the *Revue d'études palestiniennes* (1997), p. 21.
68 *Ibid.*
69 Or, more pertinently, in a Middle Eastern fashion; Juan Goytisolo, 'Le Poète enterré à Larache', in *Jean Genet et la Palestine*, pp. 87–91, compares Genet's attitudes towards those of the Sufi dervishes and such Persian poetic celebrators of young men as Rumi.
70 Quoted in Giles, p. 65.

Part III
The end of empire

12 Anti-colonialism and homosexuality

The links between colonialism and homosexuality often seem a paradigm of European men taking advantage of the colonial situation, and the benefits of foreign status, to extract sexual favours from foreign men or subaltern Europeans. Homosexuals thus appear complicit with the imperial order, and present-day commentators generally stress the more or less pronounced imperialist ideas of almost all Europeans overseas. Certainly some figures remained proudly unreconstructed and unembarrassed imperialists. Nevertheless it would be a mistake to ignore gradations of sentiment. Cecil Rhodes, Henry Morton Stanley and Nikolay Przhevalsky did not question the rightness of the colonial cause or the superiority of the white race, but nuances of opinion differentiate Europeans attracted overseas for sexual and other interests. Alexander von Humboldt rejected the institution of slavery; Roger Casement and André Gide denounced exploitation of African (and Brazilian) labourers. Herman Melville and Charles Warren Stoddard lambasted European and American takeover of Oceania. Edward Carpenter ridiculed British imperialism in India and promoted radical social change to enfranchise both European proletarians and colonised foreigners. E.M. Forster condemned the Amritsar massacre and British reaction to nationalist movements in Egypt, and *A Passage to India* indicts a certain type of Briton in the Raj. Novelists such as Louis Couperus and Claude Farrère pointed up the hypocrisies of colonial society and the social pretensions of expatriates. Marshal Lyautey hoped his proconsular rule in Morocco would represent a humanitarian administration respectful of Islamic institutions and the Maghrebin population. Alain Daniélou objected to Westernisation of India, and François Augiéras damned the effects of France's *mission civilisatrice*. Jean Genet opposed attempts to maintain French rule in Algeria and supported Palestinian nationalism.[1]

Indeed a significant number of European homosexuals overseas displayed an ambivalent attitude towards imperialism, or took an avowedly critical stance on European rule. Their renegade position as sexual heretics at home had led them to sexual opportunities in foreign countries, yet cast them in an ambiguous position. Although representatives of the 'master race' and imperial power, they did not fit into the mould of heterosexual married life (or even concubinage) and child rearing. They trespassed across boundaries of propriety by being intimate with foreign men, and sometimes making too close friends of them. Liaisons with such men could inspire a contrary perspective on the colonial world, as seen most famously in Lawrence of Arabia's memories of Dahoum. The friendships between Carpenter and Arunachalam, and between Forster and Masood, cross-fertilised political beliefs and cultural interests, making it impossible for some Europeans not to question verities of triumphant colonialism and, as well, conventions of social behaviour at home. Gide's paeans to the Maghreb in *Amyntas*, his denunciation of the situation of African labour in *Voyage au Congo* and *Retour du Tchad* and his apologia for homosexuality in *Corydon* are not unconnected.

By the end of the imperial age, as seen in the last chapter, sex and politics were even more pertinently conjoined. Activists in the gay liberation movement of the 1960s and 1970s linked demands for sexual revolution and the end of residual and variant forms of imperialism, such as American military action in Vietnam and apartheid in South Africa. Manifestos of the 'New Left' and homosexual militant groups denounced imperialism, capitalism and heterosexual hegemony. Guy Hocquenghem, the leading gay theorist in France and a founder of FHAR, the Homosexual Front for Revolutionary Action, condemned French racism at home and abroad, and exalted the 'beauty of the *métis*'.[2] Gay liberation in other countries took a similarly uncompromising stand on sexual and political revolution.

This chapter will examine several instances where connections between sexual desire and anti-colonial politics appear especially vividly. Daniel Guérin and Pierre Herbart provide examples of the conjunction between homosexual identity and socialist militancy. A third Frenchman, the *pied-noir* poet Jean Sénac, illustrates how political commitment, sexual pleasure (and disappointment) and literary creativity came together in a settler colony and during a war of national liberation.

Sexual and political radicalism: Pierre Herbart and Daniel Guérin

Pierre Herbart, born in 1903, grew up in a wealthy French provincial family; his grandfather was a Dunkirk shipbuilder.[3] In 1923, he did military service in Morocco as an aide-de-camp to Marshal Lyautey. Back in France, Herbart frequented literary circles, and also began to battle the drug addiction that periodically plagued him throughout his life. In 1929, Jean Cocteau introduced Herbart to André Gide. Much impressed by Herbart's intelligence and good looks, Gide fostered the publication of his first novel two years later. The same year, Gide introduced Herbart to Elizabeth van Risselberghe, then pregnant with Gide's daughter, and the two soon married. (They separated in 1959.) In 1931, as well, Herbart journeyed to Indo-China with Andrée Viollis, a journalist for *Le Petit Parisien*, well-known for articles and books on foreign countries. Sent to cover a tour by the French Minister of Colonies, Herbart said the journey opened his eyes to French imperialism and made him 'irredeemably anti-colonialist'.

Three years afterwards, Herbart travelled to Spain and witnessed the early stages of the Civil War, which further developed his political views, and led to him to join the Communist Party. He then went to the Soviet Union to work for a French-language communist newspaper, although he rapidly became disenchanted with Soviet bureaucracy and Stalinist thought. After a trip back to France, he nevertheless returned to the USSR with Gide and several fellow travellers (including the Dutch homosexual Jef Last). The stay caused Gide to turn against communism; Herbart tried to persuade him to defer publication of the critical *Retour de l'URSS*. Herbart also accompanied Gide to Africa, the sojourn that inspired Gide's books attacking forced labour; Herbart himself published a study of French West Africa, *Le Chancre du Niger*.

Herbart's eventful life, and political engagement, continued with service in the Second World War Resistance. He set up the first post-Liberation newspaper and, thanks to Albert Camus, obtained a position on the radical *Combat* paper. In 1946, he again visited Africa. From that time onwards, Herbart devoted himself to creative writing, although he largely lived off money provided by Gide until his mentor's death. *L'Age d'or*, published in 1953 with a preface by Camus (which hoped that readers would not be shocked by its sexual revelations), centres on Guérin's homosexual adventures. *La Ligne de force*, from 1958, discusses his political commitments to anti-colonialism, Spanish Republicanism and the Resistance. Novels, stories and memoirs followed, although by the 1960s Herbart was incapacitated by drug addiction and financial problems. He died, forgotten and near destitution, in 1974.[4]

Herbart's *Souvenirs imaginaires*, describing his stay in Africa in 1923, includes a few homoerotic anecdotes.[5] On one excursion, a servant called Mahmadou attentively washed him in the shower, and offered his son as a 'cabin boy' to the traveller – the captain repeatedly warned Herbart not to 'debauch' the handsome, nattily-dressed youth. In Morocco, Herbart remarked on Chleuh adolescents 'who sell themselves'. Later he encountered a lieutenant in the colonial army, 'the most handsome man I had met in my life'; the officer invited Herbart to stay with him, but he declined, 'and thus I lost the greatest chance of my life'. Reflecting in 1968, after most African colonies had gained independence, on this trip almost half a century earlier, Herbart lamented the puritanism of present-day leaders:

> Africa in 1923 offered to the traveller many satisfactions that today are contested. One notices that a people's accession to liberty creates a *crise de vertu*. One would have thought that these people, free at last, would say: 'At last, everyone can do exactly what he wishes.' Not at all. They declare: 'You will make love only with your lawfully wedded wife.' In a revolutionary, a petty bourgeois always lies dormant.[6]

Homosexuality appears in several of Herbart's fictional works, though seldom with a colonial connection. In *La Licorne*, the arrival of a 16-year-old *pied-noir*, whose father languishes in prison and whose sister was raped by fellaghas during the Algerian war of independence, troubles a household. Martial is attracted by young Bruno's 'incomparable eyes', his 'savage look', skin that reveals 'something suffocating, African, perhaps the desert'. Scenes of tragedy follow.[7] Several stories are set in ethnic neighbourhoods in Marseilles, and Herbart recollects a late-night encounter with a Guinean in a Paris café. A handsome French soldier in Niger (like the one he indeed met) is evoked in homoerotic terms. Herbart's ideal type was not an exotic foreigner, but a robust working-class Frenchman. He generally avoided both descriptions filled with local colour and personal confessions, and cautioned that he would not write about the 'diverse delights that I tasted' in North Africa. Even moreso than writers such as Gide, he was concerned primarily with the realities of the colonial situation.[8]

Herbart's priorities were anti-colonialism and social change, not sexual satisfaction, though attraction to Soviet workers, when he lived in the USSR, joined the politically useful and the sexually agreeable. Herbart's first acquaintance with colonialism produced 'shame' at being French when he saw a soldier intentionally trip up an Arab prostitute in Kairouan, Tunisia. In black Africa, he castigated the hypocritical sentiments of the civilising mission that overlay pure exploitation, and the duplicity of the administration claiming to protect indigenes but furthering profit-making. Herbart denounced the machinations of private companies that persuaded the state to build dams, plant cotton and allow employment of African labourers for nominal pay. He commented on lack of medical care, the practice of transporting workers indiscriminately from one region to another, the wild-eyed projects of colonial promoters. At the time, Herbart, like many leftist inter-war writers, was not opposed to colonialism as such – they hoped that it at least would spread the ideals of liberty, equality and socialism – but to the inhumane practices of private entrepreneurs and public officials. Later, however, he came to question the whole colonial system.

> The most useful work of the anti-colonialist, I wrote, did not consist in rejecting colonisation *in toto* in the name of humanitarian or social principles, but in showing in high relief, every time it appears, the opposition between the interests of the colonialising nation and one or another group of private interests which pillage the colonies. Today, I cannot keep from thinking that such an opinion leaves aside the essential question.

The question, he now felt, was the right of non-European populations to their identity and freedom.[9]

For Herbert, homosexual desires marched alongside political commitment, but his writings gave a secondary place to erotic interests. For another writer with a similar career and opinions, Daniel Guérin, the two were more intimately joined. Born into a wealthy Parisian family in 1904, and heir to the Hachette publishing fortune, Guérin rebelled against his upbringing, joined the socialist movement and throughout his long life – he died in 1988 – participated actively in libertarian, socialist and anarchist politics. After studying at the prestigious Lycée Louis-le-Grand, Guérin published his first book of poems in 1922, his verses receiving praise from François Mauriac and Colette. His military service completed, Guérin began to distance himself from the bourgeois and *belles-lettres* milieux, taking a job in a bookshop in the poor Barbès neighbourhood of Paris and associating with young proletarians: sturdy workers captured Guérin's attention both sexually and politically.

Several years later, Guérin (not wholly cutting ties to his milieu) went to the Levant as director of the Beirut branch of the Hachette book company, the sojourn in the French outpost his first experience of imperialism. 'That, very simply, taught me about the phenomenon of colonialism,' he remembered, shocked that, in the mandated territory, 'the French had often conducted themselves like brutes, like savages'. The sight of indigenes hanged for petty crimes, and of the abuses carried out by soldiers, instilled in him hatred for militarism and colonialism. In 1930, Guérin went on holiday to the Orient, his cases filled with volumes by Marx, Trotsky, Sorel, Gandhi, Jaurès and Lenin. After Bangkok and Singapore, he arrived in Indo-China, 'in a conquered country', finding himself in Vietnam during the Yen-Bay rebellion. The 'insolence of the colonials', the 'bloody repression' and attempts at 'extermination' of nationalist Vietnamese intellectuals appalled him – Guérin noted the irony of intellectuals reciting Hugo's verses as they waited to be executed. He was struck by the 'merciless exploitation' in the mines of Hongkai, the 'manhunts' directed at dissidents, and the harassment that his own renegade political opinions provoked from French colonists.[10]

Overseas experiences were thus formative influences in Guérin's deepening commitment to socialism and anti-colonialism. Returning to France, rather than settling into a middle-class environment, he took a job in a factory in Brest and joined the communist-affiliated trade union. Then Guérin moved back to Paris, to work as a typographer and live in working-class Belleville, where he found friends and sexual partners, participated in syndicalist activity and contributed to leftist newspapers – the happiest years of his life, he recalled. Becoming well known as a radical intellectual, Guérin went to Germany, just as Hitler came to power, to investigate the plight of workers, and he published books on the 'brown plague' and on fascism and capitalism. He also married and fathered a daughter; lifelong companionship with his wife never made him abandon homosexual activities. After the victory of the Popular Front, Guérin dedicated himself to trade union militancy, joined a radical faction of the socialist movement and agitated for the Republican cause in Spain.

In 1939, Guérin travelled to Oslo to co-ordinate anti-war activities, and he was in Norway when German forces invaded. Taken prisoner as a foreigner and revolutionary, Guérin was held until 1942, when he managed to escape to France. He then threw himself into writing – books on the 1789 Revolution, studies of colonialism, works on sexuality. He continued trade union activities, and made friends with other renegade intellectuals, such as Jean-Paul Sartre and Marguerite Duras.

Guérin protested at attempts to re-establish French colonial order after the Second World War, and denounced the 1945 massacre of Algerian nationalists in Sétif. He met Ho Chi Minh at a dinner in the French capital. Guérin travelled to the United States in 1946 to study the American labour movement, concerned in particular by the plight of blacks. By the late 1950s, he established links with the Fédération Communiste Libertaire, among the few French political parties to support Algerian nationalists in their war of independence. He befriended the moderate leader Messali Hadj, though also sympathising with the more radical Front de Libération Nationale (FLN). In 1958, Guérin joined many of France's leading intellectuals in signing the 'Manifesto of 121', protesting conscription for military service in Algeria. A book entitled *Au Service des colonisés*, many newspaper articles, demonstrations and petitions counted among Guérin's political activities.

After Algeria won independence in 1962, Guérin maintained interest in North African affairs, writing bitterly about the assassination of the democratic leader Ahmed Ben Bella and the institution of a virtual military dictatorship in Algeria under Houari Boumediene. More books on Algeria followed, then a volume on Marxism and anarchism, as well as a study of Cuba (although Guérin refused to idealise Castro, and rejected his revolution as a model of socialism). Meanwhile, Guérin began publicly to discuss sexuality, and homosexuality in particular, with a book on the Kinsey report and another on homosexual figures and the law. From 1956 he collaborated with the homophile emancipation organisation Arcadie (founded two years previously). Novels, plays, autobiographical writings and newspaper articles continued Guérin's manifold militant activities in the 'New Left' of the 1960s and other radical groups afterwards. Until his death, Guérin took an active part in libertarian activities, supporting anti-colonial efforts by the PLO in Palestine, the IRA in Northern Ireland and Kanaks in New Caledonia. He meanwhile surrounded himself with ideological disciples, family members (he was a proud grandfather) and lovers – at the end of his life, he had a five-year relationship with a man sixty years his junior.[11]

Guérin was a man of immense integrity, never abandoning political principles, speaking out for unpopular causes, openly assuming his homosexuality. (He also appreciated good food and wine, the comforts of privileged life to which his background and wealth gave access.) He enjoyed the life of the mind and the pleasures of the body, acknowledging that the two were not always reconciled. Guérin's sexual tastes were broad, and his appetite protean; hunky French workmen, the comrades in political struggles, most incited his physical desires and fantasies. When young, Guérin had several homosexual experiences overseas: a relatively long liaison with a French sailor in Beirut, a night with a Moroccan spahi and a tryst with a servant in a Vietnamese hotel.[12] Guérin, however, did not seek out exotic lovers. Connections between the sexual and the political – the homosexual and the anti-colonial – did not reflect so much a personal attraction to foreign partners as a wider ideological commitment.

Guérin nevertheless appreciated male beauty wherever he found it. In a 1962 text, he evoked men who had excited his sexual and political interests, the aesthetic (and catholic) appreciation of male beauty that joined with political militancy. He described passengers at the Saint-Charles rail station in

Marseilles, a veritable meeting-place of France and the empire. Pale northern tourists with rucksacks headed south for the sun and sand of the Mediterranean, while olive-skinned, dark-headed southerners caught the train to Paris and northern industrial centres. Guérin noticed soldiers, 'because this was during the Algerian war':

> strapping peasants harnessed up for the kill, uprooted for years from villages that now had no men, passive, solid and bovine, bewildered, proud and ashamed of their transformation into tigers; unaware commandos or parachutists with rosy skins and strong jaws, with the hands of killers...[and] swarms of more pacific, more decorative and less useful seamen, great thin white birds.

The troops presented a spectacle of masculinity:

> grown men and youths, rough ones and tender ones, pimps and choir-boys, beardless and moustachioed, slender, milky arms and bulging dark biceps, those who liked to kill and those horrified at doing so, those who cruised with a magnetic glance and those who, with averted eyes, avoided love.

Guérin remarked, too, on passengers from the colonies:

> Arabs arriving and leaving, a separate people, clustering together, speaking a language with guttural sounds, wary and isolated from the conquerors, more male than them, great lords reduced to the rank of subalterns but galvanised by a collective will, trudging along in their old shoes, in ances-tral fashion, with gauche gestures, jostled, badly dressed and sad, but among whom shone – made more triumphant by the contrast with this misery – the dark odalisque looks of the most handsome Alis, the most beautiful Ahmeds.

Here, too, were Africans:

> civilians and military men, one foot in their tribe and the other in the West, ebony colossuses with a dancing gait, long muscles, lips that seemed swelled by or for kissing, with childlike laughter, gentle, good and carnal, but armoured with disdainful pride at the idea of independence, and shud-dering at contact with these descendants of slave-traders separated from nature and the nourishing earth and hot sun by their too fragile skin, sweating needlessly, yet attentive to the white girls both yearning for and fleeing the black phallus.[13]

Guérin's reaction to these men – descriptions of whom, despite empathy with the oppressed, do not avoid colonialist and racial stereotypes – was sexual and political. Indeed, everywhere and throughout his life, Guérin avowed, his immediate reaction to men was sexual. Writing about himself in the third person, he observed: 'The shining bronze of the Sinhalese and the Khmers, the muscled ebony of the Africans, the stature of the Yankees and the blond Scandinavians had made him forget his "country"', even if he always kept an erotic preference for 'the Parisian street kid, the blue-eyed Breton, the robust Alsatian, the nonchalant Occitan....He could not even choose between Bob, Olaf, these pale civilised men, and Blackie, sodomitical, black and naked, in the tropical jungle.'[14] Guérin realised that the sexual, and social, relationships between a wealthy Paris intellectual and ordinary workers and poor foreigners were not uncomplicated, no matter how profound his socialist and anarchist sentiments. An imaginary dialogue highlighted the problems. Guérin's proletarian interlocutor challenges him for desiring only his beautiful body, not seeking real friendship with someone so different.

> When they [his friends and partners] came from a colonised country, when they belonged to an oppressed race, communication with them was even more difficult. He might well think of himself – he might well say with total sincerity – that he was their equal and their brother, but he nevertheless found himself in the position of the coloniser and the white man: it was not just the damnable question of money which created a chasm between them and him, but also the fact of colonialism and race.[15]

Guérin tried to overcome the great divide by political engagement. His *prise de conscience* had come aboard a ship in the Red Sea as he returned from the East, reflecting on his experiences of colonialism in Asia and, too, his sexual encounters:

> There is a formidable strength in me, which has been conferred by my homosexuality. I must commit this strength to the service of something much greater than debauchery...that is, the struggle for the liberation of the proletariat. I created a symbiosis between the two things....The two things were forever associated.

Henceforth he allied sexual and political emancipation, socialism and what he referred to as 'phallism' – a neologism invented to 'mean simply the taste, purely sexual, for masculinity'. Guérin admitted that, in crowds of workers, he noticed handsome men, rather than care-worn women. He obtained great emotional satisfaction (and sexual pleasure) fraternising with labourers in Europe or overseas, sharing rooms in hostels, drinking in cafés, attending meetings, having sex with lusty workers untroubled about sexual transgression. Sex had provided impetus to political activism, even if Guérin initially hid his proclivities from puritanical comrades in the radical movement. Books with such titles as *In the Service of the Colonised People* and *Homosexuality and Revolution* illustrated complementary aspects of his persona and his public engagement.

Guérin's personal life, including his homosexuality and his political beliefs –
socialism, anarchism, anti-racism, anti-colonialism, for he was *de tous les
combats* – were inseparable. An epigraph to one volume of autobiography
affirms: 'I believe for my part, that a single and identical vital force...has
propelled my existence, both political and carnal.' His 'revolutionary options'
and his 'amatory penchants' formed two sides of the same coin, which he had
no ability or need to separate. These embodied 'two parts of the same vital flux:
one, the priority, was aimed towards a radical transformation of society; the
other, in complementary fashion, but just as urgent, was directed at the love of
men'.[16] The moral of his apologia for homosexuality and political militancy, in
Eux et lui, was simply: 'It is necessary to change the world.'[17] That change would
emancipate workers, colonised people and homosexuals. Such ideas were not
foreign to the rebels who occupied the lecture theatres of the University of Paris
in 1968 and set up FHAR in 1970 – actions in which Guérin, by then a senior
figure in French public life, enthusiastically participated.

Herbart and Guérin led parallel lives, born a year apart into similar milieux,
first becoming aware of imperialism during trips to Arabic countries in the early
1920s, and visiting Indo-China at the beginning of the following decade. They
supported Spanish Republicans and French *Résistants*. They joined Marxist parties
and cast their lot with the proletarian struggle. Each was sexually attracted most
to working-class men, though they had occasional adventures with African, Arab
and Asian workers. They wrote in a variety of genres, although Herbart's personal
problems curtailed his literary and political work after the late 1950s. For both
Herbart and Guérin, sexual liberation went hand in hand with emancipation of
proletarians at home and colonised people overseas.

Jean Sénac

Herbart and Guérin came from metropolitan France and learned about
European colonialism during overseas travels. Their political engagement with
anti-colonialism entered into a general ideological commitment, and France
remained, literally and figuratively, the base for their actions. Another
Frenchman, Jean Sénac, came from the colonies, and was viscerally attached to
his native Algeria. His anti-colonialism grew out of lived experiences as a *pied-
noir*, and an evocation of his homeland – landscape, political conditions, culture
and young men – is omnipresent in his prose and poetry. Sénac is almost
unknown in English (none of his works is available in translation) and is only
recently becoming better known in France. In the early 1960s, he was considered the finest French-language poet in Algeria. In present-day Algeria, torn
apart by violence and political turmoil, he remains, at least to some, a symbol of
a liberal and peaceful country, and of the highest hopes of the Algerian revolution, seen too as a martyr to intolerance and the betrayal of those very ideals.[18]

Sénac is one of the most fascinating and – because of the circumstances of
the last years of his life and his death – most tragic figures in the history of
France's involvement with Algeria.[19] To begin with the end: after joining the

Algerian nationalists during the war of independence, and thus being considered a traitor by many Frenchmen, including most fellow *pieds-noirs*, Sénac lived in Algiers after 1962. He became a literary celebrity, but as the years passed, especially after Boumediene's coup in 1965, he increasingly felt that the promise of the post-colonial regime was not being fulfilled; he became more and more critical of a government that did not welcome dissent. Disciples and youthful friends gathered around as he served as a figure of political resistance and literary innovation. Sénac meanwhile lived openly as a homosexual, and his poetry adopted more explicitly erotic themes and images. In 1973, in Algiers, Sénac was murdered at the age of forty-seven. Algerian officials claimed he was the victim of an *affaire des moeurs*, killed by a sexual partner or thief. Others have suggested that he was assassinated with the complicity of authorities, angered that Algeria's most accomplished poet was a *pied-noir*, a man of European and Christian background, openly homosexual, an outspoken critic of the government and an influential figure among budding intellectuals.[20]

Sénac was born in 1926, in Béni-Saf, near Oran in western Algeria, a poor town of 12,000 miners, fishers and farmers; most of the Europeans there were Spanish settlers or their descendants.[21] On his mother's side, Sénac was of Spanish origin; his grandfather migrated to Algeria from Andalusia to work in the hematite mines. Sénac was born an illegitimate child after the probable rape of his mother, a charlady; he knew little about his father, not even his full name, other than that he was a hairdresser. (Sénac was the name of the poet's stepfather, whom his mother divorced in the early 1930s.) He mused that his father may have been a gypsy or an Arab, though without evidence. Sénac's Spanish ancestry and poor childhood bear a great similarity with the family life of Albert Camus, the most famous *pied-noir* writer, as described in his posthumously published autobiographical novel *Le Premier homme*. Camus, indeed, felt kinship with Sénac, whose early works impressed him. The two corresponded, Camus addressing Sénac as *mi hijo* ('my son' in Spanish) and aiding in the publication of his first book. They broke in 1956 because of differing views to *Algérie française*, but Sénac dedicated a collection of poems to Camus after the death of the Nobel Prize winner.[22]

Sénac's late adolescence coincided with the Second World War and the Vichy regime, during which he wrote and published his first poems, including a paean, 'A Pétain', whose cause he nevertheless quickly abandoned. After ending schooling without taking a *baccalauréat*, Sénac taught for a year in the Mascara region, and then served for two years, from 1944 to 1946, in the French Air Force, stationed near Algiers. For part of the following two years, he was hospitalised in a sanatorium, suffering from pleurisy and typhoid fever. During this time, Sénac read widely – Baudelaire, Gide and Rimbaud numbered among his favourite authors. He went through a mystical and religious phase, then a crisis of faith and probably also had his first sexual encounter. As he convalesced, Sénac made contacts with artists and writers, both Europeans and Algerians, and was influenced by the leading French Algerian writers of the day, among them Robert Randau, Edmond Brua and Sadia Lévy.

In 1949, Sénac secured a job broadcasting on Radio Alger. Over the next few years, he took part in setting up a literary group, the Cercle Lélian, and editing two short-lived literary journals (*Soleil* in 1950, *Terrasses* in 1952), which published writers such as Mohammed Dib, Kateb Yacine, Jean Daniel and Sénac himself. In 1950, having won a scholarship, Sénac went to metropolitan France for the first time, staying there for almost two years. There he met Camus and the poet René Char, his hero and model.

When he went back to North Africa, Sénac resumed his broadcasting job. But in 1954, the year the Algerian war of independence began, he was forced to resign from Radio Alger when his anti-colonialist sentiments and identification with Algerian nationalists – he sometimes wrote poetry under the pen name Yahia El-Ouahrani (John the Oranese) – became too pronounced. The same year, in a series edited by Camus, the prestigious Parisian publisher Gallimard issued the first collection of Sénac's work, called simply *Poèmes*, with a preface by Char.

With the start of the Algerian war, Sénac moved to France, and remained there for almost all of the next eight years, until the end of the conflict. He frequented the cafés of Saint-Germain-des-Près, then the centre of the Paris avant-garde, meeting philosophers, painters and other writers, as well as the young men whom he sought out for sex. He also associated with other *pieds-noirs* sympathetic to Algerian nationalism.

Sénac's activities, including work on behalf of the FLN, the Algerian independence movement, are not entirely clear; among other undertakings, he helped organise a clandestine printing press for the Algerian nationalist newspaper. In various journals, Sénac published politically committed poetry favourable to the nationalists, as well as impassioned essays in which he pleaded for fellow *pieds-noirs* and metropolitan Frenchmen to comprehend Arab Algerians' grievances, support independence and join in building a harmonious multi-racial society. 'Lettre à un jeune Français d'Algérie' and '"Pieds-noirs", mes frères' rank among the most moving documents of the Algerian war. Despite pro-Algerian undertakings, Sénac escaped harassment from the police and political authorities, probably because he never became involved in such activities as transporting money or weapons for the FLN.

In 1962, as almost a million French citizens fled Algeria, Sénac joyfully moved in the opposite direction, settling again in Algiers.[23] His poems now celebrated the achievement of independence and the Algerians who had fought for liberation, vaunting the ideals of the revolution and the new society. Sénac became involved with an association of Algerian authors, helped establish an art gallery, found employment broadcasting cultural programmes on an Algerian radio station and edited two anthologies of French-language Algerian poetry. For a while, he held a position as adviser at the Ministry of Education, and travelled on a diplomatic passport to the Soviet Union, where he participated in an international conference of writers, and made friends with Yevgeny Yevtushenko. (He also met distinguished visitors to Algeria, such as Che Guevara.)

Sénac maintained close ties with France, regularly visiting his adopted son, Jacques Miel, and friends, and staying at a house he and Miel purchased in southern France; a shepherd's lodging, the 'Maison du Berger', and the surrounding landscape figure often in one cycle of poems, *Le Torrent de Baïn*. Although he remained a French national Sénac was passionately devoted to Algeria – he asked for Algerian citizenship on several occasions, but it was never granted to him. He also never learned Arabic (though he once made an effort to do so) and showed no interest in conversion to Islam. Sénac's dream for Algeria was a nation dominated by Muslims, but a country in which Muslims, Christians and Jews, and Arabs, Berbers and the descendants of the French, Spanish, Italian and Maltese would all have their place – a vision that circumstances sadly did not allow.

Increasingly, Sénac was at odds with the Algerian government. His public statements and poems criticised political leaders for corruption, betrayal of wartime ideals and failure to address poverty and unemployment. In 1967, he resigned as secretary of the Union des Ecrivains Algériens, though he continued to be active in literary circles. Despite political disenchantment, the period around 1965 was a time of happiness in Sénac's private life. The scene turned bleak around 1967 in a climate of growing political and social intolerance, and, in Sénac's life, episodic depression and loneliness. His opposition to the Boumediene regime became more pointed, and, in an introduction to a 1971 anthology, he proclaimed: 'The Revolution seems to be on the march, but there are still profiteers, abandoned children, alienated women, oppressive taboos, errors and ambivalence.'[24] A poem written in the same year denounced the government's responsibility for the dirt and vulgarity of Algeria, the ruins of the revolution and 'hatred of difference', concluding provocatively with a line about 'long hard corteges [moving] towards green and white crematoria' – green and white are the colours of the Algerian flag.[25]

The Algerian government, in 1971, dismissed Sénac from his post at Radio Alger – just as French colonial authorities had fired him for political reasons almost two decades earlier. Financial difficulties, always present, became worse, and he had to move from a sunny, beachside flat at Pointe-Pescade to a dark, damp room in the centre of Algiers. Harassment increased, as insults and even stones were thrown at him. Sénac's mood was grim, and he told acquaintances he feared for his life. His poems foreshadowed a violent death, which came in his tiny and squalid flat in the Rue Elisée-Reclus. The government refused Sénac burial in a Muslim cemetery (as he had wished) and forbade publication of a paid death announcement in Algiers's newspaper. Sénac was interred in a European cemetery, his funeral attended by faithful friends. The gravestone was inscribed in French and Arabic, and ornamented with a drawing of the sun, the symbol Sénac used as part of his signature. Algerian police questioned thirty youths in connection with Sénac's death, and a young man was tried, convicted and sentenced to five years' imprisonment.

Sénac was a slightly built and plain-looking man who sometimes sported a long and thick beard. He enjoyed the company of well-known people, literary friends and Algerian lads. He was charming, but temperamental and proud. Disorganised in much of his daily life, he was meticulous in writing and revising his poems – often during the middle of the night, as he was very nocturnal, scribbling on odd bits of paper. He never smoked, ate little, slept much. He seldom had money, and lived on modest salaries in Algeria and hand-outs from friends, as well as from occasional temporary jobs, such as work at a horticultural *lycée* or as secretary to a professor of mathematics in Paris. By the end of his life, he was practically destitute.

Sénac's writings originally appeared in books, published in limited editions by small presses, and sometimes in rather obscure periodicals. A good deal of his poetry was published posthumously, and only recently have his poems been collected in a volume of almost 800 pages.[26] Sénac wrote many occasional pieces in prose, particularly political commentary and articles on Algerian art; some of these were gathered together in the catalogue of an exhibition held on the tenth anniversary of his death.[27] Other works, including poems, prose and letters, have recently also been collected.[28] Posthumously published have been a volume of autobiography (which he labelled a 'novel'), *Ebauche du père*, and a prose and verse journal from 1954.

Literary critics have analysed Sénac's work in terms of his place in modern French poetry, and his kinship with such other writers as René Char and Paul Eluard, as well as his place in the evolution of French-language North African writing. Sénac's *algérianité* and affiliation with classical Arabic poets have also been scrutinised. His work, and life, have been seen in terms of a great pendulum swing between an ascending cycle of hope and a descending one of despair. The *œuvre* has also been interpreted as a perpetual exile: from the ancestral homeland of Spain, from his Algerian *patrie* during the war, from the artistic circles of Paris. The recurrent theme of the illegitimate son's search for an absent father has received attention, as well as the importance of the mother figure, as symbol both of his own beloved but difficult mother and Algeria as mother-country. Commentators have isolated other threads, notably religion and painting, which traverse his work, as well as the general theme of the Mediterranean, typified in the physical and psychic images of the minotaur and labyrinth. Sénac's innovative and idiosyncratic use of language and punctuation – he invented a new 'irony mark' – has been a focus of scholarship. Discussion of his homosexuality has been more limited, as some critics appear manifestly uncomfortable with the subject, and downplay its influence in his life and work, or dissolve his lust and love for men in analyses of generalised sexual urges.[29]

Sénac's first collection, *Poèmes*, made reticent references to eroticism, and evoked Algeria, with poems about his mother and the North African landscape. The book was well received in France, and earned a review in *The Times Literary Supplement*. *Poèmes* appeared in the first year of the Algerian War, when Sénac was also living through a love affair recorded in his *Journal* and a series of poems, *Leçons d'Edgard*. Already Sénac had written several political pieces, calling on other writers and compatriots to denounce the ravages of colonialism, and condemning the killings taking place in Algeria. Now his attention turned to the political struggle.[30]

Sénac and Algerian nationalism

Sénac's poetry, especially from the mid-1950s onwards, always bespoke his political engagement. '1er novembre 1954' recalled the beginning of the war of independence. Another poem described the killing of seven Algerian demonstrators in Paris on 14 July 1953: '*Pour la fête des hommes libres / ils ont massacrés mes amis / peau brune sur les pavés gris / à Paris comme tu est triste / triste et sévère pour ma race*' ('On the festival of free men / they massacred my friends / brown skin on the grey pavement / in Paris how sad you are / sad and harsh for my race').[31] Yet another eulogised an Algerian who, after slapping a policeman, had been tortured and killed. 'Pieds et poings liés...' memorialised Algerians who died in police custody. 'Fait-Divers' evoked the slums of Algiers, and 'Honte Honte Honte' damned violence inflicted on the homeless. 'Fresque de Tilioua' was an ode to the *moujaheddin*. Other works witnessed to colonialism and revolutionary struggles elsewhere, with references to Dien Bien Phu, the Americano-Vietnamese War and Palestine, poems entitled 'Angola', 'Demain Lumumba' and 'Pour Saluer Cuba'. 'Ode à l'Amérique africaine' paid tribute to the black civil rights movement in the United States. The poems constituted statements of Sénac's political commitments, and his hopes for success of a revolutionary struggle of oppressed people throughout the world. A few, however, read as agitprop. Perhaps his most famous line, written in 1963 in the height of post-independence jubilation in Algeria, apostrophised the revolution: '*Tu est belle comme un comité de gestion*' ('You are as beautiful as a workers' management committee').[32] Fellow writers ridiculed the simile, and Sénac himself good-naturedly parodied it in later works.

Sénac's unyielding attachment to Algeria had begun as appreciation of his homeland's beauties. An essay on 'Oran ou les statues sous la peau (Mythologie des Buveurs de Sel)' lyrically represented the city in the early morning, with swimmers on the beach, old ladies going to mass, ships in the harbour, bougainvillea and ficus gleaming in the sun.[33] The childhood he recollected in *Ebauche du père* hardly predestined militantly pro-Algerian sentiment. Indeed, from Sénac's modest milieu emerged many intractable supporters of *Algérie française*: 'My childhood took place far from the Arab world, of which I was allowed to remain unaware, or when it was spoken about, it was to recount the disgusting acts of "dirty *bicots*".'[34] In describing the everyday life and poverty of his youth, Sénac wondered: 'How was our life different from that of the other poor people – the Arabs?'[35] Nevertheless, he admitted:

> We were happy in those times, I feel bad in saying it....All we had to do was to close our eyes to the misery of others. We just had to be happy with our miserable privileges. Children of the sun, drunk on its rays...bronzed right to our marrow.[36]

Gradually Sénac was politicised. Becoming aware of the social realities of Algeria, meeting like-minded intellectuals, perhaps realising his marginal position as a homosexual, encountering more Muslims after he moved to Algiers – all helped bring about the decision, unpredicted and dangerous, to support the *indépendantistes*. 'La Patrie', written in 1954 and included in *La Matinale de mon peuple*, inexorably and emblematically slides from a word-picture of the 'good life' in Algeria to a critique of colonialism:

> Mother Algeria, our unfailing love. Here the coffee is good. And it's cheap. The cuisine is rich, and the wine red. The spice adds fire even to our speech....My fathers imposed on this shore the civilisation of masters deprived of their honour and their true prestige. Were they so blind or so stupid?...Through them, we have lived in this land as nostalgic adventurers, held hostage by exile. We have defined a hypocritical 'superiority', but Virtue, grave and incandescent, took refuge behind a wall, or a veil, or in the dome of a mosque. My people surround me and are murmuring. They are preparing an awakening, relayed from their mountain-tops. Together we carry the stigmata.[37]

Here Sénac, grandson of a Spanish exile, refuses to shirk the conquest his forebears visited on Algeria, yet of which he, too, had been victim – the exile of migration, the poverty of the lower classes, the disdain with which the Spanish were viewed in Algeria. Yet, marked with the stigmata of colonialism, he pledges allegiance to Algeria, land and nation. Sénac never denied his background and proudly claimed his *pieds-noir* heritage, hoping that others would realise the merits of the Algerian cause – indeed most of his political manifestos were directed at *pieds-noirs*.

In 1956, Sénac published a 'Lettre à un jeune Français d'Algérie'. Addressed to a real or imagined friend, the son of a successful winegrower opposed to independence, it praises the settler's love of Algeria, but then accuses him:

> You have never walked around the Rue de la Lyre in Algiers at three o'clock on a December morning. You have not seen the kids who are dying of cold amidst the vermin, innocent children who are chased and kicked, stamped on the heads by police boot-heels! You have not noticed the gaping wound in the heart of your workmen. '*Bicot, melon,* good-for-nothing, thief, do-nothing, figtree-face' – words more powerful than drilling-machines, words that end up leaving holes so big that the winds of vengeance blow through them without stop. Dignity: it might be good if you admitted that all men need it and, if it is torn from them, they will end up taking it back.

The poor and colonised had now risen up. Sénac proclaimed that 'the lords and masters have lost the game in Algeria....The Algerian people have won the battle.' Perhaps colonialists could hold out for a maximum of five years, he predicted (presciently), but resistance to independence was in vain. Violence and torture committed to forestall it were proof of humiliation and frustration, defence of a lost cause. Sénac suggested an alternative to the *pieds-noirs'* promise either to die in defence of *Algérie française* or to flee – the famous option of '*la valise ou le cercueil*'. Sénac pleaded with them to help build a new, independent Algeria: 'Algeria will be made with us or without us, but if it is made without us, I feel that some of the leaven will be missing in the dough.' Changing metaphors, but in equally heartfelt and colourful language, Sénac repeated that Europeans, too, had 'a number of bricks to add to our shared dwelling' in an Algeria that would unite the Orient and the Occident: 'Algeria should be the crucible of this culture and this peaceful message.' Now was the moment to decide: 'The time has come to choose, to opt for the reality of a country over the illusions of a race.'[38]

Sénac's hopes went unfulfilled. The following year brought an escalation of violence, the 'Battle of Algiers' and reports of increasing torture by the French, as well as brutalities committed by nationalists. *Le Soleil sous les armes*, published in 1957, was the work of someone fully *engagé*, personally and intellectually, in the Algerian struggle. The book called for the creation of a 'National Front of Algerian Thought': 'Poetry and [political] resistance are two edges of the same blade,' affirmed the essay, as Sénac discussed works of young Algerian poets and the role of literature in the campaign for independence.[39]

In 1958, Sénac wrote '"Pieds-noirs", mes frères', a passionate denunciation of colonialism and the uncompromising opposition of *pieds-noirs* to an Algerian independence that seemed ineluctable.[40] He began with a powerful recapitulation of Algeria's colonial history, both an indictment and a tribute to European settlers:

> They call you '*pieds-noirs*', a phrase that already sets out an agenda. A legend of tears as well. You landed on this soil wearing your boots and polished shoes. What a black contrast with the bare feet of children in rags! These little 'rats' have grown up, washing your floors, carrying your parcels, hoeing your fields and pruning your vines. I say 'your', but I should say 'our'. My ancestors came in espadrilles. But it did not take long for them to put on little boots. Even big boots! On this soil trodden by our pointed shoes, hope nevertheless sprang up, tougher than couch-grass. But let us not talk about the past, because then, of course, we would have to talk about the expropriation of land, about blasphemous laws, about prisons and massacres – but also about marshes that were drained, poor settlers exhausted by their labours, schools and hospitals. Let the dead bury their dead. Those who have given their life for the Algerian Revolution over the past seven years have left us this precious heritage: life, yes, their life and not death.

Sénac continued that for a century propagandists and politicians had duped *pieds-noirs* by saying that Algeria was theirs alone. In a last effort at reconciliation, he solicited the *colons*: '*Pieds-noirs*, brothers....the Algerian Revolution makes you so afraid – these "assassins", "terrorists", "barbarians", but look, they

are greeting you! They are telling you that the house is big enough for all.'
Independent Algeria would be hospitable to Europeans if only *pieds-noirs* would
give up 'this insolent image…of glory and crime….the History of France, the
Colonial Empire, the Civilising Mission, churches and schools and hospitals!'
Rejecting colonialist propaganda, the exploitation of rich capitalists and the
demagogy of those ready 'to drag you anew into vengeance and bloodshed to
defend their nostalgic petty interests and superannuated visions', *pieds-noirs*, in
league with Algerian nationalists, could become 'new pioneers, as were your
ancestors, but in a more exalted adventure'.[41] Few heeded Sénac's invitation,
and his fine, but utopian, even naïve, sentiments. Fighting raged for four more
years, and, when the war against independence was lost, unreconciled *pieds-noirs*
created vigilante terrorist groups engaging in scorched-earth tactics to keep
'their' Algeria out of Muslim hands. Finally most *pieds-noirs* were 'repatriated' to
a motherland the majority had never known.

Sénac returned to Algiers in 1962, despairing that all but a few *pieds-noirs*
had rejected Algeria, but filled with hope for the future. Having won its independence, Algeria seemed a beacon in the Third World. Sénac championed the
revolution in verse and political actions, supporting policies aimed at creating a
socialist and democratic state.[42] Yet dreams for an egalitarian, free and open
society vanished as a new elite enriched itself, poverty persisted and unemployment grew, and a military junta took over the government. By the mid-1960s,
his writings openly criticised the government and lamented the failures of post-
colonial Algerian society. Nowhere, however, did Sénac abjure Algeria or
suggest that he had made the wrong choice, either in 1954 or in 1962, or when
the government began to treat him as an embarrassment, then as an enemy: 'I
have always….honestly, simply, with lucidity and fervour – and whatever price
there was to pay…– served my country and my art.'[43] In a poem published in
the mid-1960s, he affirmed:

> *Cette terre est la mienne avec son amère liturgie,*
> *Ses éclats orduriers, ses routes torves,*
> *L'âme saccagée, le peuple las….*[44]

Homosexuality in Sénac's work and life

With the exception of one affair with a woman, Sénac was homosexual. As an
adolescent, he fantasised about a Legionnaire who was briefly his mother's
partner, but, because of religious upbringing and social mores, struggled to
accept his homosexuality. From the early 1950s, he enjoyed sex and romance.
One partner, Edgard, the *pied-noir* with whom Sénac had an affair in 1954,
became the subject of a book of prose recollections and poetry; set in Algiers in
the months before the start of the war of independence, it counts among
Sénac's most touching works. Edgard was a 17-year-old, with the face of a boxer
and feline grace. Sénac recounts their walks on the beach, evenings at the
cinema and nights of love-making. Edgard proved inconstant and capricious,

however, causing Sénac pain when he failed to visit or acted fecklessly and mischievously, the dark side of his sunny adolescence that so attracted the poet. Sénac, too, was tempted, sometimes successfully, by other young men he met, even if he tired of casual sex and dreamed of 'a pure, simplified, exalted, clean, upright love, which leads us to Truth, Order and doubtless also to God'. Yet he embraced sexual pleasure with French and Algerian ephebes, 'generous, multiple, risky, unmeasured, unusual love. *L'amour fou.*' As Edgard receded, 'already here is Mustapha, young, strong, handsome, sweet…and also Slimane, a stallion [*bête à plaisir*] brimming with real affection, quick but delirious'.[45]

In Algiers and Paris, Sénac found many sexual partners.[46] He fell in love (though it is uncertain whether the relationship was sexual) with Patrick MacEvoy, the striking son of a painter, whom Sénac met in 1960. Sénac purchased the 'Maison du Berger' in the Drôme partly to be near MacEvoy, whose father despatched him to a *lycée* in the region. Other significant partners included a Parisian *métis* whose father was a French official in Asia, and an Algerian painter named Mustapha Akmoun. Not all of the young men who became Sénac's protégés and companions, however, were sexual partners.

The most important meeting in Sénac's life was, without doubt, that with Jacques Miel in 1956. Miel was a sixteen-year-old Parisian worker living from his own means. It turned out to be a fateful encounter for both men, although Miel was not at all homosexually inclined. Regardless of this fact, Sénac was determined not to lose the friendship for anything in the world, and Sénac and Miel from this time onwards maintained the relationship of a father to a son. For seventeen years, Miel was the shoulder on which Sénac would lean, and in his will he designated Miel his sole legatee.[47]

Sénac dedicated a number of poems to Miel, and many of his sexual contacts inspired poems giving voice to romantic pleasures or disappointments. Poems often set partners in context, with allusions to landscape and climate, particularly those evoking encounters in Algiers. The first, second and fifth stanzas of 'Brahim le Généreux' provide an example, as Sénac uses images of the desert and sea in hommage to Brahim Djaballah:

> *Tu m'as rendu la lumière et la paix,*
> *Le tournant de la montée abrupte,*
> *La science du puits et la pudeur de l'eau.*
> *La langue nouvelle perce entre les dents*
> *Comme le premier roseau dans la rocaille.*
> *Déjà la steppe sourit,*
> *Les arbres sont en route.*
> *De ce coeur desséché toi aussi tu fais un Domaine….*
>
> *Je suis irrigué de noblesse,*
> *Le figuier répand son visage.*
> *Citoyen du désert*
> *Il suffit que tu marches,*
> *Je n'avais jamais vu la mer aussi bleue!…*

> *Jamais la darse de l'Amirauté n'a été aussi belle,*
> *C'est parce qu'au désert la première audace a fleuri.*[48]

Sénac's poems chronicled his search for partners, often in night-time wanderings around Algiers. Some relationships and poems were romantic, others more crude, but all represented the possibility of exaltation, as in 'L'Exorcisme':

> *Le plus beau garçon possédé*
> *pour une place de ciné*
> *la plus belle fille troussée*
> *pour un dîner à bon marché*
> *la beauté se vend au rabais*
>
> *La beauté lui rendra sa justice*
> *et son éloge qui est l'amour*
> *ne plus la voir trainer de bar en pissotière*
> *à la recherche du jour*
>
> *Et que le nom soit dit une fois pour toutes*
> *Au nom du Père et du Fils et du Saint-Esprit*
> *Pour que le volcan crève la croûte*
> *Que l'eau apaise le volcan*
> *Que la terre tourne dans le sang*
> *Que la mort ne soit plus la clé de notre voûte.*[49]

The quest was not always successful, as young men refused their attentions or betrayed the poet's affection. In several lines from 'L'Abandon', using Sénac's favourite image of sun and light, the picture is one of frustrated attraction as he pursues the desired one, and day breaks:

> *Les pavés aux chevilles*
> *je marche je te cherche*
> *j'essaie d'acclimater ta fougère à ma flamme*
> *le jour n'appartient pas à l'âme qui se fend*
>
> *Je cours*
> *Qui reconnaît dans ces muscles un ange?...*
>
> *Si je t'avais trouvé*
> *J'aurais perdu la terre*
> *Troqué mon été contre ton hiver*
> *et Dieu sait si j'aime l'indolente clarté!*
>
> *Mais rien ne demeure*
> *du froid de la nuit*
> *qu'un soleil postiche*
> *qui ronge le fruit.*[50]

During the decade after 1954, Sénac's published work concentrated on politics, although explicit and implicit references to lovers, and a celebration of the beauty of Algerian youth, appear even in his most *engagé* collections, such as *Matinale de mon peuple* and *Citoyens de beauté*.[51] From the mid-1960s, poems are less overtly political, Sénac's earlier enthusiasm for the revolution tempered by the changes taking place in Algeria; sexual images become more explicit, but love is also conceived as spiritual. In *Avant-corps*, written in 1966–7, the theme of several poems is Jacob's biblical combat with the angel, interpreted by Sénac as also a sexual struggle.

'Diwân du Noûn', inspired by the symbolism of an Arabic letter, offers a sexualised dialogue between a master and his young friends. The cycle was written while looking from his Pointe-Pescade apartment at people on the beach, against a background of the sea and sun, Algiers at dawn and hot summer afternoons. The poems make reference to Algeria, Palestine and Vietnam, but evoke handsome youths, '*Adolescents dont la seule mémoire / provoque un orgasme farouche*' ('just the memory of such adolescents / provoked a fierce orgasm'). In 'Diwân du Noûn', Sénac developed a form of writing merging the body and the poem into what he called a *corpoème*: '*Tu tords ton maillot jusqu'à l'âme. / Je suis entre tes mains, ruisselant, le poème*' ('You wring your swimsuit right to the soul / I am between your hands, dripping, the poem').[52]

Later collections – including *Le Mythe du sperme-Méditerranée*, *A-Corpoème* and *dérisions et Vertige* (written between 1967 and 1972, but only published posthumously)[53] – continued to sound the poet's erotic and metaphysical desires and satisfactions, sometimes in obscure language and hermetic meaning. The title of the first brought together sex and the Mediterranean; that of *A-Corpoème* linked Sénac's new type of writing with 'A', his friend Akmoum. (Another invented word, '*spoerme*', joined sperm and poem.) A number of poems are erotic, lingering over the beauty of Algerian adolescents and sexual encounters, sometimes in explicit language. '*L'étranger me pénètre et c'est ton silence en moi qui hurle*' ('The foreigner [or stranger] penetrates me, and it is your silence that screams inside me'), from *A-Corpoème*, for instance. In the concluding poem of *Le Mythe du sperme-Méditerranée*, Sénac writes of the '*Soleil griffu plus transitoire / Qu'une goutte de sperme sur ma mâchoire*' ('A glint of sun more transitory / Than a drop of sperm on my cheek'),[54] and *dérisions et Vertige* contained a poem entitled 'L'Annuaire de l'anus'.[55] '*Ejacule-moi dans la bouche!*' ('Ejaculate into my mouth!'), from 'Drague-Appel-Doute' ('Cruising, Calling, Doubting') is certainly one of his least compromising lines.[56] The picture of Algiers is nevertheless bleaker – '*une ville de chardons*' ('a city of thistles') when angry boys shout abuse, women are cloistered in family houses and the smell of geranium and tomatoes mixes with that of urine. Frenzied quests for sex, despair at politics, self-questioning about the writer's craft and a growing blackness are only occasionally relieved by sun-drenched happiness.

'La Course', written in the early 1970s, illustrates the conjunction of homo-sexual sex, experimental and cathartic poetry, and Algeria in the work of Sénac's last, and pessimistic, years. The poem reads, in full:

> *Tu parles d'amour et d'amour. Je ne comprends*
> *Que la douleur des couilles qui n'ont que leur miroir*
> *Pour se vider. Tu parles de cheveux blonds, de poitrines*
> *Civilisées. Je ne comprends*
>
> *Que le sexe qui vrombit à vide sur les rocs.*
> *Il y a des motos énormes adolescentes qui dérapent*
> *Sur l'os iliaque. Et des continents qui*
> *Affleurent sous les tripots du cri.*
>
> *Je ne comprends*
> *Que les larmes où bafouillent des soucoupes volantes.*
> *Et des noms: Ahmed! Mahrez! Kamel! Antar!*
> *Oh, encule-moi! O Youcef, j'ai sucé jusqu'au Coran*
> *Ta course. Maintenant sur le sable*
>
> *Tu rentres dans le sablier. Tu coules*
> *A pic. Quel océan a pris ta place?*
> *Quelle planète habille ta queue?*
>
> *Le feu est invisible. Tu sais qu'il bouge aux cendres du poème. Je ne comprends*
> *Que la douleur du sexe-boomerang.*
> *Tu nous parles d'amour, d'amour, d'amour comme une momie qui déroule ses litanies d'or,*
> *Sa pustule. Je ne comprends*
> *Que l'abyssale douleur des couilles*
> *Qui refusent la déperdition.*
> *Plutôt le Vide que le Trou,*
> *Le Vide où peut croiser la Masse-Compacte-Spirituelle,*
> *Seul Présent concevable. Papa passé tu parles. Je ne comprends*
> *Que le ciel et la mer accouplés, jumeaux*
> *Bleus, licorne.*
>
> *Oooooo exil!*
> *L'abyssale douleur jusqu'à l'Os.*[57]

This elliptical and difficult poem, probably composed (like many from the period) in a moment of depression, is replete with specific references to Algeria and to Sénac's general themes. '*Papa passé*' notes the disappearance of the colonial '*Algérie de papa*', while '*cendres du poème*' may refer distantly to the burning of the Algiers library by the OAS in the closing phase of the war. Sénac's interlocutor talks about blond-headed 'civilised' Frenchmen, while the Frenchmen lust for Arabs. Exile – an ever-present theme for *pieds-noirs* – is evoked. Symbols of Algerian landscape, such as the sea, mix with those of technological modernity and consumer society, like sexy motorcycles. Sexual and metaphysical images echo through the poem: sand drips through the hourglass as the young man ejaculates on the beach. The poem rejects the love of which the narrator's erstwhile partner, or more likely a romantically inclined lover, talks incessantly. Here a sexual encounter is simply relief for discomfort in the genitals, little different from masturbation in front of a mirror – though there is intimation of spiritual enlightenment. One Arabic partner follows another as the narrator demands to be penetrated and engages in blasphemous fellatio, a race of lust. He is left with emptiness, an abyss preferable to the loneliness of solitude or a grave. At the end, sex may still be the cosmic coupling of sky and sea to produce a mythical unicorn (perhaps a metaphor for the homosexual), or for the exile from such philosophising, producing a cry of orgasmic pleasure and pain that pierces to the bone.

The sexuality that appears in Sénac's poems is important for several reasons. First, the way in which he wrote about homosexuality, particularly in the later poems, was rare in French literature of his time, displaying both lyrical evocations of carnal encounters and unembarrassed straightforwardness about the mechanics of sexual intercourse. After the allusions, euphemisms and aestheticising or historicising *mises-en-scène* of earlier authors, Sénac wrote in an open and provocative fashion. His distilled anecdotes – of cruising, meeting partners, having sex, sometimes falling in love, juggling lust and love, facing deception and depression – foreshadowed, then coincided with, a newly uncloseted sort of gay literature.[58] The up-front fashion in which Sénac wrote about homosexuality consequently caused embarrassment to nervous critics during his lifetime and afterwards.

Furthermore, Sénac placed his sexual experiences in the context of a homosexual culture, both in the Arabic and European worlds. 'Trois poèmes après Abou-Nouwas' were inspired by the Arab poet who wrote about love for youths, and a line from Abu Nuwas appears as an epigraph in another poem; Sénac evoked the Arabic tradition of love between men and ephebes – now outrageous to many Muslims – in an introduction to one anthology. Words from the Alexandrian Constantine Cavafy appear as an epigraph to another poem, as does a quotation from Rimbaud. Sénac wrote three poems about Rimbaud and Djami, his young African servant (and, as Sénac suggests, lover). Other poems are odes to Oscar Wilde, Luis Cernuda and Federico García Lorca – a poet whose themes, sexuality and death create a striking resemblance to Sénac.[59]

A second reason for underlining the theme of homosexuality in Sénac's poetry is the portrait he provides of sex in Algeria, a description without parallel in the 1950s and 1960s except in the works of François Augiéras. Sexual attitudes and behaviours in Sénac's Algeria allowed him to find casual partners and lovers in the streets of working-class Bab-el-Oued, outside the cinemas of Algiers's *grands boulevards*, at the beach of Pointe-Pescade or lounging around the Place Bugeaud. Contacts were easily established with ebullient *pieds-noirs* and sociable Arabs, coffee or a shared meal helping to bind new friendships. His 'tricks' were often teenagers who lacked access to women, but had little opposition to certain sorts of homosexual activity. The Arab partners did not consider themselves homosexual, and some even angrily refused to acknowledge Sénac in the street, or verbally abused him after their sexual rendezvous. Sénac commented that Algerians suffered from sexual troubles; an Algerian 'wants to seem…super-virile, yet has throbbing sexual problems, rooted in his traditions'.[60] However, Sénac benefited from the relatively tolerant climate of the 1950s and 1960s – ironically, before the homosexual movement was organised, and gay liberation took to the streets. Before artificial birth control became common, and in a Mediterranean society that placed a great importance on female pre-marital chastity, sex-hungry young men indulged in homosexual sex, even though they never spoke of it. A climate that encouraged young men (though not women) to live in the open, spend time at the beach and parade in the evening was propitious to homoerotic and homosocial pleasures. Sénac and other homosexuals could locate partners, adopt protégés and make friends with the Arabic *ragazzi di vita* – Sénac's Algiers was not unlike Pier Paolo Pasolini's Rome (just as Sénac's death also has eerie parallels with Pasolini's tragic end). Male camaraderie, common in Arabic society – mateship between youths of the same age, friendship between an older and a younger man – could, in practice if not in theory, veer off to homosexual dalliance.[61]

The sexual climate congenial to Sénac darkened under a more militant and prudish government by the early 1970s, as the moralistic regime became suspicious of dissidence of whatever sort. Sénac saw the new puritanism in political terms, but also as a danger to his possibilities for sexual fulfilment. Efforts to curb homosexuality, he complained, represented attempts to divert attention from more pressing concerns, including failure to provide leisure activities for youth. 'The bookshops are almost empty,' he lamented,

> and there is no need even to mention the newspapers, or the cinemas given over to the worst sorts of violent films from America or elsewhere, and there is still not a public swimming-pool in Algiers. What is left for the youth? Playing football in the street, dodging cars, and perhaps a little quick sex between boys. If they are to be deprived even of that, the country will explode.[62]

The most important reason to insist on Sénac's homosexuality, however, is because of the links between his private life, his literary creativity and his politics. 'Erotics, poetics, politics', in the felicitous phrase of Sénac's friend and fellow Algerian poet Hamid Nacer-Khodja, form an indissoluble trinity.[63] For Rabah Belamri:

> Sénac accords an equal importance to the [sexual] caress and the [political] struggle. He does not separate individual happiness from society's wellbeing. In his work, as in his life, he always showed that pleasure and

activism [*jouir et agir*] define two types of conscience, two complementarily creative attitudes: 'Revolution' and 'Love' go together.[64]

For Sénac, sex was never just sex, and a poem was not just a poem: 'I dream of bringing together, as in life, poetry, eroticism and politics, the sordid and the pure, vice and virtue, grandeur and shabbiness.'[65] Sénac's eroticised regard of young men in Algeria helped direct his perspective on the Algerian revolution. The youths – whether named Edgard or Brahim – were the ones for whom and with whom he wanted to make the revolution, make love and make his poetry. The Moroccan novelist Tahar Ben Jelloun, comparing Sénac with Abu Nuwas, pointed out the difficulty this entailed: 'How can one raise one's voice not to describe the martyred body of one's country but the nubile, delicate or virile body of the lover?' Sénac tried to resolve the dilemma: '*Si chanter mon amour c'est aimer ma patrie, / Je suis un combattant qui ne se renie pas*' ('If singing of my love is a way of loving my country / I am a fighter who does not disavow himself').[66]

In his 1954 *Journal*, Sénac responded to friends who might question the concordance between private 'vice' and publicly revolutionary 'virtue': 'Why do they not want to understand that there is no wall between my poetry and myself, that I live in my literature, that I have committed myself totally?' He added:

> This question (my country, its misery, the battle to fight, and its outcomes) preoccupies me ceaselessly....But Algerian politics, the dramas of my young motherland, are the pivot of my daily life....The role of the writer in the motherland and struggles for liberty concern me as much as love (which obsesses me right now). But is not Love just that?[67]

The view became a manifesto in the long poem that gave its name to *Citoyens de beauté* in 1967. It begins:

> *Et maintenant nous chanterons l'amour*
> *Car il n'y a pas de Révolution sans Amour,*
> *Il n'y a pas de matin sans sourire.*
> *La beauté sur nos lèvres est un fruit continu.*
> *Elle a ce goût précis des oursins que l'on cueille à l'aube*
> *Et qu'on déguste alors que l'Oursin d'Or s'arrache aux brumes et sur les vagues*
> *   module son chant.*
> *Car tout est chant – hormis la mort!*
> *Je t'aime!*
> *Il faut chanter, Révolution, le corps sans fin renouvelé de la Femme,*
> *La main de l'Ami,*
> *Le galbe comme une écriture sur l'espace*
> *De toutes ces passantes et de tous ces passants*
> *Qui donnent à notre marche sa vraie lumière,*
> *A notre coeur son élan.*
> *O vous tous qui constituez la beauté sereine ou violente,*

Corps purs dans l'alchimie inlassable de la Révolution,
Regards incorruptibles, baisers, désirs dans les tâtonnements de notre lutte,
Points d'appui, points réels pour onctuer notre espérance,
O vous, frères et soeurs, citoyens de beauté, entrez dans le Poème.[68]

The lines sum up many of Sénac's themes. There is an evocation of the seashore and the landscape of Algeria, the erotic yearning for a partner (here expressed bisexually as the reproductive body of the woman and the hand of the friend), but also the necessary conjunction of love and revolution. The poem itself becomes an embodiment of sexual desires and political beliefs, the curve of a body like calligraphy. Sénac said to an interviewer in 1971:

> For twenty years, I have devoted myself to the struggle for justice, dignity and thus [Algerian] independence. But I have never forgotten that the fight for liberty is above all making available to people the maximum possibility for happiness....If the Algerian needs bread and work, if it is indispensable in order to move forward for the Algerian woman to have the same rights as her brothers, it is necessary to preserve for ourselves the natural splendours [of Algeria], enjoyment of the beach, the delights of language and the right to full pleasure [*jouissance*]. In my wartime poems, I confronted the oppressor, and in the *corpoèmes*, I confronted different alienations, for the first time proclaiming myself, without ostentation or complacency, to be homosexual. It is not important, but simply an aspect of my being which thus ought not to be denied any more than my socialist convictions.[69]

Sex, anti-colonialism and the revolution

Sénac's sexual experiences in Algeria in the early 1950s, in some ways, do not seem all that different from Gide's encounters more than half a century beforehand. The hot climate and picturesque landscape of North Africa, whether Gide's oases or the bustling city and sunny beaches favoured by Sénac, provided the backdrop. Casual encounters took place with virile and lusty adolescents, youths who would eventually marry and raise families. Relationships might be for quick sexual pleasure or more abiding ties of friendship. Creative inspiration was one of the benefits, but a certain clash between European and Arabic expectations always loomed. Yet fifty more years of imperialism had transformed Algeria. In the 1890s, France was still 'pacifying' North Africa and staking out conquests in black Africa. Gide and his fellow travellers discovered the exoticism of kasbahs, souks and mosques, hookahs and hashish. They still existed later, but the 1950s and 1960s were the era of blue-jeans and transistor radios, moving pictures and hot-rod motorcycles. This was also the time of Arabic and Islamic nationalism, anti-colonial militancy and wars of independence. Gide was the Parisian visiting the alluring colonies; Sénac, the *pied-noir* promoting Algerian independence in Paris. *Amyntas* was a gentle portrait of the romantic Maghreb;

Citoyens de beauté and *Matinale de mon people*, insurrectionary poetic manifestos. *Le Soleil sous les armes* was not just a felicitously worded title, for Sénac's Algeria was the country of the FLN and the OAS, the Battle of Algiers and the generals' putsch, fratricidal dispute and murderous violence.

In the case of Sénac, the nexus of anti-colonialism, homosexuality and literary creation is evident and personal. He paid for political, sexual and literary dissidence with his life – ironically, in a post-colonial epoch and an independent nation that he had hoped would bring liberation to the oppressed. The fine sentiments of idealistic activists in the 1950s and 1960s did not bear fruit; regimes turned puritanical, revolutionary ardours were sapped, sexual contexts altered. Yet, his life and work capture the enthusiasm and optimism of those who, for a moment, believed in social change that would emancipate colonised peoples, the workers of the world and homosexuals.

Herbart, Guérin and Sénac (as well as Genet, and, in a different fashion, Augiéras) represent the confluence of homosexual desire and commitment to anti-colonialism and revolution. They wrote when the fight against various sorts of 'imperialism', commitment to socialism and the 'sexual revolution' coincided. They witnessed the war in Algeria, which fractured French opinion in a way not felt since the Second World War. Given their ideological orientation, veteran activists such as Guérin and Herbart could hardly avoid involvement with the Algerian struggle. For Augiéras (serving in the army and discovering his uncle in the Saharan desert) and Genet (because of his political views and through friendship with Abdallah Bentaga), the conflict had a more personal aspect. For Sénac, the *pied-noir*, the war was a question of his homeland, his family and compatriots in North Africa, his future in Algeria and France.[70]

For Marshal Lyautey, that earlier French colonial figure associated with North Africa, the homosocial camaraderie of soldiers and the homoeroticism of Arabic warriors formed part of the imperative of imperialism. For Herbart, Guérin and Sénac, public and private life, sex and politics, homosexuality and the colonies were also intimately bound together – but, for them, anti-colonialism was the imperative.[71]

Notes

1 There were undoubtedly many more lesser-known homosexual sympathisers with anti-colonialism. Rupert Croft-Cooke, for instance, mentions B.J. Horniman, one of Oscar Wilde's boyfriends, who moved to India in the early twentieth century, became a friend of Gandhi and supported Indian nationalism for thirty years through his editorship of the *Bombay Sentinel* and other activities. A thorn in the side to colonial officials, 'the British had fined him, expelled him and once on a charge of homosexuality had nearly succeeded in gaoling him. But the [nationalist] movement paid his fines' (Rupert Croft-Cooke, *The Gorgeous East: One Man's India* (London, 1965), p. 113.

2 Guy Hocquenghem, *La Beauté du métis* (Paris, 1979). See also his manifesto, *Le Désir homosexuel* (Paris, 1972).

3 Herbart's father, however, abandoned his family when Herbart was five and died a beggar; Herbart later learned that his biological father was, in fact, a Danish shipping agent and close family friend.

4 Pierre Herbart, *Souvenirs imaginaires* (Paris, 1998), with extra biographical details from the preface by Maurice Imbert. See also Pierre Herbart, *Inédits*, ed. Maurice Imbert (Paris, 1981).

5 Pierre Herbart, *La Ligne de force* (Paris, 1958) details his travels to the Far East and opposition to colonialism.

6 Herbart, *Souvenirs imaginaires*, pp. 67–71.

7 Pierre Herbart, *La Licorne* (Paris, 1998), p. 62.

8 Philippe Berthier, *Pierre Herbart: Morale et style de la désinvolture* (Paris, 1999), pp. 36, 52.

9 Pierre Herbart, *Le Chancre du Niger* (Paris, 1939), pp. 33–4.

10 Herbart, *La Ligne de force*, op. cit.

11 Much of the biographical material on Guérin in this section comes, in addition to his own writing and the other sources cited, from a television documentary prepared by Laurent Muhlheisen and Patrice Spadoni, *Daniel Guérin, 1904–1988: Combats dans le siècle* (c. 1999).

12 Daniel Guérin, *Autobiographie de jeunesse* (Paris, 1972), especially pp. 208 and 222–3.

13 Daniel Guérin, *Eux et lui* (Lille, 2000), pp. 46–8.

14 *Ibid.*, p. 30.

15 *Ibid.*, p. 35.

16 Daniel Guérin, *Le Feu du sang* (Paris, 1977), pp. 8, 10, and the special issue of *Alternative libertaire*, published (*hors-série*) in 1999. In English, see Peter Sedgwick, 'Out of Hiding: The comradeships of Daniel Guérin', *Salmagundi*, No. 58–9 (1982–3), pp. 197–220.

17 Guérin, *Eux et lui*, p. 94.

18 I am grateful to Hamid Nacer-Khodja for sending me copies of articles he published in the Algerian press on Sénac, 'Jean Sénac, d'une algérianité à l'autre', *Algérie Actualité*, No. 1,457 (14–20 September 1993), '"Awal" ou la parole à Jean Sénac', *Algérie Actualité*, No. 1,467, 23–9 November 1993, 'Retour à Jean Sénac', *El Watan* (Algiers), 3 October 1996, 'Trente ans après sa première édition, *Citoyens de beauté* est de nouveau disponible', *La Tribune* (Algiers), 26 May 1997.

19 The following biographical information comes from the books cited in this section, as well as information kindly shared by M. and Mme Jacques Miel. The most detailed chronology of his life, by Hamid Nacer-Khodja, appears in Jean Sénac, *Pour une terre possible…Poèmes et autres textes inédits* (Paris, 1999), pp. 323–80.

20 The case is put most forcefully by Jean-Pierre Péroncel-Hugoz, *Assassinat d'un poète* (Paris, 1983). Jacques Miel doubts, on several grounds, that Sénac was murdered for political reasons. At the time of his death, Maghrebin and other intellectuals were meeting in Algiers, and this would have been an unpropitious time to kill a well-known writer. Furthermore, the government had given Sénac 5,000 francs, a large sum, to organise the literary events at an international exhibition, hardly an indication of a wish to eliminate him. The way in which Sénac was killed, knocked onto a hard floor and then randomly stabbed with his own knife, did not seem the work of a professional assassin. Finally, the youth convicted of killing Sénac had earlier had an affair with him and wanted a job at the exhibition with which Sénac was connected; Sénac promised a *carte de travail* but repeatedly postponed delivering it, which may have angered the young man. Sénac told a mutual acquaintance to have him come to his flat to get the papers, and an argument may have ensued, perhaps on the subject of past or future sexual relations. In any case, on several previous occasions in Algiers and once in France, Sénac had been roughed up by tricks.

21 Association de Béni-Safiens, *L'Album de Béni-Saf* (n.p., 1988).

22 The journalist Jean Daniel has remarked that Sénac 'was literally in love with Camus' (Letter to J.-P. Péroncel-Hugoz, printed in Les Amis des Archives de la Ville de Marseille, *Le Soleil fraternel: Jean Sénac et la nouvelle poèsie algérienne d'expression française – Actes des rencontres* (Marseille, 1985), p. 142; the volume is hereafter cited as *Amis AVM*).

23 Sénac's mother remained in Algeria during the war, but afterwards moved to France, where she died in 1965. Sénac's *Ebauche du père* (Paris, 1989) contains a touching portrait of Jeanne Comma. The daughter of a miner, she managed to earn a *certificat d'études* and learn sewing. She was disgraced when she fell pregnant with Sénac and left Béni-Saf for Oran; Sénac's stepfather abandoned her for a fortune-teller, taking the small inheritance she had received from her father. Madame Sénac took a job as a cleaner, reduced to 'the lowest sort of work, the only type that she could find in a time of unemployment, an Arab's work, a Spaniard's work'. She received a tribute from her son: 'You ruined your poor little eyes sewing, and then you would wear out your knees and your hands (your cleaning-cloth, Mother, the banner of my glory, the flag of my pride)' (p. 165). Sénac also paid tribute to his mother's courage in showing his pro-Algerian manifesto, *Le Soleil sous les armes*, to her neighbours in the midst of the war of independence. Sénac had one sister, but they were not close, and eventually lost contact.

24 Jean Sénac (ed.), *Anthologie de la nouvelle poésie algérienne* (Paris, 1971), p. 7.

25 Jean Sénac, 'Cette Ville', in *Oeuvres poétiques* (Arles, 1999), pp. 709–13, originally published only after Sénac's death in *dérisions et Vertige* (Paris, 1983 [1967–72]), pp. 113–14.

26 Sénac, *Oeuvres poétiques*, hereafter cited as *OP*.

27 Archives de la Ville de Marseille, *Poésie au Sud: Jean Sénac et la nouvelle poésie algérienne d'expression française* (Marseille, 1983).

28 Sénac, *Ebauche du père*, op. cit., *Journal Alger, janvier–juillet 1954* (n.p., 1996), and '*Pour une terre possible…*' *Poèmes et autres textes inédits* (Paris, 1999).

29 *Amis AVM*, op. cit.; Rabah Belamri, *Jean Sénac: Entre désir et douleur* (Algiers, 1989); a special issue of the journal *Awal: Cahiers d'études berbères*, No. 10 (1993); and Jamel-Eddine Bencheikh and Christiane Chaulet-Achour, *Jean Sénac. Clandestin des deux rives* (Paris, 1999). See also the preface by René de Ceccatty (which discusses Sénac's homosexuality more extensively) and the postface by Hamid Nacer-Khodja, 'Erotique, poétique, politique', in *OP*, pp. 9–17 and pp. 787–802, respectively.

30 See Sénac, *Pour une terre possible*, pp. 241 ff.

31 'Les Massacres de juillet', in *OP*, pp. 262–3, originally published in *La Matinale de mon peuple*.

32 Some of the slighting feeling about what is indeed an infelicitous line seems to have come from misinterpretation of the 'tu' as a person rather than the 'Révolution', as it clearly was meant to be, although the poem mixes political and sexual metaphors. In the version of *Citoyens de beauté* published in 1967, the passage reads: 'Je t'aime. Tu es forte comme un comité de gestion / Comme une coopérative agricole / Comme une brasserie nationalisée / Comme la rose de midi / Comme l'unité du peuple / Comm une cellule d'alphabétisation' (p. 12). ('I love you. You are strong as a workers' management committee / As an agricultural cooperative / As a nationalised brewery / As a mid-day rose / As the unity of the people / As a course in literacy'.) Sénac was here trying to make poetic the new institutions of the revolution. He commented:

> Do not forget that this collection…contains almost exclusively texts that were violentlycommitted [politically]….It was not by chance that I wrote 'tu est belle comme un comité de gestion', the line that has provoked so much sarcasm from people like Kateb Yacine and Malek Bernabi….It was a question – it is still a question – of uniting, in the same gesture, lyrical beauty and the revolution in the most pointed and quotidian fashion.

> (Quoted in Péroncel-Hugoz, pp. 33–4)

33 The text is printed in *Amis AVM*, pp. 57–60. Oran was the main city of Spanish settlement in Algeria, and Sénac talks about Spanish 'conquistadors', the baroque rituals of Spanish Catholicism, and the food and dance of Iberian migrants.

34 'Lettre d'un jeune poète algérien à tous ses frères', reprinted in *Amis AVM*, pp. 28–9. '*Bicots*' was a racist epithet for Arabs.

35 Sénac, *Ebauche du père*, p. 164.

36 *Ibid.*, p. 163.

37 *Amis AVM*, pp. 55–6.

38 In *Esprit*, No. 3 (March 1956), reprinted in *Amis AVM*, pp. 61–3.

39 For an analysis of this key text, see Yvonne Llavador, *La Poésie algérienne de langue française et la Guerre d'Algérie* (Lund, 1980), Ch. 1, and 'Le Manifeste poétique de Jean Sénac: *Le Soleil sous les armes*', *Awal*, pp. 25–30.

40 At the time '*pieds-noirs*' was still regarded by many *Français d'Algérie* as a term of abuse and denigration.

41 *Amis AVM*, pp. 74–6.

42 Some of Sénac's fellow writers, one gathers, thought that he persisted in writing poems in the heroic mode of the war years rather than modifying his themes and rhetoric to accord with a new period in Algerian history.

43 Quoted in Péroncel-Hugoz, p. 144.

44 'This country is mine with its bitter liturgy / Its filthy scandals, its menacing roads / Its plundered soul, its people exhausted'. Sénac, *OP*, p. 475, from 'Ordalie de novembre', originally published in *Avant-corps* (1968).

45 Sénac, *Journal Alger*, pp. 44, 77.

46 Péroncel-Hugoz, p. 31.

47 Reminiscences kindly shared by Jacques and Françoise Miel, who also allowed me to read Sénac's correspondence.

48 'You gave me back light and peace / The bend at the steep climb, / The nature of the well and the clarity of the water. / The new language springs from your smile / Like the first reed from the rocks. / Already the plains are radiant / The trees are growing, / From this parched heart you are creating your Domain....I am inundated with nobility / The fig tree spreads its shade / Citizen of the desert / All you need to do is walk forwards, / I have never seen the sea so blue!...Never has the Admiralty basin looked so beautiful, / Because in the desert the first brave flower has bloomed'. Sénac, *OP*, pp. 439–40; written in 1966, the poem was originally published in *Citoyens de beauté*, pp. 69–71. The '*darse de l'Amirauté*' was the inner basin of the Algiers harbour.

49 'The handsomest youth possessed / for a cinema seat / the prettiest girl bedded / for a cheap dinner / beauty is sold at a discount / Beauty will render its justice / and its tribute which is love / no longer to see it dragged from bar to pisser / waiting for the day / And let the word be said once and for all / in the name of the Father and of the Son and of the Holy Spirit / so that the volcano erupt from its cone / water slake the volcano / the earth turn in flesh and blood / and death no longer be the keystone in our arch'. Sénac, *OP*, p. 187; written in the 1950s, 'L'Exorcisme' was published in *Les Désordres* (Paris, 1972), and reprinted in *Jean Sénac Vivant* (Paris, 1982)

50 'The paving-stones underneath my feet / I walk and look for you / I try to draw your leaves to my light / the day does not belong to a soul that is split asunder / I run / Who recognises in these muscles an angel?.../ If I had found you / I would have lost the earth / bartered my summer for your winter / and God knows that I love the indolent light! / But nothing remains / of the cold of the night / than a sham sun / that spoils the fruit'. Sénac, *OP*, pp. 163–4.

51 See below the discussion of the poem that gave its name to the collection, as well as 'Brahim le Généreux'.

52 Sénac, 'Troisième poème iliaque', *OP*, p. 458, originally published in *Avant-corps*.

53 *Le Mythe du sperme-Méditerranée* (Arles, 1984 [written 1967]), *Lettrier du soleil* (Paris, 1968), *A-Corpoème* (Paris, 1981 [1968]), *Alchimies (Lettres à l'adolescent)* (Paris, 1987 [1971]), *dérisions et Vertige/trouvures* (Paris, 1983 [1967–72]), *Plaques* (Paris, 1996 [1973]).

54 Sénac, 'Hyperprisme BSM', *OP*, p. 547.
55 Sénac, *OP*, p. 682.
56 Sénac, 'Drague-Appel-Doute', *OP*, p. 767.
57 *Le Mythe du sperme-Méditerranée*, pp. 8–9.
58 The *Journal* of 1954 and *Alchimies*, written in 1971, are particularly poignant accounts of love found and lost.
59 See Rabah Belamri, 'Frederico García Lorca, Jean Sénac: Influence et convergences', *Amis AVM*, pp. 123–37.
60 Quoted (from a 1973 remark) by Péroncel-Hugoz, p. 72.
61 See Malek Chebel, *Encyclopédie de l'amour en Islam* (Paris, 1998), pp. 312–16, and *L'Esprit de sérail. Mythes et pratiques sexuels au Maghreb* (Paris, 1995), pp. 17–21.
62 Quoted (from a 1970 remark) in Péroncel-Hugoz, p. 17.
63 Postface to Sénac, *OP*, pp. 767–802.
64 Belamri, p. 37. Cf. Philippe Rebeyrol, for whom, 'Politics, as conceived by Sénac, was not different from love' ('A la mémoire de Jean Sénac', *Amis AVM*, p. 155).
65 *Ebauche du père*, p. 43.
66 Ben Jelloun, preface to Pèroncel-Hugoz, p. 8.
67 *Journal*, p. 49.
68 'And now we will sing of love / Because there is no Revolution without Love, / There is no morning without a smile. / Beauty on our lips is an ever ripe fruit. / It has this very taste of sea-urchins gathered at dawn / And that you savour while the Oursin d'Or emerges from the fog and sends its call over the waves. / Because everything is a song – other than death! / I love you! / Revolution, we must sing of the ever renewed body of Woman, / The hand of the Friend, / The graceful curve [of the body] like writing on space / Of all these women and all these men passing by / Who give a beacon to our marches, / And to our heart its beat / Oh you who are serenely or violently beautiful, / Pure bodies in the inexhaustible alchemy of the Revolution, / Incorruptible looks, kisses, desires as we grope in our struggle, / Mooring-posts, real places to anoint our hope, / Oh you, brothers and sisters, citizens of beauty, enter into the Poem'. *Citoyens de beauté*, p. 9 [pp. 9–15].
69 Sénac, *OP*, p. 309.
70 For other homosexuals, too, the Algerian war, and its repercussions, mandated urgent political involvement. Pierre Hahn, a French journalist and homosexual activist, for instance 'having already studied racism in the periodical *Jeune Afrique*…wanted (in his own words) "to link discrimination against homosexuals with the discriminations that victimizes North Africans, for example"' (Michael Sibalis, 'Pierre Hahn', in Robert Aldrich and Garry Wotherspoon (eds), *Who's Who in Gay and Lesbian History: From World War II to the Present Day* (London, 2001), pp. 175–6.
71 Yet the life and work of another French writer also reflects the links between politics, homosexuality and literature. Pierre Guyotat, as a 20-year-old army conscript, was sent to Algeria in 1960. He was soon questioned by military police, and held for three months without trial, then moved to a disciplinary unit, on charges of undermining army morale and being an accessory to desertion. In 1967, Guyotat's *Tombeau pour cinq cent mille soldats* – a parable about the Algerian War – caused a scandal. Three years later, Guyotat published *Eden, Eden, Eden*; set in a desert, it pictured bordellos of women and men, as a nomad and his slave, a woman and her baby and monkey, wander around looking for the meaning of life; officials, scandalised by the work, forbade advertising or sales to minors. In 1975, *Prostitution*, written in stream-of-consciousness prose and in phonetically transcribed North African French, was set in a male brothel in Algiers.

Epilogue
After the empire

In the fifteen years from the independence of India in 1947 to that of Algeria in 1962, most of the larger colonies gained independence, and, except in a few residual outposts, the age of empire soon came to an end. European expatriates fled some of the former colonies, but happily lived on in others, enjoying the benefits of race and wealth if not political control. With the development of leisure tourism, increasing numbers of holiday-makers flocked to tropical islands, went on safari and toured exotic cities. Many looked for the pleasures of sun and sex that had attracted their predecessors to Asia, Africa and the Pacific. Some old homosexual watering-grounds, such as Morocco, continued to attract visitors, and new sites of gay tourism emerged, such as Thailand. In other countries, however, post-independence governments denounced homosexuality as an evil of colonialism, and instituted harsh laws punishing homosexuals with imprisonment or even death. Meanwhile, the Kinsey Report in the United States and the Wolfenden Report in Britain prompted a reassessment of the homosexual condition; from the 1950s 'homophile' groups organised to demand political and social rights, succeeded by the 'gay liberation movements' of the 1960s and 1970s. These trends, and then the onset of the AIDS epidemic in the 1980s, profoundly affected homosexual relations between Europeans and the former colonial world.

The decade or so after the Second World War witnessed the last surge of old-style homosexual travel to distant places, as men of money, leisure and culture travelled around the world looking for romance, or escaping discrimination that forced homosexuals in various European countries into lives of dangerous clandestinity.[1] Rupert Croft-Cooke, who had served in the British Army in India during the Second World War, and acquired an Indian secretary and companion, was arrested in London in 1953 for 'gross indecency' with two other men. After serving prison sentences for their crime, Croft-Cooke and his friend moved to Tangier, Morocco.[2] Work carried the journalist Michael Davidson around the world, where he reported wars in the Middle East and Far East. 'This is the life-history of a lover of boys,' Davidson began his autobiography, and he recorded liaisons with 'some boys' in Marrakesh and Tangier, Lahore and Rangoon, Bali and Saigon, Dakar and Timbuktu.[3] John Haylock, after being seduced by an Egyptian in Cairo during the Second World War, taught in Iraq from 1948 to 1956, and enjoyed the company of a number of young men. Haylock also went to Morocco and Thailand, and lived for years with a male lover in Japan.[4] Robin Maugham – nephew of Somerset, son of Britain's Lord Chancellor, heir to a viscountcy, Eton- and Cambridge-educated – served in North Africa during the war, and then spent the rest of his life travelling around the world. His stories 'The Boy from Beirut', 'The Tea Planter' and 'The Sensuous Soldier' explored homosexuality in far-away spots. The novel *The Wrong People* centres on the efforts of a wealthy European expatriate in North Africa to procure as a sexual partner an ideal young man from Britain through the efforts of a visiting Englishman, himself enamoured of an Arab youth. Maugham's autobiography, *A Search for Nirvana* – the title is an appropriate motto – recounts his visit to an oasis in the Libyan desert (also discussed by Forster in his book on Alexandria) where homosexual relations were supposedly guiltlessly enjoyed.[5] Most famously, the bisexual American writer and composer Paul Bowles, who took up semi-permanent residence in Morocco in the late 1930s (and lived there until his death in 1999), became the centre of a colony of homosexual residents and visitors in Tangier. He welcomed many of the Beat Generation and later celebrities who took pleasure in picturesque landscapes, hashish and men.[6] Alfred Chester and Joe Orton, among others, wrote about their adventures in sexy Morocco.[7] Bowles also encouraged young Moroccans, notably Mohammed Mrabet, to write about their homosexual experiences with foreign men.[8] By the 1950s Tangier had earned a reputation as the world's most hospitable exotic site for men seeking sexual company, generally for a price, with virile lads. Morocco attracted men from around the world, including the Frenchmen who continued a century-old migration across the Mediterranean, Roland Barthes only one of the men of letters who pursued sex in Morocco.[9]

There are many similarities between these homosexual vagabonds of the 1950s and 1960 and earlier travellers. Most came from a privileged position in European (or American) society. They left countries where homosexuality remained a crime (as in Britain and the United States) or incurred some degree of social disapprobation (as in France). They went to countries legendary for cultural 'otherness' and sexual hospitality, following in the footsteps of Gide and generally well acquainted with his works. Occasionally they ran into problems because of their encounters. Many of the 'natives' were bisexual or basically heterosexual, but willing to engage in homosexual liaisons for compensation and company. A number of the Europeans developed a great and genuine interest in the countries they visited or in which they lived – Bowles translated Moroccan tales, and his friend Brion Gysin collected *gnaoua* music. They recorded their experiences in memoirs and novels. However, the form of travel was changing, carry-on bags replacing steamer-trunks. Alternate destinations for gay pilgrimage – Castro Street in San Francisco and Christopher Street in New York – by the 1960s lured tourists away from more traditional haunts in the Mediterranean and other distant places. The new travellers more commonly affirmed their homosexuality openly 'coming out' in a way unimaginable to men such as Forster.

Gradually gay tourism became more common, as pubs and clubs opened, gay resorts sprung up and gay guidebooks were published. Western ideas of a homosexual identity and gay liberation spread around the world, and gay groups, demanding social recognition and political rights, were organised in Asia and Africa. New notions of sexual behaviour and identity replaced the old fluidity in attitudes and relationships. By the 1990s, the AIDS epidemic, somewhat contained in the West, was also ravaging Africa and Asia. Moralists campaigned about 'child prostitution', even promoting legislation to make men indictable for sex crimes committed overseas. Social observers warned about the dangers of rampant sexual tourism. Homophobic leaders, notably Robert Mugabe in Zimbabwe, mounted attacks on both local and foreign homosexuals.

Studies of non-Western sexualities multiplied, as did works on sexual tourism and the globalisation of sexuality.[10] Perhaps creative literature and art, however, best illustrate colonial and present-day international homosexual liaisons, and also show how the theme of foreign sex and romance continually reappears in Western culture, though sometimes in subverted fashion. Caryl Churchill's play *Cloud Nine*, set in Victorian Africa, satirised the sexual entanglements of Europeans. 'Friendship between men...is the noblest form of relationship,' says one character, but his upright friend is appalled: 'You don't do it with the natives, Harry? My God, what a betrayal of the Queen....Rome fell, Harry, and this sin can destroy an empire.'[11] Other writers featured homosexuality as part of the paradoxical nature of colonialism – a homosexual planter in Trevor Shearston's New Guinea, a homosexual soldier and administrator in Simon Raven's and David's Caute's black Africa.[12] Lawrence Durrell's *The Alexandria Quartet* featured a cast of expatriates enjoying the pleasures, and trying to avoid the dangers, of pre-Nasserite Egypt. Robert Liddell's *Unreal City* was set in a wartime city that was clearly also Alexandria, with a Cavafy-like Greek homosexual, an available Canadian soldier ('Antinous') and a closeted Englishman.[13] Shyam Selvadurai's *Cinnamon Gardens* drew inspiration from the relationship between Ponnambalam Arunachalam and Edward Carpenter.[14] Echoes of empire appear in Alan Hollinghurst's *The Swimming Pool Library*.[15]

By the 1980s novels featured post-colonial sexual travel, or set homosexual situations in an imprecise time in foreign places. In Andrew Harvey's *One Last Mirror*, an Englishman goes to Sri Lanka to find sex and find himself. Hervé Guibert wrote about a paedophile's trip to North Africa in *Voyage avec deux enfants*. In Dominique Fernandez's *Une Fleur de jasmin à l'oreille*, Morocco attracts a homosexual trying to sort out his emotional and sexual life, and Juan Goytisolo engages with the theme of homosexuality in Morocco in *Makbara*. Morocco, too, is the destination for a Canadian in Scott Symons's *Helmet of Flesh*. Travel goes the other way too, as a Moroccan moves to France or to the United States and gets involved in homosexual liaisons in Michel Tournier's *La Goutte d'or* and Guy Hocquenghem's *L'Amour en relief*.[16] The examples of recent novels could be multiplied because of the popularity of the theme of a search for sex overseas or at home with partners from far-away places.[17] Personal memoirs have complemented fictional works, such as Roger Bowen's recollections of growing up in

England in the 1950s and finding companionship in Thailand in the 1990s, Tobias Schneebaum's memoirs of homosexual participant–observer anthropology with Melanesians in Irian Jaya and Jack Thieuloy's unbuttoned account of his passion for Indonesians.[18]

Not only Europeans, but authors from non-Western countries, as well, are now writing about inter-racial and international encounters, providing a new perspective on contacts previously seen almost entirely from the European point of view.[19] Indeed, there has been an explosion in gay writing from the non-Western world,[20] with books presenting a more detailed and positive portrayal of homosexuality than appeared in the relatively rare writings from non-Western authors during the colonial period.[21]

It has not just been literature that has looked at the trope of homosexuals abroad. Several artists and photographers have made a speciality of homo-erotic images of men of different ethnic backgrounds, such as Robert Mapplethorpe, playing with sexual stereotypes but challenging social perceptions.[22] Silvia Sleigh's 1973 painting *Turkish Bath*, a group of naked hippie men posed in an Ingres-style hammam setting, sent up Orientalist portrayals of women odalisques.[23] Cinema has also revisited colonial icons. Claire Denis's 1999 film *Beau Travail*, inspired by Herman Melville's *Billy Budd*, uses choreography to show off the muscular bodies of French Legionnaires in Djibouti and tell the story of ill-fated homosexual attraction and obsession, while Ferzan Ozpetek's *Il Bagno Turco* of 1997 focuses on homosexual initiation and tragic death in Istanbul.

Erotic culture, both soft- and hard-core porn, returns regularly to stereotypes inherited from the colonial era. For instance, to use examples of representations of Indians, Wolf Nikolas's photographs of *Arjun* pose a lissome naked youth bathing in the sea, stretched on a hammock or draped in gauzy garments. Orion Delain's pictures, with occasional allusions to von Gloeden's photographs, show striking young men dressed in maharajah-type robes silhouetted against the Taj Mahal, wrapping their turbans, playing flutes or sitars, while skimpily clad or nude peasant lads work in the forest or frolic by the sea.[24] The Indian as exotic and seductive, whether rich or poor, in palaces or the woods, draws on iconographical and literary tropes going back to Carpenter, Forster and Stowitts. The magazine OG, standing for 'Oriental Guys', has made a speciality of photos of fetching young men from Asia. Jean-Daniel Cadinot's erotic film *Harem* brings to screen countless sexual encounters, and a budding romance, between a blond European and dark North Africans in hammam and souk.[25] Two other French pornographic films, called *Légionnaires*, purport to show men of the legendary corps in various states of undress and sexual arousal. A novel called *The Legionnaire*:

> presents an account of hot male–male sex and lust in the French Foreign Legion. Gary Cooper in *Beau Geste* gave us the romantic side of Legion life. In this erotic novel you'll read about the raunchy sex which goes on non-stop in an encampment of macho men.[26]

The myths of sexual naughtiness overseas have even inspired a French gay troupe, Les Caramels Fous, to present a self-styled 'virile and yet musical comedy'. 'Il était une fois Tatahouine' took its name from the Tunisian head-quarters of the French colonial army disciplinary brigades, the *bataillons d'Afrique*, notorious for homosexual behaviour. A European general and colonel, a sultan, a grand vizir, an Arabic prince, assorted other North Africans (some of them men in drag), the pilot of a downed aeroplane and the singer at 'Harem's Bar' gather at the desert outpost. They sing of the yearnings of colonials far from home, and the rendezvous they have in the cantonment. Edith Piaf's 'Mon Légionnaire' is redone as a duet between two male lovers, a Legionnaire and a missionary. The priest sings, 'He was young, he was handsome, he smelled of camel hair, my Legionnaire', and his partner answers, 'He was young, he was dumb, he knew only one position, my missionary one'.[27]

Novels, memoirs, paintings, art films and porn videos abound – the theme of sex with foreigners, whether in colonial or post-colonial situations, seems far from vanishing. The prologue to this book focused on a sexual travelogue from the 1890s, *L'Art d'aimer aux colonies*. It is appropriate that the epilogue conclude with a reference to contemporary collections of gay travel writing and guide-books, now legion.[28] The most famous guidebook is *Spartacus*, published every year or two. It lists bars, discos, cruising areas, saunas, porn parlours and other places for gay assignations, complete with details on the legal status of homosexuals in various countries, local political activism and paragraphs describing places visitors may go and the men they may meet. The venues, the clients who frequent them and the possible dangers to be faced are carefully spelled out with symbols and codes, an encyclopaedia of post-colonial homosexual sites. Before it became more astute, the *Spartacus* guide often implied that, in non-Western countries, many if not most men might be available for sexual liaisons, though a tourist's new friend would appreciate a small gift in return. Present-day guides underline the variety of attractions in cities such as Sydney and Bangkok, and the less openly advertised pleasures of Marrakesh or Colombo. Dr Jacobus X might have been amused.

Notes

1 Robert Aldrich and Garry Wotherspoon (eds), *Who's Who in Contemporary Gay and Lesbian History: From World War II to the Present Day* (London, 2001), provides biographical details on many of the figures mentioned below.
2 Rupert Croft-Cooke, *The Gorgeous East: One Man's India* (London, 1965), and *The Caves of Hercules* (London, 1974).
3 Michael Davidson, *The World, the Flesh and Myself* (London, 1962), and *Some Boys* (London, 1988).
4 John Haylock, *Eastern Exchange* (London, 1997); see also his novel about Morocco, *Body of Contention* (London, 1999).
5 Robin Maugham, *The Boy from Beirut and Other Stories*, ed. Peter Burton (San Francisco, 1982), *The Wrong People* (London, 1967) and *A Search for Nirvana* (London, 1975).

6 See Michelle Green, *The Dream at the End of the World: Paul Bowles and the Literary Renegades in Tangier* (New York, 1991), and Christopher Sawyer-Lauçanno, *An Invisible Spectator: A Biography of Paul Bowles* (London, 1989).

7 Alfred Chester, *Head of a Sad Angel: Stories, 1953–1966*, ed. Edward Field (Santa Rosa, CA, 1990); John Lahr (ed.), *The Orton Diaries* (London, 1986).

8 Mohammed Mrabet, *The Lemon* (San Francisco, 1969), *Love with a Few Hairs* (San Francisco, 1967) and *Chocolate Creams and Dollars* (New York, n.d.) discuss homosexual encounters.

9 Roland Barthes, *Incidents* (Paris, 1987).

10 See Dennis Altman, *Global Sex* (Sydney, 2001).

11 Caryl Churchill, *Cloud Nine* (London, 1979).

12 Trevor Shearston, *A Straight Young Back* (Sydney, 2000); Simon Raven, *The Feathers of Death* (London, 1959); David Caute, *Fever Pitch* (London, 1965).

13 Lawrence Durrell, *The Alexandria Quartet* (London, 1957–60); Robert Liddell, *Unreal City* (London, 1952). On Durrell, see Roger Bowen, '"Squalid with Joy": Scobie, sex, and race in Lawrence Durrell's *Alexandria Quartet*', *Journal of Homosexuality*, Vol. 36, No. 2 (1998), pp. 87–97.

14 Shyam Selvadurai, *Cinnamon Gardens* (London, 1999); personal communication from the author.

15 Alan Hollinghurst, *The Swimming Pool Library* (London, 1988).

16 Andrew Harvey, *One Last Mirror* (London, 1985); Hervé Guibert, *Voyage avec deux enfants* (Paris, 1982); Dominique Fernandez, *Une Fleur de jasmin à l'oreille* (Paris, 1980) – on this work, see Lucille Cairns, *Privileged Pariahdom: Homosexuality in the Novels of Dominique Fernandez* (Berne, 1996), Ch. 4; Juan Goytisolo, *Makbara* (London, 1993); Scott Symons, *Helmet of Flesh* (New York, 1986); Michel Tournier, *La Goutte d'or* (Paris, 1988); Guy Hocquenghem, *L'Amour en relief* (Paris, 1982). Two other novels about gay Maghrebin expatriates come from Norway – proof of the widespread resonance of the theme: Per Knutsen, *Svømmersken* (Oslo, 1994) and Tor Fretheim, *Om bare sola ville danse* (Oslo, 1990).

17 Examples of French-language books published include Grégory Bastien, *Khalid* (Lille, 1996), David Dumortier, *La Pioche de Salah* (Paris, 2001), Michel Giliberti, *Derrière les portes bleues* (Paris, 2000) and François-Olivier Rousseau, *Le Passeur* (Paris, 2001). One of the best English-language books is Jeremy Seabrook, *Colonies of the Heart* (London, 1998); Seabrook is also the author of *Love in a Different Climate: Men Who Have Sex with Men in India* (London, 1999).

18 Roger Bowen, 'Getting to know you', *Harrington Gay Men's Fiction Quarterly*, Vol. 1, No. 4 (1999), pp. 51–62; Tobias Schneebaum, *Secret Places: My Life in New York and New Guinea* (Madison, WI, 2000); Jack Thieuloy, *La Passion indonésienne* (Paris, 1985).

19 See, e.g., the works of Rachid O., *L'Enfant ébloui* (Paris, 1995), *Plusieurs vies* (Paris, 1996) and *Chocolat chaud* (Paris, 1998).

20 To use the illustrative example of India: a gay novel, P. Parivaraj, *Shiva and Arun* (London, 1998), a collection of stories and poems, Hoshang Merchant (ed.), *Yaraana* (New Delhi, 1999) and a memoir, *Badruddin Khan, Sex, Longing and Not Belonging: A Gay Muslim's Quest for Love and Meaning* (Oakland, CA, 1997).

21 On colonial-era writings, see Jarrod Hayes, *Queer Nations: Marginal Sexualities in the Maghreb* (Chicago, 2000), esp. Chs 1 and 3; Chris Dunton, '"Wheyting Be Dat?": The Treatment of Homosexuality in African Literature', *Research in African Literature*, Vol. 20, No. 3 (fall 1989), pp. 422–48; Lisa Kahaleole Chang Hall and J. Kehaulani Kauanui, 'Same-sex sexuality in Pacific literature', *Amerasia Journal*, Vol. 20, No. 1 (1994), pp. 75–81.

22 Among other contemporary artworks that allude to earlier images of non-Western male beauty are Arie Smit's paintings of Balinese, Ross Watson's and Donald Simonson's portraits of Pacific islanders, Cornelius McCarthy's renditions of black

men, and works by Mark Satchwill, such as *Le Petit Prince*, a seductive and almost-nude turban-wearing Arab youth. As with literature, there are new non-Western artistic perspectives on homosexuality, such as the paintings of the Indian artist Bhupen Khakhar; see Timothy Hyman, *Bhupen Khakhar* (London, 1998).

23 The painting is reproduced in Edward Lucie-Smith, *Sexuality in Western Art* (London, 1991), p. 263.

24 Wolk Nikolas, *Arjun* (Berlin, 1987); Orion Delain, 'Carnet de voyage: L'Inde', *Triangul'ère*, No. 2 (Paris, 2001), pp. 548–627.

25 Mention might also be made of non-Western films with homosexual themes, such as Nouri Bouzid's *Man of Ashes* (1986), a Tunisian film about the psychological consequences of homosexual rape.

26 Tom Kvaale, *The Legionnaire* (San Francisco, 1997).

27 Programme for 'Il était une fois Tatahouine', Paris, 1999.

28 Most concentrate on Western societies; among the best of those looking at other places is Robert Tewdwr Moss, *Cleopatra's Wedding Present: Travels Through Syria* (London, 1998). Past and present are joined with excerpts from various places and periods, including Beijing, Tangier, India, Central Africa (and Western sites) in Lucy Jane Bledsoe (ed.), *Gay Travels* (San Francisco, 1998).

Conclusion

Colonial homosexuality did not proclaim itself openly. Indeed, doing so would have been folly in an era when homosexual acts in many countries remained illegal, and when scandals, and the punishments meted out to wrongdoers, served as warnings about the dangers of indiscretion or revelation. Moreover, numerous men who did not fit the paradigm of heterosexuality, who were not fathers and husbands, would have been appalled at allegations that they were homosexually inclined. Some would have hardly been aware of the term, others would have angrily rejected the implication that they might engage in sodomical acts, and still others would not have considered their emotional attachments to other men to be homosexual. Except when arrests and trials brought explicit details of sexual behaviour into public view, or in cases where a few courageous men – such as Carpenter or Gide – discussed their own homosexual desires, traces of inclinations appear in more subtle ways.

Works dedicated to companions, such as Lawrence's poem to Dahoum, memorialise special friendships. Choice of language, as in Lyautey's repeated references to 'colonial sap', or allusions, primarily to figures of Antiquity, signal readers to particular proclivities. Novels seldom provide explicitly homosexual *mises en scène*, though such situations as the bonding between an African and a Scotsman in *Prester John* and the all-male idyll in *The Soul of Malaya* suggest relationships that it would have been too audacious to detail. Photographs and paintings never represent homosexuality *per se*, but insistence on the physical beauty of male models, the way in which subjects are portrayed and the known penchants of certain photographers or painters convey sexual seduction and lust. Those who wanted to decipher the sexual codes could do so.

The voices of colonial homosexuality are many, yet sometimes voices have been silenced or muted. Burton's wife burned the unpublished writings he left at his death, and British administrators in Nigeria insouciantly admitted that they had destroyed material relating to the homosexuality of a colleague. Homosexuality could be censored out of the record; newspapers in Malaya and Papua New Guinea, for example, simply did not publish reports on indelicate *affaires*. Often writers or artists found it necessary to censor themselves. Duncan Grant's most erotic drawings of inter-racial male couples were only published after his death. Forster discussed his relationship with Mohammed el-Adl only with close friends, and confided his sentiments about the Egyptian to a note-book that has yet to be published in full. Ackerley and Comisso published different versions of their works, giving greater or lesser space to homosexual encounters in their travels. Loti amended his diary, when he transformed his adventures in Turkey into a novel, in order to veil a homosexual flirtation. Casement wrote his secret diaries in code and kept them carefully out of sight, knowing that their discovery could bring about his downfall, as happened after his arrest. Stanley's homosexual inclinations appear most overtly in his novel. Prokosch's homosexual passions connect the countless episodes in his wholly imagined novel about Asia. Edmund Backhouse mixed a little fact with a great deal of fiction in his manuscripts on sex in China. The boundary between truth and dissimulation in Lawrence's works is impossible to discern. Gide's experiences in the Maghreb initially appeared disguised as fiction. Visual artists also disguised homosexual desire, or at least rendered it acceptable to general viewers, in the *scènes et types* postcards of Lehnert and Landrock, the tourist-style photographs of Gloeden and List, the ethnographic paintings of Stowitts and the Orientalist evocations of Day or Philpot.

Other than in the cases of Carpenter and Gide, only late in the colonial era could men speak openly about their homosexuality. Guérin's and Sénac's sentiments impelled them to take a stance on sexual and colonial emancipation. Joe Orton and other visitors to Tangier could chronicle their homosexual encounters in a way unimaginable to earlier writers, and Donald Friend could paint Ceylonese and Balinese in a fashion that would have caused consternation in prior decades. Until the 1960s, colonial homosexuality is more visible in private writings, between the lines of published works, in the suggestiveness of visual art and in the generally discreet actions of men who, with various clues, expressed their intimate friendships.

As for the voices of men from outside Europe, they are seldom heard. The letters from Masood and Mohammed to Forster, and from Athmann to Gide, count among the few documents from the colonial period providing a perspective on close friendships from the 'other side'. Only a few quotations give hints as to Dahoum's reactions to Lawrence and England, or do remarks to a biographer give insight into how bin Ghabaisha and bin Kabina remembered Thesiger. What Djami thought about Rimbaud, or how the Balinese *katjongs* viewed the scandal in the Dutch East Indies in the 1930s, can only be surmised. Even the European partners of colonials – most of Rhodes's secretaries, Przhevalsky's assistants, Humboldt's protégé von Haeften – left no recollections. Casement's partners are known to posterity only by the names and measurements he recorded in his diary. 'Natives' brought before courts for 'sex crimes' in Papua New Guinea, and offenders on trial in Australia, appear largely in judges' casebooks and often sensationalistic newspaper accounts. The 'young Arabs' photographed by Lehnert and Landrock remain anonymous and silent. The *boys*, porters and hammam attendants who proffered their services to European visitors and expatriates have merged into the background of colonial history.

The traces that remain in various genres suggest that homosexual encounters were widespread in the colonies. Men with homosexual inclinations or experiences, and whose lives and work were closely linked to the colonial world, range from some of the most famous figures in the history of European expansion to those who have left historical tracks only because of sexual improprieties. From young Humboldt going to South America in the early 1800s to Bowles growing old in Morocco in the decades after the Second World War, the European examples range across almost two centuries and all the inhabited continents. Colonial homosexual connections included both 'platonic' friendships and hotly physical relationships, brief encounters and longer-lasting partnerships. Some European men sought European partners; others preferred 'natives'. There was casual sex and abiding love, consensual pleasure and violent abuse, unreciprocated longing and brazen seduction. There is no simple model of colonial homosexuality.

Imperial circumstances, however, favoured varied expressions of homosexuality. Uncharted regions lured explorers who discovered male brothels, the ritual incorporation of fellatio or sodomy into male initiation, blood brotherhoods, 'male brides', the 'third sex' and adolescents with few reservations about certain homosexual practices. Transported convicts were crammed together, often in all-male accommodations and dangerous social promiscuity. The foot soldiers of empire were young and lusty troopers, eager for adventure and new experiences. Pioneer settlers lived solitary lives on the frontier, deprived of the company of European women. The colonies provided a refuge for those fleeing their homelands – by desire or necessity – because of reprobate desires and chequered backgrounds, and, more generally, for those ill at ease in the confines of traditional European society. The desert and kasbah, tropical islands and jungles seduced writers and artists. Foreign cultures, from the 'decadent' old civilisations of Asia to the 'primitive' life in Oceania, attracted adventurers, intellectuals and dreamers. Imperial endeavours – exploration, conquest, settlement, administration, commerce, the *mission civilisatrice* – mandated expatriation. Isolation, heat and the rigours of colonial life induced the *cafard* and tempted *dépaysé* Europeans with feverish work and idleness, hashish and opium, women and men.

Imperialism did more than just carve out new domains for Europeans. It also promoted hierarchical relationships propitious to sexual commerce. Men of power gathered agreeable young associates around them: Kitchener's 'band of boys', Rhodes's 'lambs', Lyautey's subalterns. Imperialism, even more pertinently, created new social relations between whites and blacks, colonial masters and indigenous servants, wealthy foreigners and impoverished 'natives'. Europeans had money and preferment to offer, and 'natives' had companionship and sex to barter. Sexual desires sometimes intersected. Europeans fantasised about brown skins, but indigenes might also feel attracted to white skin.

Race, self-evidently, played a role in many encounters. The physiques of overseas people fascinated, indeed obsessed, Europeans. Countries where heat and culture let men dress in revealing ways – flowing jellabas, skimpy sarongs and even less – presented a spectacle of nudity not seen in Europe. Descriptions lingered on the colour of skin and the texture of hair, the size and build of bodies. Anthropologists debated the origin of races, while sexologists measured genital endowment. Theorists hypothesised about racial characteristics and connections with sexual behaviour. The possibility of sleeping with partners so physically different could itself be an erotic lure.

Class and age also entered into the colonial sexual economy. Gide, Forster and Lawrence hailed from the educated, moneyed and respectable European elite. Their partners, Athmann, Mohammed and Dahoum, worked as a guide, a tram conductor and a servant. Middle- and upper-class European homosexuals, often of relatively mature age, bedded poor youths. Foreign artists in Bali picked up *katjongs*; colonials throughout South-East Asia, and elsewhere, enjoyed the favours of houseboys and street porters, and sometimes of pupils or parishioners. G.F. Green came to grief with a rickshaw puller. Casement had assignations with dock workers. Forster 'got off' with an Indian barber, and Gide had an encounter with a musician in Algeria. Tourists and 'expats' searched for street boys from Tangier to Port Moresby.

These relationships, from one perspective, seem emblematic of colonial domination, and many no doubt were based on crass exchange of money for sex, Europeans taking the advantages to which they claimed entitlement by race, wealth, political power and, sometimes, violence. However, that hardly tells the full story, and robs the partners of European men of their capacity to seduce, to choose bedmates, to appreciate benefits of association with Europeans – their sexual agency. It also denies that they might feel sexual desire for Europeans, or fall in love with them. Athmann's letters to Gide, and Mohammed's to Forster show genuine affection and enduring loyalty. The Europeans' actions often bespoke sincere concern – Forster saw to Mohammed in his terminal illness, Lawrence daringly crossed enemy lines in the hope of rescuing Dahoum, Rimbaud left his worldly goods to Djami, Stanley mourned the death of Kalulu. (Not just 'natives' benefited from such concern: Rhodes nursed the dying Neville Pickering and wanted to bequeath his estate to him, Rajah Brooke provided a colonial career for Charles Grant, Lyautey mentored his lieutenants.) Europeans were patrons as well as sex partners. The almost life-long links between Carpenter and Arunachalam, and between Forster and Masood, are two of the best preserved of friendships crossing the gap between colonisers and colonised. Critiques of colonialism voiced by Casement and others, and the willingness of Sénac to cast his lot with Algerian nationalists and of Genet to support the Palestinians, testify to deep personal and political empathy, not naked sexual exploitation.

The breach between cultures nevertheless always existed, though Augiéras might write as Abdallah Chaamba, and Sénac as Yahia El-Ouahrani, Lawrence might wear a burnous, and Forster don Indian court dress. 'Going native' was hardly a real option for most Europeans overseas. They returned home after their travels, back to a Parisian salon or a Cambridge college, to the British home counties or the French provinces. Some tried to take foreign friends with them, but Athmann, Dahoum and Stuart-Young's visitors stayed for only a short while. The Tunisian brought to England by Philpot turned out badly and was sent home. European and non-European ideas of sex (homosexual or hetero-sexual), marriage and love did not coincide in the long term. Politics, economics and social disapproval worked against long-lasting unions. Friendship might survive where sex did not, as distance and diverging trajectories provided challenges to intimacy. 'Only connect' proved difficult counsel.

The colonies were no paradise for 'perverts'. Tropical diseases and other hazards were the lot of all colonials. Europeans wondered in their heart of hearts about the constancy and real allegiance of foreign lovers. Blackmail, theft, violence, arrest and disgrace haunted homosexuals overseas, as well as at home. Homosexual liaisons at best might be tolerated, but were never celebrated, in the official imperial mind. British laws making homosexual acts criminal were extended to the Australian colonies and other possessions. Those who offended conventional public morals paid in prison or on the scaffold for indiscretions. Lucky ones, such as William Yate, were sent packing. Dutch colonial authorities imprisoned Spies in Bali; the British cashiered Green in Ceylon, hanged Casement in London and drove Macdonald to suicide in Paris. Reginald Poole in the distant Solomon Islands lacked the wisdom to avoid murder. In post-colonial Algeria, Sénac was assassinated.

The fates of those men show, in a tragic way, how public and private life conjoined. But those were not the only connections between the public and the private. Colonial homosexuality was seldom just a matter of sex. Homosexuality connected with colonial vocations. From Przhevalsky to Thesiger, explorers enjoyed male camaraderie on hard expeditions. Officers from Baden-Powell and Gordon to Lyautey appreciated the masculine attentions of young men and strong soldiers. Conflicts between Macdonald and Kitchener, and between Burton and Speke, may have hidden homosexual tensions. At several junctures, Rhodes's manœuvres in South Africa were shaped by his emotional ties with other men. Stanley's *Kalulu* is a homosexual wish fulfilment never quite realised in his African peregrinations. Daniélou's and Leadbeater's attraction to Eastern religions reflected erotic experiences in India, and Dinet's conversion to Islam was influenced by ambivalent friendship with Sliman ben Ibrahim. Stowitts's paintings of Orientalist dancers and men from 'vanishing India', and Day's photographs of black Americans, clearly reflected their sexual orientations. The works of a long list of novelists – Melville and Stoddard, Loti and Buchan, Couperus and Fauconnier – were inspired by homoerotic engagement with the world overseas. Carpenter's writings about his guru, and his letters to Arunachalam, and Forster's dedication of A *Passage to India* to Masood and the Maharajah of Dewas Senior, say much about cross-cultural influences. Guérin, Herbart and Sénac articulated connections between homosexuality and anti-colonialism. Colonial authorities (just as post-colonial regimes) meanwhile used sexual misdemeanours to incriminate men like Macdonald – a ranker who did not fit in with the high and mighty – who were perhaps too friendly with the 'natives' and too little respectful of the colonial elite.

The colonial world represented many things for these men. Foreign countries were refuges from the constraints of Europe. Rimbaud abandoned poetry, and Europe, for trading and companionship on the horn of Africa. Stuart-Young fled childhood horrors and prison for West Africa. The world overseas provided sexual opportunities, places where a Frenchman could be assured of the companionship of a Moroccan or Egyptian for a few coins, and an Australian could win the favour of a Papuan for a few beers. Green's 'verandahism' was a sport that could be played everywhere in the tropics. The colonies, moreover, provided places for self-discovery – friendship with Masood woke Forster from his suburban slumber. Forster lost his virginity on the beaches of Alexandria, and Gide had his homosexual awakening in the dunes of Biskra. Colonies were places of experimentation, where Europeans could join in festivals at a maharajah's court or bunk down with nomads in the Arabian Desert or the Atlas Mountains. They provided cultural inspiration, subjects for Spies's paintings and melodies for McPhee's music. One can only speculate how many *scènes et types* portraits of handsome young men of colour were stimulated by sexual interest, or how many collections of naughty drawings and photographs have been destroyed by embarrassed heirs.

The colonies were a reflection of the 'civilised' world, but also gave a different perspective on 'civilisation'. For the British, colonies were testing-grounds for manly virtues. Prison colonies could rehabilitate addicts of vice (at least in theory). Lyautey hoped that colonial experiences would revivify a degenerated nation. Some homosexuals, however, rejected the 'civilised' world. A romantic Stoddard wished that he could become a 'savage' in the South Pacific, and a disaffected Augiéras proclaimed himself the 'Occidental barbarian'. Both Augiéras and Genet expressed visceral hatred for Paris, France and Western civilisation. Anti-colonialists damned European capitalism and sham democracy, awaiting a revolution to emancipate those shackled by economic, political and sexual chains. More gently, Carpenter hoped for the triumph of a convivial and egalitarian democracy, with fellowship for all.

For many, the colonies were the new Hellas – 'Arcadia in ebony', as Stuart-Young put it, Comisso's 'equatorial Athens', peopled with 'southern gods' (like Couperus's Addy), an 'Apollo' (Prokosch's Samazeuilh), a 'dusky Antinous' (a half-Indian described by Casement), men 'like old Greek statues' (as Governor Beauchamp spoke of Australian athletes). Haeckel's Gamameda was a Ceylonese Ganymede; a Polynesian and his *tayo*, a Pacific Damon and Pythias for Melville. Ackerley's homosexual and Hellenophile maharajah dreamed of reviving ancient Greece in colonial Chhatarpur. For classically schooled Europeans, such formulations provide clues to sexual proclivities, but also dreams that the 'Socratic love' condemned in Christian Europe might be found elsewhere. For right-minded Europeans, the world overseas threatened a sexual dystopia of lascivious licence, lewd dancing, polygamy, prostitution and promiscuity, the horrors of child-marriage, the evils of the harem, the unbridled pleasures of the *Kama Sutra* and *The Thousand and One Nights*, the fright of foreign genitalia, the unmentionable vice of sodomy. European moralists created images of menacing African and Arab virility, and denigrated supposed Asian male passivity. But for 'immoralists', these stereotypes might look attractive indeed. The absence of Judeo-Christian traditions, the tolerance of contrary pleasures and the availability of willing partners made the colonies beckon as possible sexual utopias, even if they did not always turn out to be the wished-for Edens.

The colonial experiences rebounded in Europe, seen not only in the books, art, music and dance with themes of homoerotic Orientalism. Dr Jacobus X's observations seemed to confirm Tardieu's spurious theories about homosexuality, and rumours of colonial 'vice' inspired Christians to preach the Gospel. Overseas experiences also made Europeans question sexual norms at home, and suggested to some that 'unnatural' acts were actually very natural for many men. Carpenter researched the sex life of 'intermediate types' and 'primitive folk' after learning about South Asia, and Gide wrote *Corydon* after he had travelled to North Africa. Magnus Hirschfeld's trip to the East reinforced his hypotheses about Urnings. Anthropologists from Westermarck to Schneebaum discoursed on non-Western sexuality. Forster said that *Maurice* would have been different if he had already been to Egypt and India when he wrote the novel.

For many European homosexuals (as well as heterosexuals), the colonial world itself provided an erotic *frisson* or transcendental plenitude. The sight of half-clad 'natives' silhouetted against luxuriant landscapes was a sensual experience. The sounds and colours of 'heathen' and 'barbarous' ceremonies in hot countries contrasted with chilly, buttoned-down Europe. The animation of the North African souk, the sunny seashore of a Polynesian island and the elaborate temple ceremonies of India or Bali presented a theatre of sensuality. Erotic figures merge into the landscapes in Lehnert and Landrock's postcards. Literary descriptions of scenery and daily life verge on the sexual (or, in the case of Stoddard, become transparently so). Humboldt's delight in the Amazonian jungle, and the exhilaration experienced by Lyautey and Augiéras in the desert, expressed the excitement of both physical senses and the mind. The thrilling promise of the kasbah and the hammam became a cliché. For Thesiger, the desert and the expedition took the place of sex. The landscape of Algeria, the young men of Algiers and the politics of the revolution became inseparable for Sénac. Masood, the Maharajah of Dewas Senior and Kanaya were complementary aspects of India for Forster. Bali and sex were coterminous for the denizens of that island in the 1930s, and, for writers like Haeckel and Carpenter, the beauty of Ceylon and Ceylonese men were intimately intertwined.

In Europe, life was full of dichotomies – respectable versus immoral behaviour, natural and unnatural sex, homosexual versus heterosexual acts. In the colonies, things were different. Misbehaviour (so long as it was relatively discreet) would be tolerated, the global positioning of the Sotadic Zone excused misbehaviour – *infra equinoxialem nihil peccari*, there is no sin below the equator. The age of consent of a bedfellow did not seem a matter of great concern, nor was expectation of compensation for sexual favours a surprise. Beer and rum, drugs and heat lowered inhibitions. Burton and Flaubert, and then Gide and

Forster, set the style for later Europeans to discover the pleasures, and give in to the temptations, of the 'Orient'; sex appeared one of the 'musts' on the tourist's list. The camp, the cantonment and cosmopolitan port towns encouraged social intermingling and sexual interaction. Hinduism and Buddhism seemed not so obsessed with sexual propriety as Christianity, and Muslim poets like Abu Nuwas sang the praises of boys. Young men fated for marriage and fatherhood did not reject advances for homosexual sex. The colonial situation, and colonials' return home, could absolve Europeans of long-term responsibilities or momentary moral lapses. The difference between friends, protégés, foster sons and sexual partners was often vague, and the boundaries between friendship, lust and paternalism porous. Eroticised masculinity and male camaraderie issued invitations to homosexual liaisons. For homosexuals overseas, the voyage to the colonies was the search for a happy Sodom unpunished by European civilisation, a new Athens recreated in the tropics, the fulfilment of fantasies of Arabian nights, or simply an interlude on a sunny seashore with sexy young companions.

Bibliography

Unpublished sources

Australia
  Mitchell Library, Sydney
Australian Board of Missions Collection, Box 45 (6a), ABM Board Meeting Minute
    Books, Agenda, 7–9 February 1956, ML MSS 4503.

National Archives of Australia, Canberra
Correspondence concerning the Rev. H. Irving, 1957, A 452/1, Item 57/183.
Divine Word Missionaries, A 518/1, Item R838/1, Part 2.
Magwich, Rodney 'A Submission on Plantation Wages to Rural Wages Board of
    Industry', 13 May 1970 (uncatalogued).
Report on Corporal Punishment in Papua New Guinea, A 518/1, Item A 846/6/146.

National Library of Australia, Canberra
Papers of Justice R.T. Gore, Casebooks, 1948–53, MS 2819.

Belgium
Musée Royal de l'Afrique Centrale, Tervuren
Papers of Henry Morton Stanley, Notebooks, 1870–3, BL/PR 2435.

United Kingdom
British Library, Oriental and India Office Collections, London
Letters from J. Nicholson to H. Edwardes, MM Eur E 211/3.

Bodleian Library, Oxford
Backhouse, Edmund Trelawney, *Décadence Mandchoue* and *The Dead Past*, MS. Eng. Mis
    d. 1223.

Modern Archives Centre, King's College, Cambridge
Papers of E.M. Forster
Correspondence with Gamila el-Adl, Mohammed el-Adl, Edward Carpenter, Constan-
    tine Cavafy, Maharajah of Dewas Senior, Goldsworthy Lowes Dickinson, Syed Ross
    Masood – xviii.
Documents on Mohammed el-Adl – xi/10.1 and xi/10.2.
India Journal 1912–13, 1921 – xii/11.
India Journal 1945 – xii/17.
Locked Diary – Vol. 4/4.

Rhodes House Library, Oxford
Letters of Jim Allen to Robert Heussler, 16 April and 18 May 1975, MSS Brit. Emp.
480/8/2.

Unpublished theses

Fogarty, Walter J. 'Indecent connection: Notions of the development of the homosexual
in New South Wales law, 1788–1900', BA Honours thesis, University of New South
Wales, 1989.
Kerkhof, Gosse, 'Het Indische Zedenschandaal, een koloniaal incident', Doctoral thesis,
University of Amsterdam, 1982.

Published sources

Ackerley, J.R., *Hindoo Holiday* (London, 1952).
Adams, Jad, 'Was "K" Gay?', *History Today*, November 1999, pp. 26–7.
Addade, Stéphane-Jacques, *Bernard Boutet de Monvel* (Paris, 2001).
Adelswärd-Fersen, Jacques d', *Hei Hsiang: Le Parfum noir* (Paris, 1921).
Aldrich, Robert, 'Homosexuality in the French colonies', in Jeffrey Merrick and Michael
Sibalis (eds), *Homosexuality in French History and Culture* (New York, 2001), pp. 201–18.
——, 'Colonialism and homosexuality', *Thamyris: Mythmaking from Past to Present*, Vol.
3, No. 1 (1996), pp. 175–91.
——, *Greater France: A History of French Overseas Expansion* (London, 1996).
——,(ed.), *Gay Perspectives II: More Essays in Australian Gay Culture* (Sydney, 1994).
——, *The Seduction of the Mediterranean: Writing, Art and Homosexual Fantasy* (London,
1993).
——, 'Die mediterrane Besessenheit: Ein Beispiel zur Frage der Homo-Imagination', in
Maria Kalveram and Wolfgang Popp (eds), *Homosexualitäten-literarisch* (Essen, 1991),
pp. 13–21.
——, 'Weisse und farbige Männer. Reisen, Kolonialismus und Homosexualität', *Forum:
Homosexualität und Literatur*, No. 7 (1989), pp. 5–24.
Aldrich, Robert, and Garry Wotherspoon (eds), *Who's Who in Gay and Lesbian History:
From Antiquity to World War II* (London, 2001).
—— (eds), *Who's Who in Contemporary Gay and Lesbian History: From World War II to
the Present Day* (London, 2001).
—— (eds), *Gay and Lesbian Perspectives IV: Studies in Australian Culture* (Sydney, 1998).
—— (eds), *Gay Perspectives: Essays in Australian Gay Culture* (Sydney, 1992).
Allen, Charles (ed.), *Tales from the South China Seas: Images of the British in South-East
Asia in the Twentieth Century* (London, 1983).
Alloula, Malek, *The Colonial Harem* (Manchester, 1986).
Alternative libertaire, special issue on Daniel Guérin, 1999.
Altman, Dennis, *Global Sex* (Sydney, 2001).
——, 'The myth of mateship', *Meanjin*, No. 2 (1987), pp. 163–72.
Archives de la Ville de Marseille, *Poésie au Sud: Jean Sénac et la nouvelle poésie algérienne
d'expression française* (Marseille, 1983).
Arunachalam, Ponnambalam, *Speeches and Writings* (Colombo, n.d.).
Asher, Michael, *Lawrence: The Uncrowned King of Arabia* (London, 1998).
——, *Thesiger: A Biography* (London, 1994).
Association de Béni-Safiens, *L'Album de Béni-Saf* (n.p., 1988).

Association des Amis de François Augiéras, *Ecrivain-Peintre: 'Une Aventure de l'Esprit'*, *1925–1971* (Périgueux, 1985).

Atlas, Charles, *Everlasting Health and Strength* (New York, 1931).

Augiéras, François, *Lettres du Mont Athos* (Paris, 1994).

——, *Les Noces avec l'Occident* (Paris, 1981).

——, *Le Voyage des morts* (Paris, 1979).

——, *Une Adolescence au temps du Maréchal et de multiples aventures* (Paris, 1968).

Augiéras, François, and Paul Placet, *La Chasse fantastique* (n.p., 1996).

Austen, Roger, *Genteel Pagan: The Double Life of Charles Warren Stoddard*, ed. John W. Crowley (Amherst, MA, 1991).

Awal: Cahiers d'études berbères, special issue on Jean Sénac, No. 10 (1993).

Bakshi, Parminder Kaur, *Distant Desire: Homoerotic Codes and the Subversion of the English Novel in E.M. Forster's Fiction* (New York, 1996).

——, 'Homosexuality and Orientalism: Edward Carpenter's journey to the East', in Tony Brown (ed.), *Edward Carpenter and Late Victorian Radicalism* (London, 1990), pp. 151–77.

Ballhatchet, Kenneth, *Race, Sex and Class under the Raj: Imperial Attitudes and Policies and their Critics, 1793–1905* (London, 1980).

Bancel, Nicholas, Pascal Blanchard and Armelle Chatelier, *Images et colonies (1880–1962)* (Paris, 1993).

Barthes, Roland, *Incidents* (Paris, 1987).

Barua, Dilip Kumar, *Edward Carpenter, 1844–1929: An Apostle of Freedom* (Burdwan, 1991).

Bastien, Gregory, *Khalid* (Lille, 1996).

Bavin-Mizzi, Jill, '"An unnatural offence": Sodomy in Western Australia from 1880 to 1900', in Charlie Fox (ed.), *Historical Refractions (Studies in Western Australian History XIV)* (Perth, 1993), pp. 102–20.

Beale, Edgar, 'Jackey Jackey' and 'Kennedy, Edmund Besley Court', in A.G.L. Shaw and C.M.H. Clark (eds), *Australian Dictionary of Biography*, Vol. 2 (Melbourne, 1967), pp. 7, 44.

Beauman, Nicola, *Morgan: A Biography of E.M. Forster* (London, 1996).

Beckford, William, *The Episodes of Vathek*, trans Frank Marzials (Sawtry, Cambridgeshire, 1994).

——, *Histoire du Prince Ahmed* (Paris, 1993).

Belamri, Rabah, *Jean Sénac: Entre désir et douleur* (Algiers, 1989).

Bencheikh, Jamel-Eddine and Christiane Chaulet-Achour, *Jean Sénac: Clandestin des deux rives* (Paris, 1999).

Benjamin, Roger (ed.), *Orientalism: Delacroix to Klee* (Sydney, 1997).

Bennett, Judith A., *Wealth of the Solomons: A History of a Pacific Archipelago, 1800–1978* (Honolulu, 1987).

Berthier, Philippe, *Pierre Herbart: Morale et style de la désinvolture* (Paris, 1999).

——, *François Augiéras: L'Apprenti sorcier* (Seyssel, 1994).

Berthulus, Dr, 'Considérations sur les causes de dégénérescence physique et morale du peuple dans les grandes villes', *Gazette médicale de Paris*, 1847, pp. 800–1.

Beurdeley, C., *Beau Petit Ami* (Fribourg, 1979).

Bhatnagan, S.K., *History of the Muslim-Anglo-Oriental College, Aligarh* (Aligarh, 1969).

Bierman, John, *Dark Safari: The Life Behind the Legend of Henry Morton Stanley* (London, 1990).

Binney, Judith, 'Whatever happened to poor Mr Yate? An exercise in voyeurism', *The New Zealand Journal of History*, Vol. 9, No. 2 (1975), pp. 111–25.

Blanch, Lesley, *Pierre Loti: Portrait of an Escapist* (London, 1983).

Blanchard, Pascal, *et al.*, *L'Autre et nous: 'Scènes et Types'* (Paris, 1995).

Bledsoe, Lucy Jane (ed.), *Gay Travels* (San Francisco, 1998).

Bleys, Rudi, *The Geography of Perversion: Male-to-Male Sexual Behaviour outside the West and the Ethnographic Imagination, 1750–1918* (New York, 1995).

——, 'Homosexual exile: The textuality of the imaginary paradise, 1800–1980', *Journal of Homosexuality*, Vol. 25, No. 1–2 (1993), pp. 165–82.

Boone, Joseph A., 'Vacation cruises; or, the homoerotics of Orientalism', *PMLA*, Vol. 110 (1985), pp. 89–107.

Borer, Alain, *Rimbaud en Abyssinie* (Paris, 1984).

Botting, Douglas, *Humboldt, 1769–1859: Un Savant démocrate* (Paris, 1988).

Bowen, Roger, 'Getting to know you', *Harrington Gay Men's Fiction Quarterly*, Vol. 1, No. 4 (1999), pp. 51–62.

——, '"Squalid with joy": Scobie, sex, and race in Lawrence Durrell's *Alexandria Quartet*', *Journal of Homosexuality*, Vol. 36, No. 2 (1998), pp. 87–97.

Brahimi, Denise, *La Vie et l'oeuvre de Etienne Dinet* (Paris, 1991).

Braybrooke, Neville (ed.), *The Letters of J.R. Ackerley* (London, 1975).

Brett, Philip, 'Eros and Orientalism in Britten's operas', in Philip Brett, Elizabeth Wood and Gary C. Thomas, *Queering the Pitch: The New Gay and Lesbian Musicology* (London, 1994), pp. 235–56.

Bristow, Joseph, 'Passage to E.M. Forster: Race, homosexuality, and the "unmanageable streams" of empire', in Chris Gittings (ed.), *Imperialism and Gender* (Hebden Bridge, 1996), pp. 138–57.

——, *Effeminate England: Homoerotic Writing after 1885* (Buckingham, 1995).

——, *Empire Boys: Adventures in a Man's World* (London, 1991).

British Solomon Islands Protectorate News Sheet, No. 5 (1 January–15 March 1956).

Bryder, Linda, 'Sex, race, and colonalism: An historiographical review', *International History Review*, Vol. 20, No. 4 (1998), pp. 806–54.

Buchan, John, *Prester John* (London, 1956).

Buckle, Richard, *Nijinsky* (London, 1971).

Bulletin des amis d'André Gide, special issue on Gide and Algeria, Vol. 22, No. 102 (1994).

Burton, Richard, *The Sotadic Zone* (Boston, 1977).

Buruma, Ian, *The Missionary and the Libertine: Love and War in East and West* (London, 1996).

Butcher, John G., *The British in Malaya, 1880–1941: The Social History of a European Community in Colonial South-East Asia* (Kuala Lumpur, 1979).

Buzard, James, *European Tourism, Literature, and the Ways to Culture, 1800–1918* (Oxford, 1993).

Cairns, Lucille, *Privileged Pariahdom: Homosexuality in the Novels of Dominique Fernandez* (Berne, 1996).

Caradec, François, *'N'ayons pas peur des mots': Dictionnaire du Français argotique et populaire* (Paris, 1988).

Cardinal, Philippe, *L'Orient d'un photographe: Lehnert et Landrock* (Paris, 1987).

Carman, Barry, and John McPherson, *Bimbashi McPherson: A Life in Egypt* (London, 1983).

Carpenter, Edward, *Selected Writings* (London, 1984).

——, *My Days and Dreams* (London, 1916).

——, *From Adam's Peak to Elephanta* (London, 1892).

Caute, David, *Fever Pitch* (London, 1965).

Chaamba, Abdallah [François Augiéras], *Le Viellard et l'enfant* (Paris, 1949).

Chang Hall, Lisa Kahaleole and J. Kehaulani Kauanui, 'Same-sex sexuality in Pacific literature', *Amerasia Journal*, Vol. 20, No. 1 (1994), pp. 75–81.

Chebel, Malek, *Encyclopédie de l'amour en Islam* (Paris, 1998).

——, *L'Esprit de sérail: Mythes et pratiques sexuels au Maghreb* (Paris, 1995).

Chester, Alfred, *Head of a Sad Angel: Stories, 1953–1966*, ed. Edward Field (Santa Rosa, CA, 1990).

Chisholm, A.H., *Strange Journey: The Adventures of Ludwig Leichhardt and John Gilbert* (Sydney, 1973).

Churchill, Caryl, *Cloud Nine* (London, 1979).

Chylinska, Teresa, 'Szymanowski', in Stanley Sadie (ed.), *The New Grove Dictionary of Music and Musicians* (London, 1980), Vol. 18, pp. 499–504.

Clancy-Smith, Julia, and Frances Gouda (eds), *Domesticating the Empire: Race, Gender, and Family Life in French and Dutch Colonialism* (Charlottesville, VA, 1998).

Clark, C.M.H., *A History of Australia*, Vol. III (Melbourne, 1987).

Clavigny, Paul, 'L'Homosexualité dans l'armée', *Revue d'hypnotisme*, Vol. 23 (1908), pp. 39–40.

Cluny, Claude Michel and Paul Placet (eds), *Augiéras Peintre* (Paris, 2001).

Colney, Anne de, *L'Amour aux colonies* (Paris, 1932).

Comisso, Giovanni, *Jeux d'enfance*, trans Soula Aghion (Paris, 1989).

——, *Loves of the Orient* (New York, 1954).

Commonwealth of Australia, *Report to the General Assembly of the United Nations on the Administration of the Territory of New Guinea* (Canberra, 1945–75).

Cooper, Emmanuel, *The Life and Work of Henry Scott Tuke* (London, 1987).

Cooper, Wayne F., *Claude McKay: Rebel Sojourner in the Harlem Renaissance* (Baton Rouge, LA, 1987).

Couperus, Louis, *The Hidden Force*, trans Alexander Teixera de Mattos (Harmondsworth, 1992).

——, *Eastward* (London, 1924).

Croft-Cooke, Rupert, *The Caves of Hercules* (London, 1974).

——, *The Gorgeous East: One Man's India* (London, 1965).

Crowder, Michael, *West Africa under Colonial Rule* (London, 1968).

D'Alger au Sénégal – Mission Augiéras-Draper, 1927–1928 (Paris, 1931).

D'Arch Smith, Timothy, *Love in Earnest: Some Notes on the Lives and Writings of English 'Uranian' Poets from 1889 to 1930* (London, 1970).

Daniell, David, *The Interpreter's House: A Critical Assessment of John Buchan* (London, 1975).

Daniélou, Alain, *Le Chemin du labyrinthe: Souvenirs d'Orient et d'Occident* (Monaco, 1993).

——, *Le Tour du monde en 1936* (Paris, 1987).

Darling, Malcolm, *Apprentice to Power: India, 1904–1908* (London, 1966).

Dautheville, Louis, 'Le Cafard ou psychose des pays chauds', *Archives d'anthropologie criminelle*, Vol. 26 (1911), pp. 5–27.

Davidson, Michael, *Some Boys* (London, 1988).

——, *The World, the Flesh and Myself* (London, 1962).

Dawson, Graham, *Soldier Heroes: British Adventure, Empire and the Imaging of Masculinities* (London, 1994).

Delain, Orion, 'Carnet de voyage: L'Inde', *Triangulère*, No. 2 (Paris, 2001), pp. 548–627.

Delaney, J.G.P., *Glyn Philpot: His Life and Art* (Aldershot, 1999).

De-la-Noy, Michael, *Denton Welch: The Making of a Writer* (Harmondsworth, 1984).

Desbiefs, A., *Le Vice en Algérie* (Paris, 1899).

Dessaigne, Francine, *Tatahouine m'était contée* (Ivry-sur-Seine, 1996).

Dickinson, G. Lowes, *The Autobiography of G. Lowes Dickinson*, ed. Dennis Proctor (London, 1973).

——, *Appearances, being Notes of Travel* (London, n.d.).

Dollimore, Jonathan, *Sexual Dissidence: Augustine to Wilde, Freud to Foucault* (Oxford, 1991).

Downs, Ian, *The Last Mountain: A Life in Papua New Guinea* (St Lucia, Queensland, 1986).

Dugas, Guy, 'André Gide et Athmannn: Le Roman d'une amitié rare', *Cahiers de Tunisie*, Vol. 30, No. 119–20 (1992), pp. 247–65.

Dumortier, David, *La Pioche de Salah* (Paris, 2001).

Dunaway, J. Joseph, *Mandalas of the Hidden Wisdom: The Cosmos According to Stowitts* (Pacific Grove, CA, 2000).

Dunton, Chris, '"Wheyting be dat?": The treatment of homosexuality in African literature', *Research in African Literature*, Vol. 20, No. 3 (fall 1989), pp. 422–48.

Dupuy, Marie-Anne, *Dominique-Vivant Denon: L'Oeil de Napoléon* (Paris, 1999).

Durrell, Lawrence, *The Alexandria Quartet* (London, 1957–60).

Duviols, Jean-Paul, and Charles Minguet, *Humboldt: Savant-Citoyen du monde* (Paris, 1994).

Dyer, Richard, 'The white man's muscles', in Harry Stecopoulos and Michael Uebel (eds), *Race and the Subject of Masculinities* (Durham, NC, 1997), pp. 286–314.

Dynes, Wayne R., *Homosexuality: A Research Guide* (New York, 1987).

Eaubonne, Françoise d', *Eros minoritaire* (Paris, 1970).

Edwardes, Michael, *Bound to Exile* (London, 1969).

Esten, John, *John Singer Sargent: The Male Nudes* (New York, 1999).

Faro, Clive with Garry Wotherspoon, *Street Seen: A History of Oxford Street* (Melbourne, 2000).

Farr, Dennis, *William Etty* (London, 1958).

Farrère, Claude, *Les Civilisés* (Paris, 1997).

Fauconnier, Henri, *The Soul of Malaya*, trans Eric Sutton (Kuala Lumpur, 1965).

Favrod, Charles-Henri, *Etranges Etrangers: Photographie et exotisme, 1850/1910* (Paris, 1989).

Favrod, Charles-Henri and André Rouvinez, *Lehnert & Landrock: Orient, 1904–1930* (Heidelberg, 1998).

Fernandez, Dominique, *Une Fleur de jasmin à l'oreille* (Paris, 1980).

Fiji Times and Herald, 31 January 1956.

Firbank, Ronald, *Prancing Nigger* (London, 1977).

——, *Valmouth* (London, 1919).

Fleig, Alain, *Rêves de papier: La Photographie orientaliste, 1860–1914* (Neuchâtel, 1997).

Flinders, Matthew, *Personal Letters from an Extraordinary Life*, ed. Paul Brunton (Sydney, 2002).

Formes, Malia B., 'Beyond complicity versus resistance: Recent work on gender and European imperialism', *Journal of Social History* Vol. 23, No. 3 (1995), pp. 629–41.

Forster, E.M., *Indian Journals and Essays* (London, 1983).

——, *Alexandria: A History and a Guide* (London, 1982).

——, *Only Connect: Letters to Indian Friends*, ed. Syed Hamid Husain (New Delhi, 1979).

——, *The Life to Come and Other Stories* (London, 1972).

——, *The Hill of Devi* (London, 1965).

——, *Two Cheers for Democracy* (London, 1951).

——, *A Passage to India* (London, 1924).

——, *Pharos and Pharillon* (London, 1923).

Freedgood, Elaine, 'E.M. Forster's queer nation: Taking the closet to the colony in *A Passage to India*', in T. Foster, C. Siegel and E. Verry (eds), *Bodies of Writing, Bodies in Performance* (New York, 1996), pp. 123–44.

French, Robert, *Camping by a Billabong: Gay and Lesbian Stories from Australian History* (Sydney, 1993).

Fretheim, Tor, *Om bare sola ville danse* (Oslo, 1990).

Friedman, David M., *A Mind of Its Own: A Cultural History of the Penis* (New York, 2001).

Friend, Donald, *Bumbooziana* (Melbourne, 1979).

——, *The Cosmic Turtle* (Sanur, 1976).

Friend, Gwen, *My Brother Donald: A Memoir of Australian Artist Donald Friend* (Sydney, 1994).

Fryer, Jonathan. *André & Oscar: Gide, Wilde and the Gay Art of Living* (London, 1997).

Furbank, P.N., *E.M. Forster: A Life* (London, two vols, 1977 and 1978).

Garafola, Lynn, *Diaghilev's Ballets Russes* (New York, 1989).

Garafola, Lynn and Nancy Van Norman Baer, *The Ballets Russes and Its World* (New Haven, 1999).

Gard, Roger Martin du, *Le Lieutenant-Colonel de Maumort* (Paris, 1983).

Genet, Jean, 'Quatre heures à Chatila', in *Jean Genet et la Palestine*, special issue of *Revue d'études palestiniennes* (1997), pp. 7–23.

——, *Le Captif amoureux* (Paris, 1986).

——, 'Le Funambule', in *Oeuvres complètes*, Vol. 5 (Paris, 1979), pp. 7–27.

——, *Les Paravents* (Paris, 1961).

——, *Les Nègres* (Paris, 1958).

Gide, André, 'Carnets d'Egypte', in *Journal d'André Gide, 1939–1949, Souvenirs* (Paris, 1954), pp. 1,049–77.

——, *Retour du Tchad* (Paris, 1928).

——, *Voyage au Congo* (Paris, 1928).

——, *Amyntas* (Paris, 1925).

——, *L'Immoraliste* (Paris, 1902).

——, *Les Nourritures terrestres* (Paris, 1897).

Giles, Jane, *The Cinema of Jean Genet: Un Chant d'amour* (London, 1991).

Giliberti, Michel, *Derrière les portes bleues* (Paris, 2000).

Goode, John, *Rape of the Fly* (Melbourne, 1977).

Goytisolo, Juan, *Makbara* (London, 1993).

Green, G.F., *A Skilled Hand: A Collection of Stories and Writing*, eds Chloë Green and A.D. Maclean (London, 1980).

——, *The Power of Sergeant Streater* (London, 1972).

Green, Michelle, *The Dream at the End of the World: Paul Bowles and the Literary Renegades in Tangier* (New York, 1991).

Green, Richard, 'William Etty', in Jane Turner, *Grove Dictionary of Art*, Vol. 10 (London, 1996), p. 645.

Grinker, Roy Richard, *In the Arms of Africa: The Life of Colin M. Turnbull* (New York, 2000).

Guérin, Daniel, *Eux et lui* (Lille, 2000).

——, *Le Feu du sang* (Paris, 1977).

——, 'Gaugin et les jeunes Maoris', *Arcadie*, Vol. 20, No. 230 (February 1973), pp. 57–65.

——, *Autobiographie de jeunesse* (Paris, 1972).

Guibert, Hervé, *Voyage avec deux enfants* (Paris, 1982).

Gury, Christian, *Lyautey–Charlus* (Paris, 1998).

Haardt de la Baume, Caroline, *Alexandre Iacovleff* (Paris, 2000).

Haeckel, Ernst, *A Visit to Ceylon*, trans Clara Bell (London, 1883).

Hallier, Jean-Edern, *L'Evangile du fou* (Paris, 1986).

Hammond, Toby, 'Paidikion: A paiderastic manuscript', *International Journal of Greek Love*, Vol. 1, No. 2 (1966), pp. 28–37.

Hannaway, Patti, *Winslow Homer in the Tropics* (Richmond, 1973).

Hargreaves, Alec G., *The Colonial Experience in French Fiction: A Study of Pierre Loti, Ernest Psichari and Pierre Mille* (London, 1981).

Harvey, Andrew, *One Last Mirror* (London, 1985).

Hay, Bob, 'The sodomites' guide to colonial Sydney, being a guide to the principal places of shirt-lifting in Sydney Town during the convict era 1788–1843)', website (http://lemon.rainbow.net.au/fabfanny/bhay/).

Hayes, Jarrod, *Queer Nations: Marginal Sexualities in the Maghreb* (Chicago, 2000).

Haylock, John, *Body of Contention* (London, 1999).

——, *Eastern Exchange* (London, 1997).

Hekma, Gert, 'François Augiéras (1925–1971)', *Paidika*, Vol. 10, No. 1 (1991), pp. 57–64.

Henriot, Christian, *Belles de Shanghai: Prostitution et sexualité en Chine au XIXe–XXe siècles* (Paris, 1997).

Herbart, Pierre, *La Licorne* (Paris, 1998).

——, *Souvenirs imaginaires* (Paris, 1998).

——, *Inédits*, ed. Maurice Imbert (Paris, 1981).

——, *La Ligne de force* (Paris, 1958).

——, *Le Chancre du Niger* (Paris, 1939).

Herdt, Gilbert, *Guardians of the Flutes: Idioms of Masculinity* (New York, 1981).

Hervez, Jean, *Le Baiser: Baisers d'Orient* (Paris, 1922).

Heussler, Robert, *British Rule in Malaya: The Malayan Civil Service and Its Predecessors, 1867–1942* (Westport, CT, 1981).

Hilliard, David, *God's Gentlemen: A History of the Melanesian Mission, 1849–1942* (St Lucia, Queensland, 1978).

Hirschfeld, Magnus, *Men and Women: The World Journey of a Sexologist* (New York, 1935).

Hitchcock, Michael, and Lucy Norris, *Bali – The Imaginary Museum: The Photographs of Walter Spies and Beryl de Zoete* (Kuala Lumpur, 1995).

Hocquenghem, Guy, *L'Amour en relief* (Paris, 1982).

——, *La Beauté du métis* (Paris, 1979).

——, *Le Désir homosexuel* (Paris, 1972).

Hodge, Dino, *Did You Meet Any Malagas? A Homosexual History of Australia's Tropical Capital* (Darwin, 1993).

Hodges, Robert R., 'Deep fellowship: Homosexuality and male bonding in the life and fiction of Joseph Conrad', *Journal of Homosexuality*, Vol. 4, No. 4 (summer 1979), pp. 379–93.

Hogbin, H. Ian, and C. Wedgwood, *Development and Welfare in the Western Pacific* (Canberra, 1943).

Hollinghurst, Alan, *The Swimming Pool Library* (London, 1988).

Honour, Hugh, *The Image of the Black in Western Art*, Vol. IV: *From the American Revolution to World War I*, Part I: *Slaves and Liberators* and Part II: *Black Models and White Myths* (Cambridge, MA, 1989).

Hopwood, Derek, *Sexual Encounters in the Middle East: The British, the French and the Arabs* (Reading, 1999).

Hughes, Robert, *The Fatal Shore: A History of Transportation of Convicts to Australia, 1787–1868* (London, 1987).

Hugill, Peter J., 'Imperialism and manliness in Edwardian boys' novels', *Ecumene*, Vol. 6, No. 3 (1999), pp. 318–40.

Hyam, Ronald, *Empire and Sexuality: The British Experience* (Manchester, 1990).

Hyde, H. Montgomery, *The Cleveland Street Scandal* (London, 1976).

——, *The Love That Dared Not Speak Its Name* (Boston, 1970).

Hyman, Timothy, *Bhupen Khakhar* (London, 1998).

Inglis, A., *Not a White Woman Safe: Sexual Anxiety and Politics in Port Moresby, 1920–1934* (Canberra, 1974), pp. 416–18.

Inglis, Brian, *Roger Casement* (London, 1973).

Inglis, Ken, 'Mateship', in Graeme Davison, John Hirst and Stuart Macintyre (eds), *The Oxford Companion to Australian History* (Melbourne, 1998).

Jacobus X, *L'Art d'aimer aux colonies* (Paris, 1927).

Jain, M.S., *The Aligarh Movement: Its Origins and Development, 1858–1906* (Agra, 1965).

Jayawardena, Visakha Kumari, *The Rise of the Labor Movement in Ceylon* (Durham, NC, 1972).

Jeal, Tim, *Baden-Powell* (London, 1989).

Johnston, Craig, and Robert Johnson, 'The making of homosexual men', in Verity Burgmann and Jenny Lee (eds), *Staining the Wattle: A People's History of Australia since 1788* (Melbourne, 1988), pp. 86–99.

Jude, R., *Les Dégénérés dans les Bataillons d'Afrique* (Vannes, 1907).

Jullian, P., *Robert de Montesquiou* (London, 1967).

Jussim, Estelle, *Slave to Beauty: The Eccentric Life and Controversial Career of F. Holland Day, Photographer, Publisher, Aesthete* (Boston, 1981).

Kabbani, Rana, *Europe's Myths of Orient: Desire and Rule* (London, 1986).

Khan, Badruddin, *Sex, Longing and Not Belonging: A Gay Muslim's Quest for Love and Meaning* (Oakland, CA, 1997).

Kidwai, Jalil A. (ed.), *Forster–Masood Letters* (Karachi, 1984).

—— (ed.), *Khayaban-e-Masood* (Karachi, n.d.).

King, Francis, *E.M. Forster* (London, 1978).

Knox, Thomas W., *The Boy Travellers on the Congo* (London, 1888).

Koenders, Pieter, *Tussen christelijk reveil en seksuele revolutie: Bestrijding van de zedeloosheid met de nadruk op repressie van homoseksualiteit* (Amsterdam, 1996).

Kopelson, Kevin, *The Queer Afterlife of Vaslav Nijinsky* (Stanford, 1997).

Knutsen, Per, *Svømmersken* (Oslo, 1994).

Krauth, Nigel, *JF was Here* (Sydney, 1990).

Kvaale, Tom, *The Legionnaire* (San Francisco, 1997).

Lago, Mary and P.N. Furbank (eds), *Selected Letters of E.M. Forster* (London, two vols, 1983).

Lahr, John (ed.), *The Orton Diaries* (London, 1986).

Lane, Christopher, 'Volatile desire: Ambivalence and distress in Forster's colonial narratives', in Bart Moore-Gilbert (ed.), *Writing India, 1757–1990* (Manchester, 1996), pp. 188–212.

——, *The Ruling Passion: British Colonial Allegory and the Paradox of Homosexual Desire* (Durham, NC, 1995).

Larivière, Michel, *Homosexuels et bisexuels célèbres: Le Dictionnaire* (Paris, 1997).

Latimer, Tirza True, 'Balletomania: A sexual disorder?', *GLQ*, Vol. 5, No. 2 (1999), pp. 173–97.

Lawrence, Peter, *Road Belong Cargo: A Study of the Cargo Movement in the South Madang District New Guinea* (Melbourne, 1964).

Lawrence, T.E., *The Diary Kept by T.E. Lawrence while Travelling in Arabia during 1911* (Reading, 1993).

——, *The Seven Pillars of Wisdom* (New York, 1935).

Le Livre des Beaux (Paris, 1996).

Le Petit Journal Illustré, 24 April 1921.

Leonée and Richard Ormond, *Lord Leighton* (New Haven, 1975).

Liddell, Robert, *Cavafy: A Critical Biography* (London, 1974).

——, *Unreal City* (London, 1952).

Littlewood, Ian, *Sultry Climates: Travel and Sex since the Grand Tour* (London, 2001).

Llavador, Yvonne, *La Poésie algérienne de langue française et la Guerre d'Algérie* (Lund, 1980).

Lontin, Annick, *Pour François Augiéras* (Lyon, 1990).

Loti, Pierre, *Le Roman d'un spahi* (Paris, 1992).

——, *Aziyadé* (Paris, 1991).

Lownie, Andrew, *John Buchan, The Presbyterian Cavalier* (London, 1995).

Lucey, Michael, *Gide's Bent: Sexuality, Politics, Writing* (New York, 1995).

Lucie-Smith, Edward, *Adam: The Male Figure in Art* (London, 1998).

——, *Sexuality in Western Art* (London, 1991).

Lyautey, Hubert, *Paroles d'action* (Paris, 1995).

Mack, John E., *A Prince of Our Disorder: The Life of T.E. Lawrence* (London, 1976).

McClintock, Anne, *Imperial Leather: Race, Gender and Sexuality in the Colonial Context* (New York, 1985).

McKay, Claude, *Banjo* (New York, 1932).

McKenzie, John, *Orientalism: History, Theory and the Arts* (Manchester, 1985).

MacLeod, Kenneth I.E., *A Victim of Fate* (Cortland, NY, 1978).

——, *The Ranker: The Story of Sir Hector Macdonald's Death* (Cortland, NY, 1976).

McLynn, Frank, *Stanley: The Making of an African Explorer* (Oxford, 1991).

——, *Burton: Snow upon the Desert* (London, 1990).

McPhee, Colin, *A House in Bali* (Singapore, 2000).

Malgonkar, Manohar, *The Puars of Dewas Senior* (Calcutta, 1963).

Manderson, Leonore, *Sickness and the State: Health and Illness in Colonial Malaya, 1870–1940* (Cambridge, 1996).

Mangan, J.A., *The Games Ethic and Imperialism* (Harmondsworth, 1985).

Mann, Thomas, 'The Transposed Heads', in *Mario and the Magician and Other Stories*, trans H.T. Lowes-Porter (London, 1996), pp. 158–235.

Marr, David, 'After the fall', *Spectrum, The Sydney Morning Herald*, 25 November 2000.

——, *Patrick White: A Life* (Sydney, 1991).

Martin, Robert Bernard, *With Friends Possessed: A Life of Edward Fitzgerald* (London, 1985).

Martin, Robert K., and George Piggford (eds), *Queer Forster* (Chicago, 1997).

——, *Hero, Captain, and Stranger: Male Friendship, Social Critique, and Literary Form in the Sea Novels of Herman Melville* (Chapel Hill, NC, 1986).

Martland, Arthur, *E.M. Forster: Passion and Prose* (London, 2000).

Masood, Syed Ross, *Japan and Its Educational System* (Hyderabad-Deccan, 1923).

Masques, dossier on François Augiéras, No. 13 (Printemps 1982).

Maugham, Robin, *The Boy from Beirut and Other Stories*, ed. Peter Burton (San Francisco, 1982).

——, *Search for Nirvana* (London, 1975).

——, *The Wrong People* (London, 1967).

Maynard, Steven, '"Horrible temptations": Sex, men, and working-class male youth in urban Ontario, 1890–1935', *The Canadian Historical Review*, Vol. 78, No. 2 (June 1997), pp. 191–235.

——, 'Through a hole in the lavatory wall: Homosexual subcultures, police surveillance, and the dialectics of discovery, Toronto, 1890–1930', *Journal of the History of Sexuality*, Vol. 5, No. 2 (1994), pp. 207–42.

'Médecine militaire: Déni de justice', *Le Bulletin médical*, Vol. 6 (1892), pp. 65–7

Melville, Herman, *Typee* (Harmondsworth, 1938).

——, *Omoo* (London, 1893).

Merchant, Hoshang (ed.), *Yaraana* (New Delhi, 1999).

Meyers, Jeffrey, *Homosexuality and Literature, 1890–1930* (London, 1977).

Michaut, Dr, 'Syphilis et pédérastie, fumeurs d'opium et climat', *Bulletin général de thérapeutique médicale*, Vol. 61, No. 1 (January 1893), pp. 274–9.

Mitchell, Angus (ed.), *The Amazon Journal of Roger Casement* (London, 1997).

Montgomery, John, *Toll for the Brave: The Tragedy of Major-General Sir Hector Macdonald K.C.B., D.S.O., A.D.C.* (London, 1963).

Montherlant, Henry de, *Moustique* (Paris, 1986).

——, *La Rose de sable* (Paris, 1968).

——, *Encore un instant de bonheur* (Paris, 1934).

Moore, Clive, *Sunshine and Rainbows: The Development of Gay and Lesbian Culture in Queensland* (St Lucia, Queensland, 2001).

——, 'Poofs in the park: Documenting gay "beats" in Queensland, Australia', *GLQ*, Vol. 2 (1995), pp. 319–38.

Moore, Clive, and Kay Saunders (eds), *Australian Masculinities: Men and Their Histories*, special issue of the *Journal of Australian Studies*, No. 56 (1998).

Moss, Robert Tewdwr, *Cleopatra's Wedding Present: Travels through Syria* (London, 1998).

Mrabet, Mohammed, *The Lemon* (San Francisco, 1969).

——, *Love with a Few Hairs* (San Francisco, 1967).

——, *Chocolate Creams and Dollars* (New York, n.d.).

Nacer-Khodja, Hamid, 'Trente ans après sa première édition, *Citoyens de beauté* est de nouveau disponible', *La Tribune* (Algiers), 26 May 1997.

——, 'Retour à Jean Sénac', *El Watan* (Algiers), 3 October 1996.

——, '"Awal" ou la parole à Jean Sénac', *Algérie Actualité*, 23–9 November 1993.

——, 'Jean Sénac, d'une algérianité à l'autre', *Algérie Actualité*, 14–20 September 1993.

Nandy, Ashis, *The Intimate Enemy: Loss and Recovery of Self under Colonialism* (Delhi, 1983).

Nelson, Hank, *Taim Bilong Masta: The Australian Involvement with Papua New Guinea* (Sydney, 1982).

Nicholl, Charles, *Somebody Else: Rimbaud in Africa, 1800–91* (London, 1997).

Nicholl, Fiona, *From Diggers to Drag Queens: Configurations of Australian National Identity* (Annandale, NSW, 2001).

Nijinsky Dancing: From the Golden Age of the Ballets Russes (Pacific Grove, CA, 1996).

Nikolas, Wolf, *Arjun* (Berlin, 1987).

Noble, R.W., '"Dearest Forster" – "Dearest Masood": An East–West friendship', *Encounter*, June 1981, pp. 61–72.

Oja, Carol J., *Colin McPhee: Composer in Two Worlds* (Washington, 1990).

Pacific Islands Monthly, February–April 1956.

Paz Otero, Gerardo, *Vida sentimental de Alejandro Humboldt* (Bogotá, 1978).

Paine, Jeffery, *Father India: Westerners under the Spell of an Ancient Culture* (New York, 1998).

Palmer, Christopher, *Szymanowski* (London, 1983).

Parivaraj, P., *Shiva and Arun* (London, 1998).

Pearce, Barry, *Donald Friend, 1915–1989: Retrospective* (Sydney, 1990).

Peltre, Christine, *Orientalism in Art* (New York, 1997).

Peltzet, Michael, 'Ludwig and the arts', in Wilfred Blunt, *The Dream King: Ludwig II of Bavaria* (London, 1970).

Péroncel-Hugoz, Jean-Pierre, *Assassinat d'un poète* (Paris, 1983).

Peskine, Lynda Bellity and Albert Dichy, *La Bataille des Paravents* (Paris, 1991).

Phillips, Richard, *Mapping Men and Empire: A Geography of Adventure* (London, 1997).

Physical Culture, July 1929.

Pijbes, Wim, 'The artists of the tropics: The artists of the future', *IIAS* [International Institute for Asian Studies] *Newsletter*, No. 23 (October 2000), p. 37.

Pinchin, Jane Lagoudis, *Alexandria Still: Forster, Durrell, and Cavafy* (Princeton, 1977).

Placet, Paul, *François Augiéras: Un Barbare en Occident* (Périgueux, 1988).

Placet, Paul and Pascal Sigoda, *Augiéras, une trajectoire rimbaldienne* (Charleville, 1996).

Plomer, William, *Cecil Rhodes* (London, 1993).

Pohlmann, Ulrich, *Wilhelm von Gloeden – Sehnsucht nach Arkadian* (Berlin, 1987).

Pollock, John, *Kitchener: The Road to Omdurman* (London, 1998).

Pons, Xavier, *Out of Eden: Henry Lawson's Life and Works – A Psychoanalytic View* (Sydney, 1984).

Poole, Reginald, 'Introductions', *Southern Cross Log*, Vol. 62, No. 2 (May 1955), p. 52.

Porch, Douglas, *The French Foreign Legion: A Complete History of the Legendary Fighting Force* (New York, 1991).

——, *The Conquest of Morocco* (New York, 1983).

Pouillon, François, *Les Deux Vies d'Etienne Dinet, peintre en Islam: L'Algérie et l'héritage colonial* (Paris, 1997).

Prokosch, Frederic, *Voices* (New York, 1983).

——, *The Asiatics* (New York, 1935).

Purcell, Victor, *The Memoirs of a Malayan Official* (London, 1965).

Quella-Villégier, Alain, *Le Cas Farrère: Du Goncourt à la disgrâce* (Paris, 1989).

Rachid, O., *Chocolat chaud* (Paris, 1998).

——, *Plusieurs vies* (Paris, 1996).

——, *L'Enfant ébloui* (Paris, 1995).

Raven, Simon, *The Feathers of Death* (London, 1959).

Rayfield, Donald, *The Dream of Lhasa: The Life of Nikolay Przhevalsky (1839–88), Explorer of Central Asia* (London, 1976).

Rebierre, Paul, *'Joyeux' et demi-fous* (Paris, 1909).

Reed, Stephen Winsor, *The Making of Modern New Guinea* (Philadelphia, 1943).

Rees, Brian, *Camille Saint-Saëns* (London, 1999).

Renouf, Renée, '"The greatest Bohemian of all": Joseph D. Redding', *The Californians*, Vol. 12, No. 3 (n.d.), pp. 10–22.

Review on the Administration of the Dewas State (Senior), 1913–1914 (New Delhi, 1915).

Rhodius, Hans, *Walter Spies (Maler und Musiker auf Bali 1895–1942)* (The Hague, 1963).

Rhodius, Hans and John Darling, *Walter Spies and Balinese Art* (Zutphen, 1980).

Rhys, Lloyd, *High Lights and Flights in New Guinea* (London, 1942).

Rice, Edward, *Captain Sir Richard Francis Burton* (New York, 1990).

Richardson, Frank M., *Mars without Venus: A Study of Some Homosexual Generals* (Edinburgh, 1981).

Rivet, Daniel, 'Lyautey l'Africain', in *Le Temps des Colonies*, special issue of *L'Histoire*, No. 11 (2001), pp. 22–6.

Robb, Graham, *Rimbaud* (New York, 2000).

Roberts, Pam, Edwin Becker, Verna Posever Curtis and Anne E. Havinga, *F. Holland Day* (Amsterdam, 2000).

Rondeau, Daniel (ed.), *L'Appel du Maroc* (Paris, 1999).

Rorem, Ned, *Knowing When to Stop: A Memoir* (New York, 1994).

Rosenthal, Donald A., *Orientalism: The Near East in French Painting 1800–1880* (Rochester, NY, 1982).

Rousseau, François-Olivier, *Le Passeur* (Paris, 2001).

Rovsing, Leif, *I tropesol og måneskin* (Copenhagen, 1959).

Roy, Jules, *Etranger pour mes frères* (Paris, 1982).

Royal Colonial Institute, *Vanishing India: One Hundred and Fifty Paintings of Indian Types, Arts and Crafts and Portraits of Princes by Stowitts* (Amsterdam, 1931).

Royer, Louis-Charles, *Amours bizarres* (Paris, 1961).

Royle, Trevor, *Death before Dishonour: The True Story of Fighting Mac* (Edinburgh, 1982).

Ruscio, Alain (ed.), *Amours coloniales: Aventures et fantasmes exotiques de Claire de Duras à Georges Simenon* (Brussels, 1996).

Rutnam, James T., *Sir Ponnambalam Arunachalam, 1853–1924* (Colombo, 1988).

Saslow, James M., *Pictures and Passions: A History of Homosexuality in the Visual Arts* (New York, 1999).

Sawyer, Roger (ed.), *Roger Casement's Diaries – 1910: The Black and the White* (London, 1997).

Sawyer-Lauçanno, Christopher, *An Invisible Spectator: A Biography of Paul Bowles* (London, 1989).

Schehr, Lawrence R., *Alcibiades at the Door: Gay Discourses in French Literature* (Stanford, 1995).

Scheler, Max and Matthias Harder (eds), *Herbert List: The Monograph* (New York, 2000).

Schneebaum, Tobias, *Secret Places: My Life in New York and New Guinea* (Madison, WI, 2000).

——, *Where the Spirits Dwell: An Odyssey in the Jungle of New Guinea* (New York, 1988).

Schwarzenbach, Annemarie, *La Mort en Perse*, trans Dominique Miermont (Paris, 1997).

——, *Orient exils*, trans Dominique Miermont (Paris, 1994).

Seabrook, Jeremy, *Love in a Different Climate: Men Who Have Sex with Men in India* (London, 1999).

——, *Colonies of the Heart* (London, 1998).

Searight, Kenneth, *Sona: An Auxiliary Neutral Language* (London, 1935).

Sedgwick, Peter, 'Out of hiding: The comradeships of Daniel Guérin', *Salmagundi*, No. 58–9 (1982–3), pp. 197–220.

Selvadurai, Shyam, *Cinnamon Gardens* (London, 1998).

Selz, Jean, *Gustave Moreau* (Paris, 1978).

Sénac, Jean, *Oeuvres poétiques* (Arles, 1999).

——, *Pour une terre possible…Poèmes et autres textes inédits* (Paris, 1999).

——, *Journal Alger, janvier–juillet 1954* (n.p., 1996).

—— (ed.), *Anthologie de la nouvelle poésie algérienne* (Paris, 1971).

Shearston, Trevor, *A Straight Young Back* (Pymble, NSW, 2000).

Sheridan, Alan, *André Gide: A Life in the Present* (London, 1998).

Sherman, A.J., *Mandate Days: British Lives in Palestine, 1918–1948* (London, 1997).

Siemon, Rosamond, *The Mayne Inheritance* (St Lucia, Queensland, 1997).

Singleton-Gates, Peter and Maurice Girodias, *The Black Diaries: An Account of Roger Casement's Life and Times with a Collection of His Diaries and Public Writings* (Paris, 1959).

Sinha, Mrinalini, *Colonial Masculinity; The 'Manly Englishman' and the 'Effeminate Bengali' in the Nineteenth Century* (Manchester, 1995).

South Pacific Post (Port Moresby), 1953–69.

Southey, Nick, 'Cecil John Rhodes', in George Haggerty (ed.), *Encyclopedia of Homosexuality* (New York, 2000), p. 744.

Spalding, Frances, *Duncan Grant: A Biography* (London, 1997).

Spear, Hilda D., and Aly Abdel-Moneim (eds), *The Uncollected Egyptian Essays of E.M. Forster* (n.p., 1988).

Spruit, Ruud, *Kunstenaars op Bali* (Amsterdam, 1996).

Squires, Radcliffe, *Frederic Prokosch* (New York, 1964).

Stanley, H.M., *My Kalulu: Prince, King and Slave: A Story of Central Africa* (London, 1873).

——, *How I Found Livingstone* (London, 1890).

——, *The Autobiography of Henry Morton Stanley*, ed. Dorothy Stanley (London, n.d.).

Stansky, Peter, *On or about December 1910: Early Bloomsbury and Its Intimate World* (Cambridge, MA, 1996).

Starkie, Enid, *Arthur Rimbaud in Abyssinia* (Oxford, 1937).

Steinmetz, Jean-Luc, *Arthur Rimbaud: Une Question de présence* (Paris, 1999).

Stoddard, Charles Warren, *The Island of Tranquil Delights* (London, 1905).

——, *Exits and Entrances* (Boston, 1903).

——, *South-Sea Idyls* (New York, 1903).

Stoler, Ann Laura, *Race and the Education of Desire: Foucault's History of Sexuality and the Colonial Order of Things* (Durham, NC, 1995).

Stuart-Young, J.M., *The Coaster at Home: Being the Autobiography of Jack O'Dazi, Palm Oil Ruffian and Trader Man, of the River Niger* (London, 1916).

Suleri, Sara, *The Rhetoric of English India* (Chicago, 1992).

Sun-Herald (Sydney), 4 February 1956.

Sweet, Paul R., *Wilhelm von Humboldt: A Biography* (Columbus, OH, 1978).

Sydney Morning Herald, 14 and 20 February 1956.

Symons, Scott, *Helmet of Flesh* (New York, 1986).

The Government of Egypt: Recommendations by a Committee of the International Section of the Labour Research Department, with Notes on Egypt by E.M. Forster (London, 1920).

The Heritage of India (Carmel-by-the-Sea, 1986).

The London Review of Books, 2 October 1997.

The Strong Man, Vol. 1, No. 2 (July 1931).

Thesiger, Wilfred, *The Marsh Arabs* (London, 1964).

Thieuloy, Jack, *La Passion indonésienne* (Paris, 1985).

Thomas, Antony, *Rhodes* (London, 1996).

Thornton, Lynn, *Les Orientalistes: Peintres voyageurs* (Paris, 1993).

Tillett, Gregory, *The Elder Brother: A Biography of Charles Webster Leadbeater* (London, 1982).

Toullelan, Pierre-Yves, *Missionnaires au quotidien à Tahiti: Les Picpuciens en Polynésie au XIXe siècle* (Leiden, 1995).

Tournier, Michel, *La Goutte d'or* (Paris, 1988).

Trevor-Roper, Hugh, *A Hidden Life: The Enigma of Sir Edmund Backhouse* (London, 1976).

Troubat, E., *Toutes les Races: La Beauté du corps humain* (Paris, 5 booklets, 1931–2).

Tsuzuki, Chushichi, *Edward Carpenter, 1844–1929: Prophet of Human Fellowship* (Cambridge, 1980).

Turnbaugh, Douglas Blair (ed.), *Private: The Erotic Art of Duncan Grant, 1885–1978* (London, 1989).

Vercier, Bruno, Jean-Pierre Melot and Gaby Scaon, *La Maison de Pierre Loti* (Paris, 1999).

Vickers, Adrian, *Bali: A Paradise Created* (Melbourne, 1989).

Wainwright, David and Catherine Dinn, *Henry Scott Tuke, 1858–1929: Under Canvas* (London, 1989).

Wake, Clive, *The Novels of Pierre Loti* (The Hague, 1974).

Walker, J.H., '"This peculiar acuteness of feeling": James Brooke and the enactment of desire', *Borneo Research Bulletin*, Vol. 29 (1998), pp. 148–222.

Wannan, Bill, *Early Colonial Scandals: The Turbulent Times of Samuel Marsden* (Melbourne, 1972).

Weiermair, Peter, *Guglielo Plüschow* (Cologne, 1993).

——, *The Hidden Image: Photographs of the Male Nude in the Nineteenth and Twentieth Centuries* (Cambridge, MA, 1988).

Weston, Helen, 'Girodet's portrait of C. Belley, ex-representative of the colonies: In remembrance of "things sublime"', in Adrian Forty and Susanne Küchler (eds), *The Art of Forgetting* (Oxford, 1999), pp. 75–86.

White, Edmund, *Genet* (New York, 1993).

White, Stanhope, *Dan Bana: The Memoirs of a Nigerian Official* (London, 1966).

Whitton, Evan, 'Sub plot', *The Weekend Australian*, 31 January–1 February 1998.

Who's Who in France, 1963–1964 (Paris, 1964).

Wilson, Gavin, *Escape Artists: Modernists in the Tropics* (Cairns, 1998).

Woods, Gregory, 'Fantasy islands: Popular topographies of marooned masculinity', in David Bell and Gill Valentine (eds), *Mapping Desire: Geographies of Sexualities* (London, 1995), pp. 126–48.

Wotherspoon, Garry (ed.), *Gay and Lesbian Perspectives III: Essays in Australian Culture* (Sydney, 1996).

——, 'Moonlight and…romance? The death-cell letters of Captain Moonlight and some of their implications', *Journal of the Royal Australian Historical Society*, Vol. 78, No. 3–4 (1992), pp. 76–91.

——, *City of the Plain: History of a Gay Sub-culture* (Sydney, 1991).

——, 'Sodom in the South Pacific: Male homosexuality in Sydney, 1788–1809', in Graeme Aplin (ed.), *A Difficult Infant: Sydney before Macquarie* (Sydney, 1988), pp. 91–101.

—— (ed.), *Being Different* (Sydney, 1986).

Young, Robert J.C., *Colonial Desire: Hybridity in Theory, Culture and Race* (London, 1995).

Index